LZ balloons in No 1 shed, Cardington in 1937 (via R. Clarke).

The approximate geographical areas covered or to be covered by different volumes within this series

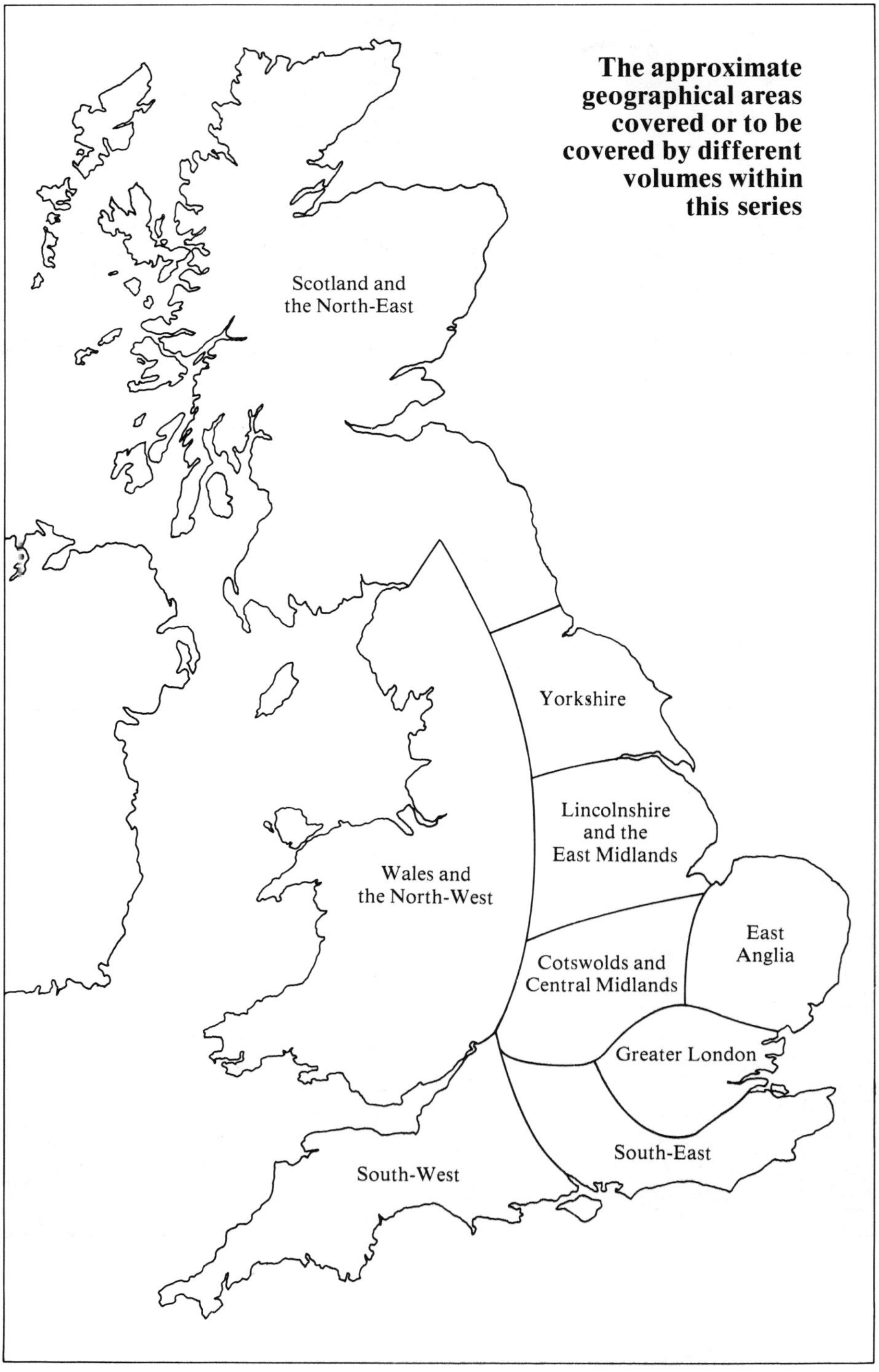

ACTION STATIONS

6. Military airfields of the Cotswolds and the Central Midlands

Michael J.F. Bowyer

PSL Patrick Stephens, Cambridge

Title Page *Spitfire,* N3249, QJ:P *of 92 Squadron crash landed at Bibury in early September 1940. It was later used by 602 Squadron and was lost during operations with 610 Squadron on February 14 1941* (RAF Museum).

First published August 1983
Reprinted December 1983

British Library Cataloguing in Publication Data

Action stations.
6: Military air fields of the Cotswolds and the central Midlands
1. Great Britain. Royal Air Force
2. Air bases—Great Britain—History
I. Bowyer, Michael J.F.
358.4'17'0941 UG635.G7

ISBN 0-85059-529-0

Text photoset in 9 pt and 10 on 11 pt Times
by Manuset Limited, Baldock, Herts.
Printed in Great Britain on 100 gsm Fineblade coated cartridge, and bound, by The Garden City Press, Letchworth, Herts, for the publishers,
Patrick Stephens Limited, Bar Hill, Cambridge, CB3 8EL, England.

Contents

Introduction	4
Glossary	7
In days of yore, soon came a war	9
Uneasy interlude	14
To battle once more	19
Looking at airfields	38
Map of the airfields for the Cotswolds and the Central Midlands	52
The airfields	54
Index of units referred to in the text	307

Introduction

'Geography is learnt through the soles of the feet', my college lecturer stated. History I knew, could be learnt through the seat of a bicycle. I know because I pedalled to many places mentioned in this book (in the prime of their days and the youth of mine), sensing and recording. When the distance was too far I used the rickety country bus, or 'Thomas the Tank Engine'. Memories of such meanderings are deeply set within these pages, mingling with emotions and countless memories.

The parameters of the region dealt with in this volume are difficult to define. The eastern edge roughly borders the A1 and, to the west, Bedfordshire, Buckinghamshire, Oxfordshire, Northamptonshire, Warwickshire, Gloucestershire and an area by Birmingham are included. The southern fringe rests along the Chilterns, twists towards Newbury, swings for Swindon then curves towards Broadway. From there the western edge wends its way to Birmingham, skirting the high scarp face, reaching 1,000 ft at Fish Hill and offering fine views of airfield sites. A line taking in Coventry and curving south of Leicester marks the northern edge.

A problem with the *Action Stations* series has been deciding upon borders for each volume, and so a final volume will include a detailed index to the entire series* to ease the problems of locating sites and units.

Geographically and geologically the area reviewed here is very mixed. Eastern parts are affected by the Ouse Valley and flood plain. To the south lies the Thames Valley. Between is an area of mixed chalk, sand, clays, gravel and oolitic limestone, making the Cotswolds beautiful to gaze upon. Workable subsoil and plateaux in a somewhat undulating region have permitted substantial, permanent airfields to be built in an area of mixed topography.

Weather is a prominent consideration in siting an airfield. In this region it is good, yet the Cotswolds, which often bake in high summer, can hide themselves from the world at the flutter of snowflakes. When the sun shines in Shakespeare's land, the scene is truly magnificent.

It is possible to visualise moments of high drama at airfields all but vanished. Highly evocative are those seeming least likely to arouse emotions, and there may be remorse that at some stations so little remains. Ancient places attract visitors in their thousands, often to sites which have only their antiquity to recommend them. Curious that these 'action stations', some the scene of

*Interested readers are invited to write to the publishers, Patrick Stephens Ltd, with suggestions for the type of indexed material they would find most useful. They are also invited to send in photographs.

tremendous events and the expenditure of colossal courage, have limited popular appeal. Barely anything at Castle Bromwich remains to remind passing youth that from here emerged thousands of Spitfires which won them their freedom.

One cannot fail to be impressed by the timeless majesty of the permanent stations. How well (by design and construction) they have withstood time and fashion, as a bold reminder of imperial yesterday. Compared with the deplorable architectural standards of recent years, the superb lines of Bicester's Officers' Mess present an image of exciting days and glamorous nights of splendour.

For this volume of *Action Stations*, I have been able to turn for assistance to many with highly specialised knowledge and great readiness to help. Some are friends of many decades, others have freshly bestowed their fellowship.

My thanks go to R.W. Mack and the Royal Air Force Museum for the help afforded with illustrations, and permission to use photographs. From the Atomic Energy Research Establishment, Harwell, I have received much help, particularly from Peter Smallbone, Harry Coles, Norman Wallis, Eric Cannings, Denis Tyler and others. Radio Oxford and the *Oxford Mail* provided facilities.

At Cranfield's Institute of Technology, Glyn Jones and Jenny Moore arranged an excellent visit and supplied fine illustrations for the book. For other photographs I am indebted to the Imperial War Museum and the Public Record Office where, within Classes Air 25 (groups), Air 27 (squadrons), Air 28 (airfields) and Air 29 (miscellaneous units) may be found detailed records appertaining to many formations stationed in the Midlands. Crown Copyright remains vested in official photographs used and some material within the text. I am indebted to the staff of the Air Historical Branch, MoD, and in particular to Eric Turner and Mr E.A. Munday, every-ready to help to answer my questions. Squadron Leader J.H. Bullock, RAF, arranged for me to visit Frank Kiernan of RAE Cardington who showed me his excellent collection of airship memorabilia. Through Mrs M.J. Neaverson I was able to obtain some photographs. Mr J.T. Breeze arranged for me to visit the tunnel site and airfield at RAE Bedford. The Luton Airport Director, Mr W.C.J. Easterbrook, and Mr D.R. Ellis arranged an excellent viewing of the airport and provided photographs, particularly of Luton's early days.

On starting this volume I visited Mrs Littler and her son at Wellesbourne where I spent some of my RAF service. They supplemented memories of that station, and lent useful items.

My thanks are due to the staffs of Bedford Central Library, Bedford County Record Office, Birmingham Central Library, Cheltenham Library and Oxford County Library. Lieutenant-Colonel Eric M. Solander arranged for the USAF Magazine and Book Branch to contribute some US Air Force photographs.

The director of the Fire Service College, through Mr D. Holland, provided a history of the fire service's association with Moreton-in-Marsh. From Martin-Baker Aircraft Ltd, through Brian Limbrey, came the interesting photograph of their MB 3 fighter.

Many people have provided written contributions which have been useful. In the forefront is Peter Corbell, an ardent recorder of airfield histories. Thank you, Peter, for help and hours of happy friendship. Thanks also to Bruce Robertson, ever-ready to help generously. To Alan Hartley, Mr A. Holt, Mr B.

Randall and Mr B. Tipping, I extend my thanks for help with the Down Ampney item, and also to Ron Clarke for some excellent photographs. Roger Dennis persuaded me that I must use his material on 1914–1918 Rendcombe. He had been helped by the late Mr Farnsworth who, at 103, was certainly the eldest gentleman to lend a hand! Alan Lowe gave specialised help, likewise Chris Ashworth. Special thanks also go to Squadron Leader Geoffrey Philips, MBE, RAF (Retired).

Writing can be a lonely task, but not in the case of *Action Stations*. The number of people ready to chat over the gates, the bars, and on the village green with an opening 'Yes, I remember when . . .' and, frequently, 'My Dad . . .', has been endless. I have been amazed at the interest these airfields retain, often among people far too young to remember them in active days. If you were one of those who chatted during my travels, thank you for making them such a pleasure.

Michael J.F. Bowyer
Cambridge,
January 1983

Glossary

AACU Anti-Aircraft Co-operation Unit.
AAF Auxiliary Air Force.
AASF Advanced Air Striking Force.
ADGB Air Defence of Great Britain.
AEF Air Experience Flight.
AERE Atomic Energy Research Establishment.
AI Airborne Interception radar.
ANS Air Navigation School.
AOC Air Officer Commanding.
AONS Air Observer and Navigator School.
ARAL Aircraft Research Association Limited.
ASI Air Speed Indicated.
A Tr DU Air Transport Development Unit.
BAT Flight Blind Approach Training Flight.
BEA British European Airways.
Bf German Messerschmitt fighter designation prefix *(Bayerische Flugzeug werke).*
BG(H) and *BG(M)* USAAF/USAF Bomber (Heavy or Medium).
C & M Care and Maintenance.
'Carpetbagger' Supply and contact operation with Resistance forces.
CFI Chief Flying Instructor.
CFS Central Flying School.
CTO Chief Technical Officer.
DFC Distinguished Flying Cross.
Do Dornier aircraft.
EFTS Elementary Flying Training School.
E&RFTS Elementary and Reserve Flying Training School.
VIIIth AF BC US 8th Air Force Bomber Command.
Exercise 'Bullseye' Night training exercise for bomber and defence personnel.
Exercise 'Eric' Day training exercise for bomber and fighter crews.
FIS Flying Instructors' School.
FSP Forward Staging Post.
FTS Flying Training School.
FTU Ferry Training Unit.
GTS Glider Training School.
He Heinkel aircraft.
HE High Explosive bomb.
HGCU Heavy Glider Conversion Unit.
Hs Henschel aircraft.
IE Initial Equipment (ie, unit strength).
IR Immediate Reserve (ie, unit reserve strength).
ITS Intermediate Training Squadron.
ITW Initial Training Wing.
Ju Junkers aircraft.
KG *Kampfgeschwader* (German bomber group).
KLM Royal Dutch Airlines.
LG2 *Lehrgeschwader* (operational training unit) No 2.
MCA Ministry of Civil Aviation.
M/F D/F Medium Frequency Direction Finding (radio).
MQ Married Quarters.
MT Motor Transport.
MU Maintenance Unit.
NAAFI Navy, Army and Air Forces Institute.
NCO Non-Commissioned Officer.
OCU Operational Conversion Unit.
Operation 'Nickel' Leaflet dropping exercise over enemy territory.
Operation 'Starkey' Feint and large scale operation in September 1943 against Pas de Calais.
OTU Operational Training Unit.
¾OTU Operational Training Unit, only three-quarter usual strength of 54 aircraft.
(P)AFU Pilots (or Pilot) Advanced Flying Unit.
PFF Pathfinder Force.
PRU Photographic Reconnaissance Unit.

PTS Parachute Training School.
Purgatory store Aircraft stored non-assembled.
QM Quarter Master.
R-101 Rigid airship 101.
RAE Royal Aircraft Establishment.
RAFGSA RAF Gliding and Soaring Association.
RAW Royal Airship Works.
RC Recruit Centre.
RFC Royal Flying Corps.
RLG Relief Landing Ground.
RNVR Royal Navy Volunteer Reserve.
R/T Radio Telephony.
SABENA Belgian Airlines.
SAC Senior Aircraftman.
SBC Small Bomb Container.
SFTS Service Flying Training School (Service to distinguish from civilian, a prefix used generally between 1935 and 1942 although some schools used merely the FTS title).
SHQ Station Headquarters.
SLG Satellite Storage area/Landing Ground.
SNCO Senior Non-Commissioned Officer.
SOE Special Operations Executive.
SP Staging Post.
STT School of Technical Training.
SWO Station Warrant Officer.
TAMU Transport Aircraft Modification Unit/Maintenance Unit.
2TAF 2nd Tactical Air Force.
TCDU Transport Command Development Unit.
TS Training Squadron.
UAS University Air Squadron.
ULAS University of London Air Squadron.
VHF Very High Frequency.
VVIP Very Very Important Person.
'Window' Metal foil dropped to distort radar image.

In days of yore, soon came a war

For almost 200 years flying has taken place from the Midlands. In 1784 James Sadler made a hydrogen balloon flight from Oxfordshire before selling his craft for exhibition in Birmingham's New Theatre. On October 7 1811, Sadler and a passenger set off from the Midlands, their balloon drifting to Heckington, Lincolnshire. Its purpose? To promote air travel.

Select Cheltenham provided an early backdrop for ballooning. On August 31 1836 Mr Graham ascended from Montpellier Gardens. Mrs Graham's turn came on September 22 1837 and, a year later, Charles Green ascended in his Royal Vauxhall Nassau Balloon from the same site. John Hampton flew the Albion Balloon from Montpellier Gardens on September 18 1838 and, a few days later, descended from a balloon by parachute. These and more ascents pleased Cheltenham's ladies by flying from Montpellier and Pitville Gardens, as well as Royal Old Wells.

The first ascent from Bedford took place in 1840 and, in 1838, Queen Victoria's Coronation was marked by one from Ampthill. Twenty tables were set for a public dinner in Church Street. Well-to-do folk donated £100 so that the less fortunate could feast upon beef and plum pudding, washed down by ale, before dancing, fireworks and witnessing the release of the balloon *Victoria*.

There were early aeroplane flights in Bedfordshire, making association with long passed days. Claude Graham White gave a flying display at Biddenham in 1906 and, a year later, an air-cooled engine was underway for Bedfordshire's first aeroplane, constructed by Mr H.P. Saunderson of Elstow, south of Bedford. He built grass cutters, but channelled his talent into making a bamboo and aluminium tractor monoplane. Length 22 ft, wing span 28 ft, it weighed 800 lb loaded. Saunderson reckoned it would fly for 200 miles. Proof that it could leave the ground was expected on October 21 1909. Hundreds of people arrived at the chosen field only to find that by 09:00 the wind was too strong for a flight. Saunderson took his aeroplane to Blackpool to fly it from the sands.

Birmingham, we used to be told, builds everything from needles to railway engines. It built aeroplanes too. First to attempt the art was Mr Alfred Maxfield—in a small workshop by Aston Road. In this and his second creation he fitted one of his 9 hp engines. The first one he wheeled in semi-secrecy to Castle Bromwich Playing Fields, much to the chagrin of the local constabulary. They need not have worried for neither this nor his second aeroplane flew. Maxfield's third did fly between September 27 1909 and October 7 1909, attaining a height of 50 ft on one hop. Later it was exhibited in Birmingham's Masonic Hall.

On September 3 1909 Mr W. Ivy-Rogers convened a meeting to consider a Midland Aero Club. The inaugural meeting was on October 13 1909, attended by Neville Chamberlain. Ivy-Rogers was able to tell him what flying was like—he had tried it, with Colonel Cody. Dunstall Park, Wolverhampton, was the club's venue for their first flying meeting in 1910. C.S. Rolls, Colonel Cody, Claude Graham White and Moore Brabazon were there, but the club did not flourish until after the war.

Much early flying took place over Oxfordshire. Oxford has an ideal flying ground—Port Meadow by the Thames. Whether they had a right to fly from there was uncertain, but early aviators used it. Most exciting of those events was surely that of May 19 1911 when Hubert Latham, a Balliol graduate, landed from Brooklands in an Antoinette Monoplane. Fearing Port Meadow could swarm with watchers, his friends maintained secrecy, clearing the ground for him on the chosen Friday. At noon he left Brooklands, with faith in a 60 hp 8-cylinder engine.

The *Oxford Journal Illustrated* of May 24 1911 records how a distant speck appeared to the watchers' great excitement. Humming, throbbing and clear to view came the 'aeroplane sailing majestically like a dragonfly'. Ladies waved hankies and men cheered before 'it gave a circuitous swoop and rapidly neared the earth'. After its 70-minute flight the machine 'came down just like a bird. People ran to it and said, "Good morning, Sir, we wish you well"'. Latham replied, 'Have you got some Luficers, so I can have a smoke?' Crowds ran, cycled, motored, to be near the machine. With hundreds watching, Latham ascended with Mr C. Gull, from a space within the crowd, for a short trip.

The *Oxford Journal Illustrated* picturesquely recorded Latham's final departure. 'The propeller whizzed round at a tremendous rate . . . With his hand on the steering wheel Mr Latham set the huge dragonfly running forward like a dog loose from the leash. Crowds cheered, and the aeroplane glided upwards in majestic fashion. Higher and higher the machine went, until it was evidently speeding along swiftly for it was soon lost to sight.' Latham sped home—at 62 mph. Leaving Oxford at 17:57 he touched down at Brooklands at 18:50, having given many their first glimpse of an aeroplane in flight.

Graham White, expected on Easter Monday 1911 to pass over Banbury, was delayed by fog at Fenny Stratford. He then followed the railway line to Birmingham via Weedon, giving many the sight of a lifetime. Other Bedfordshire residents had their first view of aeroplanes during the 1911 *Daily Mail* Air Race when aircraft landed near Barton to refuel.

As military interest in aeroplanes increased, rumour passed through Oxford that the Army wanted Port Meadow. According to the *Oxford Times* a Captain Burke, 18th Royal Ulster Regiment, headed for Port Meadow on June 14 1911, but strong winds forced his 50 hp Gnome Farman to land at Bessels Leigh polo ground. Next evening he left for Salisbury. Slowly his Farman passed over Wallingford, facing wind and rain before landing in a grass field near Heathercroft, about a mile from the town. Misfortune befell the machine, but helpers righted it. As it was taxi-ing, it hit a ditch, breaking wires and woodwork.

November 1911 was a busy and disastrous time for early aviators, for a 70 mph gale whipped across Port Meadow. Mr J. Betts was barricading the shed doors when the gale tore them 'from the ground and lifted them up 80 feet!' and 15 precious aeroplanes were wrecked. Cost of the damage—£8,000, no mean sum. The Imperial Aero Club was about to take over the sheds when disaster struck.

It was also November 1911 when Mr Perey Fawdrey's 10 ft 7 in span 30 lb ornithopter is said to have flown. Claims are that it made ten flights, Fawdrey achieving 300-yd long trips at heights up to 50 ft, take off being down a slope. Fawdrey wanted to go it alone and 'wouldn't fly with the professionals'.

Port Meadow had been selected for military use and a later military visitor was Lieutenant Parke, RN. On January 15 1912, he came from Brooklands in a 5-cylinder Avro, intending to visit Port Meadow. By the time he reached Abingdon his fuel state was low and he landed by Culham Road. Vernon Whitehead and S.V. Sippe repaired the aircraft then gave a couple of demonstration flights before flying away.

Easter Monday 1912 brought the next round of Oxfordian excitement. Frank Widdenham Gooden, in charge of Betts Aircraft, demonstrated the balloon, *Enchantress*, to 1,000 onlookers. Before the year was out Oxfordshire's residents were watching aeroplanes doing aerobatics, initially by a German at Banbury and Chipping Norton.

In early autumn 1912 another first was notched, when Mr Widdenham-Gooden flew his *Dragonfly*. A local newspaper reporter considered the 25 ft long body of 'torpedo shape', and reported that 'he dreams of travelling at the enormous rate of 360 mph'. His *Dragonfly* had a loaded weight of 650 lb, a wing area of 168 sq ft, was powered by a 35–40 hp 8-cylinder JAP engine and managed to fly at over 60 mph in the course of several flights.

The *Dragonfly* and *Enchantress* were displayed on March 1 1913. That month was memorable for the passage over Oxford on Easter Monday of the Army airship *Beta*. Carrying five passengers, and after circling Port Meadow, it flew east, the first dirigible to appear here. Wednesday, May 28 1913, brought splendid views of another airship, *Gamma*, in the area for six days of trials. At around 07:30 the airship, from Bracknell, flew along the course of the river before landing in Blenheim Park. The intention was that *Gamma* would later leave for Berkhampstead but engine trouble delayed take-off and it crept away at first light the following day.

Four aircraft sheds survived at the Wolverton/Port Meadow site. Their existence was terminated at midday on August 5 1913 when all were gutted by fire, stopping early flying at Oxford. This gave the Army an opportunity to replace the civil facilities with its own—when time was right. In September 1913 the Army held extensive manoeuvres and No 3 Squadron, RFC, made use of Port Meadow. Other landing grounds in the area were more portentous and included a field at Weston-on-the Green. Airships again frequented Blenheim Park.

Some Oxford residents had close encounters with a dirigible during these exercises. On a Friday afternoon *Delta* drifted into view, clearly in difficulties. East of the city, it descended by laboratory buildings. Under the command of Major Maitland, *Delta* had set out from Farnborough for Blenheim then Rugby, but near Oxford propeller trouble was encountered, the airship seeming likely to crash upon houses in the High Street, or to hit St Mary's church spire. Instead, it came down among tennis and croquet players who held its guide ropes whilst the occupants climbed out. At an average speed of 36 mph, and watched by a huge crowd, *Delta* left for Rugby next day.

In 1914 Ampthill polo ground became a recognised airfield. An 80 hp biplane was flying from Woburn Sands at this time, and Graham White with Mr B.C. Hucks gave a flying demonstration at Bedford in 1913. Later that year a naval aircraft crashed at Langford, two miles south of Biggleswade.

Hucks demonstrated 'stunt looping and inverted flying' at the Tally-Ho Grounds, Edgbaston, Birmingham, on February 14 1914. He gave aerobatic displays from a meadow at Whitehouse Road, Grand Pont, Oxford, between February 26 and 28 1914, raising £200 from 6,000 attenders. Passenger flights were available and Hucks had on hand two Blériots, one an 80 hp Gnôme machine with which he had won the aerial Derby around London, the other a 50 hp machine stiffened for looping. He first looped at the end of 1913 and intended to fly 1,000 loops in 12 months. Upon arrival at Birmingham on February 14 1914, he had completed 148 loops and 170 on reaching Oxford where another 27 were added to his score during the three-day show. He completed six successive loops at Birmingham and managed 11 in one flight from Oxford. Thrown in for good measure were 11 second double loops. On May 28 1914 Lord Carbery demonstrated his 80 hp Morane Saulnier, including steep banks, loops and a flight for Latham's first passenger, Mr C. Gull.

An unusual event for a land-locked region came in mid-May 1914 when Mr Raynham demonstrated 'water planing' on Edgbaston Reservoir, using an Avro floatplane. On June 20 1914 Birmingham's residents witnessed the final 'pioneer' air races, and Graham White offered joy-rides in his three-seater Farman. The action-packed race between London and Manchester and back attracted, finally, eight competitors in Moranes, Farmans, a Blériot and Harry Hawker in a Sopwith biplane. All raced for the *Daily Mail* Gold Trophy and £400 from the Anglo-American Oil Company. Brock, taking four hours 42 minutes, won easily in his 80 hp Gnôme Morane Monoplane. Alcock's Farman was the only other aircraft to finish.

Little time was left to enjoy flying for fun. Those grand days ended abruptly. A fête had been arranged for Blenheim Palace on August 3 1914, and Marcus Martin arrived to demonstrate his flying skill. Alas, it was not to be for, that morning, the Home Secretary banned all civilian flying. Martin stood in his machine proclaiming that he 'must not run the risk of damaging his machine on aerobatic frivolities while the grimmer business of engaging the Hun for the first time in aerial combat threatened', a sentiment typical of its time. Emphasis in the Midlands centred upon weapons production, recruitment and training for which Castle Bromwich found itself brought into RFC hands in 1914. It attracted many aircraft types. In Bedfordshire, Short Brothers, encouraged by the Government, began constructing an airship works in 1915. At Coley Park, Reading, a technical training school opened in 1916. The main station was at Halton Park, Wendover, opened in 1917 soon after ground was acquired at Henlow for similar use. Near Letchworth another camp concentrated on technical training.

By the Great North Road and near Stamford an airfield was built in 1916 on ground where Wittering stands. That year saw the authorities occupy Port Meadow and form No 40 FTE RS on August 21 1916. It was replaced by 17 TS whose place was taken by 1 TS in October 1917. Rendcombe, Gloucestershire, opened in August 1916.

The building of Bicester and Upper Heyford commenced in 1917, when Stamford was used for training. Promising pilots were creamed off for action in France after a few hours' flying, losses causing great imbalance throughout the RFC. Of the RFC's establishment of 1,041 aircraft, only 763 were on strength in March 1917.

Flying was also undertaken near Cirencester, where Avro 504s of 33 TS resided. There, on January 14 1918, No 8 TS formed from its predecessor. In December 1917, No 34 TS moved to Oxford from Castle Bromwich and, in August 1918, was renamed 44 TS. On April 1 1918, No 71 TS took up residence at Port Meadow, becoming part of the newcomer. At Castle Bromwich, on April 1 1918, an Aircraft Acceptance Park opened to conduct flight tests of production SE 5s and HP 0/400s. Some of the latter were built at the Birmingham and Midland Carriage Works in Middlemore Road, Handsworth.

April 1918 also saw flying at Witney, home of Nos 7 and 8 TSs, which amalgamated to form 33 TDS in August 1918. Witney, used by de Havilland for repair work in World War 2, retains aeronautical associations and in World War 1 was used for fighter combat training. One of its most colourful characters was Herbert Thomas. On one occasion he 'borrowed' a DH 6, set it down in a field near Cheltenham, purloined a bicycle and set off to visit a lady friend. Unfortunately he forgot where he had left the aircraft, and locating it was no mean problem. Eventually he retrieved it—and had then only to explain the event to commanding officer. Years passed and it seems his yearning for Cheltenham never waned. When World War 2 broke out he returned to the land of his love, joined the Air Transport Auxiliary and, doubtless to his disbelief, sometimes again flew from Witney. As a World War 1 airfield it had closed early in 1919.

The Midland contribution to victory, apart from its productive capacity and the many soldiers who took to battle from there, lay in its value as a training ground. Such activity was repeated after an all too brief interval.

Uneasy interlude

Rapid reduction of Britain's home-based forces followed the war as efforts were made to establish overseas trade. International disputes would be settled by the League of Nations.

The government soon quarrelled with Short Brothers, taking away Cardington's factory in April 1919. Military recession replaced activity in the Midlands. Stamford was placed on Care and Maintenance, Bicester closed but Henlow's depot survived to support the Empire guardians. Castle Bromwich, acquired by the Air Board in August 1919, would be the chief Midland air route station. September 29 1919 saw its use as a civil airport when the British Aerial Transport Company instituted a London–Birmingham passenger service. Austin Motors at Longbridge devoted attention to aircraft manufacture and worked on a small single-seater machine for postal, colonial and agricultural purposes. The company laid out a flying ground to include a motor track which was some 1,500 yds in diameter. From this field, years later, Austin-built Fairey Battles and Hurricane IIs were flight tested.

Defence planning ensured that the RAF policed the Empire and held reserves in Britain. By 1921 RAF strength was insufficient for even limited Army and naval support, let alone independent operations. Barely a squadron was available for home defence. Trouble could only come in the Far East—unless friction arose between Britain and France. Strategic bomber forces disbanded quickly at the end of World War 1, although the Air Staff remained convinced that the RAF should have an independent role, but eventually agreed to it providing merely air defence.

September 1922 brought to Castle Bromwich a taste of pre-war days when it was a stopping place for the King's Cup Air Race. The following July the race was repeated, 14 competitors taking part in an 810-mile race around Britain, staged through Castle Bromwich.

International squabbles were already underway with the French maintaining a larger air force than the British. It was suggested that we should match this. Building aircraft would produce a healthy industry, make commercial sense and aid civil aviation enterprises. Government plans for a metropolitan Air Force of 158 aircraft in 14 bomber and nine fighter squadrons were announced in August 1922, confirming the Air Staff belief that attack was the best form of defence while ignoring France's overwhelming strength of 600 bombers and fighters. More rapid expansion was impossible—until the French increased their strength. On June 20 1923 the Cabinet agreed to a 52 Squadron Air Force in

Britain, armed with 394 bombers and 204 fighters, all to be serving by 1929. A 1923 plan was for a 15-mile wide fighting zone, starting at Duxford, edging easterly around London then westwards to Salisbury, protecting London and the Midlands from French attack.

In 1924 the Fighting Area belt was extended, from Peterborough to Weston-Super-Mare to shelter the bomber force. New aerodromes would be built, particularly on WD property north of Oxford. Five or six new bomber stations would accommodate 14 squadrons, and a special reserve would form at Castle Bromwich. The Air Ministry offered to assist the establishment there of a light aeroplane club with a subsidy of £3,000, allowing the Midland Aero Club to equip with two DH Cirrus Moths. Club flying began from Castle Bromwich in September 1925.

At Henlow the first Officers' Engineering Course began in July 1924 and a Parachute Test Section was established in September 1925. World War 1 Stamford was renamed Wittering and rebuilt to accommodate the Central Flying School moved from Upavon now earmarked for bombers. Reconstruction of Bicester began in 1925 and, in July, Nos 25 and 43 (Fighter Squadrons re-formed at HAD Henlow.

By 1926 relations with France were improving. To show goodwill—and increase economy—rebuilding of the RAF underwent a customary slow down. The 52-squadron plan would now be completed in 1936. The opening of Wittering came in 1926, CFS moving there in August. Wessex Bombing Area, formed on April 12 1926, became part of ADGB on June 1 1926 and, in October, No 605 Squadron formed at Castle Bromwich as part of the new air reserve. For reasons of economy, RAF aircrew training would be undertaken by operational squadrons. A new Upper Heyford for night bombers opened on October 12 1927, the re-opening of Bicester following in January 1928.

February 1928 brought first talk of a Birmingham municipal airport, resulting in a long drawn-out affair leading to Elmdon Airport. No doubt the 1928 King's Cup race also excited Birmingham's interest in flying for it took place over a 1,000-mile course attracting 38 competitors.

At Upper Heyford in April 1931 40 Squadron was first to receive the Fairey Gordon day bomber based upon the Fairey IIIf. Before 1931 ended, Nos 18 and 57 Squadrons at Upper Heyford were flying Hawker Harts. Abingdon, the third new bomber station, opened on September 1 1932 and almost immediately 40 Squadron moved in.

Yet another famous bomber also entered service at this time, the Handley Page Heyford. In November 1933 it joined the RAF at 'Heyford', a few weeks after the Wessex Bombing Area had split, hiving off Abingdon, Bicester and Upper Heyford to the Central Area.

To cope with more home-based aircraft a new Aircraft Servicing Unit was formed at Cardington which, because of the *R-101* disaster, was deprived of airships. During June 1934, XV Squadron reformed at Abingdon with Harts as the government received intelligence reports confirming Germany as likely to have 576 front line aircraft in service by October 1935. This brought a new plan for the RAF—embracing in Britain 43 bomber, four general reconnaissance, four flying boat and five Army co-operation squadrons using 960 home-based aircraft.

Adoption of new, advanced machines demanded high quality manpower on a hitherto unimagined scale. Crew training by operational squadrons, detrimental to front line efficiency, was ordered to be scaled down in 1935. New style training would mostly take place in central England.

The 1914–18 war's need for thorough flying training was ever remembered. Never again would pilots enter action with 20 hours' flying to their credit. Nor would the best be creamed off to the demoralisation of others, then lost in battle. By the 1930s, pilots underwent flying training at one school where, in about a year, they experienced two five-month periods of flying, interrupted by summer leave. Initial training was on Avros—504Ns and later Tutors—then in the advanced period they flew Bristol F2Bs, DH9As, Siskins and, from late 1935, Hart variants. There was no provision for operational flying practice and a memorandum of February 1935 pointed out that pilots needed to spend much of their second year with a squadron to complete flying training and learn operational techniques. That was unsatisfactory so, later in the year, Air Commodore Arthur Tedder was appointed to re-organise flying training, making full use of all available civilian resources. Operational squadrons would have to release staff to become instructors. Elementary flying schools would be established similar to their civilian counterparts. Known as Elementary & Reserve Flying Training Schools, they would train Volunteer Reserve pilots and Regulars.

Evidence of new training plans appeared when CFS returned to Upavon in August 1935. Although earmarked for fighters, Wittering in October 1935 housed a new No 11 Service Flying Training School. Fighter aircraft were few, their control network far from ready. Some light bomber crews in the Oxford area trained at a new armament school at Catfoss.

In June 1935 No 6 E&RFTS opened at Sywell. This and other schools faced the mighty task of training 10,000 pilots needed during the first half year of any conflict. This caused the SFTS pilot course to be cut from nine to six months, thus increasing annual output from 75 to 140 pupils. A new War Plan embraced course lengths as follows: E&RFTS—100 pupil population, eight-week course including 50 flying hours, output 40 pupils per month; Advanced Flying Training School—population 80 pupils for an eight-week course including 50 flying hours, output 37 pupils per month: operational flight—population 74 pupils for an eight-week course including 40 flying hours, output 35 pupils per month.

Plans to fly balloon barrages forcing enemy raiders higher came in 1935. Choice of their development site was made—Cardington's giant hangars and large landing ground would be ideal. A Balloon Training Unit opened in January 1937, and a force of men, and later women, balloon handlers was built up.

Providing aircraft for operational squadrons was difficult enough. Finding enough for training schools seemed impossible, and forced an order for North American Harvards. As more advanced combat aircraft came along, the older ones were released (if suitable) for use at training schools. Custom-built trainers, apart from Tiger Moths, would come later.

In mid-January two squadrons of Virginia night bombers moved into Upper Heyford, pending their joining the new No 3 (Bomber) Group, at Driffield, in September 1936. They shared Oxfordshire's airspace with Overstrands, between October 1935 and July 1936, as they become the main equipment of 101 Squadron at Bicester, a station taken over by 3 Group in April 1936. On May 1 1936 No 1 (Bomber) Group formed and took control of Abingdon and Upper

Heyford. Its role was that of an advanced striking force leaving 3 Group to handle longer range operations. By now Nos XV, 40 and 98 Squadrons at Abingdon, and Nos 57 and 218 Squadrons at Upper Heyford, all had Hawker Hind biplane light bombers. Their strength increased on August 17 1936 when Bicester passed to 1 Group.

Such moves were unpublicised. Obvious though were changes overtaking the countryside of the Midlands and Cotswolds. At South Cerney, airfield construction commenced in 1936. It did so too at Harwell, at Little Rissington in the heart of the Cotswolds, at Cranfield, at Brize Norton and soon at Benson. At each quiet and peaceful village, the task of levelling large tracts and the erection of gracious living and office accommodation started. Large mess facilities were needed, also huge underground fuel stores, tall water towers and neatly disguised chimneys. Unlike today's conglomerate of pseudo-planners, those of the 1930s were motivated by ideas of fine lines and style, producing aerodrome buildings bearing Georgian gracefulness. Every attempt was made to ensure that these large constructions did as little damage to the countryside as possible. Impossible to hide were the giant steel and brick 'C' Type hangars which dominated many a skyline. Some became such a familiar sight that, when recently moved, many who have known them all their lives express regret at their parting! Hangar sides were originally left in their brick finish and later white-washed. It is currently possible to have an idea of their appearance from Benson's hangars. With war imminent and few trees camouflaging the hangars, some were painted and others covered in netting. Sizes and layouts of these new Midland sites suited them for mixed roles. In the main they were used for training purposes, three as bomber stations.

A 1937 pilot's training course laid down 29 hours' dual and 26 hours' solo at E&RFTS, followed by 22 hours' dual and 27 hours' solo at SFTS. Reserve Command, brought into being on February 1 1937, controlled the rapidly increasing number of E&RFTSs. By the end of that year 13 such schools were busy and another seven were training VR pilots only.

During 1937 a spate of new RAF stations opened—Harwell in March, Cranfield in June and South Cerney in August. Into reality, too, came an idea to alter aviation for, on April 12 1937, Frank Whittle's gas turbine engine first ran, at a test facility at Rugby. Development of jet aircraft was to be very much a wartime Midland sight and sound.

Many new squadrons equipped themselves with Hart variants while awaiting something more modern. The first came in May 1937 when Bristol Blenheims arrived at Bicester for 90 Squadron. Autumn 1937 brought the Fairey Battles, to be so terribly mauled in France during 1940. Many Battles were built at a new Austin factory at Cofton Hackett, the first machine flying in July 1938.

February 1938 witnessed Cranfield's squadrons getting Blenheims, and the first Oxfords arriving at 2 SFTS Brize Norton. In March and April 57 Squadron at Upper Heyford received its Blenheims and on April 11 1938 the first fighter station in the area, Wittering, came into use. Its task within 12 Group was to guard the approach to the industrial area around Birmingham. At first it relied upon Demon two-seater fighters of 23 Squadron and Gloster Gauntlets. At 3 SFTS South Cerney, Oxfords arrived, just before Blenheims for 34 Squadron touched down at Cranfield.

Increasingly, it was clear that the key to a good, strong Air Force lay in an effective training. Rapid technical change, very specialised training and a large output of aircrew were needed. Expansion Scheme 'L' of 1938 called for eight new flying schools. Instead, the shortage of instructors limited the number to four, making a total of 15 SFTSs. By May 1938 the training organisation could in no way meet the demands placed upon it. Only by using operational squadrons could the situation improve. So, once more, operational squadrons assisted flying training. Aircrew supply problems were such that every suitable, available trainer was being recruited.

Desperate was the need for personnel to maintain aircraft and engines—not to mention a host of other tasks necessary at every RAF station. On July 1 1938, 13,327 men were in training for technical duties, many at Halton and Henlow. By January that total was 71,300! Many new aircraft needed equipment and modifications. At Brize Norton and Little Rissington, maintenance units were formed for these purposes.

Operational training and type conversion had to be left to squadrons aided by live weapon training at summer camps. By October 1938 it was plain that more basic training was essential if pilots were to cope with modern aircraft. Volunteer Reserve aircrew would now spend brief spells at operational squadrons. The main alteration, to improve operational training, was decided upon on January 3 1939. Special centres would form known as Group Pools. They would in peacetime, hopefully, number ten—six bomber, three fighter and one coastal. In wartime each Group Pool would train SFTS output to operational standards before crews proceeded to squadrons. Shortages, though, allowed only two Pools to form before the war—and for fighter squadrons. Bomber training was instead carried out by nine of the 15 non-mobilisation squadrons. Their Anson trainers allowed operational training for regulars and for VR pilots acquiring the taste of a reasonably modern aircraft far in advance of their Hart variants.

The closing of peace came against the backdrop of desperate attempts to train as many as possible for war. It came to the Midlands against the sound of Oxfords and Harvards—and complaints about the noise of the latter. By the last evening of peace many operational squadrons were already in France. For them war had already come.

To battle once more

Spitfires by the thousand, aircrew by the ten-thousand, a cradle for the Airborne Forces; Coventry and the *Moonlight Sonata* and a night sky trimmed with vapour trails; Wellington, Oxford, the first jets—all key, unforgettable images of central England at war. There were balloons, the anti-aircraft guns and a host of different aircraft types to be seen. What I always found missing was the passage of mighty formations heading for battle within the hour, although on the eastern fringe the US VIIIth Air Force presented such a sight.

Although the war's commencement was hard to believe, prayer throughout that fateful Polish Friday was for Hitler to withdraw from Poland. Without such response full mobilisation was ordered. At the Fairey Battle bases of 1 Group, full war state came into being and on September 2 1939, aided by an exotic set of large civil air transports, the 'sailplane bombers' crossed to France at midday, landing at primitive airfields far removed from the luxury and permanence of Oxford's pre-war RAF stations. By instant metamorphosis, 1 Group became the Advanced Air Striking Force.

Vacated bomber bases were immediately used for second-line training squadrons. Whitleys came to Abingdon, Battles to Benson, Blenheims to Bicester, Hampdens to 'Heyford and 'Wimpeys' to Harwell, the latter type eventually becoming the most common bombers in the area, although for four years Whitleys frequented those skies. Operational bomber squadrons, hastened to central England as soon as hostilities commenced, scattering from their East Anglian bases lest the Luftwaffe attack them. Elmdon Airport housed 99's Wellingtons; South Cerney succoured 37 Squadron. That mere field surviving beyond most, Weston-on-the Green, provided sancutary for Blenheims of 90 Squadron. Squadrons could not operate from these stations, and long hauls back to base ceased after a fortnight, leaving the Midlands to house training and storage centres. At 8 MU, Little Rissington, on the day war broke out, 268 aircraft were in storage.

Britain held 14 Service Flying Training Schools, naval pilots training at No 7 Peterborough. Some 12 SFTSs could provide 400 pilots monthly against 1,100 needed to replace wastage and allow no wartime expansion. Little Rissington and South Cerney became crammed with Oxfords affording multi-engine experience to pilots. Brize Norton's Harvard Is gave fighter pilots a taste for the chase. Fringe-based Elementary Flying Training Schools offered initial flying courses, producing many famous fliers, and they catered for escaped Allies. At Cowley's Morris Motors, No 1 Civilian Repair Unit formed on September 11

1939, to repair aircraft and fly them from its test field.

Still a problem of increasing concern was operational training which could no longer be undertaken by operational squadrons. Bomber Command recommended, on September 5, that No 6 (Bomber) Group become responsible for all operational training, controlling a dozen second-line squadrons and that No 1 Group Pools at Abingdon and Cranfield support Field Force France where immediate losses were likely. Benson replaced Abingdon when 4 Group Whitley Pool formed. A 2 Group Pool functioned at Bicester, 3 Group Wellington Pool at Harwell and 5 Group Hampden Pool at Upper Heyford.

Normal intake was 11 pilots for each six-week course, 15 pilots at the Blenheim Pool. Pilots for heavier bombers flew 55-hour courses including 22 hours at night; the others 60 hours, 18 at night. Group Pools consisted of an Anson Flight for navigation and radio operator training, a Flight of operational-type aircraft for flying instruction and a Flight for operational training. Armament training took place at an Armament Training Camp where trainees formed crews from early summer 1940.

Pools soon needed additional flying grounds due to increasing circuit congestion. Sites chosen before the war for development as landing grounds were made fit for limited flying, and used for 'circuits and bumps' with a handful of ground personnel supervising during daylight hours. As winter deepened, intense flying turned aerodrome grass surfaces into quagmires, causing the laying of hard perimeter tracks. Contractors' machinery soon congested them, slowing flying as aircraft awaited a take-off turn. Dispersal of aircraft at training stations was also a problem. Weapons training needed to be undertaken, needing many ranges. Much use was made of Otmoor.

Headquarters Bomber Command listed the layout and functions of 6 Group in mid-October 1939. Maintenance of 34 operational squadrons needed 290 pilots, 194 observers and 324 air gunners per month. Training those heavy bomber pilots was a problem. Output of SFTSs was 1,045 pilots in six months, Group Pool capacity over the same period only 352. To meet the calculated wastage of 17 heavy bomber squadrons (initial equipment 272 aircraft) the number of IE aircraft needed at heavy bomber Group Pools must be 356, allowing 45 hours flying for each Pool pupil.

By December 1939 pupils were showing deficiencies in flying practice. Conflicting requirements were for increased front line strength and maintenance of operational strength, while the ratio would be one advanced trainer matching an operational machine. Pools would be more economically organised and, with effect from April 8 1940, be known as Operational Training Units. Their effectiveness would be examined one week later.

Fortunate for training was the calm of the air war. Remaining Reserve Command took over existing Initial Training Wings, 54 Group controlling four central ITWs formed or forming on November 19 1939. Elementary Training Flying Training Schools in the Midlands were under 50 Group, most of the SFTSs came under 23 Group. No 26 Group formed at Iver on March 27, controlling radio counter measure development.

Airfield surfaces were of increasing concern, as was lack of relief landing grounds. So great was aircraft and spares shortage that there was, in December, an incredible proposal to order aircraft from Italy for training radio operators and air gunners!

Cardington was receiving men and women for training as balloon handlers.

To Henlow went those to keep the aircraft flying, to Cardington those to fly them—if they satisfied medical and test boards. Brize Norton's MU despatched, in January, Gladiators which courageous Finns used against Stalin's vandals. Winter's icy grip had acclimatised those biplanes, leaving many an airman shivering at Midland airfields where runways were still of grass. Come springtime they were merely mud. The buildings of satellite landing grounds and small dispersal areas, where aircraft could be safely accumulated, advanced.

March 1940 estimates were that over the next two years 2,390 aircrew and 12,000 ground crew men would be needed. Between March 1940 and 1941, 351,000 personnel joined the RAF, in addition to WAAFs, many at Cardington. This prodigious expansion required large numbers of machines for operational training. Between April 1939 and March 1940 the number, nearly all around Oxford, increased from 450 to 1,250 aircraft. Training absorbed about 40 per cent of aircraft output.

Five OTUs formed near Oxford in April 1940. No 14 SFTS moved to Cranfield when Lossiemouth joined Bomber Command.

Clearly, with the German occupation of France complete, the enemy would soon attack training centres, proven on June 27 when seven bombs just missed South Cerney's flare path. Relief landing grounds and satellites were just about ready, Chipping Norton, for instance, opening on June 12 for 15 SFTS. Night flying at grass airfields for intermediate and advanced training squadrons was aided by floodlights and white Glim Lights, with gooseneck and money flares used in misty conditions. A main Chance floodlight lit the runway, red Glim lamps marked obstructions, an illuminated 'T' the wind indicator, yellow Glim lights the extremities of the safe landing run and the obstruction lights were red. Taxi-ing posts lit the direction of the flare path. Training airfields thus presented easy-to-see night targets whose lights could not be immediately extinguished. Schools had, by the end of June 1940, gathered enough complete lighting sets to use at RLGs which included Akeman Street, Bibury, Kidlington, Sibson and Windrush and soon Northleach and Witney. Aircraft could now be widely dispersed.

Another answer to attack was completed in June 1940, at Castle Bromwich—its first Spitfire. A further answer lay within the OTUs. From early June they prepared for Operation *Banquet*, repelling an attempted invasion.

No 7 (Bomber) Group controlling 16 OTU Upper Heyford and No 6 Group controlling 10, 12 and 15 OTUs issued the second phase of attack orders on August 8, thereby introducing OTUs to the art of *Nickelling*, the dropping of propaganda leaflets over occupied France. That followed Air Council orders of July 28, that operational requirements must take precedence over training.

Everywhere there was evidence of war. Road blocks were plentiful and pillboxes placed at unlikely spots. Soldiers abounded, preparing to face the invasion, but bombing in the Midlands remained sparse. Bombs aimed at Little Rissington fell three miles wide, but enemy activity forced 3 EFTS out of Hamble to incomplete Watchfield. New airfields were being built at Polebrook, Wellesbourne, Honeybourne and elsewhere, their landing grounds liberally cluttered by anti-invasion contraptions. They differed considerably from mid-1930s Expansion Period aerodromes. Usually they had only one main hangar (less to suffer bomb damage) in keeping with aircraft dispersal plans. That maintenance hangar was of the metal dome 'J' Type. Stark brick buildings lacked grace and inventiveness, not to mention permanence, and consorted with prefabricated concrete buildings with asbestos roofing. High-level Braithwaite sectional water towers balanced upon scaffolding. Nissen huts, picket posts and wood and metal Laing huts were added all widely dispersed. All airfields would have electrically lit hard-surfaced runways for heavy aircraft in poor weather, and hard standings.

August's increasing threat of air attack and invasion caused Midland training organisations to work at a frantic pace. At 6 SFTS alone, 5,435.05 a day flying hours and 287.10 hours at night were recorded, out of 23 Group's total of 43,932.90 hours. There were 90 accidents, but only seven concerned Oxfords of 6 SFTS. Flying hours in 23 Group during June had totalled 32,928 hours by day and 2,083 at night, and there had been 49 accidents. Over half came during landing, when a trainee was most vulnerable to air attack. To prevent this, SFTSs were to move to places of safety. August 1940 brought the decision to place these and other schools in Africa and the Dominions, although not until December 1940 did 7 SFTS leave Peterborough.

Sufficient faith in victory remained for Training Command to plan for the oncoming winter. With over 100 aircraft at any one station, and flying ever increasing, grass surfaces would become unusable. Runways were an answer, laying them a major task and labour was short. When lit they invited enemy attack and could cause major flying control problems. Channelling aircraft into one stream also reduced the number of possible landings, seemed likely to increase accident rates and would certainly increase wear on tyres, brakes and engines as aircraft taxied far and waited long for a take-off slot. Whilst runways reduced muddy surface conditions they had little else to commend them at training stations. Instead the Air Officer Commanding-in-Chief, Flying Training Command, obtained authorisation for RLGs to have a narrow encircling perimeter track which became a usual feature, useful in winter. Aircraft at EFTSs continued to operate from soft ground, bringing alarming control situations when up to 30 Tiger Moths could be in one circuit.

The enemy's bombing campaign considerably increased. August 9 may be seen as a milestone in the war for, upon that night, the Luftwaffe made its first major deep penetration into Britain, bombing Birmingham, Lichfield and Sutton Coldfield. Weston-on-the-Green received its first attack, 11 HEs falling in a line from Chesterton to the airfield, a further five on the landing ground causing little damage. Presumably its lights attracted misplaced attention.

On August 13 the Spitfire factory at Castle Bromwich was bombed, a 'Purple' warning being received at 22:54. Ten minutes later at least five bombers were running in from the south, so the sirens wailed at 23:18. Searchlights and AA guns went into action as 19 × 50 kg bombs were dropped on to the 60-acre factory site. Some fell on roads, others on 'F' and 'Q' Blocks, and six on 'D' Block damaged machinery. At 00:02 the 'All Clear' sounded, yet bombs were still dropping, so a second warning was sounded a few moments later. Eight workers, in all were killed, 41 were seriously injured and over 100 were minor casualties.

The attack was not particularly successful, whereas that directed against airfields on the late afternoon of August 16 was a resounding success. Already the Luftwaffe had operated over Kent and the Thames Estuary, then mounted a series of attacks on targets in Sussex and Hampshire. Late in the afternoon four groups of raiders crossed into Britain between Harwich and the Isle of Wight in considerable strength. It was cloudy, allowing enemy aircraft to penetrate deeply. In the process the forces became scattered. By intent or chance a few bombers reached Oxfordshire. At 17:45 three of them dived upon Stanton Harcourt where a Wimpey labour force was constructing a runway. Thirty small bombs fell, causing little damage but the Ju 88s strafed the airfield, killing five civilians and injuring seven, four of whom later died. No warning had been given here or at Harwell where, ten minutes later, a far more effective attack by a single raider destroyed three Wellingtons and two petrol bowsers. Two airmen were killed and five injured.

Almost simultaneously another two Ju 88s delivered a half minute attack on Brize Norton. It turned out to be the most spectacular on any British airfield during the war. Details vary within every account, but around 30 small HE bombs and a few incendiaries were dropped. They were sufficient to destroy Nos 1 and 3 'C' Type hangars and severely damage the roof of a barrack block and the Institute Building. One civilian was killed and three were injured, along with 13 RAF men. Brize Norton was crammed with aircraft at 6 MU in addition to those of 2 and 15 SFTS. Initially a staggering 38 aircraft were considered destroyed before final write-offs boosted the total to 46. There was widespread blast damage and not until darkness fell were all fires out. Nevertheless, on the following day, 6 MU—deprived of its Tutor *K3400*—despatched two Battles, three Defiants and ten Spitfire 1s.

Harwell was unsuccessfully attacked at 00:28 on August 17 but a Ju 88, on August 19, caused destruction of three Wellingtons. Such sudden ravages triggered instructions to all training stations to disperse aircraft widely, and switch night flying to satellite or relief landing grounds where possible. This allowed costly, valuable prewar stations to remain in darkness. At least four AA guns would now protect each secondary site, such need was illustrated when Windrush RLG was bombed late on August 18. Eye witnesses claimed that an Anson trainer rammed the Heinkel to bring it down. Another German aircraft crashed at Northleach, suggesting that other intruders were around.

Satellites were intended for initial operational day and night training and aircraft dispersal. Detachments of personnel could be accommodated at them, the minimum comprising two officers, two SNCOs, two NCOs and 20 men. An NCO and three men would control beacon lighting, four more the flare path. Another 34 men would feed and guard the others. Hard standing for seven vehicles was to be provided, sleeping accommodation for two officers, an ante-room and mess room for 12 officers, a 40 ft by 18 ft crew rest hut, two 18 ft by 10 ft huts for 50 men, a 40 ft by 18 ft messing hut, an 18 ft by 10 ft ablution hut and another for the guard. Small rooms would contain the armoury, night flying equipment and batteries. This establishment was the norm for bomber satellites, few of which at this time met even these requirements.

Despite the enemy activity, OTUs managed creditable performances in August, 12 OTU leading with 3,357 flying hours and 10 OTU's more complex aircraft logging 2,930 hours. All centrally based OTUs had around 17 Ansons, supplemented by 61 Whitleys at 10 OTU, 66 Battles at 12 OTU and 50 Wellingtons at 15 OTU.

The bottleneck in flying training was at night, so less expensive satellites would have to play a bigger part. Flying would continue—even during raid alerts, unless the Station Commander ordered otherwise. The normal establishment at satellites was increased to ten officers and 200 men. From the night of September 9/10, flare paths at Brackley and Stanton Harcourt would remain open, affording emergency landing facilities, irrespective of enemy activity.

Meanwhile, operational flying over the Midlands had dramatically increased. A few OTU leaflet-dropping sorties had been despatched in August but these units, not geared up for offensive activities, increasingly trained for Operation *Banquet*.

The Luftwaffe mounted fierce raids upon industrial targets in the last days of August 1940. Birmingham's third raid came on August 16 when about 60 HE bombs were distributed among Castle Bromwich, Small Heath, Erdington and the Singer Motors factory. Some 500–600 incendiaries and 22 HE bombs, aimed towards the Spitfire works on August 17/18, fell in fields at Sutton Coldfield. Early on August 24, bombs fell close to the Nuffield factory. Incendiary droppers led the operation, followed by a second wave, one of whose 50 kg bombs burst by the railway bridge on Chester Road, Castle Bromwich, causing two gaping holes. Some 22 HE bombs and a load of incendiaries rained down on to fields by Penns Lane, residential property suffering in Yardley.

August 26 brought the first Coventry raid. It was a tempting target because of its important industrial objectives. Then it was Birmingham's turn again. This time one incident dramatically scarred the old city centre. A 250 kg oil bomb pierced the roof of the 100 year-old City Market Hall, struck the floor, making a 4-ft hole, then burst in the basement designated as a shelter for 600 people but, luckily, not in use. Constructed of timber, old and dry, the famous landmark was consumed by an intense blaze which, although they arrived in three minutes, firemen were unable to quell.

Another Birmingham raid followed on August 27/28. The Spitfire factory was a target for bombs, one severing a water main to the works. The enemy aimed for the BSA factory, around which 46 bombs fell. Those intended for the Spitfire works mostly burst in Gravelly Hill which, like Sutton Coldfield and the Pype Hayes area, bore the brunt of almost every attack on the factory, damaged only once during 77 raids directed against the Birmingham area. A likely explanation for inaccurate raids is that parachute flares persistently drifted in strong southerly winds. It was easy, then, to accuse the enemy of indiscriminate bombing.

Friday August 30, was the toughest yet in the Battle of Britain. A third series of attacks developed in the late afternoon, the targets included factories at Oxford and Luton. The Oxford raid was forced to retire over Surrey, but about 20 He 111s had crossed the Essex coast. Although Hurricanes of 1, 242 and 501 Squadrons engaged them and escorting Bf 110s, the bombers of II/KG 1 penetrated to Luton after losing one of their number and destroying a Hurricane of 501 Squadron. Concentrated bombing commenced at 16:40 and was over within five minutes, during which 207 HE bombs were aimed at the Vauxhall Motors factory. Casualties were high because no siren had wailed. Indeed, the 'Red' warning was received at Luton just as the last bombs were bursting. One particularly terrifying aspect was the destruction of a main staircase within the factory, and eight nearby houses suffered damage. Bombs fell over a wide area, 23 at Caddington, 20 in Kenswick and 18 in Whipsnade Zoo. Horrific scenes followed, the casualty count totalling 59 killed and 141 injured.

Airfield building in the Midlands was well advanced. Moreton was nearing completion when it was discovered that its runways would be only 1,000 yds long. New bomber stations were to include a main NE/SW 1,400-yd runway with two others of 1,100 yds. Late 1940 brought a decision that the main runway must never be less than 1,400 yds, preferably 1,600 yds long. Others would be 1,100 yds long and 50 yds wide. Ground to either side of runways must be firm to a distance of 75 yds of electrically lit runways. At airfields without hard surface runways, the policy was for three or four mowed grass strips, 40 yds wide. In general no object in the vicinity of runway approaches was to protrude above a slope of 1:15 to the runway threshold. Bomber Command agreed, in February 1941, to accept 1,400-yd runways as the norm.

Among individual bombing sorties flown on September 26 1940, one was directed against Cranfield where bombs fell close at midday. Henlow was later attacked, eight bombs exploding on the camp, damaging two hangars. That same day a Ju 88 attacked the Standard Motors works in Coventry as the work shift was changing. One bomb burst in a machine shop, injuring 32 people. A particularly memorable event occurred at Luton, the aerial explosion of a parachute mine was quickly followed by another which detonated on a concrete road leaving a 40 ft by 10 ft deep crater and damaging 35 houses, killing eight civilians, seriously wounding five and injuring another 42. On September 25, three nights later, two more mines fell at Luton, the first exploding 600 ft from the Percival factory, yet causing very limited damage. The other penetrated the factory roof before wedging itself vertically in a lavatory ceiling, its parachute having been caught in the roof of the building. Doubtless there was ribald comment, but one may be sure that great praise was given to the bomb disposal team who defused the mine the following morning.

Another mine exploded on September 24 in a field near Cranfield and damaged houses in the High Street. By pure chance yet another parachute mine was discovered in Holcot Wood—but not until October 13 and almost certainly dropped on the previously mentioned occasion. It, too, was disposed of by naval mine experts.

Few German aircraft came down in central England. The most interesting was probably a Dornier Do 215B brought down by Hurricanes soon after midday on October 24 1940, a few yards from the *Crown* public house by the Great North Road at Wyboston, Eaton Socon. Parts of the burning engines fell on to a thatched roof at Bolnhurst Farm causing a fire. The one survivor was taken to the public house. Wreckage investigation revealed the aircraft's identity as *L2+KS* of LG2. Built at Friedrichshafen, it carried the works number *0060*. All that I was able to make out the following day was a fairly complete tail unit—a common feature of wrecked Dorniers—and evidence of yellow spinners.

The next enemy aircraft to crash in central England was a red-spinnered Ju 88 which crashed on Woodways Farm, Blewbury, Berkshire after operating over Oxfordshire on the afternoon of November 13. This, too, was a reconnaissance aircraft of LG 1 which carried the identity *L1+LS*.

Balloon barrages were flown over Birmingham and Coventry, their effectiveness questionable. They probably forced up the bombing height, but most attacks were area raids on fire markers. Late on September 16, a Ju 88 collided with a balloon cable, its bombs exploding as it crashed at Withybrook, north-east of Coventry.

For many, the German night bombing campaign became reality when, even 50 miles from London, one gazed upon its fiery sky. 'Coventry' was different. In my home town, the alert on that fateful evening sounded early. By November 1940 it was commonplace. But by mid-evening on November 16 my father and I viewed incredulously a sky laced with a multitude of contrails frighteningly lit by a brilliant moon. We watched in awe the enemy bombers performing in the *Moonlight Sonata*, heading north-west in a never ending procession, passing at a rate of one or two a minute. By late that night the sky was overcrowded by clouds formed from the vapour trails, as the de-synchronised note of Heinkels, the clatter of Dorniers and the clearer notes of the Ju 88s died away. That gap was momentary for the bombers soon returned on a south-easterly course. It was not long before we realised that a second wave was also approaching. I remember roughly plotting their course, assuming them heading for Birmingham. Breakfast news broadcasts revealed the target and the horror of the night. There was little to hide from the enemy.

Details of the great Coventry raid are well known. By later war standards it was outclassed, but this was the first of its type in Britain and aimed at a city of moderate dimensions, although perhaps a legitimate target—if there can ever be such a thing. Coventry's people, driven beyond any expectation, largely survived to see the enemy fare far worse. Armstrong Whitworth's Whitleys and Lancasters would help to see to that.

On many a cold, moonlit night, contrails abounded as the Luftwaffe headed for the Midlands. On October 24, incendiaries burnt parts of Birmingham's art gallery and town hall, but the really big attacks followed the bombing of Coventry. At 18:50 on November 19 1940 Birmingham's sirens heralded the worst of them all. Some 350 bombers unleashed 403 tons of HE and over 800 incendiary containers over the entire city, yet not one bomb was profitably placed upon the Spitfire factory.

To have experienced a heavy air raid was to acquire an indelible memory. No account of the air activity in a region where heavy raids took place can fail to mention their horrific effect.

British response to enemy activity could only be limited. Only Wittering, and briefly Luton, had fighters available for night defence. The best that could be done was to bomb the enemy, but from the Midlands only a few *Nickelling* sorties by OTUs were flown before their full effect was ordered, on December 29 1940, to be directed entirely towards training. Deep snow and the intense cold of early 1941 much reduced all flying training but, by March, things were improving.

Throughout the war training schemes were adjusted to meet operational needs and availability of trained personnel. In January 1940, for instance, it was considered that before leaving an EFTS a pilot needed more flying practice so the course was extended from eight to ten weeks. At SFTS stage it increased from 16 to 20 weeks, to be followed by a further six at a Group Pool—four in the case of a Fighter Pool. Heavy losses in May 1940 had demanded many replacement front line aircrew, the most able pilots being quickly posted from EFTSs to advanced flying courses. Reduction in course length at bomber OTUs came in August 1940. More emphasis was now upon operational flying, able trainees being sent from EFTS to OTU after only 50 hours' flying.

Immediate invasion danger passed before poor weather caused longer training courses. An alternative would have been to use more aircraft, meaning fewer in operational formations but more trained instructors. By mid-war, training programmes had produced a surplus, the ratio in September 1942 standing at 675 staff per 100 pupils. It had fallen to 420 per 100 by January 1944.

On April 12 1941, with better weather arriving, basic training programmes were again revised. Both SFTSs and OTUs would now have satellite airfields and/or RLGs. Wellingtons at OTUs would have dual controls, and synthetic training was to be introduced for bomb aimers and navigators. Intake at Wellington OTUs would be 45 pilots at each unit every two weeks, along with 40 wireless operator/air gunners, and 20 each of air gunners and observers.

An ever enlarging feature was the large number of operational aircraft types held within OTUs which were desperately needed by front line squadrons. Each OTU's holding of about 50 Wellingtons, Whitleys or Hampdens meant a reduced level of operations and, not surprisingly, there were demands that OTUs carry out operational duties. Accordingly, on February 7/8 1941, limited operational flying was resumed when two 6 Group Wellingtons scattered leaflets over Paris, Lille and Brest. On February 11 there was a further incursion into the newly designated 'Advanced Training Area' which included the towns of Amiens, Le Havre, Lille, Rennes and Rouen. This small effort continued from 6 Group stations into April 1941. A decision was then taken to make greater use of satellite stations by preparing each to hold an operational bomber squadron and 600 men. These airfields thus became far removed from their style of but a few months previously, and some became self accounting RAF stations.

With much emphasis upon night flying in Bomber Command, demand was more for competent fliers than for operationally converted crews, bringing a reversion to the 2/3 conversion flying and 1/3 operational programme at OTUs.

More *Nickelling* took place in May, by which time crew output was considerably increasing. On May 24, for example, 10 OTU posted out 40, the highest number of crews in one batch so far. Shorter, light nights made bombing operations more dangerous so 6 Group on June 8 ordered OTUs to make themselves available for leaflet dropping diversions into Unoccupied France. OTUs within the Group flew 42 successful sorties that month, some reaching Vichy.

Another aspect of training in the central area was the provision of pilots and observers for Benson's photo reconnaissance squadrons. In June 1941, pilots for PR Spitfires were trained by a small section of No 3 School of General Reconnaissance then posted to Benson for operational conversion. But when, in July 1941, Benson's first Mosquito arrived, specialised PR training was required. It became the task of 8 OTU to supply carefully chosen and trained men.

On July 9 1942, Bomber Command authorised OTUs to carry, at their discretion, 2 × 250 lb or 2 × 500 lb HE bombs on *Nickel* sorties, to be dropped only after the military nature of any target was certain. During the course of 49 sorties that month, 9,750 lb of bombs were dropped by 6 Group units.

The diminishing availability of bombers for OTUs was aggravated by the ever increasing need to back Middle East squadrons, particularly with Wellingtons. Getting the bombers positioned was difficult. The solution was to have crews trained to operate overseas after delivering Wellingtons there through hostile airspace and long duration flights. This meant increasingly heavier fuel loads so that merely getting airborne seemed problematical. The possibility of all delivery flights setting out from Newmarket Heath, with its long run, was actively pursued, but eventually a high proportion of the Wellingtons set out from Harwell, 26 Wellington 1cs making the journey in February 1941 alone. Soon, special Ferry Training Flights were formed, training a crew to handle the machine they would be delivering, probably from Harwell, Hampstead or Moreton-in-Marsh.

Considerable discussion of runways and their surfaces was undertaken between Bomber Command and RAE during July 1941. Apart from tarmac or concrete, other materials considered included rubber, pulverised wood and tan waste. Novel and attractive notions as they were, it was tarmac and concrete which remained in vogue, although building them was a lengthy, costly business.

Bomber Command's and overseas needs combined by August 1941 to indicate that there would be only enough aircrew available to man 70 per cent of the aircraft within squadrons, and OTUs were pressed to attain maximum output. *Nickel* sorties in August totalled 15 and, on August 6 1941, a Wellington failed to return from a sortie over Holland, its crew becoming POWs. By August 31, 267 *Nickel* sorties had been flown by 6 Group. That loss and diversion of effort from training caused such activities to cease.

Increasingly important was the PR organisation at Benson and Medmenham. Benson passed to Coastal Command control on August 15 1941, its satellite at Mount Farm becoming a second satellilte for busy 15 OTU Harwell. A new station, Chipping Warden, received 12 OTU. Shortly after the unit had vacated Benson one of the major events of the war was enacted from there when, on September 17, the first operational sortie by a Mosquito was flown. Until 1953, Mosquito photographic reconnaissance flights were despatched daily.

In September 1941, 120 Wellingtons were delivered by air to the Middle East, all but six arriving safely from the Midland stations. A complete examination of the state of equipment in 6 Group followed, on October 4. Each OTU had either a total of 54 Wellingtons or 48 Whitleys. Shortage of the latter because of Coastal Command use caused its lower establishment figure. A further 11 Flights were each given 18 Ansons, but there were shortages of these because of their gunnery and navigation training value. On the survey date the strength of 6 Group was as follows:

	Wellington	Whitley	Anson
Total establishment	472	100	190
On strength	360	77	86
Unserviceable	64	24	3

The survey examined the entire OTU position. Already it was apparent that some wartime airfield layouts were unsatisfactory as training stations. Widespread dispersal of bombers was a problem at a busy training station where it was customary to allocate each Flight a dispersal area. Some were badly placed from a taxi-ing point of view, and to reach the active runway often meant taxi-ing up a slope and frequently around a sharp bend so that brake pressures became quickly exhausted. Taxi-ing routes embraced a labyrinth of track, sometimes well over a mile in length. Aircraft dispersal meant spreading maintenance staff, making overall supervision difficult. At any one time about 60 per cent of Wellingtons at an OTU were serviceable and around 70 per cent of the Ansons. Flying commenced between 08:30 and 09:00, ceased for an hour's lunch break then continued until dusk when some aircraft began night flying—made additionally difficult by complicated dispersal layouts at many airfields.

Runway alignment, too, was often far from satisfactory. Westcott's main runway was orientated towards high ground whereas at Wellesbourne two of the three runways were too short to be of much value. The intersection of runways was sometimes too tight. Apart from vulnerability to air attack, it resulted in long perimeter track journeying, or back tracking. Grass surfaces, however, were quite unsuitable for heavy aircraft.

It must be borne in mind that many factors controlled airfield layouts. They included proximity of civilian areas, church spires, suitability and availability of terrain, drainage, sub-soil, balloon barrages, large factories and weather conditions. Changing basic layouts to suit a particular role was virtually impossible, and training units had to make the best of airfields put at their disposal.

In October 1941, 6 Group managed 22 *Nickel* sorties for the loss of two aircraft, before November brought special cause for satisfaction. On October 30 No 1425 Flight formed at Honeybourne, a new station, its role to carry passengers to north Africa and the Middle East for which long range Liberators were to be employed. This was a useful adjunct to the overseas ferry organisation. From this small beginning came transport flying from Lyneham, RAF Transport Command's route structure of the 1940s and the famous 511 Squadron.

A second major event was the formation, on November 1 1941, of the Airborne Forces, from which came the mighty armada which landed huge numbers of troops in France during 1944.

On November 24 1941, 21 OTU Moreton-in-Marsh was told to concentrate upon producing crews for the Middle East, the first flying out on January 1 1942. By then 15 OTU had despatched a total of 150 Wellingtons of which 23 had become en route casualties.

Repeated adjustments were still made to flying hours within training courses—the norm in January 1942 for each pilot was 45 hours at an OTU. A new feature was the allocation of particular bombers for gunnery training, Lysanders doubling as attacking fighters as well as target towers. Shock and strong words accompanied revelations that, between January 1 1941 and December 31 1941, 870 operational aircraft had been written off, or very seriously damaged, within the OTU establishment.

December 1941 brought news that a long overdue change was to overtake the SFTSs. Now that much basic and advanced flying training was undertaken within the Empire Air Training Scheme, all SFTSs in Britain would close, except that at Cranwell and one for Poles. Advanced and much basic training would be undertaken within overseas territories, a plan for 25 schools in the EATS including eight in Canada, five in South Africa and four in Southern Rhodesia. Aircrew would then return to Britain and one of the 12 Advanced Flying Units (Pilots) formed from SFTSs. They would accustom students to flying conditions prevalent over Europe, and particularly all-weather flying, before they proceeded to an OTU. Specialist instructor training was also expanded with the formation of the Flying Instructors' School at Church Lawford.

After 12 weeks' basic training at an Initial Training Wing, a pilot now flew 60 hours at an EFTS before completing 120 flying hours overseas, in a non-hostile environment. On return he flew 60 hours if a bomber pilot (30 if fighter) at an AFU(P), followed by 80 hours at OTU.

OTUs held only twin-engined aircraft so that Bomber Command pilots acquired another 30 hours' flying with four-engined bombers at one of the newly forming Conversion Units. All, for obvious reasons, were sited in forward operational areas. Before reaching an OTU a bomber pilot would have flown 260 hours, soon considered excessive and reduced. Even then the production of crews, when set against losses and force expansion, was insufficient so flying hours were again reduced. Demands upon OTUs were further increased to meet the current operational plan for 156 'heavy' and 86 'medium' RAF bomber squadrons. This meant that 43 'heavy' bomber and 14 'medium' bomber OTUs were needed to supply them. A 'heavy' bomber OTU (student population of 48 crews) had an output of 16 per month in summer and 10½ in winter. Little wonder that 6 Group managed only one *Nickel* sortie in January 1942 and none the following month.

A new commitment in which the Midlands were to play a major role was now consuming precious resources. This was the Airborne Force which Sir Winston Churchill had demanded in the summer of 1940. In terms of aircraft, gliders and men it was regarded with great suspicion. The resources it acquired were withdrawn from elsewhere, and particularly from Bomber Command. Few military gliders existed, and the only paratroop aircraft available were aged Whitleys. In January 1942, No 38 Wing formed to specialise in airborne operations. Supplying glider pilots for the Horsa meant fresh demands, particularly upon the EFTSs after the realisation that Army co-operation squadrons could not, as a sideline, train glider pilots. Specialised Glider Training Schools were needed, the first coming slowly into being at Thame during 1941. The original intent was that a GTS-trained pilot would proceed to a Glider OTU to practice operational techniques. A number of such units opened in Oxfordshire early in 1942.

There was more to mounting airborne assaults than had been foreseen. Also, the decision to use large, heavy gliders, far removed in concept from the large, eight-paratroop Hotspur, led to the glider OTUs closing and the establishment of Brize Norton's Heavy Glider Conversion Unit. There, assembly of Horsas took place within 6 MU, towing being undertaken by Whitley Vs. The HGCU formed in June 1942 with a commitment to train 800 glider pilots by July 1 1943, a task duly completed. Over those 12 months Whitley and Horsa combinations wallowed in profusion within the 'Central Gliding Area' at stated times, strictly controlled.

A fundamental change within OTUs became effective on March 29 1942. Thenceforth a heavy bomber required only one pilot. This immediately alleviated the bottleneck in bomber crew training, especially since the new Lancaster bomber needed only one pilot. Single-man operating had already been in vogue at 16 OTU because it flew Hampdens whose unusual layout prevented another system. Hampdens were outdated and, on April 25 1942, re-equipment at Upper Heyford commenced, after delay caused by the necessity to remove Manchesters from 25 OTU Finningley and replace them with Wellingtons earmarked for 16 OTU. Originally the intention was that the Midland OTUs would fly Manchesters, a scheme encouraged by the introduction of the Lancaster. Manchester problems prevented this, then orders were placed for Hercules-engined Wellingtons which equipped most bomber OTUs to the end of hostilities. It was 1944 before the last Pegasus-engined 1c finally withdrew.

Increased production of heavies released sufficient Whitleys for a new OTU, No 24, where the first course opened on May 5 1942. Progress was slowed by a need for dual controls in the aircraft. Soon there were three large-scale Whitley operators in the area—Nos 10 and 24 OTUs and the HGCU. No 24 OTU's opening followed the removal of 14 SFTS' Oxfords from Lyneham and placing 1425 Flight's Liberators there. It became the RAF's principal transport base.

May's main event became vastly famous. The arrival of Sir Arthur Harris at Bomber Command revitalised the entire bombing offensive. He came at an opportune time, for Lancasters and other four-engined bombers were arriving in increasing numbers, the Blenheims had gone and he had better trained crews. This, though, in no way diminishes his great stature as commander and leader, recognised by all at the time, and during a period of the war which was bringing great losses and soon increasing successes. Harris brought to the 1942 offensive the idea of massive, rapid assault and a skilful use of incendiary loads. To the nation he provided a tremendous tonic, and retribution for what many had endured. The moralising of recent times was totally absent then, and would have never been unacceptable to a nation at war with survival at stake. It would have shown intolerable weakness—which is not to say that, viewed compassionately and distantly, one cannot but grieve for *all* whose deaths and wounds followed.

A turn in the bombing campaign came with untold suddenness, audibly and visually over much of England on May 30 1942 when, from bases over a wide area, more than 1,000 bombers set off for Cologne. Gathering them for one master stroke was no mean achievement. Keeping them and their crews fit, many from OTUs facing battle for the first time and from strange, forward stations, was a tough problem. Harris ordered many aircraft kept in OTUs away from battle to earn their keep, on a grand scale, and it was no mean risk. He planned a raid against Hamburg for May 26 1942, considering that the getaway over the sea was easier. On that and the following night the weather was quite unsuitable. Instead, the Executive Order came on May 30 for an attack on the secondary target, Cologne. Better weather was balanced against deeper penetration.

The basic plan was for 1 Group to field 100 aircraft, 3 Group (leading) to send 160, 4 Group—130 and 5 Group—95, including a few Lancasters. This totalled only 485 aircraft, so that the remainder would have to come from other sources. Of the OTU Groups, No 91 (which was the old 6 Group, so re-named on May 11 1942) would field 200 aircraft and 92 Group (ex-7 Group) another 120. These would be supplemented by 250 Coastal machines and 21 from Flying Training Command—mainly Wellingtons from unlikely sources. This gave a total of 1,100 aircraft with 91 Group providing the biggest section.

Returns following the raid gave Command satisfying reading. No 16 OTU Upper Heyford had despatched 16 Hampdens and, although just receiving them, 14 Wellingtons. No 26 OTU Wing operated 21 Wellingtons of which three were missing and two had crashed. 92 Group had operated 114 aircraft. With the force assembled, and an unexpectedly low loss rate, a second raid was mounted, against Essen. Thick haze obscured the target, and the concentrated bombing which tortured Cologne was unrepeated. Raid reports summarised the OTU effort as: 91 Group despatching 181 Wellingtons with 24 Whitleys and 92 Group despatching 58 Wellingtons and 45 Hampdens.

The contribution by OTUs was reviewed. Using them had raised the morale of participants, breaking the monotony of training routines. Crews posted to bomber squadrons would no longer be 'freshmen'. Morale among instructors was boosted irrespective of their various misgivings, and ground crews enthusiastically greeted such goings on. Set against these points was concern that many aircraft were not modified to operational standards, that pupils had not trained as teams, that there had been stand-bys over four nights and that armament and weapons were inadequate. Each OTU had flown about 500 hours in preparing its aircraft to operate—costly, in time and money. From 92 Group, 11 aircraft had crashed. In normal training, the rate would have been one, maybe two.

These raids could not be sustained (the only repeat being a 1,000 bomber raid on Bremen on June 25/26 1942). All 92 Group OTUs operated from home stations and up to 45 crews of 91 Group were permitted to operate from No 1 Group stations. Nos 13, 16, 24 and 26 OTUs took part.

From 16 OTU, 23 Wellingtons operated and one was lost. Three of 24 OTU's 16 Whitleys failed to return and one of 26 OTU's ten Wellingtons. All operated from home bases, managing stream take-offs with one or two minute intervals, all being away in 35 minutes. A 16 OTU crew laid claim to a Bf 109, and another drove off a Bf 110. At dawn, on June 26, Blenheims of 13 and 17 OTUs flew ASR sweeps, repeating this the following morning.

June brought rumours that the 'Yanks' were coming. They had already arrived, HQ VIIIth AF Bomber Command having taken up residence at Wycombe Abbey on April 15 1942. On April 27 more American formations, sailed and arrived in Britain on May 13. The 15th Bomb Squadron moved to Molesworth and the ground echelon of the 97th Bomb Group arrived in Britain aboard the liner *Queen Elizabeth* and soon moved into Grafton and Polebrook. July 1942 saw the first operational bombing sorties by the 15th Bomb Squadron using RAF Boston IIIs, and on July 1 the first B-17E touched down at Prestwick. July 9 brought the first US fighters to fly across the Atlantic, seven P-38s, touched down in Britain. On August 17 1942, 12 B-17Es of the 97th Bomb Group from Grafton and Polebrook opened the VIIth AF bombing campaign, and, in the autumn, further bomb groups arrived in the central area.

Supply of Wellington 1cs was becoming acute, forcing OTUs to re-equip with Wellington IIIs. But because of varying problems with these, aged 1cs had to soldier on. OTU Ansons were desperately needed by Training Command, but lack of spares prevented even their delivery flights. Belief that bombing operations boosted morale at OTUs prompted more night raids against German targets under Operation *Grand National* in which the central OTUs played a part and Blenheim OTUs again flew ASR patrols. Düsseldorf, Bremen and Essen were raided.

Operational use of OTUs required more realistic training schemes, especially at night. Increased enemy fighter activity, anti-aircraft gun defences and searchlights brought about special air defence exercises named Bullseyes. The first, in daylight was ordered on July 17 1942, with London as the 'target'. Both offensive and defensive forces were combined in this large scale training exercise. The first night *Bullseye* took place on August 4/5 1942, giving London's night defences further practice. On August 15/16 a Command *Bullseye* was flown, target Westminster Bridge. Next afternoon Blenheims and Ansons mounted another daylight mock attack upon the capital. *Bullseyes* thenceforth played an increasingly important part in operational training.

By November varieties of *Bullseyes* existed. A *Command Bullseye* was co-ordinated between HQ Fighter Command and a Bomber Group. The *Command*

Special Bullseye involved a concentrated stream approach to target from a considerable distance out to sea. *Local* or *Colour Bullseye* described a small scale exercise held at the request of an OTU.

On October 16 1942 *Nickelling* was resumed using, in 92 Group, Wellington IIIs of 16 and 29 OTUs. Henceforth it would be regular training, allotted to one OTU per week. The number of sorties (usually four) would be at the Station Commander's discretion. Each aircraft would carry 20 packs of leaflets amounting to an 800 lb load, and two bombs if needed.

The enemy might have provided a welcome to the Americans—by bombing them. Although the Luftwaffe was attacking British historical cities, and casting bombs somewhat discriminately elsewhere, few raiders penetrated to central England. Late on July 23 about 30 raiders crossed the Wash, penetrating inland as far as Coventry and Leamington. Fighter Command despatched 40 patrols to intercept, as a result of which 68 Squadron claimed five raiders and 409 Squadron a probable, for the loss of a 25 Squadron Beaufighter. On the night of July 27/28, 65 to 70 bombers operated, their main target being Birmingham, although not more than ten raiders were recorded over that city and two Dorniers were destroyed.

A force around 100 strong operated in the early hours of July 30, mainly over the east and central Midlands but reaching Wolverhampton and concentrating over Coventry. Two more Do 217s were shot down, and an encounter involved a Turbinlite Havoc of 1459 Flight operating with a satellite Hurricane of 253 Squadron. Between them they claimed to have damaged a Do 217. The last major night operations came on August 3, although it was on a much reduced scale. An unusual raid was a high-level attack on Luton's railway station by a Ju 86R early in September 1942.

At the start of 1943 air activity over the Midlands came roughly under six groupings: flying training involving Oxfords and Tiger Moths; OTU activity by Wellingtons and Whitley Vs; glider training at GTSs and the HGCU Brize Norton; increasing American presence; production, overhaul and experimentation at various establishments and factories and the despatch of Wellingtons to the Middle East—general reconnaissance versions and torpedo bombers.

A highlight of January 1943 came to Lyneham's 511 Squadron whose Liberator *AL504* carried Sir Winston Churchill from Stanton Harcourt to the Casablanca Conference. February 1943 saw leaflet dropping commenced by crews from Moreton-in-Marsh, Wellesbourne and Abingdon. Five large scale *Bullseyes* were flown and 92 Group took the lion's share.

The early months of 1943 brought fresh needs in Africa, Blenheim V crews being training for the ferry flight by 307 FTU, Finmere and Turweston. April brought another revision of OTUs. The small bomber training unit at Marham, which trained Mosquito crews, moved to Finmere, dissolved into 13 OTU, then the whole unit was restructured as the Mitchell-Boston-Mosquito OTU training 2TAF crews. Complete re-organisation also overtook the medium bomber OTUs, after which their layout remained unaltered. Previously, OTUs worked at 'straight through' system, or had Flights specialising in different aspects of training. The former consisted of four identical Flights each undertaking all aspects of basic and applied operational training. Pupils remained in one Flight throughout OTU training. The second consisted of a Conversion Flight, Armament Flight and two Operational Training Flights, locations of Flights at parent or satellite being to no standard pattern.

Under the new organisation a split syllabus divided training into natural parts—basic and applied. The former was now undertaken by two identical Flights and a small Gunnery Flight, all located at the satellite and undertaking conversion training, practice bombing and air firing. Satellites thus housed target towers and fighters which bomber OTUs were to acquire. Applied training consisted of cross country flying, operational exercises and *Nickelling* by two Flights based at the parent station. Prior to any training, all crews underwent two weeks' ground training at the main base. All Wellington and Whitley OTUs switched to this layout, as well as 17 OTU which moved to Silverstone and received Wellington IIIs.

Fighter defence training at OTUs had been mainly limited to fighter squadrons being briefly affiliated to them. An abrupt change came with the arrival of a batch of Martinets for simulation of fighter attack, particularly at night. Infra-red equipment was later devised for them. Outdated Defiants and Lysander target towers were withdrawn. About once a week large numbers of Wellingtons took part in a *Bullseye*. At around 10,000 ft they formed a bomber stream, making a mock attack, often upon London. One of the most memorable took place on January 21 1944, with OTUs at Abingdon, Harwell, Moreton, Wellesbourne and Honeybourne all contributing. The stream formed over Spalding and flew via Canterbury and Dungeness towards London's Green Park, the pinpoint target. They were then to proceed to Otmoor bombing range to see a pyrotechnic display simulating a marker attack. Then they were to proceed to Start Point and south of Portland before turning for Coventry and dispersal.

The ten minute-long stream formed at 20:30, 21 OTU flying low at 10,500 ft and 23 OTU at the top, 17,500 ft. As they were running on to London, intense alarm broke out for the enemy had also chosen to attack the capital at the start of his 'Baby Blitz'. It highlighted the immense damage he could have inflicted with a few well placed night sorties. Use of metal foil—Düppel, the German equivalent of Window—upset fighter AI radar so that the danger to over a hundred Wellingtons was heightened. Some shots were fired at them, but luck was on their side.

At the end of May 1943 glider units were temporarily switched to Flying Training Command and the operational 38 Wing to 70 Group, now part of 2TAF. Glider schools were reduced from five to two in the belief that sufficient pilots had been trained. Following the Sicilian glider assault, showing the exacting nature of glider operations, it was decided that each Horsa should have two pilots. Glider schools were retained.

June 1943 had also seen a decision to increase the number of night fighter crews. 'Night fighter' is perhaps misleading, for the need was for pilots and navigators to train in the art of bomber support. No 63 OTU opened at Honiley to train these crews, pilots flying nine hours, converting via Beauforts, then 62 hours' operational training in AI IV-equipped Beaufighters, later replaced by 33 hours' Mosquito flying. During July 1943 fighter affiliation received a further boost when two Bomber Defence Training Flights formed and equipped with Tomahawks, each Flight being allocated a clutch of OTUs.

All Midland-based 92 Group OTUs now had Wellington IIIs, and Ansons were ordered out of OTUs in July. Increasing sophistication was apparent, special coloured lights being authorised to mark different aerodrome features at night. Blue lights marked taxi lane endings, orange, the outer line of taxi tracks and red identified obstructions. White lights lined the active runway, airfield outer markers and the approach funnel. These colours, standard at operational stations, were displayed at OTUs to assist crews diverted to them upon returning from operations. In July 1943 there were 54 such diversions just to 92 Group stations.

Before any Allied landing in Europe could take place the transport force, RAF and American, needed to expand. New airfields were built to accommodate 46 Group and, south of a line from Harwich to Bristol, policy demanded each major station's number of hard standings to increase from 27 or 30 to 50.

Testing the basis of the D-Day plan by mounting a feint, large scale operation named *Starkey* was mounted early in September 1943. For the last time OTU Wellingtons were ordered to make night bombing raids on ammunition dumps in the Pas de Calais. During two raids at the end of August, 92 Group despatched 33 sorties, then sent another 55 in September, the bombers carrying 500 lb GP bombs. One Wellington was lost.

After years in which camouflage was important at all airfields, mid-September brought a small change. Runway caravans would be painted overall in 4 ft black and white squares and rest upon hard standings in a manner familiar in decades ahead. Just how busy was 92 Group in 1943 is shown by the 2,167 crews it trained and the 22,844 flying hours amassed by seven OTUs with an overall accident rate of one per 446 hours' flying, a figure twice as good as in 1942.

December 1943 found the OTUs at their peak strength in Britain where they totalled 22½, the fraction denoting units only part of the usual strength of 54 bombers. In 91 Group (HQ Abingdon) there were 8¼ OTUs, in 92 Group (HQ Winslow) 7¾ OTUs. Staffing them meant 14 days' training for an instructor on Wellingtons, whose stay was then for 1½ to 2 years. Bomber OTUs with the ordered four-Flight system evoked criticism that trainees had to change their instructor half way through their course. Training had been adjusted to take account of the usual operational crew structure of pilot, navigator, signaller and gunners. Although attempts were made to fit the standard Lancaster FN tail turret into the Wellington, nothing could be done at OTUs regarding the training of dorsal gunners. Night flying became easier when OTUs acquired sodium approach funnel lights and cross bar lights leading to runways.

October 1943 saw the expansion of the tactical transport force. RAF Dakotas arrived in numbers during the winter of 1943–44. In early 1944 six squadrons of 46 Group were equipped within days. Harwell, so long 15 OTU, was taken over for two Albemarle squadrons of 38 Group. Hampstead Norris, accommodated a glider pilot refresher training unit. By March 1 1944 another 560 glider pilots had been trained and the output of HGCU settled at 40 per month. The unit moved to North Luffenham, its place at Brize Norton being taken by operational Albemarle squadrons.

Before the invasion of Normandy could be mounted, exercises of ever increasing size and complexity were flown by both 38 and 46 Groups. Paratroops were dropped at Kingston Bagpuize and Kelmscot, and glider assaults were made on Salisbury Plain until all possible facets of the operation had been practised, including casualty evacuation in which 46 Group played the vital part using Down Ampney.

It was from Oxfordshire and Gloucestershire that the first and second great airborne assaults by the British were launched, the latter for the taking of Arnhem and Nijmegen bridges. From almost the same stations as they had mounted the Normandy assault, Dakotas and Stirlings towed off Horsas and Hadrians, before supplying the troops during their faltering campaign. Losses steadily rose, the courage displayed by many during the re-supply phase being marked by the award of the Victoria Cross to Flight Lieutenant Lord.

A month after Arnhem the airborne squadrons moved eastwards to be nearer for a second Rhine crossing attempt. Gliders and transports had not left the region, though, for the HGCU fragmented into a group of similar units devised to train hurriedly replacement pilots for those lost at Arnhem. 46 Group's Dakotas remained for casualty retrieval and passenger and freight services to the European mainland, a task which continued into 1946.

In the final months of the war, considerable glider activity throughout central England mingled with the Oxford flying at AFUs and the work of OTUs. In May 1944 returns had shown that 38.5 per cent of the flying hours in Bomber Command were by the Wellington OTUs, compared with 44.2 per cent by operational squadrons. One third of all British-based operational aircraft were within the OTUs.

Early on June 13 1944 the first V-1 flying bombs were launched against southern England. Their target area was restricted by technical efficiency as well as fuel supply, but a few, fired early on June 21 1944, flew into Oxfordshire and Bedfordshire. One fell at Nuffield near Benson, one at Maiden—both in Oxfordshire—another at Streatley, causing a lot of damage in Dunstable and a fourth an hour later at Luton. On July 5, a V-1 fell at Checkendon, Oxfordshire in which county one more fell, at Stonor on August 20.

Whether any were air launched remains open to question, and seems unlikely. Surviving records indicate that about 400 V-1s were fired at Britain before mid-September from Heinkel He 111s at about 50 miles from our coast and flying low over the sea to avoid radar detection. It is almost certain that an air launched V-1 came down by Eyeworth churchyard, Bedfordshire, on September 5, and that it was one of nine intended for London.

A high proportion of the missiles fell into the water but, of seven which ran successfully on October 10 1944, one came down at Thurleigh. Another fell at Harlington, Bedfordshire, on October 12 and the following night yet another in that area, among fir trees. Deep penetration flights were unusual because of the unreliability of the weapon. The seventh to fall in Bedfordshire crashed by Glebe House, Hollesley, on November 29. Two more came down in the early evening of December 10, one at Northfields Farm, Great Barford, where electricity cables were cut and a stack was damaged, and the other not far from Letchworth. Two more were to fall in Bedfordshire, one near Silsoe on December 18 and the last in open ground near Chicksands at 03:30 on March 23 1945, six days before the final V-1 came to our shore. In addition to ten which fell in Bedfordshire another 27 penetrated into Buckinghamshire.

Although the V-2 rocket campaign included firings against London, Norwich and Ipswich, a few rockets penetrated further on journeys resulting from small alterations in the programming of the rockets' flight plan. The first of these V-2s came down at Luton at 09:50 on November 1 1944, landing within a factory area killing 17, seriously injuring 24 and causing 86 slight casualties. This was by far the most serious V-weapon incident in the central area. At 05:00 on December 14 a V-2 burst at Nuthampstead in Hertfordshire, one of 34 that fell in that county. Bedfordshire received its second at 14:20 on January 10 1945, a V-2 which fell at Henlow. The final rocket landed on Twelve Acre Farm,

Studham, Bedfordshire at 06:56, some three hours after the last V-1 had arrived.

Much interest was generally aroused whenever large scale glider training exercises took place. By the start of 1945 the glider training programme had produced ample pilots for the next venture, but they needed to keep in practice. Mounting suitable exercises was expensive and the number of tugs limited. Even by autumn 1944, 34,000 parachute troops had been trained at 1 PTS Ringway, and they also needed practice. Large scale exercises were spectacular to view, but associated problems were never solved before the treasury purse strings were pulled tight.

Closure of many training organisations came hastily at the end of hostilities. Vast numbers of surplus aircraft were in store, including Horsa and Hamilcar gliders. The latter was a Midland sight after many were erected and tested at 33 MU Lyneham. Components were Birmingham-built in the CWS furniture works.

Lyneham became one of the RAF's most important stations, a terminus for many long range trooping flights commonly called 'curry runs' to the Far East—and for the dreaded customs clearance for those coming home. From and to Lyneham, Yorks, Dakotas, Liberators, Stirlings and Halifaxes in profusion went to and fro, to places bearing exotic names.

Progressive wind-down of the British forces after the war was inevitable for financial reasons, whilst the need to protect the empire remained. Its release from British control was confounded by a monolithic state totally incapable of solving its most basic problems, yet ever ready to interfere in the affairs of others. As a result the Midland's training element was only partially dismantled. Basic and advanced flying schools were retained and more Harvards acquired. Training had to be drastically overhauled to meet the jet age—a new confrontation—and resources limited. From Percival Aircraft, Luton, came a line of new aircraft, the Prentice, Provost and Jet Provost. Brief expansion of the training layout resulted from the Korean War, aerodromes recently neglected having a further brief lifespan.

Airfield numbers fell from around 100 to nearer 20. Fear that new, heavy aircraft would need very long runways led to the joining of Wittering and Collyweston. When the Handley-Page Hastings transport first flew it did so from that lengthened runway. The Hastings forged a post-war link between the Midlands and wide areas of the world.

Let us now consider some aspects of aerodrome architecture and layout.

Looking at airfields

Airfields are no more standardised in layout than the architecture of their buildings. Those in the Midlands fall into eight categories: (a) World War 1 sites, some renewed in the 1920s and persistently developed; (b) airfields of the 1930s Expansion Scheme, including facilities for aircraft storage, some persistently modified; (c) miscellaneous civilian and specialised airfields; (d) airfields built between 1939 and 1941; (e) satellites, some becoming self-accounting; (f) much-dispersed airfields built in the mid- and late-war period; (g) Satellite Landing Grounds for dispersed storage of aircraft; and (h) Relief Landing Grounds used for intensive flying training.

The Expansion Period stations remain impressive, skyline sights evocative of so much which has passed. Typical are Cranfield and Harwell, and examination of both gives a broad idea of the layout and design of permanent peacetime stations.

Royal Air Force Cranfield, now the Cranfield Institute of Technology, is reached along narrow roads, little changed since the 1940s. Undertaking construction of an elaborate airfield in the 1930s when in adjacent fields horses still pulled a tumbrel cart, and traction engines operated the plough, was a tremendous task. Electricity was a rural novelty, residents relying upon the village well and pump for water. Into the war years cement was delivered to airfields in yellow-painted, steam-driven lorries of the Portland Cement Company. Foundations for buildings meant plentiful use of a spade, for even cement mixers were not all that common. Edward I managed to coerce his men into building great castles and doubtless the relative sophistication of the 1930s would have caused him equal amazement as labourers—Irish, and many of the ex-unemployed—set to these great tasks.

Acquiring ground for landing areas was complicated and troublesome. The best agricultural land was equally best for smooth, flat airfield use. Thus, the size of pre-war aerodromes (the term 'airfield' was a product of the mid-war years) was limited by political muscle and pacifist misguidance. When new types of aircraft were planned a major limitation was the take off run available.

Entering the 1930s stations meant passing the guardroom. Cranfield's—to pattern 4-7/35 wedded to 3/36—remains, the front graced by curved arches behind which extends a verandah. The guardroom's enquiry desk was within the front facing wall entrance hall. Woe betide any airman who passed in anything but smart condition, for the porticoed 'S.P. Sergeant' seemed ever ready to swoop. Most of his guardroom was given over to an office with a highly shining

Odeon? Regal? Certainly reminiscent of a 1930s cinema entrance, but actually the way in to Cranfield's wartime cookhouse.

One of three 'H-plan' or linked 'Q' Type Barrack Blocks at Cranfield.

Cranfield's main stores (2056-57/34), entered via doors or ramps which cater for all specialised needs.

Looking south across Cranfield, summer, 1946 (CIT).

linoleum floor. Adjacent was at least one ominous 'cooler' barred and ready for those who fell from grace.

Usually facing the 'Main Gate'—not all stations had gates but most acquired columns upon which they might be hung—was Station Headquarters (SHQ). At Cranfield the rectangular building which served in this role (2084/35) contained offices, the clerical section, pay accounts, the office of the Chief Technical Officer (CTO), the Station Warrant Officer's kingdom (ie, the dreaded SWO's office) and the office of the man really in charge, the Station Commander. Entry was generally through an unpretentious central doorway, often crowned with a curved top. These buildings were immensely strong, usually built of 2 ft thick red brick walls—all well sandbagged in wartime, in addition to which some had 2 ft brick or reinforced concrete blast walls protecting vulnerable parts. Cranfield's operations room lay to the right of the central passageway. In some it was on the first floor. An intelligence section would be close by and, quite often, a library was on the first floor.

Centrally placed within the main site was the barrack square, circumnavigated by a road. On one side was the Airmen's Mess and on at least two others were Barrack Blocks. Cranfield's original Airmen's Mess, later the NAAFI, lay on the eastern side, catering for 350 men. Its upper floor was originally the Institute (NAAFI) where snacks were available, along with a games room, writing room, etc. This unpretentious block (12922-6/38) for other ranks and Corporals was similar to Harwell's.

When Cranfield became a training camp, there were so many airmen there that a new large ORs' mess was built on the northern side of the square. Now called the Stafford Cripps Building, its style is not in keeping with those around. Entry is via steps flanked by concrete columns of pseudo-classical form.

On three sides of the barrack square were airmens' Barrack Blocks. Two faced SHQ and one was of the larger Type 'R' with planned accommodation for three NCOs and 84 airmen. This block (2277/34), like the others, has conventional sloped roofing whereas later designs had flat roofs. Cranfield's other Barrack

Above *The view north across Cranfield of the 1970s* (CIT).

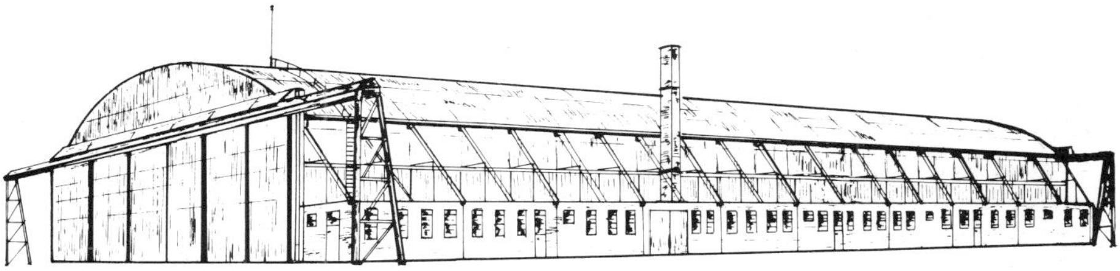

Above *Steel plate curved roofing distinguished the 300-ft long and 150-ft wide Type 'J' hangars, single examples of which were erected at a number of airfields in the Midlands. Designed in 1939 by Sir William Arrol and Co Ltd, they featured 18 bays. Gaydon-type post-war hangars are similar in appearance, but the internal girder work differs.*

Below *Aeroplane Shed, Type 'C', revised design 1934, Home Stations. A general view of the hipped roof design with a 12-bay Shed. Note that there were variations in the large side windows as regards the number of panes, not all of which were square. Further variations included the provision of offices added to the brick hangar walls, these accounting for the various pattern numbers allocated to 'C' Sheds. Earlier versions of this type had upright terminations to the roof ridges, ie, were not hipped.*

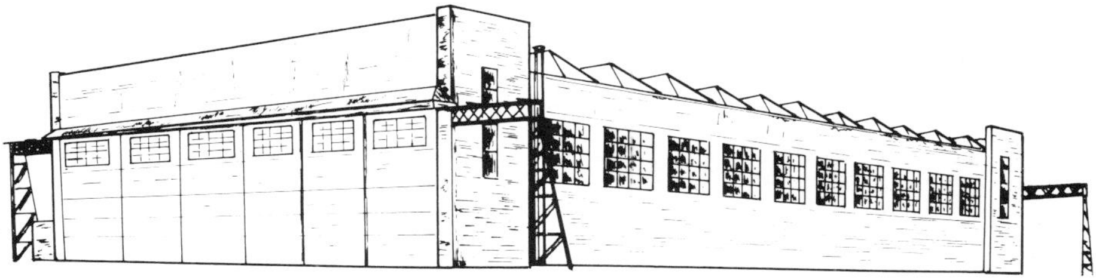

Top *Cranfield's guardroom, now the reception office.*

Above *Station Headquarters, Cranfield, little changed.*

Left *The main entrance to Cranfield's SHQ—a splendid portico.*

Blocks were Type 'Q' (2272/34) with planned facilities for 68 airmen and three NCOs. Subsequently barrack accommodation was linked by ablutions, producing three blocks, 'H' Type in plan view. One is now the Department of European Languages and Centre for Transport Studies; another the School of Electronics Systems Design.

South-west of the barrack square was the first Sergeants' Mess (1105/35, 4574/35 and further modified) with accommodation for 12 single Sergeants and up to 85 ORs. Now it is the School of Production Studies. A gracious-looking building, it proved too small when many trainee pilots passing through 14 SFTS were NCOs. A new Sergeants' Mess, now Mitchell Hall, was built in then open country north-east of the site. It has some similarity in design to Officers' Mess structures of the period.

At Cranfield, roads by the barrack square lead to a main road which, at right angles to them, crosses the operational site. Buildings to its rear housed personnel and accounting sections, those to the landing ground side forming the technical site. Positioning within a line varied, but purposes and styling were similar. Central at Cranfield was the Armoury and Photographic Block (2023/34). To its right stood Main Stores (2056-57/34), still easily identifiable even though the ramp to the large entrance has been removed and doors have been replaced by bricks. Its interior has been modified into elaborate lecture rooms but, to anyone remembering such a place in its RAF days, much is still recognisable. A central portion of the stores structure was higher than the rest, and at one time used for the storage of aircraft fuselages. A crane formed part of its equipment. Beyond the two-storey Armoury, and completing the trio, was the Main Workshop (2048-9/34), not unlike the stores in appearance.

Plans showing the typical arrangements of 'C' Type Sheds. **A** *12-bay Shed, 25-ft bays, overall length 300 ft (internal), width 150 ft, end sections, standard 37 ft 6 in seen externally as walls with door gantries.* **B** *10-bay Shed, 250 ft long.* **C** *8-bay Shed, 200 ft long.* **D** *9-bay Shed, 225 ft long. Standard width, 150 ft. Normally built hipped, both variants indicated on plans.*

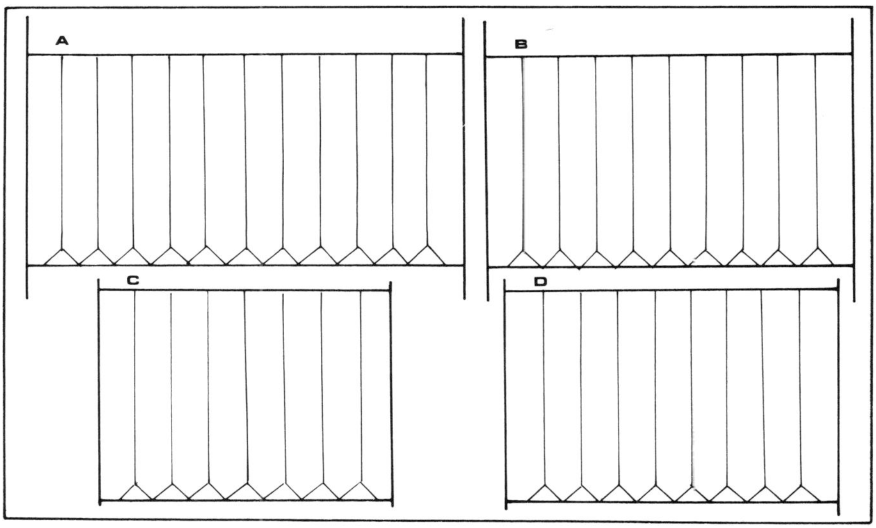

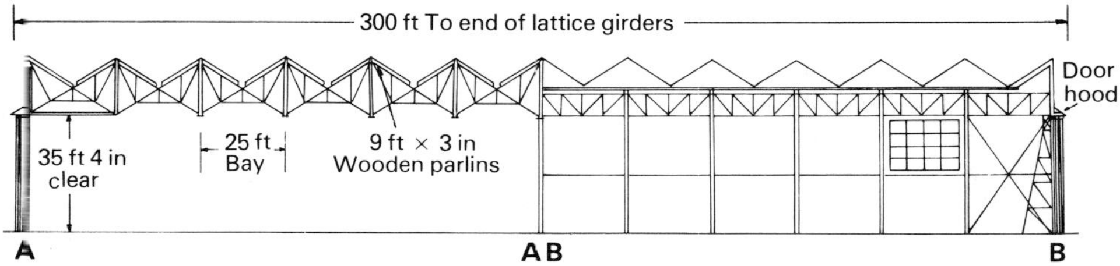

Above *Cross section and partial side elevation of aeroplane shed Type 'C', revised design 1934, Home Stations, pattern 2029/34. Portion 'A-A' represents side elevation along the hangar centre line; portion 'B-B' shows the framework incorporated in the outer wall based on the Datum Floor Level of the door rails, the latter being set in concrete foundations.*

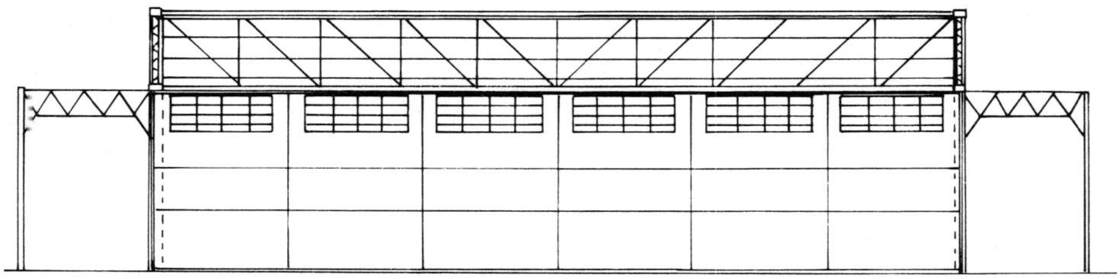

Above *Shed Type 'C', revised design 1934, end elevation (both ends alike). Six main sliding doors set in five tracks, overall width 150 ft, doors 35 ft 5 in high. Note lattice girder roof and door trestles supporting door gantry.*

Beyond lay the aircraft sheds, at Cranfield four 'C' Type with a space left at the north-east end of the technical site for a possible fifth. Hangars were built in a slightly curving position ahead of which there were lawns with slow-growing trees, affording natural camouflage to the entire site. Further towards the landing ground was a taxi area used as an apron in the days of light bombers. Broad spacing, concreted over, was left between the large sheds.

Cranfield's hangars are designated 'Aeroplane Shed Type 'C' Revised Design 1934 Home Stations', based upon pattern number 2029. Variations between Cranfield's hangars bring the three alongside the landing ground into the 2042-2043/34 style. Almost identical, they have Flight or Squadron Offices, crew rooms, radio and instrument repair rooms, flying clothes lockers, etc, the entire length of both sides of the hangars—mainly single storey. The other hangar (1583/35) is similar, but offices are different in arrangement.

Whilst the clear open width of each 'C' Type Shed remains 150 ft, the length varies according to the number of bays which range from six through eight, nine, ten, to 12. Cranfield's hangars, as at most pre-war bomber stations, are of the latter variety and measure 300 ft in length. Into the ends of each 25-ft bay is a main wall stanchion. At each end of the two hangar walls, strong vertical bracing and stiffening girders are embedded in hefty concrete foundations. Brickwork between these sections extends well above the gutter level to reduce the effects of strong winds. The 14-in thick hangar walls are of brick and are 35 ft high. Some, upon completion, were coated white and looked not unlike Benson's of the 1980s.

Piers 3 ft by 4 ft enclose lattice stanchions with 25-ft centres supporting the 150-ft span compound; lattice girders consisting of a basal main girder supporting

15-ft centre verticals. RSJ struts of the ridge girder have cross branches between the vertical struts, the overall height from the top of the wall to the top of the ridge being 17 ft. A truss system with braced steel members runs diagonally at 15 ft centres across a 25-ft span between the compound lattice girders, and constitues support for the series of 12 pitched roofs so formed. Usually their ends are hipped (ie, sloped) as on Cranfield's. Roof covering consists of asbestos cement sheeting fastened by 4-in screws over close boarding routed timber purlins, 9 in by 3 in at 5-ft centres. Half roofs at either end terminate in brick walls over each end of the doorways. Each of the alike ends have six steel door panels which slide along guide rails set in concrete at the base and, overhead, in a hooded gantry supported at either end by steel trestles.

Opening hangar doors was ordered to be possible by one man. Amazingly, it can be done, despite the colossal door weight, by one person using a primitive winding handle. This is equalled by the unlocking of the master door with the aid of a giant, ancient looking key!

An interesting feature of the 'C' hangars is their huge side windows with vertical metal glazing bars at 18-in centres holding 1/8th in thick reinforced glass. They let some light into the building but, typical of the clever design of so many of these structures at RAF stations, they had a far more subtle use. At the time of design, a hangar's ability to survive direct bomb hits was of prime importance because metal and fabric aeroplanes needed to be stored to prevent weather damage. In wartime, hangars would need to be blacked out, making artificial lighting the only option. Wiser reasoning prevailed and the large steel-framed windows were placed in the brick walls, the intention being that the windows could absorb a considerable amount of blast effect from any internal bomb burst, allowing much of the main structure to remain intact. Similar considerations contributed to the considerable height of these hangars. Ridged roofing served a variety of requirements too. Striking from certain angles, HE bombs would be likely to skip from the sloping sections, and be less likely to penetrate the roofing. Attacks upon these hangars often resulted in incendiary bombs concentrating in one position, making ensuing fires easier to cope with. None could complain about the resilience of the steel framing of the 'C' Type hangars which most resolutely resisted enemy attack.

Prior to hostilities, air traffic control was almost non-existent. Each new aerodrome nevertheless had its watch office and tower close to the apron. It contained a meteorological section, and supervised local flying from its tower. Cranfield's example (1959/34) was typical of its period and was identical at the outset to that which, in fine health, can still be seen at Bicester. Alongside the tower was normally found a fire tender shed and pyrotechnics store.

Whilst three-bay petrol tanker sheds were often sited near the hangars, the main Motor Transport Section was frequently to be found near the tall cuboid water supply tower, as at Cranfield. There the MT Section comprised five small and nine large sheds facing across a courtyard. Few RAF stations were closely linked to the railway network, Bicester and Henlow being among the exceptions.

Placed in open country, if possible, was the bomb dump comprising a variety of semi-underground shelter-like structures grassed over and linked by a road-way to the landing ground. In recent times Cranfield's weapons dump has usefully served as an engine test bed area.

At some stations the main access road passed directly through the camp, as at

Cranfield. On the opposite side of the road from the hangars was a domestic area with dwellings widely spaced. Grouped around an area, known at Cranfield as The Crescent, there were 46 houses, terraced, for married airmen and families. Slightly larger were others for NCOs, the better ones being awarded to Warrant Officers. By 1930s standards of housing for many, these married quarters were extremely good. There were also the Officers' Married Quarters at Cranfield, set on the opposite sides of the large playing field. They, included a very gracious home for the Station Commander and some Group IV or V houses for other officers.

Cranfield's Officers' Mess (now known as Lanchester Hall) is similar to many others. This example (2288-2292/34, 3600/37) consists of a central section containing an ante-room, assembly area, bar and dining room along with bedroom accommodation for up to 45 officers. Further accommodation was to patterns 397-398/36, for a dozen officers in the East Wing and 16 in the West. With a high porched entrance and superb entrance hall, these beautiful buildings have a grace rarely encountered in today's poorly proportioned structures. They tone excellently with the countryside around, and remain as compatible with a Tornado as with a Heyford. Walls, 2 ft thick, must encourage them to outlive many of the civilian monstrosities which have succeeded them.

Cranfield had no hard dispersal standings, but attacks on airfields resulted in the trainers being dispersed around the field. Had not ideas existed to use Cranfield for operations it would never have had hard surface runways. Alignment of the latter depended on numerous factors, not least the local terrain and obstructions. Wartime complaints were directed at the enemy, although screams of 'where are the fighters' came most audibly from those eager to abolish them. That remains to disturb one's peace of mind in the 1980s.

Runways were laid at Cranfield during the winter of 1939–1940 and at Harwell in the autumn of 1941. The latter was a late 1930s bomber station similar in layout to Cranfield. With four 'C' Type hangars (one 1583/35 and three 2042/34 with 2099/35 updating) Harwell differed from some stations in that it was built on one side of the supply road. First, one passed the guardroom

'C' Type aircraft sheds differ by way of office accommodation and workshops. Many have been modified but a large central side entrance remains usual. Type 2042-43/34 is illustrated here.

(3136/34) of well-known Sergeant 'Knocker' West. It was of very different style from that at Cranfield. The road then led to SHQ (8863/37 and 2984/35) which was unusually close to the hangars. The Officers' Mess, Type 2288-2291/34, faced south and Married Quarters were at the camp's extremity.

In line with the centre hangar were buildings similar to Cranfield's. Furthest away was the Sergeants' Mess (478/39 and 597/39), which replaced an earlier one (1105/35) of the type also originally erected at Cranfield. A narrow road led directly from the south-facing Sergeants' Mess to the south-facing Institute (NAAFI) Building (1422-1525/35). Across the barrack square was the Airmens' Dining Room (12922-12926/38), similar to Cranfield's. The Armoury (2023/34) was centrally placed behind the hangars. Main Stores (2057/34) lay to the east and Workshops to the west. To the rear of SHQ were the parachute stores and packing rooms, west of which was a gas decontamination centre and offices.

On eastern and western sides of the barrack square were two Barrack Blocks. Nearest to the Institute Building was a large Type 'R' 2277-2279/34. The others were Type 'Q' (2272-2274/34) as at Cranfield. A further Type 'R' faced one of the two even larger Barrack Blocks (Type 8/84) which, in plan view, resembled a letter 'H' and were to pattern 9965-9967/38. Sick Quarters was placed close to another Barrack Block variant, Type 8/56 (1159/38) situated near the original Sergeants' Mess. (The prefix in the designations of these latter Barrack Blocks denotes the number of NCOs provided for, the suffix the number of other ranks.) West of the barrack square was the nine-bay MT Section.

Harwell's grass landing ground was extended in 1940. The intersection of its three later runways was close but not so much as at Cranfield where there is no grass where the runways meet. Such layouts were mostly avoided because one attack could render all three useless.

Harwell's runway and taxi layout was very complex. Nine dispersals in the north-west area of the field directly fed runway 15/33, the shortest runway alarmingly aligned directly towards the bomb dump. Another 16 dispersals were used by the operational training secton of the OTU. A further 15 dispersals fed runway 08/26, and four more served this or runway 11/29, the main runway. To reduce taxi-ing distance the bomb dump area was linked by curved Sommerfeld Tracking. Taxi-ing from the hangars and north-west dispersal areas was complicated too. At the western end of Runway 11/29 was a complex arrangement of metal tracking. Horsa gliders were aligned from which tow ropes were laid to be attached to tugs. At 46 Group's Dakota stations, diagonal areas of steel planking were part of the initial building. Dispersal of gliders was essential, for their wooden structures made them vulnerable to incendiary attack and inclement weather.

An interesting feature of Harwell's past remains its catapult. John A. Bagley, BSc, CEng, AFRAeS, Curator of the aviation section of the Science Museum, in 1974 searched surviving RAE Farnborough records for details. In 1930 Percy Salmon, Head of Farnborough's main drawing office, developed ideas for a 'portable' catapult driven by compressed air motors working at 400 psi and with a launch capability to about 18,000 lb. It is known to have fired a Vickers Virginia, surely a sight to remember!

Design work commenced in November 1935 on a catapult to launch bombers at weights up to 65,000 lb, and known as a 'hydro-pneumatic device'. Space at Farnborough being at a premium, the RAE constructed their Mk III catapult at Harwell. It was never used because plans to catapult heavily laden bombers were

Harwell, looking north west, on July 20 1942. Wellingtons of 15 OTU are dispersed and runways are camouflaged (RAF Museum).

abandoned. This, incidentally, was a different device to that used at the RAE to launch a Heyford in August 1940 and a Manchester in July 1941.

Some details of Harwell's catapult have recently become available from Geoffrey G.J. Cooper, a wartime designer in the RAE Catapult Section. A 100-ft diameter pit was excavated close to the A34 road, the catapult gear being mounted on a turntable with a flat roof flush with the runway. Another source has suggested that the turntable was to be rotatable through 360 degrees and might have been designed for use at Gibraltar prior to construction of a runway there. Harwell's turntable could be orientated through 45 degrees for launches in one of two directions. 'It was a six ram, telescopic tube type with the largest some six feet in diameter,' recalls Mr Cooper. 'The small ram was attached to a towing hook which protruded above the ground and was intended to launch the aircraft in a tail-down attitude. The hook presented a considerable design problem and was never completed. The catapult was hydro-pneumatic, using water instead of oil for hydraulics. Pumps and control gear were mounted in the turntable and moved around with it. Power came from 12 old Kestrel aero engines, six adapted to pumps being close-coupled to the other six engines—running at the normal speed! The six modified engines had one cylinder block modified into (I think) two-stage air compressors, by packing the pistons with blocks to reduce clearance and to increase the compression ratio. The other cylinder block had a purpose-made steel unit above it, using the pistons as guides, in which slender rams operated as water force pumps. The idea was to pump air into the receivers at about 200 psi, and then bring the pressure up to 2,000 by pumping water into hydraulic accumulators. Most engineers considered this attempt at aero engine speeds was doomed to failure. All the units were worn out in testing and never did drive this catapult, started just before the war and abandoned after some years of development.'

An amusing sidelight to the catapult story has been provided by Air Commodore G.J.C. Paul, CB, DFC, who, in 1945, commanded the Harwell clutch of stations. He recalls that his Adjutant was surprised one day to see a small figure—whom he initially classified as a gnome—lift a manhole cover, fully emerge, cross to a nearby hedge, receive a pay packet, then return to his incredible lair and finally replace the manhole cover. Investigation showed that the occupant was an ex-naval stoker and RAE employee who, since 1939, had

Harwell (early 1946) with the station workshops (2048-49/34) prominent in the foreground (UK AEA).

lovingly maintained his charge and regularly received his pay packet in that most unorthodox manner! Both the Commander and his Adjutant descended the ladder to find some six Kestrel engines on 'shelves' on the walls and lots of machinery. 'There was a good deal of dripping water,' they recalled, 'and the dim light of bare electric bulbs in the far up roof the whole place resembled a scene from an H.G. Wells film.'

Suggestions persist that similar contraptions were intended for and possibly commenced at Mildenhall and Waddington. Harwell's cavern, large enough to contain a house, apparently survived until 1948 at least, according to Mr R.M. Fishenden. Hopes in 1974 that it would yield valuable Kestrels, ideal for the Shuttleworth Hind, were dashed. Maybe they were disposed of to 3 MU, Milton?

Three features commonly seen at wartime airfields were also seen at most pre-war stations. One was the elaborate watch office-cum-flying control tower. Wartime flying brought about great need for control of flying undertaken from new towers packed with radio, radar and teleprinting equipment. Harwell's wartime tower (7211/42) is now used by part of the AERE. Cranfield's, which replaced the 1959/34 tower, is used for flying control.

A second feature was many temporary brick buildings, particularly at dispersal points. Thirdly, and often associated with similar areas of the airfield layout, were steel Nissen huts usually 36 ft by 16 ft and existing in a larger 60 ft by 18 ft 6 in (5773/42) variety.

Wartime-built airfields were far less elaborate and much dispersed. Hangars ranged over five styles. There were the pre-war-designed large metal-domed 'J' Type and the prefabricated all-metal Teeside 'T' Type—transportable and existing in various sizes, the 'T2' being most common. It varied in length according to need, for additional bays could be added. Less common was the Bellman metal hangar, again of varying size. A fourth, the 'B1', to an MAP specification was readily identifiable when compared with the 'T2' by the greater angle of the roof setting. Trestles supported the door slides. These hangars were grouped variously at wartime airfields. Usually there was only one 'J' Type hangar or a 'B1', used for major servicing. Blister hangars were distributed around the airfield perimeter. Many were of the Over Type Blister Hangar. In some instances they were linked, and sometimes had one end

Above *A general view across Harwell's domestic site. The MT section is at the left-hand corner, the Barrack Blocks, Sergeants' Mess and NAAFI are central. Married Quarters are in the distance* (UK AEA).

Below *Beyond the roof are the NAAFI and Sergeants' Mess* (UK AEA).

The uninvited Lockheed T-33A 18756, *of the 514th Fighter Interceptor Squadron, 406th Fighter Interceptor Wing, Manston, which made a forced landing at Harwell. Beyond is the wartime control tower* (UK AEA).

bricked in. A further type, examples of which remain at Little Rissington, is the Lamella resembling a large grassed-over mound. Such hangars were used for aircraft storage at maintenance units.

Technical sites at early wartime-built stations were close to the 'J' Type hangars. Many temporary buildings had asbestos roofing, and some were flat-roofed. After the first Expansion period stations had been completed, a new feature was introduced, the flat roof surrounded by a two-ft high wall. In to the recess above the heavy reinforced concrete roof was poured a thick layer of sand so that, should fire bombs or cannon and machine-gun fire be directed at the roofing, the effects would be nullified.

Wartime camps usually did not have a barrack square. Their widespread living accommodation was spread over about six sites placed well away from weapon, pyrotechnic and fuel stores. This invariably meant a journey of a mile or so to the operational area. The provision of water and electricity, the latter sometimes fed from the national grid system, called for considerable ingenuity. All camps had reserve generators and back up. The water supply was ensured by the erection of high-level Braithwaite towers—large steel tanks sectionally assembled and perched upon scaffolding. Numerous examples remain of distinctive features at one-time airfield sites. Wooden and metal huts built by Laing were common features too, Nissen huts, though, seem to have been more commonly provided at American rather than British bases.

Additional to major airfields there were other types. The Relief Landing Ground consisted of suitable grassland for light training aircraft. A few tents providing living and messing accommodation were all that were needed, supplemented later with night flying equipment and power supplies. A few brick buildings were later provided. To halt the wasteful return of aircraft to their home stations, picketting facilities were made available. It was but a short step to sheltering aircraft in Blister hangars. By the middle of the war some grass surfaces had badly deteriorated and it was necessary to lay runway tracking, as at Bibury.

Satellite Landing Grounds (as opposed to satellite stations) were merely suitable grass areas on to which aircraft could be flown, and flown out in light condition. They were placed there, under good camouflage, for storage. One SLG, and surely the most picturesque, was a broad grass runway among the trees at Woburn Park. Stirlings tended by 6 MU resided there in 1944–45.

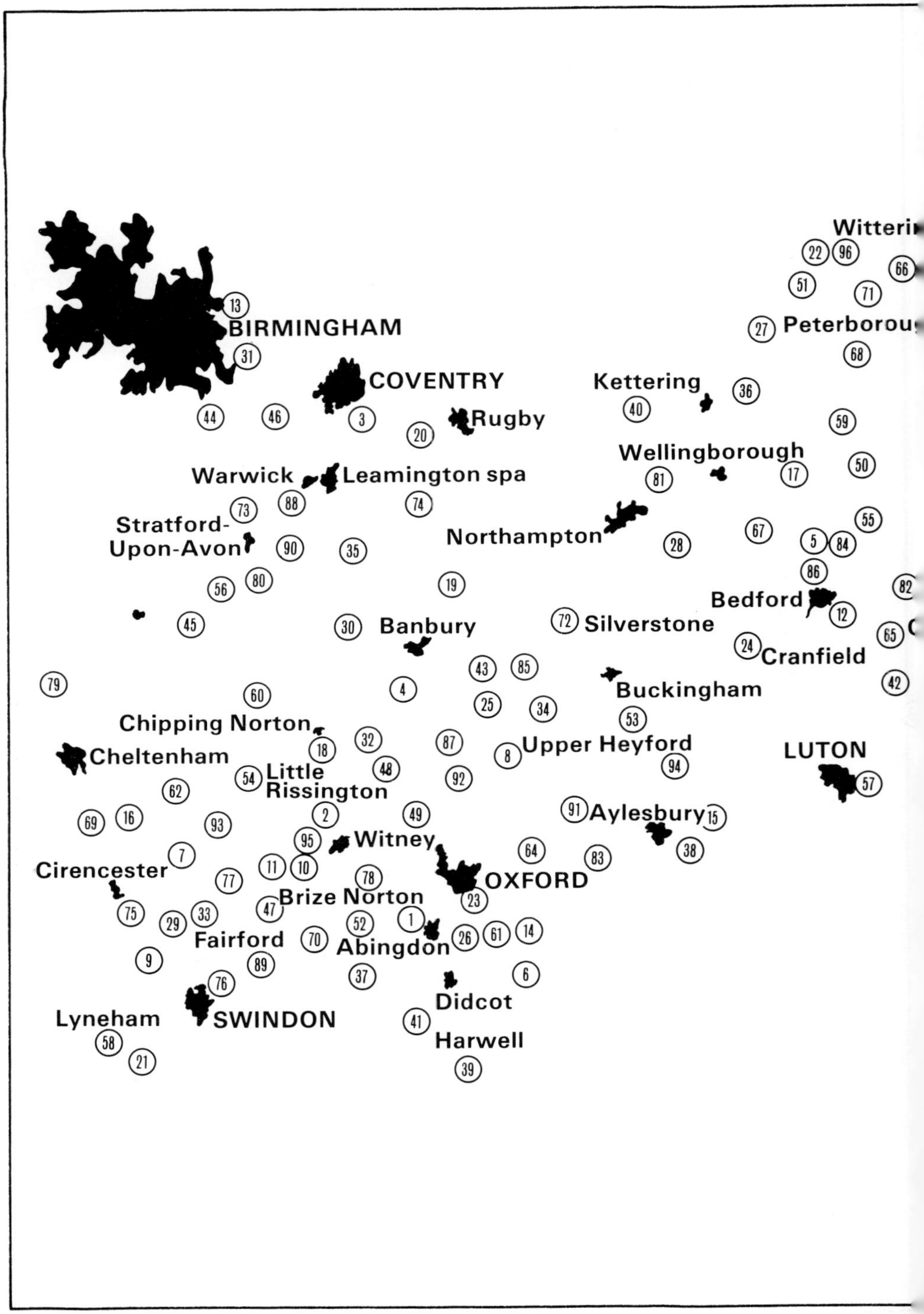
Witteri
22
96
66
51
71
13
BIRMINGHAM
27
Peterborou
31
68
COVENTRY
Kettering
36
44
46
3
Rugby
40
59
20
Wellingborough
Warwick
Leamington spa
81
17
50
73
88
74
Stratford-
Upon-Avon
90
35
Northampton
28
67
5
84
55
86
56
80
19
82
Bedford
45
30
Banbury
72
Silverstone
12
65
24
Cranfield
79
43
85
42
60
4
25
34
Buckingham
53
Chipping Norton
32
87
Cheltenham
18
8
Upper Heyford
LUTON
54
Little
Rissington
48
92
94
57
62
69
16
93
2
49
91
Aylesbury
15
95
Witney
64
38
Cirencester
7
11
10
78
83
77
OXFORD
Brize Norton
23
75
29
33
47
52
1
26
61
14
Fairford
70
Abingdon
9
89
37
6
76
Didcot
Lyneham
SWINDON
41
58
Harwell
21
39

The Military airfields of the Cotswolds and Central Midlands

1 Abingdon
2 Akeman Street
3 Baginton
4 Barford St John
5 Bedford/Thurleigh
6 Benson
7 Bibury
8 Bicester
9 Blakehill Farm
10 Brize Norton
11 Broadwell
12 Cardington
13 Castle Bromwich
14 Chalgrove
15 Cheddington
16 Chedworth
17 Chelveston
18 Chipping Norton
19 Chipping Warden
20 Church Lawford
21 Clyffe Pypard
22 Collyweston
23 Cowley
24 Cranfield
25 Croughton
26 Culham
27 Deenethorpe
28 Denton
29 Down Ampney
30 Edgehill
31 Elmdon
32 Enstone
33 Fairford
34 Finmere
35 Gaydon
36 Grafton Underwood
37 Grove
38 Halton
39 Hampstead Norris
40 Harrington
41 Harwell
42 Henlow
43 Hinton-in-the-Hedges
44 Hockley Heath
45 Honeybourne
46 Honiley
47 Kelmscot
48 Kiddington
49 Kidlington
50 Kimbolton
51 King's Cliffe
52 Kingston Bagpuize
53 Little Horwood
54 Little Rissington
55 Little Staughton
56 Long Marston
57 Luton
58 Lyneham
59 Molesworth
60 Moreton-in-Marsh
61 Mount Farm
62 Northleach
63 Nuthampstead
64 Oakley
65 Old Warden
66 Peterborough (Westley)
67 Podington
68 Polebrook
69 Rendcombe
70 Shellingford
71 Sibson
72 Silverstone
73 Snitterfield
74 Southam
75 South Cerney
76 South Marston
77 Southrop
78 Stanton Harcourt
79 Stoke Orchard
80 Stratford
81 Sywell
82 Tempsford
83 Thame
84 Thurleigh (Bedford)
85 Turweston
86 Twinwood Farm
87 Upper Heyford
88 Warwick
89 Watchfield
90 Wellesbourne Mountford
91 Westcott
92 Weston-on-the-Green
93 Windrush
94 Wing
95 Witney
96 Wittering (Stamford)

The airfields

Abingdon, Oxfordshire

SU480990. 5 miles SW of Oxford, 1 mile NW of Abingdon town

Battle of Britain Day, 1967, the end of Abingdon's runway, weather appalling. Pity, for this was the last occasion when Abingdon's Beverley sisters would waggle their tails and much more in public. Abingdon was swathed in fog so dense that flying by the last of the largest aircraft the RAF ever operated in quantity was barely visible. It was no mean thrill to stand at the runway's edge as they emerged from the mist, wing tips soaring overhead before these dinosaur-like creatures floated into the fog, their wing-tips showering water droplets. Five Beverleys soon crept in from the west and, in a style befitting a fighter, each one smoke-puffing, peeled off for a place in a stream landing. Memorable moments indeed.

RAF Abingdon has been an action station for over 50 years. Some buildings remain from 1930. Red brick, plentiful slate roofs and designs akin to army barracks of long ago, can be seen alongside assorted hangars and a large recent one built for the Beverleys. A 1925-style white-painted water tower competes with a stylish chimney of the 1930s.

Abingdon was once a simple airfield. In the plan approved (July 20 1925) only 51 buildings were listed, four of them hangars of which three remain. Intended for two single-engined day bomber squadrons, facilities were provided for a Special Reserve Squadron in wartime. After slight alterations, construction started in 1929, at the site whose surface shallow layer of loam rested upon a firm shale or clay base.

The station opened on September 1 1932 under the Wessex Bombing Area. On October 8 1932 the first aircraft arrived—Fairey Gordon single-engined biplane bombers of 40 Squadron. They had vacated Upper Heyford on July 31 1932, flying here via armament training at Catfoss, the Squadron remaining until September 1939.

On October 10 1932 the first permanent buildings were occupied, and Station Flight had an Atlas, Avro 504N and DH

A typical 'Laing Hut', complete with water tank and chimney (Laing & Co Ltd).

Abingdon's 'Building 26', the 1932-style water tower.

Moth by the end of the month. Oxford University Air Squadron moved in on November 3 for a long stay.

Central Area took control of Abingdon in November 1933. Only the Gordons were operating, but this was remedied on June 1 1934 when XV Squadron formed and soon had Hawker Harts. A year later both squadrons participated in the Mildenhall Jubilee Review. In October 1935 40 Squadron re-equipped with Hart (Special) day bombers.

January 7 1936 brought clear signs of RAF expansion. More buildings were completed on the camp, and C Flight, 40 Squadron, became 104 Squadron. The following month, part of XV Squadron became the nucleus of 98 Squadron and received Hawker Hinds, more of which were delivered, to 40 Squadron, in March 1936.

Just over 2,000 people visited Abingdon's 1936 Empire Air Day viewing, among others, a Heyford, Overstrand, Bulldog, Moth and a stripped Tutor keeping company with two Hinds. For this treat they paid just one shilling, and saw some flying too. How many would now appear at Abingdon's gates for that show?

Abingdon was so crowded that in August 1936 both 98 and 104 Squadrons left from what had, since May 1, been a 1 Group station. On January 18 1937 XV Squadron parented No 52, a new Hind Squadron. On May 3 1937, 62 Squadron arose from 40 Squadron. To make room for this latest formation 52 Squadron moved in late February to Upwood. On the 1937 Empire Air Day some 6,000 people called, and a new 12-Bay Type 'C' Hangar was to be seen.

Cranfield received 62 Squadron on July 12 1937 when Avro Tutors of the Cambridge University Air Squadron were at Abingdon. During November 1937 the Navy placed 802 Squadron on detachment here, its Hawker Nimrods and Ospreys staying until January 1938 when they boarded HMS *Glorious*. 40 Squadron shed a further Flight, on March 3 1938 when 185 Squadron was reformed and received Hinds, as did 106 Squadron, hived off from XV Squadron, on June 1 1938.

On June 13 1938, the first Fairey Battle arrived for XV Squadron which equipped with Battle IIs in June–July 1938. Seven Battles arrived for 40 Squadron on July 7 1938, others for 106 Squadron following. The latter squadron and 18 Squadron left for Thornaby in August and September.

Both XV and 40 Squadrons, operational by late September 1938, formed a Wing of the AASF. Although 103 Squadron was here in September 1938 it was not earmarked for the AASF. Lack of equipment precluded 103 Squadron from joining them. With little warning both XV and 40 were placed at readiness on September 10 1938 as the Munich Crisis developed. War peparations went ahead, short of mobilisation. With conflict seeming inevitable, Station Commanders were, on September 27, called to HQ 1 Group. Whilst they were meeting, the Prime Minister announced that war had been averted, bringing relief mixed with concern.

No 103 Squadron received Battles between late July and mid-September 1938 and was fully operational before leaving in April 1939. Through spring and summer 1939, Abingdon's squadrons trained for their role in the AASF enacted when the Battle squadrons were ordered to prepare for France when Poland was invaded on September 1 1939. By nightfall, civil aircraft had arrived to transport ground personnel. After being camouflaged these aircraft set off at around 10:00 on September 2. An hour later both squadrons followed to France as 71 Wing AASF.

War station movement brought Whitley Is of 166 Squadron, and IIs of 97

'Building 108', an Abingdon Barrack Block of 1920s design. It is still in use, sturdy and complete with a television aerial.

Squadron flew from Leconfield to Benson on September 14 and 15 1939. Two Battle squadrons were to form an AASF Pool at Abingdon, 52 and 63 Squadrons starting to arrive on September 2 1939. Benson's surface was unsuitable for Whitleys so a direct swop with Abingdon's Battles came about. Between September 16 and 18, the Whitleys arrived forming 4 Group Pool. Former buildings of HQ 1 Group were taken over now, HQ 6 Group partly controlling bomber training replaced HQ 1 Group in vacated buildings. Both later became part of HQ 91 Group.

Whitley Mk IIIs replaced 166 Squadron's Mk Is in January 1940. On March 23 1940 two visiting Whitleys landed back from the Ruhr, but the major event of the period occurred on April 2 when both Whitley squadrons dissolved into a new unit—No 10 Operational Training Unit. Whitleys of 97 and 166 Squadrons were placed in A Flight and Ansons of 97 Squadron with Whitleys of 166 Squadron formed B Flight. From May 1940 a few Whitley IVs were at the station.

Débâcle in France caused some Battles to call at their one-time HQ airfield. During the afternoon of June 15 no less than 73 AASF aircraft passed through, with six the next day.

By mid July 1940, 10 OTU's nominal establishment stood at 40 + 14 Whitleys and 18 Ansons, the former in A, C and D Flights and the latter in B. 10 OTU first operated on July 21 1940, dropping leaflets. More sorties were flown in August by Whitley IIIs and Vs. Tiger Whitleys, II and III, were then largely replaced by Mk Vs.

The designated satellite at Stanton Harcourt came into use for night flying on September 3 1940 and remained under Abingdon's control until January 15 1946. C Flight of 10 OTU dispersed there on September 10 1940 until a Whitley shortage brought disbandment in February 1941. A Flight, which converted crews on to Whitleys, replaced it.

The importance of blind approach training brought about the formation of No 1 BAT Flight at Abingdon on January 12 1941. It used Whitleys III and V and Ansons. Oxfords replaced Whitleys when 1501 BAT Flight was established in December 1941. The Flight moved to Stanton Harcourt on April 18 1943, disbanding on December 31 1943. Oxfords remained at Abingdon, within 91 Group Communications Flight.

Enemy intruders were active at dusk in the Oxford area on March 12 1941. Whilst Whitleys were night flying, a raider dropped 16 bombs putting Abingdon out of action. Damage was caused to a Whitley, and other bombs fell around the bomb dump. The Germans came again, around 21:45 on March 21 1941, dropping 26 bombs across 6 Group's HQ area. Seven offices were wrecked, ceilings and windows of another ten being damaged, in one of the few successful attacks on any

Sepulchral splendour? Abingdon's Atheneum—or simply 'SHQ (1932 Style)'—a monument to Imperial days.

HQ organisation in Britain during the war.

Orders given in May 1941 demanded that OTU output should be 40 crews a month by using satellite facilities fully. 10 OTU now made use of Mount Farm, between July 23 1941 and February 12 1942. Availability of 10 OTU for leaflet drops was signalled in June 1941, and a few operational sorties were flown from Abingdon in July 1941.

OTU strength was around four dozen Whitleys and 18 Ansons. In August 1941 Lysander target tugs were added, further aircraft of that type here at the end of the year being flown by 7 AACU.

Gradual replacement of front line Whitleys released them for alternative employment. Since late summer 1940 Whitley Vs had proven useful for ocean patrol, although the aircraft's attack profile was poor. To help to counter the U-Boats a special Whitley flight of 10 OTU formed in April 1942 and was placed at St Eval in Cornwall. Modifications to 33 aircraft enabled them to carry depth charges and carry ASV radar. Operational flying was judged good for morale for, apart from 11 *Nickel* sorties in November 1941 and eight in December, such flights were rare. Only four bombing sorties had been despatched—to Orleans and Tours airfields on November 30 1941.

Simultaneous to using Whitleys for maritime purposes, 10 OTU was to participate in the 1,000 bomber raids. This depended upon crew availability as well as aircraft. Creaming off some for Biscay patrols was no help. Therefore, the detached flight delayed its operational debut, allowing 21 Whitleys to take off for Cologne on May 30 1942. All returned, one crash landing at Manston. For the ensuing Essen raid, 22 Whitleys set out from Abingdon and one did not return. Abingdon's 20-strong contingent for the June 1,000 Plan Bremen raid was less fortunate, three aircraft being lost and one crew was snatched from the sea.

St Eval's detachment began operational flying on August 4 1942 with 26 aircraft. Each crew flew six operational patrols of nine to ten hours duration and each was credited with a third of a bomber sortie. Four depth charges were carried and, to make each sortie really valuable, two 9½ lb practice bombs were aimed at a rock off the Cornish coast! A long range tank in the aircraft's belly extended its range. Crews were ordered to ditch if they met one of the Ju 88s now patrolling Biscay. Little wonder that a popular song became questionably 'I'm dreaming of a White Whitley . . .'. Operations ceased on July 19 1943. When the detachment returned to Abingdon on July 23 1943 it had flown 1,862 sea patrols, 16,864 flying hours, had 91 U-boat sightings, made 55 attacks, damaged *U-214, U-523* and *U-591* and sunk the *U-564.* Aircraft losses totalled 33.

Participation in Main Force attacks on Germany within the *Grand National* series

and raids on Bremen, Düsseldorf and Essen had taken place in 1942. Operational training was then resumed, interspersed with a few leaflet-dropping sorties in February and April 1943.

Strength of 10 OTU in February 1943 was 55 Whitley Vs, 11 Ansons, three Lysanders and one Defiant. Earlier needs to night fly at the satellite to avoid bombing of the parent station were no longer necessary. The OTU was re-organised, A and B Flights being at Stanton Harcourt and C, D and G at Abingdon. In April 1943, Martinets replaced the Lysanders. *Bullseyes* were being flown and ASR sorties. 91 Group Air Gunners Instructors' School opened, giving a seven-day course and employing two Whitleys and two Martinets. Some of the 54 Whitleys at 10 OTU in August 1943 were Mk VIIs retrieved from St Eval. *Nickelling* was carried out in September 1943, a dozen such sorties being flown in November and 16 in December without loss.

Into 1944 Whitleys droned around Abingdon, managing 12 sorties to France in January 1944 to drop 2,266,000 leaflets. Sergeant Averill was 25 miles into France when an engine failed. All removable equipment was jettisoned before the

Whitley II, K7229, *of 97 Squadron based at Abingdon between March and July 1940. Previously with 51 Squadron, it crashed in 10 B&GS' hands on March 5 1941, during a snowstorm near Dumfries* (C.A. Nepean Bishop).

Whitley landed safely at Tangmere. During February 1944, 10 OTU flew 13 more sorties, dropping 1,656,144 leaflets, the most by one unit that month. A disturbing feature, though, was the loss of Whitley *LA787* sent to St Quentin on February 28 1944. Whitleys subsequently operated west of the north/south line passing through Paris, and only OTU Wellingtons ventured eastwards. In March 1944 another dozen *Nickel* sorties were flown.

Until March 20 1944, Abingdon's Whitleys operated from grass runways. Flying was then switched to Stanton Harcourt whilst two runways were laid. At the satellite 10 OTU bade farewell to its faithful old Whitleys, and unit establishment was reduced to three-quarters OTU. Four

Mighty Beverley, XB288, *of 47 Squadron at Abingdon in 1963.*

Hurricanes replaced the Martinets during June and, in July 1944, 10 OTU commenced re-equipping with Wellington Xs. Not until October 1944 did the last Whitley leave 10 OTU. Daylight training resumed at Abingdon on November 16 1944.

In March 1945 10 OTU's strength stood at 50 Wellington Xs, five Hurricanes and two Master IIs. Remaining in 91 Group, 10 OTU did not disband until September 10 1946. Abingdon's bomber link was broken on October 24 1946 when Transport Command took control and 525 Squadron moved in. On December 1 it was renumbered 238 Squadron. No 46, here by the start of 1947, flew Dakotas. Dakotas vacated Abingdon in December 1947 and were replaced by Avro Yorks of Nos 51, 59 and 242 Squadrons, operating overseas trunk routes. In December 1947, eight months after disbandment at Shallufa, 40 Squadron reformed at Abingdon, its ancestral home.

When the Russians blockaded Berlin, Yorks played a major part in the air lift. On July 10 1948, the first York to arrive in Berlin was one of Abingdon's 59 Squadron. The Yorks were soon sited at German airfields, reducing expense and increasing the supply rate. When the Berlin airlift ended, Abingdon was switched to an army support role, the station moving from 47 to 38 Group on June 27 1949. The York squadrons left for Bassingbourn, apart from 242 Squadron which re-equipped with Hastings. Both the TCDU and ATrDU moved to Abingdon and, in 1950, No 1 PTS came from Upper Heyford, complete with its famous parachutists' tower and captive balloon.

November 1950 saw the arrival of 30 Squadron's Valettas which stayed until May 1952. A 1951 arrival was No 1 Overseas Ferry Unit complete with Harvards, Oxfords and Mosquitoes for training. It was responsible for delivery aircraft overseas and became best known for the trans-Atlantic delivery of Sabre jets to the RAF. On February 1 1953 the OFU split into two squadrons, Nos 147 and 167, before moving to Benson in April 1953. Transport Command Air Support Flight, known from September 14 1954 as 1312 Flight, replaced them.

In May 1953 Abingdon assumed an operational role with the arrival of Hastings of Nos 24 and 47 Squadrons from Topcliffe and Dishforth. No 53 Squadron replaced No 24 on January 1 1957, then ferried troops to Kenya for anti-Mau Mau operations.

March 1956 saw the arrival of 162 ft span Beverleys, able to carry bulky loads and operate from small, rough airstrips. In February 1957, 53 Squadron received its first Beverleys and, on June 28 1963, merged with 47 Squadron, crews drawing their aircraft from a central pool. Abingdon, with over 2,000 aircraft movements a month, had become one of the busiest airfields in Britain. The long 'F' hangar was handed over to the RAF on April 30 1959, and ten years later was modified to permit Belfasts to come for overhauls.

Until October 31 1967, Beverleys of 47/53 Squadron operated world wide while the Transport Command Air Movements Development Unit carried out research into movement of heavy freight and large scale air movements.

In the summer of 1966 the station became the base for the Andover Training Flight. On December 1 1966 the first Andover Squadron formed, No 46, and was stationed here until it moved to Thorney Island in August 1970 along with the Training Flight. No 52 Squadron, Andover equipped, also formed here on December 1 1966 and soon went overseas.

April 1968 was mutely celebrated as the RAF's 50th birthday, amid ill feeling towards a government reckoned to be unsympathetic to the RAF and certainly oblivious of tradition. Whilst one intrepid soul flew by the Houses of Parliament at a low level in an attempt to wake the incumbents, others conserved their energy for HM Queen Elizabeth's visit to the RAF on June 14 1968. The venue for the event, marked by a large exhibition of historic aircraft, many destined for the Hendon museum, was Abingdon where HM Queen Elizabeth II lunched appropriately in an Officers' Mess dating back to Imperial days.

On September 1 1972 the Air Support Command Examining Unit became 46 Group Air Transport Examining Unit, Strike Command. The Joint Air Transport Establishment, formed here in 1971, moved from Abingdon to Brize Norton on December 31 1975 followed by PTS, for on January 1 1976 the station was transferred from 38 Group to RAF Support Command. The 600-ft long, 140-ft wide, 50-ft high unique 'F' hangar became the centre for Jaguar overhaul and repair by the Aircraft Production Squadron. Leconfield's 60 MU and 71 MU Bicester, had amalgamated to form

'It's the biggest, final fly past in the world', Gracie Fields might have sung. Beverleys salute themselves and Abingdon at the 1967 Battle of Britain Display.

the Engineering Wing in May 1976, and the first of many Jaguars to pass through arrived on June 3 1976. Hawks and Hunters are now handled too.

In addition to Nos 1 and 2 Aircraft Maintenance Squadron, the Rapier and Salvage Squadron is based here to maintain fixed wing aircraft in Britain and overseas. Since August 1973 Bulldogs of the University of London Air Squadron have resided here alongside Chipmunks of No 6 Air Experience Flight. In 1975 they were joined by OUAS whose Bulldogs were brought from Bicester. Abingdon has of late hosted VC-10s withdrawn from British Airways service and stored for military use.

Akeman Street, Oxfordshire

SP335140. 3 miles NW of Witney

Akeman Street took its title from 2,000 years ago when a Roman road passed across England, its line running over this wartime airfield. Akeman Street's site was selected in late 1939 for development into an RLG for 2 SFTS Brize Norton, and was available from July 10 1940. Following the bombing of Brize Norton, the Advanced Training Squadron of 2 SFTS came here and, two days after the raid, was a going concern.

By March 1941, Oxfords of 2 SFTS were also making considerable use of Southrop. An Oxford, night flying near Akeman Street at 03:30 hours on July 28 1941, was brought down some two miles north-east of the airfield by an intruder. Such incidents were, fortunately, rare.

Flying by 2 SFTS' Oxfords continued until March 1942. On March 14, 2 SFTS was re-designated 2 (P) AFU. The training syllabus changed but the aircraft remained until July 14 1942 when 2 (P) AFU closed. By then the flying field had more of the appearance of a modestly developed airfield. Living quarters, mess buildings, shelters and a small operations block had been built by Laing, with help from Thorn. Most buildings were to 1941 designs, including ten Over Type 65 ft Blister hangars (pattern 12512/41) and a large Bellman of an older style than most, (5498/36). Although small, three grass runways were closely sited on the field overlapping for much of their area.

After 2 (P) AFU closed, the airfield was allocated to 6 (P) AFU, Little Rissington,

Right *A Battle of XV Squadron flying over Abingdon before the war. The airfield is sited in the centre of the picture.*

which started using the site in July 1942 and continued to do so until October 1945 although flying ceased on August 15 1945. Still in the hands of Flying Training Command, it closed on February 1 1947. Crop sprayers sometimes now operate from the site.

Atherstone (Stratford), Warwickshire

See Stratford

Baginton (Coventry Airport), West Midlands

SP362745. 4 miles SE of Coventry

Municipal airports were contagious in the 1930s. Like Luton, Coventry relied upon an industrial tenant to help pay the bill for prestige, and knew that the Air Ministry was interested in establishing a VR school at Coventry. Land was acquired in 1935. Adjacent lay the Whitley works of Armstrong Whitworth Aircraft (AWA), with a flying field alongside for lightly loaded aircraft. The prospect of heavy aircraft using the larger nearby field appealed to AWA as much as to Coventry councillors and Baginton was born of a partnership.

Armstrong Whitworth had rarely held a production contract of much size, and not until the mid-1930s did they know real success. Indeed, their experimental and building shop was one. Now they had a chance to prove themselves with the Whitley, the Midland's bomber.

It originated from a 1934 bomber for the Czech government intended to bomb Berlin. Its cancellation left AWA with a bomber design paraded before the Air Ministry, coincidentally with the June 1934 decision to disregard disarmament agreements relating to bomber size and performance. The Air Ministry seized upon AWA's submission, produced specification B 3/34 around it and coupled a 2,500 lb bomb load with a range of 1,250 miles. On September 14 1934 an order for two AW B 3/34s was awarded. In recognition of the company's old home, the new bomber was called the Whitley.

Much design work had been completed, but AWA was also busy with the Ensign airliner based upon the Whitley, in essence a four-engined version, and the bomber's progress was slow. The first prototype did not fly until March 16 1936 and the second on February 11 1937. Concern arose over the company's ability to cope with a major production programme, although the Baginton factory came into use in May 1936.

On August 23 1935 the first production order for 80 Tiger-engined Whitleys was placed, 52 of which were to be delivered by July 1937. Production was to end in March 1939. It was December 23 1936 when the first production aircraft flew, the first delivery coming on March 9 1937. By the end of June 1937 only 14 Whitley Is had left the factory and the bomber was

already outdated. Progress with new types was slow and resulted in repeated orders for Whitleys. Whitley development was limited, but changes brought increased bomb loads from 3,000 lb to 8,000 lb. Modifications to the Tiger-engined Mk III led to it being able to carry, from August 1937, 2 × 2,000 lb bombs. The earlier Mk I and Mk II could only accommodate bombs of up to 500 lb calibre in the fuselage bomb bay. Further bombs—6 × 250 lb and 6 × 112 lb, these latter soon being made obsolete—could be carried in wing bomb cells. Fitting Merlin IVs produced the Whitley IV first flown from Baginton on April 18 1939. Only a few of the Mk Is were initially flown from Whitley works. From the Mk IV came the handful of Merlin X-engined Mk IVs before the ultimate bomber, the Mk V, appeared. It featured nose and tail FN power-operated gun turrets, delivery beginning at the outbreak of war.

Waritme production of Whitley fuselages was undertaken at Whitley Abbey works, mainplanes panelling and details at the Coventry Ordnance Works in Smith Street. Wing and final assembly was undertaken in a huge three-bay hall at Baginton.

For the purpose of observing industrial premises from the air to assess their camouflage, No 1 Camouflage Unit formed at Baginton in September 1939 and employed some unusual aircraft, including Stinson Reliants. Whitley production steadily increased, as AWA took only limited interest in their Albemarle, tested here briefly in the autumn of 1940.

Serious gaps in Midland defences were apparent by Autumn 1940. A new Fighter Group, No 9, was established whose headquarters was at Baginton. On September 25 1940, Hurricanes of No 308 (Polish) Squadron were brought to Baginton from Speke. Coventry was already protected by barrage balloons whose proximity meant that care was needed when flying near the city. Bombs first fell upon Coventry on August 26 1940. Several night raids followed before the great raid of November 14 which came six days after No 1 Camouflage Unit left for Hendon.

On November 24, a Ju 88 was shot down near Cirencester by two Hurricanes of 308 Squadron. Such activity was limited, and most enemy activity took place at night, facilities for which were so poor that night standbys had to be undertaken at Bramcote. In daylight on March 26 1941 a Ju 88, attempting to bomb the Armstrong Whitworth factory, was forced to jettison its load over Stoneleigh. Another attack, using incendiaries and made in April 1941, resulted in slight damage to a Whitley. Baginton then held a new squadron, No 403, formed in March 1 1941 and equipped with Tomahawks. As soon as it was operational in May 1941 it moved to Ternhill.

On May 29, 308 Squadron, re-equipped with Spitfires in April, left for Chilbolton.

A distinguished gathering at Barford St John. By Gloster F 9/40, DG205/G, *stand (left to right) Gloster test pilots, Crosby Warren and Michael Daunt; the firm's Managing Director, Mr F. MacKenna; Air Commodore Sir Frank Whittle and Gloster's Chief Designer, Mr W.G. Carter —pipe in hand!* (Gloster).

It was replaced by 605 (County of Warwick) Squadron. June 16 1941 brought yet another new squadron, No 457, which stayed until August 1941 when Baginton ceased to be a Sector Station, its place being taken by Honiley to where 605 Squadron moved in September. Thereafter the station became an overseas kitting-out centre. No 135 Squadron reformed at Baginton on August 15 1941, took over 605s Hurricanes then moved to Honiley. No 79 Squadron came late in December 1941 and left for India in March 1942, and 134 Squadron in April 1942.

Summer 1940 saw preparation of the Whitley for paratroop duties, and its adaptation for Costal Command leading to the Whitley VII, the first of 150 reaching the Command in August 1941. Later that year brief trials were conducted at Baginton and at Honiley to assess the qualities of the Whitley as a Horsa glider tug. A variety of non-flying units also used Baginton before 32 Squadron arrived late 1942 en route for North Africa.

Alvis, the engine manufacturer, kept a small fleet of test bed aircraft at Baginton until after the war. In June 1943, Whitley production, which had peaked at 12 examples a week, ceased. AWA was considered a weak industrial organisation, unfit to cope with a change in production type. Although at one time scheduled to build 64 Wellingtons, that plan had been abandoned in favour of production of the first Merlin Whitley, the Mk IV,

At the outbreak of war, the Air Ministry had proposed that the company should switch to building Avro Manchesters under the Group Scheme. Because the latter had done little on the Manchester, plans were then made for AWA to build Halifaxes. Again, the idea fell through then, in March 1940, an order for 300 Manchesters was placed with AWA. When Lord Beaverbrook decided to restrict production to well-tried aircraft, the Whitley was chosen, another 300 being ordered as the Manchester idea was shelved.

July 1940, however, brought strong indications that a four-engined Manchester would become reality, yet not until March 1942 was the controversy between protagonists of the Halifax and the four-engined Manchester resolved fully in favour of the latter. March 1942 finally saw the reinstatement of the Manchester order at Whitworths as a result of which, in August 1942, the first Coventry-built Lancaster was delivered from Baginton. For another ten months, though, Whitleys would be built here and over the period March 1937 to June 1943 AWA delivered 1,812 Whitleys, flew most of them from Baginton and produced for Bomber Command and others a total of 1,466 Whitley Vs.

Production next centred upon the Hercules-engined Lancaster II. Without hard runways, flight testing of heavy aircraft depended much upon the state of airfields and, to alleviate delays, facilities were obtained at Bitteswell where the conventional hard three-runway pattern existed. Both this airfield and Baginton were used for Lancaster I, II and III test flying. At the end of the war, Lancasters were being converted at Baginton to Far East standards, along with Lincolns. The latter frequently here for overhaul, was Baginton built from 1945 until 1948.

With a desire for civil business, Armstrong Whitworth boldly applied to their factory the legend 'Pioneers of Progress'. Fair comment for, in 1944, the company secured a contract for a large flying wing mail carrier, the AW52 jet tested at Bitteswell. Prototypes of the AW55 Apollo turbo-prop air liner flew from both airfields.

Association with Hawker-Siddeley led to Meteors being built at Baginton, Mk 4s then Mk 8s. Drag reduction using boundary layer suction devices led to the AWA-built Griffiths Wing for trials on a Hurricane and Meteor. Drawing boards carried AWA projects for a five-engined flying wing bomber to OR 228, which eventually resulted in the Vulcan, and a flying test bed to precede the Lightning fighter. AWA were interested in that requirement too, proposing some of the first integral wing fuel tanks. Nothing came of these, the company instead designing night fighters based upon the Meteor T7 trainer. All Meteor night fighters were built here, also the Sapphire-engined Hunter 2s and 5s. Armstrong Whitworth also built nearly all of the Hawker Sea Hawks.

There was no hard runway at Baginton prior to the opening of the mile-long runway on October 15 1950. Some jet flights were made from the grass, including the first flight (on February 10 1954) of the prone pilot Meteor *WK935*. Argosys were the last aircraft constructed here. Lacking the range for its envisaged role, the Argosy transport had a brief service career. On July 16 1965 the factory closed and

RAE Bedford has been much involved in the development of automatic and audio control using a BAC 111, XX919.

another famous name vanished.

Baginton's civilian usefulness saved it. Jersey Air Lines operated a service to the Channel Islands between 1952 and 1962, then British United flew extended services. A variety of civilian operators have used, and still use, Baginton—particularly for taxi and freight services. A wide assortment of civil aircraft are based here, on a site marked by Bellman hangars.

Barford St John, Oxfordshire

SP440340. SE of Bloxham, NW of Deddington, off the B4031 at Hempton

A well-guarded central area containing tall radio masts marks Barford as a 'communications centre'. A board near the camp entrance informs the passer-by that it is the home of a 'Transmitter Annexe' in Anglo-American hands. More thrilling moments in its life are left to imagination.

Barford came into use in mid-1941 as a small, grass Relief Landing Ground which, on June 30 1941, Oxfords of 15 SFTS Kidlington began using for practice flying. Late on August 24 an enemy aircraft dropped six light bombs on the east side of the landing ground, but it caused little disturbance.

By late 1941 a decision had been taken to develop the airfield extensively. A conventional three-runway pattern was imposed, with 'T2' hangars, and temporary wartime brick buildings. Bomber Command took control from Kidlington on April 10 1942 and made Barford Upper Heyford's satellite, reopening it on December 15 1942 with Wellington IIIs of 16 OTU. March 1943 brought Mustang 1s of Nos 4 and 169 Squadrons for their part in Exercise *Spartan.* Fast as they were, the Mustangs would have found themselves outshone had they stayed for a few weeks.

Early plans for flying jet aircraft highlighted basic problems. Gloster's airfield at Brockworth was too small for experimental aircraft whose power plants seemed likely to enforce long, problematic take off runs. The company shopped around for suitable test centres, first using Cranwell and then Newmarket Heath. Another airfield used was Barford St John.

Gloster's were afforded the use of half a hangar at Barford in May 1943, and the station became the flight test centre for the Gloster F.9/40, basis of the Meteor. To Barford came, also, the Gloster E.28/39 'Pioneer' *W4041*, the first British jet aircraft, now having the more powerful W.2/500 engine. Between June 12 and 29 1943 it managed 23 flights from Barford, and also received high-speed aerofoil section wings. *W4041* left late in 1943 for Farnborough to continue engine and aerodynamic testing.

On Sunday, May 28 1943, the Halford-

Concorde research was undertaken in Bedford's tunnels. This fibreglass model is displayed at Old Warden.

engined F.9/40, *DG206* flew in from Newmarket Heath. *DG205* fitted with W.2B engines, first flew from here, on June 12 1943. Throughout the summer both were active. F.9/40, *DG204*, with underslung axial flow Matrovick F/2 engines, arrived here in August 1943. It never flew from Barford, trouble being encountered with high idling thrust which would have made control at slow speed very difficult. F.9/40s flew from Barford until Gloster's acquired Morston Valence.

Jet flying only took place in good, calm weather. It had to be slotted into the busy training programme carried out at Barford by 16 OTU's Wellington IIIs, and later its Mk Xs. The gunnery element of 16 OTU was also placed here.

Good reserves of aircrew halted 16 OTU's Wellington Flying on December 12 1944 and brought a dramatic change, for Mosquitoes of 1655 Mosquito Training Unit—mainly Mks XX, XXV and TIII—arrived on December 30 and 31 1944 at the parent station, and at Barford where most of the TIIIs were based, accompanied by Oxfords. From January 1 1945 the unit was known as 16 OTU and was preparing Mosquito crews for 8 Group. This continued until the summer of 1945 when flying was reduced. Mosquito XVIs replaced the Canadian-built Mosquitoes in mid-summer 1945.

Positioning of lights to control traffic passing the end of the main runway at Barford received much publicity in July 1945, but within a few weeks Barford was lying rejected. The move of 16 OTU to Cottesmore in March 1946 caused it to cease being an active airfield.

Bedford (see also Thurleigh), Bedfordshire

TL040600. 8 miles N of Bedford, in open country N of Thurleigh village

On a plateau topping undulating countryside to the north of Bedford, in a sparsely populated area, lies the Royal Aircraft Establishment, Bedford. This is the largest airfield built since the war in central England. It lacks Farnborough's greatness and associations, and is clearly a product of our stark, supersonic age.

Rapid development in aeronautics demanded special post-war research facilities. Wind tunnel testing would play a far greater part, certainly for research into high-speed flight. Therefore the new test centre would need wind tunnels functioning over wide speed and pressure ranges. The airfield would require equipment and facilities for repair, major modification and trial installation work. Exceptionally long runways were thought necessary for high speed aircraft, and equipped with navigational aids in case of sudden weather deterioration. Workshops would be needed to cope with aircraft submitted for trials. For these facilities a power supply with a peak loading capacity

K7191, *a Whitley 1 outside Baginton's then-new assembly sheds, joined 10 Squadron in May 1937, passed to 166 Squadron in July 1939 and joined 7 B&GS in January 1940* (AWA).

of around 200,000 hp was necessary.

Farnborough was first considered as the site for a revised establishment, but very long runways of the type in mind could never be laid there. Alternative sites were considered in 1944 before the choice fell on a level site 275 ft above sea level north of Bedford. Electrical power for the tunnel site could be supplied by Little Barford power station. Water supplies of up to 400,000 gallons daily could be obtained from a pumping station on the River Ouse at Sharnbrook. Later, 750,000 gallons could be supplied.

What made the scheme so startling when announced in 1945 was the amalgamation of three airfields and a five-mile long concrete runway from Thurleigh to Little Staughton. A giant taxi track was to link it to Twinwood upon which vast hangar maintenance facilities were to be erected. This massive undertaking never materialised. Thurleigh was engulfed by the Ministry of Works project and giant wind tunnels were erected by Twinwood Farm.

On June 12 1946 the contract was placed for the construction of two miles of concrete road linking the Twinwood Wind Tunnel Site to the A6 road north of Bedford. Two miles of 10-in water pipes were to be laid to convey water to the site. Building at the tunnel and airfield areas commenced in 1946.

The first tunnel commissioned was the 3 × 3 ft transonic wind tunnel, the main drive for which was brought from the German research station at Volkenrode. Trials over a range 0.9 to 2.0 Mach, providing the equivalent of 1,500 mph at sea level could be undertaken in the tunnel, air pressure ranging over 0.1 to 2.0 atmospheres absolute. Drive equipment could reach 16,000 bhp. This, and the Vertical Spinning Tunnel, along with the High Speed Laboratory, were complete by 1952, when the tunnel commenced working. The spin tunnel is 80 ft high and has a diameter of 46 ft. Free fall models can be tested in it.

In 1953 the 13 × 9 ft Low Speed tunnel was completed, followed by the 8 × 8 ft Supersonic Tunnel, made ready by 1956. The 3 × 4 ft High Supersonic Speed Tunnel was opened in 1961, but has been closed for reasons of economy.

A visit to Bedford's Tunnel Site is memorable. The portion of the tunnel in which the test specimen is installed represents a very small part of the complex. The 8 × 8 ft tunnel is the largest in its Mach number range in Western Europe, and is also the largest pressure vessel. Some 90,000 bhp is required to drive the main compressor and auxiliaries when running at maximum. Little wonder, then, that the power unit resembles more the engine room of a giant ship than an item of airfield equipment. In the case of the 3 × 3 ft high supersonic tunnel, designed for Mach numbers between 2.5

and 5.0, the main drive has to be achieved from two identical compressor sets working in parallel. A total of 300,000 bhp is generated on site.

Much of the wind tunnel testing of Concorde was undertaken at Bedford tunnels, and there has been considerable work on STOL and VTOL features. Vortices occasionally form in the working section, and a dramatic photograph in one of the tunnel complexes shows them streaming from the wing tips of a model Concorde.

Bedford's airfield is set apart from the Tunnel Site, and reached by a private road. The aerodrome has a 10,500 ft runway (built by AMWD) and three smaller, subsidary runways. Its position on high ground gives it an unobstructed horizon for more than five miles, making it an ideal area for radar development work. In 1956 the Blind Landing Experimental Unit arrived from Martlesham and, more recently, the flying wing of the Royal Signals and Radar Establishment, Malvern has moved to Bedford. Its variety of unusual aircraft includes Canberras, curiously modified Meteors and two Viscounts.

The largest hangar on the site is an all-aluminium structure with a clear span of 200 ft, a clear height of 50 ft and an ovreall length of 245 ft. Radiant heating of this and other hangars reduces heat loss when the large doors are opened. The

An advert tells it all—'AWA Pacemakers of Progress' proudly recalling the 1938 Ensign against the post-war flying wing.

The Queen's Flight uses two Wessex helicopters. XV733 *is seen here after having carried HRH Princess Anne to the 1982 Suffolk Show.*

floor has a surface temperature set at 75 degrees F. Hot water radiant panels are sited along the hangar walls and heated pipes are embedded beneath the tracks to assist in cold weather door opening.

Within the Flight Area on the south-west side of the airfield are the hangars, workshops, offices, stores, laboratories, etc. On the north side is the Naval Air Section with similar facilities, catapults and arrester gear. Organisation of the Establishment has changed a number of times, but within its composition an aerodynamics testing section has remained. A recently used aircraft has been an attractively finished Gnat, employed for gust research and liberally fitted with pressure measurement equipment. General development work on helicopters, including their use in difficult weather conditions, has taken place, along with trials to improve their instrumentation. An HS 125 with a laser for radar ranging in cloud conditions has been used here.

Little evidence of Thurleigh's wartime days remain. When the Main Stores of the Tunnel Site were being built, a smallpox isolation hospital had first to be burnt down to eradicate any remaining contamination. When an old hut near the airfield was being demolished in 1974 it was found to have been used as a dormitory by the Americans. Eight wall panels bearing graffiti were carefully removed and flown to the USA for display in the Wright Patterson AFB, Dayton, Ohio museum.

As late as 1955 Bedford was referred to as the National Aeronautical Establishment, but since then it has become part of the RAE. From Farnborough the Naval Air Department and Flight Divisions were transferred that year. Within the Flight Systems Division, tests have been carried out on aids to flying, including flight simulators.

Whilst it is no part of RAE Bedford, in the town of that name is the Transonic Wind Tunnel of the Aircraft Research Association. This is an organisation combining the co-operative efforts of a number of firms in the British aircraft industry which, by contributing to the construction of the tunnel, produced one that supplements the work of the government establishment nearby. The decision to build this tunnel at Bedford was taken in 1951. The ARAL formed in January 1952 and its 9 × 8 ft tunnel came into use in the mid-1950s, building having started in October 1953.

Should Farnborough become unsuitable for flying in a busy area, British aeronautical research needs could be met by use of Bedford's excellent facilities.

Benson, Oxfordshire

SU631910. 13 miles SE of Oxford close to the A423(T)

Benson will be remembered as the home of photographic reconnaissance and the most magical aeroplane of all—the de Havilland Mosquito. Both flourished at Benson from 1941 to 1953. From there the Mosquito made its operational debut, and soon its Mosquitoes regularly roamed across Europe. They left from here to secure those famous photographs of Peenemünde, V-1s and 2s, and even reached the Balkans on unarmed sorties requiring colossal courage. Single-handed pilots of Benson's Spitfires commonly called on Berlin and snapped the shots that proved the Möhne Dam had been breached. And, most important of all, it

Above *Argosy—'a large merchant vessel once richly laden'. A fair proportion of the RAF's Argosy fleet tied up at Benson in 1969.*

Below *Typical of the numerous photographs taken by Benson's aircraft during the war as they roamed Europe, this shows the Augsburg Messerschmitt factory. Taken on April 24 1942—during a sortie to assess the effectiveness of the Lancaster raid on the MAN factory—it provided interesting shots of Me 210s.*

was Benson's crews who had the responsibility for finding just how effective the colossal wartime investment in Bomber Command was proving to be.

The building of Benson commenced in 1937 on a fine site through which a public road passes above the level of four 'C' Type hangars. You cannot easily miss these for they are painted white, as were some in pre-war days. Occupation of the station came early in 1939 and, during the first days of April, Nos 103 and 150 Squadrons brought their Battles along for a five-month stay. On September 2 1939, they left for France.

The intention was that, upon the outbreak of hostilities, Whitleys of 97 and 166 Squadrons would form 4 Group Pool here. But Benson's grass surface was found unsuitable when a detachment from 166 Squadron tried it. Therefore, on September 9 1939, plans changed. Nos 52 and 63 Battle Squadrons and a few Ansons moved to Benson and the Whitleys to Abingdon.

On arrival they found themselves alongside the Envoy *G-AEXX* of the King's Flight, for Hendon was no longer suitable for the Flight whose commander had wanted a move to Smith's Lawn in Windsor Great Park. Lacking range and defensive armament, the Envoy was the subject of concern, so, in the summer of 1939, a Lockheed Hudson, *N7263*, was chosen for the King's use. Internal modifications were made, its bulbous dorsal turret was retained and extra tanks extended the range to 3,000 miles, although only one passenger could be conveyed. Normal bomber camouflage was retained and there was no identity other than roundels and a serial number. King's Flight officers preferred using two Albatross airliners *G-AEVV* and *G-AEVW* but the suggestion was turned down. At Benson the Flight relied on the Hudson. March 1940 saw the arrival of a Percival Q.6 from Northolt for the King who shared it with the AOC Bomber Command. A second Hudson, *N7364*, held for a month early in 1940, was an unmodified reserve.

Both Battle squadrons became part of 1 Group Pool, abnormally increased by the arrival of 207 Squadron from Cranfield in April 1940. The three squadrons amalgamated to form No 12 Operational Training Unit whose Armament Training Flight was permanently detached to Penrhos for live weapons practice.

Benson's defences were rapidly strengthened in June 1940, pillboxes being constructed around the perimeter. At 23:55 on June 29 1940, 18 HEs fell in the vicinity of the fully lit station during a high level attack. It caused the satellite station, Mount Farm, to be put to use before it was intended.

July found the OTU training Battle crews to replace those lost in France. On August 13 the first Polish airmen arrived, to be trained for new Battle squadrons. As they were being welcomed as befits the brave people they have always been, the enemy also paid his compliments. A Ju 88

'Mosquito', a word almost synonymous with Benson from where Mosquitoes operated in peace and war, among them the PR Mk 1 prototype shown here, W4051 (DH).

dived out of low cloud, dropping three HEs and a hefty oil bomb. One HE fell upon unoccupied Shelter No 12 hurling debris on to the roof of the Airmen's Mess and between 'C' and 'D' hangars where an Anson was damaged. Two other bombs fell on waste ground and the oil bomb failed to ignite. Construction of a perimeter track commenced in August and September's duty concentrated upon training Poles and Czechs.

Bomber Command was eager to rid itself of the Fairey Battle. Brief trials with a Stirling showed the unsuitability of the grass airfield surface for such aircraft. There was doubt as to whether it would permit Wellington operations which, by mid-November, were intended for 12 OTU. Cranfield and Twinwood were alternative sites for 12 OTU but, by November, Mount Farm had metalled runways making this satellite quite suitable for Wellington day and night flying, leaving Benson available for maintenance duties and day flying. Benson was re-organised with effect from December 1 1940, the OTU strength changing to the equivalent of a half heavy bomber OTU. The Poles and Battles were posted.

The establishment of 12 OTU was reduced to give space to No 1 Photographic Reconnaissance Unit from Heston. Completed on December 27 1940, its arrival brought strange, unusually coloured Spitfires to Benson for work still of an experimental nature. Blenheim IVs and a few Hudsons accompanied them. Wellingtons were meanwhile arriving for 12 OTU which commenced training with them on January 4 1941, taking in six complete crews per fortnight.

A special award was now received by two soldiers, Sergeant D. Jobson and Private E.D. Gurnham, RASC. Each was given a George Medal for courage in getting a pilot from a burning Battle on July 14 1940.

Airfield extension was decided upon before January 30, when in the early after-noon, 19 HE bombs and incendiaries fell within the airfield boundary without causing damage. On February 27 1941 an enemy aircraft strafed and bombed the aerodrome and destroyed a Wellington.

By March 1941 the average intake at 12 OTU had fallen to only four crews a fort-night. Hopes for a regular six had been curtailed because the OTU was converting 1 Group Battle squadron crews to Wellingtons. Bad winter weather and the thaw played havoc with the landing ground, bringing the loss of three Wellingtons in a month, one over-running its chocks and smashing itself into No 1 Hangar.

As winter passed, Spitfire PR operations increased. On April 10 1941, for instance, a Spitfire was shot down on a sortie to Brest whilst another managed to secure PRU's first photographs of Copenhagen. Meanwhile, Flight Lieutenant A.L. Taylor was photographing Le Bourget, after which he strafed the airfield. Four days later, Sergeant W. Morgan managed quite an incredible feat when, in a Spitfire, he photographed Genoa and Spetzia before landing at Hawkinge in Kent after a seven hour ten minute flight at the end of which he had only two gallons of petrol left. He had established a record for such operations.

On the previous day, Pilot Officer S.H. Dowse had been less fortunate when four Bf 109s intercepted his Spitfire over Bergen. After escaping, he courageously turned into Germany, came out over Wilhelmshaven and forced landed, short of fuel, near Ipswich after an action-packed five-hour flight. April's successful sorties totalled 55, and a further 79 were flown in May. Wellingtons of 12 OTU in June 1941 flew a few *Nickels.* On June 17, No 1 PRU established another record for, in the course of 13 successful sorties, 37 films were run from which 6,800 prints were made between 12:30 hours and 22:10 hours. Marylands were, at this time, com-ing to Benson to be fitted with cameras, prior to operating in the Mediterranean Theatre.

Chipping Warden was chosen as the new home for 12 OTU. There the advance party moved on July 10 1941 and deprived themselves of witnessing that exhilerating moment when, on July 13, No 1 PRU received its first Mosquito. Benson's PR strength was further expanded when five Spitfires and a Blenheim IV of No 3 PRU arrived from Oakington to become part of 1 PRU which now surrendered Mount Farm to 15 OTU. By early September 1941 12 OTU had completely moved into Chipping Warden, and Benson was part of Coastal Command.

It was to Squadron Leader R.F.H. Clerke that the honour fell on September 17 of being the first pilot to take a Mosquito *(W4055)* on an operational sortie during which he called upon Bordeaux, La Pallice and Brest. Flight Lieutenant Taylor took the aircraft on its second operation, three days later, to the

Heliogoland-Sylt area. Already, the Mosquito was ranging widely.

Fast times and long duration were common to Benson's complement whose aircraft nearly always flew without defensive armament. Two long Mosquito flights, of February 12 and 28 1942, were to Danzig and Gdynia in Poland, respectively. By March, Mosquitoes were largely handling the Scandinavian commitment, leaving Spitfires to other areas. There were, though, notable exceptions such as a brave low-level run by Victor Ricketts and Boris Lukhmanoff to photograph the bombed Renault works at Billancourt. Augsburg, too, was photographed in April 1942 following the Lancaster low-level daylight raid on the MAN works. Damage assessment flights to Germany were mainly flown by Spitfire IVs, many of which differed in detail.

In September 1940 a de luxe DH Flamingo, *R2766*, arrived for the King's Flight. Alongside its RAF roundels it carried the civil registration *G-AGCC* to enable it to cross neutral territory readily in an emergency. Group Captain Fielden had pressed for a communications aircraft and, rather curiously, was offered the captured Me 108 *G-AFRN*, held at Farnborough. Displeasure greeted this and instead a Tutor, *K6120*, which had joined 63 Squadron at Benson in November 1939 and passed to 12 OTU, was put at the Flight's disposal. The Flamingo raised a number of problems, for it was an unarmed unfamiliar shape, needing a fighter escort so it was disposed of to 24 Squadron. Questions then arose about the continued existence of the Flight, along with its limited use. Eventually it was decided that the King's Flight would disband, and that the King would fly mainly in aircraft provided by a VIP detachment of 24 Squadron based at Northolt. Accordingly disbandment took place at Benson on February 14 1942. The Hudson, *N7263*, which had been used as the Royal aircraft early in the war joined 161 Squadron at Tempsford, and the Percival Q6 left for Halton in May 1942.

Another squadron which used Benson in the winter of 1941–2 was No 140. Formed to provide photographic coverage of enemy movements during an invasion of Britain, and as 1416 Flight based at Hendon, it gradually became a strategic reconnaissance unit for GHQ Home Command, controlled by Army Co-operation and not Coastal Command. It moved to Benson early in September 1941 with a mixture of Spitfires, and Blenheim IVs for night duty. Operations over coastal France commenced on October 1 1941 and, in November, night operations by the Blenheims started, during which they took photographs by the light of flash bombs. Another task was photographic support of the army within Britain, particularly of its use of camouflage. Early in 1942 the squadron began to photograph Channel shipping, until May 4 when the squadron's entire establishment and role changed. Next day it moved to Mount Farm to concentrate on army strategic reconnaissance over France, making flights leading to the Dieppe landing. The move had another purpose for, as 140 Squadron left Benson, the building of concrete runways began.

Clear, summer weather allowed a great increase in successful photographic reconnaissance operations. No 1 PRU expanded fast, frequently detaching aircraft to other bases at home and abroad. For administrative purposes it was decided to reform the PR force as squadrons rather than keep it as a series of Flights. The unit dispersed on October 18 1942, its dozen Mosquitoes forming 540 Squadron while 14 Spitfire PR IVs became 541 Squadron, an assortment of 19 Spitfires became 542 Squadron and another 15 changed into 543 Squadron, leaving a mixture of Marylands, Ansons, Spitfires and Wellington IVs to call themselves 544 Squadron.

Benson was certainly an action station, despatching sorties over the whole of Europe. At nearby Medmenham, results were analysed. The Battle of the Ruhr was daily recorded and, at 07:25 hours on May 17 1943, Flying Officer F.G. Fray set off in Spitfire IV, *EN343*, of 542 Squadron to photograph the results of the attacks on the Mohne and Sorpe Dams. Next day Flying Officer D.G. Scott took *EN411* over the Ruhr to observe and photograph the extent of flooding of the Ruhr and on the following day Benson Spitfires flew another three sorties of the Sorpe Dam. During their ever-deeper penetrations into Germany, Mosquitoes of 540 Squadron returned with photographs of Peenemünde which confirmed its use and, for the British, the development of the V-weapons. Experimental night photography using Mosquito IVs of 544 Squadron began in February 1943.

Two-stage supercharged Merlin engines led to refinements of both Spitfires and Mosquitoes. The Spitfire PR Mk XI came into use at Benson in May 1943 and a handful of re-engined Mosquito Mk IVs, redesignated PR VIIIs, had been introduced in February 1943. In June, 540 Squadron began operating PR IXs.

During October 1943, 543 Squadron left Benson. Spitfires of 541 and 542 Squadron and Mosquitoes of 544 Squadron and 540 Squadron stayed until March 1945. Before 543 Squadron vacated Benson its B Flight was hived off to form the nucleus of 309 Ferry Training Unit, also known as 309 Ferry Training and Aircraft Despatch Unit, and which held a few Master IIs and Spitfire IVs for the training of pilots prior to their ferrying reconnaissance Spitfires overseas.

Frequent attempts were made to photograph the German capital at the start of 1944 and throughout the Battle of Berlin. Then Benson began to play a vital role in the run-up to the invasion of France with 544 Squadron photographing much of northern France. Both Benson's squadrons employed pressure cabin Mosquito XVIs from the middle of 1944. The Spitfire squadrons used a few Mustang IIIs and received the first of their Griffon-engined PR Mk XIX Spitfires. In midsummer 1944 the strength of Benson's four operational squadrons was 80 aircraft. A few were detached to Dyce in August, and also to the USSR, to observe the movements of the battleship *Tirpitz* for Bomber Command.

At the end of hostilities Benson had a few very long range Mosquito PR 34s, and had despatched this aircraft's first operational sortie (by 544 Squadron) to Norway on May 7 1945. Unlike most operational stations, however, Benson had an exceptionally busy period ahead. Damage assessment flights over Europe were needed in plenty so that rehabilitation and rebuilding could commence after the tremendous destruction wrought in the closing months of the war. Photographic sorties were also flown over Britain, Malta and a variety of overseas territories. Benson became the centre to which such agencies as the Ministry of Agriculture, and of Town and County Planning, could turn for help. Techniques of war were being put to vital peacetime service.

Such was the quantity of material required that Benson's mechanical processing equipment, such as the continuous processing units coupled to fast drying techniques, were as useful now as in the closing stages of the war. Advances in survey photography had been amazing. Processing had changed from little more than hand development to machines churning out thousands of prints in a day. The value of photography for mapping purposes, particularly of uncharted areas, became an adjunct to the activities at Benson as a result of which a handful of Lancasters were acquired and, on October 1 1946, formed themselves into 82 Squadron at Benson. They spent time overseas photographing vast tracks of Africa.

No 542 Squadron disbanded on August 27 1945, and 544 Squadron on October 13 1945. On September 30 1946, 540 and 541 Squadrons were both disbanded. From them had arisen No 58 Squadron, manned and equipped by the old hands and armed with Mosquito PR 34s and Ansons modified for survey work. A new 541 Squadron was formed in November 1947 and another 540 Squadron the following month. The former operated Spitfire PR XIXs in a tactical role, the latter equipped with Mosquito PR 34s for strategic reconnaissance. For night photographic duty, 58 Squadron received a few specialised Mosquito PR 35s.

It was not only the needs of civilians which had to be answered after the war. Belligerence in the East caused all sorts of devices to be used, under the label of 'reconnaissance'. Specialised training was essential for reconnaissance crews, for which purpose 8 OTU was retained and variously flew from Mount Farm, Chalgrove and Benson. It became 237 OCU on July 31 1947 and did not leave the area until the start of December 1951, by then equipped not with Harvards and Spitfire XIXs but with Meteor 7s and 9s and Mosquito PR 34s.

Jet aircraft were late on the reconnaissance scene in Britain, the intended Meteor V proving troublesome. Later Meteors were little more than short duration tactical aircraft and not until the first Canberra PR 3s reached 540 Squadron at Benson, at the end of 1952, was the PR force moving into the new age. Meteor PR 10s had joined 541 Squadron just before it left for Germany in mid-June 1951.

At the end of October 1952, 82 Squadron's Lancasters returned to Benson, among them the famous Lancaster *PA474* which thrills us still as part of the Battle of Britain Memorial Flight. The squadron's stay was brief for, in March 1953 along with the other PR units and squadrons at Benson, it moved to Wyton. A great era at Benson had ended, and the station would never again host anything like it.

Transfer to RAF Transport Command took place in March 1953 and Benson became an aircraft despatch centre. 30 Squadron operating Valettas was briefly here before moving to Dishforth. Two squadrons with similar roles, Nos 147 and 167, arrived at Benson in April 1953 and later amalgamated to become the Ferry Squadron. An unexpected event was the reforming of No 21 Squadron here on May 1 1959, its duty reminiscent of the RAF's pre-war policing activity overseas. It trained here with four Twin Pioneers before leaving in mid-September 1959.

There had been an even more unlikely occupant in the mid-1950s. Culham being unsuitable for jet fighters, No 1832 Squadron, RNVR, set up shop here in July 1955 to fly Attackers shared with 1836 Squadron. In October 1956 Sea Hawk 1s started to replace the Attackers, but the Navy's stay was brief, for on March 10 1957 the squadrons were paid off.

Transport Command had important plans for Benson. The new medium-range, unconventional-looking, tail-loaded Argosy twin-boom freighter was being prepared, intended to be able to reach Cyprus non-stop when fully loaded. Benson was chosen as the UK base for the Argosy squadrons. Here the first Argosy for RAF service arrived on November 18 1961, for a training unit which became 242 Operational Conversion Unit before leaving for Thorney Island in April 1963.

No 114 Squadron had reformed at Benson on October 1 1961 to operate the Argosy equipment commencing in February 1962 at the same time as 105 Squadron received Argosys. It flew them from here for four months before moving overseas. No 267 Squadron began to equip in November 1962 and continued to operate from Benson until the Argosy's withdrawal. No 267 Squadron disbanded on June 30 1970. Another recipient had been 215 Squadron which worked up on Argosys at Benson between May and August 1963. With the disbandment of 114 Squadron on October 31 1971, Benson's troop and freight transport role was ended—but not that of passenger carrying.

Royal wartime flying came to be the task of 24 Squadron and later of the Metropolitan Communications Squadron. The King thought highly of their Dakotas and, in a world where flying was ever increasing, the King's Flight was reformed at Benson on May 1 1946. Air Commodore Fielden resumed his Captaincy. Originally the King's Flight was to operate a VVIP York and three Vikings, two with VVIP fit and the other with the normal passenger layout. Instead, only four cheaper Vikings were allotted, the additional one serving as an engineering support aircraft. To speed delivery, BEA surrendered two early Vikings allowing one as *VL245*—the normal passenger aircraft—to be collected from Wisley for the Flight on August 11 1946. It joined Dominie *RL951*, already in use and whose career abruptly ended in a crash at Mount Farm in November 1946. All four Vikings were at Benson by January 1947 and a month later flew to Brooklyn Air Base, near Capetown from where they operated during the South African Tour. Later in 1947 they were busy during the wedding of Princess Elizabeth and Prince Philip, and subsequently many times carried the Royal Family.

Prince Philip commenced flying lessons in 1952. Using Chipmunk *WP861*, he made his first solo flight on December 20 1952. Subsequently he flew another Benson-based Chipmunk, *WP912*, and then made use of Devon *VP961*, stationed at White Waltham from which airfield he had undertaken most of his flying training. For Queen's Flight purposes the Devon was too small, yet it was a reliable and pleasant aircraft for pilot and passengers for which reason one of its larger derivatives, a Heron, was ordered for Prince Philip.

Vikings remained very active but the little-used workshop aircraft was disposed of in November 1953 when the future of the Flight was under review. A plan emerged by which the Heron would reach the Flight early in 1954, and the Vikings be replaced by three Viscounts. With the Flight temporarily at Northolt, whilst its Benson hangar was being rennovated, discussions concerning new equipment went ahead bringing sufficient confidence for Vickers to earmark Viscount airframes in production for VIP and VVIP completion. A firm commitment was awaited for 18 months before official sanction was given for the Flight's new establishment to comprise one Viscount 700D, one VVIP Viking, a Heron and two Whirlwind helicopters. The problem ever facing the Flight was how to maintain value to set against the cost of capital equipment and maintenance over a long period. For Her Majesty to have made use of one of the finest airliners of its time would certainly have given that a prestigous boost, for which reason the purchase would have been sensible. The decision not to go ahead with the Viscount scheme, irrespective of the economics involved, cannot be concluded as wise.

September 1954 brought the Flight its first helicopter, a small Westland Dragonfly, *HC4-XF261*, from CFS South Cerney, which was intended for temporary service but resided at Benson for four years. Sanction for the Queen's Flight to operate two VVIP helicopters was given in July 1954 and the first royal helicopter journey came on September 6 1954 when Prince Philip flew in the Dragonfly from Buckingham Palace to Shinfield. Although many members of the Royal Family used *XF261*, it mostly carried Prince Philip who, in 1955, qualified as a helicopter pilot. His Heron, *C3-XH375*, joined the Flight on May 18 1955. Upon its highly burnished finish it wore an Edinburgh Green cheat line in keeping with its pilot's title. Both Devon and Heron were placed at White Waltham until July 1955 when they moved to Benson.

Summer 1955 saw Prince Philip making use of a naval Whirlwind 22, the Dragonfly being switched to route and landing area survey. Satisfied of the value of helicopters, the Air Council agreed to Whirlwinds being added to the Flight's establishment the following spring. Various delays arose and not until July 1958 was a contract for two VVIP Whirlwind 8s placed, for 1959 delivery. Meanwhile a Whirlwind 4 replaced the small Dragonfly. Trouble with the Alvis Leonides Major engine which powered the Whirlwind delayed the Mk 8s Benson debut until October 1959. Not until September 23 1960 did the new Whirlwind make its first Royal passenger flight, from Kensington Palace to Papworth.

Replacements for the Vikings were ordered in April 1956 in the form of two Heron C4s. Two years later they came into use, Prince Philip's Heron along with Vikings *VL233* and *VL246* having long borne their royal role. Not until April 22 1958 did the last Viking flight take place, then the two new Herons arrived within a few days.

Subsequently the Royal Herons—bright red overall from 1960—were used in many distant parts of the world. Their payload/range characteristics were limited and for the Royal Tour of India and the Himalayas, two Dakotas (*KN452*, previously used by the AOC Malta and *KN645*, once the transport of Field Marshal Montgomery) were acquired. Nevertheless, a fourth Heron joined the Flight in June 1961 and was used during Princess Alexandra's tour of the Far East, despite dissatisfaction with the Heron's overall performance.

In March 1964 the first of two Gnome turbo-engined Whirlwind 12s to replace the Mk 8s came into use at Benson as agreement was reached to replace the Herons by Andovers. The first two of these came into the Flight in July–August 1964.

Prince Philip flew to the North Sea rig, *Sea Quest*, in a 72 Squadron Wessex during June 1967 as consideration was being given to the Flight using such aircraft. HRH Queen Elizabeth, the Queen Mother, came to be quoted as saying that 'the chopper' had changed her life as much as it did Anne Boleyn's, but whether the use of helicopters would continue came into doubt on December 7 1967 when Whirlwind *XL487* crashed as a result of a rotor shaft snapping. Air Commodore J.H.L. Blount, Captain of the Queen's Flight, was among those killed and all Whirlwinds were promptly grounded pending a court of enquiry. Not until the end of March 1968 did the Queen's Flight resume helicopter flying.

The last Royal Heron, *XM296*, left on June 25 1968 after ten years service and an accumulation of 4,310 flying hours. Several Wessex helicopters were used before mid-1969. The VVIP Wessex HCC4's first task was to carry the Prince of Wales to his Investiture at Caernarvon. Later that year a Basset was placed at Benson for the Prince's use and also for general communications flying. It remained at Benson until September 16 1971 when it was despatched to 32 Squadron, Northolt.

The present equipment of the Queen's Flight at Benson, consists of three Andovers Mk CCOs, *XS789, XS790* and *XS793*, along with two Wessex HCC4s, *XV732* and *XV733*. These are not the only Wessex helicopters at Benson, for since 1980 those of 72 Squadron have operated from here, making way for Chinooks at Odiham.

Of all the airfields in central England, Benson is one of the most aesthetically sited. In its PR days a posting here was not universally popular. The work was hard and tedious, the hours long and the value of achievement largely unrealised as it was created. One may drive through this camp, view its domestic site, typical in design, while having to the north a splendid view over conventionally flat-roofed buildings of the 1930s beyond which, placed lower, are the hangars. It is easy to imagine the great days of the blue Spits and Mossies. Close your eyes; can you hear two fast-revving Merlins on a thick, misty day coming ever closer? Ah, memories of John Merifield, and of Victor and Boris racing home from Paris, all carrying a precious cargo able to change history. Perhaps things haven't changed all that much at Benson?

Bibury, Gloucestershire

SP115095. 2 miles N of Bibury village

Close to noon they came, three lumbering Bombay transports, protected by six Spitfires of 92 Squadron which were being brought to Bibury from Pembrey. Being August 19 1940 such a trio would have been a tempting objective were it not for those Spitfirers coming to Bibury for night stand by. Already Bibury had shown itself suitable for night fighters. Those Spitfire pilots must have thought it a primitive airfield. Situated on an extension of Ablington Down, it was remote, yet close to one of Britain's most picturesque vistas.

Whether it was that or the fighter squadrons—there was evidently some special attraction—German visitors came within some two hours of the Spitfire's arrival. Among that afternoon's marauders were Ju 88As of III/KG 51 who crept in and operated singly in the Gloucestershire area. One crew chose Bibury for an afternoon call. In their '88 they flew a fast run, bombing and strafing the airfield. A Spitfire was destroyed, another seriously damaged, three others hit by stray bullets and an airman killed. Such an impudent intrusion on a showery summer afternoon engendered rapid reaction. Two pilots jumped into their Spitfires and the chase began. They had to fly a considerable distance before catching the Ju 88. A short, sharp combat ensued over the Solent before the bomber and its crew perished in the water. The pilot of one Spitfire, *R6703*, Flight Lieutenant T.S. Wade, later to become famous as the Chief Test Pilot of Hawkers in the 1940s, subsequently had to force land and was lucky to get clear of his fighter before it exploded.

All that seems quite incongruous for Bibury village is an exquisite place—especially if you contrive to be there without fellow tourists. To leave one of the world's most attractive villages without a call, though, would mark one as soulless! Through the village passes the river Coln, into which quite huge trout escape, outwitting their breeders and many small boys. Beyond lies the line of 14th century cottages, comprising world-famous Arlington Row, once occupied by Bibury's weavers.

Bibury has another feature in that it witnessed some of the early jet flying, with which thoughts you can ascend the hill to Ablington Down where the airfield was sited. It is easy to spot, still, for it retains the appearance of a flying field. By the Northleach road there are two Blister hangars, a picket hut, various other old remains and concrete roads as recognition points.

Bibury Farm, as the camp was first known, was selected as a landing ground in April 1939 to permit increased flying by 3 SFTS South Cerney. When the first aircraft touched down seems never to have been recorded, at least officially, but the site was certainly in use as an RLG for Oxfords by April 1940. When the situation in France became alarming, orders were given by 23 Group, in whose hands the field for long rested, that it should be blocked. A number of old motor bodies then littered it for weeks. The road to the site was closed to all but official and local residents, with the LDV enjoying great, delectable power.

The initial scare passed and, at the well-placed site, night flying commenced on July 6 1940 so that 3 SFTS's more permanent home would not need to be lit, inviting attack. Presumably the residents of the houses around were none too well aware of this feature! Night flying was to continue for many months, although day training naturally took place, relieving congestion at South Cerney.

A complete change overtook the camp when, on August 7 1940, A Flight of 87 Squadron, Exeter, winged in with its Hurricanes. There was not much delight in night flying for a squadron wanting to get its own back after a battering in France, and so the claim of a quick kill of a He 111 by Pilot Officer Comillyon the night after arrival must have been a tonic. The detachment here of 87 Squadron was brief. In mid-August it was withdrawn and replaced by part of 92 Squadron, also from 10 Group. Spitfires flew a few night sorties from Bibury, the pilots including Flight Lieutenant C.B. Kingcombe.

On September 8 1940, 92 Squadron left Pembrey for Biggin Hill for which reason its detachment withdrew. On September 3 1940, B Flight of 87 Squadron replaced it, beginning a series of detachments from that squadron which continued until mid-

December 1940. The night following arrival proved ideal for night flying. Visibility was excellent, the moon bright, and Flying Officer Beaumont flying Hurricane *V7285* found a Ju 88 near Bristol with which he exchanged inconclusive fire. Next night he and Pilot Officer Jay each fired at a Ju 88, but neither had success. After a week the Flight was recalled, but it was back again for night patrols on September 10 and thereafter the two Flights of the squadron rotated, each having a week at Bibury.

Action was limited and keeping a Flight out of battle was hardly morale boosting. Thus, on the afternoon of September 30, B Flight and Flight Lieutenant J.R. Gleed went to Exeter. From there they hurried to Portland where Pilot Officer Maclure and Sergeant H. Walton ran into a group of He 111s escorted by fighters. Maclure claimed a Bf 110 and damaged a Ju 88, whilst Walton was shot down and slightly injured. Pilot Officer Cook also claimed a He 111 and damaged a Bf 109. Meanwhile, Gleed, flying above cloud, suddenly found himself about 60 He 111s to chose from. He took a rear bomber out of the formation, watching it go vertically through the thick clouds. By then the whole of the German force was turned upon him, so he had little choice but to race for safety.

Weekly rotation of 87 Squadron to Bibury continued and, on October 24, B Flight's arrival was marred by an accident when Pilot Officer Cook and Pilot Officer Jay collided when flying in formation. Jay baled out but was unable to open his parachute. The only other night engagement was, apparently, on November 24 1940 when Flying Officer Rayner saw a He 111 lit by searchlights. He fired a six-second burst before the enemy aircraft dived away. On December 18 1940 87 Squadron finally vacated Bibury.

Bibury was left to Oxfords of 3 SFTS who, by mid-January 1941, had made its surface very bad. There were many soft patches and ruts caused by pilots pivoting their aircraft on one wheel and much reducing Bibury's usefulness. The AOC of 23 Group visited the site on February 10 1941 and found the accommodation and sanitation arrangements very poor. He decided to have the landing ground extended.

South Cerney's Oxfords made use of Bibury throughout 1941 then snowy conditions in January 1942 put it out of use. From March 1 1942 it was again the scene of plentiful flying by Oxfords of 3 (P) AFU. On April 15 1943, 1539 BAT Flight formed at South Cerney and moved to Bibury on July 13 1943, flying Oxfords from there until November 5 1944. Blind approach training was centred in buildings close to the road, and near the main technical site and WAAF communal site.

Improvements to the airfield in 1942–3 resulted in the provision of two Sommerfeld tracking runways, No 1 04/22 and No 2 09/27. Buildings were of 1941–2 style and included five Over Type Blisters (12532/41) three of which were near the road by which a 'T1' of 14 bay 19 ft (9659/42) was placed between two of the Blister hangars. Accommodation in temporary brick or Laing huts was provided in four dispersed sites, three to the west of the road passing through the camp and one on the far eastern side. An instruction site was fitted alongside the limited technical facilities.

Bibury had been uplifted to full satellite status in November 1943. When 1539 Flight vacated the airfield, 3 (P) AFU was in the process of leaving too and, by the end of November 1944, flying had ceased. The station was taken over by 7 MU who held the site until its closure in 1945.

Bicester, Oxfordshire

SP595245. 1½ miles NE of Bicester town, by the A421

Leaving Bicester on the Buckingham Road one immediately sees a long-established military site where a 1934 control tower in good condition is one of the last in Britain. Bicester of the 1980s occupies Caller's Field upon which, in 1916, British and Canadian engineers—assisted by Chinese and Portuguese workers and press-ganged German PoWs—began to construct a Training Depot Station in Southern Army Command. Americans joined in, providing an electric power station, for a while the only one in the district.

The camp came into use late in 1917. In January 1918, 118 Squadron RFC mobilised here and remained until November 1918. No 44 Training Depot Station arrived at the start of October 1918. Between mid-February 1919 and September of that year, No 2 Squadron resided at Bicester and was replaced on September 19 1919 by 5 Squadron's Bristol Fighters, freshly returned from France and disbanded on January 20 1920. Bicester closed in March 1920.

Following the 1924 decision to site bomber squadrons in the Oxford area,

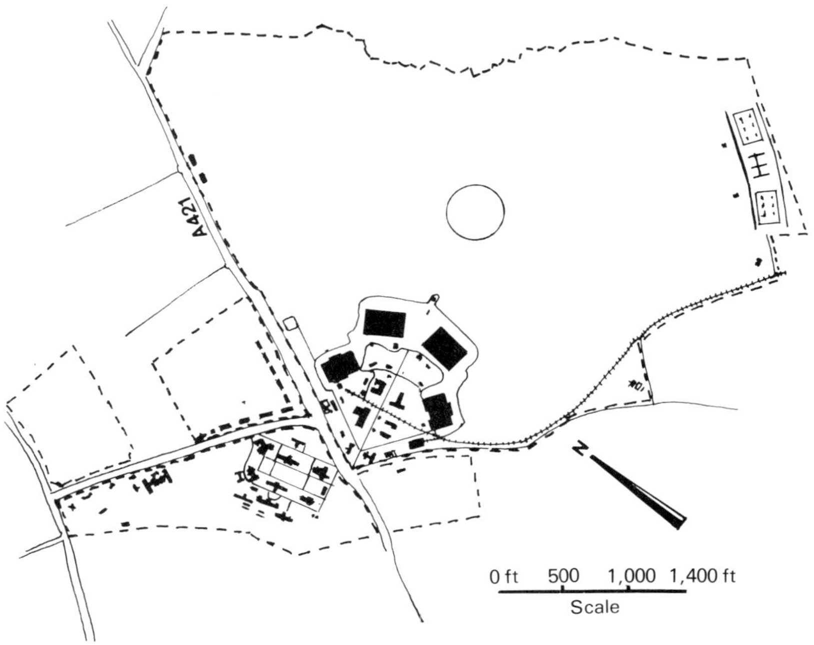

Bicester in January, 1939. The technical site lies to the east of the Buckingham road; the domestic area to west. To the left of the main road, into the technical site, lies first the guardhouse (959/25) then stores and workshops. SHQ faces the guardhouse to the east of which is the MT section. The armoury lies alongside. From left to right, the aircraft sheds are Type 'C' 1410-12/35 and 1154/27—ie, modified from 1927 design, Type 'C' 2392/37, Type 'C' 1581/35 and the other similar to that first within the arc. The watch tower stands at the apex of the apron, Type 1959/34. Across the landing ground lies the weapons dump. In the centre of the landing ground is a 4 ft wide chalk circle, 150 yds in diameter. This is a landing circle which marks the airfield clearly. Note the railway line leading to the stores, a feature of a number of airfields laid down in the 1920s.

resurrection of RAF Bicester commenced in 1925. Buildings on the technical site were placed within a pentagonal area, one hangar being on the south-west side and another on the south-east. An early layout provided for up to four more, with the original being to pattern 1154/27. A special feature was a railway link leading to the Main Stores (978/25), close to which were the MT sheds and an engine test house (702/26). Bicester's circular 30,000 gallon elevated water tank (1178/25) supplemented a 100,000 gallon reservoir. The present guardhouse retains much of the original (959/25). Provision for 192 seats was made in the Airmens' Dining Room, modified in 1925 and 1933 from its 1923 style. Original Airmen's Barrack Blocks were Type E, based on 1922–3 designs and each holding three NCOs and 80 men. Behind the 1924–5 SHQ building was the camera obscura. On the airfield was a concrete compass swinging platform with a diameter of 50 ft.

The new camp opened in January 1928 and Hawker Horsleys of No 100 Squadron winged in from Spitalgate, leaving in November 1930 for Donibristle. No 33 Squadron's Hawker Harts arrived on November 4 1930. They had a cherished place in RAF history when at Eastchurch in February 1930, they were the first to join a squadron. No 33 remained at Bicester, and in the limelight until the end of November 1934. It was replaced on December 4 1934 by the only Sidestrand squadron, No 101. Between October 1935 and July 1936 Overstrands replaced them, the first example, *K4547*, arriving on October 14 1935. These were the first RAF bombers with enclosed power-operated turrets.

Within the 1930s' Expansion Scheme, Bicester had a major face lift. Two 'C' Type hangars (1581/35, 2392/37) were constructed, supplementing the older ones, all of which remain. Barrack Blocks of the Extended 'E' Type (2489/37), accommodating one NCO and 96 men, were added, and the Watch Office and Tower (1959/34). East of the playing fields stands the Officer's Mess. By the start of 1939, nine Barrack Blocks had been built, nine Married Quarters units for airmen and another six for officers. By that time Bicester had seen plenty of RAF's expansion programme.

The first new squadron was No 48 (GR) Squadron which formed on November 25 1935 and moved to Manston in mid-December. Bicester joined the Western Area on April 1 1936 and 3 Group on April 30 1936. Transfer to 1 Group became effective on August 17 1936. Station Headquarters was established on September 21 1936 to run Bicester more effectively.

No 144 Squadron formed from C Flight 101 Squadron on January 11 1937, and left for Hemswell on February 8 1937. No 90 Squadron formed on March 15 1937. A Flight of 101 Squadron was temporarily equipped with Hinds until May 1937 when the Blenheim 1s arrived. No 101 Squadron had to wait until June 1938 for Blenheims.

The Munich crisis plunged the station into a high state of readiness giving a taste of 2 Group. For much of the war, Bicester was to feed crews into that courageous body. Maybe that sampling of 2 Group's high camaraderie encouraged the moves of 90 and 101 Squadrons on May 9 1939, to 2 Group's station at West Raynham. Two squadrons of Fairey Battles of 1 Group, Nos 12 and 142 then came from Andover, as part of Field Force France. Both squadrons left Bicester to become

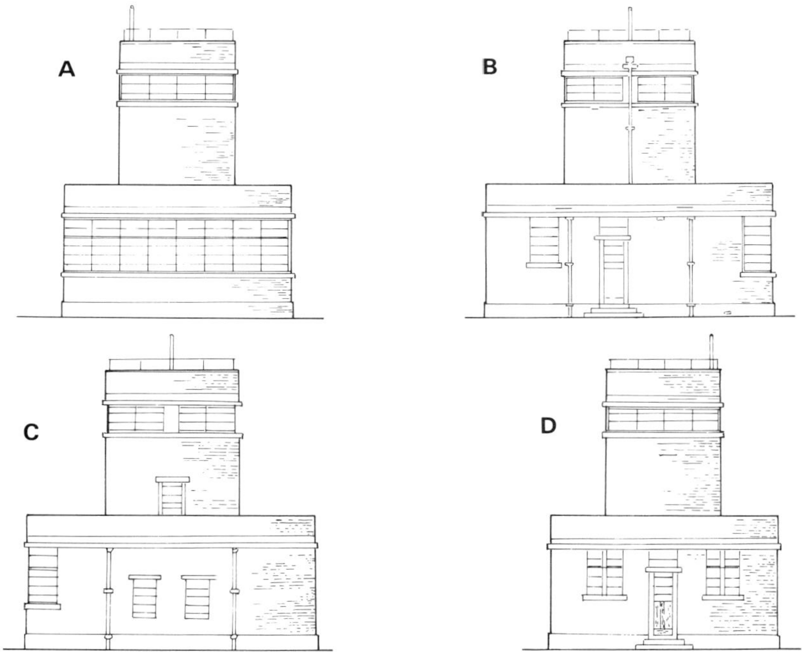

A watch office, with tower, for a duty pilot—revised design 1959/34 and 1960/34 of 1934. Four views showing the original form of the building (an example of which remains at Bicester): **A** *Aerodrome elevation.* **B** *Main entrance elevation.* **C** *Side elevation.* **D** *Rear elevation. Watch offices of this and similar designs were featured by many expansion period stations. They were generally superseded during the war by buildings offering more space. The watch office on the ground floor faced the aerodrome and, to its rear, there were toilets and a rest room. A circular stairway led to the watch tower from which a vertical ladder led to the roof upon which were placed meteorological instruments.*

part of the AASF on September 2 1939.

Once at war, the station again courted 2 Group with the arrival, on September 12 1939, of Nos 104 and 108 Blenheim Squadrons, supplemented by Ansons to form No 2 Group Pool and under 6 Group's control. Pilots and observers were recruited from flying training schools, observer schools and the RAFVR. Air gunners came from 2 Group squadrons' ground crews. Although specialised air-crew, they retained airmen ranks and, even more meanly, their old rates of pay. Training a Blenheim crew took six months.

Bicester's personnel had a morale booster on October 25 1939. Vehicles from Handley Page works at Cricklewood had conveyed a secret bomber here. In the hangar by Launton Road the Halifax bomber prototype, *L7244*, was erected and, on October 25 1939, first flew. After a few flights it left for Boscombe Down.

Bicester's two squadrons merged to form No 13 OTU on April 8 1940, then training the Blenheim crews increased to meet crippling losses during the French campaign. King George VI visited the station on July 19 1940, and many whom he met were to die in the awful punishment 2 Group sustained during the following 14 months. On July 22 1940 control of 13 OTU passed to 7 Group.

Overstrand K4561 *of 101 Squadron between old and new hangars at Bicester in 1936.*

Silent, with a million memories, Bicester's splendid Officers' Mess.

In the early 1930s, Bicester was the home of 33 Squadron and its Hawker Hart day bombers.

Bicester's satellite at Weston-on-the-Green now came into use for night flying which also started at Hinton-in-the Hedges in November. A dummy airfield at Grendon Underwood was ready to attract enemy bombs. That month Lewis gunners manning a Bicester defence post claimed hits on passing Ju 88 L1+LS which came down at Blewbury, Berkshire.

In its first year 13 OTU trained 217 pilots, 240 observers and 273 air gunners. The flying hours totalled 26,670. Demand for Blenheim crews increased for home and overseas squadrons and 2 Group's merciless anti-shipping campaign. From October 1941, Blenheim crews were trained at 13 OTU mainly to meet Middle East needs. The OTU's second year produced 32,718 flying hours and 297 complete crews, 121 of them going overseas. Bicester's bombers came nearest to participating in offensive action when they flew air/sea rescue searches after the '1,000 bomber' raids. From July 1942 a higher proportion of its output proceeded to further training and heavy bomber squadrons because of single pilot manning of new bombers.

There were changes, too, in the station's satellites. Finmere served from July 31 1942 to November 28 1942 and Turweston from October 1 1942 to November 28 1942, and again in mid-1943. On November 20 1942, No 1551 BAT Flight formed from the Blind Approach Calibration Flight and used four Ansons, three Oxfords and two Masters. On April 15 1943 this Flight became part of the Signals Development Unit.

During Operation *Torch*, the Blenheim V at last went into battle. Bisley crews were drawn from 13 OTU and replacement aircraft became urgently needed in Africa. They could only be flown there and so No 307 Ferry Training Unit formed at Bicester and, from December 24 1942, had the task of training 30 ferry crews for which seven Blenheim Vs were made available.

On the afternoon of April 5 1943, five Blenheims of 13 OTU flew a North Sea sweep, the last such operation. By April 1943 there was only 12 crews per course. Training was to switch to producing Boston and Mitchell crews who flew at the satellites because these aircraft needed hard runways.

On June 1 1943, 13 OTU left Bomber Command and joined 70 Group, Fighter Command, in preparation for the training of 2TAF crews. Nevertheless, the OTU continued to rely upon Blenheims—mainly dual control Mk Vs—for operational conversion. Some Spitfires arrived for fighter affiliation training before control of the unit passed to 9 Group on November 1 1943. Bicester then received specialised units of 84 and 85 Groups' TAF training for their roles, and became the Forward Equipment Unit for both Groups. All 13 OTU's Blenheim flying ceased on February 25 1944, the last short-nosed Blenheim 1 leaving Bicester three days later.

Bicester's backing to 2TAF became

In 1944, Blenheims were a familiar sight around Bicester. R3607 FV:E *had a long operational career—with 59, 57, 40 and 18 Squadrons—before joining 13 OTU in June 1941. It crashed on March 13 1942.*

increasingly apparent following D-Day and conflicted with the running of a busy OTU. When 38 Group vacated Harwell in mid-October 1944, 13 OTU took over that station which became its main base. Thereafter Bicester served almost exclusively as a 'non-flying' station. The Forward Equipment Unit of 85 Group became 246 MU on January 1 1945 and transferred to 40 Group, Maintenance Command. It became a transit centre for despatch of equipment to 2TAF on the Continent, and assembly point for its vehicles—in particular those radio equipped—as well as Command Centre for aero engines and vehicle spares. BAFO was supplied until September 1945, then the station served as a motor transport depot. Headquarters 40 Group arrived from Andover during February 1947, staying until 1961. A brief return to flying came during the brief stay of the Beam Approach Calibration Flight which arrived in July 1947.

No 246 MU disbanded on April 1 1949, then a parachute packing and servicing unit moved in. Between September 3 1951 and January 30 1954 the Civilian Supplies Technical Officers' School functioned here. No 71 MU opened as a 43 Group lodger unit on December 15 1953, to repair, salvage and transport Service aircraft involved in flying accidents occurring south of the line roughly joining Aberdovey to the Wash. Assistance was also rendered to incidents involving civilian aircraft. Within 71 MU were a Bomb Disposal Flight and the Historic Aircraft Exhibition Flight which restored the famous Lancaster in the RAF Museum.

Chipmunks of Oxford University Air Squadron moved into Bicester in 1959 and remained until September 1975. As part of the Strategic Reserve, No 5 Light Anti-Aircraft Wing formed here in 1967 and included No 2 Light Anti-Aircraft Squadron which had been in Malaysia defending RAF bases during the Indonesian confrontation. The Wing disbanded in 1970, by which time the RAF Gliding and Soaring Association had been on the station for seven years, and continues to make use of it.

Bicester closed as an active station on March 31 1976 and was placed under Abingdon's control for care and maintenance. Transfer to the Army Department followed on May 20 1976. Unexpectedly, the barracks became RAF Bicester again on November 22 1978 and recently the station (parts of which are being disposed of) has been used as a storage site by the Americans. An adventure school is also run here.

Bicester's remaining buildings span over 50 years of service. Thus the station is of more than passing architectural interest. What is surprising in view of its age is that Bicester, in half a century, has never despatched even one offensive sortie.

Birmingham Airport (Elmdon) West Midlands

See Elmdon

Blakehill Farm, Gloucestershire

ST 080915. 2½ miles SW of Cricklade, SE of B4040

Blakehill, close to Chelworth, took its name from the farm upon which it was built during 1943. Placed under 70 Group it passed to 46 Group, Transport Command on February 6 1944. Opening commenced on 9 February with urgency for it had an important freight and casevac role ahead. Grave concern rose over the rate of completion, and accommodation for 50 Horsas meant acquiring more land and laying roads on which gliders could be towed.

Squadron choice was unusual—No 233 which returned from Gibraltar and maritime duty. It moved to Blakehill in early March 1944 and equipped with Dakotas. Also here were two Field Staging Posts, Nos 92 and 93, to move to the Continent when practical. In March 1944, HQ Wing, Glider Pilot Regiment arrived. Its task was to place gliders in squadrons at 46 Group's three stations. On March 26 the 13th Parachute Company arrived and four days later the 1st Canadian Parachute Company. There were WAAFs here and 300 Irish labourers, so care needed to be taken to make sure that the needs of all were satisfactorily met.

During March, 233's Dakota IIIs readied themselves for exercises. The Canadian paratroops left in April and 91 and 94 FSPs arrived to train in freight loading and casevac duties before leaving on 28 April. From North Luffenham and Swanton Morley, 21 Horsas were gathered during the month and prepared for vital weeks ahead. No 233 Squadron (strength 30 Dakotas and 40 Horsas) took part in Exercises *Acorn* and *Roger*, among others, and on April 21 crews flew 22 of the 700 aircraft used in Exercise *Mush*. Propaganda leaflets fluttered into Caen from three 233 Dakotas on April 25 and next night another three crews provided reading material for the residents of Alençon.

By early May there were 50 Horsas here, tended by 11 Horsa Glider Servicing Echelon. Training concentrated upon accurate delivery of paratroops, then came large-scale glider exercises. At the close of May, the Casualty Air Evacuation Unit left and 92 FSP went temporarily to Watchfield.

On June 1 the station assumed Readiness A and from June 3 it was possible to leave camp only when clutching a station commander's permit. Next day 30 crews were briefed for Operation *Tonga*. At the final briefing General F.A.M. Browning, GOC Airborne Forces; Air Commodore Fiddament, AOC 46 Group; Air Vice-Marshal A. Collier, Deputy Commander in Chief Transport Command, and Air Vice-Marshal C.H.K. Edmonds, ADGB, attended. When all were assembled, Air Chief Marshal Sir Trafford Leigh-Mallory and the AOC, 46 Group, addressed them. At final briefing 233 Squadron was reminded that the DZ to which they would fly was the furthest inland. At 22:50 take off began with six Dakotas towing Horsas. Another 24 followed with paratroops. All were safely away by 23:11 and the drops went well. Next night panniers were dropped in Operation *Robroy*, the first re-supply service.

On June 13 1944 two Dakotas of 233 Squadron, carrying four tons of freight, made the first landings by Transport Command in France following the invasion, and returned with the first 20 air evacuated casualties. During the remainder of June an average of five daily flights to France took place delivering freight, spares, bombs, etc, and returning with personnel. A few sorties were flown from here by 575's Dakotas and a detachment of 271 Squadron operated out of Blakehill, relieving pressure on Down Ampney. Throughout July and August flights to France continued. In early September 1944, 75 US C-47s briefly called for an urgently needed load of petrol, carried in Jerry cans to advancing American forces. By then the station's Dakota strength had doubled. No 437 (RCAF) Squadron began to form here on September 4 and was ready to operate for Arnhem. In the initial assault 22 Dakota/Horsa combinations from 233 Squadron carried 308 troops and equipment, another dozen from 437 Squadron conveying a further 146 men. Next day 16 combinations from 233 Squadron and six from 437 Squadron operated. On September 20 three of the 18 aircraft representing 233 Squadron were shot down by fighters and 437 Squadron lost another four. A further supply drop on the 23rd cost 233 Squadron another machine. Typical of the incidents which befell Blakehill's crews was the shell which exploded below the tail of Flying Officer Ramussen's *KG345* as the panniers were dropped. Flight Lieutenant Reach in

KG501 had to manoeuvre violently to avoid a falling load. After Arnhem the station returned to its freight and casevac duties, and took petrol supplies to France.

Between October 15 1944 and October 21 1945, Fairford served as Blakehill's satellite, winter bringing Long Newton's Oxfords here. Practice glider towing early in 1945 interrupted flights to the Continent and, in mid-March, 233 and 437 Squadrons were ordered to Birch, Essex, from where 24 Dakotas of 233, 24 of 437 and 12 of 48 Squadrons each towed off a glider for Operation *Varsity*, the Rhine crossing.

On May 7 1945, 437 Squadron moved to Nivelles, Belgium, to concentrate upon removal of displaced persons, and 233 moved to Odiham early in June. No 22 HGCU replaced the squadrons, its varied Albemarles towing Waco Hadrian gliders, retaining American identities here until unit disbandment on October 21 1945. Blakehill received Dakotas of 575 Squadron from Melbourn, Yorkshire on November 15 1945, preparatory to moving to Italy. No 1555 RAT Flight's Oxfords arrived from Valley in mid-December along with the HQ Training Command Aircrew Examining Unit which assessed aircrew performance. No 1528 RAT Flight's Oxfords soon joined them. During January 1946, 512 Squadron was briefly here in a month memorable for the crash of Dakota *KK154* of 575 Squadron, burnt out on the Cricklade-Wootton Bassett road. Blakehill bade farewell to 575 Squadron's last Dakota on January 29 1946 and the station passed into the hands of Flying Training Command on January 21 1947 who held it in reserve for some time. The site is now marked by a variety of radio masts and aerials.

Brize Norton, Oxfordshire

SP295060. 6 miles SW of Witney

With effortless delight, *XR806* climbed away from Brize Norton's 10,000 ft runway. Alf Alderson, a long-time friend, whispered 'What a lovely way to go!'. The captain muttered something about this '. . . noise abatement procedure'. Me? For once, silent. Few joys if any, in the jet world, can remotely equal being 'up front' in a VC-10. It looks good, it feels good, it is good—just a superlative aeroplane.

Brize Norton is home for the RAF's VC-10 transports. From here the remains of the strategic reserve can be deployed. It is also the place from which important people fly, or obtain their aeroplanes—and they fly RAF in the full knowledge that its 'airline' has an outstanding safety record. Nice, too, when one leans out, to see a comforting roundel in place of the nasty, cheap colours of civilian competitors!

It's almost impossible to miss Brize Norton for it sprawls across a flat section of Oxfordshire. At times the water table must be high, but apparently the area has never been flooded. Naming the station posed a problem for it lies mainly within the Carterton boundary, a name too

Harvard 1s of 2 FTS lined up at Brize Norton in the summer of 1940. All have racks for light bombs (IWM).

A Whitley V glider tug lands over Horsas of HGCU, Brize Norton (IWM).

reminiscent of Cardington to be suitable. So Brize Norton was chosen when building started in 1935. Exceptional was the completion of five 'C' Type hangars, planned for many stations but rarely built. It was incomplete, but 2 FTS nevertheless moved in on August 13 1937. The school brought a mixture of Hawker Harts, the first of which had been received in April 1935, Audaxes, first received in May 1936, and Hawker Furies to hold the line until monoplanes arrived. First to come, on February 22 1938, was an Airspeed Oxford. Four more arrived in March, one in April after which they trickled into use, allowing realistic pilot training. A divorced group of buildings was erected, a motley collection, including 'Lamella' hangars, to house No 6 Maintenance Unit in the airfield's south-east corner. A 41 Group unit, it opened on October 10 1938, receiving its first two aircraft, Saro Cloud amphibians, on January 30 1939.

The most audible change descended upon 2 SFTS in March 1939 when ten Harvard 1s arrived. Another 13 came in June to further annoy the populace and two more in July 1939. Close by, 6 MU placed 13 in storage that month. By the time war started more Oxfords were with the FTS. Blenheims of 101 Squadron scattered here and at Weston-on-the-Green which became Brize Norton's active satellite. 6 MU early in the war supplied Gladiators to Finland and Blenheims to Yugoslavia.

The fall of France sent shudders of anxiety throughout the area. Middle Wallop, needed for fighter squadrons, had its 15 SFTS moved, Oxfords and Harvards comprising half the ITS being lodged at Brize Norton from June 11 while awaiting the availability of Kidlington. HQ 15 SFTS came along too, prior to acquiring a palatial residence, Oldner House at Chipping Norton, into which a move was made on July 10 1940.

Risk of enemy interference with flying training was proven on July 28 1940 when a 2 SFTS Oxford was shot down over Akeman Street. That the enemy really meant business was disastrously obvious when, on the afternoon of Friday, August 16, two Ju 88s wrought tremendous havoc at the station in the manner previously described (see page 23). Training aircraft had been hangared for protection against the elements, but no longer. Most of the serviceable Oxfords were dispersed, some at Akeman Street, others at Southrop, and 15 SFTS left on August 19. Although Brize Norton was attacked three more times, it suffered little further damage.

Throughout 1941, 2 SFTS trained RAF pilots while 6 MU handled a multiplicity of aircraft types. Most common were Blenheims, Hampdens, Hurricanes, Spitfires and Fairey Battles which, no longer fighting machines, languished long at Brize Norton.

November 1941, when the first EATS pilots arrived for acclimatisation flying, also saw the formation here of 25 BAT Flight. It became 1525 BAT Flight on February 18 1942 and remained here until July 13 1942. On March 14 1942, 2 SFTS had become 2 (P) AFU. Too many such units existed by the summer and, on July 14, the unit closed.

Next day Brize Norton acquired a unique role with the arrival of the recently formed Heavy Glider Conversion Unit from Shrewton. The station now became the training centre where Army glider pilots would come to learn how to handle the hefty Horsa, intended backbone of the airborne forces. 6 MU was to erect many

German jets were held by 6 MU, including this Arado Ar 234B-2.

Horsas over the next three years. After flight testing they were locally used or towed to dispersal sites on bomber bases.

Trainee pilots came from GTSs, course strength being 62 pupils. Aircraft establishment was set at 56 Horsas and 34 Whitley V glider tugs. Glider flying was no simple skill. It took time to marshal the glider, attach the tow rope and position the tug. Accidents were frequent; night training difficult. On October 21 1942 a Glider Instructors' School formed, staying until February 1944 when it moved to North Luffenham.

With very many aircraft in store, 6 MU acquired the use of 34 SLG Woburn in November 1941, relinquished in favour of No 28 SLG Barton Abbey on February 8 1943, a site taken from 39 MU Colerne. Woburn was then handed to 8 MU, Little Rissington. No 22 SLG Barnsley Park was also used.

Whitley/Horsa combinations were intractable affairs with a wide turning circle. Already the Central Gliding Area contained ample tugs and Hotspurs on daily rounds, so cross country routes were awarded to the HGCU whose Whitleys and Horsas paraded widely as single combinations well spaced. Between February 10 and April 20 1943, flying also took place from Grove while Brize Norton's runways were re-surfaced. The primary task of the HGCU was to train sufficient Horsa pilots for the Sicilian landing. Then it switched to the main task—training for the landings in Europe.

Sufficient done, the HGCU changed its strength to 40 Whitley Vs and 36 Horsas,

US Strategic Air Command operated B-47Bs from Brize Norton, including 51-2261 *of the 320th Bomb Wing.*

and moved to North Luffenham in March 1944. Brize Norton switched to an operational role in 38 Group. A new SHQ was set up on March 13 1944 and within hours Albemarles of 296 and 297 Squadrons arrived. Then they fetched their Horsas from dispersal sites, ready for the assault on Normandy. On March 20 1944, operational training commenced in earnest with the dropping of paratroops, and towing and releasing gliders accurately.

On the night of June 5/6 1944, 18 Albemarles drawn from both squadrons carried the 5th Parachute Brigade to LZ 'N', a position by the river Orne in Normandy where a landing ground was fast prepared for 17 Horsas towed out of Brize Norton. Another two, brought by 297 Squadron, landed by the Merville coastal gun site. During the early evening of June 6, 40 Horsas were towed across the Channel from Brize Norton, and carried part of the 6th Airborne Division being lifted in Operation *Mallard.*

Albemarle squadrons then flew supply dropping sorties over France, while maintaining their glider towing skill. Because of their limited range and possibilities of engine overheating, Brize Norton's Albemarles flew to Manston on September 15 1944. From there they twice operated, towing gliders to Arnhem during Operation *Market* before returning to Brize Norton. Both squadrons were then to convert to Stirling IVs and, on September 29–30, left for Earl's Colne taking with them 94 Horsas.

Arnhem's high casualty rate meant training more glider pilots for another Rhine crossing attempt. The HGCU's Whitleys and Horsas returned from North Luffenham on October 15 1944. Sufficient glider pilots could not be trained by one unit, therefore other units formed, Brize Norton becoming No 21 HGCU. Some American Waco Hadrians were added to its strength in November. An Instructors' School which arrived in October remained until December 1945.

With the increase in activity, 6 MU repossessed Woburn SLG where it placed surplus Stirlings. 21 HGCU began rearming with Albemarles in January 1945 and by February enough glider pilots were ready for another Rhine assault. Training continued against possible Far East needs.

As Europe fêted the end of hostilities, the few aircraft enthusiasts of those days were about to enjoy unforgettable moments. Over the following few weeks some 200 captured enemy aircraft were brought to Britain for detailed examination or use as temporary transports. What would the morrow bring, one asked. Where were they being taken? Mainly to Farnborough, but the support organisation was provided by 6 MU. Many German aircraft came to Britain from Schleswigland, and once here they shuttled between RAE and 6 MU, occasionally venturing further afield.

Brize Norton's first captive was, satisfyingly, a Ju 88 which landed on May 10 1945. Many exciting shapes followed, among them the Focke-Wulf Ta *152H-150168* which came from RAE on August 18 and stayed until October 22. Heinkel *219A-7* Air Min 20 came on August 21 and was followed by another, ten days later. June 30 brought Arado *Ar234B-140008* from Farnborough and a Heinkel 162 touched down on August 2. An Me 410 and *6158*, one of the two Dornier 217Ms brought for examination, were among the aircraft here by the end of 1945. 'Why did not someone save them?' you may well ask. In those days conservation was unknown, and most weathered away or were dismembered in the late 1940s.

Halifaxes replaced the Albemarle tugs before 21 HGCU left for Elsham Wolds in late December 1945. Then Brize Norton joined Transport Command—apart from 6 MU. The School of Flight Efficiency and Transport Command Development Unit arrived from Harwell, for which reason Hampstead Norris and Finmere came under Brize Norton's control.

TCDU's principle task was development of airborne delivery of mixed loads. It employed Dakotas, Halifaxes, Hamilcars, Horsas, Liberators, Stirlings, Yorks and a few Hoverfly helicopters. Later it conducted glider towing trials of the Hastings and Valetta. In May 1946 the Army Airborne Trials and Development Unit arrived, the activity here attracting American interest for which reason the exotic sight of a Fairchild C-82 Packet towing a Horsa was to be seen.

On September 5 1946, Halifax A IXs of 297 Squadron arrived and stayed until August 1947. September 1946 also brought a Douglas C-54 automatically flown here from America, whilst 6 MU was disposing of many aircraft, in particular Spitfires. In January 1948 the MU received its first Meteors. TCDU left for Abingdon on June 30 1949 and on July 4 Brize Norton came under 21 Group Training Command. A swarm of Harvards again settled, this time belonging to the Examining Wing of

Brize Norton's giant hangar could accommodate Belfasts and VC-10s (via Bruce Robertson).

CFS. They were joined in mid-August by Mosquito T.3s and 6s of 204 AFS. Once more the emphasis had shifted to training, Fairford serving as the RLG. CFS remained until May 16 1950, and the Mosquitoes left for Swinderby early in June. By then the station was being administered by 23 Group, but not for long. Just before the trainers left, news broke of alien times ahead. Bomber Command seized Brize Norton on June 1 1950 on behalf of the United States Strategic Air Command.

Embryo plans for SAC B-29 bases had existed since 1946, and Russian intransigence over Berlin forced them to be enacted. Temporary bases lay along and ahead of the eastern fighter belt. The Americans wanted bases to its rear. Final site selection was made in May 1950, Fairford, Greenham Common, Upper Heyford and Brize Norton being chosen. Each needed at least a 9,000 ft runway, revised dispersals and alert areas—and of course very secure weapons dumps. On June 7 1950 the first Americans moved here from Marham, freeing the latter for RAF B-29s. The official hand over to the USAF took place on April 16 1951, but not until June 27 1952 did the first deployment of American bombers take place and spectacular it was for it involved 21 mixed B-36Ds, and B-36Fs from the three squadrons of the 11th Bomb Wing (H), Carswell AFB. They spent 15 days at Brize Norton.

Re-organisation of facilities led to the 7503rd Strategic Wing supervising running of the SAC base. Regular SAC rotational TDYs commenced with the arrival in December 1952 of B-29s of the 301st BW (M). In March 1953, 65 Squadron, 43rd BW (M), flying B-50As, replaced the 301st, making simultaneous use of four UK bases and staying longer than usual whilst plans were prepared to station B-47s in Britain.

Following the 43rd's return to America in June, there was a break before Brize Norton received, during the evening of September 4 1953, the first of many B-47 Stratojets based here. This initial rotation brought two squadrons of the 305th BW (M) from Limestone AFB, Maine. Replacement came in the form of the 22nd BW (M) which placed one of its B-47B squadrons here. Subsequent B-47s at the base were of the B-47E variety before the summer brought more B-47Bs, this time of the 320th BW (M) which were followed by B-47Es of the 43rd BW (M).

In December 1954 the base's first tanker squadron, the 321st Air Refuelling Squadron using KC-97Gs, moved in. Their aircraft, unusually, had their 'last three' boldly displayed on their fins. By contrast the following KC-97Gs of the 310th ARS identified themselves merely by green fin tips. It was the 40th BW (M) that came next, again using KC-97Gs. They left in September 1955, flying home via Goose Bay to Smokey Hill.

Brize Norton then underwent runway repairs before re-opening in July 1956. Limited use was subsequently made by B-47s of the 307th BW (M), and in January 1957 the 384th BW (M) placed B-47Es here. It was during their stay that, on January 16 1957, the first Boeing B-52B of 93 BW (H) to land in Britain *(3395—City of Turlock)* touched down after a flight

Retired prematurely? The Falklands conflict suggested so. Brize Norton was the base of 53 Squadron's Belfasts.

from Castle AFB California.

When the 380th BW (M) arrived in April 1957 it placed its three B-47E squadrons here and after it left, runway repairs again were undertaken. Some B-47s of the 68th Bomb Wing came at the start of 1958 and were then replaced by a squadron of the 100th BW (M).

March 28 1958 brought the debut of another new type to the base when the first Boeing KC-135 tanker to visit Britain landed. Two more came on June 27, notching up record speed crossings during flights from New York. These 'flying gas stations' were welcome arrivals, unlike a B-47E on February 28 1958. Shortly after taking off from Greenham Common it developed engine trouble and both of its long range tanks were immediately jettisoned. One bounced onto a hangar at Greenham setting it on fire, the other fell onto a B-47 which exploded. In the ensuing panic the Stratojet landed at Brize Norton. Fortunately, nuclear stores were not involved.

April 1958 brought six B-52Ds of the 92nd BW (H) to participate in the annual Anglo-American bombing competition. They came to a relatively empty base for, after the 100th had vacated it early in April 1958, new policy came into enactment. Only a handful of B-47s would now be at 'Brize' at any one time, their three-week stay replacing the previous 90-day TDY rotation. This 'Reflex Alert' allowed more flexibility and less vulnerability. Sometimes as few as nine aircraft formed the detachment. For company they had, for varying periods, detachments of the 55th and 98th SRWs, flying rare reconnaissance variants of the RB-47. Also based at Brize Norton early in 1959 was one of the little seen TB-47s. When the 38th BW (M) was in Britain (late 1959) it deployed 11 B-47s at Brize Norton along with KC-97Gs.

Varied detachments continued into the early 1960s including the first involving the basing of KC-135s here. More excitement was generated when, in January 1964, a Convair B-58 Hustler, the world's first supersonic bomber and of the 43rd BW, Carswell AFB, Texas, flew in. A few more followed but never more than a handful. B-47s continued to come despite their age, although there was now a gradual swing to ICBMs for SAC and towards American-based B-52s.

On April 1 1965, Brize Norton returned to the RAF, after an interesting period to which it had attracted unusual American types such as U-2s (Gary Powers being involved), RB-47s and ERB-47s and others with all manner of intelligence capabilities. When B-47E, *53-1884*, of the 380th BW (M) left on April 3 1965, an era ended.

SAC vacated Brize Norton as Britain's transport force, strategic and tactical, was expanding. Forthcoming use of large aircraft made it essential that a base in addition to Lyneham be brought into use for the Belfast and VC-10 fleets. The choice fell upon Brize Norton, for its good facilities and strategic siting. Cargo and passenger terminals were needed, also additional housing and suitable aircraft maintenance facilities. Among the latter was a need for a hangar large enough to house half a dozen aircraft of the Belfast/VC-10 size. This, the Brize Norton

VC-10, XV107 *of 10 Squadron, climbs away from Brize Norton.*

Cantilever' MPBW Lacon 7203/64N, is an amazing 1,039 ft 6 in long and 193 ft 6 in wide. The height of the ceiling is 52 ft 3½ in rising to 88 ft 2 in at the top of the ridge. Within the structure are 11 bays alternately of 91 ft or 80 ft 6 in width. Upon completion in June 1967 this became the largest cantilever structure in western Europe, and cost nearly £2,000,000.

Despite the intensity of the work, the station was not ready in time to house the Belfast and VC-10 squadrons which instead commenced operations from Lyneham and Fairford. It was mid-1967 when 10 and 53 Squadrons moved in. August 1 1967 brought the demise of Transport Command which became Air Support Command. VC-10s of 10 Squadron were then working the trunk route to Hong Kong and supporting British commitments throughout the world, leaving the transportation of heavy items to 53 Squadron's Belfasts.

As soon as the Hercules fleet reached intended strength at Lyneham, both Britannia squadrons, Nos 99 and 511, moved to Brize Norton. 'Brits' performed excellently and were useful on account of their good field performance. The station was much in the news in the summer of 1974 when its transports lifted over 7,500 Service and civilian personnel in rapid time when trouble flared in Cyprus.

Not long after, the future for the large aircraft abruptly became bleak with a decision to phase out Britannias and Belfasts. The run down of the former force commenced in April 1975 and of the latter in June 1976. The removal of the Belfast could not have come at a worse time. Serious problems with some of the Hercules meant replacement of spars. Only the Belfast could bring them to Britain by air and replacement parts continued to be flown using *XR366* into the autumn of 1976—and even after 53 Squadron disbanded on September 14 1976. At the end of that year Brize Norton looked very empty.

Cottesmore, once in line for TSR-2, was now the choice for the Tri-National Tornado Training Unit. Argosy E1s of 115 Squadron moved to Brize Norton where, in February 1978, the last Argosy was replaced by the Andover E1. Such aircraft had been at Brize Norton for some time in the hands of 240 OCU which borrowed these and other transports from various squadrons.

In 1976, No 1 PTS arrived from Abingdon, a unit which attracts Hercules from Lyneham for paratroop practices at South Cerney and Weston-on-the-Green. It is 1 PTS which provides that superb parachuting team, 'The Falcons', for summer delights. No 38 Group Tactical Communications Wing is also based here, and the Joint Air Transport Establishment, the modern equivalent of TCDU. In recent years Brize Norton has been used for Concorde pilot training, and it has served as a major diversion airfield.

Brize Norton of the 1980s remains the home of the VC-10 fleet, one of the last reminders of Britain's Colonial responsibilities. Just how useful the VC-10s remain was illustrated at the end of 1979 when the cease-fire came to Rhodesia and a large British contingent was airlifted to monitor the event. More recently the station has figured largely as the reception centre for the Falklands' wounded, flown home in VC-10s. In so doing it has provided a reminder of events passed in this area of Britain. Its future is uncertain but seems likely to be connected with in-flight refuelling for which Vulcans and VC-10s may be based here.

Broadwell, Oxfordshire

SP250065, 3½ miles S of Burford

Perhaps to the sound of a VC-10, travel along the A361 Barford-Lechlade road. Within a few moments, fork left just beyond the Wild Life Park on to a road which crosses an open area. A few huts, the watch office and a distant Braithwaite water tower remain where RAF Broadwell once thrived.

A 70 Group opening up party arrived on November 15 1943, and Transport Command took control on January 24 1944. An advance party of 46 Group personnel arrived from Down Ampney on February 2 1944 and, four days later, the first representatives of 512 and 575 Dakota squadrons from Hendon. Aircraft and main parties arrived on February 14 1944, some bringing Horsa gliders.

Like other 46 Group stations Broadwell had a three-fold role: i) delivery of airborne forces and supplies, ii) transport runs to the Continent and iii) retrieval of wounded troops. To organise the ambulance service, elements of Nos 91, 92 and 93 Forward Staging Posts reached the station on February 29 1944, by which time 220 commissioned and 1,400 non-commissioned men were stationed there.

On April 4 1944, Broadwell took part in Exercise *Dreme*, its first major practice landing. This involved night landing of troops of the 1st Air Landing Brigade lifted in 30 Dakotas supplied by the two squadrons. Then came a major 'navex' involving 35 aircraft, and glider tow practices were also flown. April 21 brought Exercise *Mush* in which, at dawn, 248 men parachuted from 19 Dakotas. Rapidly returning to base, glider attachment and 18 Dakotas left within an hour. Dakota squadrons also undertook night leaflet drops over France, four crews of each Broadwell squadron participating on April 2 1944.

The Luftwaffe deposited three unexploded HEs on the southern extremity of the airfield on April 23. Had the Luftwaffe dropped incendiary loads upon the wooden Horsa gliders . . . luckily, the potential of such a blow was not appreciated.

On April 24 and 25 both Dakota squadrons showered leaflets onto St Lô and Vire, despatching 21 effective night sorties. May brought a rapid increase in exercises. Exercise *Exeter*, watched by their Majesties King George VI and Queen Elizabeth, included dropping of paratroops at Netheravon where radio homing beacons were set up at the dropping zone to lead in 30 Dakotas from Broadwell to drop 300 troops of the 6th Airborne Division. At the end of May spare gliders were towed away to Ramsbury by USAAF C-47s.

Tension rose quickly at the end of May for the invasion of the Continent was not far off. Orders were given to seal the station and impound all mail as from 14:00 on June 2, for Broadwell was hosting over 1,000 troops for the Normandy landing. Upon receipt of the executive order on June 5 a final briefing for those taking part was arranged for 20:00. Fifty-nine crews attended, including six spare crews, for Operation *Tonga.* Present at the briefing was the AOC, 46 Group, who stressed the vital importance of the venture before the crews and troops boarded their aircraft.

Leading Broadwell's contingent was Wing Commander Coventry of 512 Squadron who took off at 23:14. His 32 aircraft were away in 15 minutes, then came Wing Commander Jefferson with the first of 575 Squadron's crews. The whole force was airborne by 23:36, and the paradrop went well and without loss. On to the two dropping zones 952 troops had parachuted.

At 14:00 on June 6 crews of both Broadwell squadrons were briefed again, 18 from 512 and 19 from 575, for Operation *Mallard.* They were to tow loaded Horsa gliders to Normandy in daylight, protected by a massive fighter screen. Again all went well—until one aircraft had trouble which meant attaching its glider to a spare

Dakota. All returned except for one which ditched in the Channel. Additional Dakotas took part the following night in Operation *Robroy*, a special operation during which they dropped supplies.

Commencement of Broadwell's third phase on June 17 set the tone for the rest of the war. At 06:00 15 Dakotas of 575 Squadron took off for Holmsley South taking aboard 191 RAF personnel and their kit. One Dakota became unserviceable leaving the others to make history by touching down at B5 landing strip (Camilly), the first Dakota squadron to land in France in force after D-Day. Landing was chancy and two damaged Dakotas had to be left there whilst the others hurried to B2 (Bazenville), there to retrieve 254 casualties who were back in England before mid-afternoon. This was the first huge input to the Air Ambulance Pool.

Apart from retrieving the wounded, Dakotas of both squadrons aided squadron moves, then returned with casualties, often from Coulombes (B6). Such activity continued at fever pitch throughout that summer, Dakotas returning with both stretcher cases and walking wounded before mid-September brought the tragedy of Arnhem.

Broadwell's contribution on September 17 comprised 22 aircraft of 512 Squadron and 24 of 575 Squadron with one from 437 Squadron, each Dakota towing a Horsa glider. Low cloud base during take off led to five glider pilots casting off before the Suffolk coast was reached. The pilot of another glider was killed by machine-gun fire near Oustahouet. Finally, 41 gliders carrying 544 troops of the 1st Border Regiment No 1 Airborne Division along with 22 jeeps, 13 trailers, 30 motor cycles, 17 ordinary cycles, 34 hand carts and seven Anti-tank guns, were launched onto a landing zone west of Arnhem. All Broadwell's Dakotas returned safely.

Re-supply on September 18 involved 24 Broadwell Dakotas. One crew captained by Flying Officer Henry flew in error on to a southerly route towards the LZ and Henry was killed when AA guns opened up south of Turnhout. His navigator was wounded and the aircraft's rudder badly damaged before the second pilot took over. The initial intention was to turn back and release the glider over British lines. Instead, its pilots at once cast off, giving Warrant Officer Smith and the Dakota an easier chance of reaching home. He landed safely at Martlesham. A Dakota of 575 Squadron was involved in an alarming incident over the DZ when the tow rope from an aircraft overhead wound itself around the wing of Flying Officer McTeare's machine, making it very difficult to fly, before he landed at Framlingham. One Dakota of 512 Squadron did not return.

On September 19, 30 Dakotas operated, both Broadwell squadrons each losing an aircraft. Next day 31 crews were involved and 512 Squadron lost another Dakota. With the situation at Arnhem desperate it was decided to place one Dakota

Broadwell, photographed on May 31 1957 from a 58 Squadron Canberra. Only the hangar bases remain (DoE).

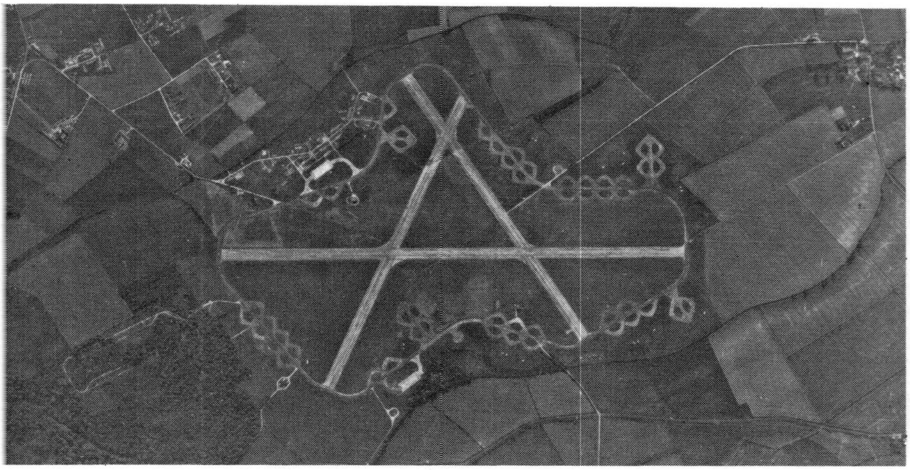

squadron much nearer to the dropping zones. One September 23, crews of 16 Dakotas of 512 Squadron found themselves taking personnel of 575 Squadron to B56 Brussels/Evere with that squadron's 18 Dakotas tagging along. Late in the afternoon 575 Squadron set out to drop food and ammunition west of Graves. About 75 per cent of the supplies appeared to reach Allied troops, so a second operation was ordered. Eventually four aircraft took off next day and faced plentiful flak.

On September 25, seven crews operated to a dropping zone west of Arnhem where nearly 800 men were desperate for supplies. This time the formation flew to Antwerp to meet its fighter escort before unloading 79 panniers of rations, 28 of medical supplies and three bundles of bedding. There was again much machine-gun fire which damaged four Dakotas. All returned except *KG449* which was hit in the port elevator and rudder, but which flew on quite well. Some ten miles north-west of Eindhoven the aircraft then ran into intense flak which put the port engine out of use. Nevertheless it flew on whilst gradually losing height and force landed near Pael, the crew having a lucky escape.

Arnhem passed, the round was again transportation of various loads to the Continent and returning with casualties. For Operation *Varsity* Broadwell's Dakotas advanced to Gosfield. After the drop they landed at B56, returning to Broadwell on March 25. No reduction in the number of sorties flown followed the end of hostilities in Europe, for troops needed supplies and there was repatriation flying to be done. The immediate post-war phase ended for 512 and 575 Squadrons when they moved to Melbourne and Holme-in-Spalding Moor, on August 6 1945. Replacing them were 10 and 76 Squadrons, here to equip with Dakotas prior to Far East service. On August 29 1945, 77 and 78 Squadrons began to arrive for similar conversion. Soon the move of 78 Squadron was halted; it was instead to go to the Middle East.

Conversion of these squadrons was rapid, 10 and 76 having set off for St Mawgan and Portreath on August 28. Training was intense at Broadwell, the two squadrons completing 720 glider tows and dropping 2,050 containers. No 77 Squadron left for India in October 1945.

On October 5 1945, Dakotas of 271 Squadron move in from Odiham, continuing scheduled services within Transport Command's extensive continental network. To ease administration Broadwell was switched from 46 to 47 Group on October 9 1945 and, by December, 271 Squadron found itself flying along the busy trunk route to India. (A 271 Squadron Dakota normally took four days to reach India.)

Broadwell was returned to 46 Group early in April 1946. Throughout that year 271 Squadron concentrated on passenger

Dakota IIIs of 575 Squadron prepare for a stream take-off from Broadwell. Horsas are parked by the trees. FZ695, *nearest, participated in the first of the squadron's leaflet raids and took part in Operations* Tonga *and* Mallard *on D-Day* (IWM).

and freight services mainly to Europe and particularly to areas where British Forces were stationed.

Closure of Broadwell was discussed towards the end of 1946, likewise a new siting of 271 Squadron. At the end of October 1946, Bicester was announced as chosen, but Broadwell had more to offer by way of accommodation—and it had concrete runways. Therefore the move was cancelled. On December 1 1946, 271 Squadron was renumbered 77 Squadron and it continued the pattern of passenger and freight services to, among others, Warsaw, Rome, Prague and particularly Buckeburg. Broadwell's end was not far off and on December 17 1946 most of 77 Squadron left for Manston. On the final day of 1946 station strength was reduced and preparations for closure began. With the rear part of 77 Squadron gone by January 9 1947, closure began. March 31 1947 marked the last day of RAF tenure of the station.

Cardington, Bedfordshire

TL085470. 3 miles SE of Bedford by the A600

'I'll hold the telescope so you can look through it. Can you see the airship, and the people?' It was midday, October 4 1930, a grey Saturday. Despite the memorable event soon to unfold, Cardington's crowd was not unduly large, although people had been aware of its imminence for many days. Dreary conditions caused a fair proportion of watchers to drift away before the *R-101* slipped its mooring. Gigantic it was, as long as an ocean liner, far greater than today's jumbo jets. A model in a showcase at Old Warden vividly portrays that comparison.

Regretfully, we left Bedford before the *R-101* sailed at about 19:00, conveying 54 people on its ill-starred Indian voyage. For some time there had been concern about the readiness of the 700 ft monster to undertake the journey. Put simply, the lift/weight ratio of the airship was worrying.

R-101 had been launched on October 12 1929 and two days later came its first flight of 5 hours 38 minutes duration during which London was treated to a view of this immense 'silver cigar'. On October 18 the Midlands glimpsed it and, in the course of a 7 hour 15 minute flight on November 1, the *R-101* paraded before King George V, then in residence at Sandringham. On November 2 and 3 a flight was made to the Isle of Wight and on the 8th and 14th local flying was undertaken. A tour of Britain followed on November 17/18 during the ship's longest flight (30 hours 41 minutes) before it was manoeuvred into Cardington's No 1 shed on November 30 1929 for six months of weight reducing modifications.

In June 1930, a contingent of airmen from Cardington and Henlow—supplemented by Bedford's unemployed—tugged the airship from its cocoon. Inherent buoyancy made the task of 'carrying' it relatively easy; the problem was to ensure

R-101 *nearing completion in her Cardington birthplace* (RAE Cardington).

that it was correctly guided. Such a task needed to take place in calm weather, at dawn or dusk. Similar conditions were also needed for ground manoeuvring and sailing.

Flight trials were resumed on June 26 1930. Their advisability was questionable, but the next day's 12-hour flight coincided with a practice for the 1930 Hendon display where, on the morrow, *R-101* was displayed. A few hours later it was back in No 1 Shed for more weight reduction treatment and attention to other snags. A drastic programme was undertaken during which the hull was cut for the central insertion of a new section in which additional gas bags would improve the lift/weight ratio. This increased the *R-101's* length to 777 ft. Its diameter was 132 ft; volume 5,500,000 cu ft.

Lavish passenger accommodation—including a lounge, dining room, sleeping accommodation and a promenade deck—was a feature of the *R-101*, in which heavy wooden features contrasted oddly with plastic cups and plates. These latter were rare and expensive in 1930. Some remain, preserved in the 1917 Headquarters building at Cardington.

Concern was now expressed at the porous nature of some gas bags, and the fact that others easily chafed against the metal. In the huge shed, assembly of the metal airship structure had taken place with the aid of steel cables hanging from a roof also containing three catwalks which can still be seen.

On October 1 1930 the 'slave labour' force again tugged out the 'Socialist airship', thus named to distinguish it from its happier capitalist rival, the *R-100.* More concern came during a long overnight flight on October 1/2 during which the *R-101* still handled poorly. Without doubt it was inferior to the Graf Zeppelin which visited Cardington in April 1930, and poor by way of comparison with the *R-100* which had recently come to Cardington after a triumphant voyage to Canada.

Competitive pressure was undoubtedly placed upon the staff and fliers of the RAW to get the *R-101* into service, as cautionary voices were raised publicly and privately. Brushing all aside, 54 people, including Lord Thomson, the Secretary of State of Air, and Sir Sefton Brancker, the Director of Civil Aviation, were aboard the *R-101* when, with little ceremony, it slipped from the 200 ft mooring mast in the early evening of October 4, circled Bedford, then set off at 1,500 ft towards the south-east and France. Although capable of up to 80 mph, adverse winds reduced its ground speed to 25 mph, its five Beadmore 580 hp diesel engines pulsating deeply. Weather forecasts, copies of which remain in Cardington's Museum, do not indicate ideal conditions. They were soon worse than expected and included strong gusts among generally bumpy, thundery conditions and rain storms. Handling the tail-heavy *R-101* was far from easy in good weather, let alone in these conditions and with a full load. The likelihood is that fabric and a gas bag tore, releasing hydrogen. Height was lost over France and a crew member later recalled that the *R-101* was at about the height of Beauvais Cathedral when it passed by about a kilometre to the north. Shortly afterwards the watch, maintained in nautical style, was changed—at 02:00 and at a very critical moment. A few minutes later the *R-101* was probably caught in a strong gust. There was a tremendous explosion as the airship fell and bounced 60 ft high on striking a hill-side near Allonne. Only six of the 54 occupants survived the conflagration.

Little materially remains of that event, but a recent acquisiton at Cardington is a heat-seared silver watch, the hands of which stopped at 02:03. Through an unusual twist of fate the RAF Ensign aboard the airship also survived. Little charred, it was found fluttering at the extreme stern of the wreck, and is cherished by Cardington's Parish Church. Among the dead were Lord Thomson, Sir Sefton Brancker and Major Scott. Their names remain commemorated by three avenues at Cardington camp.

Disaster at Beauvais spelt the end for large British airships. In July 1932 the Directorate of Airship Development was transferred from Air Ministry, to Cardington which, two months later was placed on Care and Maintenance, although the Royal Airship Works remained, in title, until 1938. The £471,000 *R-100,* was stripped of its fabric, broken up and sold for a mere £450. A better proposition might have been to have used it for public display to raise money for some other project. Cardington's mooring mast, as much a landmark as the airship sheds and built in 1926 at a cost of £150,000, was broken up in 1943 then melted down. At the time a 50 ft radio mast on the tower at the rear of the headquarters building of the RAW remained, a memorial to ghastly messages flashed there one October night.

That, too, has gone. Until the colossal airship sheds leave Cardington it is difficult to pass without thinking of those giants which seemed to fill the sky.

If you have any feeling for the past you will be overcome upon setting foot inside one of those colossal hangars, the largest of their type in the world. The bigger of the two—which differ in detail—is the northernmost hangar, the No 1 Shed built for the Admiralty and used by Short Brothers for airship building. On November 16 1930 close on 7,000 voices were raised in this sepulchral structure in a memorial service for the disaster victims. A report of the day recalled how 'the great roof echoed and re-echoed to the music of the hymns', and that 'the final chords resounded in the girders and had to be allowed to fade gradually before the service could continue. Voices were amplified and echoed from the great emptiness at either end of the shed'. That crowd only half filled the vast hangar.

The steel-framed 1916–17 shed has a cross section in the form of a three-pin arch supported on 'A' Frames. Between the pins it is 180 ft wide, overall 272 ft. Original height to the pins was 63 ft 3 in, minimum clearance at the roof centre 110 ft and overall hangar length 700 ft. The capacity of the hangar above the floor even then was a staggering 17,100,000 cu ft.

Over the steel framing was fitted ungalvanised corrugated sheeting. Annex coverings were finished with 'Hybrid' covered with cement mortar. Three rows of windows extended the entire length of the building which was finished in dark

The immensity of the door structure of Cardington's No 1 hangar is clearly shown in this photograph.

grey, colour repeatedly applied until this was recently overtaken by light green. To improve housing airships, giant screens 70 ft high and 700 ft long were erected to deflect the wind and remained until the mid-1920s.

To be commercially viable airships needed to be large. Although the spaciousness and luxury of ocean liners could be challenged, the problem of limited payload remained. Large airships needed huge sheds, one coming into use at Howden where Vickers built their *R-100.* Before the Socialists' *R-101* could be constructed at RAW Cardington, the World War 1 hangar needed enlarging. Four additional bays were fitted, adding 112 ft to the overall length. Raising the centre of the roof by 35 ft and the doors by 46 ft was far more difficult. Already those structures were very high, and the construction of the new roof by the Cleveland Bridge and Engineering Company Ltd of Darlington was no mean achievement. Liverpool Street Station would now fit into it, also a building as tall as Nelson's Column. The modified No 1 Shed enclosed 26,600,000 cu ft and covered 4¾ acres. Its internal height remains 156 ft 8 in with the height to the crown pin 174 ft 6 in, to the top ridge 179 ft 6 in. Modification, commenced in October 1924, was completed in March 1926 the hangar then being 812 ft long.

Cardington's other hangar came from Pulham, Norfolk, where it was dismantled

Opening the colossal doors of Cardington's No 1 hangar is achieved electrically and controlled from a cab.

in 1928, then re-erected as Cardington's Southern Shed. Visit Cardington and there can be no question but that one is quite overawed by the size of the sheds and no less by the truly gigantic doors at their western ends. The opposite ends are sealed. Each half door weighs an unbelievable 470 tons. Massive steel girders anchor each door to two large horizontal beams which rest upon 4-wheel bogies, themselves of no mean proportions. Each wheel supports a 33-ton load in calm conditions, twice that when the wind blows strongly. Electric power is used to close the doors, an operation taking 15 minutes. On one occasion a 70 mph gust raised a bogey from the 3 ft 6 in gauge track, which gives an idea of the vulnerability of these huge structures.

Viewing of No 1 Shed reveals seemingly unending bays, cross braced by thick cables. Six stairways lead to roof catwalks upon which the workforce spent much time when the giant airships were constructed. Ascending the ladders is for the strong willed and bold.

A 200 ft high steel-framed mooring mast, supporting a huge electromagnet, was sited in the south-east corner of the landing ground. It comprised eight columns placed on an octagonal base, 70 ft across. A 40 ft diameter passenger boarding platform, some 170 ft above the ground, was reached by a lift. The base of the mooring turret was of 25 ft diameter, and the tower could withstand a pulling force equivalent to 30 tons. In two huts at the tower's base, both still standing, were three steam winches used to pump water at a rate of 5,000 gallons an hour and gas through a 12-in pipe into the airship for purposes of maintaining its centre of gravity under varying conditions. When the water was jettisoned it was a case of run fast—or be drowned!

Without entering Cardington it is possible to observe the palatial Station Headquarters building facing the A600 road. Supported by Grecian-style columns, the façade carries the inscription MCMXVII, a reminder that Cardington has long been an action station. The entrance hall contains treasures from the station's historic past. Some walls are tiled, and the entire building is reminiscent of a stately home or Edwardian eating house. Its uniqueness is certain because it contains the ship's wheel from the *R-100*.

Short Brothers, involved in airship building, tendered to an Admiralty requirement for two rigid airships, Nos 31 and 32. The firm, lent £110,000 to purchase land and erect a 700-ft long hangar and sundry buildings, acquired suitable land at Cardington. They chose it, in 1915, because of the ample space around for development, the close proximity of the River Ouse, useful for industrial and sewerage purposes, good road and rail links and the closeness of Bedford. By 1917, 800 people were working here, 300 of them women, most of whom came from Bedford. Shorts built a housing estate, naming it Shortstown which name it retains.

R-31, launched at Cardington in August 1918, suffered a structural failure during its delivery flight to East Fortune. Its sister ship, *R-32*, entered service in September 1919 for training and experimental purposes. *R-37*, 675 ft long and 78 ft 8 in in diameter and based upon the Zeppelin *L48*, was partly built at Walney Island, Barrow, then moved to Cardington in 1917. Some £300,000 was spent before building stopped in February 1921. A second, larger airship, *R-38*—metal and rigid, too—was ordered from Shorts in September 1918.

The Admiralty were proposing to take over Cardington, leaving Shorts to run the station and build new airships there. The Company wanted better terms, and the *R-38* order was then cancelled. The Admiralty informed the Company that Cardington was to be immediately nationalised and, by April 1919, Shorts were vacating the factory.

The Royal Airship Works then came into being. Work on the *R-38* was resumed and it was completed in 1921. It was an impressive airship, with a 3,000 mile action radius and 211 hour cruise potential. Initial plans called for an airship of 750 ft long and with 3,000,000 cu ft capacity, but it would not fit any existing shed. A revised outline called for an airship 695 ft long and 85½ ft in diameter with 2,724,000 cu ft capacity and 65 hours duration at 65 mph. *R-38* encountered numerous problems during flight trials and broke in two on August 24 1921. That resulted in Cardington's Care and Maintenance state between 1921 and 1924.

Between 1923 and 1925, plans for the future of rigid large airships were further discussed, and the *R-33* was reconditioned here then test flown from Pulham. From those trials arose plans for the *R-100* and *R-101*. After its successful flight to Canada the *R-100* landed at Cardington, never to fly again.

Following the *R-101* disaster, recrimination was bitter and prolonged, and continues. Without airships what use was Cardington? In 1933 No 2 Aircraft Storage Unit was established here and supplied aircraft to the RAF until 1938. A new stage in Cardington's history was then clear to see.

The military use of balloons was long established, and the mid-1930s idea was to fly sufficient to form a barrage to force enemy bombers to fly high. Destruction of enemy aircraft colliding with a balloon cable would be a by product. No completely accurate appraisal can be made of its wartime success. An official report listed a likely total of 53 cable collisions by hostile aircraft over the United Kingdom between September 3 1939 and March 31 1941, resulting in 24 enemy aircraft crashing. Against this is a certain figure of 91 friendly aircraft hitting cables which caused 38 to crash. The first enemy aircraft to be brought down was a He 111 which collided with a cable at Billingham on June 20 1940, and the only ones to be brought down for certain in the Midlands were a Ju 88 near Coventry on September 16 1940 and two He 111s which collided with the Birmingham barrage on March 31 1941 and on April 10 1941. An enemy aircraft which hit the Birmingham barrage on July 31 1942 proceeded.

Many balloons were needed for a barrage, their testing, construction and storage being undertaken at Cardington. Just as important there was the production of vast quantities of hydrogen. SHQ Cardington formed on December 15 1936, by which time the RAW had become the Balloon Development Establishment. On January 9 1937, No 1 Balloon Training Unit formed to train handlers to control the barrages and ground equipment. The ASU left in 1938 and the Research and Development Establishment was renamed the Balloon Development Unit.

Already, Cardington was echoing to a sound that would etch itself into the memory of millions, the tramp of boots. In September 1937, No 2 RAF Depot arrived from Henlow to give basic recruit training. The intention had been that No 2 Group Pool should form here, but the idea was abandoned on January 1 1939. Control of the station then passed from Training Command to Balloon Command. Over the next decade balloons floated over the landing ground daily. No 2 RAF Depot remained under Training Command and when war commenced the station became a recruit centre.

By October 1939 plans were complete for the release of 10-ft diameter 'M' balloons over Germany from bases in France, from which would be dropped propaganda leaflets. More sinister were trials with balloons whose cables carried grenades, useful against enemy aircraft. Linkages, cables, ground equipment, all were progressively modified for the barrage.

Ever increasing numbers of recruits meant that more medical personnel were posted to the station. Balloon squadrons

Side-by-side, Cardington's original hangar and, on its right, that brought from Pulham.

formed here and, in July 1940 when camouflage painting of the sheds was completed, No 26 Maintenance Unit formed to service the balloons and their gas needs and functioned until April 1947.

Cardington remained the base of No 2 Recruit Centre. With it were the Aircrew Medical Board, Central Trade Board and later a Selection Board. By the time No 1 Balloon Training Unit closed in 1943 over 10,000 RAF and WAAF handlers had been trained in addition to 12,000 balloon operators and drivers. Squadrons continued to form until August 1944. Most of the training units moved out, then the station passed to Maintenance Command and 28 Group. The tramp of boots, though, continued to echo around the camp—No 2 RC was too firmly entrenched for that to go.

From the Balloon Training Unit the Balloon Development Unit reformed on August 1 1945 under 12 Group Fighter Command. November 1945 brought the amalgamation of the Balloon Development Unit and Training Aids Development Unit, resulting in a Research and Development Unit.

By May 1945, No 102 Personnel Despatch Centre had formed here, to demobilise wartime personnel. Call-up, induction and initial training of recruits would be events ever remembered by over 250,000 people who joined the Service here where basic drill and discipline were granted to over 100,000 men and NCOs between 1936 and 1953.

In April 1948 the RDU became the Balloon Unit which moved to Hullavington in 1966. The Balloon Development Establishment became the Research and Development Establishment in 1945, under the control of the Ministry of Supply and later the Ministry of Technology. It exists now as RAE (Cardington) under the control of MoD (PE) as an outstation of RAE Farnborough, and is concerned with weather research.

Hydrogen for the balloons is still provided by the Gas Factory established in early airship days to produce hydrogen by the 'steam-over-iron' process. Wartime needs for barrage balloons brought fast expansion, then, in 1948, the unit was named 279 MU, its task to produce compressed gasses for the entire RAF. A similar unit at RAF Wellingborough joined 279 MU in 1955, the combination becoming 217 MU.

Since 1947 the Department of the Environment has had units here, and the DoE Training Centre currently trains about 14,000 students a year. The Driving Examiners' Establishment looks after the Department's needs for driving test examiners. Their excellent quarters are far removed from the rows of wooden huts familiar to thousands of servicemen. No 2 Hangar is used as a Mechanical and Electrical Test Laboratory, carrying out trials connected with heating, vibration, ventilation and intruder alarm systems whilst the Fire Research Unit tests such items as fire resistant materials, and studies fire fighting with the aid of a full-sized house built in the hangar. The Civil Engineering Laboratory, a branch of the Directorate of Civil Engineering Development, also tests materials here.

Balloons are still seen at Cardington. KB XIs and the smaller KB XVs of RAE fly almost daily for the Meteorological Research Unit which is researching into the earth's boundary layer and recording vertical profiles of temperature and fog.

BDE has conducted considerable research into the development of fabric adhesives, and is responsible for the development of inflatables and assault equipment.

Recent years have witnessed a return of airships to Cardington. Most widely known has been the Goodyear *Europa*, a 192 ft long, 45.92 ft diameter, 202,700 cu ft shadow of former giants. Aerospace Development's *AD500*, first flown in 1979, for use in under-developed countries, was built here only to suffer a common fate when, like Lord Ventry's small airship *Bournemouth*, it was damaged beyond repair in gusty conditions.

On September 28 1981 the first flight of Airship Industries Skyship SKS 500, *G-BIHN*, took place. High hopes rest upon this latest venture and its development. Similar to the *AD500*, it is 164.04 ft long, has a maximum diameter of 45.93 ft and a volume of 181,200 cu ft. A 2-ton payload is coupled to a 600 mile range and a cruising speed of about 52 knots on a 120 hp power rating. Helium filled—which makes it much safer—it has an unusual VTOL capability offered by two swivelling ducted fans. Polyester-coated polyurethane forms the envelope and the crew and passengers occupy a one-piece plastic gondola.

One thing can never be avoided at Cardington—that haunting memory of the *R-101*. That monster, once glimpsed, became an indelible memory. In the local churchyard lies the tomb and communal grave in which the dead from that disaster were buried. Across the road in the church hangs that surviving ensign of the ship. Cardington is an extremely evocative, mysterious and, to my mind, always an eerie place.

Castle Bromwich, West Midlands

SP140910. 4 miles ENE of Birmingham

Street names have a ring of familiarity, like Tangmere Drive—but of Castle Bromwich there is barely a sign. Gone, a cradle of British aviation, beneath homes and gardens. Of the thousands of Spitfires and the great names connected with them there is barely a trace. True, the factory buildings have survived a variety of owners. Fragments of roads and a compass swinging platform are there; but the rest? Memory. Nowhere a sign that from an adjacent factory came half of all the Spitfires.

To Castle Bromwich playing field in September 1909 Alfred Maxfield transported the machine which, on the 27th of that month, became the first Birmingham aeroplane to fly. During a week of endeavour he coaxed his wonder high into the sky—well, to 50 ft anyway. Thereafter Castle Bromwich was a flying ground where in 1911 the famous B.C. Hucks, later Captain, RFC, Special Reserve demonstrated a Bleriot monoplane.

Castle Bromwich became a stopping place during many early air races. Probably the most historic was that of June 20 1914 when, during the *Daily Mail* London to Manchester Air Race, the playing fields were a port of call in both directions. Six competitors came and four proceeded to Manchester, leaving Graham White entertaining the crowd in his Farman Biplane. The War Office requisitioned the site in 1914 and established flying schools here.

No 5 Reserve Aeroplane Squadron formed on May 11 1915, and stayed until December 12 1917 by which time it had become No 5 Training Squadron. On September 1 1915, the famous 19 (Fighter) Squadron was born here, worked up using BE 2cs and Caudron G IIIs, and in late 1915 took over some RE 7s from No 5 Reserve Squadron. No 55 Squadron formed here on April 27 1916. Using BE 2cs, FK 8s and Avro 504s, it became a training unit and left in June 1916. No 38 Squadron followed, forming on July 14 1916 as a home defence squadron flying BE 12s, RE 7s and FE 2bs before leaving in October 1916. Assorted Reserve Squadron commenced existence at Castle Bromwich, including No 28 here from June 1916 to July 1918, No 34 based here during November 1916, No 67 formed in June 1917 and Nos 54, 55 and 74 here in 1918. Of these No 54 was, on July 1918, the last to leave. An aircraft acceptance park opened at Castle Bromwich in April 1918 testing locally built HP 0/400s and SE 5s. To Castle Bromwich came the remnants of 9 Squadron held here from July 1919 to the year's end. Castle Bromwich had been most active during the First World War.

Its future looked bright and, in August 1919, the Air Board acquired it. Castle Bromwich appeared to be an ideal airport site, and the British Air Transport Co opened, on September 29 1919, their first London-Birmingham passenger service.

September 1922 brought the next milestone, 17 competitors in the first round-Britain King's Cup Race. A repeat performance came on July 13 1923. Air Ministry approached the city, offering £3,000 to assist the running of an aero club. Flying clubs, they argued, could form a cheap reserve force. Some £2,000 of the money was spent on a couple of DH Cirrus Moths for the Midland Aero Club which opened in style on October 6 1925.

Further decisions led to the formation, on October 15 1926, of No 605 (County of Warwick) Squadron, part of the newly established Auxiliary Air Force. Equipped with DH 9As, the squadron displayed itself on July 16 1927 to over 100,000 people. Nearly 100 aircraft took part in that show, including Gamecocks of 32 Squadron, Horsleys, a Siskin, a Hinaidi and a clutch of RAF DH 60s. An Armstrong Whitworth Argosy biplane brought the official delegation, then gave the Lord Mayor a memorable flight. A year later the 1,000 mile King's Cup was routed via Birmingham. In 1929 it took place over an even greater distance, competitors calling at Castle Bromwich on the homeward leg.

A dozen Westland Wapitis replaced 605's DH 9As in April 1930 and Castle Bromwich became increasingly used by Railway Air Services. The GWR element extended its service to Cardiff, a 40-minute flight away when travelling in a tri-motor Westland Wessex. Steady expansion of Railway Air Services was reflected when, in April 1934, Midland and Scottish Air Ferries introduced a run to Liverpool. By that time RAS were using DH 86s. In April 1933 Bulldogs of 111 Squadron exercised here, and a year later there was talk of Birmingham having its own AAF squadron.

Hawker Harts replaced 605 Squadron's Wapitis in 1934 and were exchanged for Hinds late in 1936. Early in 1937 the go-ahead was given for £250,000 to be spent on the station over the next two years. Included was the cost of a 'C' Type hangar and a stylish Head Quarters building for the auxiliaries, built by Chester Road, opposite a huge factory site which Lord Nuffield acquired in 1938. Castle Bromwich was to train volunteer reservists at a six-aircraft strong unit known as 14 E&RFTS. In 1938 agreement was concluded with the Midland Aero Club for the latter to be a Civil Air Guard flying instruction unit, remaining when the VR school moved to Elmdon in 1939. Before 1938 ended, 605 Squadron was notified that its role would change to that of fighter.

Six Tiger Moths were delivered to the Aero Club in February 1939, and six DH Moth Minors were to follow. April 1939 brought 605 Squadron its Gladiators. Another 213 acres were added to the airfield in the expectation that Hurricanes would come to 605 Squadron. With the opening of Elmdon in May 1939, scheduled air services were switched to Birmingham council's new playground. The last pre-war air display at Castle Bromwich provided the public with its first view of Spitfires.

Come the war and Castle Bromwich's fighter squadron moved to Tangmere. In replacement came assorted ground units and balloon crews. The E&RFTS combined with Nos 20 and 44 to form 14 EFTS on September 3 1939, the school leaving for Elmdon a few days later. No 7 AACU arrived in April 1940 to co-operate with the Wolverhampton Searchlight School. Another AAC formation, No 116 Squadron based at Hendon, had a detachment here in 1941 for Anti-Aircraft gun calibration.

Wartime Castle Bromwich is remembered for its massive contribution to the Spitfire programme. Although production commenced in 1939 it was June 1940 before the first Spitfire II taxied from the factory to the airfield for the first of 33,918 Spitfire test flights here. The first Castle Bromwich Spitfire, *P7280*, was delivered to the RAF on June 27 1940, and the first delivery to a squadron took place on July 17 1940. Production reached 30 Spitfires a week with the factory long concentrating on Mk Vs and IXs and later the high speed Mks 21 and 22. Huge Spitfire orders were placed, for 1,000 on April 12 1938. In May 1942, 2,990 Spitfires were ordered, to be produced in the largest ever single order for any British military aircraft. Many came to be part of the backbone of the Spitfire squadrons in the last two years of war. Castle Bromwich works also built 50 Seafire 45s.

When the factory closed in December 1945 it had built 11,939 Spitfires, and 305 Lancasters, the first being completed in late 1943. Brooklands CRO functioned at Castle Bromwich, repairing 71 Wellingtons. From Castle Bromwich, Alex Henshow, of pre-war Mew Gull fame, flew Spitfires on test flights.

Following the war, Castle Bromwich reverted to being a training station. No 44 Reserve Centre formed on November 1 1947 and 5 RFS used Tiger Moths and Anson 21s. Also here was HQ 3605 Fighter Control Unit, No 48 Gliding School, ATC, and Birmingham University Air Squadron. No 605 Squadron's aircraft needed hard runways so it was stationed at Honiley.

No 5 RFS disbanded on June 20 1954 after re-equipping with Chipmunks.

When Castle Bromwich closed, on April 1 1958, there remained one last link with the great wartime days, Spitfire IX, *6457M* standing forlorn not far from where it had emerged as *ML427*. That item has passed on and, on the hallowed ground, now called Castle Vale, has risen a housing estate. Surely more than one of the older folk around looks and sighs for a Spitfire or a Merlin?

Chalgrove, Oxfordshire

SU635980. 10 miles SE of Oxford by the B480

Following an early breakfast on November 20 1943 a few RAF men left HQ 70 Group, Farnborough, to undertake a mighty mission. Travelling in 3-ton trucks, 30 cwt vans and two lighter ones—and superintended by the party's commanding officer in a car—they arrived at Chalgrove, a muddy mess.

Its readiness was nil. Not even a telephone had been installed to allow the news to reach a wider audience. Within a day a consignment of bicycles came from Andover. Many had flat tyres and the absence of even one pump rendered them decidedly 'U/S'. As the occupants viewed their plight, a great consignment of 'iron bedsteads' landed, complete with a vast number of 'biscuits'. Four days after opening time a GPO man came to enquire whether Chalgrove's occupants might need a telephone. A request was filed to HQ 70 Group for something akin, and for two battery radios for a station totally divorced from everything, including the world situation in which it might have to play a part.

On November 26 1943 a telephone arrived—for viewing only. In desperation, and perhaps fearing the worst, an officer completed an overland pilgrimage to Benson in an attempt to contact their padre. Surely he could enlist help for all? Indeed, his power was sufficient, and comfort came—in the form of Woodbines and rare bars of chocolate.

By Sunday equipment was submerging all and sundry. From distant Peterhead on November 30 came a new commanding officer, Squadron Leader H.A. Mockton MM. That event interested a passing Miles Magister the following morning. To encourage the inmates of 'Chalgrove-in-the-Mud' it decided to pay a call, producing a milestone in the station's history. Evidently neither it nor its crew liked what they saw for the 'Maggie' swung round and promptly left in the opposite direction to which it had landed. It was foggy so a hasty call to Benson was made. Thank goodness that the telephone was now working! The folks there fired, doubtless with great glee, a signal mortar bomb. This was memorable whenever it took place. To the surprise of all, the Maggie's pre-emptive opening of Chal-

A Royal Navy Vengeance TT IV awaits to tow away a Lines Brothers' target glider at Chalgrove.

grove raised it to international airport standard for, later that day, a Lockheed P-38 Lightning landed—and stayed. True, that stay was brief. The pilot appeared to take one glance at Chalgrove before hastily departing. He had apparently arrived where he did not want to be. Another early arrival, an Oxford which touched down on December 3, brought in a pilot who, upon enquiring where he was and being told 'Chalgrove', looked blank and said he couldn't 'find the place' on his map. He, too, fled to the comfort of Benson and, it later transpired, left to follow the railay lines towards London in order to reach Heston. Later it was discovered that the occupants were Americans who presumably had hi-jacked this RAF-marked Oxford!

The most significant event since the RAF moved in came with the arrival of Colonel F.M. Paul, US Air Service Command, bringing plans for a 9th US Air Force invasion of the station. Far more important though was the proximity of Christmas. Traditionally officers wait upon other ranks during the Christmas dinner but at Chalgrove far greater things were to overcome all. Turkey and trimmings duly scoffed, pudding—then the impossible. In Britain, racked by war shortages, each man on camp was astonished to be awarded a real, round, juicy orange. So rare was it that many in wartime Britain had never sighted one. So unusual were these bright objects that few were eaten. The suggestion was that Chalgrove's precious supply be taken home, shown to the children and, maybe, closetted in glass cases and labelled *Orangus Americanus* or something similar.

The 'locals' also had taken pity on the 'mud-men' and upon this special day braved up to inviting 17 of them into their homes to share what joy there was—and, maybe, gaze with awe and pre-war dreams, upon an orange. Not so Mrs Preston, good soul, who gave up her day of happiness to help with the washing-up at the camp and then mend some woollens.

At the fall of December a giant American airplane, a C-47, touched down with a load of Americans coming to capture this rebel outpost. Captain Hay announced that many more Americans were about to march off a big ship to revitalise this tatty British stronghold and make it great. With the announcement that 2,000 were coming, and 'many officers', there was general panic. Maybe that explains why, at this late hour in the war against Germany, although there were few enemy aircraft about, 'shelters' were dug. But, as quickly as he came, Captain May disappeared. Perhaps Chalgrove would still be a nice, quiet place when the spring came? Alas no, for January 6 brought proof of what was pending, with the arrival of a Lieutenant Colonel E. Haight to command the 9th AF Americans.

Three days later they came out of the mist . . . 400, at the unwelcome hour of 05:10. They seemed to delight in moving in great convoys, unable to resist the allure of night life except for military operations! I used to think they did it to bring fun and surprise to us all. Another curious habit they displayed was delight in leaning out of lorry cabs, as foreigners lean out of trains. It made the passage of American vehicles extremely hazardous for hapless cyclists who, whether they liked it or not, frequently became recipients of chewed (or unchewed) 'gum'.

Nature greeted the arrival by the occupying power at Chalgrove with torrential rain. These Americans had come from Culham railway station, and welcoming them to Oxfordshire was the task of Chalgrove's Adjutant who had been compelled to arise at 03:00. He later referred to his role as 'sacrificial to Anglo-US relations'. He was rewarded, though, for he soon proclaimed himself drunk on real US Official coffee. Nevertheless, he brightened sufficiently to be fully awake as the troop train pulled in. His ordeal was far from over for he had not been able to acquire an Anglo-US phrase book. There was much to conquer.

By mid-January 1944 about 1,000 Americans had penetrated Chalgrove. Some of the original RAF party had escaped to Kingston Bagpuize only to face the terror all over again! Then, at the turn of the month, there came the business end of the new world, the arrival of 45 officers and 297 men of Chalgrove's first operational unit, the 30th PR Squadron, USAAF.

Whilst the new unit sorted itself out, Chalgrove had some unlikely intruders, two intrepid Englishmen announcing themselves as Sub Lieutenant Fellows, a FAA pilot, and Mr P. Goodsir, from Thame, here to enquire whether they might borrow the airfield for the testing of model gliders built by International Model Aircraft, known universally to pre-war aviation enthusiasts as those people who produced the lovely 'Frog Penguins'. Goodsir was the gliders' designer and runways were needed for the tests. These Thame did not have. Squadron Leader Monckton agreed and on February 10 1944 two gliders arrived by road. One was quickly erected and next morning a Defiant and a Martinet came to undertake some towing.

When all was ready, 'little America' paused as Chalgrove's first International air display was about to take place. After a lot of checking a combination began to roll. Towing off needed some pluck for it was hard enough to tow away a manned glider, let alone this pilotless one. Satisfied with his preliminary checks, Flight Sergeant R. Hitchin chanced his luck and the Martinet and glider flew well away, to the delight of the audience. Landing with the target glider in tow successfully accomplished, another glider, with twice the wing span of the first, was attached to the tow rope and flew just as successfully. A feasible proposition became a certainty. International Models produced the target gliders which saw wartime and post-war service.

Already Chalgrove's first operational aircraft had arrived, P-38 Lightnings. One engaged a Spitfire in mock combat in which the lighter, British fighter totally out-performed its friend. That happened on St Valentine's Day 1944; the final stage in the marriage of the two air forces took place the next day.

The band of the US 9th AF, at the usual pace of such organisations, hurried on to the tarmac which, at a wartime airfield, was the nearest thing to a parade ground. Behind trailed the brave British warriors keeping company with Benson's Colour Party. As the national anthem sounded the RAF Ensign was lowered in colonial, ceremonial style. To suppressed satisfaction, in its place was raised a very tattered Stars and Stripes, a ceremony requiring the might of five Uncle Sams. As the Old Glory fluttered a bit, the strains of 'The Star Spangled Banner' wafted across Chalgrove's wastes, now drying out a little—and all the guards showed their arms. Chalgrove was USAAF Station No 465. The 'Yanks' had come, and a tale was ended that had been repeated many times elsewhere.

Their purpose in coming was virtually singlefold. They were here to invade and repossess France—with some outside help. All training would be fast, furious and directed to that singular purpose. Chalgrove would be the base from which photographic and visual reconnaissance of enemy forces in France would take place prior to, and following, the Normandy landings. It would provide information for attack squadrons operating from East Anglia and southern England.

The first to arrive, the 30th Photographic Reconnaissance Squadron, joined the 9th AF on February 4 1944 to become part of the 10th Photographic Group on February 21. Standard equipment became varieties of the P-38 for photo-reconnaissance. On March 23 the 31st Photographic Reconnaissance Squadron became established within the 10th, and six days later it was joined by the 34th Squadron. The Group was raised to full strength by the arrival on April 27 of the 33rd Squadron.

Assigned to the Group was a variety of PR tasks, particularly low-level operations. Photographs were secured of enemy airfields and especially coastal defences and ports prior to the Normandy landings. Damage assessment material was gathered following 9th AF attacks on airfields, marshalling yards, bridges and tactical targets. Marauder crews could study the success of their operations. The 10th's low level 232-sortie photo survey of the coast from Blankenburg to Dunkirk —a strongly defended zone—and from Le Touquet to St Vaast-la-Houge between May 6 and May 20 1944, won a Distinguished Unit Citation. By June the assortment of aircraft at Chalgrove incuded F-3s, F-5s, F-6s and light liaison aircraft.

As soon as the Allies landed in France the Group began a fast, furious campaign, photographing enemy troop concentrations, bridges, artillery posts, road and rail junctions, airfields and any enemy targets about which it was necessary to be well informed—and for neutralising resistance during the breakout from the Normandy beach-head at St Lô. On June 27 1944 the 15th Tactical Reconnaissance Squadron was transferred from the 67th Tactical Reconnaissance Group to the 10th and brought its P-51s and F-6s to Chalgrove. They replaced the 30th PR Squadron which, on June 9 1944, moved to Middle Wallop and the 67th Tactical Reconnaissance Group. With the advance well underway the 10th packed its bags and in mid-August moved rapidly to an airfield near Rennes. Chalgrove's operational span was brief but vital, and it remained in American hands.

A re-arrangement of the USAAF's PR

units came in March 1945. It brought the 7th Photographic Group (Reconnaissance) from Mount Farm to Chalgrove in the closing days of the war. On March 26 the 22nd PR Squadron flew its P-51s and F-5s here, and was followed by the 14th Squadron on April 2, the 13th on April 8 and the 27th which returned from France on April 22 after the Rhine crossing had been accomplished. In the immediate post-war period there was much reconnaissance and photographic work for these squadrons in assessing the plight of Europe from the air and providing damage assessment data for peaceful purposes. That continued until mid-October 1945 when the 7th Group split, with the 13th Squadron moving to Grove on October 13 as the 14th and 22nd Squadrons moved to Villacoublay. The 27th Squadron vacated Chalgrove for Germany on October 14 1945, but it was December before the Group HQ finally left Chalgrove.

Between August 6 and November 1945 Chalgrove held Mosquito PR VXIs of the 653rd Bomb Squadron which had been taken from the 25th Bomb Group in August 1944 to provide weather reconnaissance flights for the 9th AF. On November 21 1945 the 7th Reconnaissance Group was de-activated at Chalgrove following the posting of its squadrons overseas.

After the Americans left, the station came under Benson's control. By 1946 agreement was reached for Martin Baker to use Chalgrove. Their factory was near Denham and a suitable airfield was needed for test purposes. On July 24 1946, when flying in a Meteor at 8,600 ft and 320 knots over the airfield, Mr Bernard Lynch, a Martin Baker employee and a volunteer, made the first live ejection from a Martin Baker ejector seat. A year later the Mk 1 seat was ordered for fitment in RAF and RN fighters.

Remnants of 8 OTU, which had provided operational training for pilots and observers for the RAF's photo-reconnaissance squadrons, shared Chalgrove with the civilians. The unit arrived on July 4 1946 and left in October 1946, taking with it the three Spitfire XIs and two Mosquito PR 34s. There was still some flying from here by Benson-based Mosquitoes and Spitfires.

Since the 1940s Chalgrove has been Martin Baker's test airfield and the home of a Meteor, a Dove and, until 1981, the Company's Dakota. The two-seater Meteor permits test ejections to a speed of 450 knots. Around the perimeter is a high wire fence. There are few buildings, but a 'T2' hangar remains along with, naturally, well-maintained perimeter track and runway.

Cheddington, Buckinghamshire

SP918165, 7 miles ENE of Aylesbury, 5 miles S of Linslade and SW of Cheddington village

On March 15 1942, Cheddington opened as the satellite of No 26 OTU Wing. The first four aircraft to move in were Ansons on March 22 1942, and they began training flights on March 26. Two new Flights of the OTU, B and C, formed here on March 31 1942 and Wellington 1cs then began arriving. Both types used the station until September 3 1942. Transfer to the US 8th AAF came on September 7 1942, Cheddington passing under the administration of Bovingdon. Little Horwood replaced Cheddington as 26 OTU's satellite.

Four days after the Americans took control, personnel of the 44th Bomb Group arrived and stayed into October. On December 31 1942 the Americans left and the station returned to 92 Group which brought back the Wellingtons of 26 OTU for a brief stay in February 1943. Hotspur gliders and Master II tugs of 2 GTS spent seven weeks here before the station closed in March 1943 for extensive improvement.

Flying remained possible and, on April 13 1943, 11 Wellingtons were diverted here from Little Horwood for a five-day stay. Sundry other aircraft called, including three B-17s from Bovingdon on April 27. On the following day Squadron Leader H.C. Todd took command of the station and personnel from Bovingdon were transferred here. During May 1943 No 4263 Anti-Aircraft Flight was here briefly and on May 15 more B-17s from Bovingdon made a short stop.

On July 17 1943, No 1139 MP Company arrived. The Americans seemed ever a part of Cheddington, as on July 25 when B-24 240801 made an emergency landing. Next day brought Wellington *X3399* of 26 OTU. With starboard engine coughing, it joined the circuit, its pilot having mistaken this airfield for Wing. On landing, the Wellington overshot, damaging its propellers and ending in a belly flop near the D/F station.

August 16 1943 brought the conversion

of the airfield into USAAF Station 113 and home of a B-24 Combat Crew Replacement Centre (2nd CCRC Group). This role was performed until the summer of 1944. Earlier that year additional crew training units had arrived and in February 1944 it was put under the control of the US 8th AAF Composite Command.

A change to specialised night operations came with the arrival, on June 19, of the 858th Bomb Squadron (H) which brought B-24s from North Pickenham. Immediately they operated and continued to do so until August 4 1944. On the following day the squadron became part of the 492nd Bomb Group and on August 10 moved to Harrington. To Cheddington came the 406th Bomb Squadron (H) from Harrington followed by its sister squadron, No 36. Both under the 8th AAF Composite Command were switched to the 8th AAF Fighter Command on October 1 1944 then transferred to the 1st Air Division's on January 1 1945. They flew leaflet dropping sorties and secretive missions. The 36th returned to Harrington on February 28 1945; the 406th followed on March 16.

P-47C/Ds of the 551st and 552nd Squadrons, 495th Training Group, then moved here from Atcham staying only until June 1945 when the Americans vacated Cheddington. No 91 Group, Bomber Command, took possession returning it to 26 OTU on July 12 1945. Four days later No 1 Overseas Packing Unit opened here, also the Road Vehicle Disposal Unit which handled vehicles for public auction. From February 1 1946 other equipment was delivered here from the Vehicle Disposal Unit, Hinton-in-the-Hedges. All vehicle work ceased on February 20 1946, then the packing unit moved to RAF Drayton leaving, by March 20 1946, only a rear party. At that time the station was accommodating 75 RAF and 65 WAAF personnel working either at the Meteorological Signals Centre, Dunstable, or at the Medical Training Establishment and Depot, Halton. At the end of April 1946, Cheddington passed to Technical Training Command. It closed, as an RAF station, in February 1948. Between that date and 1978 part of the site was retained by the War Department for purposes of a secret nature.

Chedworth, Gloucestershire

SP042133. 8 miles N of Cirencester

On a fine summer's day this one-time airfield is certainly worth a call, its situation on a plateau affording splendid views to north and east. A Blister hangar remains in good condition and roads cross the site. Concrete and brick buildings remain on the north side, and fine oak trees contribute magnificently to the superb setting.

The station opened in April 1942 and in August became an active satellite of 52 OTU, Aston Down, which based Spitfire Is and IIs and Master trainers here. On December 15 1942 the AOC, Fighter Command, recommended that a training establishment be formed to train embryo squadron commanders. The proposal was for a school within 52 OTU. Half the OTU's establishment was ordered to be set aside in 1943 to provide a fighter squadron leaders' course. Air Ministry agreed, and the OTU intake was reduced. On January 15 1943 the first three-week course for fighter squadron leaders opened at Chedworth. Week one was devoted to individual section tactics, week two to squadron and wing tactics and week three to army support. The satellite's section became the Fighter Command School for Tactics. Its stay at Chedworth was brief, for on February 9 1943, at the end of the first course, it left for Charmy Down.

On February 19 1943, Chedworth came under South Cerney's control. Oxfords of both Nos 3 and 6 (P) AFUs used the airfield until October 18 1943 when the station switched to Honiley's control. Late October, after Wellingtons had arrived there, No 2 (Air Gunnery) Squadron of 63 OTU was forced out of Honiley and moved to Chedworth. There it was joined by the air gunnery element of 60 OTU and formed a combined 60/63 Gunnery Squadron, active here until January 1944.

Chedworth was next used by Oxfords of 3 (P) AFU. Between June 19 and July 9 1944 the 125th Liaison Squadron, US 9th AAF, was flying from here using mainly L-5 Sentinels. These also equipped the US 9th AAF HQ Squadron during its short stay here. On July 17 1944, control of Chedworth returned to Aston Down where No 3 Tactical Exercise had become established on July 14. A few days later, Mustangs of the unit moved to Chedworth.

A further change came on December 18 1944 when 3 TEU was re-organised as 55 OTU which subsequently stationed some Typhoon fighter-bombers here. Training ceased on May 29 1945 then Chedworth was placed on Care and Maintenance before the Admiralty took over in

A Whitley V, P5104, *about to tow the GAL half-scale Hamilcar glider, tested in 1942 at Chelveston.*

December 1945. For some time the airfield was maintained as an ELG for CFS although in the 1950s it was also being used for agricultural purposes.

Chelveston, Northamptonshire

TL015685. 4 miles NE of Rushden

Certainly it was an unbelievable sight, enough to make one assume an attack of double vision, when from Chelveston that the curious Twin Hotspur training glider undertook its flight trials.

Chelveston, on the fringe of the RAF's operational area, was laid down as a bomber station in 1940. The layout includes a 'J' Type hangar later supplemented close by with two 'T2s'. It was on August 15 1941 that Flying Officer J.B. Townsend and ten men took the station into 2 Group. Later it would pass to 8 Group, but was under Polebrook's control until September 2 1941 when it became self accounting with the opening process underway. Lengthening of the runways was then approved, the main one being extended to 2,000 yards and the other two to 1,400 yards. Installation of Drem lighting was begun, the work still under way when in December 1941 the Central Gunnery School arrived as a lodger until Sutton Bridge was ready.

Not until the end of March 1942 were the runways complete. Chelveston's future was obvious after Air Vice-Marshal Alan Lees brought General Eaker USAAF to the station. Before the Americans arrived, those new runways were in the hands of the Airborne Forces Experimental Establishment, the glider trials section of which was placed at Chelveston where its advance party arrived on May 5 1942 to test the Stirling's ability to tow a Horsa. The outcome had a grand effect upon central England's skies—and the enemy's. Glider trials did not proceed without incident, for one Hotspur broke up in the air, the crew being lucky to escape. On July 19 1942 the half-scale Hamilcar, on tow behind a Stirling, made an emergency landing at Thurleigh. But it was other landings that already pointed to the future. On June 10 the 12th TCS arrived and next day the 10th and 11th TCS, part of the 60th Troop Carrier Group. Between July 20 and 28, 48 C-47s landed and the Americans took over the responsibility of running the station, even to the extent of feeding the RAF personnel an amazing changed diet.

On August 7 1942 the 60th TCG moved to Aldermaston, making way for B-17Fs, the newest Flying Fortresses available, which began arriving August 9–10, 19 of them manned by the 352nd and 419th Squadrons. Seven of the 353rd Squadron touched down on August 16, the day upon which trials of the Twin Hotspur, still in manufacturer's hands, commenced. Another eight B-17Fs flew in on 26th and soon 352 and 419 Squadrons were fully equipped. Glider trials which, at the end of August centred upon the giant Hamilcar tank carrier, would be conducted elsewhere. Some B-17s temporarily lodged at Podington with the 352nd Squadron but on September 2 all came to Chelveston. The 301st Group commenced operations on September 5 1942 when five crews of the 352nd and seven of the 419th Bomb Squadrons set off for the engine sheds at Rouen. One of each squadron aborted leaving the rest to attack, after which bomb plots showed poor aim. Next day 13 B-17s made a diversionary raid on St Omer/Longunesse. One crew mistook Fort Rouge as the target and another bombed the rail yards at Abbeville. When 14 crews of the two squadrons were sent to attack Schiedam Docks at Rotterdam on September 7, a gunner laid claim to the Group's first Fw 190. All four squadrons of the Group set off for a raid for the first time on September 26, but poor weather brought a recall. The Group had been switched on September 14 1942 to the XIIth AF although it was still operating with the 8th.

On October 2 1942 the Potez factory at Meaulte was attacked by 18 out of 25 crews of the 301st. They were engaged by a strong group of Fw 190s, five of which they claimed without loss. Then came participation in the largest USAAF raid so far, against the Fives-Lille steel and engineering works to which the Group contributed 23 aircraft drawn from all four squadrons. Of these, 18 attacked. The RAF ASR service rescued the crew of one which force landed at sea. Another came down in East Anglia and two more were damaged in exchange for which the Americans claimed to have destroyed ten enemy aircraft. Another attack on Lille took place on November 8 1942, and it proved to be the last by the 301st before it flew to Africa. Before leaving it was honoured by a visit from King George VI who visited Chelveston with Generals Spaatz and Longfellow.

On December 6 1942 the 305th Bomb Group began to move in from Grafton whose runways needed attention. Leading the Group was Colonel Curtis LeMay whose command extended to May 18 1943. Immediately, the Group prepared to operate its four squadrons, 364, 365, 366 and 422 being briefed for Lille. Bad weather intervened, but when the attack did take place, 16 aircraft altered course too soon to bomb, and Fw 190s shot down a B-17. The next raid was against Romilly-sur-Seine, repeated on December 20 when 22 B-17s of the four squadrons operated. Tactics to be used in daylight bombing needed to be well thought out, this task particularly falling to LeMay. Not all of this tough man's ideas met with approval. In December a large scale trial used Horsham St Faith as target, Cambridge secondary, as fighters tried escort tactics with the bombers. Ideas formulated were tested on December 30 when 24 B-17s of the 305th took part in an attack on the Keroman shipyards, Lorient. Only 13 bombed and claimed six enemy fighters as engaged after the bombers faced murderous AA fire during their tightly packed run in. Enemy fighters forced a B-17 into the sea, and damaged two, one limping into St Eval and showing what could happen to a crew

Impossible? Illusion? Neither. The Twin Hotspur glider tested at Chelveston in 1942 (British Aerospace).

which broke formation. In January 1943 some P-38s were placed here to explore fighter tactics.

On January 3 1943 the target for 27 crews was the torpedo station at St Nazaire, an 85 B-17 attack led by the 305th. Heavy flak damaged half the entire force. The formation was held on the run in, the 305th claiming three enemy fighters. Lille was raided on January 13 and then came the great plunge—Germany. With the weather fine on 27th, the raid led by Thurleigh's 306th Bomb Group was ordered and 18 B-17s from Chelveston participated in this first American attack on Germany. Cloud prevented bombing at the primary target so the formation proceeded to its secondary target, the naval dockyard at Wilhelmshaven. There was cloud there, and bombing spread beyond the target. The 422nd lost B-17 *24623* last seen in the target area, the only aircraft missing on this historic occasion.

The next milestone was the Hamm raid of February 4 1943 in which 17 crews of the 305th took part. The weather was poor, pin points impossible to find and the raid cost two crews of the 305th. Bad weather marred a second attack against Hamm on February 14. Vegesack was at last found and bombed on March 18 1943, and very accurate results were obtained by the 305th when Lorient was bombed on April 16 1943. The 305th's hardest flight yet came on the following day when 20 B-17s left Chelveston for the Focke-Wulf factory at Bremen. There was ample opposition, 9/10 cloud forcing the B-17s to attack Wilhelmshaven instead. Of the 305th contingent three were lost in the biggest B-17 attack so far. Not only was that the end of the first phase of B-17 operations, Chelveston was handed to American control in April coming under Brigadier General Anderson. By the end of May 1943 the 305th had a champion 20-mission B-17 in hand, *Wham Bam*.

The 305th had won a Distinguished Unit Citation for its courage during a raid on Paris on April 4 1943; in the second half of 1943 it was to penetrate far more deeply into enemy territory, attacking a nitrate works in Norway, industrial targets in Berlin, the Merseburg oil refinery and shipping at Gdynia. An interesting and initial departure from such operations came when the 422nd Squadron switched to night bombing operations between September 8 1943 and October 4 1943. Ten days later the 305th suffered decimation when it lost 13 aircraft during the Schweinfurt raid of October 14. Assembly in cloudy conditions over Britain had placed the Group in the wrong position within the 1st AD, laying it wide open to savage fighter attack. Some measure of safety was by then being afforded to the 422nd Squadron which, between October 7 1943 and June 24 1944, carried out night leaflet dropping over Germany.

Evidence of the horrific experiences crews underwent during day raids was obvious on February 20 1944. First in the

Hamilcar prototype, DP206, *photographed at Chelveston by a 'J' Type hangar in March 1942* (RAF Museum).

305th to be awarded the Medal of Honor was 1st Lieutenant W.R. Lawley. A head-on fighter attack set one of his B-17's engine on fire, and Lawley was very seriously wounded, along with seven more of the crew. Although bombs were still aboard the aircraft, and the co-pilot dead, the crew stayed aboard, seriously injured and unable to bale out. Lawley in pain nursed the aircraft homewards, then enemy fighters set another engine on fire. At last, the crew managed to jettison the bomb load, but Lawley, having lost much blood, collapsed. Mason, another crew member, took control until Lawley revived just in time to land the Fortress at Redhill.

On April 11 1944 it was 1st Lieutenant E.S. Michael who showed great courage in a similar situation to that of Lawley. His B-17, *Bertie Lee*, was hit in a head-on attack, then spun down followed by fighters. Both pilots and others in the crew were wounded, and part of the burning incendiary load could not be jettisoned. The pilots and the wounded bomb aimer stayed aboard whilst the others baled out. Then the crew jettisoned the bombs and took cover in cloud. Although weak, Michael revived sufficiently to land the battered aircraft and was awarded the Medal of Honor.

In the run-up to D-Day, the 305th attacked airfields, V-sites and, following the invasion, tactical targets. It supported the breakout at St Lô and the airborne landings at Arnhem. Its 422nd Squadron, using H2X, was switched to a pathfinder role in day bombing attacks between March 22 and May 23 1944. Since October 1943 the 305th had been operating as a three-squadron Group, but in June 1944 the 422nd was renewed as a bomber squadron and began operations on July 6 1944 as a normal day bomber squadron within a Group continuing daylight operations to the end of the war. On April 17 1945 the 305th had the misfortune of being the last B-17 Group in the 1st AD to lose a B-17 in action. Some 337 raids had been flown when, on 25 April 1945, the last one took place.

The 305th did not return to America, it moved to Belgium in late July 1945. In October 1945 the RAF made the station a satellite for 25 MU before it was placed on Care and Maintenance. In early December 1952 the USAF took control and a long runway was laid for the 3914th Air Base Group, SAC, which tended the needs of B-47s resident here during TDY spells and between January and June 1959 serving within the Reflex Alert Force. RB-47s of the 301st SRW were briefly sited here. In August 1959, RB-66s of the 42nd Tactical Reconnaissance Squadron, 10th Tactical Reconnaissance Wing arrived from Spangdahlem, remaining until August 1962. Chelveston then became a reserve airfield. The Americans remain, in a small enclave where communications and storage centres are situated. The long runway has been attacked by demolition workers, but a hangar remains.

Chipping Norton, Oxfordshire

SP325255. 2 miles S of Chipping Norton, by B4026

Few who travel to the Cotswolds fail to discover Chipping Norton whose name derives from the medieval word, Chepynge, which describes the long, narrow market place. Of the airfield, an enhanced RLG, more remains than might be expected. Concrete huts and air raid shelters stand by the road, and an unexpected survivor in good condition is the rifle range.

First to use the landing ground was 15 SFTS. Upon being pushed out of Middle Wallop by 10 Group, Oxfords of the Advanced Training Squadron came to Chipping Norton where Headquarters 15 SFTS arrived on July 10 1940.

The airfield stood on a confined area 70 ft above sea level. Three grass runways were marked out in July 1940, the NW/SE of 1,000 yds, the E/W of 800 yds and N/S of 600 yds. The overshoot was disturbing for the land dropped away to the south-west. In 1940 two Bellman hangars and a few wooden huts comprised the technical site. Personnel were billetted in Bell tents neatly lined in one corner. Stores and messing arrangements were by the B4026 road, and main water was drawn from a temporary link to Chipping Norton's supply. All electricity was generated at the camp. During July 1940, 15 SFTS started to equip with Harvard Is, 20 being at the RLG by the end of the month. There were also 27 Oxfords here and remains of *R6266* which had crashed into a stationary Oxford *(N4580)* causing both to be burnt. Three days later Oxford *P1890* collided with *N6326* over Charlebury with shattering results. At this time HQ 15 SFTS was in Oldner House, Chipping Norton—about one mile north of the airfield.

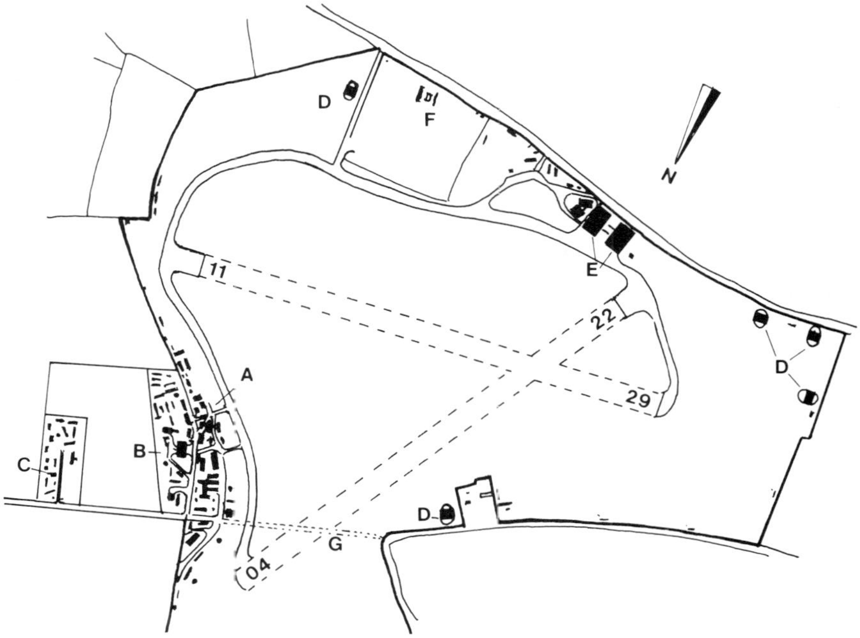

Chipping Norton in 1943 shows the features of a satellite training station with limited development. The technical site ('A') lies to the south of the road through the camp, the instruction site ('B') to the north. 'C' marks sub-site 5 (a domestic area) and Blister hangars (Extra Over Type 69 ft) are marked 'D'. That in the most southerly corner was Over Type 65 ft. Two Bellman Hangars are marked 'E'. Remaining in quite good condition are the machine gun butts (147/41). An interesting feature was the dummy road crossing Runway 04/22 (marked 'G').

On August 2 1940 the unit was informed that it was to be consolidated at Kidlington, but the Advanced Training Squadron remained some time at Chipping Norton. On August 31 1940 the squadron's return showed 41 Harvards and 15 Oxfords as based here. Headquarters staff moved to Kidlington on October 1 1940, the remainder going on October 13 when the aerodrome came into use as Kidlington's RLG. The enemy called on October 29/30 and their brand of nightlites were distributed nearby. Some high-explosive bombs were dropped a mile to the east on November 5–6.

At the end of 1940, Kidlington's RLGs were reconsidered, changes becoming effective in February 1941, releasing this RLG from 15 SFTS control. Since November 16 1940 it had been in the hands of 6 SFTS, Little Rissington which positioned Oxfords here, particularly for night flying. The Luftwaffe welcomed 6 SFTS by placing several HEs on the landing ground on 18/19 November 1940.

Extended facilities constructed in 1941–2 included a watch office (13726/41) and an instruction site to the rear of the technical area. Four Over Type 69 ft Blister hangars and a single Over Type 65 ft supplemented the Bellman hangars, and two Sommerfeld runways were laid on QDMs 11/29 and 04/22. Unusually, the perimeter track only partially circled the field. Sub Site 1 held the engine repair facilities, general maintenance, servicing and stores buildings. On Site 2 were placed the ground staff room and flight offices. Dormitory huts (2965/42) and ablutions were found at Site 5.

From November 1940 Chipping Norton was under 6 SFTS control, that unit becoming 6 (P) AFU on April 1 1942. To the end of the war it was used by their

Oxfords remaining with 6 (P) AFU until it closed on December 1945. The site was disposed of in the 1950s.

A surprising survivor at Chipping Norton—the rifle range in summer 1981.

Chipping Warden, Northamptonshire

SP493495, 6 miles NE of Banbury

Constructed to 1940 building patterns, Chipping Warden with one 'J' Type hangar (5836/39) was typical of its age. Three 'T2s' (8254/40) provided additional maintenance facilities. Buildings were mainly of the temporary brick type, and the 34 circular dispersal pads were supplemented by one loop type. Chipping Warden had three runways, No 1 07/25, No 2 15/31 and No 3 01/19. Two 72,000 gallon aviation fuel tanks and one 500 gallon were sited underground whereas the high level water tower (14285/40) held 60,000 gallons.

Completion date of the station slipped. It was incomplete when 12 OTU's advance party arrived from Benson on July 10 1941, followed on July 23 by 12 OTU from Mount Farm. Night flying commenced at Chipping Warden on July 24 1941, using a few aircraft specially flown in from Benson.

Chipping Warden was declared open for general flying on August 1 1941 under the control of 6 Group. One Flight of 12 OTU became operational on August 15 1941. By the end of the month the unit had completely moved in, to become fully operational on September 1 1941. Additional flying was undertaken at Turweston and Edgehill.

October 12 1941 brought an intruder in the early hours during night flying by the Wellingtons. Eight small HEs were dropped and a container of incendiaries, slightly damaging two Wellingtons. In mid-November 1941, preparations for aircraft diverted during night operations was made allowing for up to 20 visiting crews. December 16 1941 brought a Lysander, nucleus of a drogue TT flight for the OTU. Two Wellington 1cs had also been modified to tow sleeve targets, the three aircraft being placed in No 5 Navigation Flight.

January 1942 saw the arrival of 1517 BAT Flight's eight Oxfords, supplementing 12 OTU's 40 + 14 Wellingtons and 14 + 4 Ansons and target towing aircraft. Single pilot manning for Wellingtons came in March. Crew formation then became pilot-observer/bomb aimer and wireless operator/air gunner.

For the 1,000 Plan Cologne raid 22 Wellingtons set off from Chipping Warden, all safely returning. Only 13 of the 20 crews participating in the Essen raid on June 1 did not return. Chipping Warden's next bombing raid came on June 25/26. This time 20 Wellingtons set off to attack Bremen and four were lost. One, *L8800* flown by Sergeant Bagley, suffered a damaged fuel pipe as a result of which it was ditched 25 miles east of Cromer. The crew were picked up after two and a half hours by a minesweeper. Wellington *DV952*, flown by Pilot Officer Cowsill, was attacked near Wilhelmshaven by a Ju 88 which closed to 450 yards. The Wellington's tail gunner opened fire, saw the '88 spin away glowing red, and claimed it as probably

A familiar Midlander, a Wellington III and a special one. Z1732, FQ:S, *served 12 OTU Chipping Warden faithfully from December 1942 to January 1945* (RAF Museum).

destroyed. Flight Lieutenant Kerwan's aircraft was attacked by a Ju 88 about 45 miles north-west of Bremen, the fighter's fire being evaded.

Chipping Warden acquired Gaydon as its satellite on June 13 1942, retaining it until its transfer to 22 OTU Wellesbourne on September 1 1942. By then 12 OTU had re-equipped with Wellington IIIs, the first of which was received in July. During August the Anson flight was disbanded and a separate Gunnery and T.T. Flight formed.

A further operation in the *Grand National* series was flown on July 31 1942, 13 Wellingtons including Mk IIIs taking off for Düsseldorf and carrying mixed loads of incendiaries and 500 lb HE bombs. Some 40 miles east of Nordland the tail gunner of *T-Tommy, N2856*, spotted a Ju 88. As the fighter closed its guns blazed then the Wellington's tail gunner accurately poured his shots into the enemy which was later seen burning. The next operation came on September 16 1942 when nine Wellingtons, two of which did not return, set off for Essen. One Wellington was badly shot about and during the engagement the rear gunner baled out of the blazing aircraft. Eventually the aircraft crash landed.

A Flight 12 OTU moved to Turweston on November 23 1942. Here, instructors trained pilots and crews to handle the Wellington whilst 12 OTU's main satellite was still under construction. A startling accident befell Wellington *BK261* on November 24 1942 when a flash bomb in its chute ignited. The bomber exploded, killed the entire crew and crashed near Shotteswell, Oxfordshire. Another very serious accident came at midday on December 1 1942. Sergeant McMurchy's Wellington, *BK250*, was making its take off run when a strong gust of crosswind forced it off the runway. It swerved out of control towards the fire tender bay, then McMurchy managed to steer it clear of a group of civilians. *BK250* rammed itself into the control tower and hit a civilian car before landing on a hangar which was set on fire. Ambulance men and the medical officer were quickly on the spot and found the crew badly burned, two civililans dead and frantic efforts being made to extricate the control tower staff from burning offices. Casualties totalled 24 of which two were severely burned crew members. Whilst the Wellington's geodetic construction conferred great strength, its fabric covering burnt fiercely and extricating the crew was far from easy.

Leaflet dropping over Roubaix on November 28 1942 by four Wellingtons marked a return to operations. Another four visited Orleans on December 22/23 1942. Thereafter 12 OTU erratically participated in leaflet dropping over French towns.

Plans made for the station to accept 'cuckoos' (aircraft diverting from home bases) first were enacted on February 4 1943 when a 4 Group Wellington landed from Lorient and two Halifaxes from Turin. Such activity increased in months ahead. Edgehill, the station's new satellite, was taken over from 21 OTU on April 12

1943. The next day was also memorable in that two of the Unit's newly acquired three Martinets were lost, *HP372* crashing near Bicester and *HP373* overturning during a forced landing.

Both Flights of 12 OTU at Turweston moved into Edgehill on April 27, setting the pattern for the station's remaining wartime service. Wellington conversion flying now took place at Edgehill, operational flying training by two Flights at the parent station. Leaflet dropping over France as well as participation in *Bullseyes* and ASR Searches followed.

Four Wellingtons left to drop *Nickels* in the Rennes area on July 13/14 1943. Wing Commander Bray crossed into France some way off the intended track. He altered course for the Mortain-Domfront area, 50 miles north-east of Rennes. At about 01:20, when at 16,500 ft, heavy predicted flak burst immediately below the aircraft, causing damage to its port mainplane and engine. Bray turned for home, re-crossing the French coast over his point of entry. Heavy flak now made the Wellington impossible to handle and there was no choice but to ditch the machine. Then the crew scrambled into their dinghy, Wing Commander Bray with a broken nose and Flying Officer Parkinson with broken ribs. They were afloat for three hours before rescue came.

More *Nickels* followed and during August 1943 the first Wellington arrived. Operations continued with Wellington IIIs used as bombers when 12 OTU bombed the Foret de Hesdin and Foret de Raismes in the Pas de Calais during the run up to Operation *Starkey*. On five nights these operations took place.

Stirling *R9249* of 1657 CU was ordered to land at Chipping Warden because of bad weather on the night of October 22/23 1943. In heavy continuous rain the crew mistook the peritrack for a runway. During its landing approach the bomber clipped a tree and then roof tops in Aston le Walls before crashing and burning. Four of the crew were killed.

The final months of 1943 were busy. *Nickels* were dropped upon Chartres, Versailles, Melun, Montagris, Cambrai, St Quentin and other areas. There were *Bullseyes* too, during one of which, on December 22 1943, 12 OTU's contingent became enmeshed with German bombers operating over the London area.

Further *Nickels*, each time by four aircraft, were flown to northern France on January 14/15, February 8/9 and March 2/3 at which time Chipping Warden was beginning to receive more diverted bombers. On March 24, the OTU first dropped *Windows* during a special exercise. Even more eventful was a mission on April 24/25 by seven crews, during which the gunner in *LP456* opened fire on an unidentified aircraft with unobserved results. The same night Wellington III *BK542* was missing after being last seen losing height over the North Sea. *Bullseyes, Erics* and *Nickelling* continued, with leaflet dropping taking place around Cherbourg on May 15/16, following the loss of Wellington *LP155* on May 4 when there was enemy activity off Portsmouth. *Nickels* became fewer as the available area was limited although, on August 13/14, four sorties took the Wellingtons to Chalons, La Roche, Charlette and Monteuil/Bellay.

By the start of 1945, courses were smaller and it was increasingly difficult to meet all commitments. Training flights over France were undertaken and there were still diverted arrivals as on April 8/9 1945 when 15 Lancasters of 415 Squadron, and two others, landed from Hamburg and Lutzkendorf. Brief, totally unexpected, excitement came early on March 4 1945 when an enemy aircraft (possibly an Me 410) came in low and fast firing three short bursts of cannon fire at the airfield. The pundit beacon was on, but there was neither damage nor casualties. The enemy could still make a nuisance of himself. 12 OTU was flying Wellington Xs, Oxfords, Hurricane IIs and Master IIs with which it saw the war out.

On June 1 1945 the last cross-country detail was flown, by Flying Officer Begg and crew in Wellington X *LN158*. Over the next few days Master IIs and Hurricanes based at Edgehill (vacated on June 7 1945) were disposed of, and by the end of the month all that was left of 12 OTU's bomber force were two Wellingtons, *NC971* awaiting disposal and *LP648* awaiting repair, the unit having closed on June 14 1945.

Chipping Warden passed to 25 Group and was cared for by a party from Harwell until August 1945 when an assortment of Wellingtons and Ansons of 10 ANS arrived to stay briefly until Swanton Morley was, in November 1945, ready for them. No 1517 BAT Flight lodging here since 1942, and whose eight Oxfords were used mainly by 6 SFTS/6 (P) AFU, disbanded on December 17 1945. The station was, on January 31 1946, handed to 41 Group and became No 114 Sub Storage Unit of 6 MU Brize Norton which used it as a centre for the holding of Horsa gliders prior to their being sold off as surplus. Chipping Warden closed in December 1946, although it was some years later before it passed from RAF hands.

Church Lawford, Warwickshire

SP455355. 2 miles NW of Dunchurch by Long Lawford road, N of A45

Church Lawford was an unusual training station. Its three hard surfaced runways, legacy from an intended use for bombers, encouraged post-war retention for flying. A Type 'J' (10680/39) hangar kept company with six Bellman hangars and, across an intervening road, lay a split domestic area. Both the east-west runway and the north-south runway were about 1,400 yards long. The shorter north-east/south-west runway was used for radio approach training. Buildings were mostly 1940 temporary brick designs. There were no hard standings, trainers being placed around the perimeter by the north-west part of which were four Over Type Blister hangars and six of the Extra Over Type.

Church Lawford was ready in April 1941. An advance party arrived from Cranwell on May 1 1941 and the opening up party on May 12 1941. Since its formation on August 17 1919 the Central Flying School has been the RAF's authority on flying, and has trained flying instructors. A minimum course of two and a half months, including 78 flying hours, was maintained until the late 1930s. RAF expansion made great demands upon CFS—there was greater emphasis on night flying and fast, new aircraft to master. On March 9 1940 a decision was made to form at Cranwell an additional school for flying instructors. Its formation under Wing Commander Darvell took place on September 10 1940, equipment being a collection of Avro Tutors from 24 MU and Airspeed Oxfords. This new unit was designated No 2 Central Flying School by which title it was still known on May 30 1941 when it was ordered to leave for Church Lawford. No 1 CFS Upavon would concentrate upon training instructors for single-engined aircraft, although of each course for 45 instructors a third would learn to instruct on twin-engined aircraft. No 2 CFS would train instructors for multi-engined aircraft. Three instructors for twin-engined aircraft would be trained against each single-engined aircraft instructor.

On January 9 1941 a policy change ensured that all flying instructors could serve at EFTS if necessary. Special courses for OTU instructors were introduced in June 1941. Gone were all notions that a pilot from an operational squadron could merely be posted to an OTU as an instructor.

Church Lawford thus made an important contribution to flying training. The move here of 2 CFS was completed on June 17 1941. Oxfords and Tutors were in use, No 11 Course having just completed training. Almost immediately, flying commenced at Southam RLG, and Sibson was also used for circuit flying. At the end of July 1941 the School's strength was 10 Oxford Is, 40 Oxford IIs, 28 Tutors and a GAL Monospar. August 21 1941 witnessed the loss of an Oxford which, after taking off from Sibson crashed into a water tank, then defied all laws by burning itself out. Two detached Flights of 2 CFS, which had remained at Cranwell, in late October moved to Montrose and Dalcross taking their Tutors and Oxfords, divorcing themselves from the parent unit.

Five schools now trained instructors. On January 19 1942 they were renamed Flying Instructors' Schools. 'CFS' was retained by Upavon from which the Empire Central Flying School formed. No 2 CFS became No 1 FIS, Church Lawford, its responsibility the training of SFTS and (P) AFU instructors for twin-engined flying. Special courses were run for OTU instructors using the 24 Oxfords Is, 36 Oxfords IIs, 30 Avro Tutors and the Monospar at Church Lawford. An RLG at Warwick came into use when Peterborough acquired Sibson. Oxfords of 1509 BAT Flight were at Church Lawford from April 6 1942 until leaving for Dyce in May. By August Hockley Heath was in use as an RLG supplementing Warwick.

At the end of September 1942, with the School's strength at 20 Oxford Is, 30 Oxford IIs and 18 Tutors, No 1 FIS's training commitment was complete. During October it dissolved into 18 (P) AFU formed on October 27 1942. Still in 23 Group, and Oxford equipped, it gave twin-engined aircraft experience to pilots trained overseas. No 1533 BAT Flight, formed here on October 27 1942, operated alongside the main unit which, at the end of October, held 22 Oxford Is and 31 Mk IIs with a Tutor and a couple of Ansons for communications flying. Courses graduated each month and, at the end of May 1943, 90 Oxfords were available.

The use of a fully equipped satellite airfield was now essential. Snitterfield came into such use on May 7 1943 when nearly 100 Oxfords were at 18 (P) AFU, a total ever rising. By the end of August 1943 it stood at 136 plus four Ansons, and the eight BAT Flight Oxfords and its peak strength had still to be reached. In March 1944 it stood at 123 Oxford Is, 25 Oxford Mk IIs, four Ansons and seven Oxford Is of 1533 BAT Flight—a total of 159 aircraft, although a number were at the satellite.

Just what the enemy with a handful of fast intruders could have done to night flying was well illustrated near Church Lawford on April 27 1944. A raider entered the circuit shortly after 04:00, located Oxford I *LX196* and opened fire. There was a blinding flash, for an Me 410 had collided with the Oxford whose Canadian pilot, Pilot Officer G.S. Moore, and two others were instantly killed.

An unusual accident occurred on June 14 1944. Near Church Lawford an American AT-6 Texan was flying at 10,000 ft when its port wing broke away. The main wreckage fell at Brandon Wood Farm.

Some idea of the intensity of flying from this airfield in 1944 may be judged from the fact that in one month there were 738 visiting flights to the station. Nos 1514 and 1546 BAT Flights were making use of the station where the Oxfords on strength on June 30 1944 totalled 164 and, by the end of September 1944, 172. Two Oxfords collided over Turweston on September 25 1944 and fell on to its dispersals.

Large numbers of Oxfords remained in use in 1945, 18 (P) AFU still making use of Snitterfield and Warwick RLGs. During March, No 21 Group Communications Flight moved to the station bringing a Dominie, a Harvard and two Proctors. Church Lawford had been earmarked as a post-war station. No 18 (P) AFU would move to Ashbourne, to where an advance party was sent on March 21. Darley Moor was also chosen as a suitable base, but on March 29 the party withdrew from Ashbourne and the idea was abandoned. Instead, 18 (P) AFU moved to Snitterfield, and disbanded on May 29 1945.

No 20 SFTS was established at Church Lawford on April 3 1945 and equipped with Harvards as No 1533 BAT Flight disbanded. Although a post-war FTS was considerably smaller than a wartime one, there was ample audible flying at Harvard bases. In July 1947, No 20 FTS was redesignated No 2 FTS and in March 1948, moved to South Cerney. Flying halted at Church Lawford, and although not until the mid-1950s did it cease to have a place in the RAF.

Clyffe Pypard, Wiltshire

SU071770. 9 miles SW of Swindon

No 29 EFTS formed at Clyffe Pypard on September 8 1941 at a new rudimentary RAF station. Marshall's Flying School operated it along the lines of their 22 EFTS. It could accommodate 40 officers, 30 sergeants, 440 airmen and 208 civilians. Dimensions of the airfield were: north/south, 1,100 yds; north-east/south-west, 830 yds; east/west, 1,100 yds and south-east/north-west, 1,100 yds. A 10 ft wide perimeter track made of concrete had been laid, starting in the north-west corner and following the boundary to the south with turning points every 600 yds.

Equipped with Tiger Moths and Magisters, No 1 Course opened with 70 untrained pilots arriving from 7 ITW Newquay and one from Duxford. Training commenced on September 15 1941.

In January 1942 the snow fell deep. There were 3 ft high drifts on the airfield which was covered by a layer of snow a foot deep. Drifts 4 ft high completely cut off Clyffe Pypard from the main Swindon –Devizes road, a snowplough being used to clear a way out of the camp. It took most of a day to achieve this and cut a runway across the airfield. More snow fell on January 21 but by the 24rd a runway had been cut 900 yds long and 30 yds wide to accept necessary emergency landings.

Early in 1942 the School began to train army personnel as glider pilots, commencing with four officers and 41 other ranks from the 1st Glider Regiment here for a 12-week course.

Fresh courses, new faces, and the solo thrill leading to the pass out parade dominated life. Additional excitement involved a Liberator *AL538* from Lyneham which landed in darkness on the evening of October 18 1942 during a delivery flight from Prestwick. This was a giant arrival, and the crew who had crashed on the east side of the airfield were lucky to survive the accident.

From November 1942, 29 EFTS began using the ELG at Manningford and an RLG at Alton Barnes which permitted more intensive flying. The latter station remained in use until July 1945. It was to Alton Barnes that two instructors were probably flying when they took off without authority and, in misty weather, crashed in a wood near Roundway Hill, near Devizes, 70 miles away. The aircraft overturned, caught fire, and both were trapped in the wreckage. Another memorable event involved Stirling *BK667* 'H' of XV Squadron which came down near the aerodrome after two engines had cut and five of the crew had baled out during their return from a raid on St Nazaire.

Although the EFTS had mainly concentrated upon training RAF pilots, later in the war it trained some for the Royal Navy and continued operating until October 11 1947 when the disbandment order was received. The training commitment passed to RAF Booker, and Clyffe Pypard closed soon after.

Collyweston, Northamptonshire

TF025032. 3 miles SW of Stamford by the A43

Collyweston originally called Easton was prepared during the 1939/40 winter. On the day prior to opening, the landing ground was designated K3, K being the Sector letter and 3 the third airfield within the clutch. On the evening of May 26 1940, 266 Squadron commenced placing Spitfires here nightly and soon 32 Squadron conducted night flying training. Blenheims were dispersed here for night flying from June 1940 onwards, which month also found dispersed Hurricanes of 229 Squadron at Collyweston. No 1 Squadron Hurricanes were also to be seen here. A detachment from 29 Squadron Digby commenced night stand-bys at Collyweston in September 1940 and periodically during the summer and autumn, 266 Squadron made use of the site. As the winter deepened so Hurricanes of 151 Squadron started to use the airfield for night operations, along with the detachment of 29 Squadron. The arrival of 25 Squadron on November 27 1940 at Wittering brought more dispersals here, 229 and 1 Squadron both leaving the parent station in December 1940.

No 151 Squadron also moved to Wittering and this too used Collyweston During 1941 it came to be 266 Squadron which made the satellite its usual home, settling here in June 1941 and flying Spitfire IIs. In August 1941 the squadron received Spitfire Vs and, on October 24 1941, K3 (Collyweston) was redesignated WB3 upon the opening of Kings Cliffe, whence 266 Squadron moved that day.

On Apri 6 1942, Master IIs of 1529 BAT Flight moved in from Wittering. The Flight disbanded on November 7 1942 and 152 Squadron, which had arrived in September 1942, withdrew. No 118 Squadron dispersed here briefly in January 1943. On January 2 1943, 1530 BAT Flight's Oxfords arrived from Wittering. Over the next two years, detachments of AACU organisations used the satellite, 116 Squadron being here in April 1943 and 288 Squadron in late 1944. The main event of that period, though, was the placing of the exotic 1426 Enemy Aircraft Flight at Collyweston.

The passage of a Ju 88, He 111, Bf 110 and Bf 109, often grouped, sometimes single and unescorted, had become commonplace over the Eastern Counties. I well recall a low flying Ju 88 coming fast and head on, and my taking to a ditch near Duxford, uncertain of its ownership, then finding it unfriendly in an area where one came to expect such to be in British hands, On March 24 1943 the collection of ex-enemy aircraft left Duxford, followed, on April 12 1943, by its ground echelon, also moving to Collyweston. There all were based until the Flight disbanded. Collyweston came to house some really unusual 'RAF' aeroplanes. Initially it was the well-worn He 111H, *AW177*, Ju 88s and Bf 110, *AX772*, but expansion soon came. In June 1943 an Hs 128B-1, *NF756*, arrived, in August Bf 109F, *NN644*, and, a week later, a Fw 190A-4, *PN999*.

'Tour 10' by 1426 Enemy Aircraft Flight commenced on November 6 1943 and was being carried out by the He 111, Ju 88, *HM509*, and the new Bf 109F. The formation settled at Polebrook on November 19 1943 to give the Americans a close look at these enemy aircraft. Then came a flying display which went drastically wrong, for the He 111 and Ju 88 both commenced to take off but from opposite ends of the same runway. The Heinkel's pilot opened up powerfully but as he turned to port he developed a stall turn. Seven of the 11 aboard were killed.

Two more Fw 190s were received in December 1943, and a Bf 109G. 'Tour 11' began at the end of that month and extended to February 1 1944 during which period many stations in the Midlands were visited. On March 23 1944, Collyweston's circus set forth again, this time touring airfields in Essex and Suffolk and taking along a new Bf 109, *VX101*, which had joined the Flight on February 4 1944. Before they were back yet another Fw 190, *PE882*, had arrived. Auster AOPs of 658 Squadron which settled on March 14 1944 were merely passing through from Otterburn on their way south, where they proceeded on April 19 1944. A new resident, intending to stay longer, the Gunnery Research Unit, arrived from Exeter on April 14 1944. It brought along a Wellington X, Defiants and—most fascinating of all—a Fairey Battle *(L5776)*, one of the last to survive in Britain. Delivered to the RAF in July 1940 it joined the GRU on September 10 1941 remaining with them—apart from a two-month stay at Farnborough at the end of 1942—until it was written off on December 12 1944. GRU was here until March 1945.

A very lively performer for 1426 Flight arrived on May 6 1944, a Ju 88R-1 which force landed at Dyce and was brought along for evaluation. In pseudo-German markings it may be seen in the Battle of Britain Museum at Hendon. Three days after the Ju 88's arrival at Collyweston, 1426 Flight took over some of its aircraft to Thorney Island giving Channel gunners a chance to improve their aircraft recognition. A final tour by 1426 came in August 1944 when they liaised with 100 Group and were based at Little Snoring before getting their Ju 88S-1 in September 1944.

For the next four and a half months, 1426 Flight remained variously engaged although it was clear its days must soon be ended. That event came on January 17 1945, the unit disposing of its aircraft to CFE on January 21 1945.

Collyweston was transferred to 21 Group, FTC, on April 1 1945 and resumed its old role of satellite to Wittering. Later that year it was integrated into that station's landing ground and remains within its confines.

Coventry Airport (Baginton), West Midlands

See Baginton

Cowley, Oxfordshire

SP555035, 3 miles SE of Oxford, along the A4142

Varied were the Civilian Repair Depots, factories giant or small to which damaged aircraft were taken for repair, cannibalisation or complete write-off. Largest was No 1 Civilian Repair Unit, Cowley, which handled Hurricanes and Spitfires. Officially opened on September 11 1939, Cowley CRU was functioning by the outbreak of war, crews of No 50 MU recovering aircraft to be worked upon. From early 1940, No 1 Metal Produce and Recovery Depot assisted. All were mainly civilian manned and headed by Lord Nuffield.

Part of his Morris factory was converted into aircraft workshops. Flight test hangars were provided and a grass landing ground alongside had two runways. This superceded the use of Abingdon for flight testing in spring 1940. No 1 CRU provided vital back-up during the Battle of Britain, its civilian staff working night and day to return damaged aircraft to MUs and squadrons. Although Spitfires remained the principal wartime commodity—because of Nuffield's intended association with them through Castle Bromwich—many other aircraft types were repaired here until hostilities ceased. Then the reversion of factory and airfield to civilian state was rapid. Some buildings used by 1 CRU remain, but the airfield has long since gone and partly rests beneath the Oxford Ring Road.

Wrecked aircraft unsuitable for repair went to Cowley in vast quantities from mid-1940. From them was extracted mainly alloy, but also rubber and plastic. Giant heaps of barely recognisable items accumulated and salvage continued long after the war. By then No 1 MPRD was handling huge numbers of aircraft scrapped after hostilities, some without even a solitary day of military service. Close proximity of Nos 6 and 8 MUs led to many unusual aircraft being dismembered here.

Cowley factory played another part in the war effort—the production of over 3,000 Tiger Moths. Argument has long raged over the precise number constructed, for there were many spares items made. Certainly Cowley's wartime Tiger Moth production was considerable, and that many a 'Tiger' still flying originated at the Morris works.

Cranfield, Bedfordshire

SP945425. 8 miles SW of Bedford, S of A422, reached via a by-road from Astwood

'Stop me and buy one?' Impossible, yet here was a crowd of RAF pilots—or

Blenheim I, L1243, V, *joined 34 Squadron at Cranfield in mid-July 1938 and passed to 82 Squadron on November 21 1938. It flew to the Far East with the squadron in August 1939.*

impressed ice cream men—propelling Wall's and Eldorado tricycles around Cranfield's barrack square. It was summertime, so dark glasses were not incongruous. But, surely, something must be wrong? Nobody joined the Air Force to sell ice cream. 'We're not selling ice creams on a night fighter station in the middle of a war far from won. We're improving our night vision—under orders. Didn't you guess?' Well, yes, I was cheating, a bit. I had heard of this curious activity for which Cranfield was well known, and it is not the only reason why I remember the station well.

As our Oxford *R6350* circled it was clear that Cranfield in summer 1944 was an aircraft enthusiast's paradise. Grouped on the south side were 100 Spitfires in varied hues and many forms. Scattered among them were 15 Typhoons and about 50 Mustang IIIs, many conspicuously wearing 'invasion stripes'. Towards the north-east corner of the airfield rested Mosquito IIs, the first of which had joined 51 OTU in July. Close by were ten Beauforts and a fine assortment of Beaufighter Is and VIs. By now this night fighter OTU, training crews for 100 Group, Bomber Command, was overshadowed by No 3501 Servicing Unit's handling of hosts of front line fighters of both ADGB and 2 TAF, here for rapid servicing.

Cautiously nosing around, notebook in hand, I came across four still-novel Tempest Vs. By the tower rested a Spitfire XIV, the first production example I had seen closely. Artists' impressions of *RB174:DL-T* which appear now and then—all looking different—stem from that afternoon's activity!

Also here were Wellington XIs in Coastal colours, and fitted out as flying classrooms, aiding crew conversion to the latest AI Mk X centimetric radar. Some Beauforts wore Coastal white/grey camouflage, several had dorsal turrets and others wore standard grey/green night fighter finish. Four new OTU Hurricane IIcs and an unusual all-silver Spitfire *MJ963* were close by. Add the communications and ferry aircraft such as Ansons, Arguses, Harvards, Magisters and Proctors—not to mention a Flamingo sailing serenely by—and August 2 1944 can be looked back upon as one of those wartime days packed with interest.

Station Headquarters had opened on June 1 1937 and the aerodrome on July 1 1937 under the control of No 1 (Bomber) Group. On July 6, 108 Squadron's Hinds arrived from Farnborough. Hinds of 82 Squadron arrived two days later from Andover and on July 12 yet more, this time of 62 Squadron which was vacating Abingdon. Cranfield's operational contingent, three dozen Hinds, was complete.

When the new stations opened, Cranfield's squadrons moved. First, No 108 took up residence at Bassingbourn in February 1938, just as Blenheim Is were arriving for 62 Squadron. Blenheims came

Oxford trainers of 14 SFTS lined up at Cranfield early 1940.

for 82 Squadron during March 1938, then both squadrons transferred to 2 Group on July 15 1938. September's Munich crisis brought them to high readiness, hazardous allotted tasks including attacks on German power resources. Following the crisis, training became more realistic. Fuel consumption trials took place as did training flights over France to cement the *entente cordiale.*

Cranfield's partnership broke apart in August 1939. Ordered to the Far East, 62 Squadron's sea party left on August 12 for their troopship *Neuralia* which then headed for Singapore. Two Flights, each of eight Blenheims, left Cranfield on August 23, commencing the long journey east, followed by another eight on August 26. Some of the Blenheim Is would be hurled into an impossible struggle against the Japanese. As the last of 62 Squadron vacated Cranfield, 82 Squadron left for Watton. On August 25 and 28, advance elements of Nos 35 and 207 Squadrons arrived in Fairey Battles from Cottesmore for a training role in 6 Group.

Both Battle squadrons provided replacement pilots and observer/air gunners for XV and 40 Squadrons in France. Thirty men were trained in each six-week period. Both squadrons amalgamated on October 1 1939 becoming a 1 Group Pool although remaining under 6 Group.

The intention was that bomber squadrons in France would re-equip with Blenheims, some of which arrived at Cranfield in late 1939. Then the squadrons parted, 35 Squadron temporarily in Bassingbourn and 207 Squadron to Cottesmore. Servicing Flight remained at Cranfield from where aircraft could only take off because building of three runways had commenced. Progress was so slow that Servicing Flight had to move to Upwood on February 1 1940.

A change then overtook Cranfield. Forced out of Kinloss, the Airspeed Oxford trainers of 14 SFTS moved in and stayed for over a year. A first rate station adjacent to the operational area, and one of the first with runways, was without doubt being wasted. Consideration of changing it into a Coastal Command OTU base took place in May 1941, but because of its distance from that Command's activities the station instead became a night fighter OTU. Early in August 1941, 14 SFTS moved to Lyneham and a new unit, partially formed at Debden, replaced it. By August 3, seven Blenheims and two Oxfords were at Cranfield and by mid-month its establishment was set at 39 IE plus 13 IR Blenheim I/IVs or Havoc Is (six of the latter could come from 85 Squadron then receiving Havoc IIs), eight dual control Blenheims or Hudsons, ten Oxfords for navigation training and five communications aircraft.

The night fighters were arriving a little too late, for the enemy had first attacked Cranfield on August 27/28 1940 when incendiaries and two HE bombs were dropped to north and south of the airfield. At 21:07 on September 24 1940 a parachute mine exploded in a field damaging houses and shops in Cranfield High Street. Then, on October 13, a mine, complete with parachute, was discovered dangling from a tree in Hulcote Wood, 1½ miles south of the aerodrome, and reckoned to have fallen three weeks previously. Bomb disposal experts exploded it the following day. A story went around camp that the detonation brought about by the Station Armament Officer had demolished a ceiling in his house! As a result of winter intruder activity, an Oxford was landed by a pupil pilot after his instructor was wounded.

During August 1941, Blenheims in plenty came to Cranfield and the first of the Havocs landed on August 18. On August 25, No 51 OTU opened, offering night fighter crews courses mainly on Blenheims. This assumed major importance and Cranfield acquired a satellite at Twinwood where Blenheim Vs were brought into use in April 1942.

A major change commenced on August 8 1942 when the first Beaufighter for 51 OTU arrived. Re-equipment took place over a protracted period, and well into 1943 the unit retained Blenheim 1s. Beaufighter 1s and a few VIFs served until 51 OTU closed.

Snarling Sabres shattered Cranfield's air during March 1943 when 181 and 183 Squadrons briefly stayed during Exercise *Spartan*. More interesting was a brief American call between May and June 1943, by USAAF crews learning to operate AI Mk VIII American marked Beaufighters which equipped a few of their north-west African squadrons. Rumours that Northrop P-61 Black Widows would arrive caused a flurry of local excitement which apparently frightened them away.

Dual control Beauforts were used for twin conversion training, the unit's diverse equipment in July 1943 being listed as 78 Beaufighter IFs (AI Mk IV), four Beaufighter VIFs, four Beaufighter IFs without AI; ten Blenheim Vs (dual control), 6 Beauforts (dual control), 3 Blenheim Is, 1 Blenheim IV, 3 Lysanders, 5 Martinets (which had arrived in May), 4 Magisters and a Dominie. Additional were No 2 Delivery Flight's aircraft which arrived from Colerne on July 23 1943.

Each night fighter crew numbered about 30 men. High intensity flying reduced serviceability often to less than 50 per cent but never low enough to prevent a few operational night sorties in November 1943. During March/April 1943 seven Wellington XIs had arrived to train 100 Group Mosquito crews. No 3501 Servicing Unit was set up to handle overhauls of fighters, particularly those of 2 TAF once the invasion was underway. Included were aircraft of ADGB when the flying-bomb campaign made heavy demands upon home-based day fighters There were plenty of pilots available for flight testing because No 3501 Pilot Replacement Unit was also here until September 1944 when it moved to Middle Wallop.

On July 5 1944, Mosquito IIs started to supplement 51 OTU's Beaufighters and equipped its No 4 Squadron by September. February 1945 saw the last Beaufighters withdrawn, but many stayed here inactive. On June 14 1945, No 51 OTU disbanded and during the last week of June remaining Mosquitoes, Beaufighters and Beauforts were flown away.

A group of Canadian airmen waited at Cranfield for home passage within the Canadian Aircrew Holding Unit, under the command of Wing Commander Bob Iredale of Mosquito fame. Some 120 Australians were also waiting to go home. From July 5 1945 the station was open for flying only between 08:30 and 17:00. All Cranfield's aircraft had gone by the end of August, and 16 ACHU disbanded on 13 September 1945.

A memorable feature of this period was the extent of rumour surrounding the de Havilland Vampire jet fighter. What had become of it? A variety of snags deprived the experimental fighter of combat, and there were countless stories about it. In reality the few built were mostly at Hatfield and Boscombe Down. A story about a Vampire at Cranfield, turned out to be true because Geoffrey de Havilland Junior force landed one at Cranfield on October 15 1945. After refuelling, he set off next day and gave one of his unsurpassed Vampire demonstrations before departing the area. Jet fuel was available at Cranfield because during October 1945

Variety in a Cranfield hangar, alongside structural features.

the Empire Test Pilots' School had partly vacated Boscombe Down for its new base here, a move completed on November 16 1945. Jets became a permanent feature here.

The first ETPS course at Cranfield opened on January 2 1946 using four Lancasters, three Mosquito VIs, two Boston IIIs, four Meteor IIIs, three Spitfire IXs, three Tempest IIs, three Tempest Vs, two Oxfords, Harvards, a Dominie, a Swordfish and a Tiger Moth. Post-war needs for test pilots in Britain and many other parts of the world were increasingly met by ETPS graduates. Having them closer to the latest developments in aviation and testing techniques was desirable, so ETPS moved to Farnborough in August 1947. There followed periods when RAF Cranfield seemed ready for closure, although in 1952, 23 Group Communications Flight resided here and used an Anson 19, Provost and Vampire T 11.

Cranfield's future had been assured when, in 1946, the College of Aeronautics, a government sponsored institution, was founded. Soon it was offering advanced courses in aeronautics and engineering, mainly to post-graduates. Some of the College's original equipment came from German research establishments. Low and high speed wind tunnels were erected in a hangar, and facilities were provided for in-flight demonstrations. One-year degree courses and two-year non-degree courses were offered, studies ranging widely over project definition, structures, aircraft propulsion—for which rocket engine demonstrations were given in the one-time bomb dump, and in other associated aviation fields.

Following the harmful Sandys Paper of 1957, the College decided it must expand its work into other fields of advanced technology, its catchment area becoming world wide in the process.

At this time Cranfield housed the Fairey Development Flight for guided weapons trials using a Meteor NF 11 and a Swift F 3. It was also a Swift that was used for aquaplaning experiments along sections of a runway, flooded to a depth of several inches.

In the 1950s and 1960s, Cranfield's collection of rare museum aircraft such as the Supermarine 535, Lincoln and Tempest II prototypes and a TSR-2, attracted much interest. For reasons of space they have mostly gone. Aeroplanes for demonstration of research techniques remain, including two SAL Jetstreams. None of the aircraft flown from here, though, will be enjoyed more than Lancaster *PA474*. Rescued from its photo

A delight for millions—Lancaster PA474 *of the Battle of Britain Memorial Flight, during its stint as a research aircraft at Cranfield.*

survey days in Africa and elsewhere it acquired, above the fuselage, a hefty aerofoil section used in connection with ice accretion and boundary layer research. *PA474* was a common sight over the Midlands before the RAF repossessed it, pretended it was John Nettleton's *KM-B*, added a dorsal turret then promptly made it Guy Gibson's *AJ-G* which it little resembles!

Cranfield's runway was, on July 14 1954, the scene of a major disaster when *WB771*, the prototype Victor engaged on high speed low flying, suffered tail unit failure. Four of the crew were killed when it hit the runway.

Cranfield Institute of Technology continues to play an important part in post graduate training of aviation engineers and designers. Staff at the College recently produced their own aerobatic aircraft, the Cranfield A1, and the curious Edgeley Optica has been sited here. Roger Aviation uses one hangar for Cessnas and other light aircraft. Flight International's general aviation displays and the PFA Rally are held here so diversity is never far away. One hopes, though, that all who fly from here make a better job of it than did Michael Crawford in a well-known TV programme.

Croughton, Northamptonshire

SP561331, by the B4031 SW of Brackley

Brackley, renamed Croughton in July 1941, is best seen from the A43 which affords a clear view across the plateau upon which the landing ground was sited. As early as February 1940 Brackley LG was used by three Whitleys of 78 Squadron and on June 4 a 16 OTU Hampden crashed here, shortly before Brackley became 16 OTU's satellite, attracting the unit's Ansons and Hampdens. The most memorable event during that unit's tenure occurred on September 20 1941 when Ju 88Cs were intruding in the area. One came across Hampden *P5314* approaching well-lit Croughton. Flying at 500 ft, the enemy aircraft's cannon shot down the Hampden before eight 50 kg bombs were dropped across the airfield. Another attack was made in December 1941.

In July 1942, Croughton was chosen by 23 Group for glider training, being larger than, and preferable to, Thame. Control of the station passed to 1 GTS on July 19 1942 and on August 1 the air party of the gliding school arrived at Croughton, leaving a few personnel at Thame to form the Glider Instructors' School. No 1 GTS had 18 Hotspurs, towing being the prerogative of 14 Hectors. Master IIs began replacing these shortly after the move.

When sufficient glider pilots were available for forthcoming airborne operations, No 1 GTS was absorbed into 20 (P) AFU and, on March 24 1943, Kidlington assumed control of Croughton. Pilot-training Oxfords replaced the gliders. By July 1943 Kidlington had placed its No 2 Squadron at Croughton. Oxfords in profusion patrolled local skies, along with those of No 1538 BAT Flight which formed here on April 15 1943. Use was made of nearby landing grounds, including Mixbury Farm.

The intention was that Croughton would serve out its days as a pilot training station, but glider pilot losses at Arnhem changed that. On October 18 1944, No 1538 Flight disbanded and 20 (P) AFU retired to Kidlington, clearing the way for the rebirth of 1 GTS which took place on November 1 1944. Its purpose was to provide reinforcements for the Glider Pilot Regiment, a large number of Hotspur IIs and ample towing Master IIs being used.

Glider pilot training continued in 1945 against Far East requirements. During August 1945, 1 GTS took over Gaydon, its strength reduced, and it came under the control of 21 HGCU based at Brize Norton.

In July 1945 a Harvard II, *BD130*, came to Croughton from ECFS for consideration of its suitability as a Hotspur tug. It did not give satisfaction, so instead a number of American-engined Master IIIs were fitted out as tugs and used into 1946.

Flying ceased at Croughton on May 25 1946. Gliders and tugs—those worth preserving—were sent to Wellesbourne. Croughton was left quiet and eventually assumed its present Anglo-American 'silent' service role.

Culham, Oxfordshire

SU052958, 1½ miles SE of Abingdon, by A415

On dry land close to Oxford once rested HMS *Hornbill*, an unexpected sight where now stands Culham Laboratory, an expansive nuclear establishment. Hangars of the former occupant may be seen on its north-west side. *Hornbill* was commissioned on November 1 1944 as an Aircraft Receipt and Despatch Unit. It attracted many types of aircraft, for the RN Ferry Pool (later known as No 1 Ferry Flight) was based here, using Ansons, Fireflies, Reliants and Seafires.

Culham's principal use was as a centre for naval reservists residing between London and Oxford and the surrounds. To train them 1832 Squadron was commissioned on July 1 1947 and used Seafire IIIs, XVs, XVIIs and FR 46s. Harvard IIbs and Mk IIIs also served the squadron and Sea Fury FB 11s later. A move to Benson came on July 18 1953 as part of Culham's run down. No 1840 RNVR Squadron formed here from 1832 Squadron on April 14 1951, and operated Firefly Is, IVs and Harvards before leaving for Ford on June 30 1951.

Two further reserve squadrons commissioned on October 1 1952 were Nos 1832A and 1832B which became 1836 and 1835 Squadrons respectively in April 1953, prior to moving to the Southern Air Division Benson on July 18 1953 and taking their Sea Fury FB 11s.

An interesting small unit which formed here on May 1 1947 was 739 Squadron, known also as the Photographic Trials and Development Unit, equipped with Sea Mosquito TR 33s, Sea Hornet F 20s and PR 22s and a Dominie. Culham's aircraft carried the tail identity letters 'CH'.

HMS *Hornbill* was paid off on September 30 1953, subsequent to which the Admiralty used Culham as a store until the Atomic Energy Commission moved in during early 1960.

Deenethorpe, Northamptonshire

SE965930. 6 miles NE of Corby, by A43

Deenethorpe came into use late in 1943, one of the last airfields to open in the area under review. During the first few days of November 1943 the four squadrons of the 401st BG (612, 613, 614, 615) moved in with B-17s. Deenethorpe was of the typical three-runway wartime type with a couple of 'T2' hangars and a usual style of control tower.

Operations commenced for the 401st on November 26 1943. After even a few raids it was clear it was setting very high levels of bombing accuracy, maintained to the end of hostilities. Targets varied and included factories, submarine facilities, shipyards, marshalling yards, V-weapon sites and airfields as it took its place in the 1st Air Division's campaign. Pride of place was given to the 401st on February 20 1944 when attacks on Me aircraft

A 401st Bomb Group B-17G about to land at Deenethorpe after raiding Wilhelmshaven on February 3 1944 (US Air Force).

works at Leipzig were made, for which the Group won its second DUC, in the face of fierce opposition.

In the D-Day run up, the 401st played an active part, supporting the subsequent landings and the break out from St Lô. It took part in August's reduction of the Brest garrison, bombed Peenemünde on August 25 1944, fought in the Arnhem venture, in the Battle of the Bulge and during the Rhine crossing. From October 1944 its good bombing accuracy was put to particular use, the Group specialising in attacking oil targets. Most USAF Groups had particularly bad days—that for the 401st came on May 26 1944 when seven B-17s were lost in action. Generally, though, the Group's losses were comparatively low. When the war ended the Group had participated in 255 operations from Deenethorpe, flown 7,430 sorties and lost 95 B-17s.

Return to the USA came between May 30 and mid-June 1945. Personnel who did not fly home returned in style on the *Queen Elizabeth* and many must have felt satisfaction at sailing on both 'Queens' for their journey to Britain in October 1943 was aboard the *Queen Mary*.

Barely had they left Deenethorpe when the RAF took over, placing No 11 Recruit Centre here in June 1945. Military flying days, though, were finished at Deenethorpe for no flying unit moved in before its closure in mid-1946. Long dormant, it was almost all sold off by 1963. Part of a runway remained in use for aircraft bringing visitors to nearby Corby steelworks for which purposes Deenethorpe in recent years flew a windsock.

Denton, Northamptonshire

SP830580. 6 miles ESE of Northampton

Denton was one of those glorified meadows which came into use in the summer of 1940 as Relief Landing Grounds to expand the output of EFTSs, their Tiger Moths easy to fly from these primitive places. Their secondary night flying role allowed permanent airfields to be left unlit at night. During night flying, on July 17/18 1941, an intruder was attracted to the lights of Denton and dropped ten small bombs near the boundary. By then the parent unit, 6 EFTS Sywell, was increasingly training Free French airmen.

There was the usual round of accidents here, the most spectacular happening during night flying on December 12 1941. Flight Lieutenant E.M. Frisby and Leading Aircraftsman D.Q. May were flying a night circuit when they collieded with a 15 OTU Wellington. Both aircraft dived in, the Tiger Moth's crew dying in the collision.

During 1941 and 1942, quarters at Denton slowly improved. Blister hangars were added too. Some Tiger Moths used here were noteworthy on account of their age or origins, like the 1937 example, *L6923*, which was involved in an accident when taking off on April 8 1944. On July 25 1944, Tiger Moth *BB699* (used by Brooklands Aviation pre-war as *G-ADGY*) crashed into power cables at Turvey, the two occupants being killed. On the afternoon of April 10 1944, Beaufighter *NE480* crashed on the landing ground and was burnt out.

In late 1944 Sywell was badly flooded, the RLG then being most useful. Flying continued from Denton into the spring of 1945, and ceased on July 9 of that year.

Down Ampney, Gloucestershire

SU100965. 6 miles SE of Cirencester

'Come down, O Love divine, Seek thou this soul of mine, And visit it with thine

Down Ampney 1943. **A** *Two 'T2' hangars (3653/42) for two transport squadrons.* **B** *Glider marshalling areas.* **C** *The brick control tower (343/43) on the western side.* **D** *The technical site.*

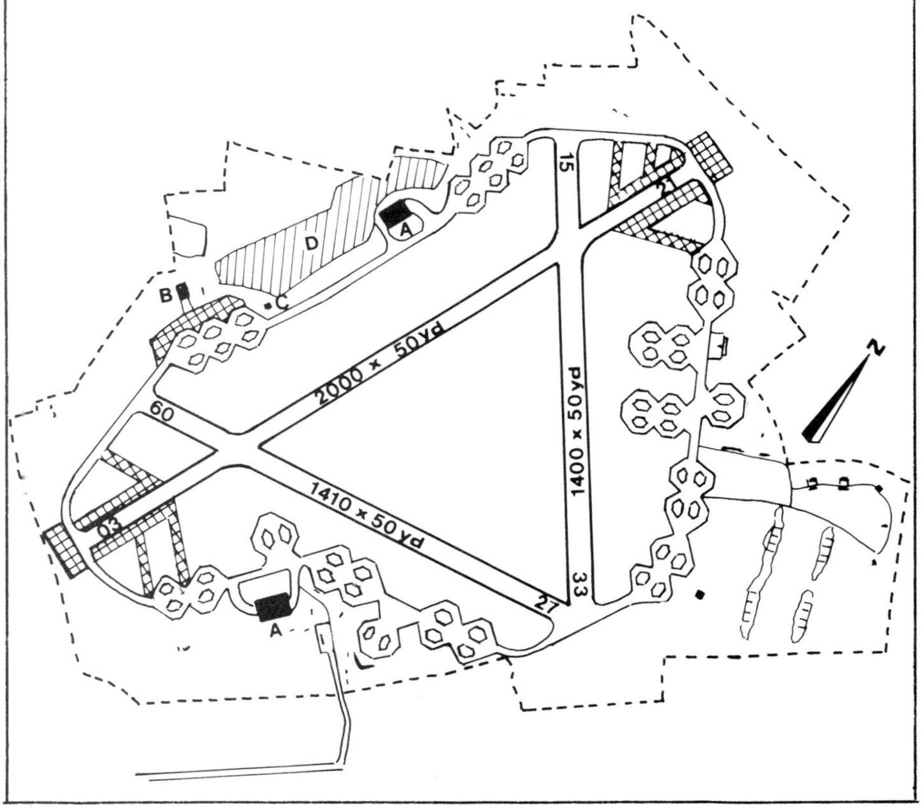

Transferring a stretcher case to a waiting ambulance at Down Ampney (F.H. Dickinson).

own ardour glowing; O Comforter draw near, Within my heart appear, And kindle it, they holy name bestowing.' Bianco da Siena whose words these are, and who died in 1434, surely never imagined they would become linked with a Gloucestershire village, the name of which would mean comfort for many in moments of anguish. For these words, Ralph Vaughan Williams (who lived here) devised that moving melody, *Down Ampney*. Viewing fields over which Dakotas once roared is surely incomplete without a murmur of that moving melody. Equally, any visit to Down Ampney is unfulfilled without a visit to the 13th century All Saints' Church, by which Ralph Vaughan Williams' father is buried, and in which, colourfully enshrined, is a bright picture of a million memories.

Upon entry, a facing window reminds visitors of the sacrifice of many who passed close by, and that of Flight Lieutenant Samual Anthony Lord, VC, DFC, killed in action during an Arnhem re-supply mission of September 19 1944. Mainly to Down Ampney the wounded came in their thousands, back from French battlefields in the 1944 summer. Succour and comfort many must have drawn during those moments at Down Ampney.

Its life as an airfield was brief like others in 46 Group. An advance party from Broadwell occupied it on February 7 1944, and to the Proctor of Air Commodore Fiddament, AOC 46 Group, went the distinction on February 18 1944 of being the first aircraft to touch down. On February 24 1944, Down Ampney's first squadron, No 48, arrived. Five days later, 271 Squadron's main party moved in. The deadline for the opening of 46 Group's three Dakota bases had been February 1 1944. Only half of Down Ampney's buildings were then completed, likewise runways and roads carved across farmland of but a few weeks past.

No 271 Squadron soon had 38 Dakotas and 19 of its allotted gliders. This provided a major problem because insufficient dispersals and essential hard standings were available. By mid-March operational training had begun. On March 16, No 91 SP arrived. April's major exercises involved Down Ampney's aircraft and gliders. On the 9th, 35 of the Dakotas were within a large formation, navigation lights blazing, which flew a spectacular night navigation tour of central England. Glider towing and careful formation flying followed. What could easily happen was clear when two Dakotas collided with grievous results.

On April 28, before the watchful, satisfied gaze of the AOC 46 Group, 40 Dakotas with Horsas took off in 27 minutes, a time soon bettered. For the forthcoming invasion, crews needed to fly very accurately at night, and perhaps face searchlights. To experience those, Dakota crews participated in Bomber Command *Bullseyes*, and took part in *Nickels* late in April relying upon *Gee* fixes over

Air Ambulance Pool personnel awaiting a call to France to escort casualties to England (F.H. Dickinson).

Normandy and adjacent areas of France.

Down Ampney's squadrons faced four tasks: freight delivery, casualty evacuation from French airstrips, paratroop drops and glider towing. One of the largest paratroop exercises was held in the early morning of April 21 involving over 700 aircraft. Just before April ended, the establishment of Staging Posts to be placed in France for casevac was practised on a wide scale. May saw a number of large scale, increasingly efficient glider landing exercises and paratroop drops. By the end of the month they were being combined with cross country night flying exercises.

Operation *Tonga* was ordered for the night of June 5/6. Seven Dakota/Horsa combinations and 39 paratroop carriers of 48 and 271 Squadrons would take part in the night landing, the gliders being released onto LZ'V' after first take off at 22:48. All the aircraft were away by 23:20, carrying the 3rd Parachute Brigade HQ under Brigadier J. Hill, DSO, MC, and the 1st Canadian Parachute Battalion under Lieutenant Bradbrook. Visibility was good, the drops went well and the Dakotas returned safely.

During the evening of D-Day, 15 Dakotas of 271 Squadron and 22 of 48 Squadron towed 37 Horsas across the Channel in Operation *Mallard*, releasing them on LZ'N'. A Dakota of 48 Squadron ditched in the Channel, two of its crew being back at Down Ampney within two days. On the night of June 7, both squadrons assisted Operation *Robroy* with a supply drop.

Casevac Dakota operations began on June 18 1944 when 11 aircraft picked up personnel of 2TAF at Tangmere and landed them at airstrip B4 in Normandy. There they were loaded with 183 casualties which they brought back to Down Ampney. Its mercy role had started, and late in the evening of June 21 90 more wounded arrived. Down Ampney's Dakotas shifted 122 Wing to B6 and, on June 25, 125 Wing from Ford to B11. On return flights the wounded were brought home, a daily average of 100.

These men had received their injuries during the previous 24 hours. Many, urgently needing surgery, had been given simple dressings. Around one third were walking cases. Many had head wounds, and most some tissue destruction. Quite a high proportion received penicillin treatment. About a third had been blinded, from all of which it can be seen that the more seriously wounded were being evacuated by air. What this meant to them can but be imagined, for many would not have flown previously. The alternative was a 3–4 day journey by land and sea. Many lives must have been saved by the aerial evacuation.

For the ground personnel at Down Ampney, stretcher bearing proved an exhausting task, however inwardly satisfying aiding the wounded became. The sick had to be fed, tended, loaded into ambulances and, by the end of June, 869 had been flown into Down Ampney, after flights of 90 minutes' duration. Over 3,000 wounded had arrived by July 20. Living nearby, HM Queen Mary came to see the tending of the wounded, inspecting Dakota *KG419* 'AV' of 271 Squadron in the process. To be greeted by that somewhat austere lady, whilst discovering her grace and great caring, must have been a memorable sensation.

As the Allies moved forward, the point of evacuation advanced and during July most flights were out of B14. Freight to the battle zone and retrieving the wounded were Down Ampney's major but not only, tasks, for they undertook supply drops, one of which was laid onto Chambois on July 21. *KG421*, flown by Wing Commander Sproule, left Down Ampney at 05:30 and met very bad weather conditions. With cloud base at 300 ft, Sproule flew low, finding his DZ lit by fires. Enemy gunners found the slow Dakota an easy target and had soon damaged its wings and engines. More enemy fire poured through the windows, hitting the navigator in the shoulder and cutting the second pilot's face. The captain had splinter wounds. First aid was given to the navigator by the wireless operator as the course was set for B14. With the rudder useless the crew tried to maintain course with engine power as the despatcher threw out disposable items. It was raining heavily, keeping height and direction being difficult. Then another burst of flak hit the batteries. The oil temperature fell, the controls were heating and, although the engines were at maximum revs, the ASI showed only 110 mph. Then, the inevitable. The aircraft smashed into the top of a tree. Wing Commander Sproule ordered crash stations before managing a skilful landing on a hill top west of Jurques. A shelter from the rain was made although the crew expected the aircraft to explode at any moment. Two soldiers aboard set off to find help, but were unsuccessful. Both pilots then left with a compass, following some tank tracks in the knowledge that they would at least be missing any mines. After nearly three hours, and with guidance from a farmer, they located British soldiers. Late that afternoon they all reached B14.

Daily, and sometimes twice a day, the casualties flowed into Down Ampney, about 20,000 having arrived by early August. With the battle intense the station was alerted on August 8 1944 to be ready for 1,000 casualties in one load—which was far beyond its capability to cope. Broadwell and Blakehill had to play their part, and eventually 527 casualties passed through Down Ampney in 12 hours. This meant providing 1,100 meals, all ranks distributing food and comfort as best they could. By 18:00 all the station's accommodation was full of wounded men. Well into the night, loading of the ambulance train took place. Not until 03:00 on the 9th was the backlog cleared.

Other squadrons began to lend a hand, 24, 511 and 525 among them, basing their effort on B14. By early September, B50 and B56 were in use and then came a break whilst the 46 Group squadrons prepared for Operation *Market*.

For the initial Arnhem assault, on September 17, 49 Down Ampney crews were detailed, each Dakota towing a Horsa, 39 of which were released at the LZ. Next day 50 Dakota/Horsa combinations sallied forth to LZ'S', then came the re-supply of September 19 by 32 Dakotas. Drops were made near DZ'V' before 27 Dakotas returned to Down Ampney. Three others were lost in action, among them the aircraft flown by Flight Lieutenant S.A. Lord and crew. The weather was poor and eight of the Dakotas suffered various degrees of damage, landings being made at Evere in the emergency. This did not prevent 20 other crews from operating out of Down Ampney later in the day to deliver petrol containers to both B56 and B58.

Lord's courage was utterly selfless. He showed total disregard for personal safety and the maximum for all others in his crew, and for those fighting for survival below. At about 1,500 ft the aircraft's starboard wing was hit twice and then the engine. It was on fire, some three minutes from the DZ. Lord came lower to ensure an accurate drop. All but two of his containers were released, then he joined the stream to drop the remainder. For eight minutes the aircraft was under intense fire, and with no hope of safe return, Lord's crew was ordered out. His aircraft crashed in flames from which only Flight Lieutenant Harry King escaped. Flight Lieutenant Lord was posthumously awarded the VC and came to be buried in the military cemetery at Oosterbeek.

On September 20 all went well for the Down Ampney squadrons; then came September 21 and what must have seemed inevitable. German fighters entered the arena, and there was no Allied fighter escort to drive them away. Pilot Officer Cuer's aircraft was blazing soon after its pannier drop. Flight Lieutenant Beddow's aircraft was damaged by fighters, the crew being lucky to survive and land at B56. Flight Lieutenant Hollom also force landed, whilst *KG512* was shot down. Flight Lieutenant Mott and crew and their four RASC despatchers baled out after fighters twice attacked their Dakota. Flak cut oil and petrol lines in Squadron Leader Duff Mitchell's machine, forcing him also to land at B56. There was tragedy aboard *KG444* too, whose pilot in later years was to become 'Mr Glum', often ready to tell his audience that he, Jimmy Edwards, was flying when Pontius was a pilot. Sad, really, that so few of those millions who enjoy his grand sense of fun knew so little of his courage over Arnhem.

Flight Lieutenant Edwards' run up to the DZ was quite satisfactory and all the panniers were dropped. After about five minutes of the return flight, two Fw 190s raced in and made six attacks on the aircraft from astern. From his place in the astrodome, the wireless operator, Bill Randall, shouted instructions to his captain, as enemy cannon fire riddled the fuselage and three despatchers were badly wounded. A further attack left the Dakota's engines blazing. With no hope of getting back, Flight Lieutenant Edwards ordered the crew to abandon as a result of which the 2nd pilot and the navigator left the aircraft. The wireless oeprator could not get out fast enough because he was wearing a harness. Flight Lieutenant Edwards was partly out of the aircraft as it crashed and he was thrown clear. All was not over, for one of the two Fw 190s then strafed the wreck and the survivors although none was hit. 'Jimmy' Edwards' injuries had now amounted to severe burns on both his face and left arm. The survivors rested, dazed, and after five minutes were cheered by the sound of English voices telling them to hide in a wood. A doctor later came and under cover of darkness they were taken to a farmhouse. There it was discovered that two crew members Harry Sorensen and Alan Clarke, had become prisoners. Next morning a car arrived and took the party to Grave and the 186th Field Hospital where their wounds were dressed.

With mounting losses, the Arnhem venture could not succeed. Before it was ended Down Ampney's Dakotas went again, 23 of them on September 23, then it was back to casevac. Numbers of casualties received fell, but often amounted to over 250 a day. Good medical

Dakota III DH:YS *of 271 Squadron on dispersal at Down Ampney* (Alan Hartley).

centres were being established in France, and Down Ampney's Dakotas frequently took blood supplies to these as well as aiding squadron moves and carrying mixed freight. On October 28 1944, for instance, blood supplies were taken to B57 and B58, and 20 casualties retrieved by aircraft of 271 Squadron—109 casualties came in all that day—whilst 59 aircraft flew a glider tug exercise. On the following day, 271 Squadron flew to B78 a load of oranges for a hospital, and 241 casualties were brought to Down Ampney where, during October 4, 291 casualties arrived. With soul destroying monotony that catalogue continued. On December 8 1944, HRH the Duchess of Kent was at Down Ampney to see the 20,000th wounded soldier arrive.

During November casualties were being sent to Stratton St Margaret's hospital, Wroughton, if they were very serious. Daily average arrivals totalled 158, there being 3,893 brought in during the month. Bad weather prevented operations on nine days. A new feature of the casualties was the number due to road accidents in bad wintry conditions. December's activity showed a further reduction in casualties with an average of 85 arriving daily and a month's total of 2,646. There was, of course, the excitement of Christmas, celebrated in good style. Officers, as customary, served the men with better fare than at many stations so that the hungry could work through cream of tomato soup, roast turkey, roast pork, sausages, roast potatoes, Brussel sprouts doubtless from Evere, boiled parsnips, cream sauce, Christmas pudding, white sauce, mince pies, apples, beer, cigarettes, music by the station's orchestra, and some of the rare oranges, consumed to strains of *God Save the King*.

Into the New Year the general run of freight and passengers, lifts to the Continent and return of wounded continued with a gradual decline in the latter. On March 24 1945, 60 of Down Ampney's Dakotas took off from Gosfield towing Horsas for a part in the Rhine crossing airborne lift. It was on this occasion that the enemy made his only attempt to interfere with the Dakotas on the ground. Just before take off, a V-1 crashed quite close to Gosfield.

For 46 Group the end of the war was a busy time with much transporting of men and supplies. A break up of Down Ampney's comradeship came on July 9 when the order was given for 48 Squadron to get glider snatch gear fitted to its Dakotas. Their move extended into August, at the close of which 271 Squadron left for Odiham. Down Ampney was still very active and hosted Canadian Dakota transport squadrons, Nos 435 and 436, the latter becoming operational on October 15 1945. Its aircraft made scheduled runs to the Continent into 1946 before the Canadians prepared for home.

For Down Ampney the end came in April 1946. Between 09:13 and 09:38 on April 22 ten Dakotas took off for

The memorial window in Down Ampney Church.

Leeming, the last to leave being *KN256*, flown by Pilot Officer Hadfield. In all 45 Dakotas had left for Canada. It but remained to wind down the depleted station. Within days, cows were grazing on the airfield.

Visit Down Ampney now and there is little to be seen of its RAF days. At the end of the runway—and on private property—there is a memorial stone recalling the station's past, some who served there coming yearly to a memorial service. Flying has not ceased. Major Robert Neasham, in whose Parish Down Ampney church lies, has placed a notice in its porch which reads: 'Our friends, the swallows, have for very many years nested in the porch on a shelf above the entrance. Perhaps you will say a prayer for them too'. On such an occasion doubtless one would also remember those thousands who prayed for peace and mercy close by in times of deep tragedy. Buried in the churchyard by the window are the ashes of Wireless Operator L. Gaydon, also a sole survivor of one of 271 Dakotas flown by Pilot Officer Len Wilson and shot down at Arnhem on September 21.

As you leave the churchyard, perhaps suitably with Vaughan Williams' setting to the hymn, *For All the Saints*, in mind, then pass through the beautifully kept lych-gateway, you may well have a glimpse of cows still grazing on meadows which were once the lair of the Dakotas. Knowledge of the present airfield owner would doubtless provoke all sorts of thoughts from H.M. Queen Mary and others. Would she approve of it being the 'Co-op'?

Edgehill, Oxfordshire

SP365435. 9 miles WNW of Banbury, near Shenington, off the A422

There's no denying it, we all like to know things we are not supposed to know. Open government and such crazy notions would do terrible damage to our imaginations. Of course, much of what there now is to know is not really worth knowing and it is in 'mumbo-jumbo'. The war years were splendid for poking one's nose into places where it might be easily cut off. Jet propulsion, in particular, was excellent for amateur spying. Ah! What happy moments you've missed if you never enjoyed such sport!

Late 1941 reports reached us from our agents commuting between Gloucester and Cambridge, confirming the existence of a small, very fast aeroplane with an amazing feature—it was propellerless. Excitement came to a climax when one of our circle met a man who had inspected it on the ground at a place 'near Chipping Norton' which we, of course, mistook to be the airfield of that name. What excited us most of all, apart from his sketch, was his emphatic—'it had a wide pipe sticking out of the back'. That clinched it, the thing must be rocket propelled. Using his drawing, which was a fair representation, we immediately had models purporting to be this 'rocketplane'. Just as Constance Babington Smith and Professor R.V. Jones had their ideas and their teams and their magic numbers to cover up what they didn't know, we had ours. 'CN/1' I called my model. True, its tricycle undercarriage was too long, the whole thing rather too large. Then came even more fascinating news. Another agent, in a cement lorry, drove close to this mysterious aeroplane and broke the news of a hole, a big one, in the nose. Derrick, always in the forefront of knowing too much, at once lectured us on the Caproni Campini CC2, the Italian gas turbine aircraft. He also seemed to be Britain's leading expert on the Coanda idea of decades past. It is, he declared, a gas turbine driven aeroplane. Of course, why had we never thought of that? Incredibly I'd often encountered in my early days a man named Whittle. If only I'd known . . .! Some rapid sawing of noses throughout Cambridge, a bash with a drill and—hey presto, we all had even better representations of the E28/39. It was to be another two years before I was awarded with a splendid view of *W4041/G*, landing over the canal at the back of Farnborough.

And why these thoughts, upon gazing over the chicken houses, vacant runways and the unusual control tower at Edgehill? Simply that this airfield is closely woven into the story of British jet aircraft development. Edgehill was completed in October 1941 as a satellite for 21 OTU, Moreton-in-the-Marsh. Although opened on October 21 1941, flights from here by ageing Wellington 1cs had begun in August. It seems that 12 OTU also made early use of the station.

On May 14 1941, the Gloster E28/39 Pioneer *W4041* first flew at Cranwell and, after ten hours flying, returned by road to Glosters for a new engine. Returning the Pioneer to Cranwell had disadvantages, that airfield being far from Gloster's home. Closer sites to Brockworth were

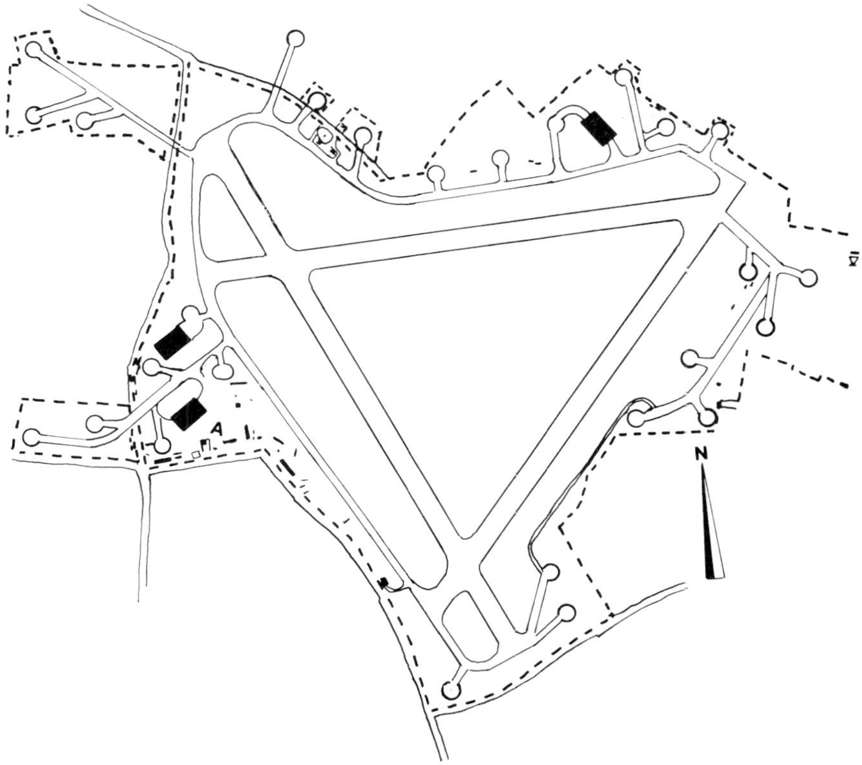

Edgehill began as a rudimentary landing ground, then was much improved into becoming a bomber airfield satellite station. Take-off towards the west meant passage over the steep scarp face, for which reason the control tower ('A') had additional height for a watch to be kept.

examined, also alternatives in reasonable reach of the Power Jets' centre at Lutterworth. Eventually, Edgehill was selected. Brockworth was too small and too close to hilly ground, for which reason Stoke Orchard was also unsuitable. Edgehill with one 1,600 yd and two 1,200 yd runways was, rather like Barford, situated on a plateau. Its position, though, was unusual because at the western end the ground fell away in a dramatic scarp face to a valley below. Nevertheless the approaches to the airfield were unobstructed so, despite that fall-away, it was reckoned suitable for the task, a special Robin hangar being erected to house the jet in secrecy. The agreement was for the Pioneer to fly from Edgehill and the F9/40 fighters from Cranwell or Newmarket during 1942.

To Edgehill *W4041* came, powered by a W.1A engine. It made its first trial taxi on February 4 1942. Flight testing began and, with this new engine, the Pioneer was quieter in flight and flew smoothly until trouble struck on March 24 1942. Part of a turbine blade broke away in flight and the aircraft hurriedly landed at Edgehill.

Wellington 1cs and Ansons of 21 OTU were very active at this time and used the airfield for training purposes. From here 21 OTU despatched a dozen Wellington 1cs for the Cologne raid of May 30/31 1942. As *DV598* was taking off, it hit a tree, and two other crews aborted leaving nine to complete their sorties. In the Essen raid 11 crews operated, and ten took part in the June 1,000 Plan Bremen attack when *X3179* failed to return.

Flight trials of *W4041* were resumed by

'Jerry' Sayer in June 1942, but not without moments of concern. Fuel starvation was encountered and a flame out also brought a quick return, among the Wellingtons, to Edgehill. Throughout that hot summer the jet was test flown and on September 27 1942 a group of visitors arrived for a demonstration, among them Americans. Just as the Pioneer was getting airborne the oil pressure fell very low and, conserving what he had while reducing power, Sayer was seen to sink below the edge of the escarpment. Great relief greeted his safe pulling away. He kept his speed low and made a neat, forced landing. Not many days later, whilst flying a Typhoon off the north-east coast, Sayer was killed, possibly in collision with another aircraft. His place was taken by Michael Daunt, although it was November 1942 before he began flying the E28/39. After four flights, *W4041* was conveyed by lorry to Farnborough for engine development work, whilst 21 OTU's Wellingtons continued to drone around the circuit. Flying was interrupted at this time by some runway resurfacing.

Since 1940, Power Jets Ltd, who built Whittle's engines, had been linked with Rover, which was to build production versions of the Whittle W.2 engine. MAP placed a contract on August 4 1940 for such work to proceed at Coventry. For greater safety it was soon switched to the Clitheroe works in Lancashire. Rover began, in 1942, the design of their jet engine, the B.26, which started running trials in November 1942. At this time Rolls-Royce took over Rover's work on gas turbines.

In February 1943 the second Gloster E28/39, *W4046*, powered by a Rover W.2B engine, was taken to Edgehill. It first flew during the evening of March 1 1943, the pilot being John Grierson. During early flight trials it reached just over 400 mph after an unstick run of 330 yards. Such success was sufficient to permit it to be flown to Hatfield on April

Edgehill, October 6 1942. Very effective camouflage has been achieved by the painting of hedgerows across runways and grass areas (RAF Museum).

The shell of Edgehill's unusual control tower.

17 1943 for a few days of demonstration flying, that 19½ minute flight being the first cross country journey undertaken, although it was nowhere near as ambitious as that of the F9/40's first such venture. Very strict flying limits were laid down for the early jets, and from Edgehill they were only allowed to venture up to five miles away or fly within a corridor two miles wide between Edgehill and Cheltenham, a distance of about 30 miles. The duration of early jet aircraft was very limited. On May 3 1943, *W4046* was taken to RAE Farnborough and the Glosters' use of it ceased. This brought an end to jet flying at Edgehill.

That event came about shortly after another period of upheaval for, on April 12 1943, No 12 OTU, based at Chipping Warden, took over the station from 21 OTU. Two Flights of the Unit under Wing Commander C.W. Scott arrived from Turweston on April 27 1943 and used Wellington IIIs. These began to be replaced by Wellington Xs in August 1943. Edgehill was used to accommodate 12 OTU's gunnery flight's Martinets and Hurricanes as well as the initial training element of the OTU, until the unit closed early June 1945.

Visit the site now and a few typical wartime airfield buildings can still be seen. Most unusual is the wartime control tower which has one storey more than usual, presumably to afford a better view of aircraft as they sped over that scarp face.

Elmdon (Birmingham Airport), West Midlands

SP181840. 7 miles ESE of Birmingham by A45

'Lord Mayor flies in Argosy, read all about it.' Before you let loose any local official or councillor with a novelty it is as well to think twice; it could result in flights of fancy and costly prestige symbols. Such is certainly true where municipal airports are concerned. The expertise needed to operate anything so complex is far removed from the world of councillors and local authorities.

Just what part in the Elmdon story that Lord Mayor's July 1927 flight over Birmingham came to play can but be guesswork but, within eight weeks, ratepayers heard of his hopes for a Birmingham airport. By February 1928 it was for a civic airport. Come November and a council committee admitted they were looking for a site and in December 1928 the scheme received council approval.

Supporters of the scheme received encouragement in September 1929 when Alan Cobham brought to Birmingham his DH Moth 'Youth of Britain', closing his campaign to engender support for municipal airports. Then in October 1929 the *R101* cruised directly over the town hall and in July 1930 the *R-100* crossed the city at night prior to its Canadian voyage. Considerable secrecy naturally surrounded the chosen site for Birmingham Airport and not until November 1930 was it revealed as being at Shirley, some six miles out of the City. Likely cost? £70,000. The intention was to develop an area by Longmore Lane. A year later the scheme was halted, economic conditions prohibiting such frivolity.

Instead it was Austin Motors that gave Birmingham a new airport. The company already had an airfield at Northfield, adjacent to their factory, and Alan Cobham brought his flying circus there on May 27 1932, National Aviation Day, to prove how safe flying was. Unfortunately, as he approached in his airliner carrying 15 passengers, rain blurred his petrol gauge forcing him to land on Row Heath Recreation Ground, Bourneville, proving the safety of flying! Northfield was only an airport for Longbridge, where Cobham's Circus returned in May 1933, reviving desires for links between Birmingham and the European mainland. Once more the Council expressed its desire for an airport. They looked around and in July 1933 found another site, which, in October, was revealed as 300 acres of magnificent meadowland and splendid trees near Elmdon.

Before Birmingham Council could operate its airport, Parliamentary approval was needed, for the council now wanted to run an airline. This the government did not like. Politics entered the arena and, by February 1935, the Council was bitterly attacking the Government attitude, stating that they wanted the best airport in the country and were eyeing 518 acres. But, during the Bill's second reading, voices were suggesting the Council drew back and a small protest lobby was deploring the felling of the trees and desecration of the land. Council officials then looked at other airports before finally committing themselves on February 4 1936, by approving £500,000 for an airport seven miles out at Elmdon, the building of which began in June 1936. When a novel terminal building was approved in July 1937 plans were for a 729 acre airfield. The estimated cost of the terminal and hangar was £89,000, and the council wanted another £68,230 for more land.

The Air Ministry wanted to open a Volunteer Reserve centre at Elmdon. When tenders were invited for the terminal block, from the sides of which protruded two 'wings', under which the aircraft would shelter when loading, there was therefore hope of government money. The provision of high speed connection from the airport to the city centre was the next problem. The proposed electric railway and monorail came to nothing. The A45 would have to suffice.

March 1939 found the large metal hangar ready and in April 1939 an aeroplane touched down at Elmdon. It was

W7434, *an early Austin-built Stirling awaiting delivery from Elmdon, joined 7 Squadron in July 1941 and was written off after a heavy landing on August 15 1941* (British Leyland).

Dragonfly *G-AEDH* of Western Airways. May 1 1939, however, was the great day. The weather was none too good when Dragon Rapide, *The Volunteer* of Great Western Air Lines, touched down, making the first scheduled flight which had left Liverpool at 08:55 and, coming via Manchester, touched down at Elmdon an hour later. The Lord Mayor was also flown in, most unconventionally in a BA Swallow. Such undignified mode of arrival was gracefully saved by the conveyance of the mayoral hat by motor car. Flying was nothing new to him, he had first taken off in 1914. Civic ceremony done, the Rapide departed as fast as decent, for Bristol and the south coast. As it did so DH Dragon, *Neptune* of LMS section of Railway Air Services, arrived from Croydon bound for Liverpool, Belfast and Glasgow. Almost ready was the unusual terminal and 215 acres of land out of the 800 acres of the landing ground had been levelled. Plans called for three 1,000 yard landing strips and one of 1,300 yards for landing in fog using Lorenz guidance. So far the airport had cost £360,000. It was officially opened by HRH Duchess of Kent on July 8 1939.

Post-war Elmdon retained the terminal building and its sheltering wings, too small for airliners such as this Viscount of BEA, G-AMOG, *photographed there in April 1961.*

The planned Elmdon Volunteer Reserve School, No 44 E&RFTS, operated by Airwork Ltd and using Hinds, had opened under 53 Group on May 1.

At Castle Bromwich on September 3 1939 Birmingham's E&RFTSs, Nos 14 and 44, amalgamated to form 14 EFTS (in 51 Group) established at Elmdon on September 7 1939. Two days later some of 99 Squadron's Wellington 1as, used Elmdon as their scatter airfield until September 15 1939. They left behind Tiger Moths of a training unit which remained here throughout the war, used Hockley Heath RLG and did not disband until February 1 1946. Elmdon had passed to Air Ministry's control on September 16 1939 and repossession would be difficult. During the war Elmdon was the airfield to which Stirlings and Lancasters, built by the Austin Longbridge works and assembled at the Marston Green Shadow Factory, were towed here for flight tests. After the war Austin were building Lancaster B VIIs in Far East trim, lines of these being eyed by Birmingham Council as they demanded the return of their airport.

The Air Ministry passed Elmdon to the Ministry of Civil Aviation on June 19 1946 and it re-opened on July 8 1946 as a startled Birmingham City Council was told that Elmdon had been nationalised. Light aircraft were soon active, the Midland Aero Club settled in, and to rub salt into the wound an MCA Oxford

arrived at the drab airport on opening day.

Not until July 16 1948 did the first post-war internal air service, flown by an Airspeed Consul, carrying six passengers, leave for the Isle of Man. Birmingham pressed for more services, particularly to the Continent and to connect with London. An MCA party in September 1948 viewed and discussed Elmdon's future and expressed doubts about the viability of even the few existing internal services. An offer by KLM to initiate a Schiphol service made no difference. Birmingham pressed again and again until in January 1949 MCA announced a daily Birmingham–Paris service operated by BEA and Air France. Swissair and Aer Lingus were soon flying here too, after a Dakota opened the Paris run on April 8 1949 and flew the first scheduled service to the Continent, an event which took 22 years to arrive.

In July 1949 the National Air Races were held at Elmdon. Squadron Leader Neville Duke rather spoilt it by winning, in the jet Hawker *P1040*, at 508 mph. Air racing could never be the same again. Sabena, at a slower speed, commenced services in July and another forward step came when on June 28 1950 the Birmingham Philharmonic Orchestra was lifted to Holland in a KLM DC-4, the largest civil aircraft to operate so far from Elmdon.

Birmingham Council again asked for their airport back, a request rejected in January 1953. A few days later DC-4s began regular services, and regular and charter flying overseas soon increased. Birmingham's Council refused to give up their struggle to own the airport which the Government disgracefully retained. When an eventual offer came, the Council pointed out that they were inheriting something quite different to the advanced airport they had been forced to surrender. As a result they were awarded an improvement grant from the MCA. On April 28 1961, HRH the Duchess of Kent came again, to open a £190,000 terminal extension. A bonanza for the Council was two hard runways, of 4,260 ft and 4,170 ft, built during the war for Stirling test flying. Prior to Elmdon's return on April 1 1960 the main runway had been lengthened to 5,006 ft, dramatically improving the airport. In 1949 18,237 passengers passed through Elmdon; in 1960 some 284,000.

A further extension in 1967 took runway 15/33 to 7,400 ft, permitting a full load operation of Vanguards, Tridents, Comets, Britannias and Cv 880s on scheduled and IT services—but it had cost around £1,000,000 to extend the runway. The second runway, 06/24, now extended 4,313 ft. Taxiways, 60 ft wide, led to 11 stands by the terminal building. At this time passenger services were increasing by 10 per cent annually. A peak of 95,111 passengers used Elmdon in August 1969 alone—630,735 that year. Birmingham acquired a link with New York, via Manchester, in 1971 by which time major airlines and charter operators were using it. During the 1970s a wide assortment of regular services and charter runs were operated from Elmdon, and on more than one occasion a lightly loaded Concorde has landed. The 1980s are likely to see major improvements at Elmdon. Whether it is ideally suited for 5,000,000 Midlanders is questionable. One might reasonably argue that a huge centre of population needs an airport, but the cost of duplicating costly operations already functioning with more sophistication at London is questionable.

One thing is certain. Had that Lord Mayor, upon stepping from his BA Swallow, set eyes upon a Concorde sitting superbly upon his apron he would have been delighted. Might he have said 'Wind it up, then, and let me have a go.'

Enstone, Oxfordshire

SP395255. 5½ miles SE of Chipping Norton, by B4030

Although Enstone opened as a second satellite for 21 OTU, Moreton-in-the-Marsh, on September 15 1942 it did not come into use until April 12 1943, replacing Edgehill. Wellington 1cs remained here until April 1944, Mk IIIs having been phased in late 1943 and Wellington Xs, February–March 1944. No 21 OTU's X Flight (Gunnery) arrived on May 17 1943 equipped with Martinets, and left for Moreton-in-the-Marsh on February 24 1944.

From Enstone, 21 OTU carried out leaflet dropping operations over France, an unusual activity from a satellite. Interesting arrivals from Stanton Harcourt, on February 26 1944, were five Curtiss Tomahawks of No 1682 BDTF, which used Enstone until disbandment on August 21 1944. From April 1944 the Flight was Hurricane equipped, Tomahawks leaving in May.

No 21 OTU had a post-war existence,

although the unit used Honeybourne from August to October 1945. Flying ceased at Enstone in November 1945 and Enstone passed to Maintenance Command on January 17 1946. On October 28 1946 it was placed under the control of Flying Training Command, and detachment of Oxfords and Harvards of 17 SFTS, Coleby Grange, arrived on November 10 and stayed until December 17 1946 when they moved to Moreton-in-the-Marsh to form the basis of No 1 Refresher School. Enstone subsequently saw limited use as Little Rissington's RLG.

Although the RAF left long ago, flying has not ceased here. An active gliding club, the Enstone Eagles, uses the control tower and a good runway, at one time used for surface trials. Microlights and light aircraft also use the aerodrome. Whereas at many airfields contractors smash concrete, at Enstone they busily make it, at an industrial area embracing the hangar and wartime buildings at the east end of the airfield.

Fairford, Gloucestershire

SP150990. 2 miles S of Fairford town

Authority was given in 1943 for a site south of Fairford to be prepared as a USAAF transport and air observation station. Eventually it became the airfield from where development and general test flying of the British Concordes was undertaken. Fairford's present day importance to the Western Alliance is in contrast to its run-down appearance, for its Boeing KC-135 tankers play a vital part in reinforcement deployment to Europe of American forces.

Fairford came into use not as an American, but as a Bomber Command, station. It was made ready for AEAF occupation by January 14 1944. An opening up party moved in on January 18 and the station entered 38 Group Transport Command on March 2 1944. Stirling IVs of 620 Squadron arrived from Leicester East in mid-March 1944 and were joined by 190 Squadron, similarly equipped, later in March. A large collection of Horsa gliders then followed. Cross country glider tows mingled with ever more extensive exercises. Both squadrons operated night sorties for SOE, taking off generally from Tarrant Rushton. On April 17 1944, Horsa *LJ263* was destroyed when it crashed into Fairford's control tower and killed its pilot. Another training accident involved two Stirlings releasing gliders during Exercise *Exeter.* Near Fairford they collided crashing near Kempsford. Both crews were killed.

On June 5 1944 the first of 45 Stirlings began to roll shortly before midnight. Aboard were 887 paratroops of the 6th Airborne Division whose task in Operation *Tonga* was to secure the Orne

RB-36F, 92708, *safe beyond Fairford's fence.*

This RAF Waco CG-4A Hadrian glider joined 22 HGCU on May 31 1945. Between June 1947 and late 1950 it was used by TCDU. Gliders of this type were to be seen at Blakehill and Fairford in 1945–46.

Bridge and an area east of that river. Three Stirlings of 620 Squadron failed to return. When the returned Stirlings were inspected, 27 of them were found to be unserviceable. By 18:00 on June 6, 25 had been made ready for Operation *Mallard*, the landing in Normandy of the 6th Air Landing Brigade in gliders. At 19:01 the first of 36 Stirling/Horsa combinations was away.

On September 16 1944, at 14:00, the station was sealed to prevent leakage of details of the next big venture. Fairford's part in the Arnhem operation was important from the start. 25 crews of each squadron were detailed for pathfinding and glider towing, each squadron operating 19 Stirlings. On September 18 another 43 Horsas were towed towards Arnhem, 37 landing on the planned LZ. Then came Fairford's big re-supply contribution. Facing the intense flak, in daylight, and at low level in a heavy four-engined Stirling, was no picnic. Although on one day 696 containers and 116 panniers were delivered, it cost two Stirlings of 620 Squadron and three of 190 Squadron. Disaster struck both squadrons on September 21 when German fighters, discovering the transports unescorted, viciously attacked them, shooting down seven of 190 Squadron's ten Stirlings and two of 620's aircraft. There were 613 daylight take offs and 669 landings by Fairford's Stirlings and visitors in September.

October's Operation *Molten* was remarkable. Sixteen crews of each squadron set out, towing 32 Horsas across France to Rome/Ciampino where, by October 10, 27 arrived safely before pressing on to Pomigliano, near Naples. Problems were many, not least the strain on crews, aircraft and engines. All the Stirling crews returned to Britain in November, but their homecoming was to a different station for, in mid-October 1944 both 190 and 620 Squadrons forsook Fairford for Great Dunmow in Essex, along with the entire station organisation and much equipment. Fairford became a satellite of Keevil where No 22 Heavy Glider Conversion Unit formed on October 20 1944 and equipped with Albemarles. Its role was the rapid training of glider pilots to replace the Arnhem casualties. Flights C, D and F of the unit were placed at Fairford with a strength of about 29 Albemarles and 23 gliders—both Horsas and Waco Hadrians. When 22 HGCU moved to Blakehill Farm in mid-June 1945, Fairford retained its equipment whilst changing its allegiance, being Blakehill's satellite until October 21 1945 when 22 HGCU withdrew and Fairford was placed on Care and Maintenance.

Early in 1946 Fairford became the base for three Flights of Oxfords, 1529 Flight being here from January 27 to mid-February 1946, 1556 RAT Flight using Fairford between January and July 1946 and 1555 RAT Flight having a longer stay—February 1946 to August 1947.

The next phase came with the return to Britain, late in September 1946, of 47 Squadron. Fairford became the main airborne forces base in England and the home of Halifax A VIIs and soon A Mk IXs. A second Halifax squadron reformed here on May 1 1947 and was joined by 295 Squadron on September 10 1947 and 297 Squadron shortly before. The four squadrons wound down in September–October 1948 by which time experimental glider flying had taken place. Yet again Fairford was, in December 1948, placed on Care and Maintenance.

Fairford re-opened in June 1950, the Americans at long last moving in to help enlarge the airfield and lengthen its runways before it became active on July 7 1950. On July 1 1951, Fairford was completely placed in American hands, control being the task of the 7th Air Division, Strategic Air Command. Strongly guarded compounds, high fencing and perimeter guards made this a typical SAC base of the period.

Just after dawn on February 7 1953, 17 B-36 bombers landed from Carswell AFB, Fort Worth, Texas. In another B-36, Lieutenant Colonel Herman Gerick got into difficulties in the circuit and the crew of 15 baled out. The incident caused no mean stir for the B-36 flew on for 30 miles eventually spiralling down out of control near Laycock, its wreckage widely scattered. Another B-36 had crashed when on its way to Gander, Newfoundland.

Memories of the B-36 are surely not only of its huge size, but also of the strange noise of the engines, like a hoard of motorcycles. Of the next type to make its debut at Fairford, one would surely remember its futuristic shape and strange undercarriage—a sort of Harrier-style of the 1950s. This was, of course, the Boeing B-47 Stratojet which became a common sight over central England in the 1950s. After a flight of 5 hours 21 minutes the first of two B-47s touched down at Fairford for a brief stay on April 7 1953. Their proving flight a success, they were followed on June 2 1953 by the first deployment to Britain of Stratojets 45 in the hands of the 306th Bomb Wing. Three B-47B squadrons (Ncs 367, 368 and 369) made their 4,500 mile homeward dash from Fairford on September 4 1953. Whilst in Britain they received another B-47 which, on August 4, flew from Goose Bay to Fairford in 4 hours 14 minutes. It made the return trip to Tampa without landing.

The 305th BW (M) from Limestone AFB then occupied Brize Norton and Fairford, placing one squadron at the latter base. When, in late 1953, the third B-47 Wing arrived on TDY, it was the first to bring B-47Es to Britain, being based at Fairford. More Bomb Wings on TDY made use of Fairford, usually basing only one squadron here. Among the interesting examples to come in 1954 were the first RB-47Es of the 68th SRW based at Lake Charles, Louisiana. A few RB-36Fs of the 5th SRW came to Fairford in July and, at the same time, three squadrons of B-47Es of the 43rd BW (M) moved in for a three-month stay. From the autumn of 1955, use of Fairford declined, but B-47s remained a common sight, and occasionally B-36s, until SAC rotations ceased.

Fairford was retrieved by the RAF in June 1964. Gnat Trainers of C Flight CFS arrived at the station and from the start of 1965 until September 1966 Fairford was the home of the Red Arrows. On November 1 1965 No 53 Squadron reformed to operate Short Belfasts and moved to Brize Norton in May 1967. During that period Fairford had been increasingly used by Belfasts and VC-10s while the runway at Brize Norton was resurfaced.

Tranquility in the summer of 1967 was brief, for in September Fairford re-opened as an independent station in Air Support Command to house the then-new RAF Hercules. Here, on February 25 1968, 47 Squadron reformed to use them, Fairford joining 38 Group on March 1 1968. A second squadron, No 30, equipped here with Hercules in June 1968. Hercules squadrons flew overseas trooping and general freighting sorties.

The designation of Fairford on April 9 1969 as the BAC Concorde flight test centre caught the public's imagination. Soon it was the home of Concorde 002 and later the test base for production Concordes. The last Hercules left for Lyneham on February 10 1971. Station HQ disbanded, Air Support Command's tenancy being terminated on April 30 1971. Fairford reverted to RLG state, and was designated a reserve airfield, a satellite of Brize Norton.

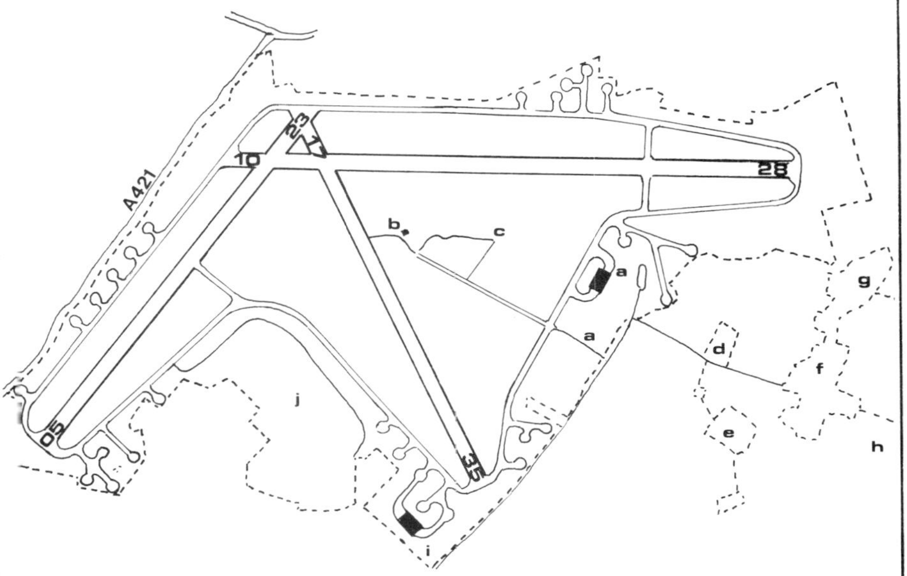

Finmere can be seen to have a most unusual layout, with runways radiating from the northern tip of the landing ground. 'A' marks the technical area, 'B' the control tower (13726/41 and modified items), 'C' the crew rooms, 'D' the instructional site, 'E' the WAAF site, 'F' the communal site, 'G' No 2 accommodation site and 'H' No 1 site. Area 'J' marks the weapons store, 'I' nearby being the 'B1' hangar still in good condition. The layout as shown approximates to that in the last two years of the war.

Concorde flying continued until the lease expired on January 31 1977. Extensive runway and taxiway resurfacing commenced in April 1977 and in September Fairford resumed its reserve role. An announcement was made in July 1978 to the effect that studies showed Fairford a suitable base for USAF KC-135s. On September 12 1978, five KC-135s were positioned here for refuelling sorties during the autumn NATO exercise. After making up to four sorties daily they left on September 28 1978. On February 1 1979 the 7020th Air Base Group (USAFE) was activated here to look after the American involvement. Control of Fairford's KC-135s was vested in the 11th Strategic Group (SAC), the overseer for brief visits by B-52 bombers. RAF Support Command placed a unit here on September 3 1979 and an RAF liaison party formed before the station was transferred to the 3rd Air Force on September 20.

Finmere, Oxfordshire

SP250300. 5 miles W of Buckingham, by A421

Finmere had a very curious layout. Runway 06/25 was parallel to the A421 Oxford road, its intersection with the other two runways at the northern tip of the former. From the air Finmere appeared to have radiating runways from a hub near the junction of the A421 and B4031 roads. Since the closure of the airfield for military purposes, the Preston Bissett road has been placed across taxi tracks leading from the east/west runway. Finmere was one of the few airfields with a watch office placed almost in the middle of the landing ground; unusual, too, was its siting close to a runway. Adjacent to the tower were the flight and aircrew offices. Bomb dumps were to be found to the north-west of where the remaining good state 'B1' hangar (pattern 11776/42) is still to be seen. There was only one other hangar at Finmere, a 'T2' (8259/40) now used by Midland Shires Farmers.

Indicative of the station's importance, particularly late in the war, was the number of huts for personnel. Officers and sergeants had living quarters in Laing or Nissen huts. Airmen were billetted in Nissen huts (9024/41). Ablutions were in temporary brick buildings.

A landing ground at Finmere was used by Blenheims of 13 OTU Bicester early in 1941, but it was 1942 before it was really established as an airfield. From the start of August 1942, the station came fully under the control of Bicester as a satellite for 13 OTU, and was used by Blenheims, both Mk I and IV. Crews trained for 2 Group and for service overseas, although Blenheims were slowly being supplanted. To supply the Blenheim V squadrons in north-west Africa at the start of 1943, No 307 FTU formed at Bicester on December 24 1942 and soon after received seven Blenheim Vs. For a week in February 1943 these flew from Finmere because of Bicester's bad state. They briefly kept company with Whitleys of 1473 Flight from Upper Heyford, at Finmere from January 1943 to September 1943. The Flight also used Wellingtons.

A foretaste of Finmere's present style was provided by 1473 Flight's communications aircraft, de Havilland Leopard Moth *AX858* (formerly *G-ACGS*). Early in March 1943, 307 FTU was notified that it was to re-arm with Boston IIIs and train crews to fly them to North Africa, the Blenheim V commitment being soon to end. The FTU moved completely to Finmere on March 18 1943 to make use of runways there. To assist in crew conversion three Havocs and a couple of Bostons were placed on 307 FTU's permanent strength. The first Boston III, *AL697*, arrived here on March 20 1943. Another, *Z2197*, was collected from West Raynham on April 16 1943 and made a trial delivery flight to Gibraltar, taking off from Portreath. The journey time was 6 hours 50 minutes.

Finmere was still in demand for Blenheim training. Relief came when 307 FTU was briefly sited at Turweston, from May 1 1943 to May 18. That unit returned as the equipment at Finmere was updated by the arrival of 13 OTU's Mitchell IIs and Boston IIIas. 307 FTU, under 70 Group of Fighter Command, busied itself ferrying Boston to North Africa, despatching its first Bostons on June 11 1943. During September 1943, 307 FTU started to receive Boston IIIas. On arrival at the FTU, crews trained on the type they would fly, before being allocated the machine which they were to ferry overseas. October 1943 saw the completion of this task and between October 9 and 27 the FTU moved to Melton Mowbray. At the start of November, control of 13 OTU passed to 9 Group. Boston and Mitchell training went ahead at some pace for the next few months.

Early 1944 witnessed a major change for in January 13 OTU began to receive, at Finmere, its first Mosquitoes. Crew training commenced on February 14, and within the next four weeks 13 OTU's remaining Blenheims were withdrawn. Finmere was now the OTU for 2 Group's Mosquito, Mitchell and Boston crews, the former gradually acquiring the leading

A 'B1' hangar remains in excellent condition at Finmere.

part. In the middle of 1944, 13 OTU had 34 Mosquitoes here, and a few Bostons.

When 38 Group vacated Harwell in October 1944 that station was taken over by 13 OTU whose Mosquitoes moved there. This left Boston IVs and Mitchells at Finmere, but not for long because the Mosquito element of 60 OTU (concentrating upon training crews for Mosquito intruder squadrons) arrived during the first two weeks of March 1945. Its Mosquitoes were stationed here, its other aircraft at Hampstead Norris. On March 3, 2 Group took control of the unit which dissolved into 13 OTU. Boston flying ceased at Finmere on March 19 1945.

Ironically, training was switched to providing up to 18 crews monthly for Mosquito squadrons—not in 2 Group, but in the Far East. At Finmere on April 30 1945 there were 47 Mosquitoes, mainly Mk IIs, in addition to eight Ansons, a Proctor, Dominie and Tiger Moth within the Mosquito Wing of the new 13 OTU. Orders were received in May for the provision of 31 Mosquito crews monthly. On May 28 1945 Mitchell training ceased and Finmere soon held the full active strength of the OTU. During June that came to include six of the then very new Tempest IIs. Contraction of the home-based air force was already under way and in late July 1945, 13 OTU left for Middleton St George taking 44 Mosquitoes, 6 Ansons, 5 Mitchells and the Tempests. Just imagine the trade that one of the frequent Sunday markets or Vintage Aeroplane Club displays at Finmere would generate if a few of those types had been left behind!

Gaydon, Warwickshire

SP355555, 8 miles S of Warwick by the A41

Gaydon's selection as the first V-bomber station was due to the existence of fighter belts to defend it, a throw back to plans of long before. One runway was lengthened and a special 'Gaydon Type' hangar reminiscent of the Type 'J' of the 1940s was erected to house Valiants and Victors. An electronics servicing block was built, something all V-bomber bases came to feature.

Gaydon came into use early in 1942 before opening on June 13 1942 as a satellite for Chipping Warden's 12 OTU. That station acquired Edgehill as its permanent satellite so Gaydon was, on September 1 1942, transferred to 22 OTU, Wellesbourne Mountford, a 91 Group station whose runways were under repair. A and B Flights of 22 OTU came to Gaydon which became the base for Training Wing's Wellingtons to the end of

Valiants of 138 Squadron, the first to be equipped with V-bombers, at Gaydon in March 1956. The signals square displays the station's identity letters, GD.

the war. Initially Wellington Ics used the station. No 22 OTU began using Mk IIIs in October 1942 and from 1943 Mk Xs were also based here.

Because of those 1942 runway repairs, 22 OTU used Gaydon as the starting point for bombing sorties within Operation *Grand National* during September 1942. In 1943 *Nickelling* sorties were flown from the station, and in the autumn a few bombing sorties, preceding Operation *Starkey*, were flown to bomb gun emplacements near Boulogne. Additionally, daylight ASR flights over the North Sea took place from Gaydon. By the end of 1943, Gaydon's Wellingtons had provided reading material to the inhabitants of Grenville, Nantes, Orleans and Rennes. During 1944 there were quite a number of diversions to Gaydon by bombers returning by day and night from operations.

Flying training by 22 OTU ceased here on July 1 1945. Control of the station, although still held by Wellesbourne, passed like that of the latter to 23 Group Flying Training Command on July 24. This resulted in the immediate arrival of 3 GTS from Exeter, bringing Master IIs, Hotspurs, Tiger Moths and an Oxford. From Croughton on May 28 1946 came the Glider Instructors' Flight whose stay was brief for Gaydon closed to flying on August 15 1946 and was put on to Care and Maintenance on August 28 1946. Although it was not in use, Gaydon was placed in 1947 under 21 (P) AFU's control as its satellite.

During 1953, rebuilding of the station commenced and, on March 1 1954, Gaydon re-opened. On January 1 1955, 138 Squadron reformed at Gaydon, becoming the first V-bomber squadron. Equipped with Valiants, it became operational prior to moving to Wittering on July 6 1955. No 232 Operational Conversion Unit opened in July and equipped with Valiants and a few Canberras. The first Valiant for 232 OCU had arrived much earlier, and the Canberra T4s were used for runway approach aid training. No 543 Squadron which reformed at Gaydon on July 1 1955 took its Valiants to Wyton on November 18 1955. Once the Valiant force had formed, aided by 232 OCU, Gaydon also began to use Victors, the first of seven based here arriving on November 11 1957. All Victor 1 bomber crews were trained at 232 OCU, alongside those for Valiants. In 1962 a 'Victor 2 Conversion Unit' was set up at Wittering, an off-shoot of 232 OCU.

V-bomber training continued until June 1965 when the Victor OCU disbanded making way for Flying Training Command and, on September 1 1965, 2 ANS and its Varsities began arriving. That unit had known a complicated life since formation at Yatesbury in September 1938 and Gaydon's ANS arose from the renaming of 7 ANS as 2 ANS. The School left for Finningley in May 1970 after becoming part of 6 FTS on April 24 1970. Gaydon remained under 23 Group until June 10 1970 when it was transferred to HQ CFS. The Strike Command Special Avionics Servicing Unit of No 1 Group lodged at Gaydon until disbanded on December 1 1971. Control of Gaydon passed to 71 MU Bicester, Maintenance Command on April 1 1972, and its station was placed under Care and Maintenance until closure on October 31 1974. British Leyland now has the site.

Grafton Underwood, Northamptonshire

SP925815. 4 miles NE of Kettering, No of Cranford on A604

Chance gave it away. This large, dull brown limousine stopped and inside was this military man in uniform unfamiliar—unlike the drawl of his request. 'Hey, fella, can you please tell me the way to the Huntingdon Road?' 'Sure,' a response necessary to fit the situation, 'right at the roundabout, left, then . . ..' 'I'm wantin' Thrapston, that's the way isn't it?'

How fortune's face can smile unexpectedly, for the question which had occupied my thoughts for a week was 'Where were the B-17Es flying from?' Now this obliging gentleman had given a possible clue, and it merely remained to find someone knowing that area in 1942 to provide an answer. It was not long in coming.

Trusting the revelations of our intelligence network, cousin Roger and I set forth early on August 5, cycled hard and by lunch time had taken the winding Slipton road off the A604, which our maps indicated (no sign posts then) would lead to Grafton Underwood. Excitement welled as US lorries passed perilously close and we had our first sighting of a Jeep. Clearly we were on the right track, although of B-17Es nothing was to be seen.

Grafton we found to be a most picturesque village, but no airfield was visible. Then—curses, the road ahead was closed, an American sentry barring its way. We retreated to a by-road to rest, bite the margarine sandwiches and to rejuvenate hope. Not a sound. On returning to the village we took to a winding path which skirted a high wall, blocking the view towards the airfield. Suddenly, a rough cough and an engine burst into life. No mistaking it, this was a Cyclone. Roger had soon discovered a loose stone in the wall. Ecstasy, for once it was removed a splendid view would appear. As he pushed I fumbled (cautiously) for the binoculars. What an incredible sight presented itself. A gigantic US 'bum' had deposited itself into the hole completley blocking it. I'm sure he did not mean to and, being an American and probably kind would certainly have moved it had I the nerve to have asked him and told him how far we'd cycled for a view of an American, albeit not this one!

He was not disposed to move, so we quietly crept away not wishing to disturb him and hopeful of another vantage point. Through a crack I spied *19038* taxiing by, its deep orange coloured serial belying the usual claims of yellow. Moments later the pilot opened up its engines and the B-17 hurried off.

We retreated to open country to plan another attack, but had to accept that a clear view of sunlit, breezy Grafton Underwood was impossible to obtain. Instead we had to be satisfied with a distant view of a stream take off by six B-17Es, our binoculars informing us that *19047* was leading. For the next hour the formation flew around low, engraving images to store for a life time. The long, hard haul home was not without incident for, while resting in the shade near Spaldwick, we had an unexpected bonus in the appearance of a USAAF P-38 Lightning, the first we had seen, scurrying northwards.

Since May 1942 there had been Americans at Grafton. They had sailed to Britain in the SS *Andes* before stepping ashore on a Liverpool dockside. These were men of the 15th Bomb Squadron, soon to take the Douglas Boston into action spearheading American bombing operations. Their stay was brief for they moved to Molesworth on June 9. Grafton had come into use in late 1941 and by the start of 1942 temporarily served as the satellite of Polebrook where 1653 Conversion Unit was acquiring Liberator IIs. American bombers were not new to this area.

On June 10, 29 officers and 412 enlisted men made a dusk arrival at Grafton to prepare for the the first Flying Fortresses. Possibly the enemy knew about it, or maybe a load of incendiaries intended for Thrapston's iron works went astray. Certain it is they fell upon a Nissen hut giving the Americans an unfriendly welcome and their first taste of war. Into Grafton the ground echelon of the 342nd Bomb Squadron moved on June 10, followed by the 414th on June 11, their aircraft following soon. Remaining squadrons of the 97th Bomb Group placed themselves at Polebrook, along with the Group's HQ, the whole coming under the control of No 1 Bombardment Wing, VIIIth Bomber Command. At last the Americans had come.

B-17Es of the 97th Bomb Group in July 1942, 19024 *'King Kondor', closest with 19043 to the left* (via Roger Freeman).

July and early August 1942 were taken up with local and cross country flying, and fighter affiliation with RAF Spitfires. By the third week of August the Group was ready to commence operations.

On August 17 1942, the battle began. First away were Polebrook's B-17s flying a mid-afternoon feint. At 16:27 the first of 12 B-17Es rolled along Grafton's runway, beginning that mighty offensive with which the 8th AF carved its place in history. Ironically that aircraft was carrying as co-pilot Major P.W. Tibbets who was to captain the B-29 from which the atomic bomb fell onto Hiroshima to all but end the war. By 16:35 the Fortresses were airborne, one from the 340th Bomb Squadron, five from the 342nd and six of the 414th. Aboard the leadship of the second formation, 19023, *Yankee Doodle*, was another who would achieve fame, General Ira Eaker.

As they made their way to Beachy Head, the exit point, hoards of Spitfires closed to give them cover. Flying high were the new Spitfire IXs of Nos 64, 401, 402 and 611 Squadrons. To the rear were Spitfire Vs of Nos 129, 131, 412 and 309 (USA) Squadrons operating from Tangmere with 133 and 307 (USA) Squadrons, Biggin-based, aiding them. Many other Spitfires busily guarded the diversion operation.

With 45 × 600 lb and 9 × 1,100 lb HE bombs aboard, the Fortresses crossed into France east of St Valéry and from 23,000 ft and between 17:39 and 17:46 bombed Rouen's Sotteville railway complex. At the coast one of the B-17s suffered flak damage, and enemy fighters were encountered just after the bombing. About 50 came up from Beaumont-le-Roger, 64 Squadron claiming two of them and 401 Squadron another, for the loss of two Spitfires. An Fw 190 was chased into the fire of a waist gunner, Sergeant West, flying in *Birmingham Blitzkreig*, and a ball turret gunner also fired at a Fw 190. When the B-17s returned to view at Grafton around 19:00 all were seen to be safe. It was a superb summer evening, but there would be many more when sunshine could never remove the sorrow.

On August 19, 'Dieppe day', 24 B-17Es of the 97th—six from each of the four squadrons—attacked Abbeville/Drucat airfield in support of the landing. Next day a dozen raided Amiens marshalling yards and, on August 21, a raid by 12 on Rotterdam proved the most dangerous yet. The bombers were 16 minutes late and escorting Spitfires could only cover them for half of the journey. Three bombers aborted, the remaining nine being ordered to turn back at the Dutch coast. Abandonment came too late and 23 Fw 190s swept in to attack. Two were shot down, but B-17E *19089* was soon in trouble. Five fighters set about the lagging bomber, killing the co-pilot and injuring the captain. A courageous crew nursed the Fortress back.

Le Trait ship yards, Avions Potez Meaulte, Courtrai/Wevelghem airfield—all were raided by the 97th by the end of August 1942. The largest raid so far came on September 7 when 29 B-17s attacked Rotterdam. Enemy fighters rose in strength, B-17 crews claiming 12 of them. At the end of the first week of September 1942 both the 342nd and 414th Squadrons moved to Polebrook making room for the 305th Bomb Group at Grafton which, by September, housed the unit's B-17Fs. In late November 1942 the 305th moved to Chelveston leaving Grafton to be much improved.

By mid-April 1943 the work was complete and four squadrons of B-17Fs of the 96th Bomb Group arrived. Their stay was brief for at the end of May they moved to Andrews Field in Essex. Immediately their place was taken by more B-17s, this time of the 384th Bomb Group which commenced operations from Grafton on June 22 1943. During the course of 314 operations the 384th ('P' in a triangle) attacked targets over a wide area—Orleans/Bricy airfield, engine works at Cologne, Gelsenkirchen coking plant, a components factory at Halberstadt, a steel works at distant Magdeburg and the ball bearing factory at Schweinfurt. Leipzig, Emden, Hamburg, Mannheim and Berlin all echoed to the crunch of Grafton's bombs. Two Distinguished Unit Citations were awarded to the 384th, one for the raid of April 24 1944 when, although greatly mauled, the Group led the 41st Wing through great opposition to bomb a factory and airfield at Oberpfafenhofen. After assisting in the softening up of French coastal targets, prior to the invasion, the 384th helped the Americans break out from St Lô, supported the Rhine crossing assaults and, on April 24 1945, was the last Group in the 8th AF to drop bombs in anger.

In June 1945 the 384th moved to France and soon the RAF repossessed the station and 236 MU arrived, disposing of large numbers of surplus motor vehicles here.

Military ownership of Grafton ceased in February 1959.

Visit Grafton now and a good view across the site of the airfield can be had. Among the remaining buildings is the operations block. The bomb dump to the east can be made out, and a memorial stone by the Geddington road reminds us of the strong association between the Americans and Grafton Underwood.

Grove, Oxfordshire

SU395900. W of village, 1 mile N of Wantage

Grove originated in a decision to build a well-equipped three-runway spare bomber airfield for 91 Group. When in 1942 Brize Norton became a glider pilot training centre instead of a bomber OTU, Grove logically slipped under that station's control. In August 1942, Wellingtons of 15 OTU had made use of the airfield for Grove was intended to replace Hampstead Norris as Harwell's satellite at the time. With so much gliding activity close by, it was inadvisable for that scheme to go forward and Grove was transferred to Flying Training Command.

Over the first four months of 1943, Brize Norton's Whitleys and Horsas used the airfield, and on March 11/12 1943 Typhoons of 174 and 184 Squadrons were here taking part in Exercise *Spartan*. Well into 1943 the airfield remained far from complete, and it seems likely that Grove had already been earmarked for American use. Different use of the station came in early May 1943 when Oxfords of K, L and M Flights of 15 (P) AFU were brought here and also temporarily used Greenham Common and Ramsbury. All were earmarked to become US 9th AF transport bases. When 15 (P) AFU arrived the runways remained incomplete, and the airfield surface left much to be desired, being amply marred by depressions and ditches. Ever increased flying made the area heavily congested too, so 15 (P) AFU moved to Andover in July 1943 and its Oxfords vacated Grove on July 3 1943.

The US 9th AAF Support Command took control and used Grove as a repair and maintenance base for C-47 Dakotas and later for C-46 Commandos. Communications flights of the 9th AAF were here in 1944, using Proctors, Oxfords, UC-64s and UC-78s.

A dramatic event took place on March 2 1944 when the exotic Vickers Armstrongs Windsor *DW506* force-landed here and was written off as a result. The accident occurred in poor weather when the large, unconventional and highly secret bomber was being flown by a pilot new to the type. A piece of metal had become lodged in the constant speed unit of the starboard inner propeller, as a result of which the engine could not be feathered. In the crash the bomber broke its back.

By the end of the war Grove had an unconventional appearance. Among the assortment of buildings of 1941, 1942 and 1943 vintage were six 'T2' hangars (3653/42) one being purely set aside for use as a store of aircraft parts. Two others were used as assembly shops, while in two Robin hangars (2204/41) parts salvaged from crashed aircraft, and also propellers, were held. The airfield had 78 dispersal standings, mainly on the east side. On the west was the bomb store, a reminder of the original plan.

In February 1946 the RAF took over the station, its excellent facilities being used both as an RLG and by 6 MU Brize Norton, then busily disposing of surplus aircraft. Visit Grove now and extensive house building will be seen to have spread onto the one-time airfield. At the time of writing, though, the airfield's unusual layout could still be made out.

Haddenham (Thame), Buckinghamshire

See Thame

Halton, Buckinghamshire

SP875010. 2 miles N of Wendover

Halton has been associated with military flying since 1912 when three aeroplanes and an airship taking part in manoeuvres, made use of the grounds of Halton House then owned by Alfred Rothschild. Halton is one of the oldest RAF stations and still plays an important part in Service life.

Prior to World War 1 technical training was carried out at CFS Netheravon. With increased demand for skilled technicians, training schools were established elsewhere, particularly at Farnborough and by 1916 at Coley Park, Reading, taken over for a riggers' and fitters' training school. As many as 1,000 men could be accommodated at the station.

Coley Park soon became inadequate and a larger training depot was established on Lord Rothschild's Estate at Halton Park, Wendover. In 1917 when the Boy's Training Centre formed there it was then decided to create a special technical training school for men and boys. On September 10 1917, the Halton School of Technical Training was established.

At Eastchurch on April 6 1918 a Boys' Mechanic Training School formed to supplement a boys' training school at Cranwell. The Boys' Training Depot at Letchworth formed in June 1918.

Cessation of hostilities brought changes to technical training. The opening of the Halton School of Technical Training (Boys) came on October 9 1919 although that nomenclature was unused until December 23 1919. The reason was probably that Letchworth's depot did not close until then when that camp site was sold. A new scheme commenced at Halton on January 1 1920, resulting in the school being again renamed, on March 1920, as No 1 School of Technical Training (Boys) Halton.

Lord Trenchard's memorandum of November 1919 laid the foundations of Halton's apprentices scheme. He thought it impossible for the RAF's need for mechanics to be met merely by recruiting skilled men. The RAF, he argued, must train its own mechanics. He decided to enlist the aid of local education authorities and others to find suitably educated boys for technical trades. Entry to courses could come only after success in examinations equivalent to the School Certificate thus ensuring a sufficiently high standard of education. The opinion was that boys should complete their apprenticeship in three years instead of five as was the custom at Cranwell and in civilian life. Cranwell's first entry under the new scheme started in February 1920. It became effective at Halton in January 1922, at the unit now known as No 1 School of Technical Training which title it retains.

After passing a medical examination, boys were allotted their trade and enlisted for 12 years' service to follow their 18th birthdays. Choice of vacant trades was allowed in order of examination success and bearing in mind any trade training they had previously acquired. Trades were fitter, carpenter and electrical and wireless trades, broken into specialist fields of armourer, airframe, engine and wireless operator/mechanic.

From August 1926 apprentices learning mechanical trades trained at Halton. Wireless training took place at Cranwell and some boys, upon changing stations, took some bagpipes with them which led to the formation of Halton's well-known pipe band. This was not the first famous Halton band for early in 1917 a brass band formed; but it was not until 1922 that a flute, drum and trumpet band was

Inside a Halton workshop during the First World War. Riggers, including Australians, are most busily engaged (via Bruce Robertson).

assembled for a part in the 1924 Olympia Royal Tournament.

Halton's training programme continued into the 1930s in relative tranquillity—apart from the very audible discipline which, for many of today's youngsters, would doubtless seem incredibly severe. In the mid-1930s expansion the problem was to find sufficient teenagers to become apprentices. Building was proceeding apace at the station and by the outbreak of war there were four Wings of apprentices, each holding 1,000 boys under its own Commanding Officer and occupying a separate block of the camp.

Within each Wing, apprentices were assigned to a Squadron and Flight. They worked for 20 hours a week in workshops, did nine hours of 'PT' and drill, had 18 hours of academic schooling and were encouraged to take an active part in sports. In their quarters they prepared for strict inspections ensuring barracks were spotlessly clean in time-honoured style. For their recreation there was a cinema, clubs and ample games facilities. Competition to join was keen, and those desiring could proceed to Cranwell for permanent commissions.

Wartime apprentice training was reduced. By the end of the war, 22,000 apprentices had passed out of Halton since 1920, and over 4,000 had become commissioned. Ex-Halton apprentices, 'Trenchard's Brats', had won over 800 decorations including a George Cross and Sergeant Thomas Gray a Victoria Cross. Over 1,800 were mentioned in despatches and, in May 1945 when No 1 STT celebrated its Silver Jubilee, Lord Trenchard inspected his ageing brainchild. A year later the intake was re-adjusted to include once more a high proportion of apprentices.

Halton's apprentices in uniform were easily identifiable. In 1918, with men and boys in the same camp, a badge was deemed necessary to distinguish them apart—to identify who should not, for instance, be smoking. The present design was adopted in December 1918. Originally it incorporated a bee motif superimposed upon a propeller boss, which the approved badge did not include. Instead, a four-bladed propeller was chosen, an emblem retained. Still the RAF apprentices' school, Halton has long been associated with other aspects of Royal Air Force life.

Halton (1939) with Blenheim Is for apprentice and general engineering training. Closest is Blenheim K7040 *once* V *of 114 Squadron and now* 1042M (via Bruce Robertson).

An RAF hospital was established at Halton in 1919 with limited medical and surgical facilities. A larger hospital opened in 1927, the ceremony being performed by HRH the Princess Mary after whom the hospital was named. During the war its facilities were heavily drawn upon. Battle casualties suffered particularly from horrific burns, so in 1940 a burns unit was established and became a leader in the field of plastic and maxillo-facial surgery. By the middle of the war Princess Mary's Hospital held over 700 equipped beds. Here in 1957 the first Artificial Kidney Unit in Britain was set up to deal with cases of acute renal failure. Facilities now exist for its rapid mobile deployment at home and overseas, for civilian as well as serviceman. Two-year nursing courses lead to Halton's students becoming State Enrolled Nurses.

With so much of its early involvement being with Empire outposts, the RAF needed specialised staff to deal with tropical diseases. A small laboratory was established at Finchley as an offshoot of the RFC Officers' Hospital at Hampstead. The tropical medicine unit moved to the new Halton hospital in 1925. Under the title RAF Pathological Laboratory it functioned until 1935 when it became the RAF Institute of Pathology and Tropical Medicine. The Institute still plays a major part in RAF medical services undertaking laboratory investigations and handling a variety of medical situations. The Department of Aviation and Forensic Pathology has the responsibility for medical investigation into the causes of fatal flying accident casualties throughout the Services, and also acts for the Department of Trade and Industry.

Halton's RAF Institute of Community Medicine is an offshoot of a long established unit known upon formation in 1919 as the Hospital Orderlies Training Depot. It was the Medical Training Establishment and School, later the Institute of Hygiene and Medical Training. Apart from running specialised medical courses, the school investigates a variety of health problems arising from noise, ventilation, heating, etc. The Joint Services' School of Physiotherapy runs courses for up to 20 male and female students from the Services and civilian life each year. Another branch of Halton's medical area concerns dental health, the prerogative of the Institute of Dental Health and Training.

Alongside the camp is a grass airfield which has served as the last landing ground for countless old warriors, time-expired aircraft brought here for technicians to be trained upon. Since 1978 some of the latter have come as electrician trainees, following the transfer of their School from St Athan in October 1978. The progression of RAF aircraft through Halton's workshops has been exceedingly extensive. The most astonishing arrival was, without doubt, a very lightly loaded Vulcan 1. Currently the School holds an assortment of Jet Provosts, Gnats, Canberras, Whirlwinds and Sea Vixens acquired as they withdrew from use. Unused wartime use of the airfield came first with the arrival in November 1940 of 112 Squadron RCAF and, later, with the formation of No 529 Squadron from No 1448 (Calibration) Flight on June 15 1943. The latter's main equipment was the Cierva C30a autogiro used since 1940 for radar calibration. Although the main HQ was at Halton, the autogiros were frequently away on detachment, supported still by a few long-life DH Hornet Moths. One of these, *G-ADKK*, is still in good condition. Earlier, its companion *G-ADKC* in the guise of *X9445* was based here as the communications aircraft of 1 STT. On August 19 1944, 529 Squadron vacated Halton for a site near Henley-on-Thames.

It is claimed that when in the late 1930s a group of senior German officers came to Halton they witnessed an amazing march past. The head of the column was so routed that it paraded around the camp to join the tail thereby providing the spectacle of a never ending body of men. Such a sight would surely gladden the heart of many a retired SNCO, as much as the tail of a Siskin or one of Halton's grand collection of Blenheim 1s would have others jumping for joy. Alas, I'm afraid we're both going to be disappointed.

Hampstead Norris, Berkshire

SU530765. 9 miles NE of Newbury, via B4009

Hampstead Norris opened in summer 1940 as Harwell's satellite. A dispersal field, it also provided a base for the initial stage of OTU day and night flying. Personnel initially lived in tented accommodation. Hampstead's value was greater than many of its type because it acquired metalled runways early in its life. The enemy must have soon known about Hampstead where three bombs fell

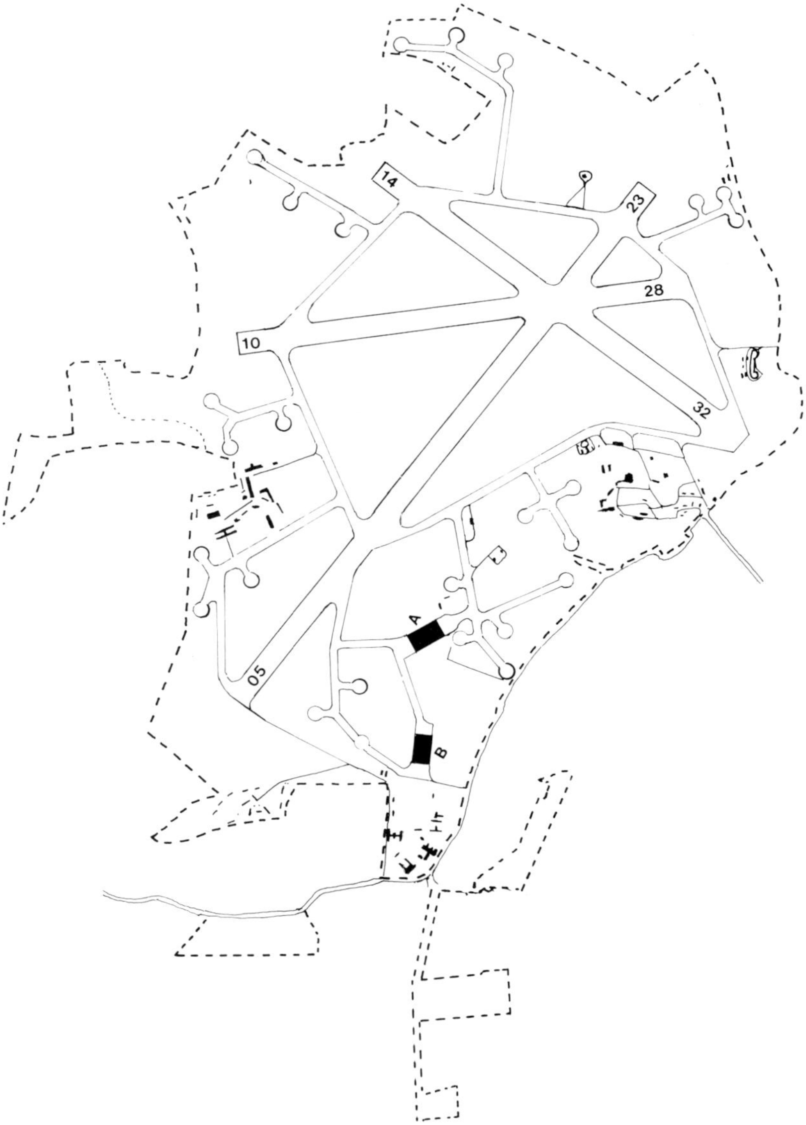

Hampstead Norris of 1945, set amidst woodland, exhibits an incredibly dangerous feature and a vulnerable one, the intersection of all runways at one point. Take off on the 23/05 runway meant immediate passage over dense woodland. Raised from a practice landing ground into a self accounting station late in the war, Hampstead represents a half-way layout with dispersed technical sites and widely-spread dispersal points which lead to complicated taxi tracks. Take-off on a 05/23 runway posed problems involving back-tracking, for the perimeter track did not encircle the field. Hangar 'A' was a Type 'T2' (3657/42) and hangar 'B' is a Type 'B1' (TP/519/43).

harmlessly on September 16 1940. Wellington 1s of 15 OTU were then active. On April 4 1941, another raider attacked Hampstead, following a Wellington in and attempting to bomb it. April 1941 witnessed generally increased use of satellites, particularly during a widespread attempt to clear the winter backlog of night flying training.

What really made the airfield important was its use as starting point for overseas ferrying of Wellingtons. The first three *(T2825, T2840* and *T2873)* left on the night of May 9 1941. They flew direct to Gibraltar averaging 8 hours 41 minutes for the first leg. Via Malta they then flew to Egypt.

Disturbed at this new venture the Luftwaffe, on May 12 1941, placed ten HEs and 100 incendiaries on the airfield, damaging both tailplane and wing of a Wellington. Damage was caused to the southern taxi track, and one bomb hit the flarepath whilst flying was in progress. It did not halt the ferry flights and on May 15 another three Wellingtons set off for Gibraltar. Such a journey, long and tiresome, remains no mean achievement. On this second occasion, though, Sergeant McManus force-landed *T2572* on a Portuguese beach, at Es Edro du Muel, where the crew burnt their aircraft. Bad weather inevitably raised loss rates, as on June 19 when *Z8722* came down off Aguiles, Spain, and rapidly sank. *X3211* ditched in the river estuary at V der Castelle, Portugal, but two successfully penetrated the disastrous electrical storms.

Heavily laden bombers were unable to use Harwell until it had hardened runways. Late in July 1941 their construction commenced, so D Flight and the Middle East Despatch Flight of 15 OTU temporarily moved to Hampstead. Only two of the 26 Wellingtons sent overseas in September 1941—22 of them Mk IIs—were lost.

Life at Hampstead Norris was more eventful than at many satellites. Pilot Officer Fenton was flying *Z5588* on a training flight on October 11 1941 when, six miles south-east of Filey, a Ju 88 opened fire on his aircraft. The rear gunner replied and two bursts warned off the enemy. That month 31 Wellingtons went overseas, 29 arriving safely, one after a flight across France to Malta. In November 1941, 25 made the journey to Gibraltar after training a newly formed Ferry Crew Training Flight. Its Wellingtons came from Kemble fitted out for the flights. The crews had additional cross country training. They were briefed, then their aircraft had a final inspection. Between May 10 and December 31 1941, 218 Wellingtons (162 Mk Ics and 56 Mk IIs) carrying 1,308 airmen were despatched from Hampstead. Four flights were made direct to Malta. Overall loss rate was 11.5 per cent with three crews being interned. By the start of 1942, transit flights started at Portreath, Cornwall.

Hampstead Norris photographed on May 19 1943, with Wellingtons of 15 OTU on dispersals. Attempts have been made to camouflage the runways which intersected in a most unusual manner (RAF Museum).

A few night diversions were now arriving, 11 Wellingtons of 214 Squadron landing from Brest on January 11 1942. This brought an influx of faces—some old, some new—as well as needs for meals, aircraft refuelling, interrogation, etc, stretching any satellite's resources.

Between January 1 and June 30 1942, 330 Wellingtons flew overseas from Hampstead or Harwell, superintended by 1443 Flight established from previous ferry organisations. A record number of 81 Wellingtons was despatched in April. By the end of 1942 a further 120 had been delivered, including Mk VIIIs and some torpedo carriers. In January 1943, 14 Mk VIIIs were despatched, but deliveries were then mainly from Harwell. Some pressure was removed from 15 OTU when, in July 1942, No 1444 FTF at Moreton, along with 21 OTU, took part of the commitment.

Hampstead remained the conversion training centre for 15 OTU, and held their gunnery section's three Lysanders. Harwell nearly lost control of the improving satellite when, in August 1942, plans were mooted for its replacement by Grove. Although 15 OTU did some flying there, such substitution never came about. Bomber Command in October 1942 reviewed Hampstead with a view to extending its runways to 2,600 and 1,400 yds whilst that month the first Ferry Command crews trained at 1443 Flight, Harwell, before flying nine Wellingtons out from Hampstead in December. On December 12 1942, six Oxfords of 1516 BAT Flight arrived from Middleton St George. The intention was that they would move to Harwell once 1443 FTF disbanded. Unexpectedly, delivery of Wellingtons to the Near East was extended, and so the BAT Flight moved instead to Pershore on April 13 1943, shortly before 310 Ferry Training Unit formed on April 30, equipped with Wellington IIs and Xs and a couple of Ansons. This unit eventually disbanded on December 17 1943.

Three Martinets replaced the gunnery Lysanders in March 1943 and both A and B Flights continued using Wellington Ics until October. In September 1943 re-equipment with Wellington IIIs and Xs started and, by November, 15 OTU had largely converted for a limited future because in March 1944 it closed. Hampstead Norris was raised to self-accounting status within 38 Group on March 1 1944. No 101 Course of 15 OTU then in training was posted to Westcott and the Wellingtons sent to Moreton and Wellesbourne.

In place of 15 OTU came the ORTU, giving refresher courses to glider pilots originally trained to take part in the airborne assault on Sicily and now being prepared for the Normandy invasion. The Operational Refresher Training Unit's equipment consisted of 33 Tiger Moths, nine Whitleys and 20 Albemarles, along with Horsas. Some elementary flying training took place at Shrewton. Use of Albemarles raised ORTU almost to operational state, and four of its aircraft performed in an RCM task during Operation *Tonga*. As company, ORTU had eight Oxfords of 1526 BAT Flight here, until it disbanded on November 9 1944.

ORTU flourished here until February 27 1945 when it moved to Matching, Essex. Hampstead reverted to being Harwell's satellite and Mosquitoes of 13 OTU arrived on March 15, mainly from 60 OTU and joined remnants of ORTU for, not until April 18 1945, was the last glider towed away. About half of 13 OTUs Mosquito IIs and IIIs were based here, staying until 13 OTU left for Middleton in July. From March 13 to July 14, Hampstead had served again as Harwell's satellite, then it was placed on Care and Maintenance. Hampstead's final use was as an accommodation centre for the Glider Pilot Regiment and redundant RAF glider pilots which role it shared with Finmere, its sister satellite.

Harrington, Northamptonshire

SP765799. 5 miles SE of Market Harborough

At Desborough 84 OTU formed on September 15 1943 with an establishment of 54 Wellington IIIs and Xs, and flying commenced on October 22 1943. Its designated satellite was Harrington, incomplete when, on September 27 1943, it received its first visitor, a Wellington of 14 OTU with engine trouble.

Harrington should have opened on November 9 1943, but failed to meet necessary requirements. The need for OTUs was, however, receding so Harrington was now to be accepted, lacking some usual features. Harrington had been built mainly by the US 852nd Engineering Aviation Battalion. Its transfer to 92 Group, RAF Bomber Command, on November 6 1943 was attended by Air Chief Marshal Sir Arthur Harris. As the ceremonial band stopped playing, three of Desborough's Wellingtons flew over, saluting the contribution of the Americans.

Not until December 26 1943 did a party come from Desborough to plan for the arrival of 84 OTU. In February 1944 the airfield remained incomplete, the intention being that this should be remedied by March 16 1944. Headquarters Bomber Command then decided that the RAF had no need of the station. All RAF personnel cleared the station before April, and 84 OTU was reduced to ¾ OTU establishment.

On March 28 1944, the 801st Bomb Group (Provisional), US 8th AAF, formed, composed of two squadrons— the 36th and 406th (Bomb) flying B-24s. The 406th arrived at Harrington on March 25 1944 and stayed until August 10 1944 when, with the 36th, it left for Cheddington to continue *Carpetbagger* operations from that station. The 801st was further expanded with the arrival at Harrington of the 788th Bomb Squadron, which left for Rackheath and the 467th Bomb Group on August 10. The 850th Bomb Squadron was also here briefly, arriving on May 11 and leaving for Eye on August 12 1944.

These squadrons had come to Harrington to support the European Resistance. They landed arms, equipment and men, and also had some C-47 Dakotas which landed, briefly, in the south of France along the lines of Tempsford's Lysanders. Previously at Alconbury, the B-24s had flown their first support sorties from Tempsford, on January 4/5, 1944.

On August 5 1944, B-24s of the 492nd Bomb Group began arriving at Harrington. This Group had incurred serious losses and its squadron numbers were now applied to units at Harrington flying *Carpetbagger* operations. Landings by Dakotas, in Vichy, France, took place in July and August 1944.

On September 16 the Group was committed to rapid delivery of cans of oil and petrol to sustain the American advance. In December 1944 the 859th Bomb Squadron moved to Italy. There was some intermittent bombing, conducted at night by the other squadrons, against airfields, oil refineries, ports and tactical targets, training for which had commenced in October. These raids began in February 1945 and continued until March 18 1945 when the Group returned to its *Carpetbagging* activity. The squadrons now employed B-24s, A-26 Invaders and Mosquito XVIs—the latter used by 856 Squadron here from September 1944 to March 1945 to drop leaflets and listen to ground signals from resistance workers. After the war the Group conveyed personnel to the Continent before returning—along with the 406th Squadron which had come back to Harrington in March—to the USA in July–August 1945.

Harrington's conversion to agricultural use was gradual before 1958. Still partly MoD property, Harrington then became a base for three Thor intermediate range ballistic missiles of 218 Squadron which, on December 1 1959, formed to operate them. Brief was the Thors' stay, bound up with their vulnerability and, one may assume, political antics. Squadron disbandment came on August 23 1963, after which Harrington was sold for agricultural purposes.

Harwell, Oxfordshire

SU465925. 5 miles S of Abingdon, by A34

Atoms and Arnhem, Wellington and Nun May, energy and excitement, turbine blades and Fairey Battles—not to mention anemometry and Ansons—all have a niche in Harwell's history. Here was sited Britain's prime nuclear research centre. Now it has become a vast, enterprising laboratory. Nuclear physics is here

AERE utilises some airfield buildings, mostly modified (AERE).

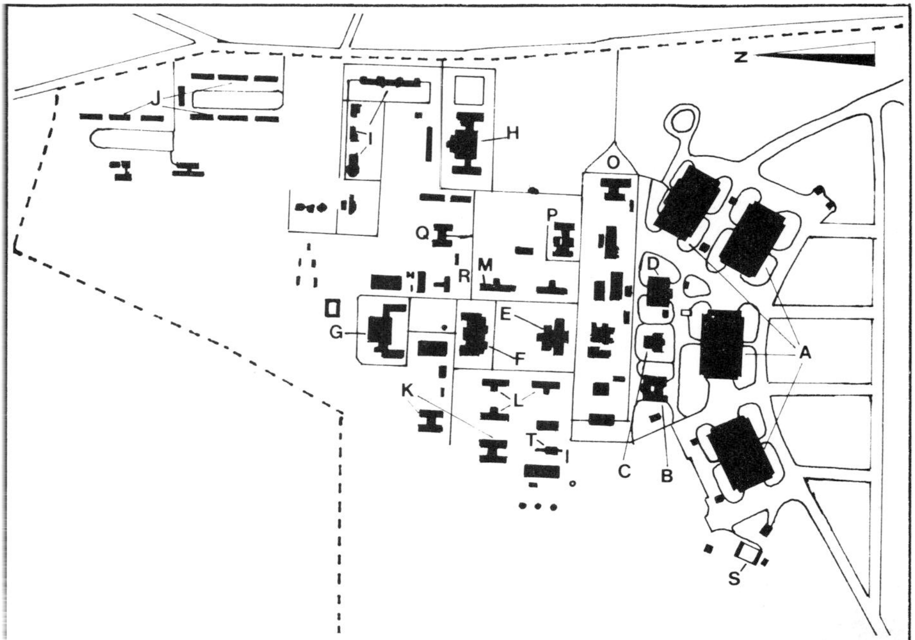

Layout of a permanent pre-war 1930s station, in this instance Harwell. The main features are: **A** *'C' Type Sheds, the most northerly Type 1583/35 having different annexes to the others.* **B** *Workshops (2048-49/34).* **C** *Armoury (2023/34).* **D** *Main Store (2057/34).* **E** *Dining Room, O/Rs and Corporals (12922-26/38).* **F** *Institute (1422-25/35).* **G** *Sergeants' Mess and Quarters (1939 design).* **H** *Officers' Mess and Quarters (288-91/34) with tennis courts alongside.* **I** *Married Officers' Quarters.* **J** *Married Airmen's Quarters.* **K** *Barrack Block Type 8/84 'H' Block (9965-67/38).* **L** *Barrack Block Type 'Q' (2272-74).* **M** *Barrack Block Type 'R' (2277-79/34).* **O** *Station Headquarters.* **P** *Former Sergeants' Mess (1105/35—single storey).* **Q** *Barrack Block Type 8/56 (11595—97/38).* **R** *Sick Quarters.* **S** *Machine Gun Range (3475/35).* **T** *Motor Transport Section.*

applied for peaceful purposes and many fields of advanced science and technology are studied. About one half of the research here is nuclear, one-third government inspired technological development, leaving the remainder of effort by the 1,000 or so scientists and engineers to be applied to meet industrial needs.

Research programmes are wide. Geothermal energy, harnessing ocean energy by use of wave energy converters, biofuels, automated rail track inspection, lasers for industrial use, submersible robots for underwater inspection of ships, even more highly sophisticated robots, research into ceramics—all and more are featured in Harwell's programmes. Aeronautical association remains, for quality control radiographic inspection, developed for the nuclear power industry, has been applied to running jet engines. Neutron bombardment of RB 211 blades has taken place in the Dido reactor to ensure that cooling fuel can flow freely within the intended blade cavities.

Non-destructive Testing (NDT) found an unusual application when, in 1976, the mechanism of the Great Clock of Westminster, old 'Big Ben', was examined. A welding failure had resulted in the heavy chiming drum being hurled across the clock room, wrecking the chamber mechanism. Harwell's investigation of the clock revealed many further flaws, including one in the hour striking mechanism. Not surprisingly the laboratory's expertise has travelled wide and variously, just as its airmen did four decades previously. As a research establishment Harwell's tasks have been widespread; aeronautically its history provides a microcosm of the history of wartime activity in the central area.

Harwell's setting is superb, with the Lambourn Hills stretching from east to west forming the southern rim. A belt of greensand combined with the close proximity of Didcot's rail link with London made fruit farming in the area viable in days gone. Official requisition of some of the Upper Chalk level countryside was followed by its use as a temporary night landing ground where, in April 1935, it was decided to build an Expansion Period bomber station. Construction commenced in June 1935 of the airfield whose features are described on pages 49-51.

Harwell came under RAF control between February 2 and 12 1937. Two weeks later, *The Times* recorded that Harwell's 220 acres had been purchased for £11,650! In April 1937, No 226 Squadron arrived from Upper Heyford with Hawker Audaxes, with which type No 105 Squadron reformed here on April 26. Both squadrons used army co-operation aircraft due to shortage of bombers. In June 1937 they were temporarily joined by four squadrons of Avro Ansons, here to participate in the Hendon Display fly-past. On June 14, Hinds of 107 Squadron moved in from Old Sarum, completing Harwell's bomber complement.

On August 18 1937, *K7571*, the first Fairey Battle to be based here, arrived for 105 Squadron which equipped fully in September, followed by 226 Squadron in October 1937. Maybe more portentous, was the November sighting of a mushroom on the landing ground.

HM King George VI and the Chief of the Air Staff, Air Chief Marshal Sir Cyril Newall visited Harwell on May 9 1938. They were received by Air Chief Marshal Sir Edgar Ludlow Hewitt, AOC-in-C, Bomber Command and the AOC 1 Group which controlled Harwell. Considerable interest surrounded the first flight of the Martin Baker MB.2 fighter at Harwell on March 3 1938.

The Battle squadrons were training realistically and, in August, 107 Squadron received Blenheim Is in time for the Munich crisis. All the Merlin 1 engined Battle 1s of 105 and 226 Squadrons were ordered to be exchanged for Cottesmore's Merlin II and Battle IIs of 35 and 207 Squadrons. These non-mobilisation squadrons were not earmarked for the AASF where Merlin I spares would not be held and, in October 1938, the switch took place. In winter the airfield became a quagmire. Surface experiments were undertaken using netting and cinders, but only concrete—or better weather—could improve it.

During May 1939, 107 Squadron moved to Wattisham, and Harwell hosted 11,000 pedestrians, 1,100 cars, 16 'charabancs' and an unknown number of German spies

Battles of 226 Squadron at Harwell (Ron Clarke).

on Empire Air Day. What they could not have discovered were the station's war plans. They were obvious, though, on September 2 1939 when the Battles now forming 72 Wing left for France.

The replacement was complete by September 17 1939 with the arrival of 75 and 148 Squadrons. Under 6 Group's control, Harwell became 3 Group Pool accommodating Wellington Is. Machine gun posts were set up around the airfield perimeter, likewise the Q-Site opened on September 3. Training featured Bomber Command's intention to operate in formation and in daylight.

By January 1940 it was clear that Bomber Command would need to operate principally at night, meaning ample navigation training for which Ansons were already in use. Conversion of some Battle squadrons to Blenheims had already commenced. Whilst it had no direct effect upon Harwell it brought exotic involvement when, on December 1 1939 with bad weather closing in, a DH 86 *G-ACVY* and a HP 42 *G-AACX* were forced to land, and proceed to France the following day. How many would flock to see an HP 42 nowadays?

Harsh realities from operational experience were relating to the Wellington trainees by Wing Commander Griffiths of 99 Squadron. He had participated in the shattering operations of December 1939 and came on January 30 1940 when it snowed heavily. The cold became intense as Harwell lay deep in snow. Rapid clearing from operational areas had been barely considered, the best means of removal being by hand and shovel. There were numerous reports on February 14 1940 of a Heinkel 111 in the area, never confirmed nor discounted. It was at about this time that Ryman and Canning devised the 'Harwell boxes', and three tall structures were built for gunnery and navigation purposes and copied at other stations.

In March 1940 the first Wellington Ias arrived at Harwell after some operational flying with 149 Squadron. On April 4 1940 both 75 and 148 Squadrons amalgamated, SHQ closed and the whole station was rejuvenated as 15 OTU on April 8 but remained within 6 Group. Its holding of Wellingtons and Ansons began increasing, an arrival of May 20 being Wellington 1 *L4265* ex-149 Squadron and one which operated against Brunsbuttel's shipping on September 4 1939. It was eventually lost without trace on March 18 1942 whilst flying a training exercise.

Action in Norway then France resulted in an expansion of operational training. It also brought, on May 24 1940, the first operational diversion to Harwell, a Whitley of 77 Squadron flown by Pilot Officer Mahaddie, later of pathfinder fame. Increased flying meant more accidents such as when an Anson, *N5186*, crashed in flames in a field near the boat dump, killing the pilot, Wing Commander Hughes.

Operational flying by 15 OTU commenced on the night of July 18/19 1940 when three Wellingtons dropped leaflets over the Dunkirk–Boulogne area. On July 23/24 three more crossed the Channel to Amiens, Cherbourg and Rouen. Dieppe, Exvreux, Beauvais and Caen were visited on July 27/28. Such activity was reckoned good for crews and recipients.

During the afternoon of August 14 some 20 Whitleys arrived from Driffield to make Harwell their point of departure and return during a long haul to Milan and back that night. Luckily they had left by the time the station received its first bombing attack, around 18:00 on August 16. The raider swept in over Rowstock and dropped four bombs. Two 400 gallon petrol bowsers caught fire, one being towed away most courageously. Three Wellingtons were destroyed and two out of seven casualties were fatal. Machine-gunning was responsible for casualties and damage. Poor station defences amounted to a few twin Vickers gun emplacements and a 3-ton Bedford lorry mounting twin Vickers guns on a Scarff ring.

Soon after midnight a further six bombs were aimed at 15 OTU, leaving neither damage nor casualties. Later that day Harwell was told to disperse aircraft and use the satellite at Hampstead, placing some AA defences there because large scale night attacks were forecast for the coming moon period. The Luftwaffe had far from finished with Harwell and during the afternoon of August 19 a Ju 88 strafed and bombed the station, destroying a further three Wellingtons. A short respite was followed by yet another attack on August 26 when bombs fell near the bomb dump. The casualties amounted to six RAF and ten civilians. That night six of Dishforth's Whitleys operated from Harwell.

These were indeed difficult days, but despite the enemy interference, and the constant invasion fears when Ansons stood ready each with 2 × 112 lb bombs, 15 OTU managed 1,594 daylight and 665 night hours of flying training, its force of 50 Wellingtons and 17 Ansons resulting in a better pupil output than larger units in 6 Group. There were many accidents, though, especially at night. Undercarriage collapse after a heavy landing was frequent, and there were bent wings, too, for night flying from grass was often hazardous. The runway was marked by about ten or so goose-necked flares, long spouted cans of paraffin fitted with thick wicks and placed so that the wind blew the flame away from the fuel reservoir. From time to time aircraft would knock them over. In addition to the lights of Harwell there were those of the large Didcot railway installation which distracted more than one pupil pilot.

In the building, now the Plastics' Technology Building, there was a bombing teacher and a Wellington fuselage for training purposes so that crews could become familiar with the aircraft's layout. Another trainer was devoted to radio aids, in all a very primitive type of flight simulator.

A Wellington 1 at Harwell in the intense cold spell of early 1940 (AERE).

Summer 1940 was a desperate period, with staff and trainees expecting the call to repel an invasion. Three Wellingtons went *Nickelling* on September 7 in a sort of defiant gesture. If any worried about balloon cables they could take comfort when, on September 18 1940, *L4322* returned safely after colliding with a cable over Yeovil. Six more *Nickel* sorties were flown, over three nights, in October 1940.

That the enemy was still around was clear on November 13 when Ju 88, *L1 + LS*, Werke Nr *6557* of LG1, which had flown across Oxfordshire, was damaged by 611 Squadron and crashed at Blewbury. Three of the crew were captured and taken to Didcot. The fourth was buried at Harwell on November 19.

King Haakon of the Norwegians visited the station on December 12. He was treated to a fly past by three Ansons one of which shed part of a cowling when pulling too steeply out of a dive. Another disaster came on March 26 1941. Sergeant Mountney and crew were detailed to take *R1243* along the Worcester–Harlech–Peterborough track, then return to Harwell. En route they were to attack sea markers in Cardigan Bay using smoke floats. As they entered the training area they inadvertently raced into sea fog.

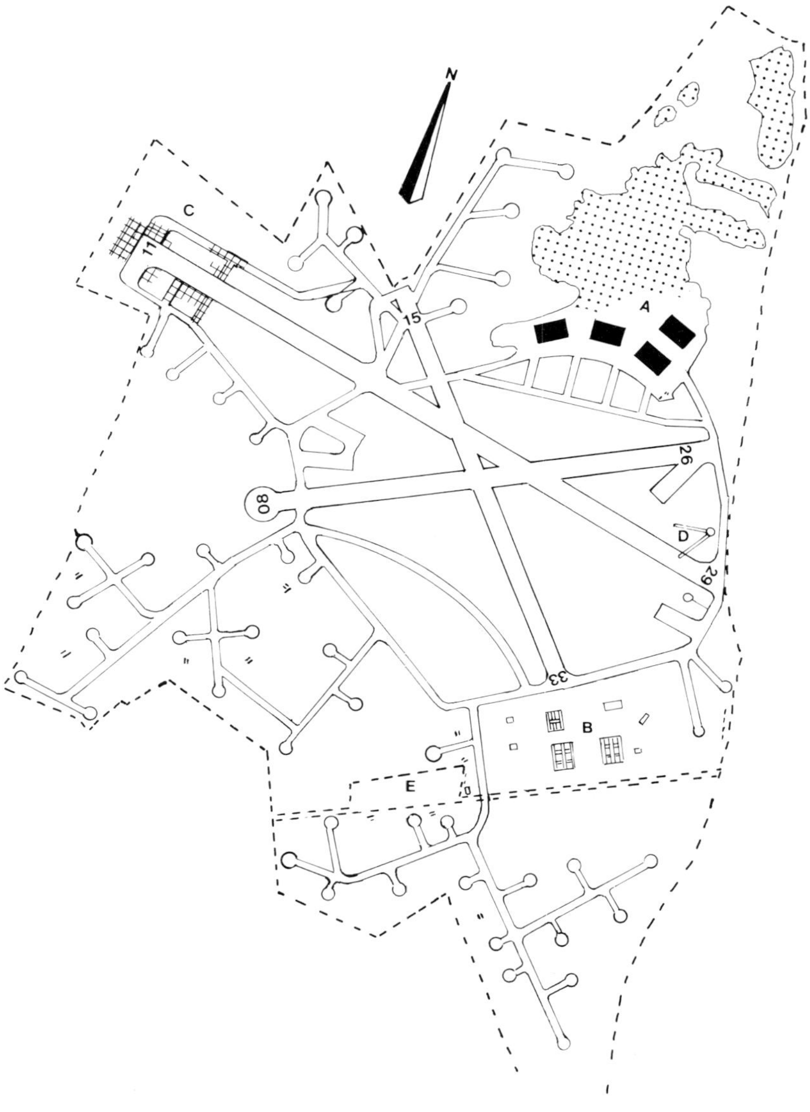

Harwell in 1945 exhibited the worst features of an OTU. The runways intersected closely making them vulnerable to bombing and highly inducive to flying accidents. The extraordinary layout of the perimeter tracking and taxi tracks, even to the extent of additional tracks leading to the hangar apron, is very obvious. The weapons dump ('B') was dangerously placed at the end of a runway—the shortest runway. Glider marshalling tracked area can be seen at 'C'. 'D' marks the position of the unusual catapult station and 'E' a civilian held farm—in no small way a hazardous position! 'A' and the shaded area is the technical site.

From Criccieth their aircraft was seen to hit the sea 1½ miles off shore. Boats were launched and two men rescued, one of whom died. Of the other four there was no further trace.

March brought two attacks on the station's Q-Site and the defences at high alert were proved on March 5. Harwell's Anson *N5078* was 12 miles north of Banbury at 20:45 when it became coned by searchlights which refused to extinguish even when the recognition signal was flashed. Therefore the aircraft's captain decided to fire the Very light colour of the day. Unfortunately the pistol discharged within the aircraft which was set ablaze forcing the crew to bale out fast.

Early on April 11 1941 the enemy came again to Harwell. After circling, a raider dived and released two bombs, repeated the action and machine gunned the station. A crew, walking between two hangars, thought they saw a cat run by. In fact it was a bomb bouncing along the tarmac which came to rest at the solid fuel dump without exploding. Another went through the superstructure on the west side of what is now Hangar 8 and came to rest unexploded under a starter trolley at the north-east corner of Hangar 9. A third bomb exploded by Hangar 2 (now No 8) while the fourth rested by the water tower. In 1946 a member of the Nuclear Physics Division dashed into Building 30 to announce that a bomb was lodged in No 8 Hangar roof. Alas, all was well—it was the tail unit of one of April's delivery of five years earlier.

Nickelling continued into 1941, the 20th operation being mounted on May 6/7. Harwell life was abruptly changed when Group HQ despatched a signal on April 30 to the effect that 15 OTU was each month to train 15 crews each of which would ferry a Wellington to the Near East. Ferrying had previously been undertaken by 3 Group squadrons who started out from Stradishall. The pattern now was for the aircraft involved to be collected from OADF Kemble by 15 OTU, and for departure to take place from Hampstead Norris from where the first three left on May 9/10 1941. On May 24 the commitment was raised to 12 crews a fortnight from the OTU, ten for ferry duty and overseas service.

June 1941 found 15 OTU the busiest in 6 Group. During 3,040 flying hours there had been 14 flying accidents and the output was 90 pilots, 40 observers and 80 radio operator/air gunners, roughly a quarter of the entire Group output.

July 18 brought news which would lead to a much improved Harwell status. Upon that day the decision was made to lay two runways of 1,100 yds and one of 1,000 yds. The station was therefore declared non-operational with effect from July 21 1941, this halting *Nickelling* until October 14 when six Wellingtons carried out Operation No 34 to central France from where *R1275* and *R1783* failed to return. The OTU had placed its A and B Flights at Mount Farm on July 24 and moved its ferrying sections to Hampstead on July 28. Flying did not entirely cease at Harwell for, while the flare path was lit, it was twice attacked on September 20. During that month 15 OTU flew 3,367 hours.

Harwell re-opened, with McAlpine's concrete runways almost completed, on November 23 1941. The Lorenz beacon lined up with the main runway, helped to maintain regular winter flying, for which Grove was to be available if ready in time.

During February 1942 the 50th Course passed out. Overseas deliveries by 15 OTU were continuing. Twenty Wellingtons set off from Harwell on the Cologne 1,000 bomber raid and two did not return. For the Essen raid 21 took off and safely returned. Bremen was attacked by 11 out of 19 Wellingtons despatched on June 25/26 and two were lost. Harwell participated in the *Grand Nationals* after which OTUs concentrated upon training—instead of operations.

The many flying accidents became memorable. In 1942 *X3209* tried a night take off, carrying a full fuel and bomb load. Half way along the runway the bomber slewed on its belly into contractor's excavations. The starboard engine burst into fierce flames whilst the crew remained inside, the aircraft too severely shocked even to leave. Wing Commander Dabinett, close by, raced to the aircraft and switched off the fuel flow, then the fire crew tackled the blaze, knowing that the aircraft had bombs aboard.

Another memorable incident involved *T2557*, returning to Harwell on August 21 1942. Its night flight about ended, the Wellington suddenly rammed into a Chipping Norton Oxford. Both showered down, a mass of flames, on to the town. Four nights later a further mid-air collision occurred. *DV595*, night flying from Harwell, collided with *N2775*, operating from Hampstead Norris and lining up for Stanton Harcourt. They collided over

Odstone Bombing Range, the pilot of *N2775* regaining control for a single-engine crash landing at Stanton. *DV595* came down near Uffington.

During summer 1942 some overseas delivery flights started from Harwell, many adventures overtaking their crews. *W5565* made an eight-hour flight from Harwell to Gibraltar in daylight on November 8 1942, then headed along the west African coast towards Bathurst but never arrived. Pilot Officer A.B. Kidson and crew had been shot down near Dakar by French fighters. In September 1942, 25 Wellingtons left Harwell for a new departure point, Portreath. Of these, 19 reached Gibraltar. One later force landed off Sicily.

Bombing raids on Italy in late 1942 attracted bombers to use Harwell as an advanced base. On November 20/21 nine Wellingtons of 420 and five of 425 Squadrons left from here for Turin. Next night they flew mining sorties. Both squadrons repeated these operations later that month. On January 7 1943 Lancaster *W4330* of 460 Squadron became the first diverted here.

Like others, No 15 OTU participated in *Bullseyes* and resumed *Nickelling* on December 4 1942. Night diversions increased, as on January 17/18 when eight Lancasters (five of 97 Squadron, one of 50 Squadron and two of 1660 HCU) landed from Berlin. 'Q' of 1660 HCU had hydraulic failure, preventing the bomb doors from opening. The load remained aboard when the aircraft landed. January 23 brought a Lancaster of 50 Squadron, from Dusseldorf. It had been intercepted by a Bf 110 which injured the mid-upper gunner.

Wellington deliveries continued into 1943; 14 setting forth in January, 20 in February. Control of the operation was by 1443 Ferry Training Flight. The 73rd OTU course passed out on February 27. A new flying control building (now containing Harwell's General Administration Department) opened on February 17 1943 as a flying and operations control centre. Watch was kept from there over the departure of 40 Wellingtons overseas as well as two *Nickelling* operations in March.

Increased sophistication failed to prevent accidents. Wellington 1c, *X3171*, on a solo cross country flight, crashed mid-afternoon on March 1 in Northumberland and the crew died. On March 3, *HF906*, practising overshoots from Hampstead Norris, was overtaken by power setting problems, then smashed into cottages at Common Barn, near Hermitage. Its crew, two civilians and livestock were killed. March 11 brought another fatal accident involving one of 15 OTU's first Wellington IIIs and, on April 3, two Wellingtons collided during circuit flying. Such an event remained unusual despite the intense activity. The risks increased during fighter affiliation and it was all too easy for a Martinet to get out of control as happened on May 11. Another problem with so many airfields about was selection of the correct runway at the right airfield. On May 19 1943, Wellington *HZ437* of 310 Ferry Training Unit, which emerged from 1443 FTF in April 1943, crashed two miles from Turweston. The wrong runway was approached and close to landing the pilot realised his error. With insufficient speed to go round again the bomber spun in.

Mediterranean departures continued from Harwell, 39 in April, 33 in May, seven in June. Operational involvement remained as in late June 1943 when 1 Group Wellingtons carried out mining, and *Nickelling* and *Bullseyes* continued into 1944. Overseas delivery flights ended in October 1943 and the FTU disbanded on December 17 1943. Still mainly equipped with Wellington Ics, 15 OTU periodically flew ASR searches. December found 15 OTU re-equipping with Wellington Xs whose stay was short for, on March 3 1944, the OTU closed.

Displaying a changed role, Harwell re-opened on April 1 1944 within 38 Group, Airborne Forces. Two Albemarle squadrons arrived, Nos 295 and 570, and with them a host of Horsa gliders, sufficient for Harwell's participation in Exercise *Dreme* on April 4. Next night ten Albemarles flew *Nickel* sorties over France and another seven on April 10. A night navigation training tour was laid on, also more sorties over France. April 16 brought Exercise *Posh*, two Albemarles of 570 Squadron acting as pathfinders, practising their part in the Normandy landings by dropping 20 troops and supplies at Winterbourne Stoke. Another three practised at Tarrant Rushton. Similar, larger exercises followed in rapid succession.

An interesting diversion was provided on May 23 by the first flight of the very fast Martin Baker MB.5 fighter, but the invasion training was paramount. By the end of May all was ready for Harwell's vital contribution to the Normandy invasion. One hour before midnight on

June 5 1944, three Albemarles from each squadron took off to spearhead *Tonga*. Each dropped ten men to set up *Rebecca* beacons to guide the main force. Another 12 Albemarles brought part of the main paratroop force, and a further 28 towed Horsas, one carrying General Gale and Divisional HQ.

Crews then rested before Operation *Mallard*, the towing of loaded Horsas to Normandy in which 38 Harwell combinations took part. SOE supply drops and further training followed. Albemarles were only stop-gap glider tugs used until sufficient four-engined aircraft were available. Harwell's first Stirling IV arrived on June 14, and a count of the aircraft available on July 11 showed 64 Albemarles, 19 Stirlings and 80 Horsas. Night SOE drop operations using Stirlings began on July 27 and continued spasmodically until early September 1944 and the next airborne assault. Before then the enemy briefly counter-attacked, using a V-1 flying-bomb which came down on August 30, destroying three grounded aircraft.

An airborne attack supporting a Rhine crossing, finalised as Operation *Market*, was ordered for September 17 1944. Shortly after 11:00, Stirlings of 295 and 570 Squadrons set off leading a giant cavalcade to Arnhem. By mid-afternoon all the Stirlings were safely home. Ground crews prepared more gliders for the morrow, a misty day forcing delay of phase II. Later, 13 Stirlings towed off Horsas and another 32 carried containers for the ground forces. Re-supply of the Arnhem force became a vital, daily task with flak taking a steady toll of the aircraft. Misty mornings delayed the operations for which extensive fighter cover was essential because the transports could little vary their routing. On September 20 fighter cover failed but Harwell's squadrons did not suffer as badly as others.

The enormity of the Arnhem failure was then clear and final supply drops took place on September 23. Fighter ground support was poor and AA guns brought down four of 570 Squadron's Stirlings. A further two had to force land. Barely had Harwell's squadrons licked their wounds when they were ordered to Rivenhall, Essex. A further stage in Harwell's history was about to unfold.

On October 12 it again hosted an OTU, No 13 under ADGB and 12 Group and the training centre for 2 Group TAF crews. Fighter-bomber Mosquito crews were to train here, but this was altered when 60 OTU merged with 13 OTU on March 1 1945. Mosquitoes were placed at Finmere, 13 OTU's satellite, and at Hampstead Norris. Aircraft of 60 OTU arrived at both satellites on March 15, and at long last 13 OTU became part of 2 Group. Harwell had housed 13 OTU's Mitchells and Bostons, flying of the latter ceasing on March 19. Harwell then held the Mitchell Wing, its strength at the end of April 1945 being 60 Mitchells, seven Spitfires and an Anson.

The last Mitchell course completed training on May 28 and 13 OTU contracted. Late July 1945 it moved to Middleton St George. On July 22, Harwell and its two satellites returned to 38 Group, the satellites being placed on Care and Maintenance. A party from the School of Air Transport arrived on July 27 but, the airfield being unready for them, they returned to Netheravon. On August 21 the School of Flight Efficiency, Transport Command, moved in followed by the Transport Command Development Unit from Netheravon on September 1. Delay had been occasioned by work on the runway intersection.

Inside the Dido Reactor at Harwell. Very prominent is the Dido rig flask for changing fuel rods, and being positioned by a travelling crane (AERE).

Barely had the units settled when they were told that Harwell was passing to the Ministry of Supply and becoming a centre for atomic research. RAF units moved to Brize Norton on December 14 1945 and the Service vacated the station on December 31.

A British atomic bomb had first been suggested in March 1940. By the end of 1942 resources and safety were more available in America to where the work was switched. By the autumn of 1944 it was obvious that Britain needed a post-war nuclear experimental establishment, the question being—where should it be? Airfields offered space, workshops, roads, water and power facilities and hangars to house the nuclear plant. Close proximity to a major university—the Clarendon or Cavendish Laboratories, at Oxford or Cambridge—was necessary.

Air Ministry listed 17 airfields which they were prepared to release, mostly with limited facilities. Preference among scientists was for a site near Cambridge with which many had associations, but Air Ministry was not keen. East Anglian airfields would retain strategic importance. When the Ministry was pressed, Duxford and Debden were offered. Radio active waste was then to be buried on site, so a low water table was essential, also ample water supply. Debden, with a high water table, was rejected, Duxford was on account of its poor water supply. Benson was considered, then Harwell. Here, the scientists decided was a most suitable area for development. Service personnel, not pleased to lose their pre-war baronial estate, were given Brize Norton to keep them happy whilst Sir John Cockcroft and his team confirmed their choice in Harwell's nearby *Horse and Jockey*.

The area and facilities seemed suitable, communications good. Perhaps with similar feelings Air Ministry produced reasons why they should not release the station. Its long runways could be used for Brabazon flying, they claimed, then the Thames Conservancy expressed concern about effluent discharge. Eventually it was agreed, Harwell it must be. On January 1 1946 the scientists took control.

A stupendous future lay before Harwell, study ranging from particle physics to large reactors. Nuclear fuels would be studied, also the production of radio isotopes for medical and industrial purposes.

By the mid-1950s, Harwell had 94 buildings, only 34 from RAF days. The large 'C' Type hangars would be used for purposes far beyond anything their originators had in mind, one now housing a large reactor. By 1957 the Atomic Energy Research Establishment had grown quite vast, so parts were hived off. The National Institute for Research into Nuclear Sciences used the original Harwell buildings. On an adjacent site was the Rutherford Laboratory under the control of the Science Research Council. In 1959 at Winfrith a new site was built to explore power reactor development. Fusion research would now be studied at Culham Laboratory whilst, at Grove airfield, research was to take place into industrial applications of isotopes until this task returned to Harwell in the 1970s. A more recent off-shoot from AERE has been a Medical Research Council unit researching into the protection of human tissues from radiation. AERE employs about three-quarters of the Harwell workforce.

Flying did not cease in January 1946, for there was an alarming episode some years later. A USAF T-33 jet trainer in trouble mistook Harwell's closed runway for an active one and landed. Once down, could he now leave? RATO bottles were strapped in place and the intrepid soul tried. Alas, the aeroplane just could not make it.

Although much work here is connected with technological development, one inevitably associates Harwell with atomic physics. For the uninitiated in a nuclear environment there is a sense of foreboding and concern at what takes place unseen. A visitor to the Dido reactor first views a model of a fuel cell along with cutaway and sectional drawings. Plastic shoe coverings are donned before entering the reactor area within which many of its functions are recorded and observed within a control room. Experiments recently run included neutron bombardment of an RB 211 turbine blade. When the proximity of anything nuclear raises all sorts of comment, wise and foolish, it is surprising to find that item so uncontaminated that it could almost be handled almost immediately after exposure. From an upper gallery one observes the apparatus needed to remove a fuel cell from the reactor which requires the rod to be encased, mechanically of course, in a lead container.

As I left the reactor chamber a device pronounced me fit and uncontaminated. Maybe I looked apprehensive because a scientist close by said to me 'I've worked here for 30 years and I've never been in trouble. I'm sure it is safe'. I think that is generally right. What use man makes of nuclear energy is his concern. He has not proved to be a very sensible being and this gift of untold power seems to be beyond the wisdom of many, let alone their comprehension. I came away from Harwell feeling that as I pass Sizewell and frequently Dounreay I shall feel a trifle more easy, just a trifle.

Henlow, Bedfordshire

TL165365. 5 miles NNW of Hitchin

'Heard the news? They've sunk *Ark Royal.*' 'Not again!' 'Yeh, it's true this time,' my friend said. For our family it held alarm, for one of 'us' was on *Ark Royal.* Luckily hardly a man was lost, a hurried visit to our relatives confirming that 'he' was safe and very soon he was with us and had a good tale to tell.

'I was in an alleyway when there was a heavy, muffled bang. I rushed onto the flight deck and at once knew the ship had been torpedoed. What surprised me was the calm way everyone was acting. One chap, though, was very excited. As the ship began to list he jumped overboard. As far as I could see he was our only casualty. I then put on as many warm clothes as I could, and made sure I had my money. Then, with many others, I lined-up on the flight deck. Some aircraft were pushed overboard to lighten the ship; others slid off, for soon she was listing badly although she wasn't sinking. In an orderly manner, we were transferred to other ships. What amazed me was the discipline shown. After what we'd been through on HMS *Furious* during the Malta runs all this seemed less frightening.'

What, you may reasonably ask, has this to do with Henlow? Well, from there those precious Hurricanes, which did so much to save Malta, set out on their gun-running carrier journeys to make world headlines and unheralded heroes out of those who made the dash—including airmen of 13 MU, Henlow.

Henlow's selection for an Eastern Command repair depot dates back to 1917 when a flat area with good communications, and near industrial Luton, was chosen. Construction started in April 1918, the first service personnel moving in on May 10 1918. They came from Farnborough to establish No 5 Eastern Area Aircraft Depot and within three months were overhauling Bristol Fighters and de Havilland aircraft. In October 1918 some 100 Americans came to work here, leaving soon after the armistice. At this time 300 women were fabric working or doing clerical work.

Soon after the armistice, repair work

Henlow Camp, in a First World War photograph, retains much the same appearance in the 1980s (RAF Museum).

was halted. Much of Henlow's equipment was to be scrapped, aircraft selling at 10s for a small one, £1 for a bomber. Just imagine their worth now! Some went to Australia, many were scrapped. Henlow hit the headlines on April 1 1919 when airmen about to be demobbed mutinied over increased working hours. Long jail sentences followed for some of the 56 tried by Court Martial.

The decision to keep the site was emphasised in February 1920 when a further 161 acres were purchased from a farmer, for a flight test airfield. March 16 1920 saw the station become the Inland Area Aircraft Depot which, by the close of 1921, was dealing monthly with about 15 engines and ten aircraft. Into Shed 186 went aircraft arriving for repairs, overhaul or modification. Engines were dealt with in Shed 187, metal work in 188 and assembly and checking prior to flight test in 189.

A wide variety of aircraft passed through the station workshops, including Fawns, Flycatchers, '504s, Grebes, Snipes, IIIFs and Vimys. From a Handley Page Hinaidi, fitted with a public address system for use in colonial territories, were once heard Shakespearean utterances which, penetrating the clouds, mesmerised Henlow's neighbourhood. Remaining at Henlow from those days is a building with a curious past. There are claims that it was intended for a 'pickle factory' built at Hendon, and that it was erected at Henlow in error instead of Northampton. Within it, large Handley Pages used to be repaired.

From Farnborough the Officers' Engineering School arrived in April 1924. Three months later the first course commenced within the Engineering Instruction Section which, variously renamed, functioned almost to the 1970s. It represented an extension of Lord Trenchard's plan in which, after five years of flying, an officer pursued a ground trade for two years.

Changes in home air defence resulted in new fighter squadrons. Suitable stations were few but, despite its poor strategic position, Henlow was chosen. On July 1 1925, No 23 and 43 Squadrons reformed, using Snipes. In April 1926, No 23 became the first Gamecock squadron. Before leaving for Kenley in February 1927, No 43 re-equipped with Gamecocks in Spring 1926, and left for Tangmere in December.

Henlow, now under 21 Group, became the Home Aircraft Depot on April 4 1926. In September 1925 the Parachute Test Section formed and in October 1926 was joined by Northolt's Parachute Training Section. This combination became the Parachute Test Unit and used Vimys. To test a parachute an airman hung on to the bomber's interplane struts, faced the direction of flight, streamed out his parachute, then allowed himself to be pulled away. This was reasonably safe, whereas a delayed parachute opening was far more hazardous. A violent death overtook LAC Dobbs of the PTU. Using a balloon to assist in lifting him over low obstacles when near Henlow, he was carried into an 11,000 volt electricity system.

On October 1 1930, Henlow's airmen pulled the *R-101* from its Cardington hangar for its fatal flight. A week later 800 of them lined Bedford's streets or took part in the funeral of those killed. Airships were linked with failure whereas the opposite was true of young Flying Officer Whittle who joined the engineering course in August 1932. This he completed in less time than usual. Whilst here his theoretical work upon gas turbines continued, planned thinking which would lead to experiments within central England bringing Britain into the forefront of gas turbine technology. In mid-1934 Frank Whittle entered Cambridge University for a two year engineering course. By chance one of his fellow officers, later Commandant at Henlow, was within our family circle. I first met him in 1933 and, while my friends were just playing, I was being indoctrinated into the world of Harts, Hendon and Henlow! It was he who brought along friend, 'Frank', for afternoon tea. Just what I would have thought had I known what device he was contemplating defies my imagination, but I can at least say that for a while we were on Christian name terms!

There is another memory I hold dear from those days as far as Henlow is concerned. Thursday brought a half day for Cambridge schools and shops providing a regular spotting time when activity was ever increasing. One windy afternoon a Henlow Virginia raced across, at a snail's pace, displaying a strong fawn tint to its supposed green finish. I watched as the big, drifting biplane turned into wind, making a very wide turn. On its reciprocal course it made slow progress and to my fascination, momentarily halted before being blown backwards for some moments before it found enough strength to head for Henlow at such a slow speed that it took over 15 minutes to pass from sight. From discussions I have had with those who flew 'Ginnies' and their cousins I know that this sort of delight was, for them, not all that uncommon. But I can only recall seeing one 'Ginny' brave a gale!

By August 1935 the RAF Expansion Scheme was making considerable demands upon ground technician provision and the Home Aircraft Depot became an airframe riggers' school. No 1 Wing trained machine tool operators and Fitter 1, Nos 2 and 3, the flight riggers and flight mechanics. New accommodation was erected in the north-west corner of the station and other huts between the road through camp and Henlow village. Training of MT drivers and operatives began here in January 1937. Next, a cookery course opened at Henlow. An offshoot of the RAF Depot, Uxbridge, was established in July 1937, an initial training unit to introduce over 1,000 men to Air Force life. There were now so many troops at Henlow that basic trainees were housed in tents. Two months later ITU moved to Cardington where huts had been erected for the 'rookies'.

By 1938 Henlow's pupil population reached 5,000 men, and Henlow had forsaken its repair role. The Parachute Test Unit remained and, since December 1936, the engineering school had been known as the RAF School of Aeronautical Engineering. Additional were three Training Wings, the MT Training School and the Pilotless Aircraft Section.

Plans called for Henlow to revert, in wartime, to being a repair depot. In September 1938 two thirds of the Training Wing moved to St Athan, and No 2 Mobilisation Pool formed to allow an increased repair role. The Home Aircraft Depot became 13 MU in October 1938 and, in April 1939, No 1 Wing moved to Halton. Only small training units remained at Henlow. Shortage of space for new squadrons caused No 80 to come from Kenley on March 15 1937 with Gauntlet IIs and to receive Gladiator 1s before moving to Debden on June 9 1937. The PAS came in October 1936 from Farnborough, its Queen Bees from January 1937 being handled by the Base Training Unit. Queen Bee Flight situated in Hangar 186A was responsible for test flying Queen Bees preparatory to their use for gunnery training. This unit moved to Hawkinge on February 22 1940.

No 13 MU was undertaking aircraft modification, manufacturing replacement parts and handling armament tasks when war began. Suggestions for a No 6 Group Pool here did not materialise, but No 21 Aircraft Depot formed and moved near to Nantes in France on September 26 1939. When the British were forced out of France, 21 AD withdrew through St Nazaire. In June 1940 some 3,000 of its officers and men re-assembled at Henlow.

Many immediately worked long hours modifying and repairing Hurricanes, about a dozen a week during the Battle of Britain. Another task was unpacking, assembling and testing Canadian-built Hurricanes.

Over 6,000 personnel were at Henlow within 13 MU, 14 School of Technical Training, the School of Aeronautical Engineering, test flying section and station staff in the summer of 1940. No 13 School of Technical Training had on role over 2,000. Soon it became 14 STT for having two 'No 13s' on the station brought problems. Enemy action against Henlow was limited but, on September 26 1940, a bomb fell between two hangars. Two houses in Station Road, Lower Stondon, were demolished and three servicemen killed. In another raid a bomb passed across the roof of Hangar 530 and into soft ground.

In 1941, 13 MU prepared for Operation *Quick Force*. Parties of fitters, numbering between 50 and 100, served on aircraft carriers—in particular HMS *Furious*, their task to dismantle Hurricanes for shipment to Malta. About 30 men sailed with the Hurricanes and prepared them for flying off the carrier's deck when it was about 300 miles west of Malta. The last of these voyages was aboard *Ark Royal* when she was torpedoed by the *U-81* on November 14 1941. Seven survivors reached Henlow on November 22 1941.

Parachute trials had long taken place at Henlow so, when an airborne troop force was formed, authorities looked here for instructors. For parachute testing the three ancient Virginias were not replaced until 1941 when Whitleys arrived. Later development work involved Dakotas and a Halifax for trials of the delivery of material and weapons to resistance forces.

No 13 MU maintained and modified many aircraft, in particular Hurricanes, Mosquitoes and Typhoons. Between June 1940 and October 1943, 1,004 Canadian Hurricanes were erected and tested at Henlow. Many Bristol radial engines were handled and modifications to Halifaxes made, among them the fitting of rectangular fins and rudders and, to some aircraft, 'Z' Type noses. During March 1943 a Whitley IV was modified to enable it to snatch personnel from the ground by means of a long line. Another 13 MU idea was the mobile link trainer for Continental squadrons. Three satellite sites were used, one built in 1939 north-west of the camp, a second close to Meppershall water works and a third near Clifton village.

When I visited Henlow on April 19 1944 a mixture of Mosquitoes was spread around the field, keeping company with Hudsons—among them a grey/green example from Tempsford. I noted a half yellow Blackburn Shark—dusty, complete, wings folded, the last example I was to see. Adjacent were two Hawker Fury biplanes, an 'all silver' Hind, a Gladiator and a Fulmar. Plenty of Mosquitoes were flying, and a few Typhoons too.

Henlow's post-war status as a technical training centre was enhanced before it became involved with radio engineering. Accommodation for the 1948 Olympic Games contestants forced the Signals Development Unit to vacate West Drayton and, on October 19 1947, move to Henlow where it functioned from August 21 1948 and was renamed the Radio Engineering Unit on January 1 1950. Other changes at Henlow had taken place, the School of Aeronautical Engineering becoming the Technical College on August 15 1947. Courses were given for senior engineering officers. Then 13 MU began to close, also closing was No 3 Ferry Pool, another 24 Group unit here.

The association with RAF Debden commenced on October 20 1949 when its Empire Radio School became Signals Division, RAF Technical College—which moved to Henlow on April 8 1960. Its Armament Division at Manby, once the Empire Armament School, moved to Lindholme in 1949 and to Henlow in February 1951 to become the Engineering and Armament Division, Technical College, renamed yet again in March 1951 as 'Henlow Division'. No 1 Recruit Centre was here for a year, prior to returning to Cardington. It had held 1,000 men, and, by the time it left, was No 1 Recruit Training Squadron. No 14 STT amalgamated with 10 STT Kirkham on June 6 1952. Vacant space was taken over by the Technical College which had barracks converted for technical training. The Sergeants' Mess became students' quarters and huts remaining from 1918 were providing modernised accommodation. From April 1951 the school offered courses in guided weapons technology.

Henlow was raised to Group status, under an Air Commodore, in June 1953. When Debden Division arrived in 1960, Technical College embraced HQ and five Wings—Basic Studies, Mechanical Engineering, Electrical Weapons Systems, Engineering and Cadet Wing. This was short lived for, on December 31 1965, it amalgamated with the RAF College, Cranwell.

Thenceforth Henlow's use was varied. It undertook work for the RAF Museum and had a part in the Battle of Britain film and in *The Magnificent Men in their Flying Machines*. RAF bandsmen have brought joyful notes to the camp, while the positioning of the English Electric *P:1-WG760* was an incongruous sight by buildings housing the Officer Cadet Training Unit which arrived from Feltwell in 1966. By 1970 only four original wooden huts remained, three being used for messing and social purposes. A much reduced Parachute Test Unit provided another link with the past.

Officer cadet training here ceased on April 24 1980 and a depleted station passed, on March 21 1980, to the Radio Engineering Unit which, on January 1 1975, had celebrated its 25th year at the camp which it shares with the Land Registry.

Henlow 1983 presents a trim image of days far gone. For thousands it remains the place where they learned their 'trade', did their 'square bashing', worked staggering hours to prepare aircraft vital for Britain's survival and that of Malta, too. For some it will recall the 1914-18 days; for me it will be the place through which my interest in the RAF was born.

Hinton-in-the-Hedges, Northamptonshire

SP545370. 2½ miles W of Brackley

Hidden among its hedges, this airfield is named after Sir William and Lady Hinton who lived in manorial style in the 1300s. What the incumbents would have made of the goings on of the 1940s defies imagination! The airfield is most easily reached by a narrow road off the A422, about four miles west of Brackley. Sharp left and right turns lead into another narrow lane which wends it way to

Walltree Farm, once part of the airfield of which a few battered buildings remain. The hangars have gone, but the shell of the control tower remains with parts of the peritrack and runways.

Hinton's remoteness may be the reason for its usefulness. It opened in November 1940 when 13 OTU's Bicester-based aircraft used it. Between March and May 1941 the airfield was not used. On May 5 1941, D Flight of 13 OTU placed its Ansons' navigational trainers here. Blenheims from Bicester flew circuits and, in October 1941, A Flight brought its Blenheim IVs.

In July 1942 Hinton became the satellite of 16 OTU Upper Heyford when Croughton was transferred to Flying Training Command. Finmere became 13 OTU's new satellite. Hinton's alliance with 16 OTU's Wellington 1cs was somewhat brief for, in April 1943, its A Flight left Hinton for Barford St John. Most unusual things followed.

July 1942 had seen the formation at Upper Heyford of 1473 Flight which also used Finmere for an assortment of radio trials. No 1478 Flight, an offshoot, formed at Hinton on April 15 1943 as part of the Signals Development Unit. The flight's role was highly specialised, it would employ five Whitley flying radio stations over a battle area whilst assault troops went into action. Equipped with point-to-point VHF, R/T, M/F D/F and R/T, radio contact with forward troops could be made and details of the battle situation relayed to rear areas.

The prototype radio station Whitley V, *BD286*, was with 1473 Flight Finmere when 1478 Flight formed. Operational aircraft came to Hinton where Marshall of Cambridge fitted the radio installations. The first two aircraft modified, *Z6977* and *Z9165*—the latter a veteran from 51 Squadron—were set aside for training. *Z6977* had aged Merlin engines and quickly became unusable. The Whitley was an excellent aircraft for the intended purpose, being able to operate from small airfields even at maximum weight. That included radio gear such as Types 9, 11 and 14 Radio Stations. Eventually only Type 9 was fitted because the weight of petrol-driven generators was high. These Whitleys sprouted numerous radio aerials, otherwise they externally resembled normal examples. On April 18 1943, *BD286* arrived at Hinton, and was soon joined by *BD203, LA854, LA887* and *LA889*. Long-range tanks were installed in their bomb bays and, early in June 1943, the four production machines left for Portreath. They vacated Cornwall on June 12 for North Africa, *LA889* encountering trouble over the Bay of Biscay so some radio gear to be discarded. After refuelling at Marrakech it left to help control the ground situation from off Algiers, a task also undertaken by others reaching the area via Casablanca and Oran. Whitleys are not generally associated with the Mediterranean war; and this was a rare event. The Flight consolidated itself at Maison Blanche before disbanding on June 30 1943.

A taste for the unusual remained Hinton's to the end of its active military days, with the Signals Development Unit on the station using mainly Ansons and Beaufighters. The Unit, which arrived in mid-1943, had absorbed 1551 BAT Flight on April 15 1943 and had in its A Flight Masters, Oxfords and Ansons for development of beam approach systems. B Flight undertook calibration duties. At the end of July 1944, SDU moved to Honiley and Hinton was put on to Care and Maintenance. Flying continues, the Aquila Gliding Club operating from a site which is mainly agricultural land.

Hockley Heath, West Midlands

SP155735. W of Hockley Heath, by A34, 10 miles SSE of Birmingham

Hockley Heath, a small grass Relief Landing Ground, came into use in 1941 for training organisations. Four Laing huts (1032/41) afforded barrack accommodation for NCOs and men. Another served as officers' accommodation and their Mess. Flight offices were in a Nissen hut. There was a water tank and a 4,000 gallon fuel tank, and most buildings were in the south-east corner of the airfield. There were six Blister hangars, one a Double Blister. The landing ground had diagonal runs of 4,000 ft and had an area of 3,000 square ft.

First to use Hockley Heath was Church Lawford in 1941-2. During 1942-3 it was 14 EFTS Elmdon's satellite landing ground. Between February 1943 and November 1944 5 GTS used Hockley. The Glider Instructors' School used the RLG until early February 1945. Harvards of No 20 FTS operated from the site in mid-1945. Hockley Heath was abandoned in 1948.

Honeybourne, Hereford and Worcester

SP025300. 2 miles NW of Weston Subedge by A4035

Follow the A46 Stratford road out of Broadway, at Weston Subedge turn sharp left to Honeybourne. Turn left at the first cross roads and Honeybourne is to the right, retaining a 'J' Type hangar and a variety of buildings. Honeybourne, of 1941 style, had buildings of temporary brick and 1940 design, including the existing control tower. Little is to be seen of the three runways, No 1 05/23, No 2 11/75 and No 3 17/35, and little remains of the 31 circular dispersal pads. Most lay on the west and north-west sides of the airfield. There were four 'T2' hangars (12705/40 pattern) at Honeybourne.

Some wartime Laing huts (14887/40) for 32 men and an NCO have survived. Identical buildings served as Officers' Quarters, but each then contained six officers and 'two servants'. Maybe officers physically require more space than other slimmer ranks! In similar buildings resided up to 27 air women and a lady NCO. Strange because one expects WAAFs to be of more slender form than airmen, at least for much of the time!

The main entrance to the camp was on the eastern side, still easily recognisable. Two aviation fuel dumps each contained 72,000 gallons, and there were three EWS tanks, each of 20,000 gallons capacity. In front of the hangars were four ground defence 'trenches' known as 'Oakington Pillboxes'.

As early as December 3 1940 the station's future was decided. It would be a 6 Group OTU, using nearby Long Marston as its satellite. In October 1941 the RAF arrived. Unexpectedly, the initial occupants were units of 44 Group responsible for ferry duties.

In November 1941 the Service Ferry Squadron at Kemble became the Ferry Training Unit, moved to Honeybourne mid-November and, on November 18, commenced training crews to ferry Hudsons and Beauforts.

For company the FTU had 1425 Flight which had formed at Prestwick on October 30 1941 to operate a ferry service for passengers and freight to the Middle East, with a trans-Africa route preceding return from West Africa. The Flight moved to Honeybourne on November 16 1941 with an establishment of three rare Liberator Is. Three crews were trained to fly them, and operated under the command of Squadron Leader N.M. Boffee, DFC. Since both were units of Ferry Command they were lodgers at Honeybourne, remaining until a planned OTU formed. Flying training using Liberators commenced on November 25 1941, crews for '1425' being aided by experienced members of 120 Squadron, some of whose aircraft at Prestwick, awaiting conversion into maritime Liberators, would revert to being transports.

A typical Maycrete hut near one of Honeybourne's 'T2' hangars.

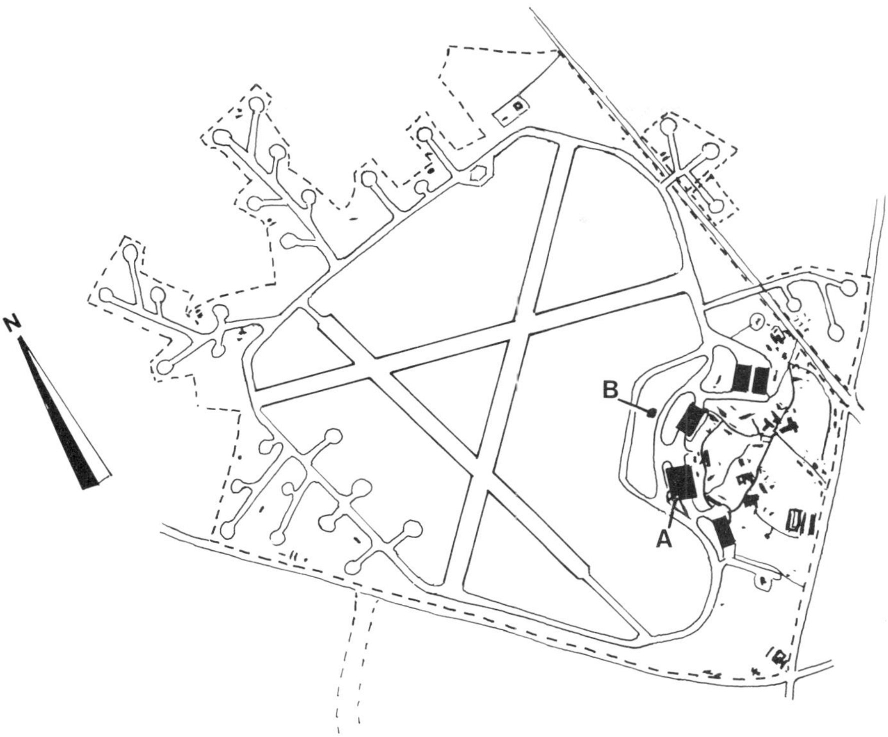

Honeybourne during the last year of war exhibited many standard features on an airfield of 1939/40 vintage with a main (roughly NE/SW) No 1 Runway and a 'J. Type hangar ('A') and four 'T2s'. The early style of brick control tower is marked at 'B'. The track leading off the map southerly leads to the weapons store. Dispersal areas were far better sited here than at many stations, involving the minimum of taxi tracking and easy parking after landing on most days—at a time when crews were most vulnerable to accidents.

January 1 1942 brought to Honeybourne *AM913*, 1425's first Liberator 1. On January 6 came *AM922* the second, not fully equipped as a transport. Introduction of the service had been delayed, the provisional date having been December 15 1941. Snow fell throughout January, the FTU managing only 14½ days of flying that month. February was little better.

Liberator sorties started from Hurn, to where *AM913* was despatched on January 9 1942 and left that evening, commencing the runs with a modest load of one passenger and 2,500 lb of freight. Return to Hurn came on January 28 1942 after the inaugural round trip. *AM919* had arrived at Honeybourne on January 24 1942, but flew no operational sorties whilst based here. The second trip was by *AM922* which left Hurn on February 10. Before any Liberators went to Hurn they flew a height/range fuel consumption trial ensuring sufficient endurance.

Just as services were underway Squadron Leader Boffee was, on February 26 1942, called to Lyneham to discuss a move to this station. He could have travelled by Miles Monarch *X9306* of the Station Flight, an aeroplane surviving as *G-AFJU*.

During March, while the Liberators

Honeybourne's 'J' Type hangar, still in good condition.

made lengthy journeys, the FTU trained crews to ferry aircraft overseas, before beginning to move to Lyneham on March 10 1942, and finally vacating Honeybourne on March 28 1942. No 1425 Flight moved to Lyneham in early April 1942, that station having taken on Hurn's role.

Whilst the FTU was moving, Honeybourne's 24 OTU came alive, forming on March 15 1942. Instead of Wellingtons it equipped with Whitleys, five of which at once floated in. By the end of April 1942 the Unit had only ten Whitley Vs and two Ansons and was unable to participate in the Cologne 1,000 bomber raid. Whitley strength increased in May–June, A Flight aircraft identifiable by FB coding and B Flight by the letters TY. Sufficient Whitley Vs were available for 16 to participate in the Bremen 'Thousand Plan' raid, a costly venture with three Whitleys being lost, *BD379* coming down in the Netherlands. Mainly fire bombs had been carried amounting to 50,494 lb of small incendiaries, 288 × 30 lb incendiaries and 22 HE bombs.

A second operation came on July 31 1942, when 24 OTU's Whitleys attacked Düsseldorf, losing two of their number. Output from 24 OTU, using 54 Whitleys and five Ansons, was 14 crews per fortnight. On June 21 1942, Battle *L5416* was assigned to Honeybourne then, in August, two Lysander target towers arrived. The Battle flew away in October, but Lysander strength was maintained until May 1943. On October 14 1942, three C-47s flying from Burtonwood to Keevil, had to land at Honeybourne due to bad weather. A pernicious fate overtook Whitley *EB389* on the night of December 9/10 1942. It exploded in flight falling in pieces near Shipston-on-Stour.

Spasmodically during 1943 Whitleys dropped leaflets over France. Five sorties were flown in January, but February's weather prohibited such activities and forced Avro Tutor *K4817* to land here on February 7 1943. Returns to HQ 91 Group in March showed the Unit's strength as 55 Whitleys, 11 Ansons, a Defiant and two Lysanders. These target towers were replaced on April 28 1943 by three Martinets. Doubtless the latter were as disappointed as we not to have been spotting at Honeybourne on March 11 1943 when Bermuda *FF557* put down for refreshment on its way to a time of trial at Boscombe Down.

Five *Nickels* were flown in May then, on June 2 1943, the inevitable happened. High ground to the east of Honeybourne is very apparent, and hillside crashes expected. Such fate befell *Z6639* in cloud and rain at night time and the crew perished.

Six *Nickels* were flown in June, seven in July, for the loss of one aircraft. By August, 24 OTU had a few Whitley VIIs surplus to Coastal Command's needs, maintaining establishment at 40 IE plus 14 IR aircraft. To enjoy the sight of them—and doubtless write down their serials and maybe peep to see if there really were 27 slim WAAFs in each barrack block—the AOC winged in on August 21 1943 in his 91 Group CF Monarch, *W6464*, once *G-AFJZ*. Ten days later a visitor arrived in more alarming circumstances. On approach, Wellesbourne's Wellington *XN-I-HE356*, hit electric cables near Honeybourne church and burst into flames. All the crew escaped, only one having serious injuries.

By September 1943 Whitleys were participating in *Bullseye* exercises. *BD368* failed to return from *Nickelling* on September 3 1943, 91 Group's only loss that month.

Only a few powered Hamilcar Xs were produced, and stored at both Honeybourne and Lyneham (British Aerospace).

In October, 12 leaflet dropping sorties were despatched and ten in November. Of 91 Group's December effort of 78 *Nickels*, 21 were flown by 24 OTU which still had some Mk VIIs. In January 1944, the OTU flew 16 of the Group's 85 *Nickel* sorties and dropped 756,880 leaflets out of the Group total of 9,871,258. On January 21, 24 OTU took part in the most alarming *Bullseye*, with Green Park in London as target to be followed by a demonstration of target indicators at Otmoor. Six OTUs took part, 24 OTU flying at 13,500 ft when the Luftwaffe also attacked London.

Adding incentive to *Nickelling*, OTUs were authorised in March 1944 to carry bombs. Both 10 and 24 OTU would each make a dozen Whitleys available, half carrying SBCs and the remainder each carrying 4 × 500 lb GP HEs additional to leaflets. In March 1944, 24 OTU flew 20 *Nickel* sorties and, on March 24/25, took part in a *Bullseye* routed over France, a diversion for an attack on Berlin.

On February 8/9 1944 Whitleys dropped *Nickels* over Versailles and Paris. One crew had a lucky escape when their aircraft was badly damaged by enemy fire. With wings, rear turret and fuselage shot about, the aircraft was guided safely to Exeter. Poor weather reduced *Nickel* sorties to 11 in April, additional to *Bulls-*

Some of the first Liberators to operate from Britain were based at Honeybourne.

eyes and two diversion sweeps flown over the North Sea.

Whitley replacement was long overdue. With ample Wellingtons available, the switch came in April, the establishment changing to 54 Wellington III/X on April 20 1944. By June strength equated establishment, with four Hurricane IVs replacing the Martinets of C Flight, although it was August before they left. The last Whitley vacated 24 OTU in July, but Ansons soldiered on to the end of the year.

Disbandment of the OTU came on July 24 1945. Wellingtons of 21 OTU, nudged out of Enstone due to runway work, were at Honeybourne from August 11 to October 6 1945. Honeybourne then passed to 8 MU under the title 107 Sub Storage Unit. With so many Wellingtons to tend, 8 MU placed many of them here and, in January 1946, some 50 Hamilcar gliders joined them, awaiting the same fate as Honeybourne.

Honiley, Warwickshire

SP300395. 1 mile NW of Honiley village by A4177

Honiley was intended to be a training station but its strategic situation led to a change of plan. In mid-May 1941 some Defiants of 96 Squadron needed an advanced base for night fighter patrols, and Honiley was chosen.

On June 1 1941, 605 Squadron, significantly the County of Warwick Squadron, replaced 308 Squadron at Baginton and used Bramcote as a satellite for night operations. Late July the squadron began using the landing ground which 96 Squadron had used, known as Ramsey, renamed Honiley on August 3 1941 and held by 9 Group. No 457 Squadron's Spitfires made brief use of Honiley before leaving for Jurby, Isle of Man, on August 7 1941. As 605 Squadron re-equipped with Hurricane IIbs, it passed its Mk IIas to 135 Squadron.

Late August 1941 marked the start of the new moon period and 605 Squadron positioned itself at Honiley for possible night operations. Honiley, now fully open, was far superior to Baginton and by September 5 1941, 605 Squadron had moved in along with SHQ Baginton. No 135 Squadron followed.

During October 1941, 605 Squadron moved overseas, Midlands fighter cover being provided by Atcham's aircraft. When 135 Squadron proceeded overseas in November its place was taken on November 7 1941 by 16 Hurricanes of 257 (Burma) Squadron from Coltishall, control being vested in High Ercall. No 257 day fighter squadron changed its role to night defence. On November 24 1941, No 1456 (Turbinlite) Flight formed and received Havocs fitted with airborne searchlights. Much effort was devoted to the Turbinlite which was already outclassed by AI radar. Attempts to reap some reward continued and, by January 1942, Hurricane IICs had joined 257 Squadron, to fire at raiders lit by the Havocs' searchlights.

By March 1942, training for AA gunners and searchlight crews was being afforded from Honiley by B Flight of 285 AAC Squadron. No 56 Squadron had a Typhoon detachment here briefly, under famed 'Cocky' Dundas. Hurricanes of 79 Squadron were now responsible for day operational states at the station, but the main occupants remained 257 Squadron and the Havoc Flight. On March 27 1942, 134 Squadron staged through on its way overseas. Baginton remained Honiley's satellite.

Squadron Leader Wykeham-Barnes took command of 257 Squadron on May 1 1942. Enemy night activity had increased with the *Baedeker* raids to challenge which A Flight 257 Squadron went to Hibaldstow.

Honiley became busy on May 30 1942 as 255 Squadron started to move in, its Beaufighter VIf night fighters coming on June 6 1942 as 257 Squadron and the Havocs of '1456' moved to High Ercall. Possibilities of sharp attacks on Birmingham prompted the Beaufighters' arrival, but the Sector remained remarkably quiet while crews were at readiness and flew defensive patrols. Early on June 25 1942 Flight Sergeant Kendall and Pilot Officer Hill of 255 Squadron fired at a raider NE of Coventry making theirs the first Honiley guns to fire in action.

A sharp attack on Weston-Super-Mare was mounted on June 29 and Honiley's Squadron patrolled without doing trade. The nearest it came to success was on July 28 when between 20 and 30 enemy aircraft operated widely over the Midlands, scattering incendiaries and high explosives. Flight Sergeant Kendall in *X7931* sighted a raider and received six German bullets for being too inquisitive.

From Cherbourg, in the early hours of July 31, more enemy aircraft operated

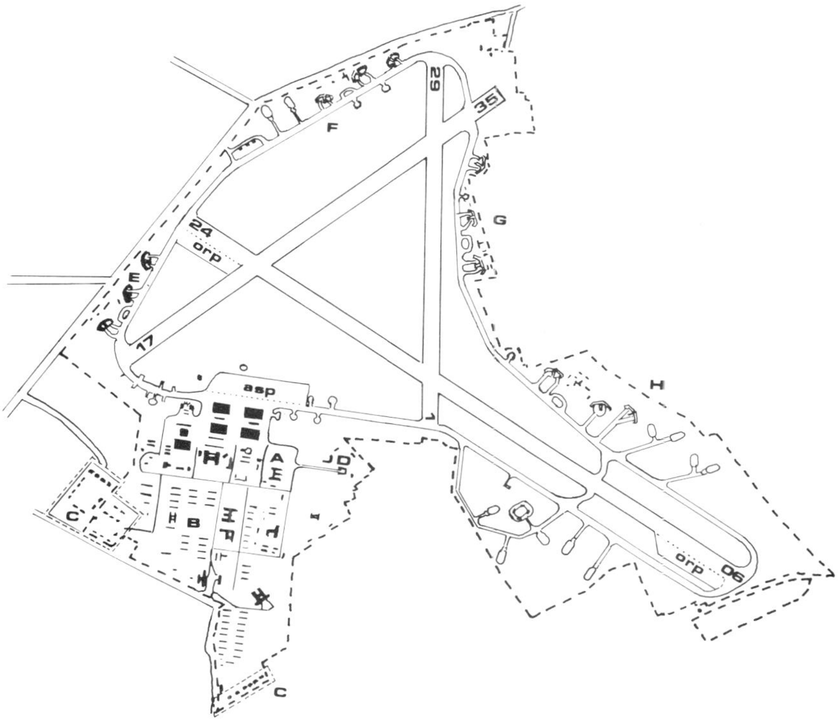

Honiley was a fighter station developed from an intended bomber OTU station—hence the typical rectangular layout of the technical site and, to its rear, the domestic site. The wartime typical three-runway layout has been altered by the extension of the 24/06 runway to the north-east. Operational readiness platforms have been built (in concrete) at either end, and an aircraft servicing platform added in front of the hangars, so that Honiley became a typical 1940s/60s fighter station. Four dispersal areas (marked 'E', 'F', 'G' and H,) were added, complete with protecting revetments and post-war style pans, the latter being skilfully placed at the end of the main runway to enable very rapid reaction. 'A' marks the technical site, 'B' the lines of hutted accommodation, 'C' Married Quarters, 'D' the firing butts.

over the Midlands. Flying Officer Wyrill, piloting *X7933* in the Gloucester area, saw a raider, closed to 200 yds and fired as the enemy returned the compliment. Luck was out again. Both 285 Squadron's B Flight and part of 116 Squadron were still training ground defences.

At 01:00 on August 5 1942, 20 enemy aircraft were located flying north-west off Cardiff. Again 255 Squadron was ordered to intercept without success. This and the AAC squadrons stayed awhile, joined by Beaufighter IIs of 96 Squadron's A Flight on June 9 1942. Hurricanes joined the circuit on September 9 1942 when 32 Squadron came for a brief stay before going overseas on October 19 1941. Briefly here was 41 Squadron at a period of rapid squadron changes which brought the remainder of 96 Squadron to Honiley in October, complete with newly received Beaufighter VIfs which were at readiness by the time 255 Squadron left for North Africa in mid-November. Next month witnessed the passage of yet more Beaufighters, this time of 153 Squadron transferring from Ballyhalbert to Gibraltar via Portreath.

Few raiders over the Midlands prompted the question of finding useful employment for 96 Squadron. On April 14 1943, four crews flew to Ford from where, during the new moon period, they operated *Ranger* Flights over France and attacked locomotives before returning to Honiley on April 23. A similar detachment took place between May 15 and 23, and 21 *Ranger* sorties were flown by the Honiley based squadron over the two periods.

Honiley provided the lair for a completely new sound at this time. On April 20, 91 Squadron arrived with Spitfire Vbs. The following afternoon three Griffon-engined Spitfires touched down and 91 Squadron commenced re-equipment with Spitfire XIIs next day. Their stay was brief for, on May 9, the squadron's seven Mk XIIs, three Mk Vbs and a Tiger Moth moved to Wittering.

May brought along Beaufighter VIfs dressed in USAAF markings, part of the 414th Fighter Squadron, VIIIth Fighter Command, here for night training before leaving for Portreath and north-west Africa on June 30. July was a month of moves too. No 96 Squadron hurriedly left the line and 130 Squadron's Spitfire Vbs arrived. On the 10th ground personnel of 234 Squadron arrived in three Harrows from Church Stanton.

The first task for the Squadrons' pilots was to fly fuel consumption tests, led by Mitchells of 98 Squadron also unexpectedly ordered to be at Honiley by July 15. Here the force stayed for two weeks, unaware of what was secretly afoot. Intelligence sources had scent of a German attack on Portugal to meet which this special group had formed. The main problem was how to get it into Portugal in a hurry. By early August the scare had passed so the Spitfires went to West Malling, the Beaufighters to Church Fenton and the Mitchells back to 2 Group.

Honiley was quickly filled by a new OTU, No 63, formed in 9 Group on August 17 1943 to specialise in AI training. Initially it had a nominal strength of 34 Beaufighter IIs, ten Beaufort IIs, a couple of Blenheim Vs (*AZ897* and *BA156*), three Martinets, two Magisters and a Dominie. Opening day was August 24 and the unit was strengthened in October 1943 by five Wellington XI AI 'flying classrooms' for navigators' use. These specialised and closely guarded aircraft—serial numbers *MP529, '533, '535, '546,* and *'562*—were here only briefly. Sufficient AI observers were soon trained, 63 OTU closed on March 21 1944 and the Wellingtons moved to Cranfield on March 31.

To make room for these Wellingtons, No 2 Squadron (Air Gunnery) of the OTU had moved to Chedworth and returned to Honiley in January 1944 when No 1 Squadron of 63 OTU closed. A night conversion course for single-engined fighter night duty commenced in February 1944 but closed in March.

Removal of the OTU freed Honiley for operations once more, the Honiley Sector opening on March 31 1944. Mosquito XVIIs of 219 Squadron briefly sojourned here and, now that the Sector was open, the station began accepting aircraft diverted from home bases during night operations.

On May 10 1944 a Typhoon detachment from 3 Tactical Exercise Unit, Annan, began moving. Around D-Day, 3 TEU was detached to Acklington to prevent air attacks in that area and to free Honiley for any urgent use during the invasion period. On July 14, 3 TEU left for Aston Down and, next day, Honiley was transferred to 26 Signals Group, Bomber Command. By the end of July the Signals Development Unit was moving in from Hinton-in-the-Hedges. From this the Signals Flying Unit formed here on July 20 1944 using Ansons, Beaufighters, Wellingtons and Oxfords which together comprised the Signals Development Wing.

Its task was radio calibration, development of new radio aids and trial installations of special equipment. More portentous was the work of the Ground Controlled Approach Wing whose mandate was to develop talk-down approach procedures mainly for the rapidly expanding Transport Command, and to train crews in its use. Much of the work was conducted with Wellington XIIIs. Such specialised work attracted assorted aircraft types including Stirlings, Venturas, Hudsons, Spitfires and Mosquitoes. A controlling Sector Room was retained until December 1944 in case of emergencies.

Until the summer of 1946, SFU used Honiley then left for Watton. Reserve

Command took control on August 31 1946 and Honiley became the home of 605 (County of Warwick) Squadron reformed on May 10 1946 and given a few Mosquito NF 30s. Vampire 1s began replacing them in July 1948, No 605 becoming the first RAuxAF squadron to fly the type. After three years these were in May 1951 replaced by Vampire 5 fighter bombers.

Bramcote was unsuitable for Jets so 1833 RNVR Squadron moved to Honiley to complete conversion via Sea Vampires to Attacker FB 2s with which it was re-armed by October 1955. Doubts about the future of reserve squadrons arose over the cost and there were complications in training part-time pilots to operate complex aircraft. As a result both reserve squadrons disbanded on March 10 1957. Honiley closed to flying, passed on to Care and Maintenance on April 15 1957 and closed on March 1 1958. It was subsequently administered by Gaydon until it was sold in July 1961.

Kelmscot, Oxfordshire

SU240980. 2½ miles SE of Lechlade

Immediately north of Kelmscot village, land was requisitoned for an 'L'-shaped landing ground. It had further strange characteristics for, in its prime of life, it attracted only 11 buildings in a small group on its north-west side. They included one Over Type Blister hangar (12512/41), a dining and recreation hut and two Handcraft Type airmens' barrack huts (2886/42). A 36 ft × 16 ft Nissen hut served as a dispersal hut and another (10024/41) served as a control building in lieu of a control tower. Kelmscot, Watchfield's RLG, was used for beam approach training.

Two miles east of the Faringdon–Barford road was the outer marker, an inner marker being sited at the threshold to No 1 Flying Lane. The main beacon lay west of the landing strip. There were no runways in the usual sense, but instead a flying lane (vector 09/27) or grass landing strip 1,400 yards long and 50 yards wide. Two other very short flying lanes were roughly orientated north/south and north-west /south-east. The long lane was used by Oxford pilots practising blind approach techniques. For this purpose Kelmscot came into use on October 17 1942, remaining on hand for No 1 Blind Approach School until the end of 1946.

It knew one other period of different usage. For a week in May 1944 it was closed to flying and used as a dropping zone for paratroops brought overhead in Dakotas of 46 Group. These drops, last minute preparations for the Normandy assault, commenced on May 7 1944 with Exercise *Noggin*, an early morning drop of the 1st Polish Parachute Brigade, from 18 of Down Ampney's Dakotas. On May 8, 50 Dakotas in Exercise *Nark*—ten from each of five squadrons—brought troops of the 1st Polish Brigade in greater number. Release was lower and in one case from an aircraft too low. As a result a stick of paratroops overshot the DZ incurring casualties, four of which were fatal.

May 10 brought Exercise *Noggin II* in which 50 Dakotas delivered troops of the 2nd Polish Brigade. On the following day Exercise *Nark II* took place here. This time 49 Dakotas provided the airlift in addition to which five acted as pathfinders. Operating from Down Ampney, the troops were again of the 2nd Polish Brigade. Exercise *Nark III* mounted on May 12 comprised 27 Dakotas and two pathfinders, the aircraft being drawn from Nos 48, 233 and 271 Squadrons. These were relatively small exercises compared with some others, but made good use of Kelmscot which could, briefly, be said to be taking a part in the invasion preparations.

Kiddington (also known as Glympton), Oxfordshire

SP438230. 5 miles NW of Woodstock, off A34, 1 mile NE of Glympton

Kidlington's RLG opened near Glympton in the summer of 1940, and Harvards and Oxfords of 15 SFTS used the field in 1940–41. Further use was made by Kidlington's glider OTUs in 1942. Early in 1943 it came under 20 (P) AFU which used it, spasmodically, until June 1945.

Kidlington, Oxfordshire

SP475153. 6 miles NW of Oxford, by A34(T)

Kidlington has a varied history for a city airport, wartime expansion into a rectangular array of huts and roads having brought it into line with training establishments. It came into use in 1938, No 26 E&RFTS opening here on June 24. First to arrive was Audax *K7552*, the School's strength merely amounting to a couple of

Audaxes and four Hinds at the outbreak of war when it closed.

On September 9 1939, Battles of 52 Squadron dispersed here for a few days since Kidlington was now Abingdon's satellite. They left when their parent unit moved to Benson, Kidlington coming under 4 Group Pool, Abingdon.

Late 1939 control passed to 6 SFTS, Little Rissington. That station became waterlogged and, on January 8 1940, E and G Flights of 6 SFTS, along with F and H servicing parties and the Advanced Training Squadron HQ, moved to Kidlington. The latter became unusable following heavy snow on January 27. Barely was it fully serviceable when, in mid-March, it had to close again.

Kidlington was operated then as an RLG under 6 SFTS until that unit abruptly withdrew its complement in mid-August 1940. Bombing of Brize Norton caused a rapid dispersal, half of the ITS, 15 SFTS and ground staff quickly moving into Kidlington on August 19 1940 to reduce the large number of vulnerable aircraft at Brize Norton where 6 MU also used Kidlington, still a rudimentary site although major expansions had started. Air Training (Oxford) had two hangars in which they had switched from their pre-war flying school activity to undertaking aircraft overhaul. Campsfield House was requisitioned for dormitory use. The movement of 15 SFTS from Brize Norton increased Kidlington's importance within 23 Group, added to when, on August 31

An aerial view of Kidlington on August 21 1940 (Public Record Office).

1940, the remainder of ITS 15 SFTS arrived from South Cerney where it had lodged when Middle Wallop became a fighter station. A count on August 31 1940 showed that Kidlington held 56 Harvard 1s and two Oxfords.

Headquarters' staff of 15 SFTS arrived on October 1 1940, the remainder of 15 SFTS following on October 17, with over 100 Harvards on charge and wartime building well advanced. On November 1 1940, 15 SFTS acquired Weston-on-the Green as its second RLG.

Need for ample dispersal was audible at 15:15 on November 3 1940. In low cloud and rain, a Ju 88 swept in from the north east, raced low over the technical site and dropped five bombs. One ricochetted its way through the station armoury and another hit a hangar before bouncing back into the armoury and exploding. Two others burst on the landing ground where the fifth rested unexploded. The Ju 88, machine guns blazing, scurried into cloud flying south-westerly. One person was killed, two seriously injured. The armoury and Hangar 4, along with an Air Training Co hangar, were all seriously damaged, and two Harvards burnt.

Throughout the winter of 1940/41 Harvards and Oxfords used Kidlington. February 27 1941 brought the appearance of another Ju 88, flying at around 300 ft

A recent view of Oxford Airport, Kidlington, home of OATS (via Squadron Leader G.M. Phillips).

along the Woodstock road. A Kidlington gun post crew opened fire and, returning it, the raider retreated.

Surface state was hindering flying so, on February 28 1941, a Flight from 15 SFTS moved at Watton. On March 8 use of that operational station increased when two separate Flights, each of five aircraft, moved there for flying training. The need for detachments was alleviated when, on June 30 1941, a new RLG, at Barford, opened.

Kidlington was in an increasingly busy area which added to the risk of accidents. At 16:03 on May 22 1941 an Oxford of 15 SFTS hit a balloon cable and fell in Beechwood Avenue, Coventry. The switch from Harvards to Oxfords had taken place over several weeks, at the start of 1941.

Oxford flying training continued during 1941. Concern that winter would bring a poor surface resulted in the start of runway laying in autumn 1941. On December 23, with the customary two Sommerfeld track runways available, Oxfords of J and K Flights 15 SFTS returned from Weston, forced out because 2 GTS formed there. On the day after their arrival a letter reached Kidlington confirming that 15 SFTS was to close. A new 'No 15', called 15 (P) AFU, was to form at Leconfield in January 1942. Intake at 15 SFTS ceased, but courses completed flying programmes and Oxfords of the School continued to fly from here until April 11 1942.

On January 1 1942, No 1 Glider OTU controlled by 70 Group formed at Kidlington, for after a GTS course a pilot would acquire operational skills at an OTU. Before this scheme became effective, the Horsa had been selected as the assault glider and the Hotspur relegated to training duties. A few OTUs were formed, a glider pilot after leaving GTS finding himself flying a Hotspur towed by an antique Hector as before. A second glider OTU formed at Kidlington in February 1942, and both were renamed 101 and 102 OTUs soon after. They functioned until June 1942 when the HGCU opened at Shrewton.

From Kidlington a party proceeded to Shobden on May 28 to form 5 GTS. Then, on July 13, the remaining Hotspur organisation and SHQ Kidlington combined to form 4 GTS. Kidlington had lost its RLG at Barford St John on April 10 and now switched to using Kingston Bagpuize. No 4 GTS retained Kidlington as its busy home until it amalgamated with Nos 1 and 2 GTSs to form No 20 (P) AFU on March 10 1943, to use Oxfords and to make use until November 1944, of Croughton. Flying also took place from Kiddington and Hinton before disbandment on June 21 1945. A non-flying unit then formed at Kidlington, No 1 Aircrew Holding Unit, and stayed until

September 1945. No 265 MU was also here and at Grove between October 1945 and 1948.

After the war the Oxford Aeroplane Club formed. In 1959 considerable expansion commenced after the Oxford UAS departed. Kidlington became an outlet for Piper aircraft and in 1961 the first Commercial Pilot Licence students arrived for training, and British Executive Air Services, part of Pressed Steel, ran courses leading to Private Pilot Licence standard. The Oxford school in May 1964 became the first to be CAA approved for the training of CPL students. Eventually it evolved into the Oxford Air Training School.

Kidlington's present control tower was built in 1964–5, an upper room being added in 1969–70. Some wartime buildings remain, including the Officers' Mess, complete with frontal drive and small lawn. A celestial training dome survives, although its interior gives no clues as to its use for astral navigation and gunnery training. Kidlington is an active airfield with a variety of civil aircraft coming and going.

Kimbolton, Cambridgeshire

TL105695. 1 mile N of Kimbolton, on the Kimbolton to Spaldwick road

Kimbolton was prepared in 1941 as Molesworth's satellite and on November 29 received Molesworth's first aircraft, a Wellington IV destined for 460 Squadron. Thereafter Kimbolton and Molesworth shared 460 Squadron's Wellingtons until early January 1942 when they left for Breighton.

Many Midlands airfields were being surveyed for American bombers, inspection of Molesworth and Kimbolton during January 1942 resulting in agreement that both should be offered to the Americans. Agreement reached, both stations were to be ready for B-17s by summer.

An opening-up party arrived at improved RAF Kimbolton on July 31 1942 and, on September 13 1942, Americans reached their new base. They were personnel of the 91st Bomb Group bringing some of the first B-17Fs to arrive in Britain, in appearance quite different from B-17Es. Whereas those had 'splodges' of dark green and brown irregularly applied upon their olive drab upper surfaces, these mostly had single tone bronze-green finish. Under surfaces were a darker shade of grey, and fin serials yellow instead of orange as hitherto. B-17F noses had increased clear transparency areas and a more pointed shape.

Brief was the 91st's stay. Placing Bassingbourn's Wellingtons within the inland training area released their elaborate station, recently provided with hard runways, for offensive duty. These facilities were readily accepted by the comfort-conscious visitors who left the huts of Kimbolton for the permanence and splendour of Bassingbourn during October. Transit personnel on their way to Operation *Torch* and Algeria replaced them. Statements that the 91st Bomb Group left Kimbolton because its runways could not withstand B-17 operations are only partly true. The main reason was to allow general expansion. To accommodate a four squadron USAAF bomber group required a much improved Kimbolton.

On March 30 1943 the station was again divorced from Molesworth and received Americans on May 20. They comprised 11 officers and 1,646 men who had disembarked from the *Aquitania* at Glasgow and formed the complement of the four squadrons of the 379th Bombardment Group. Additionally, there were support personnel for the 82nd Service Group, 171 QM Company, 1094 and 1773 Ordnance Companies and the 379th Servicing Squadron. On May 21 another 115 officers and 203 enlisted men moved in. Six days later more came from AAF Station 109, Podington, then came B-17Fs on May 21 for the 379th BG. At noon on June 1 1943, Kimbolton was transferred to USAAF control, the necessary documents being passed to Colonel M. Preston by Squadron Leader H.W.C. Davies.

The 379th BG, whose operational debut had taken place the previous day, was to fly 330 operations, more than any other Group in the 8th AF BC. Its operational debut came during an attack on U-Boat installations at St Nazaire. Operations by the Group included attacks upon a variety of strategic targets such as factories, oil plants, storage depots, submarine pens, airfields, communications centres and industrial items in distant Poland and Norway. Special raids in which the 379th participated were mounted against the IG Farben chemical plant in Ludwigshaven, an aircraft factory at Brunswick, the ball bearing works at Schweinfurt and synthetic oil plants at both Merseburg and Gelsenkirchen. The 379th played its part in the 1st Air Division's operations leading to the Normandy landings, the Arnhem assault, the Battle of the Bulge and the Rhine crossing and flew its final sorties on April 25 1945. For its excellent operational record between May 1943 and July 1944 the 379th was awarded a Distinguished Unit Citation. A second such commendation followed a courageous operation without fighter escort, mounted against an aircraft factory on January 11 1944.

At the termination of action the tally of operational sorties reached 10,492, the bomb tonnage dropped 26,459 and the number of operations, the record 330. Of the 379th 'K in a triangle' marked aircraft, none became better known than B-17G *42-40003* 'WA-H' named *Ol' Gappy* credited with 157 operational sorties.

The 379th vacated Kimbolton on June 16 1945, for Morocco and Casablanca. After the Fortresses had gone, the runways and perimeter track echoed to the sound of marching by RAF new entrants posted to the recruit training centre here. Silent, Kimbolton's two 'T2' hangars saw little further use. The airfield hit the headlines in November 1971 when an abortive attempt was made by a Syrian flying a Piper Cherokee to smuggle immigrants into Britain, an exercise brought to a dramatic end by a farmer. Little remains of Kimbolton's wartime days.

King's Cliffe, Northamptonshire

TL025980. 6 miles S of Stamford, ENE of King's Cliffe village by the Wansford road

Wicked looking? Spiteful? Such adjectives traversed the mind upon confronting a high-flying Spitfire VI, the first of which resided, initially, at King's Cliffe. Commonly called Wansford, officially 'K2', this site was acquired early in 1940 as Wittering's satellite and took its designation from Fighter Sector 'K'. Wittering differed from most fighter stations in that it housed a number of squadrons and an additional satellite was needed. What use was made of it in 1940 remains uncertain, but in July work commenced on building its perimeter track with the intention that this and runways be complete within three months. Wimpeys were given the contract and it was 1941 before King's Cliffe was a really active station, dispersal airfield for Spitfire IIas of 266 Squadron.

In August 1941, 266 Squadron acquired Spitfire Vbs and, on October 24, completely moved in from Wittering. Now the airfield was called WB2 King's Cliffe, which came into use late 1940. No 266 Squadron had vacated WB3 Colly Weston preparatory to a move to Duxford and conversion to the Typhoon. One of those, *R7590*, touched down at King's Cliffe on January 25 1942. Next day it fled to Duxford and, on January 29, Spitfires of 266 Squadron joined it.

Their place was taken by Spitfire Vbs of 616 (County of Yorkshire) Squadron whose crews, arriving in sleet and snow, found King's Cliffe a poor substitute for Kirton-in-Lindsey. February 1942 was cold and cheerless, so HRH The Duke of Kent called, when the news was grave. Adding to low morale came February 12 1942 when German capital ships sailed through the Straits of Dover unchallenged. Too late the British reacted, ten of 616's Spitfires racing to Matlask and six subsequently supporting Whirlwinds of 137 Squadron searching, without success, for the German ships.

King's Cliffe was too far from France to permit Spitfires to operate over the Continent. Instead, 616 Squadron joined 12 Group's Wing which would fly to West Malling early, refuel, then operate from there returning to King's Cliffe in the evening. On April 12, 35 Spitfire Vbs of 412, 609 and 616 Squadrons gathered at West Malling for the first 1942 Circus involving King's Cliffe. It took them to Hazebrouck and two of 616s Spitfires failed to return.

Next day 616 Squadron participated in a Rodeo and on April 15 operated twice. During the afternoon the 12 Group Wing (411, 609 and 616 Squadrons) covered eight Hurribombers attacking Desvres. Enemy fighters challenged and Flight Lieutenant Johnson damaged a Fw 190 before Sergeant Millar, also of 616 Squadron, ditched off Dungeness and was rescued. Two days later, during the Lancaster dash to Augsburg, 616 Squadron's Spitfires diverted enemy attention. By the close of April, 616 Squadron had flown seven offensive sweeps in a Wing generally led by Wing Commander Jamieson. On April 29/30 six pilots tried their hands at night fighting during the bombing of Norwich.

April 22 1942 excited 616 Squadron, with the arrival of the first Spitfire VI, *A-Apple*. Pressure cabin insulation made full flying gear entry difficult. The cabin temperature was high at lower altitudes and on the climb and, although the engine had a higher altitude rating than others, it

Lockheed P-38J-10-LO KI:N *of the 55th Fighter Squadron, 20th Fighter Group, King's Cliffe* (Merle Olmsted).

was far from the desirable Mk 61 two-stage variant. The Mk VI was heavy, and propeller refinement much needed. Planned four-bladed propellers remained in short supply and some Mk VIs at first had inferior three-bladers. But 616 at least had their first high flier with which to endure combat at great heights.

May 1942 was a busy month at King's Cliffe with Mk VI training, some at Boscombe Down. Five sweeps using Spitfire Vs were flown, two on May Day when Pilot Officer Brown claimed a probable Fw 190. Another sweep took place on May 4 whilst 616's fourth Spitfire VI touched down at King's Cliffe. Rodeo 19 was flown with 19 Squadron on May 6 before on May 9, 616 Squadron took two Mk VIs on a sweep along with ten Mk Vs and Spitfires of 411 Squadron. These joined 48 Spitfires of the North Weald Wing, all returning without seeing combat, then 616 Squadron was taken off operations to concentrate on Mk VI flying. On May 24, 14 Mk VIs were on strength.

During the rainy afternoon of May 25, coastal radar plotted a Dornier 217 east of Mablethorpe, flying southerly. After it flew over the Wash and inland, two Spitfires of 411 Squadron were scrambled, then four of 616 Squadron. The Dornier flew to about 15 miles east of Bramcote at between 7,000 to 10,000 ft before 616 Squadron engaged and probably damaged it near Leicester. The event was sad for 616 Squadron because return fire from the Dornier damaged Perspex in a Spitfire, pieces of it causing Pilot Officer Brown to lose the use of an eye. The Do 217 dropped four bombs near Belton, Rutland, before its exit over the Wash. It was not the expected baptism of fire for the high altitude fighter.

Conversion complete, 17 Mk VIs in hand, 616 Squadron resumed operations over France, making a diversionary sweep with 610 Squadron in the Le Touquet–Boulogne area on June 3, and another two days later with Nos 610 and 611 Squadrons. These were the only two operations from King's Cliffe in June 1942, excessive heat in the tightly enclosed Spitfire cockpits halting operations until June 15, after which only training took place.

On July 3, 616 Squadron was detached to West Malling, reinforcing 11 Group during an intended commando assault on the French coast. On July 7 it returned to WB2 (still commonly called Wansford) only for an overnight stay. The Squadron moved to Kenley the next day.

Its place was taken by Spitfire Vbs of 485 (NZ) Squadron from Kenley making a direct swop. The squadron came to rest, but moved forward to fly four operations during the Dieppe landing. Then '485' busied itself supporting US 8th AAF B-17s and RAF day raids from advanced bases.

On September 8 1942, No 93 Squadron's Spitfire Vbs arrived from the Isle of Man to prepare for service in north-west Africa, quitting the station mid-October. 485 Squadron moved temporarily to Kirkeston, Northern Ireland, on October 24. On November 23 they returned, leaving for West Hampnett on January 3 1943.

Their brief absence was to make way for Americans awaiting to participate in Operation *Torch*. Instead, it was December 8 1942 when USAAF Bell P-39 and P-400 Airacobras of the 347th Squadron, 350th Fighter Group, arrived. For three weeks Airacobras in British colours and wearing US insignia were seen and heard for, as the aircraft climbed, their Allisons noisily hauled the fighters aloft in a sound peculiar to their breed. On January 4 1943 they started on the long journey to Africa to find their ground echelon. Almost immediately the 56th Fighter Group arrived soon receiving P-47C Thunderbolts. King's Cliffe's facilities remained poor. One squadron, No 63, lodged at Wittering, leaving the 61st and 63rd at King's Cliffe.

With the airfield non-operational, this was an ideal time to improve it by building better runways, blast pens and additional accommodation. By May 1943 what had been little more than a large meadow with a few Blister hangars was now an airfield of moderate sophistication. Early April 1943, the 56th Fighter Group moved to Horsham St Faith. The RAF re-possessed King's Cliffe and, in May, No 91 Squadron's Spitfire XIIs arrived before leaving for Hawkinge on May 21. Commencing on June 14, No 7 (P) AFU came for two weeks. No 349 Squadron returned from overseas, was then assembled at Wittering and, with one Spitfire V, moved to King's Cliffe on June 29, worked up using Spitfire Vbs and left for Wellingore early in August.

The most active period at King's Cliffe now commenced. On August 26 1943 the 77th and 79th Squadrons, 20th Fighter Group, USAAF, brought along the new Lockheed P-38H Lightning fighters and, in early September, the USAAF completely took over. There was still shortage of accommodation, so that the Group's 55th Squadron was detached to Wittering. Not until May 27 1944 did the 55th find room at King's Cliffe.

The P-38s suffered from engine and supercharger problems. To clear these the 20th's P-38Hs went to the 55th Fighter Group, Nuthampstead, more able to use them than the 20th which was far from ready for operations. Replacement aircraft arriving in October, were P-38Js recognisable by deep air intakes accommodating radiators ahead of engines and which had been shifted from the wing leading edge. Additional fuel tankage was installed and, with a 150-gallon drop tank, still-air non-combat radius of action rose to over 600 miles. For operations about 400 miles was a realistic figure.

The 20th Fighter Group cautiously commenced operations on November 5 1943 when eight P-38s of the 79th Fighter Squadron tagged along with P-38s of the 55th Fighter Group. Full-scale action from King's Cliffe commenced on December 28 1943. Troubles were far from over and to the end of its operational career with the 20th Fighter Group the P-38 proved difficult. There were aerodynamic problems, and the Lightning was a complex single-seater. Nevertheless its range made it useful and P-38s saw seven months of active service at King's Cliffe.

April 8 1944 was a day the 20th would always look back upon with pride. Cheated by misty conditions of joining a main bomber force operation, the Group secured permission for a special, one-off strafing mission. Forty-eight P-38s set out from King's Cliffe, their target area being around Salzwedel, about 80 miles from Berlin. This was a highly successful venture and, for the loss of two Lightnings, the Group claimed 21 enemy aircraft destroyed on the ground and four in the air along with much rail traffic. P-38s had mainly been used for bomber support, low level strafing by a fighter fitted with turbo-superchargers seeming strange, especially as that equipment gave much trouble. That forced P-38s to be used for lower level operations.

What also transformed the P-38s' value was the novel fitment of a clear nose in which a bombardier could, just, be accommodated. As bombing leader he could mark the target for attack by other P-38s within his formation. There were few of these 'droop snoot' P-38s, but the 20th had one by April 1944 and used it first during an attack on Gütersloh, afterwhich more airfield attacks were attempted.

Late on May 5 1944, King's Cliffe's P-38s commenced their Normandy invasion task of patrolling over Channel shipping in daylight hours, helping huge convoys to advance slowly towards France.

Come July 1944 and P-51 Mustangs began arriving at King's Cliffe. The 20th Fighter Group had lost 87 P-38s but had claimed 80 enemy aircraft shot down. On July 20, the 20th's P-51s first went into action from King's Cliffe then mounted bomber escorts, fighter-bomber raids and low level locomotive strikes in the months ahead. They were busy during Arnhem and Ardennes battles and the Rhine crossing. One of their more unusual bomber escort missions came on September 11 1944 when they escorted B-17s and, after the bombing, proceeded to the USSR. Then they protected the bombers flying home via Hungary and Italy before landing back at King's Cliffe on September 17 1944. At base the Group recorded that the biggest opposition they had encountered during the entire operation was, pathetically, Russian.

The last of 312 operations flown by the 20th Fighter Group from King's Cliffe took place on April 25 1945, the 20th returning to the USA the following October. King's Cliffe became a Holding Unit for German PoWs awaiting repatriation, under the control of 28 Group. That Unit closed in July 1947. King's Cliffe was held on Care and Maintenance and later served as an ammunition storage area. The RAF vacated the site in January 1959 and it was sold for private use later that year.

Kingston Bagpuize, Oxfordshire

SU410965. 5 miles W of Abingdon, S of A415

Kingston Bagpuize, on flat land south of the village, had excellent approaches. Between January and May 1942, 3 EFTS used Kingston as an RLG, then from March 9 1942 to July 19 1942 it served as a satellite for 1 GTS Thame whose Hotspurs and tugs undertook circuit training. When a glider pilot refresher school for those trained already and not flying very much was suggested, Kingston and indeed Thame, were considered. Nothing came of this and, between January and April 1943, Kingston was used by 4 GTS. On March 10 1943 it became a satellite of 20 (P) AFU whose Oxfords operated from here. No 20 (P) AFU withdrew on July 28 1943, plans to enlarge the airfield being then implemented.

When a 70 Group party arrived on January 30 1944 to take over from the contractors, they found that the USAAF had already moved in. On February 7 1944 an advance party of IXth AF also arrived. American interest was not so much in operating from the station as in trying a wire mesh covering on the original runway surface. The Commander IXth AF came to inspect this on March 10, observing rapid refuelling and rearming of 50 P-47s from the 368th Fighter Group, Greenham. Next day the Group mounted three operations from here, testing the efficiency of the novel runway surface. They again used Kingston on April 13 1944.

An intensive day's flying to test the runway further came on May 6 1944 when P-47s repeatedly landed showing that frequent repairs were necessary. A B-17, short of fuel, visited briefly on May 25, and on June 15 circuits by C-47s trying out the runway showed little wear on its surface. Late June 1944 the experimental wire mesh was removed, and all trial work was deemed complete by August 1944. Kingston lay dormant until December 14 1944 when 3 MU took over the site. The sub-site which 3 MU had established was eventually closed on June 14, 1954.

Little Horwood, Buckinghamshire

SP795315. 2½ miles NE of Winslow

As the Americans took over Cheddington, Little Horwood replaced 26 OTU's lost satellite as the main centre, for conversion training, on September 3 1942. Also here was the OTUs Gunnery Section and 92 Group Communications Flight which came from Bicester on September 16 1942.

Of Little Horwood little remains. Apart from Wellington IIIs and Xs of 26 OTU, few other aircraft used it. On January 23, 1943, however, Chelveston's B-17s were received when returning from Lorient, with fuel short and the weather bad. On May 31 1943, Wellington *BJ977* was burnt out on dispersal. Tomahawks equipped No 1684 Bomber Defence Training Flight which formed here on June 5 1943 and transferred to Wing, the parent station, on July 17 1943.

On August 26 1944, 26 OTU ceased flying at Little Horwood upon being reduced to ¾ OTU status. This left 92 Group Communications Flight in occupation with an Oxford, Anson, Tutor and Proctor. Full establishment returned

This formation of pre-war CFS aircraft depicts training aircraft used at Midlands airfields (RAF Museum).

to 26 OTU in October 1944 and on November 1 various parts of the OTU came back to Little Horwood including the gunnery section's Hurricanes. Despite the end of hostilities, 26 OTU, in a contracting air force, survived until March 1946. Not so Little Horwood, where flying ceased on November 30 1945, although the station was administered by 26 OTU until January 15 1946.

Little Rissington, Gloucestershire

SP215190. 4 miles S of Stow-on-the-Wold, by the A424

Unfortunately we live in an age of pseudo planners. Unsightly concrete blemishes win prizes, shared with designers whose competence is surely shielded by misleading titles. Their more curious creations inevitably lead to conclusions that many confuse the Golden Section, which they have not experienced, with some sort of tele-confection. Not so the architects who devised the buildings—gracious in form and simplicty—which adorn British 1930 Expansion Period permanent aerodromes.

Bearing lines of fine symmetry, these functional, strong structures of undating design would pleasantly tone in many a graceful city. Designed for war, they would fit satisfyingly into many a peaceful place. Unlike the tasteless civilian and military edifices of recent decades these majestic monuments with strong Georgian overtones have come to blend most satisfyingly with the countryside around them. Their creators must surely feel most content upon seeing them harmonise as well with yesterday's Hart as today's Tornado. Such affinities between form and utilisation have been nowhere more apparent than at Little Rissington, the highest placed British airfield of recent times.

When the Fine Arts Commission and the Council for the Preservation of Rural England were requested to advise upon the design of military aerodromes in the 1930s they stipulated that, as far as possible, these massive creations should not harm the countryside. The agricultural lobby, not noticeably concerned with national defence, was eager to ensure that as little land as possible slipped into Air Ministry hands. That caused greatly increased expenditure, and profoundly effected aircraft design.

Little Rissington stands upon a 750 ft high plateau. It gazes upon a delightful collection of 17th and 19th century houses in the village from which it takes its name. Dominating this part of the Cotswolds is the Windrush river, making Bourton-on-the-Water a precious attraction, and one

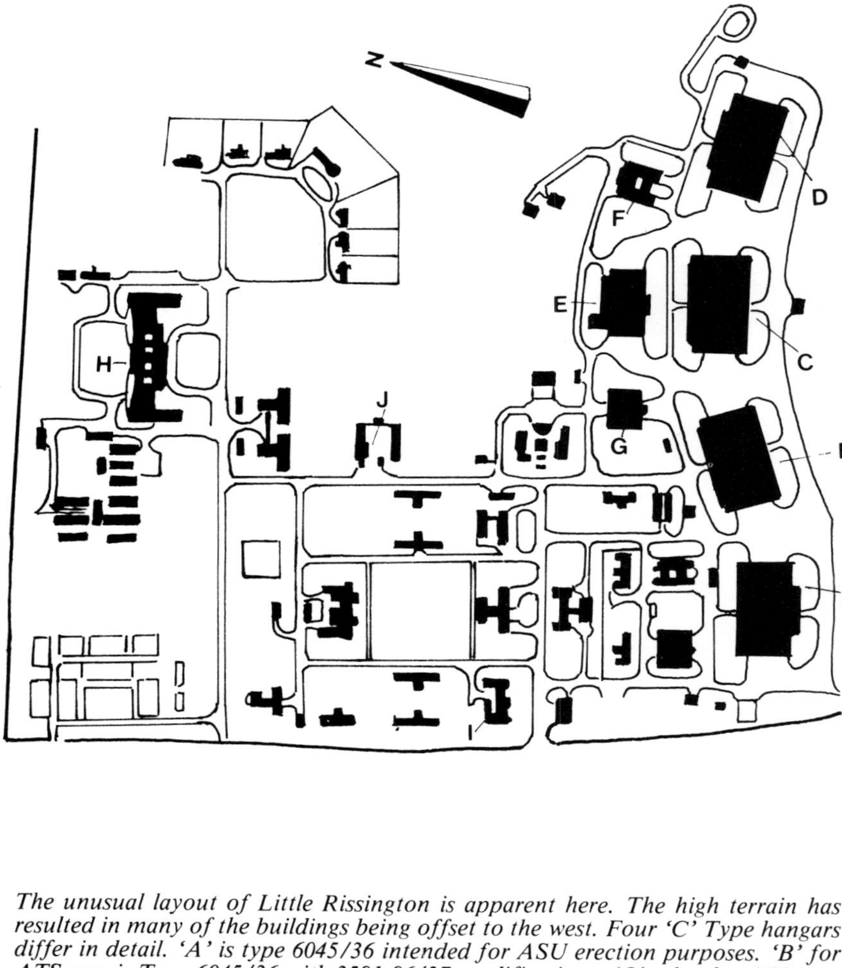

The unusual layout of Little Rissington is apparent here. The high terrain has resulted in many of the buildings being offset to the west. Four 'C' Type hangars differ in detail. 'A' is type 6045/36 intended for ASU erection purposes. 'B' for ATS use, is Type 6045/36 with 3591-96/37 modifications. 'C', also for ATS use, is Type 6045/36 with 2557/37 additions. 'D' is Type 6045 and 1751-56/36 and is for the FTS to use. An interesting building, of which another existed at Wittering, is the aircraft repair Shed (6116/36) marked 'E'. Letter 'F' marks the workshops (2048/34) and 'G' the main stores (2056-61/34). Barrack Blocks P,R, and Q, are around the barrack square overlooked by the Airmens' Dining Room and Institute. The 1937 style Officers' Mess ('H') could accommodate 108 officers. The Sergeants' Mess is marked 'I'. The MT yard is 'J'. The layout is for the pre-war period only.

Little Rissington on July 10 1942. Hangars of 8 MU and a number of Wellingtons are in the foreground. Black 'hedges' have been imposed upon the landing ground. The main buildings are on the right of the picture (RAF Museum).

whose aeronautical connection in recent years has been Frederick the pelican, quartered in Birdland, and the personification of the pelican within the badge of the Central Flying School so long associated with Little Rissington.

Pass the camp and one notices the use of Cotswold stone in its construction. The wall around the entrance is of such material, which may also be seen used in some buildings. Little Rissington's four 'C' Type hangars (6045/36) flank a double curved apron. When the station opened, its Aircraft Repair Shed (6116/34) was behind No 3 hangar, in front of which was the Watch Office and CFIs Office (5740/36). Most buildings were to the rear of Nos 1 & 2 Hangars, sloping ground to the east preventing development. Main Stores (2056-61/34) and Workshops (2046/34) were to the rear of the No 1 Hangar. Barrack blocks were of three types, Type P (2363/37, for 52 men and three NCOs), Type Q (582/36, for 64 men and three NCOs) and Type R (2277/34, for 84 men and three NCOs). The Sergeants' Mess (102/55) could accommodate 65 SNCOs, with quarters for 12. To the north of the parade ground was the Airmen's Dining Room for 450 men, combined with the Institute (5062-66/36). The Officers' Mess (566/37, 1459/37) for 108 officers was built on the northern edge of the camp.

Little Rissington came alive between August 20 and 25 1938. When 6 SFTS moved in from Netheravon it brought Harts and Audaxes, received in October 1935, a few Hawker Furies and soon had a few Ansons. During June 1939 the pernicious notes of Harvard engines began shattering the sky. With this assortment 6 SFTS went to war.

There were already other aircraft types on the station because, on October 11 1938, No 8 MU had formed under Squadron Leader D.W. Dean. From small beginnings it became an important unit, handling many Spitfires and Wellingtons. In the south-east corner of the airfield were its Lamella hangars and other buildings akin to MUs. On September 3 1939 there were 268 aircraft in storage. Wellingtons of 215 Squadron briefly scattered here for safety when the war started.

Organisation of 6 SFTS comprised an Intermediate Squadron, training pilots following their elementary course and flying Harts and Audaxes, and an Advanced Squadron of Harvards and Ansons and from which pilots proceeded to operational training. Limited operational training was afforded to pilots during brief detachments to Penrhos in October–November 1939, and again in December 1939–January 1940, this time at Hullavington.

Jet Provosts flying from Little Rissington.

Then came major trouble. Snow fell fast and settled deeply over the exposed Cotswolds where very deep drifts formed in what proved to be a very cold spell. This did not stop 8 MU helping the courageous Finns defeat the Russians, 8 MU despatching Blenheims for the Bristol Aeroplane Co to prepare for that distant conflict. Both 8 MU and 6 SFTS found themselves in a very difficult position. Flying was barely possible from Little Rissington, so E and G Flights, along with two servicing parties and the Advanced Squadron HQ, fled to Kidlington. They fared better, but only for a week for, at the end of January 1940, Kidlington was put out of use by the thaw which extended into February. At Little Rissington only the southern and western areas of the landing ground could be used, and only for essential flying. Kidlington was briefly out of use again in March but, by the close of that month, all was well at both stations. Armament training then took place at Warmwell and was next used in May 1940, by which time other schemes were in play.

Dispersal of large numbers of aircraft held by an SFTS, and around the perimeter of the landing ground, demanded adquate anti-intruder/sabotage defences. Fencing off large areas and patrolling them was virtually impossible. Instead, many aircraft had to be taken into hangars—particularly biplanes susceptible to inclement weather. Anti-invasion devices included a Crossley heavy tender sprouting machine-gun mountings. Trip wires were slung between poles embedded in likely landing fields in the vicinity to bring disaster to uninvited Ju 52s. Such defences were placed on many sites earmarked for airfield developments too. In May 1940, 8 MU had about 350 aircraft on hand, and all closely packed in mainly grass clad hangars.

With things looking bad, the OC 8 MU arranged, on June 24 1940, for a Spitfire to be available to Staff Pilots of 6 SFTS in case it was needed for local defence. With over 400 aircraft on Little Rissington's strength in mid-1940 it was a highly vulnerable target. Not all the aircraft, though, were on the station. Some trainers remained at Kidlington, and in July first use began to be made of Rissington's RLG at Windrush. As for 8 MU—which, on a day in June 1940, counted among its occupants 58 Battles, 39 Hampdens, 21 Magisters, 30 Spitfires and 21 Tiger Moths—it temporarily dispersed some aircraft to Watchfield, Worcester, Stoke Orchard and Great Shefford. Stored, dismantled aircraft were held at Luton (from 1940 to 1942) and Portsmouth (1940 to 1941). Arrival of close on 100 Blenheims in July 1940 added a new dimension to a worrying state. Just how disastrous it could become was evident on July 29 when a raider dropped 17 bombs, harmlessly, in fields 3½ miles away. Safety was then increased by the use of Windrush RLG for night flying. Complete blackout at Little

Rissington was vital to prevent night bombing.

For an enthusiast with the courage to view it at this time, Little Rissington would have provided much fascination. In August, for instance, some 14 Mohawks arrived and three of the rare Curtiss Cleveland biplanes. To help guard the station, 60 civilians working in the SFTS, and others at the MU, formed on August 28 a Home Guard battalion. Three days later an invasion alert brought the immediate manning of the 14 brick block-houses and 14 concrete pill boxes around the airfield, by troops armed only with primitive equipment.

As autumn set in there was mounting concern at increasing accident rates at training schools which harmed programmes. A serious accident occurred on September 20 1940 when Anson *N9821* collided with Oxford *P9039* of 2 SFTS, three miles south of the station, killing all the aircrew. On October 29 1940, two Ansons, *N9737* of 11 AONS Watchfield and *N5285* of 6 SFTS collided ten miles north of Stow-on-the-Wold. Such serious accidents were relatively rare although, on May 23 1941, two Oxfords of 6 SFTS collided over their home station.

Using Windrush helped particularly at night and acquisition of a second RLG, Chipping Norton, where 6 SFTS commenced circuits on November 16 1940, eased flying congestion. Additional to the problem of many trainees in the circuit was the integration of mixed aircraft types handled by 8 MU whose storage problems ever increased. These were partly alleviated in 1940 when use commenced of Satellite Landing Grounds at Great Shefford, Pembridge, Watchfield, Worcester and at Stoke Orchard where the Gloster Aircraft Co established a sub-factory.

In summer 1940 SFTS became a Twin Engine Training School. Courses for twin and single-engined aircraft had previously been run but now the Harvards were replaced by Oxfords. Biplanes had been phased out in early 1940 and during June 1941 remaining Ansons were withdrawn. Between then and the end of the war strength of the Unit increased dramatically so that over 150 Oxfords were eventually assigned to it.

Further changes to SLGs, of which an ever enlarging 8 MU had control, also came in 1941. In February, No 3 SLG Middle Farm came into use and No 28 Barton Abbey acted as a sub-station from February 1941 to August 1942. By October 1941 over 90 aircraft were in storage at Middle Farm. Control of 8 MU had been switched to 52 Wing on April 21 1941 and on June 30 the MU's Little Rissington stock included 27 Hampdens, 10 Mohawks, 39 Proctors, 37 Spitfires and 120 Oxfords.

Ever increasing RAF night bomber strength made instrument flying training increasingly essential. Equally important was the growing need for improved bad weather landing approach training. In

Aircraft of CFS Little Rissington have included Prentices, one of which is illustrated.

October 1941, No 23 BAT Flight formed, became No 1523 BAT Flight in January 1942 and equipped with eight Oxford IIs. It functioned at Little Rissington until November 1945.

The role of 6 SFTS was altering because of the extent of flying training undertaken overseas. In line with others No 6 SFTS changed, on April 22 1942, into No 6 (Pilot) Advanced Flying Unit. Using Oxford IIs it provided the finishing touch to pilot training overseas by bringing it into line with European flying needs. By June 1942 6 (P) AFU's establishment stood at 115 Oxfords and four Ansons. Further expansion took place when an additional 34 more Oxfords, previously on 2 (P) AFU's strength, were received on July 14 1942. At the same time Akeman Street RLG was acquired. Additional Oxfords arrived conveniently for, during the previous month, 6 (P) AFU had been assessing the possibilities of using Blackburn Bothas as advanced pilot trainers. That type proved unsuitable and 6 (P) AFU's Oxfords continued droning around the circuits at Little Rissington, Chipping Norton, Windrush and Akeman Street.

With extra landing space available, runway building was undertaken at Little Rissington during 1942. Night flying was now acceptable at the station because of reduced enemy night activity. Little Rissington's triple runway pattern was also useful to 8 MU for Horsa gliders erected here, also Hotspurs, which were to be towed away by Whitleys. The main aircraft types handled by 8 MU in 1942 were Hampdens, Oxfords, Spitfires and, increasingly, Wellingtons. Aged biplanes including Harts, Hinds, Hectors and Audaxes, useful for glider training schools, came for overhaul.

By early 1943 Spitfires predominated at 8 MU where there were Hampdens, Wellingtons, Tomahawks, Halifaxes, Typhoons and a few Kittyhawks. March 1943 saw No 8 MU take over administration of No 34 SLG, Woburn Park. Alongside the MU 6 (P) AFU's Oxfords proliferated and, in May 1943, the Unit's establishment rose to 163 Oxford I/IIs, 4 Ansons and a Tiger Moth serving a pupil population of 350 who still trained at three RLGs as well as at the parent station.

In April 1944, personnel of 8 MU, put ten Hengist gliders into purgatory storage at Rawcliffe Paper Mill. At that time the MU held 520 aircraft and had another purgatory store at Northolt. Increased BAT training became available to 6 (P) AFU in May 1944 when 1516 and 1517 BAT Flights at Pershore and Chipping Warden respectively commenced assisting in the training of pilots. Although the intensity of flying training was high, the aircraft holding of 8 MU still increased dramatically, particularly in regard to the number of Wellingtons. The MU was, in November 1944, ordered to concentrate its energy upon the dispersed storage of at least 600 Wellingtons and more to follow. At the end of 1944 the Unit had on charge 757 aircraft including many Wellingtons Mks III, X, XIII and XIV. A year later strength had swollen to a staggering 1,388 machines for which reason No 107 Sub-Storage Unit at Honeybourne and No 108 at Long Marston were also established.

Right to the end of European hostilities, use continued to be made of Little Rissington's three RLGs. When training ceased on November 26 1945 at 6 (P) AFU, records showed that 5,444 pilots had been trained at the station, and that its pupils had received 705 awards for gallantry including four Victoria Crosses.

On December 17 1945, 6 SFTS was reformed, its new strength being 54 Harvard IIBs, two Ansons and a Magister. Control of Little Rissington remained with 23 Group which had for long been in command. On April 25 1946, 6 FTS moved to Ternhill. Its place was taken, during the first two weeks of May 1946, by the RAF's most prestigious training formation, the Central Flying School from Hullavington. Blind approach training continued to be provided, until February 1947, by 1537 Flight based here.

From 1946 to 1976 Little Rissington was the home of the Central Flying School, its task the training of instructors. Basic flying instruction was given using Tiger Moths, replaced by Chipmunks and next by Bulldogs. Advanced training instruction was undertaken using Harvards, then the Prentices, the first of which arrived in July 1947 and, from 1953, by Provosts. These remained in use until 1960 when Jet Provost T3s replaced them. Earlier jet flying had relied upon the use of Meteor T7s and Vampire T11s. Multi-engine training courses had earlier been run using Mosquito TIIIs, and much later Varsities. In 1958, CFS formed 'The Pelicans' using a few Jet Provost T1s which were soon replaced. Later the School formed a light aircraft team, 'The Skylarks' with Chipmunks. Although part of CFS, the 'Red Arrows' were never based here but instead lodged at Kemble.

In the 1970s, CFS Little Rissington was mainly equipped with Jet Provost T3s, 4s and 5s and SAL Bulldogs. Because of its importance, CFS had Group status but, on February 9 1974, that was withdrawn and the School passed under the control of 23 Group. For Little Rissington this marked the commencement of the close-down procedure and, on April 12 1976, HQ CFS, the Examining Wing and Jet Provost Squadron all moved to Cranwell. The Bulldogs flew to Leeming, and Little Rissington closed as a functional station in Training Command. On August 31 1976, SHQ Little Rissington disbanded and the RAF vacated the station which was handed to the Army Department on September 1 1976 and became Imjin Barracks. During 1982 the Americans arrived to establish a medical centre here.

Little Staughton, Bedfordshire

TL120615. 4 miles W of St Neots, N of Bushmead

Pforzheim was rarely attacked. A raid by 250 aircraft of 1 Group and 50 of 6 Group was thus an unusual event. Additionally, 8 Group, the Pathfinders, fielded another 53 aircraft as well as eight Lancasters of 582 Squadron, Little Staughton. One was flown by the Master Bomber, Captain Edwin Swales, DFC, South African Air Force. Barely had his *M Mother PB538* reached the target area, when a fighter engaged the Lancaster. Although the rear guns were put out of action, Swales continued his task. A German fighter then repeatedly attacked rendering a second engine useless.

Swales, his task completed, set course for home in an almost defenceless aircraft. By the time friendly territory was reached it became clear the aircraft could never land safely. Swales decided that his crew must bale out, which meant flying the aircraft steadily. Moments after the last man parachuted away *PB538* crashed at Chapelle au Bois, near Monchaux in France and Swales was killed. For his action he was posthumously awarded the Victoria Cross.

From Little Staughton in the last year of the war 582 Squadron was at the helm of many a bombing raid. Even more importantly, it was from here that the *Oboe* Mosquitoes of 109 Squadron marked targets, sometimes for all Bomber Command.

On December 1 1942, 475 American airmen and 28 officers arrived at Little Staughton to prepare the Advanced Air Depot, 1st Bombardment Wing, which positioned B-17s at this airfield, alias AAF Station 127. Little Staughton had previously attracted a variety of aircraft, the first to land being an Anson from Finningley which called on December 7 1942. By February 1943, three T2s were in place, and on May 1 1943 it passed into American hands, some Robin hangars had been added—unusual in this part of Britain.

Throughout 1943 the base was a maintenance depot. An agreement to place RAF Bomber Groups within clutches led on March 1 1944 to Little Staughton, passing to No 8 Group, PFF, Bomber Command. On April 1 a Flight from 7 Squadron and another from 156

On dispersal at Little Staughton, an Oboe *Mosquito BIX of 109 Squadron.*

Squadron arrived to amalgamate as No 582 Squadron, Lancaster equipped. The next day much of 109 Squadron, PFF, arrived from Marham where runway building was to commence. Mosquitoes of 109 Squadron had been marking invasion targets and undertaking extensive diversion and nuisance raids on Germany. On the night of April 4/5 1944, 109 Squadron opened Staughton's impressive operational record, with raids on Essen where 'Cookies' were dropped on Cologne, Krefeld, Aachen and Rheinhaussen. That first night was one of the few occasions when an *Oboe* Mosquito failed to return. 'S Sugar' had crashed in the North Sea.

Lille marshalling yards on the night of April 9/10 1944 were 582 Squadron's first target, seven crews operating. On April 10/11 they bombed Laon and next night, Aachen. By the end of April they had visited Cologne, Düsseldorf, Karlsruhe, Essen and distant Friedrichshafen, suffering their first loss on April 22/23, *JA933* which was one of two aircraft attacking Laon. By the end of April 1944, 582 Squadron had flown 120 sorties and No 109, 190. May was busier, 320 sorties being flown by 109 Squadron and 173 by the Lancasters of 582.

An unusual event took place early on May 23 1944. At 03:00, Anson *LT476* of 13 OTU, on a cross-country flight, was attacked by an intruder, hit by cannon fire and forced to land at Little Staughton. One of the crew had baled out, the pilot had serious abdominal wounds and the navigator a thigh injury.

For both squadrons the opening of the Normandy invasion brought a busy night marking coastal batteries. During July 1944, 628 sorties were flown from the station and, in August, 620, which gives an indication of the activity level.

Although losses were lower than at many bomber bases, operations were far from uneventful. On May 22/23, for example, Squadron Leader H.W.B. Heley, flying at 18,000 ft in *JB417-R*, had an incendiary bomb hit his Lancaster's port rudder. Another lodged in the port outer engine before exploding. Heley completed his bombing run, then ordered the crew to prepare to bale out as flames were now trailing behind the wing. A searchlight picked out the bomber and it was seven dangerous minutes before the flames went out. Between Cologne and Gladbach predicted flak hit the Lancaster, yet it still made England.

Near Mepal, Heley switched on his navigation lights because there were many aircraft about. Moments later an intruder attacked the Lancaster from below and astern. With the rear turret out of action, *JB417* was highly vulnerable. Although enemy fire raked the bomber none of the crew was injured. Despite the loss of hydraulics, *JB417* made an emergency landing at Little Staughton after which the crew discovered that a 500 lb GP bomb had 'hung up'. An eventful sortie indeed.

The first day raid for 582's Lancasters came on the evening of June 30 1944 with Villars Bocage as target. No 109 Squadron also took part. Thereafter daylight operations became quite common with 582 Squadron concentrating upon them during the first half of August. Both squadrons took part in tactical bombing raids, including Operation *Tractable* on August 14, and Lancasters of 582 Squadron marked for a day raid on the Ghent–Terneuzen Canal on August 18. In early September 582 Squadron helped to reduce Le Havre's garrison to submission, before Calais and Boulogne received similar treatment. On October 3 the target was West Kapelle with Group Captain P.H. Cribb as Master Bomber in 582's *ND750*.

Rarely did enemy fighters successfully engage Bomber Command's heavies in daylight, but an exception came on December 23 1944. To attack Cologne's Grimberg marshalling yards 17 Lancasters of 582 Squadron and a 109 Squadron Mosquito set out in fine weather. Intense flak on the run in damaged 11 Lancasters, a mixture of Bf 109s and Fw 190s then swept through the fighter screen, engaging the bombers over the target. Lancaster *T Tommy*, flown by Captain Swales, was attacked by eight Bf 109s and a Fw 190 which one of his gunners claimed. Wing Commander Clough's crew fought it out with a Messerschmitt. Twelve of the Lancasters placed their bombs at the southern end of the rail yard. But it was costly for Little Staughton, five Lancasters and a Mosquito failing to return.

Barely had the returning Lancasters touched down when four Mosquitoes of 109 Squadron took off to join another 36 attacking Seighburg. Four more were among the 58 sent to Limburg. During December, 582 Squadron lost seven Lancasters, and by the close of the year, it had flown 1,588 sorties—147 in December during which 109 Squadron lost five Mosquitoes in the course of 284 sorties.

Nine crews of 582 Squadron participated in the notorious Dresden raid, four as blind illuminators, one a blind marker, one a blind skymarker, one a primary visual marker and two as visual centres, all of whom returned safely. Complexity of pathfinder operations is well illustrated by even this small portion of the force. On the same night six other crews of '582' marked the synthetic oil refinery at Bohlen for 200 bombers of 4 Group and 115 of 6 Group. Chemnitz was twice 582's target at this time. Operations by 109 Squadron included a daylight raid on March 6 when Wesel was bombed by six Mosquitoes leading other 8 Group Mosquitoes. The leader of the first formation collided with a Mosquito off Southwold, leaving Flight Lieutenant Carnegie to force land his Mosquito at Woodbridge.

Offensive operations by Little Staughton's three-Flight squadrons ended on April 25 1945. Only one of 109 Squadron's aircraft was able to mark the Wachenfels SS Barracks at Berchtesgaden, the rest having technical problems, then came the final fling. Wangerooge's guns were targetted for 25 Lancasters of 582 Squadron and eight crews of 109 Squadron were marked. Both squadrons participated in food drop operations for the starving Dutch in Operation *Manna* in early May, and 582 Squadron retrieved PoWs in Operation *Exodus* particularly from Juvincourt and Lübeck and brought them back to Westcott.

Cook's tours of damaged Germany followed. Mosquito crews continued training, their squadron being earmarked for retention. Some of their practice raids were experimentally intercepted by Meteors. The end for 582 Squadron came on September 10 1945, its Lancasters being flown away to Mepal and Wyton. On the afternoon of September 28 all of 109 Squadron's Mosquitoes left for Upwood, ending Staughton's operational days.

On October 19 1945, Typhoon *RB390* of the Station Flight crashed nearby, five days before Transport Command took control of the airfield which, on October 10 1945, was declared non-operational. Tempsford billetted 300 of its men here from late November. Flying had not entirely ceased for, on November 28, a Dakota landed and, on November 30, an Anson. But during December 1945 Little Staughton was placed on Care and Maintenance.

There was considerable discussion as to whether this and Thurleigh could be linked by a long runway for the NAE, it being reckoned that high speed aircraft would have long take off runs. The idea was abandoned although RAE Bedford has had links with Little Staughton. The airfield has seen post-war use by Brooklands Aviation who handled Valettas, Varsities and target towing Mosquitoes here. A visit to the airfield in the 1980s reveals assorted light civil aircraft including crop sprayers. The control tower, hangars, dispersals and runways remain, and are easy to view from adjacent roads.

Long Marston, Warwickshire

SP170480. 6 miles N of Chipping Campden, by A46

Long Marston had the customary three runway layout, one runway remaining in quite good condition. A large domestic site to the ENE retains many of its buildings. The airfield came into use in late 1941 for brief use by the Ferry Training Unit. In March 1942 under 91 Group it became satellite station for Whitleys of 24 OTU whose Gunnery Flight formed here in November 1942. From April 20 1944, 24 OTU functioned with Wellington III/Xs, conversion flying being taken here until July 1945. Wellingtons of 23 OTU also used the airfield during 1943 and, on March 8 1944, No 1681 Bomber Defence Training Flight's four Tomahawks arrived from Pershore and within days Hurricane IIcs replaced them.

After the war 8 MU used the airfield as a sub-storage unit. After a period of Care and Maintenance, Long Marston was resurrected as an RLG for Oxfords of 10 Advanced Flying Training School, Pershore, which specialised in the training of National Service pilots. The airfield closed in 1954 and was transferred to the War Department.

Part of the aerodrome has recently been re-activated, for civilian flying. A new hangar has been erected, housing a variety of light civil aircraft. Gliding also takes place from Long Marston, and among the unusual aircraft based here of late has been the Spartan Arrow *G-ABWP*. Microlight aircraft also have a home here. Long Marston secretly appeared in the ITV series, *Crossroads*, for it was here that the motel fire was staged to mark Meg Mortimer's going.

Luton, Bedfordshire

TL120210. 2 miles E of town, off A6129

'What on earth is that awful din?' Father said. 'Never heard anything like that before.' I agreed, fascinated. This was an aeroplane for which one waited—you could hear it coming for ages, adding to the excitement. 'It' was certainly worth waiting for, something like an enlarged, pregnant Piper Pawnee. Wings like thick wooden planks supported as unstreamlined a form as man could devise. A speed of almost nil was accompanied by an incredible din emitted from this flying pantechnicon.

What on earth could it be? With brown and green camouflage underpinned by trainer yellow—certainly experimental. Yet for what purpose? One of 'us' consulted a friend who consulted another who naughtily devised a means of consulting that most attractive volume presumably printed to give the likes of us temptation and pleasure, *AP 1480X*. A precious copy of the handbook of silhouettes of experimental aircraft had been lodged, entrustingly, into military hands. Most things are possible and after a deft and rapid piece of fast tracing—how useful a photo copying machine would have been in the fun days—we had a good drawing of Experimental Aeroplane No 103.

With the tracing came news that the aircraft had not come from Duxford—unlike the drawing. Yet it staggered from Cambridge in that direction. Deliberations and a map suggested its lair to be Farnborough where all good things were said to reside. It would, though, have taken that aeroplane a mighty long time to reach the RAE—and why would it have come so far, and approach from the east? By the end of that week, during which it had exhibited itself again, we had discovered that it was from Luton where Napier had their flight test facility. That noisy engine was the mighty 2,000 hp Sabre built to deliver twice the power of a Merlin and probably the most troublesome production engine of all time. The aeroplane we later learned, was a Folland '43/37' flying engine test bed. How utterly removed from the present Luton international airport although 'tis true that quite noisy aeroplanes, some with pregnant forms and strange sounding engines, may still be seen.

Luton has long been far more than a hive for Monarchs, 737s, 'Brits' and Court Line, for this was the place where Percival aeroplanes, *real* aeroplanes were made. Prior to the present site, a landing ground existed 2½ miles to the north-west until it was outflanked by Luton town's ribbon development. In its place came a new grass aerodrome officially opened on July 16 1938. Luton Corporation's desire for a municipal airport differed from Birmingham's, and was on a much firmer financial and economic base. Council eagerness to attract new industries to their town resulted in Captain Edgar Percival vacating his Gravesend factory and moving his production base to Luton. Percival had achieved considerable

Among aircraft tested by Napier, Luton, was the Annular Tempest, NV768.

Impressive because of noise, bulk and its ability almost to hover—the Folland 43/37 engine test bed. P1774 *by a Luton hangar* (Folland).

success with the Gull series and the Mew Gull racers.

The airfield, on high ground east of Luton, was constructed where conditions were usually clear whereas the low lying town was often misty. Thoughtful positioning makes the present airport well sighted and has often made it a diversion airfield. Percival's factory lay to the north of the adjacent industrial site and to the left of the approach road.

A Sabre-powered Firebrand naval fighter at Luton (Napier).

The company moved to Luton in 1936–7, building and levelling of the aerodrome taking place in 1936. The Company's Gull first flew in December 1935 and, during the move, further Gull variants were being planned. Work was also being undertaken on the twin-engined six-seven seat Percival Q.6, the last new pre-war design, first flown in 1937. Vega Gull and Q.6 production occupied the firm in 1938. Fifteen Vega Gulls were supplied to the RAF and a specialised military variant followed.

The Air Ministry desired to open an Elementary & Reserve Flying Training School at Luton. This was discussed in 1936, and Marshall of Cambridge offered in April 1937 to run the school to which the Council agreed. Ten days after the air-

Above *At pre-war Luton, hangars and a rudimentary club house are being built. A Heston Phoenix is close by. The large oddly sited house still stands* (Luton Corporation).

Below *By 1945, Luton airport was adjacent to a large factory complex. In the foreground are the Percival factory and flight sheds, Napier lay beyond. A few Mosquitoes are on the aerodrome* (Luton Corporation).

field officially opened, two Hawker Harts, *K2979* and *K3054*, landed to be available for 29 E&RFTS which opened on August 1 1938. It was never a large School, but the airfield attracted a wide variety of light aircraft in pre-war days and many famous fliers sampled the delight of a Gull or the sight of that beautiful, turquoise Q.6, 'EYE'.

Percival's military Gull, the Proctor, first flew from Luton on October 8 1939, by which time Captain Percival had left the Company. Proctor 1 deliveries commenced in March 1940, and some also went to the Royal Navy. Proctor 1 production at Luton totalled 222 aircraft and, as work on the Mk II was underway, much else happened. Into the western area of the airfield, where some 'T2' hangars had been erected, moved a small, secretive organisation, the Napier Flight Development Unit. Napier's factory was in Acton and the firm had managed to establish the Napier Experimental Engine Installation Unit at Northolt in 1937, to carry out flight trials of their H-type Dagger engine, testing of which was underway in 1938. That year witnessed bench running of the mammoth 24-cylinder 'I' inline Sabre engine. An output of 2,000 hp seemed colossal at that time, making it favourite choice for a multitude of new aircraft types. Problems with the engine were endless, often insurmountable, but the need for the Sabre made cancellation impossible and forced its development to acceptable levels. Eventually only two fully operational wartime aircraft were Sabre-powered, out of over 30 designs for which it was considered.

To test the power plant a Fairey Battle, *L5286*, was taken to Northolt on August 18 1939 to have the engine installed. Another Battle, *K9240*, fitted with a Dagger, flew mostly from Farnborough.

Whilst the Battle was suitable for a variety of engines, it lacked space for comprehensive measurement equipment and was a makeshift test bed. Napier's flight facility was pushed out of Northolt, by Fighter Command needs, to Luton during March 1940. From there the fixed undercarriage Battle was busily flown, testing its Sabre until March 1941 when RAE took charge in an attempt to improve the engine.

Others were about to move too. Short Brothers operated two E&RFTSs, one at Rochester (No 23), the other at Belfast (No 24). At the outbreak of war the two amalgamated at Sydenham as No 24 EFTS. Pre-war training of personnel for the Fleet Air Arm continued. The 1940 collapse of France led to Battle bombers being placed at Sydenham to prevent a German attempt to land in Ireland, and 24 EFTS was forced to find space elsewhere. Leicestershire airfields were reviewed, but choice finally fell upon under-used Luton to where, on July 17 1940, the EFTS moved. Two courses underway had to live under canvas, and servicing the unit's Miles Magisters was undertaken in the open. Each course trained about 30 pupils. trained about 30 pupils.

By the end of August there had been limited enemy action near Luton. The climax came in the late afternoon of August 30 when a score of Heinkels bombed Luton's factory area. Although 28 bombs fell within the airfield boundary there was little damage and no very serious casualties. A parachute mine one night penetrated the roof of the Percival factory some 25 yds from where RAF Luton's Orderly Officer was on night duty.

Luton had meanwhile established another link with Northolt. Fame came as fast as it went to No 264 Squadron, the first to operate Boulton Paul Defiant turret fighters. Losses forced its withdrawal to safer skies, and the Battle of Britain further proved it outmoded. Then 264 Squadron switched to night fighting, for which B Flight moved to Northolt on September 12 1940. Seven days later, Squadron Leader Garvin moved his Flight to Luton and used sick quarters as the operations room. Tents in the north-west corner of the airfield were for the duty crews. On the night following arrival, the Defiants commenced night patrols west of London under Northolt's control. Nightly operations were punctuated by a spectacular accident. At around 05:30 on October 7 veteran Defiant *L7018* was commencing its take off when, as it raced along the flare path, it hit the wing tip of a stationary aircraft, setting the latter ablaze. The Defiant, momentarily airborne, crashed into a large tent, the whole bursting into flames. Amazingly, the three tent occupants escaped with slight injuries.

Greater excitement, was afforded to Pilot Officer Hughes and Sergeant Green who, flying *N1621*, shot down a Heinkel 111 near Brentwood at around 01:30 on October 16. This was 264's first night success, and the only occasion when a Luton-based aircraft successfully engaged

An early product of Percival at Luton was the Vega Gull.

the foe. B Flight left Luton on October 29 for Rochford.

Through the Battle of Britain the Sabre Battle, *L5286*, was active. It logged over 1,000 flying hours during four years of active service which ended on December 7 1943. Between May 10 1940 and August 17 1941, a Hereford was also at Luton helping to solve oil problems plaguing the Dagger. More important, though, was the arrival in late 1940 of *P1774*, the first Gloster-built Folland test bed, used for Sabre 1 flight trials. Over the next four years it was joined by four others. *P1774* served as a Sabre II cooling test bed, *P1776* arrived at Luton on March 29 1942 to help test the Sabre II and various radiators before it crashed on August 28 1944. *P1780* served at Luton from January 1943 to August, and *P1778* was used for trails of the E 118 Sabre and its ducted radiator. *P1779* was used for development of the Sabre V and VII.

Napier's test facility attracted Sabre-powered operational aircraft, the first in the summer of 1941, being a Typhoon Ia for engine oil pressures and temperatures, cylinder tests and engine cooling investigations. Meanwhile 24 EFTS flew long hours using Magisters, some of which, from the summer of 1940, used Barton-in-the-Clay RLG for circuit flying. One of the highlights of the stay of 24 EFTS came on May 23 1941 when Sir Winston Churchill and a famous retinue visited. Their opinions of the Sabre will probably always remain secret!

At Luton, 24 EFTS concentrated upon training pilots for the Fleet Air Arm. There were 99 pilots undergoing

The beginnings of a grand venture—Avro Yorks by a primitive Luton control tower (Luton Corporation).

instruction when the School left Luton and its Magisters, and moved to Sealand on February 7 1942.

In 1941 Percival's drawing office designed the Proctor III. Only its prototype was built here. Instead, the Company constructed 775 Airspeed Oxford Is, 575 Mk IIs and six Oxford Vs in its much enlarged factory. Wood working skills were even better utilised, building 195 Mosquito XVIs and 50 Mosquito PR 34s at Luton whilst Messrs F. Hills & Son of Manchester built the Proctors. A further Proctor re-design during 1942–3 led to the four-seater Proctor IV radio trainer. Only eight were Luton built.

The second type to have a Sabre was the Blackburn Firebrand naval fighter, the prototype of which, *DD804*, was at Luton in 1942–3 for 200 hours of flying in an attempt to clear its 2,250 hp Sabre III. The Sabre required a large radiator, and a novel manner of reducing its drag was tried on Typhoon *R8694* which arrived at Luton in August 1942 to have a radiator wrapped around its Sabre IV in annular style. Such a radial change would have upset production lines far too much, although in August 1944 a Warwick III arrived for similar fitting, and trials lasted into post-war years.

The development of a two-speed supercharged Sabre was an obvious progression. Napier's went even further and designed the E.118 three-stage Sabre in connection with which Folland *P1778* did some flying. The final wartime main Sabre work revolved around making it a going concern for the Tempest V, the first of which, *EJ518*, came to Luton on May 29 1944. Napier, keen to push the annular radiator on the Sabre VI, fitted an example to this aircraft. When it force landed in late 1944, Napier continued their work using Warwick C III *HG248*.

Napier held up to 20 aircraft at one time in 1944 for engine development. One tricky problem was to add wing root oil cooler to allow the Tempest VI to operate in hot climates. Another Tempest, *NV768*, had an annular radiator. This was the unusual looking Tempest, later fitted with a drag-reducing ducted spinner adding 15 mph to top speed. This was to be a standard post-war fitting to the Naiad turbo-prop engine, test flown in the noses of two Lincoln bombers, *RF402* and *RF530*. At Luton a Bristol Phoebus was installed in the belly of another Lincoln, *RA643*, and the Napier-patented electrothermal Spraymat de-icer system was first tested on Viking *VL229*, which served for seven years, and then on a Lincoln. Another Lincoln, *SX973*, had a Napier Nomad, a large compound engine intended for very long range ocean patrol aircraft. Its ultimate rejection was a bitter blow to Napier, and when the Eland-powered Rotodyne was also cancelled Napier's future was bleak. Some success attended the Gazelle engine for the Bristol 192, and the Double Scorpion rocket motor in

Napier's icing research Lincoln carrying a Sud Aviation Caravelle test section (Napier).

Further step in Luton development—a new tower, large apron and additional hangars have been added, along with some large civil transports. Napier has now suffered a demise (Luton Corporation).

Canberra *WK163* hurled the aircraft fast and high in spectacular scenes. Another Canberra, *WH793*, was in 1955 modified to become the PR Mk 9 prototype. Lack of orders ended Napier's engine work before the 1960s.

Hostilities over, Percival put the Proctor V—a civil version of the Mk IV—into production at Luton, selling it at home and abroad. Even more important was the three-seat trainer design to Specification T.23/43, the RAF's post-war intermediate trainer, the Prentice, produced at Luton between August 1947 and August 1950.

Recalling their elegant Q.6 airliner, Percival designed a new five-eight seater, the Merganser. It first flew on May 9 1947 but its Gipsy Queen engines gave insufficient power. Re-design resulted in the Alvis Leonides powered eight-ten seater Prince, and the military Pembroke. Varieties of both types were built and more projected, but it was the Provost trainer which brought success when it was accepted as the replacement type for the RAF's Prentice. All Provosts were Luton built in the large hangar and works to the left of the approach road at the entrance to the airport site.

Vaguely resembling the Provost and retaining side-by-side seating for instructor and pilot, the Jet Provost was a natural development. All the Mk 1s and 3s were built at Luton but, during production of the Mk 4, Percival became Hunting-Percival and then Hunting Aircraft was overtaken by the British Aircraft Corporation. At that time the company had, in a building on the opposite side of the road to the production line and strongly guarded, a mock-up of an elegant P.107 airliner which BAC acquired and from which in part the BAC One-Eleven was devised.

Alongside Percival's, Luton Flying Club with its pre-war origin operated from the end of the war. Much publicity surrounded the news that the notorious Neville Hume, who cruelly murdered for sexual satisfaction, flew with the club and did so during its first post-war air display on June 10 1946. Hunting, much associated with Luton, had two Proctor Vs on view. Others were being overhauled for the RAF and keeping them company was Jean Batten's Vega Gull still registered *AX866* (and presently at Old Warden as *G-ADPR*). Hunting Aerosurvey displayed their Dragon Rapide, *G-AEAL*. By Hangars 3 & 4, used by the Napier Installation Experimental Establishment, were two Typhoons, the aged *R7712* keeping company with *RB450*. Warwick III *HG248* still retained its wartime grey-green-blue transport finish, beside which Tempest *NV768* looked immaculate. During the show a Tempest VI *EJ823* was demonstrated, making this a small yet memorable display. There was not the slightest portent of what would overtake the airfield.

Luton acquired its asphalt runway after the war, although not before Eagle Aviation obtained hangar space and, in the early 1950s, kept some of its Yorks here. Expansion of charter operations was slow, the mainly ex-military aircraft being costly to maintain and having low load factors.

Luton Council decided, in 1958, cautiously to expand their aerodrome, devising Luton International Airport at the time when Napier was floundering and Pervical's future was none too assured. Before the decade was out Derby Aviation was running scheduled internal services from Luton, and in 1960 charter operations were commenced by Autair using the 5,532 ft runway and departure buildings which, as part of the briefing and operations area, remain in use at the base of the unusual shaped control tower.

Indications of the rapid growth of Luton Airport can be appreciated from the fact that in 1961 there were 580 commercial movements whereas in 1980 they totalled 26,358 with a peak in 1972 of 31,257. Expansions followed the runway extension to 7,054 ft in 1966. Another £750,000 was spent on a new passenger terminal, then the new combination eroded Southend's tourist trade.

Autair became Court Line in 1969 and entered the inclusive tour market, undercutting fares and introducing Lockheed TriStars. In 1972–3 3,145,658 passengers passed through the airport. Then in August 1974 came the catastrophic collapse of Court Line, at the height of the summer traffic. Luton's passenger total fell dramatically, to 1,920,275 in 1974–5. Since then it has built up and, in 1979–80, some 2,230,568 passengers passed through the airport.

Well sited, and with a flight path which takes the aircraft to the south of the town, Luton Airport suffers from a tedious feature. Taxiways to the runway join the latter someway along its length, requiring backtracking prior to take off, this reducing the speed of operation. Approval for improvements has never been forthcoming from the Government—linked, perhaps, with hopes that Stansted could snatch away Luton's success. In the league of passengers passing through, Luton stands in fifth place in Britain, Stansted eighteenth. Elmdon, which has suffered from ambitious schemes of long ago, currently occupies sixth place, with some quarter million fewer passengers but more general aviation use than Luton.

Since the Court Line disaster, Luton has been largely the home for Britannia Airways, Monarch Airlines and McAlpine which handles a lucrative and mainly VIP charter business. The 1970s have seen operators here switching from first generation jets to the quieter, more economic Boeing 737. Some boost to Luton has come from the decision of the Post Office and Air Ecosse to use it as the base for the distribution of Datapost during night flights. Over 90 airlines used Luton during 1979–80 and flights were made to 65 countries. With every confidence in the future Luton Council, in late 1979 approved a plan for a much enhanced terminal building. This will cost at least £6m to produce but, bearing in mind that the airport makes a healthy profit, and that the future looks encouraging, this is a worthwhile risk.

Quite a lot of the old wartime, and even pre-war, Luton remains. The large hangar by the west side of the apron comprises the two pre-war hangars, joined and modified. Some of the 'T2s', still in use, once held the Typhoons and Follands. Pervical's factory is now part of Vauxhall Motors. Two grass runways on the north side of the field, 18/36 and 06/24, lead to the light aircraft section sited where once Defiants dispersed.

'Luton' will have provided delight for millions setting off for a place in the sun and, maybe, venturing to some far away place. Luton provides a far more intimate service than many airports, and in a highly competitive field. The two old hangars have been updated to house Boeing's new wide-bodied 757s and 767s. Some difference from that noisy old Folland!

Lyneham, Wiltshire

SU015785. 3½ miles SW of Wootton Bassett by A420

With a clear sunlit summer eve as a backdrop, I 'borrowed' a Comet and flew it

Lyneham on September 25 1943. Central is the transport base area supplied with Albemarles and Liberators (RAF Museum)

over the Atlantic. It was outward bound from Lyneham and when we turned for home, darkness was encompassing base. Part of Britain's outline appeared as a pale glow, punctuated by millions of bright, minute lights before thick haze obscured their magic. Over Cornwall we flew, high and contrailing.

Let down started, night circuits commenced, and *XK696* was still mine as I banked around the lights of Swindon. Then the thrill of flying this exhilerating aeroplane ebbed away when the captain took over. When I regained control some circuits later we were racing along the runway, tremendous force coursing through my fingers. 'Not so much power, Mike,' called the captain—by which time we were ferociously hurtling into the night sky. Comet, at that time, was synonymous with Lyneham which, for over 40 years, has been the major RAF transport centre.

Lyneham was never intended for such use. RAF transport aircraft were almost non-existent when Lyneham emerged with two 'J' Type hangars and ranks of huts and single storey buildings which graced many a Midland training centre. Allied to School facilities were Lamella hangars for 33 MU, which opened on May 18 1940 and handled assorted types of aircraft. In mid-August 1941, the 41 Group station passed to 23 Group, Flying Training Command. Oxfords of 14 SFTS arrived from Cranfield and stayed only until February 1942 when the School left for Ossington.

Ferry Command possessed Lyneham on February 14 1942. A ferry unit sited by an MU made sense, and Honeybourne's Ferry Training Unit reached Lyneham in March 1942. By then that unit had become important. No 1 Flight operated Beauforts, Hudsons, Marylands and Wellingtons, No 2 Flight trained crews to ferry these to the Middle East and No 3 Flight trained test pilots for ASUs in 41 Group. The latter left for Filton in June 1942.

No 1425 Flight concentrating on courier services to Africa, brought four Liberator Is from Honeybourne to Lyneham in April 1942. In June, No 1442 Flight arrived. It flew overseas ferry deliveries from Bicester, and was joined by No 1444 Flight, lately ferrying Hudsons to the Far East, and a Flight of Liberator IIs, No 1445, concentrating upon the delivery overseas of that type.

Lyneham's 1425 Flight within a few weeks found itself carrying some of the world's most distinguished leaders. *AL504 Commando*, the famous British Liberator with special VIP interior, joined the Flight in May and, on August 1, left Lyneham carrying Sir Winston Churchill to the Middle East. It was followed, on August 8, by *AM914*, conveying General Alexander and proceeding to Teheran, whilst *AM911* followed with Lord Alanbrooke, General Wavell and Air Chief Marshal Sir Arthur Tedder. *AL504* visited Moscow prior to landing back at Lyneham on August 24. A month later another famous Liberator, *AM922*, brought

General de Gaulle to Lyneham.

Responsibility for maintaining 1425's aircraft switched to Lyneham Maintenance Wing in September 1942. On October 10 1942 the aircraft became part of a new squadron, No 511, which received a few Liberator IIs. The squadron continued its predecessor's role in 1943, conveying important passengers and vital freight to and from Africa. Its equipment also included a few special Albemarles for a service to Gibraltar sometimes extended to Africa. On October 1 1943, Squadron Leader J.F. Sach, with the Flight since its start, inaugurated a regular Transport service to India. More sombre was the misfortune which, on July 5 1943, overtook Liberator *AL523* when carrying the Polish leader General Sikorski. Shortly after taking off from Gibraltar, it crashed into the sea in mysterious circumstances.

Lyneham's FTU had been restructured on November 3 1942 as No 301 FTU, flying Blenheims, Beauforts, Hudsons and Liberators in addition to aircraft for overseas delivery. Within A Flight (previously No 1) were Blenheims, Beauforts, Beaufighters and Wellingtons. B Flight, formed from 1444 Flight, handled Hudsons leaving C Flight (ex-1445 Flight) to deliver Halifaxes and Liberators. Throughout 1943, No 301 FTU trained ferry crews to deliver multi-engined aircraft, via No 1 OADU Portreath, to the Middle East. No 33 MU mainly dealt with Spitfires, 250 being held at one time. At the end of 1943, 33 MU started assembling Hamilcar gliders, an association lasting till the end of the Hamicar's days and including maintenance of powered Hamilcar Xs until December 1951. The MU mainly concentrated upon servicing jet fighters, particularly Meteors, after the war.

To Pershore, 301 FTU moved mid-1944, ending Lyneham's ferry commitment. The station passed to Transport Command on July 24 1944, and became its main UK passenger centre. No 525 Squadron arrived in February 1944 with Warwick Transports. In June–July 1944 it equipped with Warwick IIIs and from November 1944 until its departure in July 1945 flew Dakotas.

Dakotas were first based at Lyneham in October 1943, four Mk Is having come from 512 Squadron for No 511. On November 10 1943, 511 Squadron took on charge its first Avro York, the VVIP-*MW100*, joined by *MW101* on November 22 1943. Dakotas replaced 511 Squadron's Albemarles in December. The special Yorks were soon replaced, supplemented by more standard Yorks in mid-1944 and joined by a dozen Liberator VIIs, serving with 511 Squadron from June 1944. On July 21 the first York scheduled service to the Far East began and in August Liberators replaced Dakotas on the Middle East Runs. Close partnership existed with BOAC whose aircraft were frequently at Lyneham.

Britannia C2 Canopus *alongside a modified 'J' Type hangar at Lyneham. The centre cut-out allows tall-finned aircraft to enter the hangar which has modifications to its doors and their rail hoodings.*

Proud were the Comet crews of 216 Squadron, Lyneham, and with justification, for theirs was the world's first military jet transport squadron.

By autumn 1944, Lyneham was extremely busy, with over 300 daily movements by Dakotas, Liberators, Yorks and by an increasing proportion of Stirlings. Early in 1945 a Halifax Development Flight began to work out possible roles for that aircraft in Transport Command. Passengers streamed through Lyneham's primitive lounges, whilst through the VIP facility came the famous, to such aircraft as Skymaster *EW999* and York *LV633, Ascalon*.

Cessation of hostilities in Europe resulted in increased activity. Large numbers of Liberators, hastily modified into troopers and freighters, staged through Lyneham to the Far East, the war ending as the big lift came under way. Liberators were then switched to returning an army, and maintained contact with British overseas territories in both the Middle and Far East until, in mid-1946, Yorks took over and a route structure was established with regular flights.

October 1945 had brought Mosquitoes of 1409 Flight to gather details of weather conditions along trunk routes. This was important work because transport aircraft were unpressurised and needed to avoid bumpy conditions to ensure passenger comfort. On December 1 1945, No 1389 VIP Flight formed, operating fast courier flights overseas using Lancastrians. It left on February 25 1946 for Bassingbourn.

A serious accident took place on November 23 1945. Stirling V, *PJ904*, touched down in poor visibility alongside a runway, careered into an assortment of buildings including a civilian canteen then smashed into the operations block causing serious casualties. A new Operations Section had to be established temporarily in a 'J' hangar.

Commonly seen here in 1946 were Avro Yorks. No 511 Squadron used them on the Far East route and other users' aircraft staged through daily since passenger flights operated from and to Lyneham.

Indian independence reduced route flying but in a post-war plan the reformation of Nos 99 and 206 Squadrons took place at Lyneham on November 17 1947, and both equipped with Yorks. The Berlin Airlift further reduced trunk route flying as Lyneham's squadrons operated to Germany. No 242 Squadron arrived in mid-June 1949 and, between August and October of that year, Nos 99, 242 and 511 Squadron re-equipped with Hastings. No 206 retained its Yorks until disbandment on February 20 1950. Diminishing need brought about the end of 242 Squadron on May 1 1950 and by 1951 route flying was in the hands of the Hastings squadrons. Between November 1950 and February 1951, 24 Squadron operated that type from Lyneham. It was replaced on February 9 1951 by 53 Squadron which flew

Falklands bound, a Hercules C1P, XV298, *with its in-flight refuelling probe prominent*

Hastings 1s and 2s from here until January 1957.

No 216 Squadron came to Lyneham in 1955 after 38 years service overseas. In June 1956 it became the world's first military jet transport squadron, flying Comet C.2's equipment with which was completed in May 1957. These aircraft were useful in the 'aeromedic' role. No 99 Squadron started to re-arm with Bristol Britannias in summer 1959, 511 Squadron following suit late that year. 'Brits' were popular aircraft on account of their comfort and economical performance, both squadrons using them until June 1970 when they moved to Brize Norton.

February 1960 brought to 216 Squadron its first Comet C.4. Whereas the C.2 carried 44 passengers, the stretched version could accommodate 94. Sometimes these aircraft operated in a VIP role, and also served as medical transports. In 1966, 216 Squadron's strength began to fall, the last C.2 being withdrawn from service in March 1967. C.4s continued operating until 1975, the squadron disbanding on June 30.

During the 1960s Lyneham's aircraft stood ready to carry the army's Strategic Reserve to troublespots, having over 20 Britannias and nine Comets available. Route flying to Hong Kong via Singapore, and less frequently to Australia and Africa, was undertaken. Support flights were often made to Malta and Cyprus, in support of the British presence there.

On April 5 1967, Lyneham's splendid terminal building opened, replacing the primitive wartime accommodation used by thousands. A superb new Officers' Mess also opened, offering comfort and facilities akin to a luxury hotel. The 'J' hangars had already been modified to permit aircraft with tall fins to be taken in for servicing. Although not based here, VC-10s of 10 Squadron staged through Lyneham awaiting the opening of Brize Norton's passenger terminal. At the end of 1967, No 33 MU closed.

No 36 Squadron moved to Lyneham on August 1 1967 to introduce the Hercules to the RAF. More squadrons followed until the Wing comprised six. Defence cuts resulted in No 36 disbanding on November 3 1975 and 48 Squadron closing on January 7 1976. This left the current four, Nos 24, 30, 47 and 70, along with a Hercules training unit. Following the Falklands conflict, tanker and in-flight refuelled Lyneham Hercules transports have provided the only air link between Ascension and Port Stanley.

Molesworth, Cambridgeshire

TL008775. East of Thrapston, best seen from B660 near Old Weston, N of A604

Molesworth! A place of delight for any

Hercules C1, XV290, *airborne from Lyneham for the Queen's Jubilee Review of the RAF in July 1977.*

protester. Mention the magic words 'Hell's Angels'—a group which fought gallantly from here, laying down many lives for our freedom, in a manner far more likely to secure it than the antics of some today—and the odds are that it will mean precisely nothing. All history proves beyond any doubt that freedom is for those, and only those, with the courage, means and determination to retain it. Whether the storage of cruise missiles at Molesworth is a good idea, or whether we all would be better safeguarded by the stationing of B-1s or 'Stealth' bombers with their accompanying noise, are arguable points. What is not in doubt is that Molesworth has an interesting and unusual history.

Planned in 1939 and built in 1940–1 as a bomber base with a single 'J' Type hangar, with associated services close by in serried rows, it is similar to Polebrook. An RAF opening party arrived on May 15 1941. It was intended to be an RAF Liberator base but, on November 15 1941, a new Australian squadron, No 460, formed here for C Flight of 458 Squadron armed with American-engined Wellington IVs. Kimbolton was already Molesworth's satellite and indeed the first Wellington for 460 Squadron placed itself there on November 29. No operations were flown before 460 Squadron left for Breighton on January 5 1942. Molesworth's first association with operational flying came three days later when a Wellington of 9 Squadron landed here from operations.

Molesworth's next occupants were crews of 159 Squadron who had learnt to use Liberators at Polebrook. Their 'aircraftless' stay was brief for, on February 12 1942, they left, in two trains, from Thrapston. Next day 13 Blenheims of A and B Flights, 17 OTU, came because Upwood was unserviceable. Some returned home on February 17, the remainder in March.

On February 27 1942, General Ira Eaker brought along four of his staff to view the station for possible American use. Major improvements followed, including runway extensions and additional dispersal areas. More accommodation was built and two 'T2' hangars added. Another unexpected interlude began on March 13 1942, 13 Master IIIs of 5 SFTS Ternhill arriving for a month's stay along with three Hurricanes.

In May 1942 preparations raced ahead for the establishment of No 2 Depot. On May 10 the station was placed on Care and Maintenance then, during the evening of May 12, trains arrived at Thrapston bringing foreigners under the command of Major M.C. Carpenter. Throughout May more Americans moved in, and early June ground personnel of the 31st Fighter Group were briefly here, and in mid-June some of the 5th Photographic Squadron. The greatest excitement greeted the arrival, on June 9 1942, of the 15th Bomb Group, which came to operate and that day received a couple of Boston IIIs and a helpless Tiger Moth.

Crews of the 15th had come to discover how to use Douglas A-20s in a night fighter/interdictor role. Outdated, the aircraft had been switched to day bombing and the Amerians decided to see how it performed such duty. Having no operational aircraft of its own, the 15th borrowed Boston IIIs from the RAF and was attached to No 226 Squadron RAF, Swanton Morley. Crewing one of their aircraft on June 29, a Molesworth crew, headed by Captain Kegelman, carried out the first USAAF bombing raid on a European target, the Hazebrouck marshalling yards.

One of the most famous early Fortresses, B-17F 41-24577, Hell's Angels, *of the 303rd Bomb Group photographed at Molesworth on October 10 1943. 43 bombing sorties are recorded on the nose and claims to nine fighters* (US Air Force).

Some Bostons were acquired in July from the RAF and decorated in US star insignia. More personnel arrived on July 14; their crusade, the effective operation of their vaunted Flying Fortress, and the target was Germany.

Of the date of the arrival of the first B-17F Fortress there seems uncertainty, but I first recorded one there on August 5. The 5th Photographic Reconnaissance Squadron left on September 10 and the 15th Bomb Squadron three days later. All was now clear for the arrival of the 303rd Bomb Group which left Biggs Field, Texas, and began moving in on September 12 after a five-day Atlantic crossing in the *Queen Mary*. By the end of the war in Europe the 303rd was to fly more operational sorties (10,721) than any other 8th AF Group, and in the course of 364 operations.

On November 17 1942, 16 B-17Fs of the 303rd flew their first operation, the target being U-boat pens at St Nazaire. Bombs were brought back for, on arrival the target was thickly cloud clad. Next day they tried for La Pallice, bombed—and discovered that they had hit the previous day's target! A few days later they redeemed themselves as the only Group to bomb Lorient during a difficult operation.

Committed to operations, 'Hell's Angels' joined in most major attacks by the 8th AF including the Wilhelmshaven raid of January 27 1943, when the 8th AF introduced itself to the residents of the Fatherland. They visited Hamm on February 2.

It was March 18 1943 when the courage suddenly demanded on operations was dramatically displayed. Lieutenant Jack W. Mathis was bombardier in *The Duchess*, a B-17F of the 358th Bomb Squadron. As the aircraft ran in on target a shell burst close to the nose, hurling Mathis back into

the fuselage. Horrifically wounded, he summoned the courage to drag himself back to the bombsight and released the bomb load before he died. He was posthumously awarded the Medal of Honor.

Raids on Germany took the group to well-known targets including Huls synthetic rubber factory, Bremen's shipyards, Hamburg, Frankfurt and Schweinfurt. Many targets in France were attacked both prior to, and following, D-Day, by which time another member of the 303rd had been awarded the Medal of Honor. Technical Sergeant Forrest L. Vosler, also of the 358th, was aboard *Jersey Bounce Jr* and ordered to bomb Bremen on December 20 1943. Heavy flak was encountered after which German fighters pestered the damaged Fortress. Vosler, seriously wounded, continued with his task, aiding the defence of the B-17. Eventually the aircraft ditched in the Channel. Despite terrible wounds, Vosler held another member of the crew aboard until both were transferred to a dinghy. After ten months treatment Vosler was invalided out of the Air Force.

As well as courageous men, Molesworth was the base of famous Fortresses. One was the B-17F *Hell's Angels, 41-24577* of the 358th Bomb Squadron, the first B-17 to complete 25 operational sorties over Europe. Another was *Knockout Dropper*, the first B-17 to manage 75 sorties—the equivalent to three crew tours. As *41-24605* it had arrived in Britain in October 1942, joined the 359th Bomb Squadron, became *EN-R* and brought its crew home each time without any being wounded. During the Oschersleben raid of January 11 1944, when the 303rd was leading the 1st Air Division, ten B-17s were shot down by intense fighter onslaught. The courage of all won the group a Distinguished Unit Citation. Molesworth remains a place of caring pilgrimage—but not for the weak willed.

The 303rd, making its final operation on April 25 1945, bombed Pilsen in Czechoslovakia. In early June the Group moved to North Africa for transport duty. The RAF repossessed Molesworth on July 1 1945. Affinity to things American continued, Nos 441 and 442 Canadian squadrons bringing their Mustang IIIs and IVs on July 16. On July 27 1945 a rare sight and sound arrived as Meteor IIIs of 1335 Conversion Unit came in from Colerne. They were to convert piston engined fighter squadrons to jet aircraft.

Both Canadian squadrons disbanded on August 10, and were replaced by 234 Squadron from Hutton Cranswick. On September 7 1945, Mustang IVs of 19 Squadron moved in. Whilst here they managed to acquire blue and white nose chequerboard markings, despite official frowning.

In March 1946, Spitfire XVIs replaced 19 Squadron's Mustangs, the squadron leaving on June 28 1946. Spitfire IXs of 129 Squadron had arrived from Brussels on November 9 1945 and left for Hutton Cranswick on December 3. No 124 Squadron, here from August to October 6 1945, flew Meteor IIIs. In late October 1945, 222 Squadron came from Weston Zoyland to convert to Meteors. October 15 1945 brought the first accident to a Molesworth Meteor. Short of fuel, it came down two miles from Polebrook.

In November 1945 the first of several foreign delegations came to see the Meteor. Whether they knew of November's highlight is doubtful. At about 01:00 on November 20 a guardroom Corporal heard an unexpected roar. A Meteor was making an unauthorised flight. The roll call showed Pilot Officer J.E. Adam missing, along with *EE316*. The general hullabaloo brought the special investigation branch along and 12 Group held a court of enquiry.

On December 11 1945, 222 Squadron left for Exeter. Following a winter break, 234 Squadron came in mid-February to convert to Meteors, leaving for Boxted in March. Between September and October 1946, Tempest IIs of 54 Squadron were based here, then the station was placed on Care and Maintenance.

Molesworth's very open approaches and generally good weather record led to it being improved, and re-opened, for the USAF, in July 1951. A long, single runway was laid, superimposed upon the conventional three-runway site. The base opened for flying in February 1954. Unusual were the new occupants for, when the 582nd Air Re-supply Group arrived late that month, it brought a dozen B-29As, four Grumman SA-16A amphibians, three C-119Cs, able to use RATO gear, and a C-47. The B-29s' role was hidden under security wraps and said to include 'supply dropping and giving assistance to crews who had come down in difficult terrain'. A few B-45s of the 47th Bomb Wing briefly were at Molesworth in mid-1956 whilst their home base had runway repairs.

On October 25 1956 the 582 ARG dissolved into a new 42nd Troop Carrier Squadron (Medium) directly controlled by USAFE through HQ 3rd AF. Gone the B-29s, their places taken by C-119Cs, a few C-54s. C-47s and SA-16As merely switched owners. This unit's stay was brief for, on May 31 1957, it came under Alconbury's control before being de-activated there on December 8 1957. Transport aircraft continued to call for some time because Molesworth was a supply depot for the USAF as well as a reserve airfield. A few Boeing WB-50s made use of Molesworth in the late 1950s. The large 'J' hangar remains for storage purposes and presumably there will be a lot of burrowing to accommodate storage bunkers for the Tomahawks.

Moreton-in-Marsh, Gloucestershire

SP230350. 2 miles E of Moreton-in-Marsh

During the war Moreton-in-Marsh was considered an amusing name for an obscure airfield, and 'Much-Binding in the Marsh' stemmed from it. Similarity there ends, for this Cotswold airfield, in post-war years, presented a very smart appearance. Moreton-in-Marsh lies on the Fosse Way. Why the town is so-called is uncertain; it could be because of marsh-land around, or its situation on a 'march' or county boundary where Gloucestershire and Oxfordshire meet. Fast growing trees shield the airfield site from view. Behind the greenery lies the Fire Service College.

The building of Moreton took place during 1940. Although the runways were well advanced by October, they were 1,000 yds long and judged too short. One was extended to 1,400 yds, the other two to 1,100 yds. January 21 1941 saw the arrival of the RAF on to a truly sodden marsh befitting the airfield's title and upon which the runways remained incomplete. Likewise unfinished was the roofing of the 'J' hangar, and only frame-work for two 'T2' hangars was being erected. Foundations of the other two had so far been worked upon. It was not unusual for a new airfield to be occupied by the Service prior to completion.

Wartime airfields were often very muddy in winter, whilst in summer many presented parched plains, grass taking a while to become established. Areas 75 yds to the side of main runways were usually rolled hard in case aircraft swung off them, or needed to make 'soft' ground belly landings.

Before Moreton-in-Marsh opened it had been allocated Edgehill as its satellite. The first aircraft of 21 OTU, based here throughout the war, were three Wellington Ics and two Ansons, the latter for navi-gation training. No 1 Course commenced operational training on March 1 1941.

Evidently the enemy was soon aware of the existence of Moreton-in-Marsh, although only twice—on April 3 1941 when two large HE bombs fell on the landing ground and on May 8 1941 when incendiaries fell on the west side of the airfield—was any attack delivered. On April 28 1941, 21 OTU despatched Wellingtons for leaflet dropping over Paris. Such activity, though, was very limited. The OTU's task was to train Wellington crews rather than conduct operations.

November 24 1941 brought a directive to seal 21 OTU's activity for much of the war's remainder. It was to train crews exclusively for Middle East Wellington squadrons. The first group of crews for the Middle East completed their training on December 14 1941. Followng a week's leave they spent ten days in Despatch Flight before making a night flight across France on January 1 1942, then landed on Malta. Such journeying was not new, it had taken place from Stradishall, New-market, and Harwell. Effort was now being concentrated at Harwell and Moreton. After operational training, Wellington crews would specially prepare for a long ferry flight to Malta—later Gibraltar—and thence to Egypt or beyond. For a crew with limited experience such an undertaking was surely faced with some concern. There was, though, no other feasible way of delivering the aircraft apart from their being taken by crews of operational formations in Britain, and loss rates proved quite low. From Moreton the second seven crews set off on January 15 1942. Thereafter the pattern was to despatch 15 crews a month rising to 18 in April and then 20 monthly. By then 1446 Flight, formed at Bassingbourn, had arrived to control despatching of crews after ferry flight training. Take-off accidents were often serious as at Moreton on May 6 1942. As it was taking off, a Wellington Ic suffered a tyre burst, then swerved, ramming *X9934* on dispersal and being armed. Both aircraft burst into flames, personnel in *X9934* clearing the aircraft before its bombs exploded. Three men were, however, injured.

As with many OTUs, No 21 contributed to the 'Thousand Plan' attacks. From Moreton ten Wellingtons operated against Cologne on May 30/31 1942 and, for the Essen raid, 17 set out. Three crews made early returns and Wellington *W5618'W'* did not return. Moreton despatched seven aircraft for the Bremen raid in which *T2974* returned to Honington after being attacked by a night fighter.

Establishment of 1446 Ferry Training Flight took place in May. It became operational in June 1942 and first despatched a set of Wellingtons for Nos 99 and 458 Squadrons, after which it took over half of the commitment of 1443 Ferry Training Flight, Harwell. From July 1942, and for safety reasons, all Wellington flights to the Middle East went via Cornwall on a route taking them over the Atlantic. The exceptions were Wellington GR VIIIs whose range problems meant shorter flights. In July 1942, 1446 Flight sent 36 Wellingtons overseas.

Between July and September 1942, 21 OTU bombed German targets, but thereafter such activity ceased as Bomber Command's strength increased and OTUs concentrated upon training. In October 1942, in keeping with other 91 Group OTUs, Moreton resumed leaflet dropping, five sorties being sent to the Paris area on October 24/25. A second such operation was mounted on November 18/19 during which engine trouble forced down *T2574* at Lysse, near Petersfield, Hampshire, the crew of four being killed. That month 22 Wellingtons were despatched from Moreton-in-Marsh to the Middle East.

In December 1942, No 1446 Flight, which held 12 Wellingtons as well as Ansons and Oxfords for ferry crew training, despatched 13 Wellington VIIIs, and 21 OTU dropped reading matter to the residents of Nantes. Such activity was repeated in February 1943 after leaflets had been distributed to Parisians. The Ferry Flight that, on May 1 1943, became 311 Ferry Training Unit continued moving Wellingtons—soon of superior types—to the Middle East. Such duty continued from Moreton-in-Marsh until 311 FTU disbanded on May 1 1944.

Spring 1943 found 21 OTU's establishment set at 54 Wellingtons, 17 Ansons and four target towers and found the unit taking part in many *Bullseyes.* The first two Martinets received on April 27 1943 moved to Enstone which had become 21 OTU's satellite from April 12. At the end of August, and during the first week of September 1943, 21 OTU briefly resumed bombing operations, targets in the Pas de Calais being attacked during the *Starkey* period.

Change now overtook Moreton-in-Marsh and other OTUs as the fitment of a second navigator's table in Wellingtons—still the aged Mk Ics here—meant that Ansons could be dispensed with. Two *Nickelling* operations were flown in mid-September 1943, but bad weather prevented a repeat in October by which time 21 OTU was ordered to provide a dozen *Nickel* sorties monthly. In November, 13 were despatched when the OTU was contributing to six *Bullseyes* a month.

Perhaps the most surprising thing about 21 OTU was that into 1944 it was still flying operational sorties using Wellington Ics, many of which were beyond retirement age. It seems likely that the last British-based Wellington Ic operational sorties were flown, and from Moreton-in-Marsh, on February 6 1944. Prior to that three certainly dropped leaflets on January 22. On February 6, among the six Wellingtons operated over France were *R1523*, once with 311 Squadron, *X9818*, earlier used by 101 Squadron, *Z8840* with a long front line career, and *DV844* and *DV896.* Survival rates of some of the Wellingtons at Moreton were quite remarkable. Participants in the leaflet dropping operations on January 14/15 1944, for instance, included *L7890* which entered OTU service at Pershore on April 9 1941, progressively serving Nos 22, 21, 15 and 21 OTU between December 2 1943 and February 22 1944. Operating, too, that night were *R1523,* used by 3 PRU from March 30 1941 until July 27 1941, and *N2736,* delivered to Hendon in January 1941, passed to 221 Squadron in May 1941 until it went to Moreton-in-Marsh on January 8 1942. *R1523* survived the war and was not struck off charge until March 1946.

Changeover to Wellington IIIs and Xs came during January 1944, Mk Xs first operating from Moreton-in-Marsh on January 14/15 and soon from Enstone too from where sorties were flown in March. Early that month unit strength quickly rose, partly because 35 Wellingtons had come to 21 OTU upon the closure of 15 OTU at Harwell. Moreton-in-Marsh was congested with Wellingtons until the trusty old Ics were ferried away. An increased number of newer Wellingtons brought the number available for operations to 20, two being the Type 423 variant so that 21 OTU could, if necessary, drop 4,000 lb bombs. Normally their aircraft could carry up to 500 lb bombs. *Bullseyes* continued and in March the first Exercise *Eric* was flown. Sixteen *Nickels* were mounted in April 1944, including leaflets warning the French to expect heavy attacks on transport targets. Diversion feints were flown over the North Sea in May, to mislead German night fighter controllers.

For a year Martinet target towers had doubled up as fighters, giving gunners training. From April 26 1944, Hurricanes replaced the Martinets. All Wellingtons here were Mk III/Xs, the nominal strength still 54. Operatonal flying ceased after July 1944.

Unlike many OTUs, No 21 did not disband at the end of hostilities but moved to Finningley in November 1946. Moreton-in-Marsh was taken over in December 1946 by No 21 (P) AFU from Wheaton Aston, which brought a fleet of Oxfords. No 21 Group, Flying Training Command, controlled the station from December 9 1946.

No 1 Refresher School arrived from Enstone on December 17 1946, the Oxford population rising to 62 aircraft. Seven Magisters and 15 Harvard IIbs were added in January 1947. Heavy snow falls soon halted flying, not resumed until April 9 1947. A drastic reduction followed as half the Oxfords were declared surplus.

On August 6 1947, 21 (P) AFU and No 1 Refresher School combined becoming No 1 (Pilot) Refresher Flying Unit. A Flight used 11 Oxfords, B Flight ten Wellingtons, C Flight nine Harvards and seven Spitfire XVIs. On January 10 1948, the unit was ordered to Finningley, leaving Moreton-in-Marsh to Care and Maintenance.

An RAF medical school then opened, a 'medical flying squad'. The school closed in 1951, being replaced by Harvards of No 1 Flying Training School. It trained pilots and provided acclimatisation for those trained overseas and, in December 1951, was the last to re-equip with Prentices. Little Rissington and Valley aircraft made use of Moreton-in-Marsh, but its runways were too short for safe jet flying. No 1 FTS closed in 1955, the station again entering Care and Maintenance. Later that year the Home Office commandeered it for training RAF 'H' Class reservists in fire fighting techniques in a nuclear war. This task continued until 1959.

Civilian and auxiliary fire service training then commenced, and Moreton-in-Marsh became an annexe to the Fire Service College at Dorking. On June 14 1966, it was announced that the Fire Service Technical College was opening at Moreton-in-Marsh to train middle rank fire service personnel. Training has taken account of increasing problems and hazards facing the fire services, particularly toxic materials and chemicals, and complex problems arising in fighting industrial fires. For economy reasons, Staff College Dorking closed on June 30 1981, senior staff courses commencing at Moreton-in-Marsh on July 1 1981 when the Fire Service College re-opened.

Mount Farm, Oxfordshire

SU578963. E of Berrisfield, by A423(T), 8 miles SE of Oxford

Ground purchased for Benson's satellite became known as Mount Farm. Battles of 12 OTU began using the airfield in July 1940 for initial flying training by day and night. There was no fixed accommodation, troops guarding the site using tented accommodation.

Following the attack on Stanton Harcourt, a few light machine guns came to protect Mount Farm which, by mid-August, because of its good situation, was already undergoing major development. Concrete runways were being rapidly constructed in the hope that they would be ready in mid-September 1940. Completion was retarded and it was two months later before the runways were fully open.

Policy changes relating to satellites had come about. Now they were for dispersing aircraft and, in September 1940, for reducing bottle necks arising in night flying training because of enemy interference with training programmes. Long outdated, the Fairey Battle was now to be phased out, its place taken temporarily by Wellingtons of 12 OTU. Benson's grass surface had stood the tempo of wartime training well, but was unsuitable for Wellington night flying training. Mount Farm's runways, on the other hand, were suitable for day and night flying Wellingtons. Extension of these by 300 yds was ordered, when feasible.

On December 1 1940, 12 OTU was reduced from a Battle armed OTU to a half strength Wellington OTU, flying from Mount Farm and Benson. The reason for reduced strength was the decision to place the PRU at Benson in December 1940. January 1941 found 12 OTU training Wellington crews, a task briefly interrupted in the early afternoon of February 27 1941 when an enemy bomber, using low cloud cover, penetrated the Benson area. It dropped two bombs about half a mile from Mount Farm whose LAA guns fired unsuccessfully as the raider hastened off to bomb Benson. A second attack, during night flying, resulted in 13 50 kg bombs being dropped on Mount Farm. One cratered the north-east/south-west runway and two burst on the peritrack. An NCO was killed, three men injured and damage caused to two Wellingtons and a Magister. A third attack came on May 12 1941 when a large bomb caused a 50 ft diameter crater, again on the main runway, which was further damaged by a smaller bomb. Another bomb fell on the perimeter track and 15 on waste ground. Such attacks were more of an annoyance than a major disaster.

The prime role continued until the OTU moved to Chipping Warden. Then 15 OTU Harwell took control of Mount Farm, on July 23 1941, making it a second satellite. Just how fully fledged Mount Farm was at this time could be seen by operational diversions here, nine Hampdens of 61, 106, 144 and 408 Squadrons and two Wellingtons of 218 Squadron on July 10 1941, returning from attacks on Aachen and Osnabruck.

On September 5 1941, Benson received No 1416 Flight which became 140 Squadron on September 17 1941. It was mainly equipped with PR Spitfires, and a handful of Blenheims for night reconnaissance. To accommodate PR aircraft, Benson re-possessed Mount Farm in January 1942, 140 Squadron placing four of its Spitfires there on January 23 1942. Operations continued from Benson. In the event of a German invasion of Britain, 140 Squadron would have mounted a visual and photographic watch upon it, for which reason 140 Squadron had a higher establishment than most PR squadrons.

Mount Farm served as a dispersal airfield for Benson's PR Spitfires until May 4 1942 when both A and B Flights of 140 Squadron moved here whilst Benson's concrete runways were built. Into Mount Farm came up to ten PR Spitfires, variously known as Mk 5G, Type F and Mk 1a, along with six Blenheim IVs and a Tiger Moth. From Mount Farm the Blenheims flew night reconnaissance flights, using photo flashes for photography. Spitfires flew daylight PR sorties over France. The Dieppe landing was being prepared, that area becoming much photographed by 140 Squadron. After postponement, a second busy period came in the run-up to the raid. Between August 15 and 22 1942, 63 of the 75 Spitfire sorties were successfully flown, many to Dieppe. On August 17 1942, a busy day when the squadron flew 22 Spitfire sorties, many covered Dieppe among them *R7115*, flown by Pilot Officer L.G. Smith who flew six runs across the port and obtained pictures from 30,000 ft.

Blenheim operations became increasingly dangerous. Twice towards the end of June 1942 crews reported seeing night fighters, and Blenheim sorties ended a night reconnaissance to the Cherbourg Peninsula on August 15 1942.

On March 15 1943, 140 Squadron moved to Hartford Bridge and Mount Farm's future immediately changed. Gearing up for a tactical PR role was the 13th PR Squadron, USAAF which arrived at Podington on December 2 1942 and was awaiting an operational base. Mount Farm provided it and, on February 16 1943, the 13th Photographic Squadron arrived, bringing some L-4 Piper Cubs, although it was mainly equipped with P-38 and F-5 Lightnings. During 1943 reverse Lend-Lease Spitfires played an ever increasing part in the squadron's equipment and were used to obtain target and damage assessment photographs for 8th AAF Bomb Groups.

Second to arrive was the 14th PR Squadron (Light) on May 12 1943. It operated P-38s, F-4s and F-5s and later Spitfires. The 22nd Photographic Squadron (Light) reached Mount Farm June 8 1943 and also equipped with P-38s and Spitfires.

PR flights by the 13th Squadron commenced from Mount Farm on March 28 1943 with the 14th joining in during July. The squadrons became part of the 7th Photograph Group on July 7 1943. Activated on May 1 1943, the 7th Photograph Group almost at once became the 7th PR and Mapping Group until redesignated, on November 13 1943, the 7th Photograph Group (Reconnaissance). A fourth squadron, No 27, joined the Group on November 4 1943, and commenced operations on December 20 1943. It, too, used P-38s, F-4s and F-5s. March 6 1944 brought the first PR sortie to Berlin by a Spitfire from Mount Farm. Maps for ground forces and air forces were produced by the group which observed enemy transport movements, installations and gathered weather information. L-5s were used for close support work. In the run-up to D-Day, airfields, towns, French ports and targets in the Low Countries were all watched by the 7th.

During July 1944, attention was diverted to V-1 sites and, in August 1944, to gathering information for up-dated maps for the fast advancing army. Photographs were also provided for September's airborne assault and, in December 1944, for the Battle of the Bulge. In the last months of the war, P-51s assigned to the Group escorted its reconnaissance aircraft. On November 9 1944, 27 Squadron left for France and later Chalgrove. The other three squadrons disbanded during December 1945 after flying post-war damage assessment flights.

The headquarters of the 7th moved to Chalgrove on April 8 1945, soon followed by the three squadrons. Mount Farm returned to RAF on May 1 1945, becoming Benson's satellite again from June 22 1945 to October 19 1946. No 8 OTU was here until July 4 1946 when it moved to Chalgrove. Mount Farm became a depot for surplus military vehicles. It was being used for farming by 1949 and was finally sold in 1957. A gravel excavation site marks the position of the airfield.

Northleach, Gloucestershire

SP110155. 10 miles NE of Cirencester, via A429

An RLG near Northleach was planned in 1940, its use commencing with the arrival, on November 2 1942, of a Flight of Master GT IIs and Hotspur gliders from 3 GTS Stoke Orchard. The poor winter state of the airfield's surface soon caused them to return to Stoke Orchard, until better weather permitted their return in 1943. The RLG, raised to Satellite level in May 1944, was still administered by Stoke Orchard. Between October 21 and 23 1944, No 3 GTS, forced to leave Stoke Orchard because the grass airfield there was in poor state, moved to Zeals. Northleach passed from activity.

Nuthampstead, Hertfordshire

TL435345. 2½ miles ESE of Barkway, off B1368

B-17Gs of Nuthampstead's 398th Bomb Group (IWM).

October 23 1943 broke as a rainy day, but it needed more than that to deflect Alan Wright and I from our purpose—to see the reported P-38s at the 'new' Nuthampstead airfield. There was plenty of activity in the morning mist, reconnaissance aircraft presumably trying to discover what we were up to! Duxford displayed 58 grounded Thunderbolts, and Beaufighter 1s flew around, probably from 51 OTU. By 13:45 we had climbed Royston downs to reach Nuthampstead where, to our glee, a P-38 zoomed around, confirming the rumour. More engines soon burst into song as the afternoon detail prepared for flying. There were many engines soon running, for one of the tasks current then was the clearance of countless engine bugs which were wrecking operational prospects. All that afternoon one could hear run-ups of offending Allisons.

Thunderbolts in increasing numbers intruded upon the scene and commenced low attack training and soon the fighters were engaging in combat practice above our heads. A delectable moment came as P-47 *QP-V* was chased over very low by P-38, *17245*, of the 343rd Squadron. As it banked, white vapour streamed from the wing tips. On reflection, and judging by the animations in my diary entry, this must have been the first time I had noticed anything quite like that. Certainly the P-38s showed surprising manoeuvrability. Seconds later P-38, *CY-S*, which I noted as *267066*, slipped in overhead, revealing its vital long range tank racks.

Time to go brought a fine send off as eight 'CY' coded P-38s roared away spectacularly. Going home delighted, with a notebook of memories, we were serenaded by the 'pop stars' of our day, a Beaufighter 1 with an escorting Martlet and P-47. A Spitfire Va with clipped wings and yellow under surfaces passed. What can our late breed of markings experts tell us of such impossibilities? Among parading UC-78s crept a smart Barracuda, and moments later, 'a Mustang 1 in USAAF colours and markings'. No doubt, for it circled twice. Presumably to reassure myself at this unusual sight I noted in my diary that evening that it 'sounded like an Allison engined Mk 1, too'.

Meanwhile the P-38s had attracted a Mosquito II of 157 Squadron, an all-black Mosquito in use long after that scheme had been superseded. As dusk closed in, a low flying Cierva C-30a, whirring its way westwards, closed an enjoyable day. For all their problems, Lightnings were grand to watch.

Not everyone who knew Nuthampstead enjoyed it at this time, for it was a ghastly mess of mud, chalk mud, the worst of all. It must have been memorable for the US Army engineers who produced Nuthampstead in 1942–3. The RAF took over the airfield in May 1943.

American fighters came in September, air and ground crews manning three squadrons of the 55th Fighter Group equipped with assorted camouflaged P-38s. Twin booms made these aircraft look very racy and highly unconventional. Work up took a month, by which time the P-38Hs among them were declared operational, flying their first sweep, off the Dutch coast, on October 15 1943. The P-38 had good range, American bomber losses were heavy and only fighter protection could reduce them. Therefore, the P-38 was commited to Europe here and at King's Cliffe. Priority was given to the Nuthampstead Group as regards delivery of available P-38Hs.

The P-38s' action radius with two drop tanks was about 400 miles and gave little room for manoeuvre. Participation in sweeps and B-26 escorts over France took place from Nuthampstead in October. Then, on November 3 1943, the 55th set off in support of heavy bomber operations. The target for the B-17s was Wilhelmshaven over which the P-38s engaged enemy fighters operating in its defence. An encounter came about, the 55th claiming six enemy aircraft and being credited with three.

Two days later came a repeat performance, around Munster to where B-24s had been shepherded. Operating in four-finger formations, the 16 P-38s claimed five enemy aircraft without loss, but all was not well with the P-38. Its two engines, which should have conferred additional safety, were troublesome, particularly in low temperatures. Cockpit heating was extremely poor and, despite the vaunted turbo-supercharger, engine performance fell off rapidly above 20,000 ft, making the aircraft highly vulnerable in combat at this frequently flown height. Around 15,000 ft the P-38 was a fine performer so it came to be accepted as an interim fighter. Just how vulnerable the P-38s were was apparent on November 13 1943 when 48 escorted B-17s to Bremen. Seven did not return and eight were damaged in combat. By the end of November, the two P-38 Groups had lost

18 aircraft, some without doubt partially as a result of engine malfunctions.

Little improvement came with the longer ranged P-38J, a theoretical radius of 640 miles if two 150 gallon drop tanks were carried, in reality being little over 400 miles. One special prize nevertheless fell to the 55th during its Nuthampstead days when, on March 3 1944, it became the first USAAF fighter Group to fly over Berlin. The bombers it had supposed to be escorting, though, had aborted near Hamburg!

The arrival of Merlin P-51s meant the P-38's days were numbered, except at lower altitudes. A bright idea was to fit a transparent nose into which was crammed a bombsight and a bombardier. Such 'droop snoot' P-38s would lead others into the attack from around 20,000 ft, other pilots releasing their bombs as the leader's fell. The first such operation at 20,000 ft was mounted in April 1944, each aircraft carrying a 1,000 lb HE bomb and a drop tank. After 28 bombs had been aimed at Coulommiers airfield, the P-38s strafed the ensuring confusion. Defenders skilfully fired, bringing down the 'droop snoot'. Six days later, the 55th Fighter Group moved to Wormingford.

During February and March 1944, the 50th Fighter Squadron was here briefly, after helping to defend Iceland. It moved to the 802nd Group at Cheddington in mid-March and appears never to have had any aircraft here or at its next base, where it stayed until August 1944 before returning to the USA.

On April 22 1944, the last to join the 8th AAF, the 398th Bomb Group (Nos 600-603 Squadrons inclusive) moved into Nuthampstead bringing all-silver B-17Gs. It arrived as the invasion build up was intense and participated in sustained attacks on V-weapons targets—one of which, the site at Sottevast, was on May 6 1944, intended to be the group's first target. Too late in formation, the 398th had to abort. Subsequently, it was to participate busily in operations to places near and far. Its target manifests included Berlin, Kiel, Merseburg, Munich, Munster Saarbrucken and, of course, Normandy. It fully supported field operations, flying its last sorties on April 25 1945 whilst raiding an airfield near Pilsen. Thereafter it transferred PoWs from Germany to France before pulling out of Nuthampstead in late May 1945. The 398th's personnel made the homeward journey in the liner, *Queen Elizabeth*. Behind them lay 195 operations and the loss in action of 58 B-17Gs.

Nuthampstead returned to the RAF on July 10 1945 for weapons stores of 94 and 95 MUs. On October 30 1954, it was placed on Care and Maintenance. The site was closed in March 1959, some of its concrete dissolving into the M1 Motorway. There is still aeronautical activity from remnants of the airfield, in the form of crop spraying. There was some prospect of much more when the curious notion arose to make this the site of a third London airport. Much of the clamour seems to have been a mixture of camouflage and diversionary kite flying for it is reasonable to suppose that the aim was to build upon Stansted or Maplin.

Oakley, Buckinghamshire

SP640110. 8 miles ENE of Oxford, near B4011

Oakley will be remembered by many a prisoner of war who, after release from the Continent, first stood upon the soil of freedom as he stepped on to Oakley. Its position is in a flat, damp, wooded area. In its Service days, Oakley was a three-runway airfield whose main runway remains largely intact like a 'T2' hangar retaining its wartime black finish. Temporary brick wartime buildings stand alongside and Oakley holds one special feature, a well preserved 'B1' hangar which must have meant much to many.

Intended as Westcott's satellite, Oakley was ready before its parent so, when it opened on a May 27 1942, it was as Bicester's second satellite. August 1942 saw it switched to its intended status. When 11 OTU moved to Westcott in September 1942, Oakley became that unit's satellite where it placed some of its Wellington 1cs. In autumn 1943, Hercules-engined Wellingtons came increasingly into use, the OTU's air gunnery training section being at Oakley. From March 1943 it flew Martinets, one of which, *JN587*, force landed near Aylesbury on February 7 1944. A few Hurricane IIcs reached Oakley in March 1944.

Being a fully fledged bomber station by size and layout, diversions were accepted during night bomber operations, as on April 5 1944 when eight Lancasters of 106 Squadron landed from Toulouse. At 02:30 on June 7 1944 a Halifax was on its approach from the south when the crew baled out, then the bomber crashed near Benson. A more distressing accident

happened at Oakley in the early evening of June 9 1944. Wellington *LP252* was making a low approach to runway 025 when it touched a hedge and then a passing army lorry. It successfully landed, but a soldier in the lorry was killed and four men were injured.

Conversion training for bomber crews was Oakley's primary role which continued to the end of the war during the final year of which most personnel were trained for overseas squadrons. After the end of hostilities in Europe, orders were received to clear the 'B1' hangar and fit it for the provision of refreshment and succour to hundreds of repatriated PoWs brought here during May 1945. Oakley closed to flying in August of that year. It remains very visibly a wartime airfield.

Lancaster PB726 *of 467 Squadron after overshooting Oakley's runway during Operation* Exodus, *on May 12 1945* (via P.H.T. Green).

On dispersal at Oakley—a Wellington X of 11 OTU.

Old Warden, Bedfordshire

TL160445. 2 miles W of Biggleswade

Few aeronautical shrines are as special as Old Warden. Here, verdantly surrounded, resides the world's finest collection of antique aeroplanes. Unique, too, because many still enjoy the thrill of flight. What is more, on a still summer's day, they like to perform within an atmosphere little removed from that they once knew well. Sometimes it is to the scent of castor oil, often to a coughing engine and nearly always to gorgeous sounds of days long gone. Here displayed is a world of biplanes, of wood, of dope and petrol combining to provide that smell so much part of a proper aeroplane.

We must be grateful indeed to the Shuttleworth family who built this collection. Sad, too, that Richard Shuttleworth never survived to enjoy the success of youthful dreams. Born in July 1909, and endowed with ample charm, handsome appearance, considerable ability, certain courage and delight in mechanical things, fortune also endowed him with considerable wealth. Educated at Eton and afterwards in France, Richard Shuttleworth passed through Sandhurst acquiring, during his army career, an interest in aged vehicles. He also learnt to fly, but he never lost his love of unusual vehicles and delighted in conquering their fastidiousness. Motor racing he enjoyed, but most of all he adored old aeroplanes.

Money available, he bought a Moth. In 1932 a small airfield was laid out on part of the large family estate. It was named Old Warden and sheep safely grazed when there was no flying. Richard Shuttleworth equipped his aerodrome with a tiny Comper Swift and a couple of Desoutters. To these he was able to add a DH 84 Dragon, once the transport of HRH the Prince of Wales. Although his father died when Richard was only three years old, it was not until July 1932 that he succeeded to his father's estate.

Richard Shuttleworth heard of an air race to be run in India. Enjoying a challenge, he set off on January 28 1933 to participate. His mode of transport would still evoke considerable comment for he chose to travel in his diminutive Comper Swift. Another one was flown by a friend. In this extraordinary aircraft he crossed France, traversed the length of Italy, flew to North Africa and then took the long route to Persia, arriving in Delhi 12 days after setting out, an amazing achievement. Participation in the air race, however, was less successful, and Shuttleworth returned conventionally.

In the mid-1930s Shuttleworth came to know Mr A.E. Grimmer, an Ampthill garage proprietor. Grimmer had a 1909 Bleriot XI and a 1910 Deperdussin Monoplane, both of which had been flown at Hendon prior to the First World War and then were stored. Although both machines were in unhappy condition,

Ah! the whistle of wires as Old Warden's Avro 504 E3404 *whirrs overhead.*

De Havillands to the fore, and Roger, the voice of Old Warden, coming from the control room roof, tells the crowd all they will ever need to know about the Rapide!

Shuttleworth wanted to restore them to flying state and Grimmer, knowing they would be getting a good home, let Richard have them. The famous Shuttleworth Collection had commenced.

Bringing both aircraft to flying standard was a tremendous challenge but both flew often before World War 2, by which time a 1912 Blackburn Monoplane had been acquired from a barn near Wittering. Not until 1949, though, did this—the oldest British aeroplane still airworthy—make its flight.

With World War 1 a clear memory, Shuttleworth added aeroplanes of that vintage to his stock. Included was a Sopwith Dove, a post-war two-seat version of the Pup fighter. This he converted into the latter and, as *N5180*, it is frequently demonstrated. Restoration and conversion work needs great skill and patience as found in Mr A. Jackson who became Chief Engineer and Manager at Old Warden. An ample income is also needed, for which the Warden Aviation Company was formed to carry out overhaul and charter services.

With the international signs ominous in the late 1930s, Richard Shuttleworth joined the RAFVR. At the outbreak of war he went to Upavon and then Ternhill before being posted to 12 OTU Benson. The intention was that he would join the accident investigation branch. He was still managing the Shuttleworth Estate, and friendly with a fellow officer, that well-known figure at modern Old Warden, Air Commodore Alan Wheeler. To him was entrusted the care of Old Warden following the war. The reason for that came from tragedy for, in the early hours of August 2 1940, Richard Shuttleworth was killed when flying in a Battle, *L4971*, which crashed at Ewelme, Oxfordshire.

That event could have so easily halted flying at Old Warden, but surely Richard Shuttleworth would never have wished for that. His small airfield played its part in the war as an overhaul depot for Harvards, Proctors and Miles Magisters, and an example of the latter *P6382*, still flies from here.

Following the war, a Trust ran the estate. More recently it became an educational charity. By the end of the 1940s it was very much a going concern. Most of the aircraft were tightly packed in the hangar near the gate area, or in a small hut adjacent. A visit, which I paid on April 11 1950, revealed, amongst others,

Above *Very much a Midlander in its hey-day, a Hawker Hind. This example, beautifully and lovingly restored at Old Warden, bears Afghan Air Force markings.*

Below *Where, other than at Old Warden, would one be likely to see a sight like this Rapide and Dragonfly formating so closely?*

the fuselage of Queen Bee *LF858*, some Auster Vs, a 1912 Blackburn, a Bleriot XI, a 1911 Deperdussin and a dismembered Pup. The latter commenced its civilian life as *G-EBKY* in 1925 and Warden Aviation acquired it in 1936. Also resident were a DH 60X Cirrus Moth, *G-EBWD*, in a blue and silver scheme, a red and silver DH 60, *G-ABYA*, Dessoutter Mk 1 Coupé, *G-AAPZ*, and Alan Wheeler's Slymph *G-ABOI* from which much was missing. The Bleriot, 1912 Monoplane, Pup and Moths remain active and much has been added.

Included are replicas of a Boxkite and an Avro Triplane built for the film *Those Magnificent Men in their Flying Machines.* Often flown is an Avro 504K and the SE 5A, *F904*. The Collection owns the only surviving LVG C VI, now cautiously flown sometimes with the Bristol F2B *D8096*, which once served the RAF in Turkey and was restored for the Collection by the Bristol Aeroplane Company in 1950–51.

Inter-war years are represented by a fleet of de Havilland aircraft and in 1980 the sole Parnall Elf resumed flying. The Avro Tutor, *K3215*, at Old Warden has links with CFS, and 2 FIS, Church Lawford. A Gladiator, formed from the remains of two such machines, is always a popular performer, and these are but a few of the Shuttleworth Collection's beautifully maintained old aeroplanes.

The Collection is open daily to visitors, apart from a few days at Christmas, from 10:00 to 17:00, but closes a little earlier in winter. Close viewing of many aircraft and other exhibits is possible. On the last Sunday of month, between spring and autumn, the Collection flies its treasures and, in 1981, such delights were extended with the first flight of the sole remaining Hawker Hind. It is hoped that the DH 88 Comet *G-ACSS* will fly again. Documentation relating to its spectacular performance in the 1934 MacRobertson Air Race is displayed in a hangar. Other such items include a metal panel from the Brabazon 1. A recent addition is a wind tunnel Concorde model from RAE Bedford. In a case may be seen a model of the *R-101* dwarfing to the same scale, a model of a Boeing 747.

Old Warden is idyllic for dreaming, for delighting in the sights and sounds of long ago, in surroundings which always reveal to perfection the beauty and skill of the Red Arrows at the summer show. At such events famous fliers mingle with famous aeroplanes. Soaring with them is the voice of Old Warden, that of Roger Heflin

Below *Avro Tutor,* K3215, *presently with the Shuttleworth Collection. Cranwell-based from July 1933 to December 1939,* K3215 *joined CFS on August 28 1941 and was used by No 1 FIS from March 17 to August 23 1942. Later it served with 41 and 61 OTUs, the latter from June 1944 to January 6 1946 and was sold for civilian use on July 4 1946.*

whose informed commentary and humour have come to be so much a part of these enjoyable afternoons. One memory which certainly brings delight is of a hot air balloon engulfing the commentator who continued to commentate, proving that nothing could daunt his spirit! Variety and the unexpected are hall-marks of Old Warden.

Peterborough (Westwood), Cambridgeshire

TF165002. 2 miles NW of the city, now an industrial estate

Westwood's situation as a busy flying training school close to Peterborough was unusual, even more so was its post-war use. Before the Second World War, autogiros had been suggested for mail delivery and trials were undertaken in London in 1934. Plans existed for them to land on Post Office roofs, but hostilities halted the idea, and resumed at Peterborough in revised form.

After the war, MCA purchased some helicopters for mail carrying trials over a 115-mile circuit from Yeovil using an S.51. The helicopter proved reliable—essential for mail duty—and BEA decided upon trial East Anglian Services, basing their S.51 and Bell 47B3 at Peterborough.

Flying commenced on May 12 1948; the regular mail service on June 1 1948. Its circular route from Peterborough took it in daylight to King's Lynn, along the coast to Cromer then to Norwich, from where it returned on a more southerly route. On the initial journey the S.51 left Peterborough at 09:55 carrying 13,000 letters, and reached Great Yarmouth at 12:49. The return journey commenced at 17:48, touch down at Peterborough being at 19:30 after a journey of 272 miles—one repeated 96 times before trials ended on September 25 1948. The BEA Helicopter Unit found the Bell 47 too small for mail carrying, although it was reliable. The larger Sikorsky S.51 was fairly reliable but too expensive to operate. BEA also conducted night flying trials from Peterborough between October 17 1949 and April 15 1950, the service running to Norwich. Tests were made using Downham Market at a time when helicopter night flying was in its infancy and being explored along with blind flying equipment and navigation aids. From Peterborough a total of 283 S.51 flights were made and 95,000 lb of mail was carried.

On December 2 1935, No 7 SFTS formed at Peterborough, a most unusual station, to which the previous month 17 Hawker Hart (T)s *(K4983–4999)* had been posted. For company they had Avro Tutors, Furies, Audaxes received in February 1936 and Harts two months later. The first course assembled in

A late wartime flier from Peterborough's 7 SFTS—Harvard IIb, FT212.

Post-war Peterborough was BEA's base for Westland S51s and Bell 47 helicopters.

January 1936 and at the end of March the Advanced Training Squadron formed. Students undertook a three month flying course, spending another three months studying applied flying, weapons training, formation flying and tactics. A boost came on January 17 1939 when the first Oxford arrived. Eight more came that month, seven in February and three in March. One, *L9689*, was written off when on March 10 it crashed into a hangar.

Major upheaval in the training programme took place between May and July 1939, the station being at half strength as it switched to training FAA pilots. The flying course was reduced to four months at the outbreak of war. A further alteration came during October 1939 when the School switched to single-engine aircraft courses and the Oxfords left. Nominal strength was 24 Hart (T) and eight Audaxes in the Initial Training Squadron with 24 Audaxes and eight Hart (T) in the Advanced Training Squadron. January 1940 brought a new shape when the establishment altered to include 29 Battle Trainers, 34 Harts (T) and 21 Audaxes. In summer of 1950, 7 SFTS was ordered to hold in readiness 12 Harts for bombing duty within Plan *Banquet* for which the operational base would have been Stradishall.

During July 1940 7 SFTS started using Sibson RLG for night flying training, short lived because the School was ordered in August to prepare to leave for Canada, one of seven units told to make the Atlantic crossing. The first echelon left on August 29 1940 to join No 31 SFTS Kingston, Ontario. With 15 FAA Course having completed its training, the fourth and last echelon left in January 1941.

Peterborough was switched to 50 Group on December 20 1941 and 13 EFTS moved from White Waltham by January 11 1941. It brought a swarm of Tiger Moths. Their stay was, however, brief for, on May 31, 72 'Tigers' flew to Booker to form the basis of 21 EFTS. On June 1 No 25 (Polish) EFTS formed in 21 Group at Peterborough and also used Sibson. Again its stay was short and, with only 57 of the scheduled Tiger Moths in hand, it left for Hucknall in mid-July 1941. Yet another Tiger Moth school replaced the Poles—No 17 EFTS which arrived from North Luffenham on July 15 1941 and remained at Peterborough until disbandment on June 1 1942.

Replacement came the same day with the birth of 7 (Pilots) Advanced Flying Unit. Miles Master I and II equipped, this refresher school expanded fast soon placing two Flights permanently at Sibson. By April 1943 it had up to 130 Masters (mainly Mk II) and four Ansons, the pupil population similarly increased from 90 to 211 pilots. A further two Flights then formed. To answer the need for night fighter pilots, night flying commenced at King's Cliffe on June 25 1943, the three stations now in use allowing a constant pupil population of 150 to be flying. King's Cliffe, though, was required for operational flying and 7 (P) AFU vacated it in July.

A visit to Peterborough afforded a sky packed with Masters of various types and in conflicting markings, a state which continued into 1944. A Flight of some 15 Hurricanes was added to the Unit in March 1944, at the time when command passed to the well-known Wing Commander J.M. Foxley-Norris.

In August 1944 the use of Sibson largely ended. On August 8, Sutton Bridge came into 7 (P) AFU hands as its satellite where, since June 1944, the unit had been night flying. No 7 (P) AFU was re-organised into two Advanced Flights, a Gunnery Flight and two Battle Flights. At Sutton Bridge 22 Oxfords arrived during September 1944 for the opening of a new 7 (P) AFU, soon a fully fledged and new SFTS, still under Peterborough's control. As a result of the change, eight Hurricanes were promptly taken from Peterborough and plans were made to retire the 95 Masters on roll and replace them, in the spring of 1945, with Harvards (which came into use in May 1945) and supplement those with a few aged Spitfire IIs.

At Peterborough, 7 SFTS was reborn on December 21 1944. The training pattern called for one-third of the pilots to pass out as single-engined trained. Many pupils were French for their newly-formed Air Force. Instruction by the spring was undertaken, using 47 Oxfords, 29 Harvards and four Ansons. No 1 French Course of 32 pilots passed out in February while the Masters were still in use and as the Spitfires were being removed. Night flying was undertaken at Wittering.

In June 1945, with Wittering and Sutton Bridge still in use, the last Master on strength, *AZ497*, was ready to leave. In the immediate post-war period, training continued with Oxfords and Harvards until, on April 4 1946, the main party of 7 SFTS left for Kirton there to join 5 SFTS, after which Peterborough was put on to Care and Maintenance. Apart from its use for helicopters, the airfield saw very little post-war use and has now been overtaken by an industrial estate.

Podington, Bedfordshire

SP955605. 3½ miles S of Rushden

Podington was one of the first airfields in England fully occupied by the Americans, and accommodated a larger assortment of units than most. Opened in August 1942 as Chelveston's satellite, it remained thus until Chelveston passed to the USAAF on April 19 1943 and Podington became a full station. Construction was still under way when ground echelons of the 352nd Bomb Squadron, 301 Bomb Group, arrived, preventing over crowding at Chelveston. They lodged here from August 18 to September 2 1942, replacing C-47 Dakotas of the 28th Troop Carrier Squadron, 60 TCG, the first USAAF unit to briefly use the base—from July 29 to August 7 1942.

Podington was much involved with the 12th AF and Operation *Torch.* Boston IIIs of the 15th Bomb Squadron (L), forced out of Molesworth by B-17s, were here between September 13 1942 and November 13 1942 when they left for North Africa. Personnel of the 5th Photographic Reconnaissance Squadron were at Podington from September 10 1942 to October 29 1942 when they left for Algeria. Their place was taken by the 13th Photographic Reconnaissance Squadron, 3rd PR Group, here between December 2 1942 and February 16 1943.

Squadrons had been flying from an airfield in much need of expansion and runway lengthening before fully loaded B-17s could operate safely. The early months of 1943 found Podington out of operational use whilst 50 dispersal standings were completed and runways extended. Nevertheless, between August 1942 and May 1943, the VIIIth BC CCRC used the station. With ten dispersals incomplete, three squadrons of the 100th Bomb Group arrived on May 30 1943 for a brief stay. With 32 B-17s on hand, the 100th left for Thorpe Abbott on June 8. Construction work continued into the summer then the 92nd Bomb Group's B-17s arrived from Alconbury on September 11–15 1943. In May 1943 it commenced operations, taking a major part in the 1st AD's bombing campaign.

During November 1943 the 479th Anti-Submarine Group arrived from Dunkeswell and soon disbanded here, its squadrons forming the nucleus of Special Operations Squadrons. The '92nd' participated in 1st AD operations to the end of the war. To increase effectiveness of attacks against reinforced concrete fortifications, the 92nd Bomb Group undertook trials using Disney rocket bombs, two of which could be carried beneath each B-17 mainplane. Only two operations were flown using them, the close of hostilities rendering the weapons unnecessary.

In mid-June 1945 the 92nd left Podington for Istres, France. In the summer of 1945, RAF airfield construction units were based at Podington which closed in 1946. The site was sold in 1961 and is presently known as the Santa Pod Raceway.

Polebrook, Northamptonshire

TL095870. 5 miles ESE of Oundle

'Come quickly,' my mother called. I hurried into the avenue, querying the reason for such fuss. 'Look at that,' she said. There, brilliant against a clear blue sky, was a broad band of white cloud. Through binoculars it resolved itself not as one streak but four bright trails. Heading this swathe was . . .? Its identity puzzled me. This was May 1941 and a high flyer might be an unheralded, new type of aircraft. But, as it proceeded slowly overhead, there was no mistaking its identity, this was one of America's vaunted 'Flying Fortresses'.

My interest in its passing was far from lonely, for a crowd was watching a phenomenon, the origin and nature of which had experts puzzled until the year previously. During the summer of 1940 we became accustomed to narrow fighter trails which often drifted north drenching the evening sky with high cloud. This, though, was quite different; typical of big America. When I muttered that I thought its producer was a Flying Fortress a neighbour cried 'The Yanks have come. You won't see one of Oakington's Stirlings making a smoke trail like that'. Smoke trail? Well, everyone called them that until some know-all announced 'vapour trail'. Contrail is a recent invention.

The arrival of a handful of useless Fortress 1s—for the RAF, because the Yanks still weren't coming—was a novelty for all concerned. Initially these bombers sojourned at Watton, West Raynham, Bodney and Gt Massingham, all of which were 2 Group Blenheim stations. None had hard runways, which Fortresses needed. A search was initiated and Polebrook, building of which began in autumn 1940, was a chance suggestion. Pat Webster, leader of 90 Squadron which used the 'Forts', took an aerial look at Polebrook and reckoned it quite suitable. To this new base, 90 Squadron took its bombers between June 27 and 29 1941.

Polebrook, land for which was acquired from the Rothschilds, was one of those 1939 style airfields with one Type 'J' hangar (pattern 5836/39) later supplemented by 'T2s' (8254/40). Three runways and a compact technical site, north of the main hangar, were featured. Parts of the technical site remain, also the hangar, although the latter was damaged by fire in 1979.

Placing camouflage netting over large aircraft was time consuming and far from easy. This photograph (of May 26 1943) shows B-17F, 230006, *of the 92nd Bomb Group being camouflaged at Polebrook* (US Air Force).

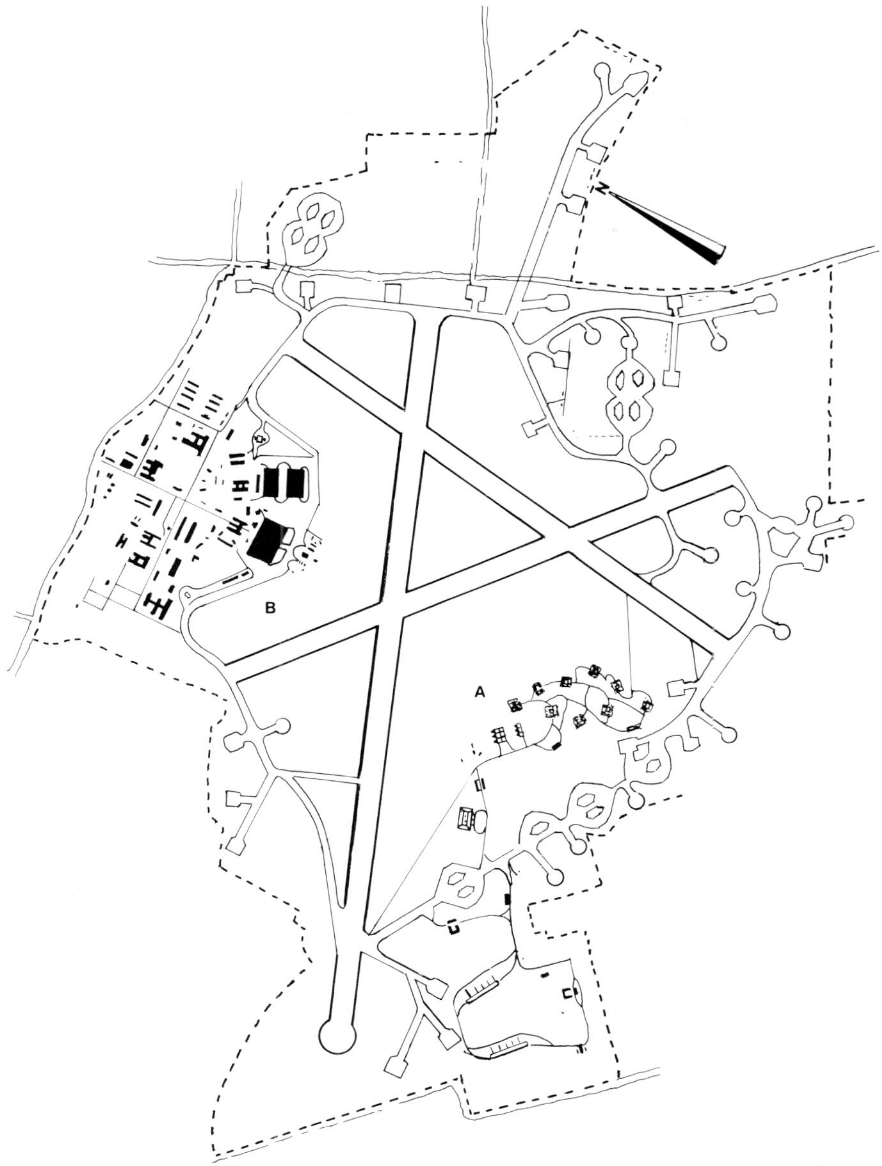

Polebrook in 1944 exhibits many of the features resulting from a major face-lift in 1942–43 to permit the accommodation of a USAAF Bomber Group. Runway lengthening has imposed a most unusual array of southern dispersals and taxi ways. A curious assortment of dispersal pads have been built and the enlarged bomb dump ('A') has been replaced between the runways. 'B' marks the position of the Type 'J' hangar—the other two were 'T2s'. To their rear is the technical site, domestic quarters being at dispersed sites.

Work complete, the B-17 is hidden—but not the netting! As the RAF discovered early in the war, removing it made the effort not worthwhile (US Air Force).

In the winter of 1940, and before completion, Polebrook was a dispersal airfield and later a satellite for 17 OTU Upwood, a sleeping role retained until September 1941 when Warboys replaced Polebrook. Group Captain A.C. Evans had arrived to open the station as self accountating on May 26 1941, following which it came to be one of the first airfields in Europe from which USAAF B-17s operated. Thus Fortresses were here for longer than at any other airfield.

Operating those early B-17Cs was fraught with problems. The Americans advised that the RAF should not employ them operationally but as trainers in advance of refined versions. Troubles likely during lonely, stratospheric flights were rightly forecast as enormous. To the Prime Minister they were challenges to be mastered. He was eager that the British should encourage the Americans to back them to the hilt so that making the Fortress a success seemed very worthwhile. Bombing Hitler, in Berlin, from a great height and in immunity—a notion which delighted Churchillian enterprise.

To operate from over 30,000 ft needed a well-heated aircraft, ample oxygen and clear weather for bombing accuracy. Huge gun ports in the aircraft's sides, when open, flooded the fuselage with air as cold as -50 degrees C. No pressure cabin meant an elaborate oxygen system, portable bottles and heavy clothing. Hand traversed guns and ample hazy weather further branded the bomber as of limited value. What was never in short supply was the courage and will to attempt to make the Fortress a going concern.

Operations commenced on July 8 when three Fortresses set off for Wilhelmshaven. Conditions were quite good but only two bombers reached the target area and only one attacked. Enemy fighters were spotted—and the Fortress waist guns had frozen to their mountings. Survival came because the fighters turned away. A layer of ice, seven inches thick, on the tailplane of the third aircraft had forced an early return to base.

The possibility of reaching Berlin in daylight to deliver a puny load could never boost morale and, because of the risks, Fortresses operated mainly against fringe targets. Had the weather been clearer, Berliners might have witnessed white vapour trails from aircraft which would surely have attracted wrath and vengeance.

On July 24 1941, 90 Squadron's Fortresses led a daylight assault on German capital ships in Brest. Nuisance raids followed, limited by unserviceability, hazy conditions and other criteria. An attack, on September 8 1941, on the *Admiral von Scheer* in Oslo docks virtually ended operations, two out of the four Fortresses

A handful of RAF Fortress Is of 90 Squadron operated from Polebrook. Despite persistent references to the contrary, those with Deep Sky under-surfaces had grey and green upper camouflage (IWM).

being shot down. No 90 Squadron, on October 26, sent a detachment to the Near East. In December 1941 it was admitted that successful Fortress 1 daylight raids were almost impossible. Suggested night operations, too, were abandoned. High altitude bombing, if resumed, would be by Wellington VIs with pressurised cabins. No 90 Squadron disbanded at Polebrook on February 12 1942.

On January 8 1942, Liberator IIs arrived from Snaith to train crews of Nos 159 and 160 Squadrons. They were for the newly formed 1653 Conversion Unit which was to build to a strength of 16 + 2 Liberators, and use Grafton Underwood as its satellite station. After converting crews for two overseas bomber squadrons, its task was also to provide crews for No 1 Group whose Wellingtons were at this time intended to be replaced by Liberators. During the first six months of 1942, training of Liberator crews was undertaken at Polebrook but, in June 1942, all aircraft of 1653 CU flew to Burn.

Whereas in June 1941, Americans went to Polebrook as businessmen, now they arrived for battle. The Yanks had at last come, and to Polebrook. They brought the first Fortresses to Britain. On June 11, 20 officers and 450 other ranks moved into Polebrook, followed by a further 31 officers and 465 men on June 12. A new State of America had been founded, men from these postings were soon establishing themselves as the 340th and 341st Bombardment Squadrons of the 97th Bombardment Group whose headquarters were set up at Polebrook. There, on July 6, the first B-17E to come to Britain for operational purpose landed. By July 31, 38 B-17Es were shared between Polebrook and Grafton. For them there were 47 combat crews who, between them, had flown over 500 hours in training since arrival.

For Americans accustomed to flying over wide, open spaces, crowded eastern England took some getting used to and they did well to be ready early in August. The 97th, at Polebrook and Grafton, was alerted for action on August 9 and again on 12th, but on both dates poor weather prevented operations. August 15 brought a visit by General Spaatz and Lieutenant General Eisenhower, but it was August 17 that became the most auspicious day.

Polebrook's part was limited, if important, and two small diversionary operations were mounted from the base. An hour ahead of Grafton's bombing effort, three B-17Es of the 340th Bomb Squadron, escorted by a swarm of RAF Spitfires drawn from Nos 121, 242, 331 and 403 Squadrons, under North Weald control, Nos 111, 308 (USA) and 350

Squadrons, under Kenley, and Nos 71, 124 and 232 Squadron, controlled by Debden, flew some 25 miles out to sea and towards Dunkirk. Further support came from nine radio-jamming Defiants operating from Northolt. German fighters at St Omer and Courtrai were ordered to engage too late. By then the diversion had turned for home.

Another three B-17s, of the 341st Bomb Squadron, flew a feint towards Alderney to attract fighters from the Cherbourg Peninsula. The B-17 crews were exposed to more risk than intended because they had taken off 15 minutes too soon and the six-Spitfire RAF escort was not available. The only problem the Americans encountered came from a flock of pigeons which intercepted a B-17 near Marlborough. Some crashed into the bomber and injured its navigator.

On August 19, a dozen B-17s of the 340th and 341st Squadrons, supporting the Dieppe operation, bombed the Abbeville/Drucat airfield. Later that day a Pecival Q.6 touched down with General Eaker, here to find out first hand about the latest operation. Another visitor was *12354*, one of the first B-24s in Britain.

Bombing raids from Polebrook included attacks on Amiens/Longeau on August 20, Le Trait on the 24th when Fw 190s damaged several B-17s, Wilton's Shipyards at Scheidam on 27th and Meaulte on the 28th. On September 5, Polebrook's contingent and others raided Rouen/Sotteville. Return to the Potez Meaulte factory, on September 6, brought the loss of B-17 *124450*, piloted by Lieutenant Lipsky, 340th Bomb Squadron. This was a B-17F, which the '97th' received late August.

An Ibsley P-38 called on September 7, its suitability as a fighter bomber carrying a 1,100 lb bomb being considered. That day the '97th' returned to Wilton's shipyard. September 8 brought consolidation when the 342nd and 414th Squadrons moved in from Grafton. On October 2, using only B-17Fs, Meaulte and St Omer were attacked. A week later, 22 B-17s participated in the largest US raid yet on the Fives-Lille's steel plant and Hellemmes railway works. On the 21st the Group suffered its heaviest loss yet, three B-17s missing from a Lorient raid.

On November 18, the 342nd and 414th Squadrons left for Hurn and thence North Africa, followed by the 340th and 341st on November 25 1942. Polebrook was then extensively modified to accommodate four B-17 squadrons. One runway was extended to almost 2,000 yds, the others to 1,400 yds, and an unconventional taxi track was added.

Selected for Polebrook was the 351st Bomb Group which came to Britain by sea during April–May 1943. The first B-17F to arrive was *229411*, bringing the advance party on April 15 1943. Four squadrons (508, 509, 510 and 511) followed and commenced operations on May 14 1943. Thereafter an intensive round of operations took the Fortresses to Schweinfurt and Berlin, Hamburg's oil refinery, a locomotive factory at Hannover, communications targets in Koblenz and Mayen, factories and railway installations in Cologne and harbours, V-weapon sites, submarine installations and tactical targets in France, Holland, Belgium and Norway. A famous visitor to the 351st was Clark Gable who flew in several operations whilst making a training film at Polebrook in the summer of 1943.

Probably the most meritorious event during the 351st Group's stay came on February 20 1944 when Leipzig held the target. One of the B-17s was badly crippled, its co-pilot killed and the pilot seriously wounded. The damage did not bring the aircraft down, so Second Lieutenant Walter E. Truemper, the navigator, and Sergeant Archibald Mathies, ball turret gunner and engineer, decided to nurse the B-17 home. The aircraft was righted to allow some of the crew to bale out. Then the bomber was heroically flown to Polebrook. After circling, those aboard tried to land it. That proved very difficult and after their splendid effort in bringing their wounded pilot home, the entire crew was killed during their third landing attempt. Mathies and Truemper were each posthumously awarded the Medal of Honor.

By the end of the first week of June 1945, the 351st, its last combat mission flown on April 25 against a Czech target, started returning to the USA. American tenure of Polebrook ceased on July 10 1945 and the RAF's 273 MU moved in to store Stirling IV and V transports and Mosquito VIs and XVIs, ferry duty being carried out by No 3 Ferry Pool's Ansons. Polebrook's flying days ended late in 1947, closure coming in October 1948.

After ten years of dormancy the unexpected came, a Thor missile squadron, No 130, formed here on December 1 1959. The three missile launch pads were under North

Once a rifle range, this long building, in fine condition at Rendcombe, serves as a barn.

Luffenham's control until squadron disbandment on August 23 1963. The Polebrook site returned to the Rothschild Estate in January 1967.

Rendcombe, Gloucestershire

SP350850. 1½ miles NE of North Cerney, by White Way

Close to Chedworth lies a recognisable First World war airfield. True, imagination is needed to raise the sloping meadows to their former glory, but the sight is worth viewing. The aerodrome lay to the east of White Way with the North Cerney to Calmsden road forming its southern edge. Here, 48 Squadron became the first to equip with Bristol Fighters, making Rendcombe hallowed RFC territory. The aerodrome is thought to have opened in early 1916 and it was active in June 1916 when 48 Squadron brought its BE 12s from Netheravon. Bristol F.2As arrived in February 1917 and left for France and the 1917 spring offensive on March 8. Posted to 48 Squadron were some of the most able RFC personnel. Captain Leefe Robinson VC, was leading when the squadron entered battle.

In August 1916, No 21 Wing established its HQ at Cirencester, No 38 Reserve Squadron forming at Rendcombe on August 1. Renamed 38 Training Squadron in May 1917, it was equipped with Bristol Fighters. On July 17 1917, No 62 Squadron arrived, converted to 'Brisfits', and left

Two large huts of First World War vintage remain at Rendcombe—on private property.

Home with a view—across what was once the very busy RFC Rendcombe aerodrome.

for St Omer on January 29 1918. No 110 Squadron formed here on November 1 1917 and, with BE 2c/d light bombers, left on November 12.

No 38 Training Squadron apparently became 45 Training Depot Station which opened here in mid-1918 comprising elementary, advanced and operational squadrons. It is likely that 48 Reserve Squadron was briefly in residence in 1916 with DH6 elementary trainers before settling at Waddington. No 59 Training Squadron is reputed to have brought DH6s and F2Bs to Rendcombe on February 1 1918 and was locally accommodated. One of its Flights had a Home Defence role. Certainly in 1918 an assortment of aircraft was here, including BE 2cs, F 2Bs and RE 8s. In February 1919, cadres of 45 and 46 Squadrons arrived, disbanding in late 1919. Rendcombe closed soon after, dismemberment of the camp taking place in 1920–1. It did not however, completely disappear.

Mr Malcolm Farnsworth, a dairy farmer, is occupant of Rendcombe Buildings and owner of the one-time aerodrome site. It was his father, who recently sadly passed away aged an incredible 103 years, who transported by horse and cart the wartime YMCA hut to Chedworth where it became the village hall and served until very recently. Between 1964 and 1976 Chedworth's villagers fought for an overdue replacement in the face of 'bureacrats united', eventually overcome sufficiently for the erection of a new hut, albeit for £72,000!

As elderly Mr Farnsworth gazed across the road to grassland opposite he could recall from days long gone a water tower from where the 48th used to be watched by 'brasshats', and which has recently surrendered. Not so three northerly hangar plinths lurking beneath the soil, slots in their concrete mark positions for vertical timbers. Tarmac roads and portions of apron remain between aged buildings. Station Workshops are still there, with double doors resting upon runners. Alongside the private road to Rainbow Barn stands the rifle range. Further east are four brick huts in varying states of decay, remnants of a domestic site. In one hut remains a sink and a small stove—what stories they could unfold! By Chalkhill Wood the squash court markings remain on a wall beneath a battered roof. Ivy covered, the machine gun butts survive at the south-west corner of the wood.

Worth visiting is Rendcombe churchyard containing reminders of the First World War activity. One stone bears an RFC emblem marking the grave of a one-day-old child, John Kenneth Lester Jones,

Village churchyards sometimes contain features of aeronautical interest. At Rendcombe is the grave of a baby. His father was a local RFC officer.

buried July 30 1918 and whose father was an RFC pilot, billetted in the house of the local blacksmith. In 1939 the Air Ministry inspected Rendcombe with a view to its re-opening. South of Nordown were tall radio masts so the authorities decided, instead, to build an airfield near Chedworth.

It is said that the Ministry of Defence still holds seven 'Bessoneaux' hangars, one being visible at Halton. Imagine one or two being placed on those bases at Rendcombe, and some of Old Warden's treasure alongside . . . .

Shellingford, Oxfordshire

SU325940. 4 miles E of Faringdon, by A417

Many wartime EFTSs originated in pre-war organisations. No 3 EFTS, Shellingford's wartime user, began as the Reserve Flying School, Hamble, which opened on

Other First World War buildings can also be seen at Rendcombe.

April 1 1931. It became 3 E&RFTS, equipped mainly with Hart variants.

In 1940 flying training around Southampton Water was hazardous and in July the unit's unusual, civilian marked Avro Cadets flew to Watchfield. There, 3 EFTS ran into more problems. Mixing blind approach training with elementary pilot training was hardly ideal.

The search for a practice landing ground to relieve Watchfield commenced. Kelmscot landing ground, available for Brize Norton, small and irregularly used, was proposed, but 50 Group showed little inclination to settle for it. In August 1940, 3 EFTS managed 1,935.40 flying hours, having only two accidents. The search for a landing ground continued and the choice fell, in October, upon a small area near Shellingford, four miles east of Faringdon. Judged to be a good site, surface preparation was needed whilst its main attraction lay in the ease of possible enlargement.

December 1940 brought proposals from FTC that 3 EFTS take over Wanborough RLG, dormant and awaiting use by Lyneham's SFTS. Wanborough, claimed 3 EFTS, was unsuitable because its grass surface could not accept winter activity. Due to increased flying at Watchfield, 3 EFTS decided, in May 1941, to accept Wanborough. Command's response was that the site was now earmarked for Lyneham, and 3 EFTS was authorised to use Kelmscot for practice forced landings. No Tiger Moths were based there for the site was unguarded. At night it was obstructed by an odd collection of vehicles placed there by a local farmer on behalf of Air Ministry.

Closure of 11 AONS at Watchfield during July 1941 brought suggestions that 3 EFTS stay there. Since early 1941 3 EFTS's choice of an area near Shellingford had interested higher echelons, and planning was going ahead to acquire it. Orders were received by 3 EFTS on September 6 1941 that, because upgrading of Kelmscot was unlikely, and because a third Flight was added to the EFTS, a move must come. The new C Flight would be detached to Shellingford until that airfield won full station status.

Shellingford was soon fit for use, obstructions littering it being removed. At a dispersal site pupils had dormitory accommodation from which they were conveyed by motor coach. As yet there were no cooking facilities, meals for the defence force permanently stationed there being brought from Watchfield. Tiger Moths of C Flight dispersed on the airfield, but inspections were carried out at Watchfield.

September 1941 brought instructions from 50 Group that EFTS pupils should have night flying experience to relieve pressure on SFTSs. It commenced at Watchfield on September 25 1941, only for instructors. Pupils began night flying at Shellingford on October 15 1941. A Cranwell-type flare path proved satisfactory, and 3 EFTS night training was undertaken there.

On December 18 1941, with sufficient

A daily sight over Shellingford, and many a grass-surfaced RLG, a DH Tiger Moth whose pilot is completing a solo flight.

buildings erected, 3 EFTS moved its 56 Tiger Moths to Shellingford. The technical site had four hangars along with stores, lecture rooms, a Link Trainer, transport section, armoury, flight offices, crew room, parachute section, administration block, nine Nissen huts, three Laing huts for the defence force and a collection of 'latrines—bucket seat type'. A communal site was established at Stanford in the Vale, where the Officers', Sergeants' and Airmens' Messes were, along with the NAAFI, and central ablutions. Officers' and Sergeants' quarters were at dispersed Site 1, each with three sets of huts. Other sites were soon in use and sick quarters was placed at No 5.

In January the use of RLG Kingston Bagpuize was authorised. By mid-January 1942 enough accommodation was available for 30 cadets, and 3 EFTS started to use it as an RLG. Kingston Bagpuize was only briefly available to 3 EFTS so, on May 16 1942, a detachment went to RLG Wanborough, no longer needed by Lyneham which was making itself a base for heavy transports. Wanborough, though, was too far away from 3 EFTS to be of much value.

Army pilots first joined 3 EFTS in July 1942, for pre-glider flying training. They had to complete 80 hours' dual and solo flying before posting to a GTS. Glider pilot courses were an important part of Shellingford's activity into 1943. Some measure of activity at 3 EFTS may be judged from the 3,472.45 hours flown in March 1943, 209.05 of them at night.

A steady flow of trainees passed through 3 EFTS in 1943 and Tiger Moths were a common sight here. Training of army pilots continued spasmodically and, in September 1945, a period of glider pilot refresher training took place.

Shellingford resumed its association with Watchfield after the war, messing being switched to the latter station. In 1946, Royal Netherlands Air Force pilots trained at Shellingford. With the gradual wind down of the RAF, 3 EFTS, like Shellingford, closed on March 31 1948.

Sibson, Cambridgeshire

TL095960. 7 miles SW of Peterborough, by B671, S of Wansford

Some airfields most unlikely to survive do so against all odds. Sibson certainly lies in this category. Close proximity to Wittering mitigated against survival, but the ever increasing size of Peterborough helps Sibson. Visit it and one finds a grass airfield smaller than when the RAF used it.

Sibson's grassland became an aerodrome by addition of a few tents, and portable flares for night flying. Use as Peterborough's RLG began in July 1940 and it was bombed the following month. At this time it was being used for the training of naval pilots using Harts and Audaxes.

In January 1941, Sibson was transferred to Cranfield control. Oxford pilots trained here until 14 SFTS left in June. On June 15 1941, No 2 CFS Church Lawford acquired the use of Sibson for Tutors and Oxfords, which flew from here until mid-January 1942. This unit shared Sibson with Peterborough which regained control in July 1941. Use had been made of it by Tiger Moths of 25 EFTS, replaced by others of 17 EFTS which did circuit training here until the school disbanded on June 1 1942.

That date coincided with the formation of 7 (P) AFU at Peterborough, a unit which equipped itself with many Master IIs. Controlled by 21 Group, it placed its A and B Flights at Sibson on a permanent basis in August 1942. By mid-1943 there were two day-flying Flights and a night-flying Flight at Sibson. Increased flying brought about improvements and enlargements to a once spartan site which were needed to cope with its increased use. A 'T1' (14) hangar (9659/42) was erected and existing buildings changed into SHQ (3825/43), and Main Stores which was sited in a Romney Hut (11279/42). A rest room was converted into a lecture block (745/41) whilst the control tower remained (13726/41). Two Sub Sites existed, No 1 in the south-west corner dominated by a 'T1' (14) hangr. There was a Blister hangar here, and High Leys Cottage accommodated flight offices and the rest room. Sub Site No 2 also had a 'T1' (14) and flight offices. A 24,000 gallon fuel tank was placed nearby. Beside the main site was the instructional site. Four enlarged Over Type Blister hangars (12532/41) were added to the landing ground which ultimately had three runways.

Throughout 1943 and into the summer of 1944, the Master IIs of 7 (P) AFU were ever active in the area and, occasionally, a Hurricane of 7 (P) AFU. There was intense operational flying around Sibson. This and the amount of mixed flying from Wittering was hardly conducive to pilot training. Accordingly, 7 (P) AFU relinquished its hold on Sibson on August 8 1944, moving to long established Sutton Bridge where the facilities, although antique, were far superior to Sibson's.

Some flying continued at Sibson to the end of 1944 then, early in 1945, it was placed on Care and Maintenance. Its proximity to Wittering rendered it a possible dispersal site. Sibson closed on May 21 1946 and was placed under Care and Maintenance in the hands of Flying Training Command. Fighter Command took over the station on July 8 1946 before it closed on October 1 1946.

Since the 1960s Sibson has been a centre for civilian flying and has become the Peterborough Parachute Centre. It is the only airfield in Britain where the lanky Pilatus Turbo Porter may be seen regularly. Visible from the A1 is a grounded Varsity, so that all links with military aviation have not been severed.

Silverstone, Northamptonshire

SP675420. 6 miles SW of Towcester

Stirling Moss, Jack Brabham, Froilan Gonzales, Guiseppe Farina—names to thrill when Silverstone was a circuit around a converted airfield. From the start it was a mecca for personalities whose none-too-powerful cars proudly displayed each driver's name. Then, all was for pure delight. At the old Silverstone, King George VI and Queen Elizabeth attended the British Grand Prix in May 1950 and drove along the perimeter track-cum-racing track, in a superb car on a lovely day.

Silverstone's opening commenced on March 20 1943. Upwood's 17 OTU had concentrated upon training Blenheim bomber crews. By 1943 that need had passed and HQ 92 Group, on April 10 1943, ordered 17 OTU to Silverstone to equip with Wellington IIIs on a ¾ OTU basis, and Upwood's occupants moved in mid-April.

On May 6 1943, two Wellington Ics arrived from Westcott. These, the first bombers to land at Silverstone, were ending their flying lives and about to be converted into instructional airframes. Next day a Wellington III touched down. By mid-May 10 Wellingtons were here. Training commenced on June 1 and No 62 Course changed role in mid-stream. OTU strength was set at 30 IE plus 10 IR Wellington III/X, raised on June 26 to 54 bombers. Among others were four Ansons, three Martinets, two Lysanders and, briefly, a Defiant.

On July 30 1943, the first *Bullseye* was attepted, but the four participants were soon recalled. Three days later, B Flight moved into the satellite at Turweston as four crews flew the unit's first Exercise *Eric* from Silverstone. The following night brought the unit's initial offensive sorties, four crews scattering leaflets over Arras, Lille, Roubaix and Tourcoing. Thereafter *Bullseyes, Erics* and *Nickelling* took place according to 92 Group's rota.

Late August 1943 brought increased activity. On August 28 a Halifax of 434 Squadron landed back from Nuremburg. Two nights later, Silverstone despatched its first bombing raid, two Wellingtons dropping 12 × 500 lb bombs on the Fôret d'Eperlecque. Over the nights leading to the climax of Operation *Starkey*, two more night raids, eight sorties, were successful. *Bullseyes* played an increasingly important part. Sergeant Shearing, flying *HE264* one night, was intercepted by two enemy aircraft and was lucky to escape. A Gunnery Flight formed on November 24 1943 at the satellite. Equipment now consisted of Wellingtons and Martinets.

By the end of 1943, 17 OTU had despatched 33 leaflet dropping sorties. No 71 Course passed out on January 2. Operational aircraft were occasionally diverted to Silverstone when returning from operations, as on May 22 1944 when 16 Halifaxes landed from Bourg Leopold. Another 14 came on July 26, and some of the 100 diverted to 92 Group airfields on July 30. When 17 Halifaxes came here on September 21 most still had bombs aboard.

Leaflet dropping ended on August 14 1944 with quite deep penetrations into France. Thereafter 17 OTU flew diversionary sorties to confuse enemy radar. The round of events changed little before the war ended. During August 1945, when courses 10–115 were being trained, the OTU vacated Turweston which closed as satellite on September 23 1945. No 17 OTU remained intact during the initial post-war wind-down. In September 1946, attempts were made to find suitable replacements for Hurricanes which, in 1944, replaced the Martinets. The Tempest V was too fast, whereas the Harvard was too slow, so Spitfires and Masters were to be used. News then reached Silverstone that 17 OTU was to move to North Luffenham in November

1946. Swinderby was then chosen and, after 17 OTU left in November, Silverstone was put onto Care and Maintenance, and sold in 1947. In 1948 the first RAC Grand Prix was run here and, in May 1949, the British Grand Prix. Flying has not ended for, on race days, light aircraft arrive for the excitement, and often bring famous personalities.

Snitterfield, Warwickshire

SP195600. 3 miles N of Stratford-on-Avon, Snitterfield. Bearley road crosses the site

Snitterfield, built for bombers, never fulfilled its role although it was, for long maintained for operational use. Supplementing the usual three-runway pattern, '04/28' as main runway, '09/27' the No 2 and '16/34' No 3, were 12 circular dispersal pans on the south side, nine of the north and another nine in the north-west corner. Technical Site 'A' was on the western side of the airfield and within it were two 'T2' hangars (8254/40), workshops, the main store, MT sheds, armoury and squadron and Flight offices. The watch office was to pattern 12779/41 and the 80,000 gallon water tower, pattern 9526/41.

Technical Site 'B' on the eastern side served as the main aircraft maintenance area. An unusual, later feature here, for use of training aircraft, was the siting of six Double Blister hangars (Type EO—12532/41) upon dispersal pans. Most buildings were of temporary brick in addition to a few Nissen huts.

Snitterfield came into use early in 1943 as the satellite of 18 (P) AFU, Church Lawford. From May 7 1943 to April 3 1945 it was a hive of Oxford flying activity. The RAF (Belgian) Initial Training School was here from January to October 1944 (when it moved to Snailwell) and trained personnel for a post-war Royal Belgian Air Force. On April 3 1945, 18 (P) AFU moved from Church Lawford to Snitterfield where it disbanded on May 29 1945. Meanwhile 20 FTS had formed at Church Lawford on April 3 1945 and used Snitterfield as an RLG. It closed in 1946.

Southam, Warwickshire

SP430615. E of Southam, S of A425

On Southam Fields lay a grass area which in 1940, was snatched for use as a Relief Landing Ground from which Tiger Moths of 9 EFTS Ansty flew until it disbanded at the end of March 1944. Southam was also used in 1941 by Church Lawford's Tutors and Oxfords.

Southam was very small, its few 1941-style buildings positioned at the southern tip of the landing ground. Some Laing type huts served as Barrack Blocks and for a combined Officers' and Sergeants' Mess—an unusual feature. These were to pattern 1032/41. The medical section was housed in a Nissen hut. Both the Flight office and the crew room were situated in wooden huts. On the east and west perimeters were a total of four small Blister hangars. A small technical site was built at the southern extremity of the landing ground. Included was a maintenance hangar comprising a couple of joined 69 ft EO Blister hangars. One end was bricked in; not unusual. Closure came on March 21 1944, after which Southam was used by Airfield Construction Units. On December 18 1944 it was transferred to the Ministry of Works.

South Cerney, Gloucestershire

SP045985. 3 miles SE of Cirencester

When recently driving into Cirencester my wife directed my attention to a group of soldiers being persuaded into completing a lap of South Cerney's perimeter track. I know that feeling, I thought. Most of them looked unlikely to be battle crazy types . . . indeed, they looked quite worn out, and—well, that is the impression South Cerney portrays. Gone the years of the smart, training camp image. Three 'C' Type hangars and a white, unusual-shaped control tower remain, monuments to an active past.

Aerodrome construction commenced in autumn 1936 of a custom-built camp for 3 SFTS. The Grantham-based school was in an area of operational stations and a move was necessary. There was haste to use South Cerney and, when the opening up party arrived on August 16 1937, the camp was far from ready. Only one aircraft shed was available for the Hawker Audax trainers. The Intermediate Training Squadron and workshops occupied it, leaving Audaxes of the Advanced Training Squadron outside until cover became available. From August 7 to 23 1937, 3 SFTS vacated Grantham between training courses. Personnel found facilities at South Cerney most inadequate, although fine summer weather brought some cheer. Whether this weather had anything to do

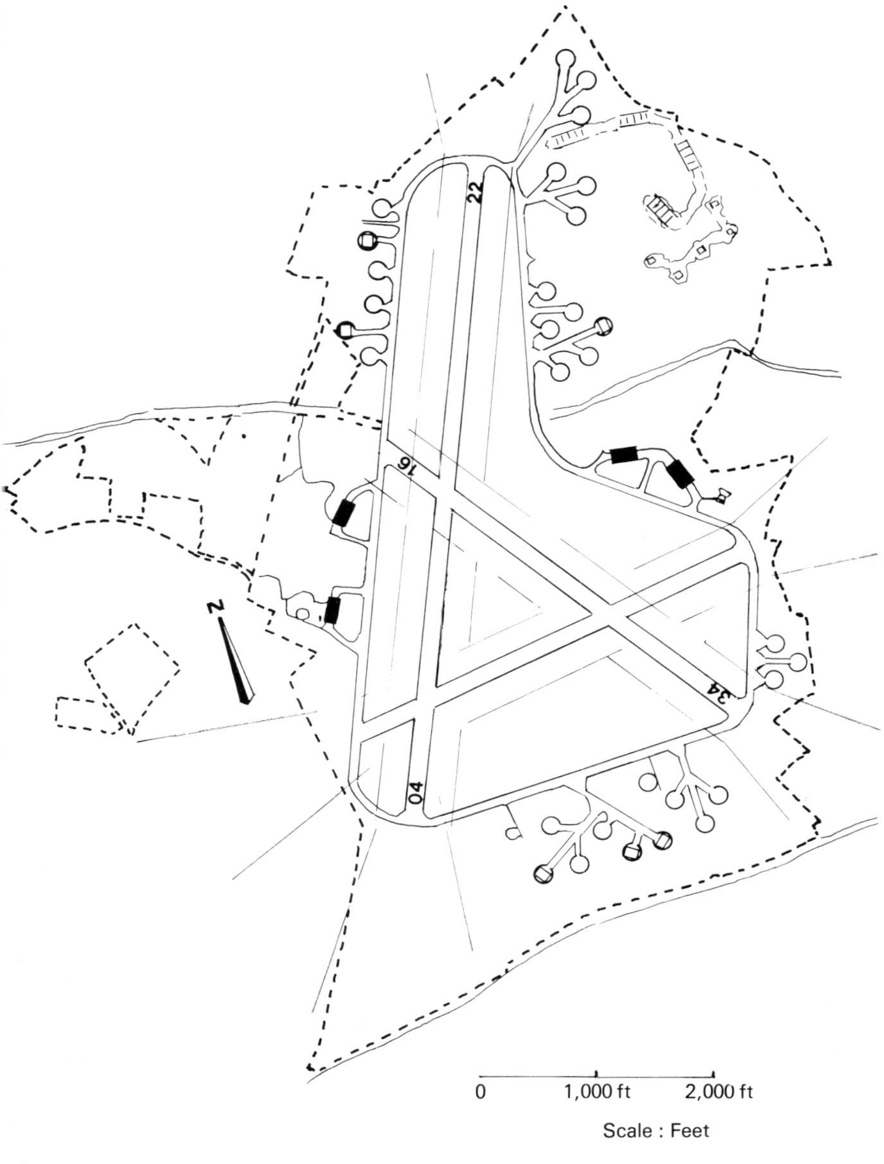

Snitterfield was laid down as a bomber OTU station with many dispersals conveniently sited at the north-east corner close to the weapons stores. Two 'T2' hangars (9254/40) were placed on the east side, and two more of the same type on the western side, next to which was the second technical site. With the arrival of Oxfords in considerable numbers, six Double Blister hangars, type E0 (12532/41), were built upon dispersal site bases.

with a hangar fire, on October 3 1937 which damaged an Audax, is unknown.

Audax trainers had joined the School in October 1935. Main deliveries came between February and August 1936, supplementing Hart trainers, the first of which came on charge in August 1935. Not until summer 1938 did modern aircraft reach 3 SFTS, the first attractive looking Airspeed Oxford twin-engined trainer for the RAF reaching South Cerney on June 14 1938. Re-equipment of 3 SFTS commenced on June 17 1938 and, by the end of July 1938, ten Oxfords were at South Cerney, sufficient to permit No 24 Course to begin using them on July 25. Those on that course became the first of thousands to learn multi-engined aircraft flying skills using Oxfords. Between July and September 1938, 3 SFTS shared deliveries of Oxfords with Nos 2 and 11 SFTSs, then a further ten Oxfords brought 3 SFTS strength to establishment. Training of Short Service Commissioned Officers could then proceed. From 1938 to the end of the war, South Cerney's Oxfords were a daily sight, and often there were over 150 of them with 3 SFTS.

A brief change overtook the station on September 8 1939 when Wellingtons of 37 Squadron arrived under Scatter Plan 3 Group. The Wellingtons' crews and mechanics lodged at Kemble, before returning to Feltwell on September 20 1939.

In September 1939, HQ, 23 Group, controlling advanced pilot training, moved into the old, temporary Mess at South Cerney. Audaxes remained in limited use at that time. Some cheer at least could be derived from a visit by HM King George VI. (His mother, Queen Mary, resided in nearby Badminton House during the war.)

As the 1940s' weather improved, flying increased, like the tempo of the war. Its seriousness was clear on May 31 when families were ordered away from married quarters. Within a few hours troops back from Dunkirk took their places as mechanical diggers, churning up fields likely to afford landing grounds for invading Ju 52s.

In June 1940, part of ITS, 15 SFTS, driven out of Middle Wallop by Fighter Command, began a temporary stay. Its aircraft, along with those of 3 SFTS, were night flying when an enemy aircraft arrived over South Cerney shortly before midnight. No warning had been received and five 50 kg bombs and some incendiaries fell, without causing damage or casualties, 400 yds from the flare path. A 100 kg bomb exploded not long after dawn. Raid warnings followed on the next three nights, interrupting night flying. On June 29/30, 22 bombs fell parallel to the Cirencester-Cricklade road between Swindon and Down Ampney.

Throughout July the station maintained advanced readiness to propel any invasion attempt. A second bombing raid came on the early afternoon of July 25 when two Heinkel 111s dropped sticks of bombs across the landing ground, about 500 yds from the apron. One raider was believed to have come down in the Bristol Channel.

At the end of August 1940, 15 SFTS moved out as invasion fever built to its crescendo. Instructors stood by to fly bombing operations for Plan *Banquet* with 23 Group. As hours of daylight shortened, the state of alarm receded. The enemy seemed less active in the area, although a Ju 88 came down at Coates Manor, near Cirencester, on November 24. The crew was brought to South Cerney, prior to burial in Coates churchyard.

Autumn 1940 brought a major change in the flying training syllabus. No 3 SFTS was instructed to run an intermediate instead of advanced training programme. There was no let up in flying, though, and throughout 1941 the pace ever hastened both here and at the Bibury RLG. A further role change came on March 14 1942 when the flying programme altered as the unit became 3 (Pilots) Advanced Flying Unit, giving refresher flying training courses whilst concentrating on acclimatisation flying and beam approach training for pilots trained overseas. Bibury remained the RLG until November 1944 when Aston Down replaced it.

On April 15 1943, No 1539 BAT Flight formed here, received Oxfords and moved to Bibury on July 13. A second BAT Flight, No 1532, operated from mid-1943 at South Cerney. A third such Flight, No 1547, ceased its attachment to 3 (P) AFU on December 4 1945, by which time the parent unit was closing. It disbanded on December 17 1945, on the day that No 3 Flying Training School formed from within it, re-established itself and moved to Feltwell in April 1946. South Cerney now held Charmy Down, on a Care and Maintenance basis, as its satellite.

South Cerney's post-war career commenced on May 24 1946 with the arrival of assorted aircraft of the Flying Training Command Instructors' School from Wittering. October 1 1946 saw the removal of HQ 23 Group, to Leighton Buzzard. FTCIS survived only to February 1947 when CFS took over its commitments.

Another interim phase came with the opening here of the Central Link Trainer School, the Aircrew Transit Unit and the Aircrew Allocation Unit where Command Clerk and general duties courses were held. March 1948 witnessed the arrival of No 2 Flying Training School whose Tiger Moths and Harvards vacated Church Lawford to provide basic flying training courses here which continued until May 1952.

Central Flying School (Basic) Squadron opened at South Cerney in May 1952, absorbing much of 2 FTS, using Harvards and Prentices, and then piston-engined Provosts were joined in June 1954, by the helicopters previously forming CFS (H) Detachment, Middle Wallop. In August 1954, CFS (helicopter Squadron) formed, using Dragonflies, Whirlwinds and Sycamores—the first RAF unit organised to teach helicopter instructors.

Provosts of CFS (Basic) Squadron moved to Little Rissington in May 1957. On July 22 1957, the Aircrew Officers' Training School (previously No 1 Initial Training School) arrived from Kirton-in-Lindsey bringing a few Chipmunks and Ansons. CFS retained control of South Cerney until August 10 1961 when CFS (H) left for Ternhill. In July 1965 the Primary Flying School formed and, using 21 Chipmunks, gave initial flying instruction to newly-commissioned pilots when the all-through jet flying training scheme was abandoned.

South Cerney's RAF days were ended when the PFS left for Church Fenton in January 1967. The Aircrew Officers' Training School held its last pass out parade on December 22 1967, then moved to Church Fenton on January 21 1968. South Cerney was placed in the hands of Air Support Command for use as a dormitory site by Brize Norton and Fairford. On July 1 1971, the station was transferred to the Army Department, leaving messing arrangements and some married quarters for RAF use. No 625 Gliding School remained, although South Cerney's days as an RAF station had passed.

South Marston, Wiltshire

SU184880. 4 miles NE of Swindon

A 'shadow factory' for large scale production of Phillips & Powis trainers was erected here in 1939–40. The bombing of Short's Rochester factory in 1940 changed that and at South Marston that

South Marston was the post-war production and testing centre for Supermarine. Their Type 508, VX135, *was built there.*

company established a major Stirling production line. Nearby, at Stratton St Margaret, Short's established drawing office facilities. The company used the factory and adjacent airfield until the end of hostilities.

Vickers-Supermarine was looking for a site where it could establish post-war production lines. During the war that company had production centres widely spread between Birmingham, Southampton and Salisbury. In 1945, South Marston was acquired and production of Spitfire 24s (from parts built for Mk 22s at Castle Bromwich) was initiated. A similar process resulted in the output of Seafire 45s, 46s and 47s. Work was also undertaken here in the refurbishing of Spitfire IXs for foreign air forces.

Production of Attackers for the Royal Navy was followed by Swift production, the first being delivered in March 1953. Scimitars were produced before the aviation works closed, leaving a good airfield with two runways, one 01/19 tarmac surfaced and of 5,997 ft and the other of concrete, 3,839 ft long. In October 1977 a link with past days came when Spitfire 21, *LA226*, arrived to guard the Vickers gates. South Marston remains an airfield, its industrial complex attracting civilian aircraft.

Southrop, Gloucestershire

SP190035. 2 miles NE of Fairford

To the south-west of Southrop village was a small grass airfield. For an RLG it was quite elaborate with two runways—05/23 and 15/33. In its south-west corner was Sub Site 1, the main servicing area, including two 69 ft Blister hangars and a 4,000 gallon aviation fuel tank. Sub-Site 2, in the south-east part of the landing ground, contained another seven 65 ft Over-Type Blister hangars (12532/41). Technical and Instructional Sites were at the north end of the LG, the former comprising buildings of 1941–2 vintage, many of temporary brick construction or adaptations of Laing huts. Within the Technical Site was the main hangar, a 'T1(14)19' (9665/42). There was a two-bay MT shed, a fuel compound and a brick control tower (13726/41). The Instructional Site of 1942 design contained such features as the intelligence library, photographic block, armament training facilities and navigation training rooms. Within the area known as Macaroni Wood were four dispersed domestic sites, the Sick Quarters site and the WAAF site.

Each of the four male domestic sites contained living accommodation in Laing huts suitably laid out to accommodate six officers and two servants, or 14 Sergeants, or a Sergeant and 14 men.

A communal site contained the Officers' Mess Type '68' (3440/41 and 10216/42), Sergeants' Mess Type '159' (3441/41, 10217/42) and Airmens' Type '673' (3445/41, 10218/42). The NAAFI block and games room, etc, (3446/41), had facilities for 104 corporals and 625 men showing a flourishing camp, whose high level water tank (Type 20/41) held 50,000 gallons.

First to use RLG Southrop was 2 FTS in August 1940. This continued until March 14 1942 when the School became 2 (P) AFU. When the latter closed, on July 13 1942, the station passed to 3 (P) AFU, South Cerney, which used it as a satellite station until January 22 1945.

Southrop's position on a hill top offers a splendid view of the south-east. About six huts remain at the junction of the B4033/A413 roads, and in places the perimeter track can be glimpsed—along with Greenway Farm's broiler houses.

Stanton Harcourt, Oxfordshire

SP415050. W of Stanton Harcourt village. 3½ miles S of A40 at Eynsham.

Late in the afternoon on August 16 1940, when civilian workmen were busy on one of Stanton Harcourt's hard runways, three enemy bombers suddenly swooped, strafing and bombing. Five of the Wimpey work force were killed and later another four died of their wounds. As a result Anti-Aircraft defences were installed at developing airfields.

Work on Stanton Harcourt, little damaged in the raid, was hastened. On September 3 1940, No 10 OTU, whose satellite Stanton Harcourt became, commenced night flying here. Until January 15 1946, when Stanton Harcourt closed, it reflected 10 OTU's activities. Whitleys of C Flight moved here from Abingdon on September 10 1940, concentrating on night flying training. Shortage of aircraft caused the Flight to disband in February 1941, then A Flight, converting crews to Whitley flying, replaced it.

Stanton Harcourt had an unusual layout in that its three runways were placed far apart. The proximity of the

Stoke Orchard photographed on November 14 1942 (RAF Museum).

River Windrush made flooding ever a possibility. Weapons were stored in the south-east of the airfield, main dispersals being on eastern and western sides. Personnel were accommodated in dispersal sites north of the village beyond the 'T2' and 'B1' hangars. Most buildings were of 1940 and 1941 vintage. The runways were put to good use in July 1941 when Halifaxes of 35 and 76 Squadrons attacked the *Scharnhorst*, in La Pallice, from Stanton.

Whitley V operational trainers provided most of the air activity throughout 1942. January 12 1943, however, brought a most auspicious event. In great secrecy Group Captain van der Kloot brought the famous Liberator, *AL504, Commando*, from Lyneham for Operation *Static*. Early on January 13 *Commando* left, carrying Sir Winston Churchill to the Casablanca Conference.

Re-organisation of 10 OTU came in February 1943. A and B Conversion Flights were positioned at Stanton Harcourt and gunnery trainers joined them. From April 18 1943 until December 31 1943, Oxfords of 1501 BAT Flight, were here and a 'B1' hangar was erected. On March 20 1944, 10 OTU's flying was switched to Stanton Harcourt while two runways were laid at Abingdon, and was reduced to ¾ OTU strength in May. Soon after, Hurricanes replaced the fighter-affiliation Martinets. Wellington Xs began to replace Whitley Vs in July, 10 OTU bidding farewell to its last Whitley Vs in October 1944. On November 16 1944, daylight flying was resumed at Abingdon and most of the unit moved there by early 1945. Stanton Harcourt retired from active use in the summer of 1945. Parts of the airfield have become busily worked gravel pits.

Stoke Orchard, Gloucestershire

SO925275. 2 miles W of Bishop's Cleeve

There are two vantage points for viewing Stoke Orchard. One is from Cleeve Hill at the foot of which the low flat land of the Severn Valley spreads far to view. An alternative is from a railway bridge by the side of this one-time airfield, revealing a scene little different from when Stoke Orchard was an airfield.

I first visited the station on August 22 1945. By then flying had ceased. Nevertheless it was a satisfying afternoon with interesting aircraft flying over, indicating the variety at that time. Barely had I left Bishop's Cleeve, my diary relates, when a Mosquito IX flew over alongside two camouflaged Mustang IIIs. Soon I recorded an Anson 1, more Mosquitoes probably from Defford, a Tiger Moth, Wellington X, Oxford and a Mitchell III. More uncommon was a grey-green-Sky Barracuda carrying an aluminium cylinder outboard of the undercarriage below the port wing. Chasing it was a Lysander, followed by another Oxford and a 'silver' B-17G. Recalling Stoke Orchard's former days came a quartet of Master IIs towing Hotspur gliders. A turreted Liberator VI circled, then one of those wartime delights appeared—an impressed civil aircraft, a genuine Puss Moth still camouflaged. An Avenger passed, then a trio of Mustang IIIs. Then it was a sign of the times as a Wellington X in night bomber colours displayed *PF962* in white below the port wing—obviously in the process of being painted. A Dominie trudged across, then a Wellington X could be seen playing around with a white and grey Beaufort 1 over Tewkesbury. A Wellington XIII came to observe me and, by the time I was back in the 'bus queue at Bishop's Cleeve, a naval Reliant, *FL163*, had paid its respects. Just a normal afternoon, I suppose, in the middle of which I had sandwiched a look across a very pristine Stoke Orchard.

Here was an unusual airfield. Four Bellman hangars (6411/39) and rows of assorted huts filled the south east corner. Barrack huts Type X or Y (9003/40) each accommodating an NCO and 57 other ranks, 16 sergeants or eight officers were close by. WAAFs were billeted in 60 ft long, 18 ft wide, Laing huts, or in Seco huts (3497/43). The Sergeants' Mess could accommodate 122 RAF Sergeants and five WAAFs (9002/40) and the Officers' Mess. 50 RAF and five WAAF officers. Workshops, stores, SHQ and MT Section were placed in temporary brick buildings of 1940 style. Around the airfield were assorted Blister hangars, the largest a Triple E0 (12532/41). There were six Double E0s, one single E0, two standard Doubles (12494/41) and three standards. A 30 ft compass swinging platform was provided.

July 1941 brought a decision that 10 EFTS, Weston-Super-Mare would move to Stoke Orchard when that airfield became available, expected to be in September. To Stoke Orchard the first of the Tiger Moths moved on September 23 1941 then 38 Course on September 27. By then 54 Tiger Moths had arrived where already Gloster Aircraft had a dispersed factory site. Under 50 Group still, 10 EFTS closed on July 21 1942 after plans for the airfield had been discussed.

Required expansion of glider pilot training brought concern in 1941. Selection of suitable airfields for glider training so that such activity would not interfere with conventional flying was difficult. It needed to take place away from operational airfields—yet brought complications to regions reserved for training. Glider training routes were studied and Stoke Orchard appeared a possible choice, although there was concern over the dangerous proximity of Cleeve Hill. To assess the situation a Hector brought a Hotspur to Stoke Orchard. Fully loaded, the glider was flight tested on March 10 1942 and there seemed no reason why a glider training school should not operate from here.

Before that came about 10 EFTS trained intensively. An alarming accident befell the crew of *N9492* which hit HT cables at Boxham Ferry before crashing in the River Severn, an accident which the crew survived.

Stoke Orchard was, on June 19 1942, informed by FTC that the EFTS's closure would be followed by the formation of a new No 3 Glider Training School, which could absorb some personnel. Formation commenced on July 21 1942 and Hotspur IIs arrived over the next few days. For towing, the unit equipped with Master GT IIs so that from inception 3 GTS proved more efficient than some schools.

Airfield surface conditions and intense flying, caused detachments of the GTS to operate from Northleach, Aldermaston and Wanborough. Training was all the time taking place from Stoke Orchard and continued, using some Hotspurs modified into Mk III trainers, until mid-January 1945 when 3 GTS towed itself to Exeter leaving Stoke Orchard to be held on Care and Maintenance until closure late 1945.

Stratford (Atherstone), Warwickshire

SP215515. 3½ miles S of Stratford-on-Avon

Authority for a satellite station to be prepared south of Stratford was given on June 18 1940. An advance party from 22 OTU opened the site on July 5 1941, flying by Wellingtons starting a week later. An error had been made in siting, for aircraft taking off from the parent station at Wellesbourne frequently passed directly over the main runway at Stratford. The station's name was changed, because of the existence of another airfield, known as Atherstone.

Wellingtons of 22 OTU used the airfield until November 15 1942 and were briefly here in larger numbers due to runway resurfacing at Wellesbourne. The station was then passed to 23 OTU Pershore, a ¾ OTU whose establishment amounted to 42 Wellington Ics. When Gaydon opened for 22 OTU, pressure on 23 OTU was relieved after the unit was nudged out of Defford in April 1942 when that station joined 10 Group.

Once 23 OTU held Pershore and Stratford, its establishment rose to full OTU level, maintained until January 15 1944 when it again was reduced to a ¾ OTU, mainly because of the need for major works to be done at Pershore. Stratford returned to 22 OTU on March 7 1944, remaining under Wellesbourne's control until December 15 1944. This permitted Wellesbourne to increase to 1½ OTU level from March 15 1944, giving it a strength of 81 Wellington III/Xs, 33 inherited from 23 OTU so that, although the name and markings changed, many of the Stratford residents remained the same. When 22 OTU vacated the station it was transferred to the Signals Flying Unit at Honiley in whose control it remained until flying ceased in late 1945.

Sywell, Northamptonshire

SP825690. 6 miles NE of Northampton off A43(T)

Many a sizeable town in the 1920s and 1930s attracted to itself an aerodrome, Northampton being no exception. Sywell's siting by Holcot Lane proved wise, allowing plentiful flying in a non built up area, permitting it to continue when larger aircraft used the airfield.

The first landing on the field which became Sywell took place on June 12 1927, its opening as an aerodrome coming in September 1928 at a ceremony presided over by Air Vice-Marshal Sir Sefton Brancker, Director of Civil Aviation, Northamptonshire Aero Club attracted DH Moths and air pageants here and famous fliers performed. Financial problems arose in 1932 and when resolved resulted in an expanded airfield and a smart clubhouse complex, completed in 1934 and still used.

Military Sywell was run by Brooklands Aviation. On June 10 1935 it began operating, under Air Ministry contract, an RAF pilot training school employing a few DH 60s and, soon after, Tiger Moths. In April 1937 five Hart variants were added for the training of RAFVR pilots, by which time the school had become 6 E&RFTS. In June 1939 the 20 Tiger Moths were supplemented by three Ansons, the syllabus extending to include the training of air observers and air gunners.

Unit strength in September 1939 included 25 Tiger Moths and 16 flying instructors. The observer/navigator training role switched to No 8 Civil Air Navigation School. Pilot training was now undertaken by 6 EFTS concentrating upon *ab initio* flying, using Tiger Moths, a role basically pursued throughout hostilities. Until the first War Course opened on October 23 1939 the school provided short courses for flying instructors. Establishment had then risen to 50 aircraft and 24 flying instructors.

Clearing the way for large scale elementary training, the navigation school became No 8 AONS on November 1 1939, lost its civilian status and, on November 25, was absorbed by 9 AONS Squires Gate. The civilian status of 6 EFTS also changed and, on January 1 1940, all flying instructors were called up for RAF service. This placed Squadron Leader R.W. MacKenzie as Officer Commanding 6 EFTS where previously he had been CFI as well as Manager of Brooklands Aviation. Aircraft establishment stood at 54 Tiger Moths.

By the summer of 1940, 6 EFTS was using an RLG at Denton. The school had an enviable record, there having been no serious injury to any pupil to the end of August 1940. Billeting increasing numbers of pupils caused problems and from the start of October 1940 they lived in Northampton, United Counties buses conveying them to and from Sywell.

This allowed quarters at Sywell to be occupied by airfield defence personnel guarding against '5th columnists' penetrating anti-sabotage defences. Road closures were common around airfields and anyone without an identity card—serviceman or civilian—could be faced with quite frightening moments. This facet of life continued well into 1942 and made the pleasure of observing wartime activities a trifle hazardous.

November 1940 brought a sudden scare to the EFTSs. An instructor was diving Tiger Moth *N6804* to restart the engine which had stopped during a slow roll and the leading edge of its upper starboard mainplane collapsed. However, the skilful instructor managed to land. There had been similar failings at the other EFTSs and 33 Sywell Tiger Moths were grounded for AID inspection. The conclusion was that the trouble was attributable to moisture permeating into the structure when aircraft stood at dispersals in all weathers—and particularly in winter. This was something Schools would have to live with while observing diligently. With each course standing at 60 pupils, all from ITWs, there had to be high levels of aircraft utilisation. Flying accidents were surprisingly few considering the combination of weather, congestion in the circuit and malfunction.

Free French pilots began training at Sywell in early 1941 and it became a wartime feature. Despite the high quality of training there were accidents as, in September 1941, when Tiger Moth *T6342* was gliding in to land and was suddenly struck by Oxford *V3980* from Kidlington. Both aircraft dived to the ground, killing their occupants.

In the summer of 1940 Brooklands Aviation began an important contribution to the war effort by opening a CRU on the south-west side of the airfield for the overhaul of Wellingtons—1,841 passed through its hands. In 1944 some were converted into special transports.

An additional Flight was added to 6 EFTS in March 1942 and 18 more Tiger Moths were allocated to meet increased pupil establishment which rose by 30, raising the School's establishment to 210, met by the use of 126 Tiger Moths. On May 7 1942, the new Grading Scheme was introduced. After 12 hours' flying, pupils were awarded marks according to their flying ability. Arrangements were made to remove from the School, by May 13, all *ab initio* cadets and re-organise 6 EFTS into six Flights of Graded Pupils. This pattern of instruction continued during 1943. Training of Frenchmen enticed General Vallin, Commander-in-Chief French Air Force in the UK, to visit his men on February 8 1944.

Opposite the airfield in a large factory Armstrong Whitworth Aircraft was to assemble Whitleys then Manchesters. Both plans were changed before, in 1943, assembly of Lancaster IIs commenced. They were flown away from Sywell for testing, the airfield grass having been increased in area in July 1943.

Evidence of operational activity around was apparent as B-17 formations assembled overhead in the early morning

Also at Sywell, David Cyster's famous Tiger Moth G-ANRF *following its epic Australian flight.*

Tiger Moth G-ADGV—restored in Brooklands colours of red, black and white—at a Sywell PFA Rally.

before setting off for distant targets. Their return was often a sobering sight. One B-17, *229860*, crashed at Sywell on December 31 1943. Lost in cloud the crew force landed at Sywell, clouting a Wellington's wing and knocking its own tail off. Forty minutes later *229888* also put down, short of fuel, and smashed its way through the boundary hedge.

To the end of the war Sywell was occupied by 6 EFTS and Wellingtons were overhauled. Post-war the work covered Wellington T.10s. Brooklands overhauled Valettas and, between 1957 and 1971, Varsities. Repair and refurbishing of Mosquitoes, Vampires, Chipmunks and conversion of Mosquito 35s for target towing was also undertaken. Lack of a hard runway limited Sywell's value but did not prevent Dakotas being overhauled here during the Berlin Air Lift. Most of the Varsity work and some Mosquito work was undertaken at Little Staughton. A few Vampire T.11s made use of Sywell's grass.

Soon after the war the EFTS was reduced to four Flights, training of Frenchmen ceasing on January 8 1947. Since February 15 1941 Frenchmen had come to learn to fly RAF style, both Army and Navy personnel, at what was often called the French EFTS where a total of 1,932 Frenchmen—1,707 from the Army—were trained.

The final Course was posted out from 6 EFTS on April 21 1947, the School closing upon transfer to Reserve Command on May 12 1947. Some exchange of Tiger Moths was effected and, as then customary, a few Anson T.21s joined the School for navigation training. Chipmunks replaced the Tiger Moths and Prentices briefly served at 6 RFS before its closure on March 31 1953. For the training of National Service pilots, No 4 Basic Flying Training School operated Chipmunks from Sywell and, to improve flight safety levels, a new conrol tower was built before the School closed in 1953.

Civil flying had resumed at Sywell in 1947. The Northamptonshire Aero Club reformed and Sywell became a prominent post-war light aviation centre. Such activity continued through the 1950s and 1960s. Between 1959 and 1965, Marathons, and later Dakotas, of Derby Aviation ran scheduled air services from Sywell, and in 1969 the first 'Flying for Fun' pageant took place. For the 1973 display the Popular Flying Association took over responsibility, making the airfield a yearly venue for all light aeroplane enthusiasts. With around 400 visiting aircraft during a weekend, these occasions, in aesthetically satisfying surroundings, will surely come to be viewed with intense nostalgia. Something of that was present when Tiger Moth *G-ADGV* visited in Brookland's colours the final PFA Sywell Rally. After initial use here pre-war *G-ADGV* served for four years at Clyffe Pypard and later with the Navy. Further excitement came when David Cyster brought his Tiger Moth to the same rally.

Brooklands suffered a take-over in 1974 and in 1977 decided to dispose of their Sywell interests. In any case the PFA had outgrown Sywell's space. On a fine summer day a Sywell PFA Rally was a delightful place to be. Pity those days have gone forever.

Tempsford, Bedfordshire

TL185140. 3 miles N of Sandy

Approach from Everton village, pause on the brow of the escarpment and a splendid view across Tempsford is yours. Only recently has much of this famous airfield been taken away, leaving the outline easy to make out. Proceed down the hill, passing on the left remains of a camp site. Moments later a bridlepath sign lies on the right. The path is really a wartime concrete road, barred by a wooden gate and then a rusted metal one by which a picket post once stood. To the left an assortment of huts marks the one-time Technical Site into which the main camp entrance led.

You can now tread hallowed ground. A fair proportion of the adjacent south-west/north-east runway remains in good health —useful for the inevitable crop sprayer. Beyond the runway rests a remaining 'B1' hangar of which a good view is obtainable from the main road. A brown object beyond, though, is the object of your interest.

Old, delapidated, but luckily supported by interior brickwork is the famous barn. On its north side is a noticeboard placed there by the East Anglian Aviation Society informing the passer-by that this was once part of the vanquished Gibraltar Farm. This was the place to which Special Operations Executive agents came to be equipped and kitted out before setting off on perilous drops or adventurous landings in Occupied Europe. Few barns in our entire history can have meant so much to both so few and yet so many.

Tempsford is a special place with a past eclipsing that of many a picturesque castle. Imagine, as you cross the runway, a Halifax swinging on to the threshold as agents quickly clamber aboard—faceless in the darkness, nameless to the crew and supremely brave. Surprising it is that, at the time, quite a lot of what was taking place was quite widely known. When the

Tempsford, from the south, on October 13 1942. The dark line on the left is the railway track to Scotland, presumably used regularly by enemy agents (RAF Museum).

'NF' Whitleys and Halifaxes were at Tempsford, and easily observed climbing over the old A1, they were accepted as merely continuing secret activities in more seclusion than at Newmarket.

Tempsford was positioned upon somewhat marshy ground forming part of the Astell Estate of which Tempsford Hall remains a major feature. Construction of the airfield commenced in late 1940. It opened in late summer 1941, under 3 Group, responsible for SOE flying activities until 1945. First to lodge upon the station were Wellington Ics of 11 OTU, here from December 16 1941 until

Above *Although Tempsford based, Lysanders used to land SOE agents in Europe operated from forward bases.* V9367:MA-B *of 161 Squadron is seen in overall black finish at its home station in August 1942. It joined the squadron on February 18 1942 and crashed on December 17 1943. Lysanders and Hudsons of 161 Squadron naturally dispersed by the railway line!* (Public Record Office).

Below *In 1944, 138 Squadron converted to Stirling IVs for supply drops, using them in particular over Scandinavia in 1945* (J.T. Breeze).

April 1942 while runway construction took place at Bassingbourn.

Radio and radar navigation aids were being skilfully developed for Bomber Command at this time on a number of RAF stations in this region. Tempsford became involved when, on January 19 1942, the HQ and Wireless Development Flights of 109 Squadron brought in their Wellington Ics. Spring 1942 found 109 Squadron experiencing the unique misfortune of being the only squadron to attract Wellington VI high flying pressure cabin bombers. *W5801* and *W5802* were here for a fortnight testing their suitability as *Oboe* radio carriers, a task eventually given to Mosquitoes. Tempsford, with its approach roads sealed, was ideal for secret goings-on. With 109 Squadron was No 1418 Flight whose four Wellington IIIs arrived at the start of March 1942 for a five-week stay and were used to develop radio navigation aids, before removal to BDU Gransden.

Important as this was, Tempsford's fame would come through its association with 138 Squadron. It arrived on March 14 1942, mainly flying Whitley Vs but also having a handful of Westland Lysanders whose modifications by Fairfields included a fixed fuselage ladder and a belly, long-range fuel tank. These were the Lysanders used to land and retrieve agents in France and Belgium on nights when the moon was high and discretion permitted some risk.

At Newmarket, from whence 138 Squadron, No 161, formed on February 15 1942 under the command of Wing 1942 under the command of Wing Commander E.H. Fielden. Barely existent, the squadron moved to Graveley on March 1 1942 before settling at Tempsford in mid-April 1942.

Prior to arrival at Tempsford, 138 Squadron's Lysanders were involved in nine pick-ups in France and one in Belgium, eight of them being successful. By the end of 1942 the Lysanders had set forth, usually via Tangmere, on a further 38 such sorties. Until October 1942 the main equipment was the Whitley V. Such was the importance of the task that in March 1942, although still rare, 138 Squadron was awarded a few Halifax IIs which began to replace Whitleys in both squadrons the following October. Part of one Flight of 138 Squadron was manned by Polish airmen who, in September and October 1942, made particularly gallant attempts to penetrate deep over Poland. One crew managed, on October 29, to deliver supplies to Warsaw, only to have run out of fuel which necessitated a ditching off Sheringham. This happened at a time when three Liberator IIs were attached to 138 Squadron for Polish sorties. They were soon placed in a special

Whitley Vs from Tempsford flew long range supply dropping and bombing attacks. Z9428, photographed in August 1942, flew with 138 Squadron between April 24 1942 and October 30 1942 (Public Record Office).

One of 138 Squadron's first specially modified Halifax IIs, NF:W, *photographed in December 1942. Note the absence of a dorsal turret and additional window aft* (Public Record Office).

301 Flight which became 1586 Flight and which, in July 1943, proceeded to Brindisi, Italy, from where flights to the Polish Resistance movement were undertaken.

Of the brave associated with Tempsford, surely no one became better known than Wing Commander P.C. Pickard. One of his moonlight exploits took place on November 22/23 1942 when he and Flight Lieutenant Bridges operated together to a field near Chateroux, flying in two agents and six packages and returning with three others and their luggage.

Most of the squadrons' work consisted of very accurate low-level supply drops to resistance forces. A triangle of red lights was lit on the ground and a white code identity letter flashed downwind of the apex. Landings were later aided by a Rebecca homer and an 'S' telephone link, allowing the pilot to contact the reception committee. An extension of pick-up operations came with the delivery of Lockheed Hudsons to 161 Squadron. Whereas the one-man undefended Lysander could operate within a rectangle of 250 × 25 yds, the Hudson took a greater run. But it permitted much deeper penetration flights, as on November 25/26 1942 when Group Captain Fielden flew *FH406* to Avignon, a 7½ hour flight, made only to find no reception committee able to great him.

November 1942 found A Flight, 161 Squadron, converted from Whitley Vs to Halifaxes. The squadron also had a special detachment flying two Albemarles at St Eval for shipping co-operation sorties. Detachments from Tempsford were common and at the end of 1942 some crews operated within the Mediterranean Theatre. Another diversion from the usual SOE employment came when Lysanders and Whitleys of 161 Squadron made bombing raids, thus providing diversion activities whilst the usual operations were taking place.

Throughout 1943, when the moon was bright and conditions favourable, Lysanders of A Flight, 161 Squadron, operated, 111 out of 157 pick up sorties being successful. Part of 138 Squadron was detached to operate in support of guerilla forces in Libya whilst four Halifaxes spent a short time in Russia. Wing Commander Pickard left Tempsford in May 1943, by which time a number of pilots had become skilled at pick-up operations. One of the most successful months for operations was August 1943. Within that month 66 agents were dropped, also 194 packages and 1,452 containers in the course of 184 operations. October 18 1943 witnessed the first double Hudson pick-up, both aircraft becoming temporarily and alarmingly bogged. Wing Commander R. Hodges, commanding officer of 161 Squadron, landed first and picked up ten people. Flying Officer J. Afflick, who followed him in, airlifted out another ten. Years later Hodges was to discover that one of his then un-named passengers was a Mr Vincent Auriol, later President of France. Hodges became well known in the post-war RAF, and at one time was station commander at Marham, whilst John Afflick spent some time as a BEA Viscount pilot.

Double operations were fraught with great danger, only too apparent on December 16/17 1943 when two Lysanders collided during a blind landing. A very special operation took two Halifaxes to Norway, a ten-hour journey to deliver paratroops whose task was to attack a heavy water plant, an operation prompting the Telemark film. On May 28 1943 a new unit, 1575 Flight, equipped with Halifaxes and Venturas, formed here before proceeding overseas a fortnight later.

During February 1944 the first mail pick-up was attempted. The Lysander used the antiquated pick-up hook with which it had been born and which had hitherto seemed so outdated in an era of radio contact.

Short Stirlings first came in numbers to Tempsford in February 1944 when a detachment from 149 Squadron took up

Set within fields in wartime, Tempsford's famous barn may now be visited by following a footpath. Within its hallowed walls, many a famous person obtained equipment for an SOE Mission. Racks for assorted supplies remain in place.

residence for SOE dropping training. For effective SOE operations it was essential that ample, regular radio communications be maintained with resistance forces. For that role Hudsons were used, to fly 296 so-called *Ascension* Operations mainly off the Dutch coast, and at around 20,000 ft. Prior to the use of Hudsons, a few Havocs were employed for an evening ritual in the summer of 1942. One or two would climb on an easterly track arriving high to make widespread contacts.

Immediately prior to D-Day both 138 and 161 Squadrons supplied war material to resistance forces throughout Europe. Poland, Austria and Yugoslavia were most easily reached from the south and Tempsford's crews flew to the Mediterranean Theatre to undertake drops in those countries.

On August 11/12 1944, 138 Squadron flew its last Halifax sorties from Tempsford, 13 aircraft supplying the Maquis. Lysander pick-up flights now ceased. Between November 1942 and September 1944, Hudsons made 36 successful pick-ups out of 46 attempted.

Rapidly 138 Squadron converted to Stirling IVs fitted with long range tanks. No 161 Squadron flew its final Halifax sorties on the night of September 1/2 1944 and began operating Stirlings on September 8/9 1944, 138s having gone into action on August 28/29.

By September 1944, drops were mainly to the Belgians, Danes, Norwegians and over a few areas of south-east France. By the end of 1944 they were also being undertaken over Germany, using Hudsons. The last agent landing flight was despatched on February 3 1945. Low flying made SOE operations hazardous, as on March 20/21 1945 when three Hudsons, despatched to Germany, failed to return.

No 138 Squadron's association with Tempsford ended most abruptly when it moved to Tuddenham and re-equipped with Lancaster bombers. During its Tempsford operations it had delivered 995 agents, 29,000 containers and 10,000 packages in the course of 2,494 sorties and for the loss of 70 aircraft. No 161 Squadron operated from Tempsford to the end of European hostilities, completing its commitment when, on June 3 1945, a Stirling flew to Brussels. Disbandment came on June 14 1945. Tempsford crews had brought hope and succour throughout enslaved Europe.

As 161 Squadron disbanded, No 1 Transport Aircraft Modification Unit formed, a centre for the conversion of

Tempsford from Everton hill, a vantage point in wartime. **'A'** *marks the remaining 'B1' hangar,* **'B'** *the remains of the main site,* **'C'** *the main runway,* **'D'** *the SOE barn and* **'E'** *indicates the start of the footpath to the barn.*

Coastal Command and bomber Liberators into transports. When this work finished 1 TAMU moved, in February 1946, to Honington.

In mid-June 1945 Tempsford was switched to 47 Group under whose control 426 Squadron rapidly converted to Liberator troopers for the Europe to India run, a short lived task since the squadrons disbanded on December 31 1945. A Proctor and an Anson of 48 Group Communications Flight were here before the unit disbanded on May 15 1946. A detachment of 53 Squadron's Liberators arrived on December 9 1945 and returned to Gransden Lodge in March 1946. No 102 Squadron also had a detachment of Liberators at Tempsford from early January 1946 to February 28, when it was dissolved into 53 Squadron.

Removal of the Liberators left Tempsford quiet. Maintenance Command took over the station on August 7 1946, Polebrook's 273 MU establishing a sub-storage unit at Tempsford. Briefly, a considerable number of Harvards and some Mosquitoes were here in the spring of 1947. Tempsford reverted to Care and Maintenance in June 1947 then transferred to Technical Training Command in October. On April 12 1961 many remaining buildings were sold and, in February 1963, 648 acres of the site were bought by the Astell family. Land to the east is owned by Francis Pym; pity he could not have somehow discovered a Whitley or two when he was Minister of Defence. He might even have been able to show a profit by flying it from this most historic place.

Thame (Haddenham), Buckinghamshire

SP755090. 6 miles SW of Aylesbury, NW of Haddenham village

Imagine the reaction had it happened but yesterday! There would have been much crashing of shutters on cameras with monstrous lenses everywhere. Instead when, on April 27 1941, two of the seven remaining, aged Avro 504Ns impressed for unusual military service arrived at Haddenham, nobody seems to have clicked a Brownie. These remnant designs of the previous war had retired from a reserve training role in 1933! Some went to civilians, among them *J8533* which became *G-ADET,* and *K2353* alias *G-ADBP.* Yet, here they were again, serving King and Country, disguised as *AX875* and *AX874* respectively.

An astonishing scheme had previously been devised for these antiques, the towing of wooden sailplanes part way across the English Channel for release not far from the French coast, although they would not then operate from Thame. The reason for such sport? To discover whether radar could detect wooden gliders. Such escapades could never become one of life's most carefree ventures, that's certain.

Following the fall of France, the decision was taken to form a British glider-borne paratroop force. A start followed using sailplanes and training gliders hauled aloft by a collection of light aeroplanes based at Ringway where a glider training school formed on September 19 1940. Operating this alongside experimental activities was undesirable so a training site was sought. A strange choice was Side Hill, grassland on the east side of Newmarket where horses canter. Lysanders occasionally joined them and at least one Whitley indulged in the sport of kings. Glider pilot training in a busy operational area, with the enemy nosing around, was hardly an apt choice. The formation calling itself the Glider Training Squadron arrived at Side Hill on November 21 1940 and left on December 28, setting up shop at a small aerodrome known as Haddenham, later known as RAF Detachment Thame.

Opening Thame gave its new occupants plenty to enjoy. Upon arrival, GTS found the landing ground strewn with obstructions to discourage airborne forces. This rubbish had to be removed quickly and burnt in preparation for the impressive arrival of Britain's mighty airborne army.

When it came it did so complete, almost, and in formation. Composition? Five Tiger Moths which made an assault landing in an astonishing one minute, thus setting a target time for future airborne ventures. Crew shelter was found in a room of Yolsome House prior to the occupation of more expansive accommodation at No 8, Church Road, Thame. This residence was conveniently adjacent to the other ranks' billet in a tithe barn. All the troops were in their billets by January 3 1941. Nothing short of incredible is it, that the mighty force which skilfully moved into Normandy in 1944, and fought with such colossal courage at Arnhem, should have virtually been born in these pathetic circumstances. Such, though, is the manner by which the

British have always gone about their fighting business and always will. That we are quite incapable of altering this is frighteningly proven by present day antics.

The glider forces' arrival at Thame was understandably, not featured by the media of those days, particularly as the gliders came in over-sized suitcases. 'Gliders' does not describe them for these were five Kirby Kite sailplanes which, by January 5 1941, had been prepared for flight. Snow put an end to such notions, and ice often needed to be swept from the wings of the aircraft.

Construction and improvement of the airfield was underway and, on January 11 1941, a Bessoneau hangar was completed, along with three huts. Total flying time to January 11 amounted to 25 hours 33 minutes. Doubtless 70 Group was pleased that a start had been made.

To satisfy himself of the value of airborne forces the General Officer Comanding in Chief visited Thame on January 6. An impressive parade of 'Tigers' and Kites awaited him. Soon they were flying in a wide formation as far as Hartford Bridge. They turned, crossed White Waltham for the benefit of aviation enthusiasts in that area (were there such people?), then returned to Thame, gliders casting off for a stream landing.

The vulnerability of glider trains was disturbing. Surely fighters could easily pick them off? This needed investigation, so a ground party left for Duxford on January 17 1941 while another group acquired a Viking sailplane for trials. Five Kirby Kites, letters A to E, were towed to Duxford by the 'Tiger Club' and, on February 10, the exercise was flown, five combinations being engaged over Royston Heath by AFDU fighters whilst Wing Commander Vasse observed from a Gladiator. During a repeat performance a Defiant from GRU Exeter had, as his unlikely 'gunner', the famed Professor Melville Jones. All satisfactory, the gliders returned to Haddenham.

It was all very well having a glider school; what was needed were gliders and not sailplanes. Between February 15 and 18 1941, personnel from Haddenham were at Farnborough inspecting four real gliders available for trials. Squadron Leader H.J. Wilson of the Aero Department explained that originally the idea was to release troop carrying gliders at 20,000 ft and 100 miles from their target, leaving them to approach silently. Tests revealed a very creditable 83 miles glide by a Hotspur 1, released from 20,000 ft. General Aircraft Limited had designed and built its prototype in three months. The method of tow was uncertain, the glider having towing hooks in the extreme nose, under the belly and in the tail to allow another glider to be attached, thus forming a train. Wind tunnel tests showed this impossible because of the dynamics involved.

The Hotspur 1 was extremely elegant, its superb fuselage aerodynamics being derived from the profile of the *R-100* airship. A moulded, transparent streamlined cockpit hood covered the two pilots seated in tandem behind which six troops sat in line astern. On landing they jettisoned the cabin roof, deplaning in a few seconds after the glider landed on its fuselage skid. Shortly after take off the wheeled undercarriage would have been jettisoned. Twelve Mk 1s were completed but before then a policy change meant that gliders would be released at the landing zone and steeply descend to land. To control descent, a braking parachute was experimentally fitted to a Hotspur.

Meeting the new requirement caused the aircraft's wing span to be reduced from 61 to 46 ft and removed nearly all its gliding capability. No longer was the fuselage top to be jettisoned, doors for paratroop or ground troop exit were built into the fuselage. A new cockpit canopy was designed as well as bench seats for the troops. Gliders were now to be expendable after one operation, this effecting their means of operation—not to mention life span and durability.

BV134, the prototype Mk 1, first flew in December 1940 and displayed poor aileron control. Indeed, its ailerons had four inch wide strips added to their trailing edges, to help remove some four inches of dead control column area. *BV135*, the second machine, had enlarged ailerons and they were still not powerful enough. *BV136* had Frise ailerons, and now control was being over-complicated since the pilots' controls were duplicated. A trimming tab was not powerful enough to remove the tail heaviness of the aircraft. Flaps were too small and strength of the structure was so critical that the 8-seater GAL 10/40 intended to carry eight armed men could safely carry only six. The towing quick-release hook on the glider's nose had to be repositioned because of centre of gravity problems, the cure for which became a bifurcated tow rope.

BV137, the fourth Hotspur, was the first with shortened span and enlarged ailerons. A variety of modifications made this preferable to others for the designated role, although it had a longer landing run, higher stalling speed and no brakes. The Hotspur saga faced another watershed in March 1941 when the decision was taken to establish a huge glider force, equipped with 25-seater Airspeed Horsas. Hotspurs would be used almost exclusively for training purposes—for which they were far from ideal.

Twelve army pilots reported, on March 3 1941 for training at Haddenham. Suggestions that they be trained as a side line by squadrons of Army co-operation command had been discarded. They would learn to fly Tiger Moths and then sailplanes until the Hotspurs were available. On April 6 the first example for GTS arrived by road, was erected then flown on April 9, being towed off by Hotspur *K8119*. Finding suitable Hotspur tugs was another problem and Malcolm were instructed to quickly modify 25 unsuitable, unwanted Hector Biplanes.

Haddenham's sailplanes and Tiger Moths had twice been to Ringway for important demonstrations. Another took place on May 15 1941 for the local Home Guard as the first long distance Hotspur tow, of *BV135* from Ringway to Haddenham, took place. This was useful preparation for a cross-country flight to White Waltham on May 24. Next day PTS and the GTS mounted a display in a field near Windsor, for the King and 5,000 Home Guard personnel. Following a paratroop drop from a Whitley, three of Thame's Kirby Kites were released from Tiger Moths. The climax was the arrival of a Hotspur brought along by a Hector.

Building the GTS was a protracted process and there was certainly no room for the slightest complacency. By September it was reckoned that for each three men trained, one Hotspur would be written off.

October 14 1941 saw the arrival of Haddenham's first Hotspur II, *BT498*, and, on October 22 the layout of GTS was specified thus: Tug Towing Flight—16 Hectors, along with a Hind trainer upon which tug pilots flew their conversion course, and two Tiger Moths; two Glider Flights, each supposed to have 8 IE and 7 IR Hotspurs, high reserves allowing for expected wastage. Actually the unit held 11 Hectors, three Hinds, 12 Tiger Moths, those two Avro 504Ns (both sent to 71 MU on December 12 1941 for disposal to ATC squadron—*AX875*, going to No 1458 at Deal, and *AX874*, to 1813 Squadron at Merthyr Vale) but only 8 Hotspurs. A further six Hotspurs had, on October 13, been allocated to the Ground Training Unit. All needed erection and rigging at Haddenham, a tricky task complicated by continuous control problems and tail heaviness for which no cures had been devised.

Formed on November 4 1941, No 1 GTS Thame (the name of which was thus altered at the start of December), held 16 army pilots forming No 1 Hotspur Course which opened on December 1 1941 under the control of 23 Group, Training Command, and no longer 70 Group. With much faster gliders becoming available now the outline of an ideal Hotspur trainer was formulated after Thame's experience. It would need a low sited nose hook to prevent the glider climbing too rapidly, effective dual controls and instruments, wheel brakes and ballast load. *BV134* was modified to Thame's ideas. Meanwhile limited flying showed that the Hotspur was not robust enough for training purposes. Wing and tail stresses had been underestimated and there was excessive wear on the undercarriage for a glider intended always to land upon its skid.

Another problem concerned suitable tug aircraft. Whilst loaded Hotspurs needed the pulling power of a Hector on take off, Thame's run was not long enough in emergency conditions. One possibility was to operate from Kidlington, the gliders carrying ballast. As these deliberations were under way, the first glider operational training units had formed. These needed Hectors which meant that GTSs would have to use Audaxes.

Nothing in the sphere of military gliders was ever simple, and none more so than the task of fitting them into the available air space in the busy Midlands. On long tow, Hotspurs, and soon Horsas, were difficult to turn. Therefore around Kidlington was established, in March 1943, the Central Area, within the bounds of Barford–Thame–Kidlington. Some lengthy glider routes across the Midlands were also prescribed as, for example, Thame–Olney–Kettering–Barford and return, Kidlington to Tetbury or to Shrewton via Netheravon and a long route, Barford–Pershore–Shrewsbury–Northwich–Ringway, along which flights could be made to heights of 12,000 ft. Ample notice was needed by all Commands of such flying.

Glider activity rapidly expanded in 1942, so much so that 1 GTS needed RLG Kingston Bagpuize, used between March 9 1942 and July 25 1942. This did not remove Thame's unsuitability, particularly for possible larger gliders. Training Command searched for a better airfield, eventually chosing Croughton. No 1 GTS began to move there on July 22, completing the change on August 3 1942. A small portion of 1 GTS remained at Thame, becoming the Glider Instructor's School whose role was to train pilots to instruct others to handle military gliders. Five months later the GIS closed, its task transferred to a smaller unit at 5 GTS Shobden.

For a while Thame was without towing activities. Early in 1943, though, the Royal Navy Air Experimental Department was formed here to develop equipment for target towing and suitable targets. This brought an assortment of aircraft, including Martinet, Defiant, Swordfish and Vengeance target towers.

An interesting series of experiments concerned the Lines Brothers' towed small aircraft targets. Lines were famous for their Frog Penguin plastic models and now found themselves producing the real thing for naval gunners. The RNAED was replaced in May 1945 by the RAF. The 3rd Reception Centre was here until October 1945 when it left for Ludham, leaving Thame in the hands of RAF radio engineers, and an overseas packing unit, here until the station closed on April 30 1946.

Civilian aircraft engineers followed the RAF and, in 1948, Thame was, perhaps surprisingly, the lair of a handful of civil Stirling Vs. Since those days it has attracted an assortment of small aircraft and engineering concerns with part of the site now being an industrial estate. Light aircraft still use the airfield which is operated by Airtech Limited as an unlicensed aerodrome where sailplaning takes place at weekends.

Thurleigh (see also Bedford), Bedfordshire

TL042601. 6½ miles N of Bedford, now part of RAE Bedford

January 1 1942, a fine, warm, clear day. Very good for winter flying, ideal for spotting. Mid morning brought one of those wartime highlights for, flying low and northerly came a scrumptious, fully turreted Liberator II bomber. Such fare was rare in England and my immediate question was—where had it come from? Local rumour associated it with an airfield near Bedford called Thurleigh, where Lancasters were also said to have been seen. Clearly the place was worth looking at. When we arrived it was in a ghastly mess, one mass of mud and a few Wellingtons. Certainly 160 Squadron, reformed on January 16 1942 and which briefly stayed at Thurleigh, used Liberators. Whether they flew them from here remains doubtful. Our sighting was probably of one from Polebrook.

Thurleigh's opening party had arrived on July 24 1941. By the end of the month the perimeter track, two runways of 1,600 yds and 1,100 yds and three groups of dispersal points were complete. On October 9 1941, the station was switched from 2 Group to 8 Group, an event which was celebrated at 02:00 by the arrival of Wellington *R1234* of 12 OTU which damaged its wing and undercarriage in the process. This switch in loyalties reveals all, for such changes were the fate of stations set aside for the Americans, a group of whom visited Thurleigh on October 28, before going to Little Staughton.

On February 12 1942, eight RAF officers shepherded no less than 524 obedient men of 160 Squadron from Thurleigh to their port of embarkation. This left 96 men to represent 160 Squadron, among them 58 aircrew with another five 'AWOL'.

On February 16, personnel of 18 OTU arrived, the remainder of 160 Squadron leaving for Polebrook and, eventually, 120 Squadron. Among new Thurleigh residents were 127 Polish airmen, part of 18 OTU's detachment which opened for business on March 1 1942. On May 18, during night flying, Wellington *DV783* crashed on the aerodrome. The five Poles aboard were all killed. Almost simultaneously, but miles away, another Polish crew died when *N2806* crashed. Its crew was buried at Newark two days later. On June 3 1942, five Wellingtons arrived from Bramcote to take 18 OTU's detachment. Others set off in lorries, leaving 2813 Airfield Defence Squadron to guard the airfield

Work proceeded on improving the station for its main role which commenced in the early hours of September 7 1942 with the arrival of some 1,700 officers and men of the 306th Bomb Group, USAAF. After a brief rest they paraded to greet 18 B-17Fs of the 367th and 423rd Squadrons. Alas, there was disappointment because the incomplete runways prevented landings and, after an impressive formation tour of the area, the Fortresses put down elsewhere. This was only a brief diversion and, in two formations, the B-17s of the 423rd, 367th and 369th Squadrons made an even more impressive spectacle as they settled on September 11. Two days later the Fortresses were out and about learning to fly in formation and proving to the arriving 368th Squadron that the 306th was already active.

For the Group, October 9 1942 was the big day, indeed for many it would be a morning to remember. This was the first occasion when a large number of American bombers was to be seen literally drenching a clear sky with contrails as they roamed around getting into battle formation for the biggest USAAF raid so far. Take off by Thurleigh's two-dozen B-17s began at 07:32, for Target Z183, the Fives-Lille steel works. Flying with the 11th CCRC, the 306th performed very creditably, 19 crews claiming to bomb the target from around 22,000 ft between 09:38 and 09:46. Enemy fighters were very active and the Group's crews had a clear, chilling view of *124510*, of the 367th Bomb Squadron, being shot down.

The 306th next operated on October 21, 20 B-17s setting off for the Karoman shipyards at Lorient, an operation halted by poor weather resulting in the bomb load being jettisoned in The Wash. In November the 306th attacked Brest on the 7th, Lille on the 8th, St Nazaire on 9th and La Pallice on 18th. On the latter occasion the 306th operated with 12 B-24Ds, 18 B-17s of the 303rd BG, 18 of the 91st BG and had 12 of their own B-17s in the formation. Flak was intense and in one B-17, an engine disabled and six of the crew were injured. Bad weather in December reduced the bombing effort, Rouen marshalling yards being attacked on the 12th and Romilly-sur-Seine on the 20th.

At the start of 1943 the US 8th AAF had four Groups of B-17s operating from Britain, the 91st, 303rd, 305th and Thurleigh's 306th now the most experienced. Eighteen of its Fortresses set off for St Nazaire on January 3, the 367th losing *124469* and the 369th, *124470*. Two more B-17s were lost when Lille marshalling yards were raided on January 13 and another attempt to bomb Karoman on January 23 brought three early returns, matched with a claim of three enemy fighters.

Field Order No 90 of January 26 1943 brought the news that all knew must come, the start of the US daylight onslaught on Germany. It informed the 91st, 303rd, 305th and 306th Bomb Groups that their next target would be the U-boat building yards at Vegesack, with Wilhelmshaven the reserve target. Fighter escort would, of course, be impossible. The layout of the operation was for the 101st CBW to lead with 32 B-17s of the 306th and 91st BGs followed by the 102nd CBW with 18 aircraft from the 305th and 303rd BGs. B-17s in the former formation would assemble in a line east of Peterborough–Bedford, make for St Ives and thence King's Lynn, arriving there at 10:10, by which time the 102nd was to swing into line behind them. On a steady climb they would reach bombing altitude 35 miles from Baltrum Island, the 101st at 23,000 ft, the others at 25,000 ft. Orders were that, after bombing, they should turn left, crossing out between Wesermünde and Cuxhaven. Each B-17 would carry 5 × 1,000 lb bombs. Colonel Frank Armstrong, who led the first Rouen raid, led this one in a B-17 of the 306th BG.

A formation of 16 B-17s set off from Thurleigh for their part in the operation. Before the target, two crews turned back and, as the others ran in towards Vegesack, they found the target cloud-clad and attack impossible. They pressed on to Wilhelmshaven where the first American bombing attack on Germany was delivered. Some flak was encountered, and a few fighters. From the following Group, the 305th, a B-17 was seen to be shot down, and a Fw 190 was observed burning.

Once launched, there was no holding back the B-17s. On February 4 1943, Thurleigh's Fortresses bombed Hamm, headed for the Focke-Wulf factory at Bremen on February 26 but, because of cloud, had to settle for Wilhelmshaven. On April 5 the 306th suffered its first major defeat when, although five enemy fighters were claimed, five B-17s were shot down when attacking Antwerp.

These were a prelude to increasingly tortuous days ahead when Thurleigh's Fortresses struck deeply into Germany and beyond. What agonies and horrific hours their crews endured were vividly illustrated on May 1 when the 306th attacked St Nazaire. The interception was fierce and First Lieutenant L.P. Johnson's B-17F, *229649* of the 423rd Bomb Squadron, was hit. Fire broke out in the waist section and radio compartment. Sergeant Maynard H. Smith was his ball turret gunner, occupying a position wherein one curled oneself in great discomfort whilst attempting to train two massive-looking guns. Only with the necessary physique could one even squeeze into that position. Sergeant Smith's turret was soon out of action and when he crawled into the aircraft's fuselage he first fought the fire aft. He discovered three of the crew had abandoned the aircraft and the rear gunner needed much assistance. Smith, realising someone was still controlling the bomber, set about tackling the fire forward. Then he helped the rear gunner before tackling the forward blaze once more—and whilst Fw 190s were shooting at the bomber. Blazing ammunition boxes were thrown out of the aircraft by Smith as escaping oxygen from bursting bottles fed the fires which he fought for 90 minutes while helping the tail gunner. Johnson managed to get the stricken B-17 back to Britain and landed at Predannack. Sergeant Smith on his first operational sortie displayed courage which resulted in him being awarded the Medal of Honor, the first to the US 8th AAF. Personnel of the 306th won many awards, the Group receiving a DUC when, in poor weather, it bombed an aircraft assembly plant at Bernberg on February 22 1944. Losses were sometimes heavy, as during the Schweinfurt raid of October 1943 when ten B-17s were shot down before the target. Thurleigh's 306th was in continuous action over a longer period than any other in the 8th AF. Also, it stayed on one base longer than any other and, at the end of hostilities, had completed 342 operations. Its final sorties were on April 19 1945. Despite this it was not the best known of the B-17 Groups even though it had within its 367th Bomb Squadron the British Sovereign's daughter's name sake, *Rose of York*, a B-17 christened by Princess Elizabeth and which flew 62 successful missions. When returning from Berlin on February 5 1945, it came down in the sea taking with it a BBC war correspondent. At the end of the war the 306th BG had despatched 9,614 sorties and lost 171 aircraft in action.

Unlike most, the 306th detached its squadrons to the Continent and overseas before moving to Giebelstadt, Germany, during December 1945. In 1944 the Government had decided that a new aeronautical research establishment would be built embracing Thurleigh. Building commenced in 1946 and wartime Thurleigh became engulfed in a new airfield generally known as Bedford. A few buildings of wartime Thurleigh remain on wartime sub-sites but Thurleigh aerodrome of those days has been completely absorbed within the new aerodrome, sometimes known by its predecessor's name.

Turweston, Northamptonshire

SP615384. 3 miles NE of Brackley

Remains of this wartime airfield lie to the north of Turweston village, close to a picturesque wooded area. The airfield is best viewed after passing Whitfield, reached by a right turn off the A43 (T) about 2¾ miles north of Brackley. The name Turweston may be in memory of a Danish soldier of times long past. Beyond Whitfield the road crosses a small stream which later swells into the bold River Ouse. Climb the plateau and the collection of brick huts seen to the right are part of a domestic site. Beyond each, and placed separately, is its associated latrine, an unusual layout. Across farmland, firing butts in good state may be glimpsed. The road passes close to the control tower (pattern nos 13726/41 and 15683/41). Parts of the perimeter track runway are visible, and huts and shelters remain near the tower.

Turweston has a surprisingly involved history. In August 1941, No 12 OTU moved its Wellington Ics and Ansons from Benson to Chipping Warden. Gaydon served as satellite until Turweston replaced it with the arrival there of A Flight of the OTU on November 23 1942. In mid-April 1943 the elements of 12 OTU moved to their permanent satellite at Edgehill. Turweston then became a second satellite for 13 OTU which, on April 30 1943, moved its Mitchells here. No 307 FTU's Bostons were also here between May 1 and May 18 1943. Turweston became Silverstone's satellite on July 3 but Bostons and Mitchells remained until early August. They were replaced by Wellington IIIs of 17 OTU's conversion and general handling squadrons. On November 24, 17 OTU's Gunnery Flight formed, with Wellingtons and Martinets.

In late July 1945, 17 OTU's Wellingtons were withdrawn from Turweston and the bomber defence training flight during August. Turweston closed on September 23 1945, all flying halting on November 2 1945. On January 21 1946, the station was transferred to the War Office, and army vehicles soon littered the airfield awaiting public auction. Turweston is now farming land and sections of runway form the bases for a number of chicken broiler houses.

Twinwood Farm, Bedfordshire

TL035550. E of A6(T) 3½ miles N of Bedford

'They should never have gone, they should never have let that plane take off,' said the tall American in his 'pinks'. 'What Goddam idea entered their heads, we'll never know.' True, true indeed. Weather at take off time was too bad for Thurleigh to be used. Instead, the USAAF UC-64, Norseman, on December 15 1944, positioned itself at Twinwood (Twinwoods as it was coloquially known), and awaited a famed, most popular passenger. By then the whole wide world knew of Glenn Miller, about to be flown to Paris to arrange accommodation for the American band of the AEF.

What happened over the icy cold Channel remains conjecture. The Norseman, ever noisily present in East Anglian skies at this time, sounded like a Harvard throwing a tantrum whilst resembling some ugly Soviet contraption. A most rugged beast, this giant single-engined aeroplane looked as if it could fly through a 5-ft thick wall and emerge unmarked. On Christmas Eve 1944, news broke that Glenn Miller had failed to arrive in Paris. His Norseman had not even been tracked over the French coast. Somewhere off the Cherbourg Peninsula it came down in the sea, perhaps due to severe icing, lost without trace. A tragic end for one who, in the gloom of war, brought pleasure and dreams to millions.

Twinwood Farm, named after the place upon which it was built, was in use as a landing ground long before it became a fully fledged concern. Before the war it had interested Bedford Councillors as a possible site for a municipal airport. By mid-1941 Cranfield's SFTS was using it, continuing to do so until the Oxfords moved to Lyneham in August of that year. Twinwood then had a major face lift whilst remaining under Cranfield's control. No 51 OTU formed there in August 1941 to train night fighter crews. Twinwood opened as its three-runway satellite on April 9 1942. Thereafter it served 51 OTU until June 1945, populated by Blenheims and then Beaufighter 1s. Crews used them during type-conversion training.

In March 1943 it enjoyed a brief period of intense fighter activity when a succession of Mustang 1 squadrons paraded through during Exercise *Spartan*. Nos 164, 169, 239, 268 and 613 Squadrons were all briefly here. The OTU, of which the station was a part, closed on June 14 1945 and Twinwood Farm seemed finished. Seemed, at least, but behind the scenes the decision had been taken to make this airfield part of a grandiose dream. To the north would be built a massive research establishment, a sort of Farnborough with a gigantic runway which, it was reckoned, would be needed for flight testing the Brabazon 1 airliner. The two intended examples were so large that, it was contended, a special maintenance area would be necessary. This would be built on Twinwood Farm and linked to the research station by a mile or so of wide tracking.

To achieve this meant crossing a busy road. Travelling between Thurleigh village and the RAF Tunnel Site, the motorist now discovers, in a deep recession, a stretch of completely unexpected 'dual carriageway'. Over this point the wide concrete taxiway would have passed. Like the Brabazon itself, the scheme never came to fruition. Twinwood, though, cemented its link with Thurleigh another way for their flying club uses a Blister hangar there where part of the runway is, from time to time, shared with crop spraying and other light aircraft.

Upper Heyford, Oxfordshire

SP515260. 5 miles NW of Bicester, near A43(T)

'Come in Number One, your time is up,' almost crackled the call to the Thunderbirds' leader over Upper Heyford on June 19 1971. Well, maybe. There were six fliers, each of whom, after touch down, positioned his Phantom in front of the open house crowd. At the simultaneous tweak of a switch each cockpit canopy rose and the aircraft's occupant stood to accept half-hearted rapture. Whilst arms were at the salute the object of the exercise became all too obvious. The Might of Uncle Sam was being confronted by the Curves of Uncle Hefner who had kindly

A Handley Page HP 24 Hyderabad (J9293 of 99 Squadron) based at Upper Heyford.

provided a warren of Bunnies for lunch. Introductions came fast and cuddly, after the warriors had, understandably, hastened down the ladders from their aircraft to be snatched away, probably to a fate as audacious as conceivable.

Not far away the 'Red Arrows' were taxi-ing in. Their greeting was, in a way, similar if not identical. Power off, canopies up and to each Red Gnat also hurried a figure as well proportioned and as aware of the world as any Bunny Girl. There was one clear difference, for the thick brown overalls of the RAF Chiefies were in direct contrast to the lack of attire favoured by the girls. Closely cocooned by RAF Police and ground crews, the Arrows' pilots were soon secured in a grey RAF bus, with faces long and envy clear as the Bunnies were whisked off in London taxis bound for some playpen . . ..

Placing America's F-111 swing-wing bombers at Upper Heyford seems incongruous for they squat sometimes in hangars of the 1920s on a station born in the 1910s as a training ground for war in France. Whether there were any bunnies around in those distant days one can but muse, but certainly these surroundings could not be further in style from 'smart' bombs, jeans and jammers.

Upper Heyford was laid down in 1916. A year later Canadians arrived for the formation, on January 20 1918, of No 123 Squadron which equipped itself with Sopwith Dolphins before changing its name to No 2 Squadron, Canadian Air Force, early in 1919. Then it left for Shoreham. A second such squadron, also Dolphin equipped, was No 81, formed on November 20 1918 and later known as No 1 Squadron, Canadian Air Force. This moved to Shoreham in March 1919. First World War Upper Heyford closed in 1920.

Selection of the First World War airfield site for development followed the 1924 Defence Review. Although incomplete, Heyford re-opened, as a bomber station, on October 12 1927. Station Headquarters formed on October 25 and also the Oxford University Flight which acquired three Avro 504Ns. It was renamed Upper Heyford Station Flight on November 4 1927.

From Bircham Newton, on December 12 1927, came the advance party of 99 (Bomber) Squadron to prepare Upper Heyford to receive a dozen Hyderabads on January 5 1928. As companies they would have 10 Squadron reformed two days previously. Upper Heyford was starting its long career as a bomber station where, on January 25 1928, 10 Squadron took on charge its first three Hyderabads. Equipping was a long drawn out process,

Hawker Harts of 57 Squadron which was based at Upper Heyford in the 1930s.

the usual plea of money shortage abounding. Not until October 15 1928 did its second Flight form, also with Hyderabads, but on April 26 1930 the squadron still had only six aircraft.

During 1929 the first Hinaidis reached 99 Squadron. Apart from their Bristol Jupiter engines they differed little from the Hyderabads. During 1930 the squadron began to receive later metal Hinaidis. Production remained pathetically slow and into 1931 Hyderabads were still with 99 Squadron. The first Hinaidi for 10 Squadron reached Upper Heyford on December 9 1930 and by April 1931 it held five. A change in emphasis came when, after its formation on April 1, 40 Squadron—the first to have Fairey Gordons—led to 10 Squadron moving to Boscombe Down.

No 18 Squadron was resurrected on October 20 1931 and supplied with Hawker Harts. Its two other Flights, formed on March 31 1932, were joined by Harts of 57 Squadron on September 5 1932. Both squadrons became the core of the station's bomber force to the outbreak of war. Abingdon's availability brought space to Upper Heyford for 40 Squadron, repositioned there in October 1932.

Re-equipment long overdue, 99 Squadron soldiered on with its antiques until November 14 1933 when it took on charge the RAF's first two Handley Page Heyfords. In sombre green, the Heyford had a distinctive shape, making clambering aboard a memorable experience. Curious indeed seemed the attachment of the fuselage to the underside of the upper mainplane, causing fuselage entry to be made by means of a steep, narrow ladder leading from the lower mainplane on to which one had first to scramble. The peculiar arrangement allowed a dustbin turret to be fitted under the narrow cross section fuselage. Strange, too, were the very narrow tyres set within huge spats. After a crawl along the fuselage one emerged into an open cockpit high above the ground in this 'poor man's Stirling'. A few wriggles more and one was situated in splendid isolation in the nose gunner's position, albeit being able to turn for company to the pilot close behind. A year to the day from receipt of its first Heyfords, 99 Squadron commenced moving to Mildenhall. That move made space for Harts of 33 Squadron from nearby Bicester. A year later they hurried to Egypt, answering the Italian attack on Abyssinia.

Harts of 18 Squadron temporarily vacated Upper Heyford in January 1936 and were replaced by two lodger squadrons of Vickers Virginias nudged out of Worthy Down, Nos 58 and 215, awaiting

Above *Virginias periodically floated into Midland airfields, the example here is of 58 Squadron, Upper Heyford.*

Below *Wellesleys of the Long Range Development Unit based at Upper Heyford.*

Hawker Hind K5471 *served with 18 Squadron at Upper Heyford from April 1936 to June 1939.*

Driffield's opening in September 1936. No 18 Squadron then returned, Hind equipped. Bomber Command had then formed and Upper Heyford was in No 1 (Bomber) Group.

New squadrons came from Flights, 218 Squadron from 57 Squadron on March 16 1936, the parent squadron re-equipping with Hinds in May. Then, 57 Squadron surrendered its B Flight on January 4 1937 to become 108 Squadron which left for Farnborough the following month. B Flight of 57 Squadron then changed into being 226 Squadron which moved to Harwell in April 1937. Another Hind squadron, formed here on May 18 1937, was No 113 which went to Grantham in August.

An event which received wide publicity was the formation here in January 1938 of the Long Range Development Flight. Five much-modified Wellesleys, able to carry 1,290 gallons of fuel for their special Pegasus engines, joined the LRDF, commanded by Wing Commander O.R. Gayford of Fairey Long-Range Monoplane fame. A 32-hour flight was made in July 1938 from Cranwell to the Persian Gulf. In November, two aircraft made a spectacular record flight from Egypt to Australia non-stop in 48 hours, unbeaten for eight years.

Upper Heyford's bomber squadrons were ever changing. Hinds of 218 Squadron left in April 1938, making way for the monoplane era. It began with Bristol Blenheim 1s and soon the station became one of their most prominent bases as 57 Squadron rapidly worked up with the wonder-bomber in March–April 1938 with 34 Squadron joining the sport in July. That had vacated Lympne and left behind its Hinds.

In May 1938, 18 Squadron received Blenheims, the three squadrons during the Munich Crisis awaiting to become part of the 2nd Echelon, AASF, France before the crisis passed. January 1939 found Upper Heyford placed in 2 Group which, in February, shifted 34 Squadron to newly opened Watton. Upper Heyford faced the coming storm with some stability, the base for two front-line Blenheim 1 squadrons. Their role within 70 Wing, Air Component, BEF, was to provide aerial reconnaissance for the British Army in France.

At the commencement of hostilities, Upper Heyford and its satellite field at Brackley (later known as Croughton) were immediately placed in No 6 Group and into a training role. Both Blenheim squadrons left for France as planned, 18 Squadron going to Amy and 57 to Roye, both on September 24 1939.

On the day previous to that move, SHQ Finningley arrived, bringing two Hampden squadrons, Nos 7 and 76, to become the 5 Group Pool. No 76 was half Hampden equipped, its other Flight using Anson

navigation trainers. This training establishment ran until April 22 1940 when SHQ closed and 5 Group Pool became 16 OTU within 6 Group. Steady expansion followed and, on May 7 1940, the OTU received the first of 19 troublesome Handley Page Herefords. A month later more Ansons arrived. August 13 1940 brought a spectacular midday crash. Two Hampdens, *L4138* and *P4339*, barely airborne, collided in a gruesome smash when taking off from different grass runways.

On July 25 and 27 1940, handfuls of Hampdens set off on leaflet dropping sorties, carrying out the station's first offensive action. An operations order of August 8 called for up to eight such sorties weekly, in response to which Hampdens of 16 OTU visited Caen, Rennes and Brest. Croughton landing ground began to be much used in July, accommodation

Above *Fairey Gordons were often seen in the early 1930s flying from both Abingdon and Upper Heyford.*

Right *A Hind of 40 Squadron releases a practice bomb.*

Below *A Blenheim 1,* L1145, *of 57 Squadron beside one of Upper Heyford's hangars.*

40
K5426
K5426

being at Rastwick and Rectory Farms for ground crew controlling the busy night flying procedures and equipment. More leaflet drops took place in October, then operations stopped.

Throughout 1941, Upper Heyford housed 16 OTU, training up to 24 one-pilot crews for Hampdens each month. The OTU was using widely spread accommodation, in Aynho Park, Fritwell Manor, Fucott House, Middleton, sundry stone cottages and in Nissen huts which decorated the area around the station.

In April 1941, due to their poor serviceability record, the Herefords were posted away, to 5 B&GS. The established strength at that time was 49 Hampden/Herefords, 13 Ansons, 12 Oxfords and sundry light aircraft.

Barford St John replaced Croughton as satellite in 1942, use also being made of Hinton-in-the Hedges. Another advance came in April 1942 for by the end of that month, 16 OTU had received 23 Wellington Ics. Only the course underway flew Hampdens. The first Wellington joined the OTU on April 25, the first crew output being made on June 5 1942.

May 1942 found 16 OTU half equipped with Wellingtons, sufficiently so for 14 of them and 16 Hampdens to take part in the Cologne 1,000 bomber raid from here. For the Essen attack of June 1/2, 30 crews operated, again in a mixed force. Hampden *P2080* was attacked by a German fighter, in exchange for which the crew claimed to shoot down another. Twenty-three crews operated Wellington Ics in June's Bremen 1,000 bomber operation. More bombing raids were flown in July, August and September.

By March 1943, the OTU's strength had risen to 57 Wellington Ics, 6 Ansons, a Defiant and two Lysander target towers. Alongside, enveloped in great secrecy, was 1473 Flight whose origin lay within the RCM Flight of 109 Squadron. That formation broke away on July 10 1942 from the organisation which achieved fame as a result of its so-called 'beam bending' activities in 1940. It was now an independent unit under Flight Lieutenant C.F. Grant, DFC, controlled by 80 Wing and administered by 92 Group. Using Ansons and Wellingtons, it monitored German radio beam activity whilst participating in *Window* trials for Bomber Command before moving to Finmere in 1943. No 1505 BAT Flight's Oxfords, also within 92 Group, provided beam approach practice from Upper Heyford between December 17 1942 and its disbandment on February 20 1943. Wellington IIIs came into use at 16 OTU in September 1942,

That hangar at Upper Heyford now houses F-111s of the 20th Tactical Fighter Wing, two of whose swing-wing bombers are here seen climbing out on an exercise.

their improved performance causing 92 Group to issue an order in November that four *Nickelling* sorties be flown per fortnight. From Upper Heyford leaflet dropping was resumed on November 27/28 with drops in the Nantes area. In between *Bullseyes*, propaganda leaflets were dropped on Paris on December 20/21 1942.

Such activities continued throughout 1943, in the autumn of which Wellington Xs joined the OTU in increasing proportion. In 1944, too, the pattern of activity was all but the same. At the end of December, No 1655 Mosquito Training Unit arrived with an assortment of Mosquito bombers and trainers along with a selection of Oxfords. The old 16 OTU disbanded, its title at once being conferred upon the new arrival which also used Barford St John. For training bomber crews for 8 Group, 16 OTU's nominal strength in March 1945 stood at 45 Mosquitoes of Mks 3, 4, 6, 20 and 25 supported, for navigation and light bombing training, by as many as 32 Oxfords, all under 92 Group control and shared in positioning with Barford. Immediate post-war days witnessed a reduction in strength before 16 OTU moved to Cottesmore in March 1946. In its place came Dakotas of the Parachute Training School. Also brought here was the famous parachute training tower which came from Ringway and moved to Abingdon in 1950.

The reason for that move was that the Americans were coming in June 1950. They took over four Barrack Blocks and the Airmens' Mess, using facilities for a US Engineer Aviation Battalion, a Maintenance Company, Ordnance Company, Engineer Depot Company and the Base Support Company. These units, which soon increased in strength, had come to support the expanding SAC force moving into East Anglia and the Midlands. Barford St John remained Upper Heyford's satellite, like Middleton Stoney. Weston-on-the-Green which, since 1946, had been under Upper Heyford's control, became the home of the Air Position Plotting Unit on August 9 1950 and, at the end of April 1951, was transferred to No 62 (Signals) Group, RAF. On May 15 1951, control of Upper Heyford passed completely to the USAF, formal handover from 3 (Bomber) Group being staged on June 1 when the 7509th Air Base Squadron took control.

Upper Heyford's main runway was some 6,000 ft long and 150 ft wide, the Americans' first task being to lengthen it to some 10,000 ft. By the end of 1951, with the 7509th ready to support operational units, the first TDY element arrived, the 93rd Air Refuelling Squadron flying Boeing KB-29Ps from Castle AFB at the start of December 1951 for a 90-day stay. On January 10 1952 the 3918th Air Base Group took over the running of the base where the RAF's PTS held lodger unit status.

American construction of specialised facilities for use by SAC included three nose docks for large aircraft and a new maintenance building. Among the units based at Upper Heyford in 1952 was the 98th Smoke Generating Company, there to provide a smoke screen in the event of a air attack. Further airfield defence was soon to be provided by light Anti-Aircraft guns of the 4th AA Artillery Battalion. By then Upper Heyford had hosted KB-29P aerial refuellers of the 97th, 509th and 2nd BGs as well as KB-29Ms whose role was in-flight refuelling of B-29s of the 301st BG. Sundry sections of KB-29s and B-50Ds were temporarily stationed at Upper Heyford before, in June 1953, the first B-47B Stratojets in Britain began using the base. Thenceforth many B-47s and RB-47s were to be seen here. On February 5 1954, a B-47 was involved in a spectacular crash in Stoke Wood, 1½ miles from the end of the main runway. Not long after, some of the first B-47Es in Britain were based here.

Mid-1954 witnessed the first landings at Upper Heyford of RB-36H reconnaissance aircraft of the 5th SRW whose main base was Fairford. Principally, it was nuclear-armed Stratojets that made Upper Heyford their home—until March 31 1965 when the SAC mission ended and the base was transferred to USAFE. Upper Heyford then came under the care of the 7514th Combat Support Group who maintained it as a Dispersed Operating Base (DOB). That status terminated on September 1 1966 with the arrival of the 66th Tactical Reconnaissance Wing from Laon, France. The 7514th was de-activated and Heyford became a Main Operating Base housing RF-101C Voodoos until their unit was de-activated on April 1 1970, a year after RF-4Cs had been placed in the 17th Tactical Reconnaissance Squadron.

Their place was taken by the present residents, F-111Es of the 20th Tactical Fighter Wing. Its assignment meant a complete change of mission for the 20th and extensive modifications to the base, resulting in the station being the largest of its kind in Europe. On September 12 1970, the first two F-111E swing wing bombers touched down at Upper Heyford, the 20th having its full complement by July 29 1971. By September 1980 the F-111Es had flown over 55,000 training sorties.

Warwick, Warwickshire

SP270635. 1½ miles Sw of Warwick, N of A429, A46(T) crosses western edge of site

Just beyond the western edge of Warwick a large, picturesque meadow by the Stratford road lay for a long time. This was RAF Warwick, a Relief Landing Ground opened in December 1941 and which came into use in 23 Group during January 1942. Initially Church Lawford used it for Oxfords and Tutors in use for flying instructor training.

On October 1 1942, the emphasis at Church Lawford changed, and by the end of that month the unit there had become 18 (P) AFU which retained the Tutors and Oxfords but which soon was equipped with only the latter and some Ansons. Warwick RLG remained with Church Lawford until the end of May 1945 when it was placed on Care and Maintenance.

Apart from the grass landing ground there was never much to be seen. Two Blister hangars (Over Type) were by the road, one serving long after the peace began. Two more were in the south-west corner, along with six Laing huts (1032/41) for personnel. Two Nissen huts contained stores, and there was a fuel compound and water supply.

Watchfield, Oxfordshire

SU240900. 6 miles N of Swindon, by A420

Watchfield's contribution to the winning of the war is impossible to assess, but it played an important part in improving the safe return of many an operational crew. The availability of the station in July 1940 brought along Tiger Moths of 3 EFTS, a unit formed at Hamble on January 1 1940 from the pre-war 3 ERFTS and forced out of its siting by Southampton Water when the Battle of Britain was unfolded. At Watchfield the School arrived on July 20 1940 as Ansons of 4 AONS were arriving from Ansty and others of 11 AONS were fleeing from Hamble. Watchfield was over-populated, yet more occupants would follow. The intention was for No 1 Blind Approach School to form here on August 2 1940 but lack of suitable equipment delayed this. Instead the School commenced activity here on October 28 1940 and was operated by AST, a subsidiary of Hawker Siddeley. Four Ansons, with two in reserve, were placed at the unit, along with three wheel-type link trainers. The task was the training of

Welcome to RAF Watchfield, School of Air Traffic Control (G. Phillips).

pilots in blind approach flying techniques, increasingly important as night flying increased.

Blind approach training had commenced at Mildenhall in March 1939, first using Anson *L9155* fitted with blind approach receivers (R1124/1125). Commanding the small formation was Squadron Leader R.S. Blucke, AFC. In July 1939 the Anson was allotted to 24 Squadron, Hendon. VHF blind approach equipment was then in full use at Boscombe Down. The precious Anson was taken from Hendon on September 1 1939 and placed at CFS Upavon, pending the establishment of a blind approach training development unit at Boscombe Down to where the Anson was transferred on September 22 1939. More Ansons were then fitted with blind approach equipment and, by May 1940, the 20th short course was underway.

On June 6 1940, orders were received from 23 Group to close the school, and Wing Commander Blucke was posted to HQ Bomber Command. On June 13 1940, the unit re-opened, but for a totally different purpose. The establishment was raised to eight Ansons and three Whitleys, the new task was to investigate unusual enemy radio signals code named 'Headache'. Operational control was vested in Fighter Command, the unit having five Ansons with suitable equipment. Pilots from the old BATDU were posted to the new unit and included Flight Lieutenant H.E. Bufton who arrived from 214 Squadron to command. Two days later he took Anson *N9945* to Wyton to commence radio investigation into the German use of radio beams for navigation purposes and target marking. Such operations were soon busily engaged upon.

In October the unit's role had so far altered that, on the 14th, its name changed from Blind Approach Training and Development Unit to Wireless Intelligence Development Unit, a title which had been in colloquial use since September 30 1940. Meanwhile the need ever increased for specialised blind approach training. No longer could formation of a specialised unit with such needs be overlooked. On October 20 1940, Watchfield received two Ansons from the WIDU, *R9828* and *R9830*, both carrying blind approach equipment. On the following day, *R9829* and *R9837* joined them and initial equipment was complete for a Blind Approach School. If an element of secrecy was needed it was easy to achieve since navigation training Ansons were busy in the circuit.

Ground equipment for blind approach training was in short supply. Main beacon, as well as the inner and outer marker beacons, were of a type made by Philips in Holland and no longer obtainable and more advanced than the British standard type. Its main beacon had a system of phased aerials which reduced the twilight zone. Only at Schiphol Airport in the

Watchfield's unusual control tower (G. Phillips).

Netherlands had such advanced equipment been installed and Watchfield's had been shipped to Britain before the Netherlands fell. All the Ansons now at Watchfield had receivers working with this system, already used at Boscombe Down.

Six pupils arrived on October 28 1940 at the commencement of the first two-week course. That involved 12 hours' flying to a schedule laid down by Wing Commander R.S. Blucke. Training commenced with time on the Link Trainer, during which they listened to blind approach notes in headphones and had the figure-of-eight flying procedures demonstrated.

From the start it was obvious that there would be considerable flying training problems at this busy station. Tiger Moths of the EFTS were ever active on circuit and Ansons setting off on longer flights. Control of the flying, from the tower, was vested in an instructor of the Blind Approach School who saw to it that when an aircraft was on blind approach a red light on the tower was switched 'on'. This indicated to EFTS pilots that the incoming aircraft was at 100 ft in the direction of the main beam, irrespective of the wind direction. All aircraft on the ground had to remain stationary when the red light was 'on'.

During the winter, training proceeded satisfactorily, despite a visit by the enemy on the evening of February 27 1941. Incendiaries fell, along with a stick of five HEs along the south-east boundary of the airfield. Even less successful in display was the blind approach equipment when the Inspector General, Air Marshal Sir W. Mitchell, arrived in his Cygnet on May 19 1941. As he was about to watch the demonstration a resistance burnt out in the main beacon, putting everything out of use!

By mid-1941, installation of blind approach equipment had been extended to units in other parts of Britain. Reliability of the equipment and its accurate calibration needed to be regularly checked so, in May 1941, the Blind Approach Calibration Flight formed at Watchfield, equipped with three Oxfords, the first aircraft of that type to be used for any blind approach duties. Over the next month, three more—*V3888, V4026* and *V4027*—arrived. Any slight increase in flying at Watchfield brought problems, so it is hardly surprising that No 11 AONS closed on July 19 1941 and No 4 on August 30 1941.

Mid-August saw discussions into the means of considerably increasing the output of trainees. Existing flying programmes called for 18 hours' flying each day, 24 hours being deemed impossible to maintain because of enemy activity, unserviceability, etc. A scheme to train 1,100 pilots a year was to be put in hand, which meant an increase in aircraft establishment from six to 15 and of instructors from seven to 16. On September 1 1941, as an interim measure, the establishment changed to 12 Ansons, an event soon overtaken. Blind Approach training would now be part of the training syllabus at SFTSs, where the standard aircraft type was the Airspeed Oxford. To achieve standardisation it was decided to re-equip No 1 Blind Approach School with Oxfords, a decision made on September 16 1941 to help dispel a generally held and erroneous notion that blind approach training could only be effectively carried out using Ansons, and that the Oxford was less well mannered. On the following day, three more Oxfords, *V4051, V4052* and *V5054* arrived at Watchfield.

Another alteration became effective at Watchfield on September 26 1941 when night flying throughout the hours of darkness commenced. It depended upon a Cranwell type flarepath, power for which was supplied from the floodlight beacon. Flying took place every night so that new training programme demands might be met, for the rate of trainee arrivals was now 12 every four days for a 12-day course. In the 12 months ending October 28 1941, 405 pupils were trained, 60 per cent for night fighter duties. An enviable flight safety record had been achieved for there had been merely one forced landing brought about when a pupil knocked off some switches upon changing seats. No other accident had marred the School's record. Additionally, pilots of the School had, since March 13 1941, been training wireless mechanics. Introduction of the 24-hour flying scheme, on September 8 1941, improved the pupil output rate. In October 1941 the unit was redesignated No 1 Beam Approach School.

From Brasenose College, Oxford, the Regional Control School of Bomber Command moved into Watchfield on December 15 1941, becoming the School of Flying Control. Lecture rooms for the School were available after the departure of 3 EFTS to Shellingford on December 18 1941. Trials of the Bell and Bobbitt trailing wire device, intended to inform

Anson NK273 *of the School of Air Traffic Control* (G. Phillips).

the pilot accurately of his height, were conducted in January 1942.

February 2 brought the first serious flying accident involving *AT775*, flown by Sergeant C.M. Rustron. January had ended with snow and very cold weather which extended into February. As this Oxford was approaching, ice accretion on the wings seriously increased and snow obliterated the pupil's vision, forcing him to make a very difficult blind landing. A stall developed, the port wing dropped and the aircraft side-slipped in from about 15 ft.

Four Dominies were allocated to BAS on February 9 1942 to give SFC pupils air experience. On the following day the first attempt to locate a suitable satellite airfield site for blind approach training was undertaken. Firstly a landing ground at Bushy Barn, Pusey, near Burford was inspected, but it was quite unsuitable.

By mid-March 1942 another Flight was needed in order to train 1,450 pilots a year from April. Trials on April 22 1942 proved it was possible for an Oxford to be landed every five minutes if a revised holding pattern was introduced. By that time three Dominies—*X7491, X7492* and *X7493*—had arrived and, in May, Oxfords from Docking's BAT Flight were posted in to equip the new, additional Flight. To simulate night flying in daylight, synthetic night flying was tried using Oxford *V4051*. On May 16 1942, the aircraft was flying with blue window panels, its pilot wearing special goggles.

The association with the SFC had, by July 1942, brought along a new RAF trade, airfield controller. Things moved fast, the first trainees arriving on July 18 1942, comprising 34 ORs here for a two-week course. A few days previously, Oxfords of the Calibration Flight moved to Bicester, easing some pressure from Watchfield. By November, use of existing beam approach equipment at nearby stations was being made. Those at Boscombe Down, Abingdon, Harwell and Little Rissington were used, and equipment at Watchfield's new satellite, Kelmscot, came into use on October 17 1942. Each course now lasted a week because the other beams were available.

Sudden changes in weather posed major problems in this busy area, as when general weather deterioration came quickly on January 6 1943. One pupil landed safely at Kelmscot meaning that an overnight guard had to be placed on the aircraft. Flying Officer Hutchison, flying *V4049*, was over Otmoor when ordered back to base. His homing equipment failed and when he eventually arrived over Watchfield he discovered that the undercarriage would not lock in the 'down' position, so the aircraft had to be abandoned.

Flying was drastically reduced for a period of six weeks early in 1943 while contact lighting was installed, and at a time when the airfield surface was very wet and the laying of a flare path impracticable. Some flying was possible at RLG Kelmscot.

Operational aircraft as well as others were kept well away from busy Watchfield, except in emergencies. One such came on the night of June 10 1943 when, at 01:43, the Duty Flying Controller heard a large, low-flying aircraft. There was soon an explosion, and flames poured from the wreckage, a mile north-west of the airfield. They marked where a Lancaster from Lindholme crashed, killing the crew of seven.

By July 1943, the second RLG, Wanborough, was in regular use, mainly for training airfield controllers. Up to 110 pupiles at a time trained there, each course spending half its training period at this RLG. Kelmscot RLG was busily in use whilst a few personnel manned Watchfield's Q-site at Kingston Warren.

It was Flight Lieutenant James in Oxford 'H' who, at 17:25 on October 22 1943, gave the station warning of startling, impending disaster. Using his R/T he reported something akin to a whirlwind approaching the airfield from the south. Moments later it was possible to see from the tower a mass of *nimbo stratus* coming from the direction of Shrivenham, and with a dark funnel hanging from it. Two Oxfords about to take off were ordered to taxi quickly back to the tower. The violent disturbance passed across the airfield towards the NNE, snatching a metal sheet off a hangar and depositing it in the middle of the landing ground. Oxford 'S' was lifted ten feet into the air, swung around then dropped. Its undercarriage collapsed and the port wing crumpled. Two others were damaged before the intense storm died suddenly away.

At the end of 1943, the Beam Approach Technical Training School moved to No 1 RS Cranwell. On December 18 1943, the training of airfield controllers was transferred from Wanborough to Watchfield and Kelmscot, allowing 3 GTS to place one Flight at Wanborough because Stoke Orchard was temporarily out of use. Wanborough was vacated by the School of Airfield Controllers on December 2 1944 due to the poor state of personnel accommodation there, although the School still made some use of it.

By March 1944 the area around Watchfield was highly congested by the influx of transport aircraft—and worse, by gliders taking part in ever increasingly large exercises. With flying control becoming ever more important, a master flying control for the whole area was set up at South Cerney. Although Kelmscot was to remain the RLG for Watchfield into 1947, during 1944 it was used a number of times for parachute troop training exercises on a grand scale. Not until after D-Day was the BAS able to use the RLG.

A new BAT syllabus was introduced on August 30 1944. Full cross-country flying in cloud was now to be practised at (P) AFUs by pilots undergoing BA training. During 1944 the course undertaken by a pilot at No 1 BAS consisted of three unhooded introductory exercises: i) familiarisation and orientation, ii) a figure-of-eight flown at constant height and iii) normal approach procedure. During this 'hooded' training he again flew the 'eight' at constant height, the normal and back beam approach, visual and oral signal approaches, QDM homing procedures, homing without QDM, cross country and, finally, engaged in night flying. In addition to 1 BAS, several beam approach and radio aids training flights used Watchfield: 1500 in 1943; 1547, which formed on June 1 1945 and was here into 1946; and 1557, also formed June 1 1945 with double the normal eight Oxfords of these Flights, and quickly transferred to 6 (P) AFU.

No 1 BAS disbanded on January 1 1947, having latterly used a few Harvards as well as Oxfords. In its final months it trained pilots with the aid of two beams operated at Watchfield and Kelmscot, and used other beam systems within a radius of 100 miles. During six years of existence, 1 BAS aircraft had flown little short of 100,000 hours, some 8,500 pupils passed through the School and only one flying accident involving injury had come about during QBI conditions. An amazing record, for sure.

After the war, Watchfield settled to being the centre for the training of airfield control personnel, the School of Air Traffic Control forming from the School of Flying Control during April 1946 and remaining until January 1950. In the 1950s a new use was found for Watchfield—parachute training, and as a dropping zone for heavy loads from RAF transports.

Wellesbourne Mountford, Warwickshire

SP265548. 5 miles E of Stratford-on-Avon, off B4086

'Postings are through. I've got Kinloss, you've got Wells-something; I've never heard of it.' A look at the list in Movements revealed Wellesbourne Mountford. I knew little of it, but soon that would be

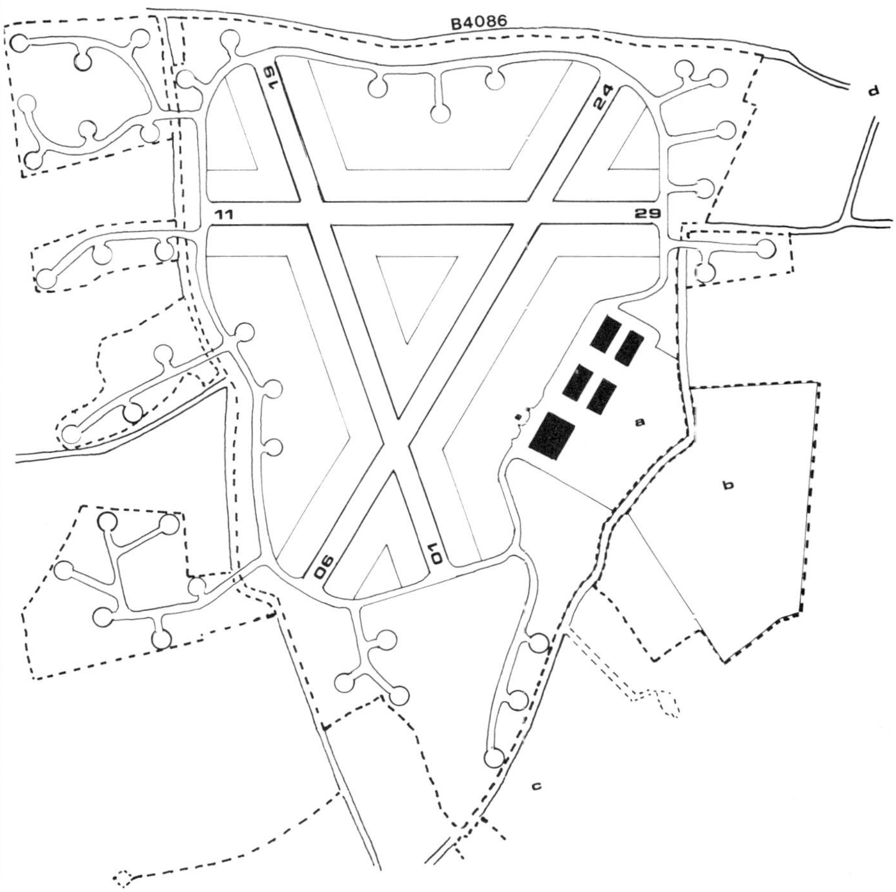

Wellesbourne Mountford in 1944—a typical layout for a Midland bomber OTU with conventional runway pattern, one large 'J' hangar and four 'T2s'. Circular dispersals date from 1940/41. High terrain lay to the south and in the path of runway O1/19. 06/24 was lined up with the Stratford's main runway. The technical site is marked as 'A', the domestic area—mainly wooden huts—is 'B'. The weapons store area is 'C' and the village 'D'.

remedied. I had been spoiled at Manston with its flexi-hours, ample lay-ins, late breakfasts and long lunch hours in which to enjoy the exotic visitors. Johnny Luck, whose popular Polish belief 'Vat you do not do today you do another day' was to the liking of all. A climax to days there was a fly-past comprising a French AAC1 (Ju 52 in Gallic disguise), a French Air Force Baltimore and an Aeronavale Barracuda. Containing one's excitement on such occasions was difficult but necessary for, in those days, no serviceman admitted the slightest interest in his Air Force let alone aeroplanes. I was almost unique.

My arrival at Wellesbourne emphasised one thing—nobody was even welcome there. I always felt that even its 'stationmaster' avoided the Main Gate where the foe was ever close to hand. 'He' all but resided in 'his' guardroom frequenting, with glee, its little white portico in which 'he' readily displayed his bold white teeth

Wellesbourne Mountford, looking north east. The control tower can be seen, a 'J' hangar and four 'T2s'.

pre-empting Sergeant Major Williams of more recent vintage. 'He' is inaccurate, for there were really two of them working in apparent affection and unity, sentiments which they failed to bestow upon the remainder of the camp. Both had cultivated splendid moustaches which they twitched with ready abandon. One was ever to be observed, even on the hottest summer's day, parading his leather gloves and magic wand whilst watching, eagle eyed, for a tiny trip from grace which with delight he would bring to the attention of the unfortunate 'little man'. Ever impressive was the scant regard he seemed to hold for those of higher rank, many of whom were distinctly nervous of him. It was widely whispered that he owned the camp barber's shop—certainly he provided it with plentiful trade, spreading a wry smile across those brilliant teeth as he uttered his war cry, 'Am I 'urtin' you laddie? I'm tredin' on yer 'air'. I dread to think what he would have said had one muttered a 'No', fear to imagine his response upon facing a set of skinheads—and regret that he was never thus tested. Mind you, in an emergency, I'm sure one would have been grateful for his courage. Of course, that was Wellesbourne immediately after the war. Things had not changed all that much, though, for Wellesbourne was born within a burst of official bullying.

Summer 1940 brought extensive airfield building to central England and an abrupt order to the Littler family, in whose hands peacetime Wellesbourne resided. They were ordered immediately to remove their dairy herd, and thus much of their livelihood, in a matter of hours. They had no choice but to obey, their total movement being fast followed by the arrival of airfield contractors working to plans similar to those resulting in Moreton and Polebrook, all of which had a 'J' Type hangar as centrepiece. Three runways were laid by the contractors, John Laing & Co.

Wellesbourne hosted No 22 OTU, formed here on April 14 1941 and equipped with Wellington Ics, supplemented by Anson navigation trainers. The strength built to 40 IE + 14 IR Wellingtons and 14+4 Ansons.

Before the OTU was a going concern, the enemy paid his respects, four attacks being made during May 1941. In the first, 11 bombs fell, slightly damaging the fire tender building. Three bombs fell near No 1 Dispersal in the second attack and, during the third, a dozen bombs were dropped in the north-east corner of the airfield, damaging two Wellingtons and an Anson. On May 10, a raider, believed to be a Heinkel 111, fired upon a dispersed Wellington and attacked the active runway and flarepath. A stick of three bombs overshot on to a field by the village.

By the end of May 1941, in which 22 OTU managed a creditable 414 flying hours, the Unit was set to train three crews per fortnight, an output soon doubled. Further interruption to flying came early on June 5 when a 500 kg bomb smashed a dispersal hard standing. As if in resultant spite, orders were received on June 12 that the OTU might reply by *Nickelling*. Not until June 23 1941 did practice bombing commence, making use of Prior's Hardwick range. Flying hours in June rose to 946, in a month bringing three day and two night flying accidents. In August came Lysanders for target towing and general gunnery training. By this time Wellesbourne's satellite at nearby Atherstone, later renamed Stratford and which had opened on July 12 1941, was relieving pressure on the parent station. C Flight moved there entirely on September 14 1941 to carry out day and night type conversion flying.

With the satellite in use, and Wellesbourne very active, an appraisal of the station was made by 6 Group, and serious dissatisfaction was expressed. Only one of the three runways was of much use, one too short for night flying, another downright dangerous for it led directly towards high ground. Equally disturbing, the single runway at Atherstone—satisfactory for day and night flying—was in line, almost exactly, with one of Wellesbourne's. Only 3½ miles separated the airfields so that, on take off, aircraft invariably overflew one of the other fields and quite low. Little could be done to alter this, so a keen lookout and careful control were essential.

In December 1941 the average serviceable aircraft strength at 22 OTU reached 23 Wellington Ics, 3 Ansons, a Lysander and a Magister. February 1942 saw flying hours total 1,796, showing that the OTU, whilst trailing behind others in 6 Group, was making progress. It did little to aid the training programme, though, when Wellington *X9640* crashed and severed the main electricity supply to the station.

Within weeks of opening, Wellesbourne Mountford started to receive aircraft returning from operations—diverted or making emergency landings. These increased in 1942 and later in the war reached higher numbers than at most stations in the area. As the flying multiplied so the accident rate rose. A bad crash came on March 17 1942 when *X9964* hit the A Flight crew room in a corner of No 9 hangar, the Wellington's crew escaping unhurt.

Prior to the Cologne 1,000 bomber raid, some Wellingtons left for Elsham Wolds. On May 30 1942, 22 OTU fielded 14 Wellingtons from Wellesbourne, 11 from Stratford and 10 from Elsham. At the time of take off from Wellesbourne, there was torrential rain. From the operation four Wellingtons (three from Wellesbourne) were missing, two returned early (one of Wellesbourne's) and another from the parent station only reached Zeebrugge.

For the second 1,000 Plan raid, No 22 OTU fielded 34 Wellingtons, 12 of them setting off from Wellesbourne. This time all safely returned. Against Bremen, on June 25/26, Wellesbourne despatched 12 aircraft, one of which did not return. Wellingtons from Wellesbourne also participated in the *Grand National* raids. Only two of the 15 crews ordered to bomb Hamburg on July 28 took off. They failed to receive the recall message and were not heard of again. Next night the enemy replied by showering incendiaries near Goldicote House used as a WAAF billet.

On September 1 1942, Wellesbourne's new satellite, Gaydon, came under its control. Until mid-November, when Stratford passed to 23 OTU Pershore, 22 OTU had two satellites. It was now one of the busiest OTUs in the country, its strength updated on October 8 when its first Wellington III arrived. Two months previously, Defiant target towers had replaced the Lysanders. Most flying at this time was being undertaken from the satellites, both being temporarily retained whilst the main runway at Wellesbourne was resurfaced in preparation for increased flying by the heavier Wellington IIIs.

Although earlier alerted, 22 OTU had not yet been *Nickelling* but when, in November 1942, it was resumed by 91 Group—which had taken over the station—No 22 OTU was ordered to start in December 1942. Thereafter it was the climax for crews reaching the end of their operational training.

By this time 22 OTU was flying *Bullseyes* and taking part in 91 Group's Exercise *Reduce*, a fighter affiliation exercise in daylight flown over sought-west England in co-operation with 10 Group. Another activity, begun in August 1942, was that of flying ASR searches looking for ditched bomber and Coastal Command crews.

March 1943 took *Nickelling* crews to Clermont Ferrand and, in April, the target for four more was Limoges whilst another flew to Le Mans. One of those on the Limoges operation had a very eventful journey, for their aircraft was hit by flak. It put the port engine out of use and, at 13,500 ft, the engine burst into flames. It was hoped that when the fire died down the engine might re-start. That was forlorn. Nevertheless the crew dropped their load in the target area by which time the rear turret was out of use. The pilot decided to come home at around 5,000–6,000 ft to minimise chances of fighter interception. He was soon flying far lower—as low as 300 ft—and on one engine. Then the intercom failed and the directional gyro became unserviceable. More flak was encountered as the aircraft crossed over an enemy airfield. With fuel low, the radio operator sent an SOS as he crossed the French coast. The main petrol supply and hydraulics had been severed over Le Mans and now the crew were guided by searchlights into Warmwell. Without R/T functioning, the pilot made his way in, setting the aircraft down to a belly landing without injury to the crew. A splendid effort indeed.

A further five *Nickelling* sorties were flown in May, then in June the monthly commitment rose to seven *Nickel* sorties which involved the dropping of special leaflets over Brest and St Nazaire. The aim was to discourage U-boat crews. Further sorties of this nature were undertaken on July 9/10.

On July 11 1943, No 312 Ferry Training Flight was established at Wellesbourne, to train Wellington crews prior to their ferrying of their aircraft overseas. The Unit remained here until December 17 1943. For the August–September series of night raids on the Calais Peninsula during the run-up to Operation *Starkey*, crews set off from Wellesbourne and Gaydon. The first raid was directed against an ammunition dump in the Fôret de Raismes. Half the 91 Group's effort of 36 sorties over this period was flown by 22 OTU before *Nickelling* was resumed, usually to areas around Angers, Argentan, Granville, Le Mans and Rennes. By this time some Wellington Xs had arrived to supplement the Mk IIIs. Wellington Ics had been phased out in the closing weeks of 1942.

In September 1943, trials were carried out at Wellesbourne with a Wellington fitted with a hood in place of a nose turret, and also a 1 lb increase in boost pressure for its Hercules VI engines. Both features were successful alterations but, whereas the go-ahead to remove nose turrets from Wellingtons followed, permission to alter the boost was withheld. Some 89 hoods were almost immediately obtained for Wellingtons, 30 of them being fitted to Wellesbourne's aircraft.

January 1944's returns showed that 22 OTU flew 2,221 hours that month, the third highest in the Group. *Nickelling* was at its peak and, in January, 22 OTU despatched 18 sorties and delivered a record 2,788,000 leaflets. For those in Occupied France it warned of heavy raids to come on communications targets.

On March 7 1944, 22 OTU took control of Stratford, retaining it until December 15 1944. The reason was the disbandment of 23 OTU Pershore. Many of its Wellingtons were transferred to Wellesbourne, as a result of which, from March 15, the unit became a 1½ OTU by way of strength. It was now the largest OTU and held 81 Wellington III/Xs and six target towers. Changes to courses resulted in two weeks' ground school and eight weeks' flying. The intake was 24 crews every fortnight, raising crew population to 120 and output to 46 crews monthly.

Increased operational employment was ordered for all OTU Wellingtons, including those without front turrets. As a stand-by invasion reinforcement measure, up to 20 aircraft were to be regularly available. At Wellesbourne this included four Wellington Type 423s, each able to carry a 4,000 lb bomb. Not surprisingly March

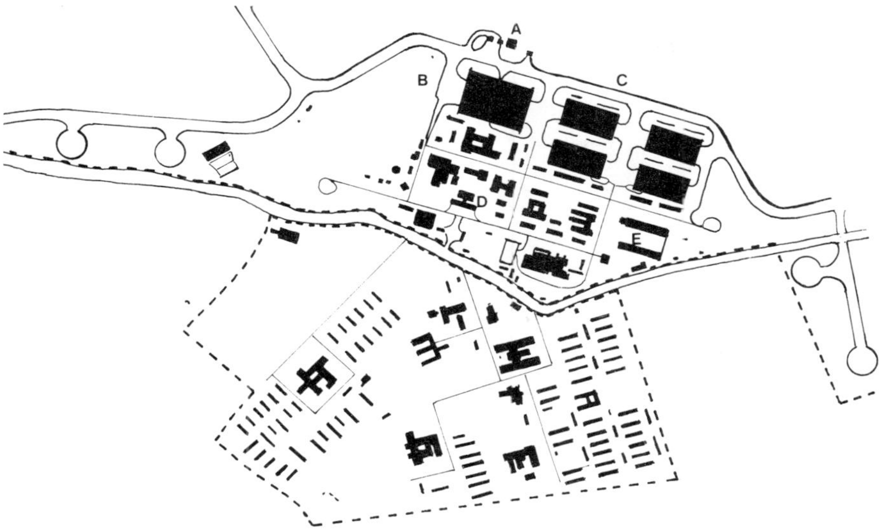

The technical site and domestic site at Wellesbourne Mountford. **A** *Control tower.* **B** *Type 'J' hangar.* **C** *Four 'T2' hangars.* **D** *SHQ.* **E** *MT Section.*

1944 saw a further upsurge in 22 OTU's *Nickelling* effort and, in the course of 20 sorties, 3,180,000 leaflets were delivered. The OTU also participated on March 24/25 in the special *Bullseye* routed over France to provide a diversion whilst the Main Force attacked Berlin.

At this time Wellesbourne was ever attracting diverted operational aircraft. On April 5, for instance, 12 Lancasters of 61 Squadron, Coningsby, came after bombing Toulouse. June 7 was also a busy night when eight Halifaxes of 420 Squadron landed after attacking Coutances and L/429 Squadron arrived from Conde-sur-Noireau. On June 14, three Halifaxes came here following their mining operations off Lorient and St Nazaire. August 25 brought ten East Moor Halifaxes to Wellesbourne after they had bombed coastal batteries at Brest. These were but a few of the diversions at this time.

After four months, when accidents averaged one per 1,000 flying hours, the OTU achieved an excellent rate of 3,600 hours accident-free flying in October 1944 before the following month showed far less favourable results, including Wellington *LN460* which exploded over Broadway on November 20 1944. An hour and a half later, *MF509*, flying from Stratford, crashed in the Welsh mountains killing the entire crew and, two hours later, *MF505* was in trouble at Wellesbourne with engine problems. Winter weather also brought many more diversions, one of the largest in February 1945, resulting in the arrival of 24 B-17s. To the end of the war this continued, 15 Halifaxes of 415 Squadron, for instance, homing in on April 14.

Hostilities ended, wind-down at Wellesbourne was rapid. On July 1, No 91 Course completed its training and upon that day all flying ceased at 22 OTU. This was not the end for Wellesbourne for, on July 24 1945, both this and Gaydon were taken over by 3 Glider Training School for its Master IIs and Hotspurs. This unit functioned here until closure on December 3 1947 when Wellesbourne was set aside as a site for technical training.

First to come was the School of Photography which vacated Farnborough in the spring of 1948. It was necessary to install special equipment for the School, delaying the resumption of training until the following autumn. In May 1948 the

Anson NK340 TWM:A *used at Wellesbourne by the School of Photography.*

School of Education arrived, remaining until the end of 1950. Its coming was surrounded by considerable ill feeling, SNCOs taking a jaundiced and understandable view of school leavers with Higher School Certificates rising, literally overnight, to the often hard-won rank of Sergeant. Even more ill will was directed at those who, having somehow secured a university place prior to military service were, upon joining the RAF, instantly elevated to the lofty realms of pilot officer.

Inside the 'J' hangar two war-weary aeroplanes made themselves available for camera fitment. One was Spitfire XI, *PL837*, which had served with 400 Squadron, the other a Mosquito XVI, *NS551*, which had sacrificed itself in order to show the Americans what a real aeroplane was like. These shared the vast emptiness with an Auster J/4 *G-AIJT* of the Spa and Warwick Timber Company which had achieved the impossible, in those days, by basing its executive transport on a military aerodrome. Pale blue, and never looking very happy, was the unique Burgoyne Stirling Dycer, a light plane of the PFA type. The only military aircraft that flew was a solitary Anson 'TFAB', at one time *NK312* and another, *NK340*, used by the SOP for aerial photography—rarely.

Whether the military preparedness, or lack of it, among Wellesbourne's martial men encouraged the Soviets or not we shall probably never know. But when the Cold War temperature fell it brought quite dramatic changes at a Wellesbourne still in excellent condition. An Advanced Training School was established in May 1950 and became, in 1951, No 9 Advanced Flying Training School, amply equipped with Oxfords which functioned until 1954. The School of Photography stayed until 1964. With the removal of SOP came the departure of the Airfield Construction Branch based here since September 1958.

With rich memories of Wellesbourne, I returned some 30 years after I had left. It is a camp I recall set in a most attractive rural environment. I called on Mrs Littler who, with her son, explained that Wellesbourne was a shadow of itself although it was hoped that there would be a considerable revival of flying in future. From their home I glanced across to the dispersal where I had 'courageously' refused to burn a pile of Hotspurs—long after official records indicated that they had been disposed of! Next day some soulless character drenched all 20 with petrol. Well, I did try, honestly I did! Nearby was the den where my friend, Peter Jackson, resided, unofficially, whilst preparing for his post Air Force chemical career. His ordered task was the painting of a large number of fire extinguishers—over a long period when a few moments would have sufficed. For his meritorious service he all but received a good conduct medal.

I motored on and soon I had reached the . . . but, my goodness, where was it? Where was the guardroom where *they* reigned supreme? Gone, all gone, into a messy pile of junk like so much more of the old place. As I stood there surveying the remnants I thought of the many

Oxford DF336 *represents 9 AFTS, Wellesbourne, at Odiham during the Coronation Review of the RAF in 1953. Only very smart Oxfords had wheel guards, astro domes and a Wing Commander to guard them.*

characters I'd come to know there. It had attracted, by its role, the artistic and the articulate, quite a fair proportion of whom delighted in Stratford where for a 'bob' one could stand through *Hamlet*. And I thought, too, of Baber and his music interests and of Henshaw who was forever slipping off to his naval homestead on unauthorised leave. There was that magic moment when the SWO announced that his beloved Mess (gone, all gone, overgrown by a housing estate) might win the Jolliffe Trophy until some nameless fool spoilt it all with gigantic white foot marks across the wretched red floor. Years later I chuckled merrily when, in a rather more privileged stance, I attended the presentation of that item to RAF Waterbeach, which in no way matched Wellesbourne's 'Palm Court'. What, I wondered, was Harris up to these days? Tall, blonde, a private person, he used to slip away alone each evening. Determined to discover his secret, I followed his track to Wellesbourne Church. My initial assumption was that he went there to pray

A formation of Oxfords of 9 AFTS.

Above *A northerly view over Wellesbourne Mountford, across the technical site and runways to three distant dispersals.*

Below *A complete view of Wellesbourne. In the foreground the Sergeants' and Officers' Messes. Central is the main domestic site comprising only single storey buildings. The largest in the centre of the picture is the Airmen's Mess.*

Wellesbourne's 'J' Type hangar and typical brick/concrete/asbestos hutting.

but, just as I opened the door, he released the organ into an orgy of splendour. His secret revealed, he soon admitted that he knew the organ 'at Windsor' and was 'keeping his hand in'.

I took a quick wander around the hangars before it was time to go. Thousands of machinery parts were in store, and my guide then pointed to some Russian, yes *Russian* script on the wall of the old parachute section. It was, he said, applied by workers of a tool company who had used it for storage. I thought to myself 'hm, the old SWO won't like that!'

We next stood where once the lawns of the grand entrance smiled, where a low line of huts called themselves 'SHQ' and kept company with the Ensign. There was one last thing to do—to take, for keeps, a little piece of that guardroom. As I did so I smiled to myself at the pleasure someone derived from an unregistered firm 'Passes Unlimited'. If *that pair* had known—but they've all been knocked down and nobody needs the guardroom any more. Knocked down . . . none of us would have ever gone to such lengths—I think.

Against the odds Wellesbourne has of late come alive again, its light aircraft and 'pterodactyls' being joined by a branch of the Confederate Air Force. Its future, though, is uncertain.

Westcott, Buckinghamshire

SP711540. 10 miles ESE of Bicester by the A41

Between September 28 1942 and early October, 11 OTU claimed Westcott as its new home, quickly resuming its bomber crew training role using Wellington 1cs. This move resulted in 11 OTU joining 92 Group and participation in *Bullseyes*, the first of which took place on January 26 1943. Average strength of 11 OTU was 52 Wellingtons and an assortment of aircraft for gunnery training. The latter machines were based at Oakley, the satellite station. For communications purposes, an Avro Tutor was on strength until November 1943. Ansons were withdrawn early in 1943. Westcott, in the spring of 1943, also provided a base for the ECDU, 92 Group, which used four Wellingtons for its radio trials.

Hercules-powered Wellingtons, including Mk Xs, first joined 11 OTU in September 1943, releasing some 1cs—in increasingly short supply—for 14 OTU, although it was many months before all had gone. Leaflet dropping over France was resumed in December 1943 after a long break, for by then the Hercules Mk III/X were fully integrated into Westcott.

The main dispersal of the remaining Wellington 1cs came in February 1944, by the end of which month the unit's strength stood at three Mk IIIs and 50 Mk Xs. Conversion flying was being undertaken by A and B Flights at Oakley where the Gunnery Flight remained. *Bullseyes* and *Nickelling* sorties were flown from Westcott where operational training was undertaken.

At the end of March 1944 ground equipment began to arrive from Harwell whose OTU had closed. Westcott took over much of its training commitment, most crews now being trained at 11 OTU for overseas theatres. Since early 1943 bombers were diverted here on returning from operations. Early on April 5 1944, Westcott played the role of host to famous 617 Squadron when 18 Lancasters landed from Toulouse. A returning Lancaster, which overshot on landing just before 03:00 on May 31 1944, brought an alarming situation for aboard was a 13,000 lb bomb load. After crossing the A41, the bomber came to rest near the D/F station and the occupants quickly got out. Flight Lieutenant E.C. Bulmer, Flying Control Officer, went to the scene and was there when at 03:30 the bombs blew up, taking his life.

On D-Day Westcott received diverted Halifaxes. *Nickels* were continuing, as on July 19 1944 when four crews dropped leaflets on Le Mans, Angers, Nantes and Leval. From March 1944 Hurricanes were used for gunnery training in addition to Martinets retained to the end of the year. It was during a cine gun affiliation exercise on July 30 1944 that a fighter pilot returned to state that, when five miles north of Westcott, he was horrified to see the wings torn off a Wellington taking evasive action.

To the end of hostilities, 11 OTU Westcott continued the training of bomber crews, its strength in March 1945 being 50 Wellington Xs, about half of which were based at Oakley where there were four Hurricanes and a Master II. An abrupt change came in May 1945 when Westcott became a reception airfield for receiving repatriated Allied prisoners of war. Seven Dakotas landed on May 3 with the first load. Such became a daily event, a very large number of men passing through to freedom. On June 2 1945, 15 Liberators touched down, true to name, bearing prisoners of war from Italy followed by more next day. When, on June 15 1945, 92 Group closed, the station passed to 91 Group under whose control it was when 11 OTU disbanded on August 3 1945.

Westcott's useful days were far from passed. German advances in rocket technology caused a Guided Projectile Establishment to be set up at Westcott in

Wellington X, ME954 TX:I, *of 11 OTU Westcott, summer 1944* (J.A. Bolt).

A familiar scene over Oxfordshire—Hawker Hectors towing Hotspur training gliders (IWM).

April 1946, in buildings wherein 11 OTU personnel had worked. This new establishment would be responsible for development of ground launched missiles. In 1947 its title changed to Rocket Propulsion Department, Royal Aircraft Establishment, its role narrowing to development of rocket propellants and concentrating on liquid bi-propellant rocket engines after the German style. Engines for the RTV I and RTV II were developed between 1946 and 1951. Work on solid propellant motors commenced in 1949 for which purpose the Solid Propellant Laboratory was created and an experimental filling factory completed in 1952. Plastic propellants were then introduced. In the 1950s, work was instigated into various other chemicals, materials and combustion processes for which further facilities were built.

Rolls-Royce contracted in 1955, to build the liquid bi-propellant RZ1 engine using liquid oxygen and Kerosene for Blue Streak. Runs of the engine, far more powerful than any hitherto seen here, commenced in 1958. By 1960 over 500 firings had taken place. After the cancellation of Blue Streak in 1960, work continued on the engine for use in the rocket Europa 1. Upper atmosphere research followed the development of the 17-ft long Raven Motor between 1955 and 1956, a component of the Skylark research vehicle.

The link with Farnborough ceased in August 1958. Westcott became the Rocket Propulsion Establishment when a variety of scientific programmes were initiated, satellite propulsion interest remaining until 1973. By the late 1960s, attention was also being devoted to the problems of liquid propellant storage by the Armed Services.

Not all Westcott's work has military overtones. After the wreck of the *Torrey Canyon* in March 1967, RPE was asked to carry out tests on the disposal of oil spillage by burning. Progress by November 1970 was such that in a major test 175 tonnes of crude oil were burnt.

The Rocket Propulsion Establishment became the responsibility of the Procurement Executive of Ministry of Defence in 1971 and in January 1973 it merged with the Explosives Research and Development Establishment, Waltham Abbey. The Rocket Motor Executive moved to Westcott in 1975, further merging bringing the ERDE and RPE together as the Propellants, Explosives and Rocket Motor Establishment (PERME) in February 1977.

Recent work has involved boost motors for Sea Wolf and Sea Skua, propellants for anti-tank weapons and air launched cruise missiles and static firing trials. Their purpose is to find possible points of failure during operations, or in man-

handling. PERME has a site of 623 acres and a staff of about 700.

Of wartime Westcott the runway and perimeter tracking remains, along with buildings including a 'B1' hangar. PERME's Social and Sports Club uses an assortment of brick and concrete wartime structures sited in the south-east corner, outside the security fence.

An excellent view over Westcott can be obtained from high ground between Westcott and Ashendon. Just how hazardous flying from Westcott must have been for trainee crews is at once obvious. The ground rises rapidly to the south, reaching its greatest height almost in line with the runway. The wonder is that there were not more accidents.

Weston-on-the-Green, Oxfordshire

SP535205. 3½ miles SW of Bicester by A43(T)

Weston's survivability is amazing, particularly as it never has been much more than a large field. Even more surprising, it has been quite important and must, in several respects, be unique. Additionally, it is one of the few airfields retaining concrete evidence of First World War days—albeit little more than foundations.

Apparently the ground was acquired for military use in 1916. By whom it was

Hotspur II gliders and Audax tugs at Weston-on-the-Green in summer 1942. Across the field, Master II glider tugs are dispersed (IWM).

first used seems now uncertain. Surviving records state that No 28 Training Depot Station opened here on July 27 1918, arising from an amalgamation of Nos 61 and 70 Training Squadrons. Rotating Clergets of Sopwith Camels therefore rent the peace of the area, along with Avro 504Ks. Ground attack Sopwith Salamanders replaced the Camels before No 28 TDS closed in 1919. Establishment figures suggest that as many as 72 aircraft may have resided here, where six aircraft sheds and a repair shed were provided. Remnants of 18 Squadron came from Germany. No 2 Squadron disbanded here on January 20 1920, activity ceasing at the site in 1921. Under whose control it was placed remains uncertain, but before the outbreak of war in 1939 it was in the hands of RAF Brize Norton whose satellite it then became. During the intervening years it was grazing land.

On September 2 1939, upon the order to scatter, No 90 Squadron (and probably 101 Squadron) hurriedly brought its Blenheims to Weston. Next day both squadrons were repositioned at Brize Norton, although some activity connected with both squadrons continued at Weston-the-Green until mid-September. Bicester then used Weston for its Ansons and Blenheims. When 13 OTU formed in April 1940 it came under control of that unit, remaining within 7 Group.

Weston-on-the-Green was, on August 9 1940, the first Oxfordshire airfield to be bombed. Late that night a stick of 16 HEs was released in a 2 mile long line extending from Chesterton to the landing ground upon which five of the bombs exploded without causing damage. A second attack came on August 25/26 when a lot of incendiaries were scattered. The following night the Germans came again, to make seven more holes on Weston's flying field. Persistent Luftwaffe attacks were quite remarkable for on September 2/3 another five HEs fell near Weston and one on Otmoor bombing range. It was almost as if someone was waging a personal war against this small, inoffensive little airfield, instead of the large ones nearby.

In the summer of 1940, 13 OTU obtained more suitable satellites and on November 1 1940 the station became an RLG for 15 SFTS, Kidlington. Harvards and mainly Oxfords flew daily and often by night. Early in 1941 part of that unit moved to Weston where a detachment of 30 men, to service the aircraft now based here, came on February 20 1941.

Considerable local concern arose when,

Weston-on-the-Green in July 1941—a motley collection of old and new buildings, evidence of First World War foundations, all in the hands of 15 FTS (Public Record Office).

just after midnight on August 12 1941, an intruder entered Weston's airspace and joined night flying Oxfords of No 24 Course. After engaging one, the intruder came upon another, opening fire upon it when flying at 4,000 ft. *W6629* promptly burst into flames and both Flight Sergeant Julin-Olsene (Norwegian) and Leading Aircraftsman C.P. Blair were killed. Wreckage fell near Sturdy's Castle. Then the raider dropped six light bombs on the airfield. Seven Oxfords on the landing ground were damaged by strafing.

The protracted closure of 15 SFTS to clear way for glider training at Kidlington resulted in the contraction of the SFTS and withdrawal of J and K Flights from Weston on December 23 1941. By that date No 2 Glider Training School was already functioning at Weston-on-the-Green.

Hotspur II training gliders at Weston-on-the-Green in 1942 (Flight International).

Orders for its formation as an off-shoot of No 1 GTS were received at Thame on December 4 1941. Over the following few days, Weston's state was examined. It occupied six accommodation sites, in addition to a technical site where about 160 personnel resided. The communal site was 1½ miles away and the dormitory site a further mile from it—such was wartime dispersal for which the bicycle provided the ideal means of transport. A rapid decision was made, a party to open No 2 GTS arriving on December 8 1941. Airmen and NCOs would be accommodated in huts whilst officers resided comfortably at Kidlington. On December 22 1941, No 2 GTS was transferred from 70 Group

Army Co-operation Command to 23 Group, Training Command.

Shortage of Hotspurs, Hector tugs and tow ropes was matched by that of flying instructors. Training started early in January 1942 after conversion of pilots from Netheravon who had Hawker Hart experience and who would now fly Hawker Hectors. By the end of December 1941, No 2 GTS had eight Hectors, four of which were swopped for two dual control examples at Thame. Another two, without towing hooks, were suitable for pilot training. Maintenance was a problem with these ageing biplanes and their Napier Dagger III engines, further complicated by a shortage of suitable maintenance equipment. Such features ensured an inauspicious start for 2 GTS.

Gliders were slow in coming, the first four arriving as a late Christmas present from 15 MU Wroughton. Assembly, with the help of General Aircraft, commenced on December 29 1941. This was none too easy for tailplane warping was discovered and two gliders had to be borrowed from Thame to help with initial flying. Nevertheless a general start had been accomplished and, on December 28 1941, the first trainees reported to Weston-on-the-Green for flying training, where a few Hawker Hinds were now also to hand. Although 15 SFTS had left, one Over Type 'Blister' hangar was set aside for the use of any night flying Oxford which might need servicing during limited use of the aerodrome.

Shortage of tugs for training gliders resulted in a Fairey Battle being tested for the task at Weston in mid-December, and promptly being found unsuitable. In January 1942 winter conditions brought a steady deterioration for the airfield surface which was soon too wet for Hectors. These aircraft performed poorly in winter, whilst the Dagger's characteristics indicated that it would easily overheat in summer during towing activity. This brought about further search for a replacement, resulting in a Kestrel XX engined Hawker Audax, *K5152*. This type, which when towing a Hotspur, needed an 820-yd run to clear 50 ft, was far preferable to the Hector, and Audaxes were acquired as fast as possible for glider towing attachments to be fitted.

January 1942 also witnessed the completion of the 12-bay Bessoneau hangar with another nine bays being constructed. Two more Over Type Blister hangars were being erected, along with another eight Hotspurs to fill them. Establishment was currently for 30 Hotspurs, 12 + 4 tugs, two Tiger Moths and a Hind (T). The first six-week glider pilot's course commenced on January 2 1942, pass out coming on February 17. Despite the poor surface, up to six tow lines were then in operation simultaneously, two of these being temporarily made available to 1 GTS whose base at Thame was even more unsuitable for flying than Weston.

Five Audaxes arrived on March 7 and others later that month although they did not entirely replace the Hectors, a few of which remained for full load towing. Two more 'Blister' hangars were erected in April 1942. In March 1942 the projected Hotspur (T) became the Hotspur III and, in April 1942, all Hotspurs were ordered to be completed as training gliders. Some 370 had been built by then and plans were for ten to be much modified to Mk III standard per week. Cost, and ever changing requirements, led to only 52 Mk III being produced fully modifed for glider schools.

Now that the Hotspur II was in service some modifications were very necessary. Tail skids gave trouble and new designs were produced by various agencies, among them Weston's staff. A modification eventually adopted involved backward extension of the foot of the skid which was also made more flexible and able to withstand heavier shocks during landings. There were three more serious accidents in May 1942. One involved a glider which entered a very steep climb just after take off and stalled as the tow rope was released. Then a high point tow developed as another Hotspur took off and had to be released quickly for a forced landing. Trouble with another glider's canopy opening in flight brought futher hasty touch-down.

Throughout the month, night flying was also carried out here by Hotspurs of No 102 (Glider) OTU, Kidlington. Search for more suitable landing grounds for glider training schools was underway and 2 GTS conducted trials at Long Newton with the idea of its being used for 1 GTS in place of unsuitable Thame. There was also a constant desire to improve the Hotspur's performance. Gliders being built or in preparation depended upon a bifurcated tow rope which meant that extra time was needed in hook-ups. Nose point towing was developed and, by the end of May 1942, Hotspurs were being modified to have the nose towing point, featured by four gliders here by the end of the month.

Using outdated Hawker biplanes to tow the gliders was far from satisfactory. Various replacement aircraft types were again considered for the task, including an Oxford tested here in May before the choice fell upon the Miles Master II. On June 16 the first arrived at Weston for towing equipment. Three dual-control Master IIs arrived on June 28 and conversion training was undertaken with the assistance of instructors from 9 (P) AFU. Two Hotspurs with nose towing points were in regular use.

The Hotspur was far too tail heavy for the Master tug. Ballast had to be carried to ease the problem before research at CTSs and RAEs eventually led to a change in the glider's tailplane incidence. By August the glider establishment had doubled and the tug strength set at 40 aircraft. On a fine day it was now possible to achieve as many as 80 tows out of Weston. Towing a Hotspur, the Master needed a 900 yd run to reach 50 ft. Standard Manilla tow ropes were 2½ in thick and were suitable for 35 launches.

On September 2 1942, Master *DL425* was towing *HH518* off from Weston and little height could be gained. Within moments the combination smashed into the steeple of Witney's church. Survival of the occupants was amazing, although their injuries were serious.

Intensive glider pilot training continued into 1943. Conditions at Weston at the start of February were so bad that the unit was detached to Cheddington from where flying took place until March 20 1943 when return to Weston came. Drastic changes were then underway. Air Ministry Works had, in February, decided that it was essential that Sommerfeld Tracking runways and peritrack be laid at Weston prior to the next winter. Another decision had been taken to the effect that all glider pilot training at 4 GTS would cease, an order becoming effective on March 10 1943. The existing 4 GTS became, that same day, retitled 20 (P) AFU. Next, it was the turn of 1 GTS to close, this unit also dissolving into 20 (P) AFU on March 24 1943. Its Croughton base then became a satellite of Kidlington. Finally came the turn of 2 GTS, Weston, which ceased to function on April 6 1943 to emerge the very same day, and at Weston, as yet another satellite of 20 (P) AFU. Before that date new occupants arrived and soon three dozen Oxfords were based here. In March, 20 (P) AFU had received 76 Oxfords and three Ansons and later its strength would be double that figure.

Weston had become a satellite of Kidlington and soon came the training accidents which afflicted all such places. On May 15 1943, Oxford *T1100* crashed into the roof of a cottage on the airfield boundary, an accident from which, luckily, the pilot was extricated.

AMWD were as good as their word and laid Sommerfeld Tracking in September 1943. Thereafter by day—and particularly by night—Oxford flying took place until it was forcibly halted by the disbandment of 20 (P) AFU on May 31 1945. Weston remained in 23 Group until October 1 1945 when it came under 3 MU which held it until March 15 1946. Control then passed to Upper Heyford, a 38 Group station and a part of Transport Command. As soon as 1 PTS reached that station, Weston-on-the-Green began to be used as a dropping zone for parachutists. They were also able to jump from a basket suspended below an LZ Kite Balloon which, for many years, drifted daily above Weston.

The Korean War brought weeks of high tension to many British airfields and Upper Heyford was no exception. On June 10 1950, Weston was placed at the disposal of Bomber Command which held the station until August 9 1950 when the Air Positioning Plotting Unit arrived. That was part of 62 Group under whose command Weston remained until April 20 1951 when the site was placed into a Care and Maintenance state.

With so much transport activity in the area, it was not long before Transport Command repossessed the airfield for use once more as a dropping area for exercises run by 1 PTS. Weston has been used as a DZ for parachutists descending over the years from Valettas, Beverleys, Argosys, Andovers and Hercules. During 1976 the parachutists' captive balloon was removed to Hullavington. Since that time a lot of free fall parachute jumping has taken place, both civil and military, and has included jumps by the RAF Sport Parachute Association.

Weston-on-the-Green houses the Oxford Gliding Club, and the RAFGSA Chiltern Gliding Club which also functions from Bicester. It seems that, come what may, Weston is determined somehow to serve its country.

Westwood (Peterborough), Cambridgeshire

See Peterborough

Windrush, Gloucestershire

SP180120. 4 miles W of Burford

It happened at the end of a day when the fight to the south was at its fiercest. Kenley had been smashed, Biggin battered, Gosport, Croydon and Manston, too. Not long after twilight passed on a double summertime eve, some 50 German bombers made their way inland. A number of rudimentary landing grounds were being used for night flying, lit both to aid crews night flying as well as to divert German bombs away from costly, major airfields. A strip of lights marking the grass runway at Windrush beckoned to the crew of a marauding Heinkel, one of several in the area, late on the evening of Sunday, August 18 1940.

Maybe they stood off, assessing the activity whilst planning their attack. Maybe it was chance. As they lined up on the field that called itself Windrush they must have seen ahead of them another aircraft. Ten 50 kg HE bombs fell close to the airfield, one without exploding. As the bombs burst, the Heinkel 111 then closed on the aircraft ahead—Anson *L9164* of 6 SFTS. Both aircraft were flying at about 1,000 ft and, as the Heinkel closed from 200 to 150 yds, its front gunner opened fire. Sergeant B. Hancock in the Anson immediately switched off his navigation lights, banked to port and in a flash the German bomber rammed itself into the trainer. Eye witnesses maintained that Hancock had deliberately turned into the bomber's path. Whatever the truth, two blazing infernos shattered within seconds to fall over fields some two miles south west of the LG. The hours surrounding the event were the most action packed that this small landing area would know for, not long after, another enemy aircraft came down near Northleach. Later on the 19th, Harvard, *P5788* of 6 FTS, crashed at Haselton, killing one and injuring the other member of its crew while on a low flying sortie. At midday on August 19, Windrush was taken from 15 SFTS and placed in the hands of 6 SFTS who tended it, as their RLG, until its use ended on July 12 1945.

Windrush came into use early in summer 1940, and was being very busily used by mid-June, as an RLG for the aircraft of Little Rissington's 6 SFTS as much as for its parent unit, 15 SFTS. Both the ATS and ITS of this latter unit trained here, by day and night, for which purposes they were allocated, at an early stage, three Nissen huts on the camp for ground crews stationed here on detachment.

Between July 27 1940 and August 19 1940, care of the RLG was vested in 15 SFTS, after which it was returned to 6 SFTS which had earlier looked after the station. Windrush's bright runway lights seem to have been irresistable to the Luftwaffe for, on September 2 1940, it returned depositing some small HEs, which failed to explode, a mile from the airfield. Another ten were dropped shortly after midnight on September 11 1940, a mile or so to the north-east of the site. Windrush was diverting the bombing, as intended, and not getting too hurt in the process.

During 1941, trainers from 2 SFTS also used the RLG, but mainly it was Little Rissington's Oxfords which monopolised the circuit. On April 22 1942, 6 SFTS was re-organised as 6 (P) AFU. Although the training programme was amended, the aircraft were the same, and the sight too. Nine Blister hangars were then in position on the western side of the landing ground which was encircled by a perimeter track. Buildings clustering in the north-east corner were used for instructional purposes, whereas those in the north-west corner formed the communal site. By the summer of 1942 two Sommerfeld Tracking runways had been laid, No 1 being the 19/01 runway, No 2 running 25/07. Four collections of huts along the A40 road formed the living quarters.

A few brick huts mark the airfield which stands out clearly against a vast sky. On a fine, clear day its plateau situation affords a vista of county after county beyond. It rests upon a landscape hard to beat.

Wing, Buckinghamshire

SP860240. 7 miles N of Aylesbury, W of village of Wing

Clyffe, Foulness, Cublington—attempts have been made to transform all into international airports. None has succeeded, and when the Roskill Commission suggested Cublington (alias Wing), in 1971, as a site for London's third airport there was the customary furore. No such opposition was voiced

when the site was acquired in 1940 and opened on November 17 1941. People were different then.

Under 7 Group, 26 OTU formed on January 15 1942. It was March before all runways were clear of obstructions and first to land was, on March 18, a Tiger Moth. Thereafter Wellington Ics were posted in.

No 1 flying training course commenced on April 25 with eight Ansons, and Wellingtons for conversion flying, at Cheddington. On May 11 1942, control was switched to 92 (Bomber) Group. Orders came for operations on May 31, 20 crews setting out from Graveley, Huntingdonshire, for their part in the Cologne 1,000 Plan raid which cost 26 OTU three crews. Of the remainder, 15 took part in the following Essen raid and one more failed to return. Wellingtons of 26 OTU also participated in the June 1,000 Plan raid on Bremen. By August 1942 the average strength of the OTU stood at 34 Wellingtons and eight Ansons. Two Lysander target towers and a Wellington were being used by E (Air Firing) Flight.

Residents of Wing now had a rare treat. Few interested in wartime 'new types', as they were colloquially called, failed to peep into a closely guarded copy of *AP 1480X*, a handbook of silhouettes of experimental aircraft. They would then know of a racey looking six-cannon,

Refuelling the Martin Baker MB 3 fighter at Wing. The bowser identifies itself as belonging to B/92, ie, 92 Group. The control tower is behind and Wellington 1c, WG:B, *taxies by* (Martin Baker).

fighter listed as Experimental Aeroplane No 120 and rumoured to be called the 'Whippet'. Seeing is surely believing, but nobody ever seemed to find anyone who had seen that fighter, although lots laid suspicious claims to having been successful. It was in reality one of the line of unusual aircraft from Martin Baker, well known for ejector seats and that other superb flyer, the MB-5. This other one was the MB-3, ordered to Wing for its long overdue flight trials. It first flew on August 31 1942 in the hands of Captain H.V. Baker. Sadly its existence was too brief for, on September 12 1942, its Sabre engine failed and in the ensuing forced landing Captain Baker lost his life.

During September 1942, 26 OTU participated in further bombing raids including attacks on Düsseldorf, Bremen and Essen, all flown from Wing where, in October, the OTU's average total strength had risen to include two Wellington 1s, two Wellington Ias, 49 Wellington Ics, six Ansons, three Lysander target towers and a Defiant. Equipment changed little until February 1943 when the first ten

Wellington IIIs were received to supplement 52 Mk Ics on strength. A further 16 Mk IIIs came in March and the re-equipment programme was completed in May 1943 although Mk Ics remained long after at the station. It was August 1943 before a full switch to Hercules Wellingtons was made.

During April 1943, three Martinets replaced the other gunnery trainers. More fascinating would have been the fruition of plans for Wellington VI high altitude bombers to be stationed at Wing. Various ideas were proposed to make use of the 60 or so available, but they were too specialised for anything other than their primary role. Instead, 26 OTU started receiving Wellington Xs during July 1943, by which time only one Mk 1c was left at Wing. That month was auspicious for, during its course, 26 OTU despatched six effective *Nickel* sorties over France, the unit's first such venture.

In mid-July a few Tomahawks of 1684 Bomber Defence Training Flight moved in from the satellite, Little Horwood. They remained for longer than expected due to their general unacceptability. In mid-1944 three were still at Wing although the Flight's main equipment was then six Hurricane IIcs.

Bombing had briefly been resumed on August 30/31, September 2/3 and 8/9 1943. These raids were directed against ammunition dumps in the Fôret d'Eperlecques and were part of the build up to Operation *Starkey*. They cost 26 OTU one crew. About 20 per cent of the OTU's equipment now consisted of Wellington Xs. The remainder were Mk IIIs one of which, *X3790*, was involved in a memorable accident on August 7 1943. It first hit a tree then crashed onto the roof of a house in the High Street, Winslow. Then it careered across the street, clipping the top of *The Chandos Arms* before demolishing four cottages. Four of the crew died, along with 13 civilians.

During the last three months of 1943 the OTU despatched 26 *Nickel* sorties from Wing. *Bullseyes* attracted far more effort and during one of these Wellington *BJ978* off course over the London IAZ was hit by Anti-Aircraft fire, at a time when enemy aircraft were active.

A mixture of Wellington IIIs and Xs equipped 26 OTU almost to the end of the war. Half a dozen Hurricane IIcs replaced the unit's Martinets at the satellite in April 1944. In June, 26 OTU's overall strength was 26 Wellington IIIs and 13 Mk Xs, four Martinets, four Hurricanes an Oxford 1 and two Mk IIs.

June 1944 was a busy month with Wing accepting operational bomber diversions. The highlight, though, was far more sombre. A Wellington X, *HE854*, was involved in a disastrous collision with another parked Wellington, two '60-footer' low loaders and a hangar. A serious fire ensued, three WAAFs with the lorries, and the Wellington's co-pilot, being killed. Take-off swings as result of wrong power settings, engine problems and undercarriage troubles were all frequent misfortunes at OTUs.

Crew requirements were constantly changing and, on August 26 1944, 26 OTU's state was reduced by a quarter. Elements at the satellite were withdrawn and 1684 BDTF disbanded. This reduction was temporary for, in October, 26 OTU increased again to full strength. Two Warwick IIs were received, *HG349* on November 18 and *HG350* on November 30, for assessment as to that aircraft's suitability for OTU employment, particularly as this and the Centaurus-engined Buckingham seemed likely to play an increasing part overseas and in the post-war Air Force. Wellington Xs formed three-quarters of the main equipment. By February 1945, 26 OTU had 52 Mk Xs and only 7 Mk IIIs, and was still conducting Warwick trials. Both examples remained until autumn 1945.

The end of the war in Europe brought hectic activity to Wing, chosen to receive home-coming prisoners of war. The first came on April 9 1945 in 33 Dakotas, and totalled 819 men. By the end of April 1945, 14,794 ex-PoWs had passed through the station, chosen because of its central position. On May 8 no less than 750 were landed here, arriving in 61 Lancasters and eight Dakotas. May 15 saw no less than 132 Lancaster landings at the station. Of the 1,269 aircraft which brought PoWs here in May, 518 were Lancasters. But tragedy once struck in what must have been momentous days for, on May 10, a Lancaster carrying 31 PoWs crashed on landing.

On June 15 1945, with the disbandment of 92 Group, 26 OTU became part of 91 Group and the following month the Gunnery Flight returned again from Little Horwood. Post-war training was on an ever reduced scale and, on March 4 1946, 26 OTU closed. Maintenance Command took control of Wing on May 4 1946 and the site was disposed of by April 1960.

Witney, Oxfordshire

SP330095. 1 mile W of Witney, S of the old A40

Witney First World War RFC flying training school was sited on the west side of the town. Training in fighter tactics was undertaken here where, on March 30 1918, No 8 Training Squadron arrived from Netheravon to be followed by No 7 a month later. Their equipment was mainly Avro 504Ks, F2Bs and DH 5s which, on August 5 1918, combined to form No 33 Training Depot Station here until disbandment in 1919.

Witney remained dormant until the 1930s when civil flying commenced. The main office block of the pre-war flying school was by the old A40 road. On the outbreak of war the airfield was taken over by Brize Norton, 2 SFTS using it as an RLG for Oxfords, one of which, *F6796*, crashed on the airfield on February 2 1940. In the spring of 1940 de Havilland opened a Civilian Repair Unit here. The company acquired the site to relieve the main Hatfield works of repairing the multiplicity of types of de Havilland light aircraft doing war service, also Hurricanes.

On November 22 1940, at 05:30, an attack was made upon Witney, a raider releasing two bombs, one of which fell behind a brewery and the other in the church grounds. Some 200 houses were damaged, army vehicles on the church green were burnt and many shop windows in the high street fragmented. The damage was out of proportion to the bomb load. Witney works, though, was unscathed. Making maximum use of the site, an RAOC Depot was built in 1941 on its western side.

By then work particularly centred upon the de Havilland Dominie and impressed Rapides. Some production work connected with the former was undertaken here. In September 1942, Brush Electrical secured a contract to build Dominies, the DH Witney staff playing a major part in initiating production. Witney works at this time was completing much of the final DH contract for 150 Dominies.

During 1943 some Brush-built aircraft were transferred to Witney for completion and at the end of the war a number of Dominies, built at Loughborough, were brought to Witney for conversion to civilian Rapide specifications. Witney also converted military Dominies to civil standards, and generally gave in-service backing.

Witney, in 1918, graced by a line of Bessaneaux hangars (RAF Museum).

Avros, BEs, 'Brisfits'—all types represented in this ground shot of Witney (Bruce Robertson).

The factory closed in 1946. In 1951 Smiths Industries established a factory on the one-time airfield. A surviving First World War hangar, complete with Belfast Truss roofing, was then demolished. Some First World War relics remain—among them the MT depot, and airmen's hospital and the stop butts.

Wittering, Cambridgeshire

TF045025. 3 miles S of Stamford by the A1

'Royal Air Force Wittering, Home of the Harrier'. Certainly both are assured a special place in RAF history, and for me Wittering recalls many exciting moments. April 10 1944 was a typical wartime day, fair enough for Alan Wright and I to pedal away from Cambridge to the grumble of P-47s and B-17s also airfield-bound, and more offensively than us. Before reaching Huntingdon, Oxford *V4024* 'BN', a B-26, 16 slowly climbing B-17s, Lancaster *OL-O* from Wyton, three Stirlings of 199 Squadron, a B-24J and a leisurely plodding Whitley V glider tug had all presented their compliments. Over Huntingdon passed a Spitfire Vb and a Wyton-based Mosquito IX of 1409 Flight. From the PFF NTU Warboys came Lancaster *QF-T*, and then commenced one of those daily Anson 'migrations' directed by budding navigators, and Anson *EF904* of a BAT Flight intruded upon them. A UC-78 chattered towards Alconbury (recall its sound?) and Lancaster *TL-E* circled Graveley.

Lined up at Alconbury were 15 camouflaged B-24s wearing unadorned white fin discs and yellow fin letters beneath, 'P' for instance being 128778. More to my liking was Mosquito PR *XVI-MM338-G* carrying a yellow serial on its fin. Three USAAF Dominies, three UC-61s, three UC-78s, 15 unpainted B-17Gs and a camouflaged example, *231142-X*, stood by a lonely C-47. Just imagine that lot for viewing at the next Alconbury open day!

But I digress; it's Wittering we're heading for, pestered by Master Is and IIs unsure whether to live at Peterborough or Sibson. A fuselage from a sick Typhoon, *MN943*, passes through Sawtry on a '60-footer' as, overhead, chugs Oxford *DF306* on air test from Cambridge. Then we are saluted by a Whitley V tugging a wallowing Horsa, presumably on an airing from Luffenham. More Masters, a Mosquito II, some Hurricanes and then we are level with Sibson where I counted 25 Master IIs, a Typhoon and Blister hangars. Overhead pass increasingly more C-47s for we are now on the fringe of the US IXth AAF troop carrier zone, and the cluster of buildings that form Wittering—little changed still—appears on the hilly skyline. It had taken five hours hard cycling to get here—and every moment now proved worthwhile.

Wittering is unusually sited, the grass area rising away from the A1 towards a plateau making viewing from the road difficult. The station retains a wide assortment of structures, some close to the road being very old. The pre-war style 'twin box' watch office and tower was built in front of the three nine-bay 'C' Type hipped

During the September 1938 Munich Crisis, camouflage was applied to Demons of 23 Squadron at Wittering.

hangars, one of which in 1944 remained in an awful mess as a result of the 1941 bombing. Two remain, supplemented by a post-war large one and, more recently, a small hangar.

Wittering in April 1944 was an enthusiast's paradise. Close to the road rested the captured Focke-Wulf Fw 190A-3, *PM173*, camouflaged dark earth and green and having yellow under surfaces and a light blue spinner. Clustered around it were a Wildcat VI with a tiny fuselage serial, possibly *JV684*, Barracuda *P9917* festooned with ASV aerials, Hellcat 1 *JV124*, an early clipped-wing Seafire and Fulmar *DR716*. Although all were with the Naval Air Fighting Development Unit based here, the fighters sported a most unusual finish of dark green and a very dark shade of grey on their upper surfaces and medium sea grey under surfaces. Either they were in the process of passing to the Fighter Interception Unit based here, or they were in an unusual naval night fighter scheme.

Hoots of delight came from us as we enjoyed the sight of a rare white Coastal Command Hampden, *AE373*, perhaps audible in the Station Commander's office! This was the last complete Hampden that I ever saw and a memorable one for, on its grey-green upper surfaces, it carried an assortment of 'white' stripes which I later learnt were night flying formation aids. By that Hampden was the old Boston III, *AF-Z*, a momento of AFDU's Duxford days.

Extending our scan we spied a Corsair 1 curiously painted in dark earth and dark green with yellow under surfaces. Its four-bladed propeller was unusual for the three-blader was then normal. A second look at a Spitfire revealed it to be fitted with contra-rotating propellers. Surprised, I made a careful check and certainly it had six blades and a closer look revealed it to be *RB179* resting among a group of AFDU Spitfires. One was the unusual Mk Vc dive-bomber *BR372* later to be credited with five enemy aircraft. *MH413-ZD-M* was also there, and a couple of Mk IIbs, *AF-I* and *AF-E—P8252*. Beyond them towered the oft-mentioned Grumman Avenger *FN785* whose *YØ-P* identity letters were bright yellow. It was to end its life in the Wash.

During the afternoon 16 P-38s trundled around the peritrack from their south-west corner dispersals, revealing KI coding, yellow noses and spinners and white fin triangles. Their take-offs in fours remains memorable. Consuming margarine and peanut butter sandwiches by a gateway still in evidence, and being unsure whether that gift from the 91st Bomb Group was all that tasty, we enjoyed a procession of C-47s and Whitleys depositing Horsas onto Luffenham as BAT Flight Oxfords commenced circuit flying at Wittering interrupted by an arriving RAF Hornet Moth. A C-47 tugged a Waco *CG-4A* across before a bevy of Mosquitoes of FIU, joined by some Beaufighters, began local flying. An Auster IV *MT214*, Lancaster *CF-P* and a Barracuda wearing a sky band around its rear fuselage arrived. As the latter crossed the A1, it dangled its arrester hook. Then the contra-prop Spitfire took off amid, for those days, no mean din.

Come 16:15, with an action packed afternoon to look back upon, it was time for the hard haul home. Mind you, there was still much to enjoy such as a passing C-47 with a glider snatch device fitted below the fuselage. The seven B-17s which did a stream take-off from Alconbury were rated as not worth bothering to watch, for that was a daily sight in 1944. A couple of B-24s joined them, *128778* and *128787*, and a Mitchell passed before exhausted—more mentally than physically—I slumped into bed too weary even to face a morsel of rationed food. A visit to Wittering, like a wartime trip to Farnborough, is something still to look back upon with sheer delight.

Throughout its long history Wittering has been an interesting station. The site of that name came into use during the First World War as Stamford. Between December 1916 and November 1917 it housed FE 2bs of A Flight, No 38 Home Defence Squadron. The 35th Wing Headquarters at Stamford included No 1 Training Depot Station, here between August 1917 and May 1919. It had for companion C Flight of 90 Squadron (formed from 38 Squadron) from September 1918 until its demise in 1919. Stamford had by then been home for mainly Avro 504s, Camels and Pups. At the end of 1919 it became a storage depot until placed on Care and Maintenance in January 1920.

Stamford's resurrection followed the air defence review of the 1920s. Its name was changed to Wittering in May 1924, arrangements being finalised on May 1 for the removal of the RAF Central Flying School from Upavon to Wittering because the former station would be in an operational area. Wittering rebuilt, the advance party of CFS arrived from Upavon on

An all-black Hurricane night-fighter, DZ-D, *of 151 squadron at Wittering in 1941* (RAF Museum).

July 21 1926 and during that summer remnants of the school arrived to open at Wittering, complete, on October 17 1926. Many of Wittering's existing buildings date from this rebuilding period, a typical example being the guardroom whose structure is typical of the 1920s.

Wittering then had two hangars, an Aircraft Shed Double (322/17) reconditioned and half serving as a storage area, and a similar shed half used as a workshop. Much of the old station had been remodelled including Main Stores and SHQ (191/24). In a new Sergeants' Mess 68 SNCOs could be accommodated and, in each of the four Barrack Blocks, New Type 'C' 242/23, three NCOs and 64 airmen. Station Offices (1799/25) and a Guardhouse (84/24) were other additions, likewise a 1924-style Officers' Mess. Airmens' Married Quarters were of 1922 design whereas the Watch Office was to pattern 1926/27.

The main purpose of CFS was the training of flying instructors. Introduced by E Flight in 1927 was the standard refresher flying course. New training schemes were studied, in particular blind flying techniques. Instrument flying courses introduced in 1930 became a standard part of the CFS flying instructors' course. Within its nine years here, CFS operated many aircraft types. Between 1926 and 1931 these included the Bristol F2B, *DH9A*, Lynx, Snipe, Grebe, Gamecock and Siskin. In 1931–2 Fairey IIIFs and Bulldogs were used and a Vickers Victoria floated in. Further changes in 1932–3 brought Bulldog Trainers, Hawker Tomtits, Hart day bombers and Armstrong Whitworth Atlases before CFS commenced its return to Upavon on August 1 1935 and completed the move on September 2 1935. Removal came because Wittering had been selected as a fighter Sector Station guarding northern East Anglia and extended towards Digby, barring entry to the Midlands.

A new FTS, No 11, formed at Wittering on October 1 1935 and was here until the fighter expansion programme permitted new squadrons to form. No 11 FTS equipped with Audaxes, used Tutors, had Harts from September 1936, Gauntlets and a few Hawker Furies.

Station Headquarters within Fighter Command formed on April 11 1938. Establishment was for one single-seater squadron and one multi-seat fighter squadron. No 11 FTS left on May 13 1938, having been a lodger on a 12 Group

Blenheim 1fs fast replaced 23 Squadron's Demons at Wittering in late 1938. YP-O, *possibly* L6738, *is pictured at snow-clad Wittering in early 1940.*

Frequently seen at Wittering, one of 266 Squadron's Spitfires by the pre-war control tower (RAF Museum).

station. By this time Wittering's appearance had changed again, as a result of its conversion into an operational fighter station. A 1935 contract required one 1917 hangar to be retained and three small 'C' Type Aircraft Sheds to be constructed. Main Stores (2108/37) were erected in the centre of the Technical Site. AMQs to 1922, 1931, 1932 and 1933 specifications were retained and additional examples built in 1934. There was a small southern extension to the camp and on to the flying field was laid a concrete taxi track to which, in 1939, were linked ten dispersal points around the edge of the flying ground. For all personnel, improved accommodation was available.

Wing Commander D.V. Carnegie assumed command of Wittering on May 16 1938 as 23 Squadron's Demons arrived. Two days later, 213 Squadron's Gauntlets moved in from Church Fenton. In August, 64 Squadron's Demons were here for the annual air defence exercise.

New shapes appeared in October 1938 when 269 Squadron's Ansons were affiliated to 23 Squadron whose camouflaged Demons were seen intercepting the newcomers. A winter conference held by Fighter Command at Wittering brought squadron Spitfires and Hurricanes together for the first time. News was given that 'as a temporary measure' 23 Squadron would arm with Blenheim 1f fighters, each having a four machine gun belly tray. They joined the squadron with alacrity, for it was fully re-armed by the end of the year.

Companion squadron, No 213, received its first Hurricanes on January 16 1939 and reached its establishment of 16 on March 3 1939. Within a matter of days the biplane era had passed from Wittering. Numerous tactical exercises followed, including involvement of French bombers which 213 Squadron intercepted during a mock attack upon Birmingham on August 17. A few days later, mobilisation was ordered and, at 08:00 on September 3 1939, with German withdrawal from Poland unlikely, machine gun posts sited around Wittering's perimeter were manned. Fear of attack caused a dummy airfield to be devised at Moxey, west of the station. Detachments from 213 Squadron moved forward daily to West Raynham to undertake convoy patrols off Norfolk. Blenheims of 23 Squadron commenced night standbys in October

Much use was made of Wittering for emergency landings. This Lancaster, reputedly QR:F *of 61 Squadron, crashed there on September 28 1942 after its 14th operational sortie.*

1939, one Flight being at readiness while the other trained at Digby.

Chester's auxiliary squadron, No 610, arrived to help with east coast patrols on October 8 and, ten days later, there was a scramble for a possible 'bogey' off Wells. Following winter weather and little enemy activity, flying increased when on March 21, 264 Squadron started detaching Flights of Defiants for training here. On April 4 1940, 610 Squadron left for Prestwick. Further detachments of 264 Squadron were rotated but April's main event was the arrival on the 7th of 266 Squadron whose ground crews arrived stylishly, in an Ensign air liner. Three days later, 266 Squadron joined the convoy patrol business.

Sudden German attack in the West resulted in the Defiants at once leaving for action. On May 16, B Flight, 213 Squadron hurried to France via Manston, ground crews following in a Bombay and Ensign, themselves chased soon after by the squadron's other Hurricanes. Early on May 17, B Flight flew to Merville in France and it proved a busy day for the Wittering squadron. B Flight joined 3 Squadron for an early morning patrol during which a group of Do 17s were attacked with uncertain results. Mid-morning A Flight arrived, and further sorties were flown alongside 79 Squadron with patrols into the evening. Next day was busy too then, at midday on May 19, Merville was bombed and the Hurricanes there were scrambled as much for safety as anything else. One was brought down—by 'friendly' Anti-Aircraft fire, and some Ju 88s were engaged. More patrols took place next day then, early on May 21, A Flight returned to Manston to operate over France from there and Biggin Hill to where the entire squadron moved on May 26 to escort Blenheim raids and help cover the evacuation of the BEF, returning to Wittering on May 31. The station then had open its first satellite, at Easton alias K3 where, from May 26, No 266 Squadron nightly dispersed its Spitfires with 32 Squadron using the site for night flying.

With the Dunkirk evacuation underway, 266 Squadron's Spitfires moved to Martlesham, earmarked for a possible move to France. Then they reinforced the Duxford Sector whilst that station's squadrons

Focke-Wulf Fw 190, PN999, *and Ju 88S-1,* TS472, *dispersed in the Collyweston area of Wittering when both were in the hands of 1426 (EAC) Flight* (IWM).

were away. It was June 2 before, operating from Martlesham, the Wittering Spitfires first patrolled over the retreating BEF, and claimed a Bf 110 shot down and two Bf 109s damaged for the loss of two Spitfires.

Possibly knowing of the station's French involvement, the Luftwaffe first directed its attention to Wittering on June 6 1940. Lights were on at the Q-site when raiders arrived and dropped 11 bombs near Etton. On June 9, 213 Squadron went again to Biggin Hill, returned briefly to collect belongings on June 18, then left Wittering for Exeter, moving not long before Wittering's Blenheims drew first blood.

Around midnight on June 18/19, a handful of KG4's Heinkel He 111s, operating ironically from Merville, crossed the Norfolk coast near Wells, were soon in the Wittering Sector and headed for airfield targets. Blenheims of 23 Squadron were ordered to intercept—easier said than done. Duxford's Spitfires were also despatched, and without radar aids the two stations achieved surprising success in bringing down four Heinkels, two of which fell to 23 Squadron, one to Squadron Leader J. O'Brien and the other to Flying Officer H. Duke-Woolley.

Wittering's Q-site was attacked again on June 25, bombs falling half a mile away at North Borough. Air raid sirens wailed next night, more bombs falling nearby, after 229 Squadron and its Hurricanes had arrived from Digby. On June 29, Pilot Officer Williams of 23 Squadron claimed an enemy bomber in the Norwich area.

During the Battle of Britain Wittering was too far away for direct involvement although its squadrons gave reinforcement support to 11 Group, and 266 Squadron joined that Group on August 12. It was replaced by 'Sailor' Malan's 74 Squadron at Wittering for a rest. When, on August 21, 66 Squadron returned from Hornchurch, among its Spitfires were some aged Mk 1s with two-bladed wooden Watts propellers. No 74 Squadron was ousted north to Kirton, whilst 23 and 229 Squadrons made use of K3.

Each day during the summer of 1940, Wittering's squadrons were at readiness. On August 31, for example, a day of busy activity north of London, 64 Squadron

A Victor B2 climbs away from Wittering. Nestling in the weapons bay is a Blue Steel stand-off bomb.

strengthened the Wittering Sector when 229 and 266 Squadrons operated within the Debden and Duxford Sectors, returning as usual to their base during the evening.

Long overdue was replacement of 266 Squadron's aged Spitfires. It came in the form of Castle Bromwich-built Spitfire IIs, first taken into action on September 7 when two pilots over Yarmouth spotted a high flying raider. They gave chase, later claiming to have shot it into the sea. A further change came on September 9 when 229 Squadron moved to Northolt, exchanging places with No 1 Squadron. Then 23 Squadron moved to Ford and Middle Wallop on September 12, night readiness at K3 subsequently being provided by detachments of 29 Squadron, Digby.

Although enjoying some respite, No 1 Squadron was still available for action. On September 15 it provided rear support to 11 Group, patrolling Duxford Sector

Hunter FGA 9, XF431, of 45 Squadron at Wittering by the Gaydon-type hangar.

during a day of intense fighting. Although there were some alarms, September 1940 passed without Wittering being bombed. Two Hurricane pilots damaged a Ju 88 near South Cerney and another pair chased a bomber out to sea, leaving it smoking. A trio of 1 Squadron's Hurricanes engaged a Do 17 near Banbury and on October 27 others damaged a Do 17 near Feltwell.

In late October 1940, 266 Squadron gave up its precious Spitfire IIs, reverting to Mk 1s. Early on October 28, four small bombs fell in a field near a Bofors site by the A1. Next day was even more eventful when eight pilots of 266 Squadron, operating with 12 Group from Duxford, engaged 11 Bf 109s. Blue Section that day shot down a Do 17 not far from Cambridge, but return fire pierced the coolant system of a Hurricane forcing it to crash near Peterborough. A chase by 1 Squadron near Sutton Bridge on the following day resulted in the destruction of Ju 88A-4 *L1+GS*.

Sorties by lone raiders relying upon frontal weather were becoming an annoying feature of life in the Eastern Counties. One pass by a single bomber could bring destruction and alarm out of all proportion to the effort mounted. Combatting nuisance raiders was difficult, sounding public alerts playing the enemy game. Yet without the warning siren, morale could suffer. On October 31, with cloud base too low for fighter interception, German bombers maurauded over a wide area. At Wittering five alarms were sounded that day and in the afternoon a delayed action bomb fell in St Leonard's Street, Stamford, where there was machine gunning and two casualties.

By November 1940, the day after the battle in the south was won, the future could be viewed with a little more confidence. From Wittering, as from many fighter stations, much effort was now devoted to protecting coastal shipping. The appearance of a Wittering Wing comprising Nos 1 and 266 Squadrons was important. They trained with 19 Squadron at Fowlmere to form a 12 Group offensive, Wing able also to engage German fighter-bombers over the south-east. At night 29 Squadron still maintained standby forces at K3 where 151 Squadron placed part of its strength from November 12.

For a variety of reasons German bomber crews, returning from prime targets, released varying loads over wide areas of Britain. Sixty bombs fell near Wittering on November 20 1940, some at Barnack. Routes for enemy night bombers were now often passing over or near Wittering as the Luftwaffe headed for the Midlands. No 25 Squadron moved in from Debden on November 27 to engage them and was joined, three weeks later, by 151 Squadron which brought its Hurricanes along from Bramcote. For the day fighter role, 229 Squadron's Hurricanes replaced those of No 1 Squadron on December 15 1940 and, in the midst of these squadron moves, command of the station passed from Group Captain Harry Broadhurst to Group Captain Basil Embry. No 229's stay was brief for it moved to Speke shortly before Christmas so that, in the New Year, Wittering and K3 housed Nos 25 (Beaufighter), 151 (Hurricane and Defiant) and 266 (Spitfire) Squadrons.

January 1941 was extremely cold. Heavy snow fell on four days, icy conditions making fire fighting very difficult. A German bomber crew delivered a New Year's Day gift of four 50 kg bombs to the rear of 25 Squadron's hangar, damaging the boiler house and coal compound. A clear, cold night with full moon, January 16 was ideal for fighting—if one could withstand the cold. Contrails from enemy aircraft were that night clear to view over a wide area and Pilot Officer Stevens of 151 Squadron scored his first success, Do 17Z *5K+DM*, Werke Nr *3456*, of 4/KG 3 shot down near Brentford, Essex. After refuelling and rearming, his Hurricane was off again and Stevens shot down He 111H-5 *A1+JK*, Werke Nr *3638*, of 2/KG53 in the sea off Canvey Island.

March 14 1941 was another clear night. The moon was high when, at about 23:00, a German bomber raced low across Wittering unloading six 250 kg bombs and about 100 incendiaries on to the camp. The first bomb penetrated the roof of 25 Squadron's hangar, smashed through the wing of a Beaufighter but did not explode. A second bomb burst in the hangar roof, causing widespread damage. The third hit the airmens' cookhouse and the fourth exploded by the gas decontamination centre. A fifth went off by the Officers' Mess, shattering the Card Room and living accommodation above. The sixth burst on the squash court. Incendiaries set a hangar on fire, and burnt the station cinema and two barrack blocks. Surprisingly, although fires raged for an hour and a half and there was considerable enemy activity overhead, no more bombing took

Hunter T7 of 58 Squadron in Wittering's Gaydon-type hangar, a modern form of Type 'J'.

place. Three men were killed and 17 injured, two of whom died later. By noon next day the station was fully operational. On March 23 it responded to the attack when, for the first time, Spitfires of 266 Squadron participated in an offensive strike using a forward base.

At night both 25 and 151 Squadrons were very busy and when Commander-in-Chief, Figther Command, Air Chief Marshal Sholto Douglas, visited the station on April 10 1941, intensive operations were underway. Whilst he was there Sergeant Bennett of 25 Squadron destroyed a Ju 88, 151 Squadron scored a victory and Flight Lieutenant Armitage of 266 Squadron a possible. In all, seven enemy bombers were destroyed during that night's raid on Birmingham.

The end of the night blitz was approaching and a switch to offensive operations increasing. On April 15 1941, transition was apparent when 266 Squadron joined 65 and 402 on a 12 Group Wing sweep over France. Emphasis at Wittering, though, remained on night fighting. Whereas previously night fighter operations had largely been mounted from the satellite to protect the main base, the opposite policy was now in force. Sophistication of night fighting and radar gear demanded even more elaborate facilities.

Although the night campaign against British cities was soon to cease, not so the bombing of Wittering. On May 7 nine medium sized bombs were laid across the parade ground and on to a corner of a barrack block, five men being killed and ten injured. That night the enemy suffered more, 25 Squadron claiming three raiders. Enemy response seemed swift, too, because, on May 8, Wittering was twice attacked. In fine, clear conditions, a diving intruder dropped ten HEs and incendiaries killing Pilot Officer Carlin of 151 Squadron and damaging a number of aircraft, one of which was burnt. In the second attack of the night, five HEs and incendiaries fell by the watch office. Wittering's night fighters were meanwhile very busy, laying claim to two bombers and engaging three more.

Undaunted, the Luftwaffe returned the following night and dropped four HEs. A burst water main was soon repaired. One bomb fell on a hangar hitting a girder but failed to explode. Pilot Officer Picknet of 25 Squadron landed soon after, he claimed to have shot down 'possibly a Fw 200'. And still the attacks were not over. On May 10, recorded as the last night of the major German night blitz, four HEs and incendiaries were aimed at the camp, but they overshot close to Wittering village. The station's pilots that night claimed five enemy aircraft, although confirmation was not possible. German records list seven aircraft as missing.

As RAF activity over France increased, 266 Squadron was more and more drawn into the fighting, operating mostly from the satellite. On June 27, for instance, Sergeant Lewis claimed a Bf 109, but it cost two of the squadron's pilots. A fast fight developed on July 3, two 109s being claimed and five damaged. In mid-July 1941, Lord Nuffield was entertained at the station to which some of his earliest Spitfires had been despatched. Next month 266 Squadron re-equipped with Spitfire Vbs. Autumn 1941 witnessed the opening of the second satellite, at King's Cliffe, to where 266 Squadron moved.

Defiants of 151 Squadron and Beaufighters of 25 Squadron were here at the start of January 1942. No 266 left the Sector and was replaced by 616 Squadron, but there was no successor to 25 Squadron which moved early in January to Ballyhalbert. Room had been made for 1529 BAT Flight which formed in January and moved to Colly Weston (alias K3 and WB3) in April. Enemy night activity was mainly devoted to shipping operations. Defiants of 151 Squadron patrolling over the sea on February 19 1942 came across some Do 217s, one of which was shot down by Squadron Leader Smith's gunner, Flight Lieutenant Beale. That night three more Do 217s and a Ju 88 were engaged.

For circus and escort operations No 486 (NZ) Squadron came from Kirton on April 9, permitting 616 Squadron to stand down for conversion to Spitfire VIs. It also had an unusual night defence role for a Spitfire squadron, since it was affiliated to No 532 Squadron, Wittering's Turbinlite organisation.

On July 10 1941, No 1453 (Turbinlite) Flight, the third of ten, had formed at Wittering with a nominal strength of eight aircraft. Its mixture of Havocs and Bostons each carried an airborne searchlight in the nose, the first patrol being flown on October 22 1941. At first the Flight operated with the aid of satellite Hurricanes of 151 Squadron whose task was to shoot at any illuminated enemy aircraft. On September 4 1942 the Flight became 532 Squadron whose Turbinlite force comprised two Havoc Is (T) and six Boston IIIs (T) in mid-October by which time it had its own Hurricanes. Operations had, however, ceased after the squadron participated in experimental flights during which attempts were made to illuminate enemy aircraft by dropping flares. Disbandment came on January 25 1943, by which time Wittering had achieved distinction for very different reasons.

Basil Embry, never one to be left behind or out of excitement, was greatly thrilled when, on April 6 1942, the first Mosquito II for 151 Squadron touched down. Only 157 Squadron at Castle Camps had hitherto received Mosquito fighters and Embry was determined that one from his station should draw first blood. Whether this was achieved will probably never be proven. No 151 Squadron began Mosquito operations on April 30, the first claim to success being made on May 29 when, at dawn, Flight Lieutenant Pennington engaged what was listed as a Heinkel 111 over the North Sea. Eventually he was recorded as damaging the bomber. Irrespective of total success or not, 151 Squadron achieved an enviable reputation as a night fighter squadron. Re-equipment had come as the *Baedeker Raids* were under way, Wittering's fighters seeking, off their Sector, raiders tracking along the coast. That the Luftwaffe had still not forsaken Wittering was clear when on, June 25 1942, flares lit the area as bombs fell wide at Stamford. For much of the remainder of 1942, though, the night sky was largely free of enemy aircraft.

A new BAT Flight formed here on November 23, No 1530 which left for Colly Weston in January 1943. That month witnessed the arrival of the 56th Fighter Group USAAF at King's Cliffe. Insufficient accommodation was available for the American taste and the 63rd Fighter Squadron, under Major Toky, lodged at Wittering along with its P-47s until March 1943 when the Group left for Horsham St Faith. This move took place within a general re-arrangement of Allied squadrons in East Anglia following the departures to the Mediterranean Theatre and arrival of many Americans. One of the decisions made was to pass Duxford to the USAAF, the aged station being of little operational value to the RAF.

This entailed the removal from Duxford of an assortment of organisations, each an enthusiast's joy to perceive. First to leave was 1426 Enemy Aircraft Flight which, although based at Colly Weston, made daily use of Wittering. On March 25 the Main Party, Air Fighting Development Unit, under Wing Commander E.S. Smith, and the Naval Air Fighting Development Unit, commanded by Lieutenant Commander B.H. Kendall, between them saw to the movement of their exotic aeroplanes. With armament, tactical and handling trials in plenty, there was little room for an operational night fighter squadron and, on April 30 1943, 151 Squadron fled to Colerne. Almost at once it was replaced by 141 Squadron's Beaufighters from Predannack. They had come to institute a highly secret series of operations code named *Serrate*. Using aged radar they operated over enemy territory at night trying to engage German night fighters, carrying out the first attempts to protect British night bombers. Wittering, into the bomber world for the first time, served increasingly as a diversion base. One of the first arrivals was Lancaster *JA691* which landed following an aerial collision with an enemy fighter.

Spectacular fighter operations were not a thing of the past though, as was shown on June 29 1943, when a very long range daylight penetration into France was carried out by two Mustangs of AFDU, flown by Squadron Leader McLachlan, DSO, DFC, and Flight Lieutenant Paige who between them claimed six enemy aircraft.

August 1943 found the Americans once more using Wittering. Accommodation problems remained acute at King's Cliffe when P-38s of the 20th Fighter Group arrived in late August so the 55th Fighter Squadron positioned its aircraft at Wittering where they remained until April 1944, participating in many operations, including

Wittering's most famous inmates—the Harriers of No 1 Squadron and the Harrier Conversion Unit, prior to the toning down of their markings.

an escort during the first attempted USAAF Berlin raid of March 3 1944.

Wittering, wartime home for many famous RAF figures, came to be associated with Wing Commander D.R.J. Braham, DSO, DFC, a very successful night fighter pilot involved with *Serrate* trials in 1943. Yet not all of its heroes were men. Late on October 24 1943, Wellington *DV839* of 14 OTU crashed and burst into flames. Corporal A. Holden of the WAAF was quickly at the scene and, despite the danger, managed to drag the rear gunner from the aircraft before the fire crew arrived. On March 31 1944 she was awarded the British Empire Medal.

During October 1943, No 141 Squadron re-equipped with Mosquito IIs and moved to West Raynham and 100 Group in December. As the Americans left in April 1944, the Fighter Interception Unit was arriving from Ford, bringing Beaufighters and Mosquitoes for experiments with equipment and techniques. Involved was some operational flying. By that time Wittering held an amazing assortment of aeroplanes, including some of the first Tempest Vs, a Meteor 1, Douglas Dauntless and the Ju 88C-6, now to be seen in the RAF Museum. Only Farnborough and Boscombe Down could compete where assortment was concerned. Crashes were commonplace for the station attracted battle damaged aircraft. Flapless, brakeless, seriously damaged aeroplanes with engines out of use and seriously wounded aboard, the station faced all such situations in 1944.

Shortly before the invasion's final build up, Wittering hosted Auster IVs of 658 Squadron, the first of which touched down on April 1 1944, the squadron leaving after a three-week stay here and at Colly Weston. April 14 marked the arrival from Exeter of another unusual organisation, the Gunnery Research Unit which brought along one of the last Fairey Battles, and accommodated itself at Colly Weston.

Summer 1944 brought more crippled aircraft to Wittering and into an area packed with American transports. These latter were involved in impressive night exercises, bringing the bizarre wartime sight of large formations ablaze with navigation and station keeping lights. Even that was insufficient to prevent accidents and, late on July 28, two C-47s collided north-west of the airfield, crashing at Ketton with heavy casualties. Wittering was used as a night landing ground for paratroops, leading to more accidents. Between the many activities here, 1530 BAT Flight continued flying until disbandment on August 1 1944. Beaufighters and Mosquitoes, along with Fireflies and Fulmars, served with the FIU and, at the height of the flying bomb assault, tested interception techniques. To place them more ideally the Unit moved to Ford on August 23.

On August 5 1944, the day that NAFDU lost its Avenger in the Wash, a most unusual event took place. An attempt was being made to establish a long distance record free flight for a military glider, the trip from the south to terminate at Saltby. Luck ran out and the glider came down at Wittering.

Removal of the FIU meant that, for the first time since 1938, Wittering did not house multi-seat fighters. Instead it became the centre for all advanced fighter training. On August 3 1944, Air Marshal Sir Roderic Hill, AOC, ADGB, proposed the formation of the Central Fighter Establishment embracing day and night fighter wings, to the Air Ministry. Liaison with day fighter units would be undertaken by the Day Fighter Wing ensuring the latest technical developments and tactics were appreciated. It would include a 'Fighter Training Unit', arising from the existing Fighter Leaders' School and use Spitfires and Martinets. Also within DFW would be the Typhoon-equipped Fighter-Bomber Wing of FLS. An Air Support Development Unit would be formed, and the existing AFDU re-established to comprise six twin-engined and 20 single-engined aircraft. In the Night Fighter Wing would be a training unit, also the FIU established at 20 twin and five single-engined aircraft. Authority for CFE to form was granted on September 4 1944 and FLS began moving into Wittering on October 6. Command was vested in an Air Commodore when HQ CFE opened at Wittering on October 26 and AFDU became the Air Fighting Development Squadron, the layout of the Establishment being somewhat different to that originally envisaged. In February 1945, the elements of CFE gathered at Tangmere.

Although the flying bomb campaign was largely over when CFE formed, nuisance launches from He 111s flying low over the sea continued, and caused great concern when, on Christmas Eve 1944, the V-1s were directed towards Manchester. To guard against extension of such manoeuvres, 68 Squadron moved into Wittering on February 2 1945, flew its last Mosquito XVII and XIX sorties from Wittering and before moving to Coltishall on February 27 re-equipped with the troublesome Mosquito NF XXXs. With the squadron's departure, the operational wartime career of Wittering ended. Claims by the station's squadrons stood at 151½ enemy aircraft destroyed, 50 probables and 61½ damaged. The FIU laid claim to 82 V-1s. Before Flying Training Command took control of the station, on March 31 1945, NAFDU moved to Ford and the Enemy Aircraft Flight to Tangmere. Wittering then passed to 21 Group.

The European war had ended when Wittering received a talented visitor, Mr Martin of Martin-Baker Aircraft. He sought permission to use Wittering's runway for trials of his ejector seat idea using a Defiant, the best aircraft he could prise from the authorities who, suspicious of the firm, offered him a particularly poor example—as he expected they would! In any case, he needed a speed of at least 400 mph to test his device and therefore abandoned the Wittering trials.

Summer 1945 found Wittering quieter than at any time since the early 1920s. On the station were some Americans of a fighter control unit, shortly to leave for New York. PoWs were temporarily here pending rehabilitation. Wittering's first runways had been built in 1941, fighter operations being less affected by major works programmes than bombers. With two satellites to hand, it was easier than at most stations. With the war ended and jets thought certain to need long runways, the decision was taken to marry wartime Wittering with close-by Colly Weston, and a long runway was built in 1945–6. On December 17 1945, the Flying Training Command Instructors' School arrived from Brize Norton, staying until May 24 1946, by which time Fighter Command had repossessed the station, forcing the FTCIS to South Cerney. Fighter Command regained Wittering on May 1 1946.

On April 15, 41 Squadron's snarling Spitfire 21s arrived and on, May 1, 219 Squadron's Mosquito NF 30s. They were preceded by road by an important new shape, the Handley Page Hastings, the prototype of which, on May 7, flew for the first time from Wittering making use of the station's long runway for reasons of safety.

Spitfire XVIs of 19 Squadron moved in on June 22 after 141 Squadron reformed here on June 17 and received Mosquito NF 36s. A third night fighter squadron, No 23, reformed in October 1946 and equipped with the older Mosquito NF 30, replacing No 219 which had left early in September. On January 23 1947, both 23 and 141 Squadrons vacated Wittering for Coltishall. The other two day fighter squadrons moved to Church

A Harrier of 233 OCU on the Aircraft Servicing Pad at Wittering.

Fenton, also in 12 Group, in mid-April 1947. No 19 Squadron had re-armed with Hornet 1s late in 1946.

On April 20 1947, 264 Squadron arrived to be Wittering's sole occupant and to free Linton-on-Ouse to become the base for a second Hornet Wing. Its Mosquito NF 36s were at Wittering until mid-January 1948 when they moved to Coltishall. Flying Training Command resumed control of Wittering on February 20 1948, the second post-war phase opening when No 1 Initial Training School occupied the station and stayed until April 6 1950 after which activity fell to a low ebb, but with good reason. Wittering had been earmarked for improvement and use as a bomber station. The 0/26 9,052 ft asphalt runway was strengthened and a new 'Gaydon' Type hangar erected. During the end of rebuilding, the Central Servicing Development Establishment was here, from December 1952 until March 1953.

Wittering passed to Bomber Command in 1953 and, early in August, Lincolns of 61 Squadron arrived, along with others of 49 Squadron. Little was seen of these aircraft for, in November 1953, a 49 Squadron detachment moved to Africa and, on return, went to Upwood. From March to June 1954, 61 Squadron's Lincolns were in Kenya.

The jet age had by then overtaken Wittering for, on December 12 1953, No 76 Squadron reformed here equipping with Canberra 2s. On February 25 1954, No 40 Squadron's Canberras arrived from Coningsby and, in April, No 100 Squadron moved in. In August 1954, No 61 Squadron re-armed with Canberra 2s to complete the Wittering Wing.

This third post-war phase was brief because Wittering had been selected for the V-Force, for which specialised building took place. No 61 Squadron left for Upwood in July 1955, and No 76 in November went to Weston Zoyland and was earmarked for specialised duties like 100 Squadron which was held at Wittering until disbandment on September 1 1959. The movement of 40 Squadron to Upwood came about in November 1956.

Although a fully operational station, new techniques and trials were traditionally undertaken at Wittering, the Bomber Command Development Unit (a latter day sort of AFDU) moving in during July 1954, at the same time as No 1321 Flight formed for a major part in Britain's nuclear weapon tests.

At the start of July 1955, the V-Force in the form of the Valiants of 138 Squadron, arrived to make Wittering the prime operational V-bomber station. No 49 Squadron followed in May 1956. In the autumn of that year, 138 Squadron (detached to Malta) carried out devastating, accurate attacks on Egyptian airfields during Operation *Musketeer.* The task of participating in the Christmas Island nuclear weapons trials during 1956–7 had meanwhile fallen to 49 Squadron. BCDU wound down in March 1960, and 7 Squadron brought its Valiants here from overcrowded Honington in September 1960.

The disastrous discovery that Valiants were suffering from metal fatigue ended this phase in Wittering's career. On June 26 1961, No 49 Squadron disbanded, followed on April 1 1962 by No 138 and, at the end of September 1962, by 7 Squadron which ended the Valiant's service here.

Replacement had already come about. Apart from the Navigational Bomb Sight Development Unit, also based here was the Victor 2 Trials Unit from which 139 Squadron formed on February 1 1962. On May 1, No 100 Squadron reformed, also with Victor 2s for which the Blue Steel stand-off cruise missile was prime weapon. Soon followed the decision to operate Victors at low level, despite concern about the effect of strong turbulence on their structures. Blue Steel was phased out because of its limited low level strike capability. No 100 Squadron disbanded on September 30 1968, followed by 139 Squadron on December 31, Victor 2s being judged more useful as in-flight refuelling tankers than bombers.

Wittering was placed in the hands of Air Support Command on February 1 1969, the resident Strike Command Armament Support Unit becoming the RAF Armament Support Unit on October 1 1971. By then the whole tenor of Wittering's activity had dramatically altered. The first signs of a vertical take-off era accompanied the arrival, in March 1969, of Whirlwind HC 10s of 230 Squadron. Control of the station by then was in the hands of 38 Group.

On July 18 1969 No 1 Squadron arrived. Some Hunters were brought along, but the squadron's main task was to discover the potential of the Harrier, pilots for which would learn to fly the exceptional aircraft of 233 OCU which opened in

October 1970 and originated in the Harrier Operational Conversion Unit. Harriers had little need for Wittering's long runway and soon established themselves as world famous for they were the world's first operational V/STOL combat aircraft.

In November 1971, No 230 Squadron commenced, re-arming with Puma helicopters before moving to Odiham at the start of 1972. To make fuller use of the station, Hunter 9s of No 45 Squadron arrived from West Raynham on September 29 1972, and No 58 Squadron reformed as its offshoot on August 1 1973. These squadrons, on September 2 1974, formed a Hunter Wing which had both training and operational commitments. It disbanded on July 26 1976, leaving the Harriers in the prime position they currently occupy.

And so *Action Stations 6* ends appropriately at Wittering, whose Harriers were active in the Falklands conflict, and where life has been as busy as at any RAF station. Architecturally it spans the years from draughty wooden hut to specially-heated, dust proof caverns of the 1980s. Resting silently by one of the remaining two 'C' Type hangars is a Spitfire 21, neatly coupling the history of the station, a sort of half way shape between the early era and the new fast jets. Pass Wittering on a working day and one sees Harriers hovering incredibly, perhaps a helicopter in support and trying a similar trick—and maybe a Tornado doing a 'touch and go'. What must those aged buildings think as they ponder upon all that they have witnessed?

Index of units referred to in the text

Luftwaffe
II/KG 1 - 24
4/KG 3 -
III/KG 51 - 76
2/KG 53
LG 1 - 25
LG 2 - 25

Royal Air Force
FLIGHTS
301 - 248
1321 - 204
1389 - 204
1409 - 204
1416 - 212
1418 - 247
1425 - 29, 31, 170, 172, 203
1426 - 117, 118, 302
1442 - 203
1443 - 153, 154, 162, 210
1444 - 153, 203
1445 - 203
1446 - 209, 210
1453 - 301
1456 - 174
1473 - 143, 169, 264
1478 - 169
1501 - 56, 240
1505 - 264
1509 - 115
1514 - 116
1516 - 190
1517 - 112, 114, 190
1523 - 190
1525 - 86
1526 - 154
1529 - 117, 141, 301
1530 - 117, 301-303
1532 - 237
1533 - 115, 116
1538 - 124
1539 - 77, 237
1546 - 116
1547 - 237
1551 - 81, 169
1555 - 84, 141
1556 - 141
1586 - 248
1681 - 193
1682 - 138
1684 - 184, 289

Flying Schools
E&RFTS/EFTS
3 - 21, 194, 231, 232, 266
6 - 16, 126, 242-244
9 - 235
10 - 241
13 - 222
14 - 101, 137, 169
17 - 222, 233
20 - 101
21 - 222
23 - 197
24 - 197, 198
25 - 222, 233
26 - 177
29 - 116, 117, 197
44 - 101, 137

FTS/SFTS/(P) AFU
2 - 17, 23, 60, 85, 116, 189, 238, 239, 290
3 - 17, 76, 77, 106, 235, 237, 239
5 - 217, 222
6 - 22, 60, 106, 110, 114, 145, 178, 187-189, 190, 287
7 - 19, 22, 183, 221, 222, 233
11 - 16, 294
14 - 21, 31, 120, 202, 233, 257
15 - 21, 23, 66, 85, 110, 148, 177, 178, 237, 283-285, 287
17 - 139
18 - 115, 116, 235, 266
20 - 116, 124, 169, 177, 179, 194, 286
21 - 145, 211

MISCELLANEOUS UNITS
7 AACU - 57, 101
4263 AA Flight - 105
AATDU - 87
16 ACHU - 121
21 AD - 167
2813 ADS - 254
6 AEF - 60
AFDS - 303
AFDU - 302
204 AFS - 88
9 AFTS - 276
1 AHU - 179
Andover Training Flight - 59
2 ANS - 145
10 ANS - 114
4 AONS - 266, 268
8 AONS/CANS - 242
9 AONS/CANS - 242
11 AONS - 189, 232, 266, 268

2 ASU - 98
ATrDU - 59
BAC Flight - 82
BAS - 177, 268-269
BATDU - 267
1 BAT Flight - 56
23 BAT Flight - 190
BCDU - 305
4 BFTS - 244
5 BGS - 264
Cambridge UAS - 55
1 Camouflage Unit - 62
CFE - 118, 303
CFS - 16, 75, 88, 106, 115, 141, 186, 190, 191, 238, 267, 293
2 CFS - 115, 233, 234
1 CRU - 19
1335 CU - 208
1653 CU - 146, 227
1657 CU - 114
1660 CU - 162
ECFS - 124
ETPS - 122
3 FP - 168, 228
1 FIS - 115
FIU - 303
FLS - 303
FTCIS - 238, 304
FTU - 170, 203
301 FTU - 203
307 FTU - 81, 142, 256
309 FTU - 73
310 FTU - 154, 162
311 FTU - 210
GIS - 254
1 (G) OTU - 179
Group Pools - 20, 80, 120, 261
48 GS - 101, 179
1 GTS - 123, 194, 251-254, 284
2 GTS - 105, 179, 284, 285, 286
3 GTS - 145, 213, 241, 275
4 GTS - 179, 194, 286
5 GTS - 169
625 Gliding School - 238
Halton S of TT - 149
HGCU - 30, 31, 35, 85-87, 179
21 HGCU - 87, 124
22 HGCU - 84, 140
Home AD - 166, 167
Inland Area AD - 166
King's Flight - 70, 72, 74
2 LAA Squadron - 82
5 LAA Squadron - 82
LRDF - 261
1 MPRD - 118
1655 MTU - 265

Maintenance Units
3 - 184, 286
6 - 23, 51, 85-87, 115, 118, 148, 178
7 - 77
8 - 19, 86, 118, 174, 187-190, 193
13 - 163, 167
15 - 285
24 - 115
25 - 110
26 - 99
33 - 37, 202, 203, 205
39 - 86
60 - 59
71 - 59, 82
94 - 215
95 - 215
217 - 99
246 - 82
265 - 180
273 - 228, 251
279 - 99
NAFDU - 292, 302-304
NBSDU - 305
1 OADU - 203
OADF - 161
OFU - 59
1 OPU - 106
ORTU - 154

Operational Conversion Units
232 - 145
233 - 305
237 - 73
240 - 90
242 - 74

Operational Training Units
8 - 73, 105, 213
10 - 21, 23, 27, 31, 56-59, 90, 239, 240
11 - 215, 246, 279, 280
12 - 21, 23, 28, 70, 112-114, 132, 144, 211, 212, 218, 254, 256
13 - 32, 80, 82, 142-144, 155, 163, 169, 192, 206, 256, 283
14 - 154, 279, 303
15 - 21, 23, 28, 29, 35, 148, 153, 154, 158-162, 210, 211
16 - 21, 30, 31, 32, 67, 123, 169, 262, 264, 265
17 - 32, 34, 226, 234, 256
18 - 254
21 - 29, 34, 114, 132, 133, 135, 138, 153, 174, 209-211
22 - 144, 241, 242, 273, 274
23 - 34, 242, 273, 274
24 - 30-32, 172, 173, 193, 204
25 - 30
26 - 31, 32, 105, 106, 184, 288, 289
51 - 119, 121, 214, 257
52 - 106
55 - 106
60 - 144, 155, 163
63 - 34, 106, 176
84 - 154
101 - 179
102 - 179, 285
Oxford UAS - 55, 60, 82, 258
(P) AFUs - see under FTS
PAS/Queen Bee Flight - 166
PERME - 281
PFS - 238
1 PRU - 71, 72
3 PRU - 71, 210
1 PTS - 37, 59, 90, 285, 286
PTU - 166
Queen's Flight - 74, 75
RAE - 28, 68
RAF (Belgian) ITS - 235
1 (P) RFU - 211
5 RFS - 102

6 RFS - 244
RN AED - 254
RPD - 281
RPE - 281
1 Refresher School - 139, 211
SDU - 81, 169
SFC/SATC - 268, 270
SFS/FTU - 170
SFU - 176, 242
SoE - 276
SoP - 275, 276
3 SLG - 189
22 SLG - 86
28 SLG - 86, 189
34 SLG - 86, 190
10 S of TT - 168
14 S of TT - 167
107 SSU - 174, 190
108 SSU - 190
114 SSU - 115
3501 SU - 119, 121

SQUADRONS
(Royal Air Force)
1 - 24, 117, 298, 299, 305
2 - 77
3 - 296
5 - 77
7 - 191, 261, 305
9 - 100
10 - 205, 258
12 - 79
XV - 15, 55, 117, 120
18 - 15, 17, 259, 261
19 - 100, 208, 299, 304
21 - 74
23 - 17, 166, 295, 298, 305
24 - 59, 72, 74, 267
25 - 117, 299, 300, 301
29 - 298
30 - 59, 74, 141, 205
32 - 63, 117
33 - 78, 259
34 - 17, 261
35 - 120, 157, 240
36 - 205
37 - 19
38 - 100, 293
40 - 15, 17, 54, 55, 59, 120, 305
41 - 304
43 - 166
45 - 230, 306
46 - 59, 141, 205
47 - 59, 141, 205
48 - 79, 84, 127-131, 177, 205, 229
49 - 305
50 - 162
51 - 59
52 - 55, 56-59, 70, 178
53 - 59, 90, 141, 204, 251
54 - 208
55 - 100
57 - 14, 17, 259, 261
58 - 73, 261, 306
59 - 59
61 - 211, 274, 305
62 - 55, 119, 120, 229
63 - 56, 70, 72
64 - 147, 295, 297
68 - 303
70 - 205
71 - 227
72 - 75
74 - 297
75 - 158
76 - 93, 240, 261, 305
77 - 93, 94, 158
78 - 93
79 - 63, 174, 296
81 - 258
82 - 73, 119, 120
85 - 121
87 - 76
90 - 17, 19, 79, 224, 226, 282, 293
91 - 176, 183
92 - 76
93 - 183
96 - 174-176
97 - 55, 56, 162
98 - 55, 176
99 - 90, 137, 158, 204, 205, 210, 258, 259
100 - 78, 305
101 - 78, 79, 85, 210
102 - 251
103 - 55, 70
104 - 55, 80
105 - 55, 74, 157
106 - 212, 215
107 - 157
108 - 80, 119
109 - 191-193, 247, 264
110 - 229
111 - 101, 227
113 - 261
114 - 74
115 - 90
116 - 101, 117, 175
118 - 77, 117
120 - 170
121 - 227
123 - 258
124 - 208, 228
129 - 147, 208
130 - 176, 228
131 - 147
133 - 147
134 - 63, 174
137 - 181
138 - 145, 247-249, 305
139 - 305
140 - 72, 212
141 - 302, 303, 305
142 - 79
144 - 79, 212
147 - 59, 74
148 - 158
149 - 249
150 - 70
151 - 117, 299, 300, 301, 302
152 - 117
153 - 176
156 - 191
157 - 214, 301
159 - 206, 227
160 - 227, 254
161 - 247-249
164 - 257
166 - 55, 56, 70
167 - 59, 74
169 - 257
174 - 148
184 - 148
190 - 139, 140
206 - 204
207 - 70, 120, 157
213 - 295, 296
214 - 153
215 - 74, 187, 261
216 - 205
218 - 155, 212, 261
219 - 176, 304
222 - 208
226 - 157, 207, 261
229 - 117, 297-299
230 - 305, 306
232 - 228

233 - 83, 117
234 - 176, 208
238 - 59
239 - 257
242 - 24, 59, 204, 227
255 - 174, 176
257 - 174
264 - 197, 296, 305
266 - 117, 296, 298-301
267 - 74
268 - 257
269 - 295
271 - 93, 94, 127, 129, 131, 177
285 - 174
288 - 117
295 - 141, 162, 163
296 - 87
297 - 87, 141
308 - 62, 174
331 - 210
349 - 183
350 - 227
401 - 147
402 - 147
403 - 62, 227
408 - 212
411 - 182
412 - 147, 181
415 - 114
420 - 162, 274
425 - 162
426 - 251
434 - 234
435 - 131
437 - 83, 92
441 - 208
442 - 208
457 - 62, 174
458 - 206, 210
460 - 162, 180, 206
485 - 182, 183
486 - 301
501 - 24
511 - 90, 203, 204
512 - 91, 92, 93, 203
529 - 151
532 - 301
540 - 72, 73
541 - 72, 73
542 - 72, 73
543 - 72, 73, 145
544 - 72, 73
570 - 162, 163
575 - 84, 91, 92
582 - 191-193
605 - 63, 101, 174, 177
609 - 181
610 - 182, 296
611 - 147
613 - 257
616 - 181, 182, 301
620 - 139, 140
658 - 118, 303
1 TAMU - 250
3 SGR - 27
TCAMDU - 59
TCDU - 59, 87, 163
3 TEU - 106, 176
ULAS - 60
Victor 2 Trials Unit - 145

Royal Flying Corps

5 Eastern Area Aircraft Depot - 165
5 RAS - 100
5 RS/TS - 100
28 RS - 100
38 RS/TS - 229, 230
40 RS - 12
48 RS - 230
55 RS - 100
54 RS - 100
67 RS - 100
74 RS - 100
1 TDS - 293
28 TDS - 282
33 TDS/TS - 12, 13, 290
44 TDS - 77, 230
1 TS - 12
7 TS - 290
8 TS - 12, 290
34 TS - 12, 100
59 TS - 230
61 TS - 282
70 TS - 71
71 TS - 282

Royal Navy/Fleet Air Arm

HMS *Hornbill* - 124

SQUADRONS

739 - 124
1832 - 74, 124
1833 - 177
1836 - 74, 124
1840 - 124

United States Army Air Force/USAF
Bomber Groups/Wings

2 - 265
11 - 88
22 - 88
25 - 105
40 - 88
43 - 88, 141
47 - 208
68 - 88
91 - 180, 255, 292
92 - 89, 223
96 - 147
97 - 32, 146, 147, 227, 265
100 - 89, 223
301 - 88, 107, 108, 223, 265
303 - 207, 208, 255
305 - 88, 108, 109, 110, 141, 147, 255
306 - 141, 254, 255
307 - 88
320 - 88
351 - 228
379 - 180
380 - 88, 89
384 - 88, 147
398 - 215
401 - 124
467 - 155
492 - 106, 155
509 - 265
801 - 154

Bombardment squadrons

15 - 32, 146, 207, 223
36 - 154
65 - 88
340 - 147, 227, 228
341 - 227, 228
342 - 146, 147
352 - 107, 108, 223
353 - 107
358 - 207, 208
359 - 208
364 - 108
365 - 108
367 - 141, 255
368 - 141
369 - 141, 255
406 - 106, 154
414 - 146, 228

419 - 107, 108
422 - 108, 110
423 - 255, 256
508 - 511 (inclusive) - 228
600-603 (inclusive) - 215
612-615 (inclusive) - 12
653 - 105
788 - 155
850 - 155
856 - 155
858 - 106
859 - 155

Fighter Groups
20 - 183, 302
55 - 214
56 - 183, 301
350 - 183
368 - 184

Fighter Squadrons
50 - 215
55 - 183, 302
61 - 183
63 - 183
77 - 183
79 - 183
307 - 147
308 - 227
309 - 147
343 - 214
414 - 176
551 - 106
552 - 106

MISCELLANEOUS UNITS
3914 Air Base Group - 110
3918 Air Base Group - 265
7020 Air Base Group - 142
93 ARS - 265
310 ARS - 88
321 ARS - 88
582 Air Re-Supply Group - 208
479 Anti-Submarine Group - 223
2 CCRC - 106
7514 CSG - 265
852 Engineer Aviation Battalion - 154
802 Group - 215
125 Liaison Sqn - 106
3 Photo Group - 223
7 Photo Group - 105, 212
10 Photo Group - 104
13 Photo Squadron - 212
14 Photo Squadron - 212
22 Photo Squadron - 105, 212
27 Photo Squadron - 105, 212, 213
30 Photo Squadron - 103
31 Photo Squadron - 104
33 Photo Squadron - 104
5 Photo Reconnaissance Squadron - 207, 223
5 SRW - 141, 265
55 SRW - 89
68 SRW - 141
98 SRW - 89
301 SRW - 110
60 TCG - 107, 223
10 TCS - 107
11 TCS - 107
12 TCS - 107
28 TCS - 223
42 TCS - 209
20 TFW - 265
67 TRG - 104
495 Transport Group - 106
15 TRS - 104
17 TRS - 110, 265
42 TRS/10 TRW - 110

Valiants of 138 Squadron, the first to be equipped with V-bombers, at Gaydon in March 1956.